FOOD FUNDAMENTALS

FOOD FUNDAMENTALS

TENTH EDITION

Margaret McWilliams, Ph.D., R.D.
Professor Emerita
California State University, Los Angeles

PEARSON

Boston   Columbus   Indianapolis   New York   San Francisco   Upper Saddle River
Amsterdam   Cape Town   Dubai   London   Madrid   Milan   Munich   Paris   Montreal   Toronto
Delhi   Mexico City   São Paulo   Sydney   Hong Kong   Seoul   Singapore   Taipei   Tokyo

Editorial Director: Vernon Anthony
Senior Acquisitions Editor: William Lawrensen
Editorial Assistant: Lara Dimmick
Director of Marketing: David Gesell
Senior Marketing Manager: Thomas Hayward
Assistant Marketing Manager: Alicia Wozniak
Senior Marketing Assistant: Les Roberts
Production Manager: Holly Shufeldt
Senior Art Director: Jayne Conte
Cover Designer: Bruce Kenselaar
Cover Image: Shutterstock
Full-Service Project Management and Composition: Integra Software Services Pvt. Ltd.
Printer/Binder: Edwards Brothers
Cover Printer: Lehigh-Phoenix Color

Credits and acknowledgments borrowed from other sources and reproduced, with permission, in this textbook appear on the appropriate page within text.

Many of the designations by manufacturers and sellers to distinguish their products are claimed as trademarks. Where those designations appear in this book, and the publisher was aware of a trademark claim, the designations have been printed in initial caps or all caps.

Library of Congress Cataloging-in-Publication Data
McWilliams, Margaret.
    Food fundamentals / Margaret McWilliams.—10th ed.
      p. cm.
    ISBN-13: 978-0-13-274773-8 (alk. paper)
    ISBN-10: 0-13-274773-1 (alk. paper)
    1. Food.   2. Cooking.   I. Title.
    TX354.M28 2013
    641.3—dc23
                              2011048701

10 9 8 7 6 5 4 3 2 1

ISBN 10:   0-13-274773-1
ISBN 13: 978-0-13-274773-8

Brief Contents

Contents

6
Fruits 107

7
Salads and Salad Dressings 131

8
Fats and Oils 153

9
Carbohydrates: Sugar 173

10
Carbohydrates: Starches and Cereals 189

11

Proteins: Milk and Cheese 217

12

Proteins: Eggs 247

13
Proteins: Meats, Poultry, and Fish 277

14
Leavening Agents 319

15

Basics of Batters and Doughs 329

16

Breads 345

17

Cakes, Cookies, and Pastries 363

Preface

The food scene today is dynamic and evolving. Emphasis is not only on eating less to achieve and maintain a healthy weight but also on changes in menu choices. Attention today is focused on eating more fresh fruits and vegetables, substituting olive and other oils for solid fats and reducing total and *trans* fats, choosing more seafood and poultry and less red meat, shifting to whole grains, and reducing sodium and sugar. Increased physical activity and awareness of food safety are the other changes recommended to promote good health. I have written this tenth edition to focus on these priorities.

The nation's focus on weight control makes this a particularly appropriate time to be preparing for a career in the world of food. Considerable attention is being directed toward the safety of our food, its preparation and consumption, and ultimately its effect on health and well-being. Not surprisingly, such a broad field has many specializations and career objectives, but they share the common objective of preparing foods to bring optimum health and pleasure to consumers. Few areas of study afford people such broad opportunities to be of service and benefit to others. Yet another benefit is that the strong academic preparation for careers involving food can be the basis for making personal lifestyle choices that promote healthy and fulfilling lives.

Professionals in any aspect of the food industry need to know the fundamentals of foods and their preparation. Whether your future career will include responsibilities for feeding individuals or large groups of people, research and development of new food products, marketing, or oversight, you will need to use the broad range of information covered in this book. This foundation provides an invaluable perspective for approaching and solving the challenges you will face in your career.

This text provides a broad foundation for studying and working with food. The scientific bases for practices and procedures are integrated with discussions on ingredients as sources of nutrients and as components of products. The effects of preparation techniques are discussed in the context of the science underlying various aspects of preparation: manipulation, ingredients and ratios, effects of heat and cold, storage, preservation, and evaluation. In today's world, this curriculum needs to include foods from cultures around the world. A broader cultural perspective is provided by the feature "Cultural Accents" and by illustrations of exotic foods from distant countries.

Several study aids are included to assist you in your study. A chapter outline and "Key Concepts" introduce each chapter and provide a road map to the subjects that are discussed. Key words defined in the margin and an extensive glossary are aids to expanding your professional vocabulary. The "Science Note" boxes are of particular interest to readers wishing to develop a deeper understanding of the science that underlies what is happening in the laboratory. The "Industry Insight" feature brings some industrial applications into the picture. Numerous illustrations enhance understanding of various topics throughout. "Judging Points" for many products are included to emphasize the importance of product evaluation and the knowledge needed to improve them. Web addresses are included to guide students to accurate, pertinent information on the various topics being studied. The summary at the end of each chapter provides a review of the key topics discussed. Study questions reinforce the learning process.

Chapter 2 (Nutrition and Food) has been revised based on the 2010 *Dietary Guidelines for Americans* and MyPlate. These recommendations regarding changes in food choices and improvements in assuring safety have been incorporated in many of the chapters, particularly Chapter 3 (Food Safety). Emphasis on eating a variety of foods underscores the importance of building a broad base of knowledge about less familiar ingredients. Many new black and white as well as color photographs have been added to translate unusual food names into reality. Information on healthy food choices and labeling is incorporated in appropriate chapters (e.g., vegetarian diets in Chapter 13 and gluten-free products for people with celiac disease or severe allergies in Chapter 15).

Just in case you are hungry for real food as well as for information about it, you will find my laboratory manual *Illustrated Guide to Food Preparation*, Eleventh edition, to be a useful ingredient in your study and a treasure in your kitchen. You might also enjoy my book *Food Around the World: A Cultural Perspective*, Third edition. These are also Prentice Hall publications.

—Margaret McWilliams
Redondo Beach, California

Acknowledgments

Once again, it is a real privilege to say a heart-felt "thank you" to Pat Chavez. Her sharp eyes and professional expertise helped greatly in eliminating the confounding typos that can so easily pop up in the bound book. She also teamed with me to prepare and photograph some of the new pictures in this edition. Her ideas, culinary skills, and artistic sense are evident in the salad photos.

Special thanks for their very helpful suggestions go to my excellent reviewers. They are Alexandria Miller, Northeastern State University; Sarah Murray, Missouri State University; Marci Smith, Brigham Young University; Jay Sutliffe, Chadron State College; and Mary Wilson, Eastern Kentucky University.

FOOD FUNDAMENTALS

Section One
Foundation for Food Study

Thai shrimp arranged on a petal from a banana blossom are a healthful, tempting dish. Courtesy of Plycon Press.

1
Food for Today

Chapter Contents

Key Concepts

1. Food professionals coordinate knowledge of food behaviors (e.g., nutritional needs, health issues related to diet) with preparation and evaluation of foods that meet consumer preferences and needs.

2. Food that is prepared well and presented attractively appeals to all the senses and adds significantly to the pleasure of life.

3. People have a wide variety of choices regarding what, where, when, and how much they eat (e.g., food prepared at home, carry-out items, and commercial establishments ranging from fast-food franchises to fine restaurants).

4. Food choices have a significant impact on people's health over a period of time.

5. Subjective (sensory) and objective testing are key components of developing products and evaluating food.

6. Various career paths based on food are available to today's graduates.

INTRODUCTION

Are you eating to live or living to eat? Your answer probably indicates that both of these choices play a role in your life. Of course, it is necessary to eat a diet that supports health, and it also is possible for that food to bring considerable pleasure and added interest to your life. Our global food supply and the ways in which these ingredients are prepared have greatly expanded menu choices. Never before have there been so many opportunities for creating menus and dishes to enhance the joy of the dining table.

Your study of food and the science underlying its preparation will lead to culinary success and set the stage for a lifetime of good eating. It also will broaden your knowledge of ingredients and products to provide a strong foundation for your professional career. Clearly, this is a win–win course of study.

The ultimate goal of food preparation is to create dishes that please diners while providing the nutrients needed for good health. This may sound simple, but success comes from applying scientific principles to the procedures and techniques used in cooking. Ingredients of high quality in the hands of a creative chef are the prelude to dining pleasure (Figure 1.1). Well-prepared food satisfies all the senses and adds pleasure to the day. On the other hand, eating can seem boring or simply a matter of survival if the quality of preparation is poor.

Unfortunately, food can even threaten survival if viable hazardous microorganisms are present. Food must be prepared in a sanitary environment with careful attention paid to personal hygiene habits of workers, cleanliness of work surfaces and utensils to avoid **cross contamination**, and temperature control. Food-borne illnesses (Chapter 3) have been traced to a wide spectrum of sources ranging from produce contaminated in the field to outbreaks due to inadequate heating and/or refrigeration. All food handlers need to be vigilant to maintain food that is safe, whether in a commercial setting or in the home.

cross contamination
Introduction of microorganisms to a food when it comes in contact with a surface contaminated previously by another food.

Figure 1.1
Chefs are often a source of creative menu ideas. Courtesy of Plycon Press.

FOOD PATTERNS

Food professionals need to be in tune with the way people are choosing to eat, so food in the marketplace and in commercial venues will meet expectations for palatability and safety. Because patterns and preferences change, there is a continuing need for surveying and reviewing the food scene on an ongoing basis. This chapter highlights various aspects that shape and modify what people select to eat, changes that significantly influence food preparation and selection.

Americans have a remarkable number of choices when they eat (Figure 1.2). Their patterns are extremely varied in number of meals and snacks, setting where eaten, and both the types and the quantities of foods. Conformity definitely is not the rule.

Lifestyles and the economy are strong influences on how and what people eat. The hectic pace and demands on time that are placed by jobs and school often limit choices to grabbing food at any opportunity or to carrying it from home. Even airline passengers may need to buy a portable snack to avoid starvation as they race from flight to flight. Income or budget also has an important influence on where and what a person eats. The rapidly rising cost of food is causing many people, particularly those on limited incomes, to be increasingly restricted in the foods they buy.

Health problems or concerns play an important role in food selection for many shoppers. Some people with dietary restrictions due to problems such as diabetes, high blood pressure, or lactose or gluten intolerance are avid label readers as they seek suitable products. Issues such as nutrition and food safety are prominent in the minds of many as they shop for food to promote their health and well-being.

Individual food preferences also determine food choices, and many of these favorite foods reflect family eating patterns. Not surprisingly, a special treat for one person may be a food that is shunned by somebody else (Figure 1.3). People clearly are entitled to their personal tastes. However, students preparing for careers centering on food need to think about it from a very broad perspective, not simply from the limited viewpoint of what, where, and how they personally choose to eat.

Figure 1.2
McDonald's and Starbucks, ubiquitous competing food outlets, vie for consumers and their money on opposite street corners across from a high school. Courtesy of Plycon Press.

Dining Venues

The recent economic downturn has increased the numbers of people eating meals at home, especially breakfast and dinner. Meals at home provide an excellent opportunity for family members to coordinate and catch up with the happenings of the day. Conversation there can be easier than in a noisy restaurant where the din frequently makes it impossible to be heard. The advantage of this sociability at home may be offset a bit by the effort and time required to prepare a pleasing, healthful meal unless cooking is a cooperative project.

Dishes from the deli section of the grocery store or a takeout order are time-saving options chosen by some people wishing to eat at home. Some use convenience foods extensively in their meal preparation, particularly during the week. Others prepare their own food, not only for family meals but also for special occasions. The creative opportunity provided by food preparation is viewed as a delightful challenge by some, while others cheerfully buy prepared foods. The results in terms of dining quality vary greatly from household to household.

Figure 1.3
Breakfasts featuring fried eggs and bacon and lunches highlighting comfort foods tend to draw customers who are focused more on flavor than health. Courtesy of Plycon Press.

People frequently eat meals away from home in a wide range of situations, even in the car while driving to work or school. These may have been prepared at home, or they may be purchased from a commercial food operation. Fast-food outlets are popular, particularly among young people and families with young children and limited income. Convenience, low cost, efficiency, and food choices geared toward their clientele are all factors that have contributed to the success of these chains. The competition between various chains is great, but the leaders have been successful in adapting to consumer wishes (e.g., low-carbohydrate menu options) over the years, and their fans continue to come in for both snacks and meals.

Schools, hospitals, and other institutional settings usually have cafeterias or dining rooms where people eat, either through choice or necessity (Figure 1.4). The quality of food served varies considerably from place to place, ranging from acceptable to excellent. The price also ranges from free school lunches for children who qualify under the federal program to $1500 or more per day in a special hospital unit catering to wealthy clients willing to pay for gourmet meals prepared by a highly trained chef.

Figure 1.4
Lunchtime at the U.S. Naval Academy. Courtesy of Plycon Press.

CULTURAL ACCENT
FLAVORS FROM ABROAD

America's immigrants have created a wonderful opportunity for everyone to gain experience and savor the excitement of eating special dishes from other cultures. European dishes have long influenced food choices because of the roots of many families who arrived long before the 20th century. In the Southwest, foods from Mexico have been a part of the scene for centuries. Immigrants in the latter half of the 20th century arrived from countries with very different food patterns that have also expanded dining pleasures for many Americans.

Ethnic restaurants can be found in urban centers throughout the nation. Asian dining opportunities have expanded beyond the Chinese restaurants that have long been familiar and now include Korean, Japanese, Vietnamese, Indonesian, Cambodian, and Thai restaurants. The adventures do not stop there. Indian, Sri Lankan (Figure 1.5), Middle Eastern, Ethiopian, and Moroccan flavors are offered in other restaurants. Even Tibetan restaurants can be found during the search for food adventures.

These unique dishes and flavors can be savored at home, too. Many stores now carry the exotic spices, herbs, and other ingredients needed to create authentic dishes. Regardless of the venue a diner chooses, foreign flavors can add delightful accents for dining adventures.

Figure 1.5
Naan, dal, lamb saag, beef vindaloo, lamb khorma, and raita are favorites on Indian dinner menus. Courtesy of Plycon Press.

Restaurants are the venue selected by many people when dining out rather than a fast-food operation. For special occasions, the choice may be an upscale restaurant that features beautiful food presentations and very attentive service. Families seeking a simple meal and a change of place may choose more economical, less formal restaurants. People seeking food adventures may opt for a restaurant that guarantees an unusual dining experience with foreign or exotic foods.

Food Choices

People choose the foods in their diets for a variety of reasons. Those that have been familiar since childhood usually continue to be favorites throughout life. These and other choices are influenced by such factors as ethnic heritage, resources (time for preparation and money), personal preferences, and health. If families merge, the variety of foods served may broaden, too.

The ingredients available in grocery stores today provide tempting invitations to try new food experiences. Whether selecting frozen foods, convenience foods, or fresh produce, shoppers have innumerable opportunities to opt for new food adventures as well as old favorites. Items from all around the globe are found in virtually all American supermarkets. The adventurous cook has only to decide what to prepare.

Diners make choices with their forks when they eat. Favorite foods quickly vanish from the table at dinner, but other items may be destined to become leftovers, or even may be thrown away. Unpopular dishes may never appear on the table again because cooks like to make items that will generate praise rather than criticism.

IMPACT ON HEALTH

Excess weight and obesity are an ever-increasing threat that is creating a national health crisis due to poor food choices and too little exercise. The influence of overweight and obesity on health is well recognized; the risks of heart attacks, strokes, and diabetes increase significantly when people are too heavy. Among the causes cited for this national health risk are the escalating portion sizes, choice of foods high in fat, and frequent snacks high in calories and low in nutrients. Dietary habits throughout life contribute to a person's physical condition, but it still is possible to alleviate some of the problems that have developed over the years. By eating balanced, colorful meals featuring fresh ingredients, in amounts that help to achieve and maintain a healthy weight, people can promote personal well-being. However, responsibility for eating to achieve and maintain a healthful weight rests on each individual.

Although the matter of how much to eat is a personal issue, people preparing food can quietly help by reducing the amount of fat used in cooking, planning menus that

www.fmi.org
—Website for the Food Marketing Institute.

national organic program Legislation defining the production standards for produce (at least 95 percent of produce must not have been treated with sewage-sludge–based or petroleum-based fertilizers, conventional pesticides, ionizing radiation, or bioengineering) to be labeled organic.

genetically modified organism (GMO) Plants (and food) that have been modified by genetic engineering to enhance desired characteristics.

www.cfsan.fda.gov/~lrd/ biotechm.html
—The FDA's biotechnology website.

www.cfsan.fda.gov/~lrd/ biocon.html
—Bioengineered foods approved by the FDA.

INDUSTRY INSIGHT
FOOD FOR HEALTH

The food industry monitors consumer attitudes, desires, and practices on an ongoing basis, tailoring its research and development efforts to bring new products to market shelves successfully. Today's consumers desire food products that are easy to prepare in a very short time. They place a priority on items that can be prepared in 15 minutes or less and with little effort or cleanup. Food products that can quickly be heated in their own bag are one approach that the food industry has developed to fulfill consumer desires.

In addition to the emphasis on convenience and speed, consumers are becoming increasingly concerned about eating for good health. Vegetables and fruits are viewed as being important in promoting health, and some consumers are seeking foods labeled as "organic." Produce and other foods labeled "organic" must meet the criteria for this designation required in the **National Organic Program**.

Apparently, concern over pesticides has caused some consumers to gradually drop their opposition to **genetically modified organisms** and to support genetic engineering that reduces the need for pesticides during crop production.

Awareness of the potential protection against cancer that some phytochemicals (e.g., various carotenoids) provide has heightened consumer demand for foods containing them. The food industry is incorporating various nutrients and substances with recognized health benefits because of the increased interest in healthful eating.

National concern over the incidence of obesity has added impetus to the interest that consumers have regarding the role of food in promoting health. *Light* and *lean* are important designations that may attract those who are trying to lose weight. High-protein food products are very popular among the many people who are attempting to follow a high-protein, low-carbohydrate regimen to lose weight.

emphasize fruits and vegetables, preparing less food, and serving smaller portions. Creative cooks can find many ways to help reduce the calories in their menus and provide appetizing meals. They are in a position to subtly promote more healthful dietary patterns for their clientele and/or family.

DETERMINANTS OF PALATABILITY

Aroma

aroma Volatile compounds perceived by the olfactory receptors.

The **aroma** of some foods is evident even before they are seen. Odors wafting from the kitchen hint of the pleasure to come. Bakeries sometimes deliberately vent the aroma from their ovens outside to lure potential customers. Sniffing the air can be a favorite pastime when bread is baking, steaks are being grilled, or a turkey is roasting. Conversely, the aroma of boiling cabbage usually generates far less enthusiasm for the treat being prepared. Clearly, aroma helps to define the palatability of some foods, either positively or negatively.

Taste

taste Sweet, sour, salt, bitter, and umami; basic tastes detected by the taste buds on the tongue.

umami Savory quality that contributes to the taste of some foods.

Remarks about how good a food tastes often are made around the dining table because taste is one reason that food is so enjoyable. However, **taste** is actually quite a limiting term. Four basic tastes—sweet, sour, salt, and bitter—plus **umami**, a savory quality sometimes also classified as a taste, combine to give sensory messages about food in the mouth (Figure 1.6).

Color

The colors of many foods are visually exciting and contribute significantly to palatability. Fruits and vegetables are often colorful, especially when served raw in salads and desserts. If vegetables are cooked, they should be prepared to optimize their colors. Ham and corned beef are meat choices that can add color to a meal; the golden brown skin is an attractive color when roast turkey is carved at the table. Good menu planning incorporates color as a consideration in selecting specific recipes and foods.

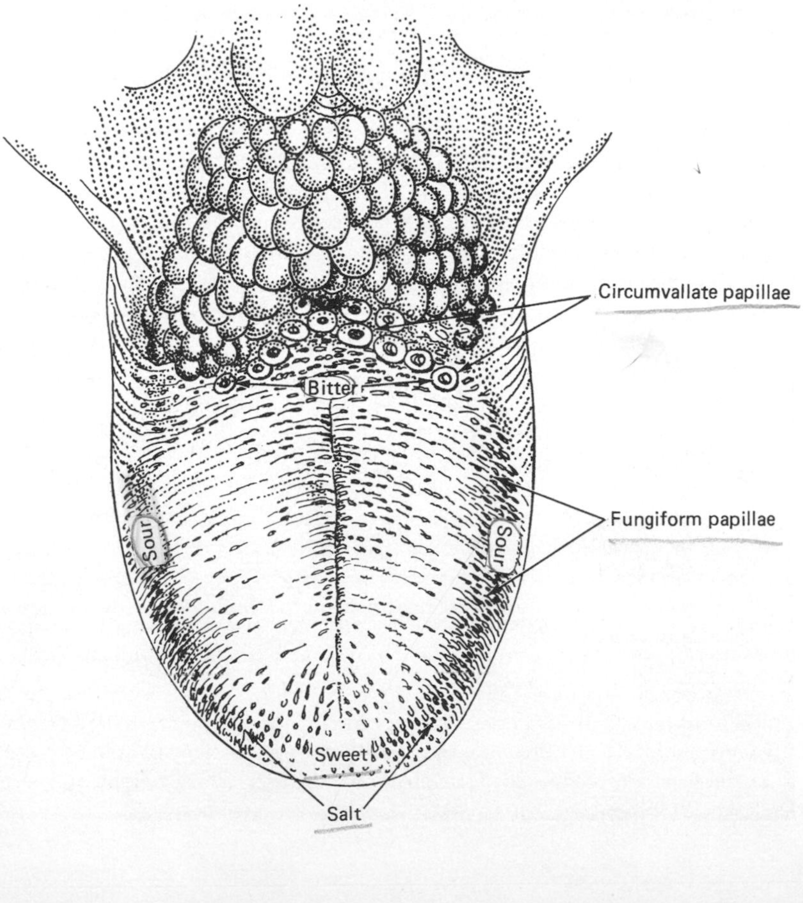

Figure 1.6
Diagram of taste receptor sites on the tongue. Courtesy of Plycon Press.

SCIENCE NOTE
ANATOMY OF FLAVOR

Flavor is perceived as a combination of taste and aroma. This sensory experience involves blending the messages the brain receives from the olfactory receptors in the nose and the taste buds in the mouth. Even before a bite is in the mouth, olfactory receptors detect aromatic compounds in the vapors from the food, especially if it is hot enough to vaporize some of the volatile compounds.

When a bite is being chewed, saliva mixes with the bits of food to help distribute them all over the surface to taste buds on the tongue. These sensors, located in various regions on the upper surface of the tongue, are capable of detecting dissolved substances, such as sugars and salt. Sweet is detected primarily across the tip, salt along the forward edges, sour farther back on the edges, and bitter across the rear.

While food is in the mouth and then being swallowed, the aromatic substances continue to reach the olfactory receptors. The messages of aroma from these receptors mingle with those from the taste buds on the tongue in the **trigeminal cavity** (space including olfactory receptors, taste buds, and the oral cavity) where flavor is perceived.

flavor Combination of aroma and taste perceived in the trigeminal cavity.

trigeminal cavity Space including olfactory receptors, taste buds, and oral cavity, where flavor is perceived.

www.ffs.com
—Website for Flavor and Fragrance Specialties.

Texture

Texture (called **mouthfeel** by food professionals) can add greatly to the pleasure of eating. Crisp bacon, smooth ice cream, a crunchy cracker, and a slippery bite of mango are examples of specific textural characteristics different foods provide. Good menu planning considers texture and utilizes foods that provide interesting contrasts in mouthfeel. Optimal preparation of the foods in the menu results in meals with pleasing textures.

mouthfeel The term food professionals use to describe textural properties of a food.

Overall Appearance/Presentation

Diners form their initial assessment of food quality based on the overall appearance and presentation of a food or a meal. Although their criteria may not be articulated, all of the factors (aroma, taste, color, and texture) discussed earlier contribute to the perception of food quality. The techniques used in preparing foods determine the final appearance of a food and/or a meal.

The principles of food preparation that are discussed throughout this book provide guidance on achieving food products with an overall appearance that is pleasing and of high quality. Promotion of a pleasing flavor in cabbage and other vegetables that have the potential to alienate diners requires that preparation minimize strong odors and flavors. Retention of bright colors in fruits and vegetables and desirable browning in baked products are essential to achieving optimal quality in these foods. Meats need to be heated to a safe internal temperature, but not so long that texture is negatively affected (e.g., they become dry and tough).

Presentation is the term used to describe the way the food is displayed for the diner. A cold bowl of vichyssoise may be more appealing if it is garnished with a sprig of fresh dill or minced chives. Chefs in expensive restaurants often do elaborate presentations that may include painting the plate with a colorful sauce to enhance the entrée or dessert. These suggestions illustrate the importance of a beautiful presentation to enhance the perceived quality of food.

JUDGING FOOD

Food quality is determined by ingredients and their preparation, and the final results need to be examined so that possible changes can be identified to create even better products subsequently. Evaluation is an important aspect of study when preparing to be a professional in this field. Foods can be evaluated subjectively and objectively. **Subjective (or sensory) evaluation** is done by people using their senses as instruments to evaluate such qualities of a food as appearance, aroma, flavor, and mouthfeel. **Objective evaluation** is conducted using a variety of machines to measure various physical aspects such as volume and tenderness.

subjective (or sensory) evaluation Evaluation using the senses.

objective evaluation Evaluation of physical and chemical aspects using equipment for measuring specific aspects of a food.

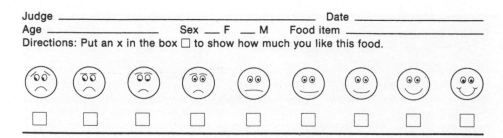

Judge _____   Date _____
Age _____   Sex __ F __ M   Food item _____
Directions: Put an x in the box ☐ to show how much you like this food.

Figure 1.7
The Smiley scale is convenient for judges doing sensory evaluation to determine how well a food sample is liked. Courtesy of Plycon Press.

Subjective (Sensory) Evaluation

Subjective evaluation is done using a panel of people who are given samples and a scorecard for evaluating the product. For testing during research and development, panelists may be trained in the use of the scorecard. Food companies sometimes do product testing, using consumer panels that have not been trained.

Aroma is evaluated by sniffing to draw the volatile aromatic compounds up through the nose to contact the olfactory receptors. Taste is noted by moving a bite of the food all over the surface of the tongue so that dissolved compounds encounter the various taste buds that detect sweet, sour, salt, bitter, and umami. Flavor can be judged by breathing in and exhaling immediately after swallowing or while a bite is held in the mouth with lips closed tightly so that the volatile substances blend with taste sensations.

Vision and touch also are used for sensory evaluations. Color and texture are key characteristics of appearance that can be evaluated by panelists. Color is an important aspect of food that judges may be asked to evaluate, either for differences between samples or to indicate a preference. Texture can be detected by touch or feel in the mouth, characteristics that may be noted on a scorecard by such descriptions as tenderness or mouthfeel. If qualities such as crunchiness or crispness are important in a product, sound may also be evaluated.

Panelists may be asked to analyze products in tests that are designed to describe or to discriminate. Descriptive testing utilizes panelists who are thoroughly trained in flavor or texture profiling. Laboratory testing to discriminate sometimes tests a judge's threshold to detect a specific taste; the ability to determine the difference can be measured using paired comparison, duo–trio, triangle, and rank-order tests.

Affective testing is of special importance to food companies developing products for the marketplace. Scorecards are designed to determine preferences and acceptability. **Hedonic** ratings by consumer panels can guide researchers toward the goal of a product that will be accepted and enjoyed. The Smiley scale is an example of a scorecard that communicates easily and quickly with consumer respondents (Figure 1.7).

Objective Evaluation

Physical and chemical methods may be used to measure various aspects of food in a laboratory. Physical methods include measurements of volume, specific gravity, moisture, texture, rheology (flow and deformation), color, and cell structure. Chemical tests are used for nutrient analysis, proximate analysis, and to measure pH, sugar concentration, saltiness, and compounds comprising aroma and flavor.

Numerous machines and techniques have been developed to be used in objective testing of food. Some examples of machines for physical testing are the Warner–Bratzler shear for measuring meat tenderness, the penetrometer (Figure 1.8) for tenderness of gels, and the farinograph for measuring gluten development in batters and doughs. Chemical testing devices may include such varied equipment as a pH meter, high-pressure liquid chromatograph, infrared spectrophotometer, and mass spectrometer.

hedonic Pertaining to degree of pleasure.

Figure 1.8
A penetrometer can be used to measure tenderness of gels and some other foods objectively. Courtesy of Plycon Press.

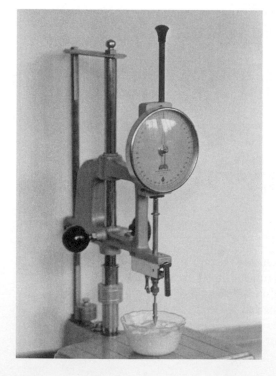

CAREER OPPORTUNITIES FOR FOOD PROFESSIONALS

The preceding discussions of such diverse aspects as where, why, and what people eat provide the context for exploring the field of food, its preparation and evaluation using sensory and objective methods. Not surprisingly, the breadth and depth of studies in this field can prepare specialists for challenging and interesting careers.

Professionals working with food include people working in quite diverse careers. Some food scientists may conduct their research in their laboratories in universities; others work in the research and development units in food companies to create new products to enter the consumer marketplace. Quality control is another area of importance to scientists in food production facilities. Some people in the food industry focus on specific areas, such as additives, to develop and market ingredients to the food industry. Government regulations of food and food products at all levels from national to even local trigger the need for food professionals, both in production and the marketplace; these regulatory specialists may represent either the industry or government. Academic preparation required for these varied positions includes a minimum of a baccalaureate degree with a major in food science, dietetics, or other food-related program. Course requirements include several chemistry courses, physics, microbiology, and mathematics, in addition to major courses in food science.

Dietitians and nutritionists are professionals who use food as the basis of their work with clients to improve their health. Career opportunities include clinical and administrative dietetics (based in hospitals, health care facilities, and private practice), nutrition specialties (e.g., sports, diabetes, weight management), research (based in university or industry), and sales. Academic preparation for these careers requires a strong science background in biochemistry, anatomy, and physiology to understand the ways nutrients from foods function in the body. Organic chemistry and microbiology provide important background for developing the knowledge about food that is needed for effective diet counseling. In addition to the required academic program, it is necessary to complete an approved clinical internship or experience to qualify to take the registration examination for dietitians. Upon passing the examination, a person becomes a **Registered Dietitian**. This title is a requirement for many professional positions in dietetics and nutrition. A graduate of an approved two-year dietetic technician associate degree who passes the dietetic technician registration examination becomes a **Dietetic Technician, Registered (DTR)**. DTRs often work under the direction of an RD in hospitals or other health care settings.

Food-service careers may be based on administration of food service or on food preparation in institutions (e.g., in hospitals, dormitories, prisons) and in the hospitality industry (e.g., hotels, tourism, restaurants). Some positions combine administrative and food preparation responsibilities. Academic requirements for professional positions in food service usually require a baccalaureate in the field, with emphasis on business and foods courses.

Although these various career paths encompass distinctly different responsibilities, professionals on any of these tracks are required to have a broad knowledge of food. They need to be familiar with the broad inventory of ingredients available today to meet the needs of a culturally diverse population. Basic preparation techniques are essential tools for today's food professionals so they can prepare and evaluate the broad range of foods their clients wish to eat. Knowledge of safe food handling practices is essential to professionals working with or educating others about food.

Food professionals possessing this broad foundation then can build on it to tailor advanced study of foods toward the specifics required for the positions they will be seeking. Although they may not be required to prepare food, they will need a solid understanding of its preparation, handling, and evaluation. Whether developing new products, teaching people how to eat for optimum health, planning diets for patients, or managing food service in an institutional setting, food professionals rely on their knowledge of food and food preparation to help them be successful in their positions. Restaurateurs continue to work directly with food as they pursue their careers.

---

http://www.ift.org/ knowledge-center/learn-about-food-science/ become-a-food-scientist/ approved-undergrad-programs.aspx
—Directory of food science programs approved by the Institute of Food Technologists (IFT).

www.foodproductdesign. com
—Website for *Food Product Design* journal.

www.worldfoodscience.org/
—Website for *World of Food Science*, published jointly by the Institute of Food Technologists and the International Union of Food Science and Technology (IUFoST).

registered dietitian
Person who has passed the registration examination after completing an approved baccalaureate or master's program in food and nutrition and clinical experience.

dietetic technician, registered (DTR)
Graduate of an approved two-year dietetic technician associate degree who passes the dietetic technician registration examination.

http://www.eatright.org/ students/getstarted/ highschool.aspx
—American Dietetic Association site outlining the requirements for becoming an RD or DTR.

http://www.restaurant.org/ careers/education/schools/
—Overview of colleges and universities with programs in restaurant and hospitality management.

www.culinology.com
—Website for Research Chefs Association.

SUMMARY

Americans today follow many different eating patterns that are influenced by lifestyles and income, as well as personal food preferences. Many meals are eaten at home, although the food may be carryout or very simple preparation during the week. When people dine away from home, the venue often is a fast-food outlet or an institutional dining area, such as a school lunchroom. Restaurants also are popular, particularly for business meals and special occasions.

Ethnic foods are growing in popularity as immigrants from other parts of the world have brought along their food traditions. Ethnic restaurants and the availability of ingredients needed for making dishes of other cultures have generated broad interest in eating a great variety of foods. Nevertheless, foods that were popular during childhood usually remain prominent in dietary patterns of adults. Time, money, and health also influence food choices.

Aroma and taste are sensory perceptions that combine to produce flavor when food is eaten. The basic tastes of sweet, sour, salt, and bitter may be enhanced with umami, a savory quality. Many volatile compounds in foods contribute to aroma and ultimately to the flavors of different foods. Color is also a vital part of the visual appeal of foods. Texture (mouthfeel) adds to the sensory qualities when food is eaten. Overall appearance and the presentation add to palatability and quality of food preparation.

Food professionals need a basic knowledge of food safety and preparation as a foundation for their future careers, whether as food scientists, dietitians, nutritionists, or chefs.

STUDY QUESTIONS

1. Keep a record of where you eat each meal and snack for a week. Summarize (a) how many meals and snacks you ate each day and (b) where you ate them. Compare weekend days with weekdays. How would you describe your eating pattern?

2. Compare your eating pattern with the pattern of someone else in your class. What are the differences? Why do the patterns differ?

3. Visit a supermarket to answer the following questions:
   a. What ethnic ingredients are available?
   b. What deli foods are displayed?
   c. Identify at least three different potato products. Compare the cost and the preparation time required for each of them.
   d. Record the ingredient labels on four different cereal packages. Compare the nutrients and the amounts added to each.

4. Survey the ethnic restaurants in your community. Are the patrons generally of that ethnicity? Do other people eat in them? What foods have you tried from each of the ethnic groups in your community?

5. What are your five favorite foods? Explain why each one is a favorite. Describe how each is prepared.

SELECTED REFERENCES

Berry, D. 2010. Heat-and-eat meals go gourmet. *Food Product Design 20*(10): 32.

Bren, L. 2003. Genetic engineering: The future of foods? *FDA Consumer 37*(6): 28–34.

Bugusu, B. 2009. Nanoscale science creates novel food systems. *Food Technol. 63*(9): 36.

Bugusu, B. 2010. Exploring food nanomaterials. *Food Technol. 64*(10): 44.

Camp, D. B., et al. 2010. Paradox of organic ingredients. *Food Technol. 64*(11): 20.

Decker, K. J. 2011. Healthier fried foods. *Food Product Design 21*(1): 42.

Demeritt, L. 2010. Consumer trends in wellness 2010. *Food Product Design 20*(10): 84.

Duxbury, D. 2005. Sensory evaluation provides value. *Food Technol. 59*(5): 68.

Foster, R. J. 2005. pHood phenomena. *Food Product Design 14*(11): 61.

Gerdes, S. 2004. Perusing the food-color palette. *Food Product Design 14*(9): 94.

Getz, J. G., et al. 2010. Nutrigenomics and public health. *Food Technol. 64*(2): 28.

Griffiths, J. C. 2005. Coloring foods and beverages. *Food Technol. 59*(5): 38.

Hon, G. 2009. Harmonizing sweetness and taste. *Food Technol. 63*(12): 20.

Katz, P. H. 2004. Designing better weight-control bars. *Food Product Design. Functional Foods Annual.* Sept.: 45.

Klahorst, S. J. 2004. Nutrigenomics: Window to the future of functional foods. *Food Product Design. Functional Foods Annual.* Sept.: 5.

Kuesten, C. 2004. Designing for demographics. *Food Product Design 14*(4): 30.

Kuntz, L. A. 2010. Natural colors for beverages: A rainbow of possibilities. *Food Product Design 20*(11): 36.

Land, D. 2010. Optimizing bioactive ingredients. *Food Technol.* 64(10): 50.

Leake, L. 2006. Electronic noses and tongues. *Food Technol.* 60(6): 96.

Luff, S. 2005. Organic identity preservation. *Food Product Design* 15(7): 107.

Marcus, J. B. 2005. Culinary applications of umami. *Food Technol.* 59(5): 24.

Massengale, R. D. 2010. Biotechnology: Going beyond GMOs. *Food Technol.* 64(10): 30.

Newsome, R. 2010. Feeding the future. *Food Technol.* 64(7): 49.

O'Hagan, P. 2004. New technologies: Why measure particle size? *Food Product Design* 14(11): 120.

Pszczola, D. E. 2010. 2010: Beginning a new decade of the ingredient odyssey. *Food Technol.* 64(9): 56.

Remig, V., et al. 2010. *Trans* fats in America: Review of their use, consumption health implications, and regulation. *J. Am. Dietet. Assoc.* 110(4): 585.

Rodriguez, N. C. 2005. Communicating sensory information to R & D. *Food Product Design* 14(11): 86.

Rudolph, M. J. 2003. Nutraceutical food ingredients: Function for the future. *Food Product Design FFA.* Nov.: 5–13.

Sloan, E. A. 2010. Giving consumers what they want. *Food Technol.* 64(9): 52.

Stouffer's. 1999. *Consumer Attitudes on Meal Preparation and Packaged Meals.* Stouffer's. Solon, OH.

Tseng, M., and R. F. DeVellis. 2001. Fundamental dietary patterns and their correlates among U.S. whites. *J. Am. Dietet. Assoc.* 101(8): 929.

Wiecha, J. M., et al. 2001. Differences in dietary patterns of Vietnamese, White, African-American, and Hispanic adolescents. Worcester, MA. *J. Am. Dietet. Assoc.* 101(2): 248.

Zoumas-Morse, C. D., et al. 2001. Children's patterns of macronutrient intake and associations with restaurant and home eating. *J. Am. Dietet. Assoc.* 101(8): 923.

Vegetables are important sources of vitamins, minerals, and antioxidants. Courtesy of Plycon Press.

2
Nutrition and Food

Chapter Contents

Key Concepts

1. Food can provide all the nutrients (carbohydrates, lipids, proteins, vitamins, and minerals) needed for good health.

2. Carbohydrates, fats, and proteins are the nutrients that provide energy, while vitamins and minerals perform many unique functions (e.g., vitamin D and calcium are essential for bone growth and maintenance).

3. Recommendations for eating for good health include the Dietary Reference Intake values (DRIs), designed for professionals to use in assessing dietary adequacy; *Dietary Guidelines for Americans*, 2010; and MyPlate, a nutrition education tool designed to help the public know what to eat for good health.

4. Good nutrition can be promoted by buying a variety and an appropriate quantity of food and preparing it to be appetizing and nutritious.

macronutrients Nutrients needed in large quantities: carbohydrates, lipids (fats), and proteins.

calorie Unit of energy provided in a food. One calorie (also called a *kilocalorie*) is the amount of heat energy required to raise 1 kilogram of water 1°C at sea level.

nutrient density The amount of nutrients in relation to the calories in a food; high nutrient density means a food is high in nutrients when compared with its caloric content.

NUTRITION, THE ULTIMATE APPLICATION OF FOOD

Food brings dining pleasures to the mind and nutrients to the body. The nutritional merits of various foods and the implications that preparation techniques have on nutritive value are featured throughout this book, for the ultimate purpose of food is to provide nourishment. Knowledge of the essential roles of nutrients in foods provides motivation to prepare healthy and pleasing food.

Everyone needs energy to do work, even simply to maintain life itself; children also must have energy for their dynamic growth. This energy is provided by the **macronutrients**: carbohydrates, lipids (fats), and proteins. Carbohydrates and proteins provide 4 **calories** per gram, less than half as much energy as the 9 calories per gram available from lipids. Although it is true that all people need energy to live, one of the most challenging and frustrating facets of food for many people is eating an appropriate quantity to get the right amount of energy.

Too many calories (or kilocalories) provide more energy than the body uses, and the surplus is converted into fat and stored. Overweight and obesity are so prevalent in the United States today that they are considered to be an epidemic that is raising major health concerns. The tendency is for some Americans to make unhealthy food choices, eating too much and choosing too many foods with low **nutrient density**.

Many people follow eating patterns that result in body weights that are within the range considered to be healthy. On the other hand, eating too little will cause people to be too thin. The amount of calories eaten regularly, day after day, can be controlled appropriately in relation to energy needs through wise food choices and also through use of sound principles of food preparation.

The preoccupation of the general public with the subject of dieting and weight control often tends to overshadow the fact that other nutrients are essential for a wide range of specific chemical reactions and other key functions. For example, some minerals are necessary to form the structure of the body, while certain minerals and vitamins are essential to catalyze innumerable chemical reactions and to synthesize vital compounds.

Figure 2.1
Sugars are tempting
carbohydrates because
of their sweet taste. Courtesy
of Plycon Press.

starch = polysaccharide + monosaccharide

Carbohydrates

Carbohydrates (e.g., sugars, starch, fiber) are primary sources of energy and comprise a significant part of the diet (Figure 2.1). The sweet taste of sucrose and other sugars adds appeal to many foods. In fact, part of the obesity problem in America is related to the high consumption of candy, sweetened beverages, and desserts. These foods seem to sing a siren song to many people, tempting them to indulge beyond their physical needs.

Not only are carbohydrates valued for their energy content, but certain polysaccharides are important as **fiber** or roughage in the diet. Cellulose, pectic substances, and several gums from plants are polysaccharides. However, these carbohydrates are not digested and absorbed in the small intestine, as is the case with sugars and starch. Instead, these particular carbohydrates serve as irritants to the gastrointestinal tract and help to keep the food mass moving on through the body. Although cellulose and the other polysaccharides comprising fiber are not incorporated into the body to serve as sources of energy, they nevertheless are key dietary components for good health.

Carbohydrates considerably larger than the disaccharides are common in some foods and also are good sources of energy. These compounds, called polysaccharides because of their size, include starch and dextrins. Starch is actually the substance in which plants store energy. The human body can digest the starch in potatoes and other foods, breaking it down into smaller and smaller components until the monosaccharide glucose is produced and absorbed for use in the body. Dextrins are quite similar to starch, but they are somewhat smaller molecules.

fiber Components of food not digested and absorbed; cellulose, pectic substances, and gums are plant carbohydrates contributing to the fiber content of the diet.

Lipids

Lipids are fatty substances that are a concentrated source of calories (9 kcal/g compared with 4 kcal/g from carbohydrates). In addition to being sources of energy, they carry the fat-soluble vitamins (vitamins A, D, E, and K) and provide the essential fatty acid, linoleic acid, and omega-3 fatty acids (Figure 2.2). Not only do fats make foods taste good, but they also add to the feeling of satisfaction after a meal because they take longer to digest.

http://www.umm.edu/
altmed/articles/omega-
3-000316.htm
—Discussion of omega-3
fatty acids and the
Mediterranean diet.

Proteins

Proteins are essential for their amino acids, which are needed to synthesize many important components of the body. Muscle tissue, connective tissue, blood, antibodies, and many other substances contain proteins, each of which is made to meet specific physical requirements. It is not possible to eat the specific proteins needed for a particular function. Instead, protein molecules in meats and other protein-containing foods (Figure 2.3) are digested and the individual amino acids are released in the small intestine and absorbed. Remarkably, the body can use these individual amino acids to synthesize the needed proteins.

More than 20 amino acids are required to make the various proteins the body needs. Each of these amino acids has a slightly different structure, but nitrogen (in combination with hydrogen as an amino group), carbon, hydrogen, and oxygen (forming an acid) are found in all amino acids. To make proteins in the body, many individual amino acids must be combined in the appropriate sequence for a specific product.

Figure 2.2
Oils and shortenings are concentrated sources of lipids. Courtesy of Plycon Press.

Some of the necessary amino acids can be produced in the body, which is why they are termed *non-essential amino acids*. Others must be available from food that is eaten because the body needs them but cannot make them. These are **essential amino acids**. There are nine essential amino acids, and these must be eaten in adequate amounts if a person is to be nourished adequately and maintain good health. In order to be sure to get an adequate intake of them, the diet needs to include food from animal sources (meat, poultry, fish, milk, eggs) and/or plants (legumes, cereals, nuts). If no animal sources are eaten, at least two of the plant sources should be included in the same meal to provide an adequate blend of complementary amino acids. The recommended balance of calories from carbohydrate, protein, and fat for people of different ages is presented in Table 2.1.

Minerals

Food contains many other components besides the nutrients that yield energy. Although they are present in much smaller quantities than the energy-yielding nutrients, **minerals** are widespread throughout the food supply in sufficient quantities to meet physical needs if a wide variety of foods is eaten. Actually, there are many different minerals. Those found in the largest amounts—calcium, phosphorus, potassium, sulfur, sodium, chloride, and magnesium—are termed *macrominerals*. The

essential amino acids Amino acids that must be provided in the diet to maintain life and promote growth; unable to be synthesized in the body.

minerals Natural elements in foods that remain as ash if a food is burned; many are essential nutrients.

[handwritten margin note: if no meat need 2 plant sources in meal]

Figure 2.3
Fish are important sources of protein and also omega-3 fatty acids. Courtesy of Plycon Press.

TABLE 2.1
RECOMMENDED MACRONUTRIENT PROPORTIONS BY AGE

	Carbohydrate (%)	Protein (%)	Fat (%)
Young children (1–3 years)	45–65	5–20	30–40
Older children and adolescents (4–18 years)	45–65	10–30	25–35
Adults (19 years and older)	45–65	10–35	20–35

Source: United States Department of Agriculture.

micronutrient minerals include iron, zinc, manganese, selenium, copper, and iodine, as well as some other minerals in minute quantities. The various minerals play different roles in the body, but they do not yield energy (Table 2.2). Because of the diverse functions and the wide range of foods providing significant sources of these minerals, it is essential to eat a varied diet.

vitamins Organic compounds needed in very small amounts by the body and that must be included in the diet to maintain life and promote growth.

Vitamins

If ever the general public viewed a group of nutrients as being pure magic, surely **vitamins** would be the group. Many people feel that swallowing a vitamin pill will solve all of their nutritional

TABLE 2.2
OVERVIEW OF FUNCTIONS AND SOURCES OF MINERALS NEEDED BY HUMANS

Mineral	Functions	Selected Food Sources
Calcium	Promote bone structure and maintenance, structure of teeth, blood clotting, muscle contraction	Milk and milk-containing products, including cheese; broccoli, greens
Chloride	Form hydrochloric acid in stomach, fluid balance, acid–base balance	Salt, meats, milk, cheese, eggs
Chromium	Promote glucose uptake in cells	Fruits, vegetables, whole-grain cereals
Cobalt	A component of vitamin B_{12}	Meats, organ meats
Copper	Catalyze hemoglobin formation, form connective tissue, energy release	Meats, cereals, nuts, legumes, liver, shellfish
Fluoride	Strengthen bones and teeth	Fluoridated water
Iodine	Form thyroxin to regulate basal metabolism	Iodized salt, ocean fish
Iron	Form hemoglobin and cytochromes for transporting oxygen and releasing energy, respectively	Meats, organ meats, dried fruits, whole-grain and enriched cereals
Magnesium	Promote energy reactions (ATP formation), bone maintenance, conduct nerve impulses	Milk, green vegetables, nuts, breads and cereals
Manganese	Develop bone, amino acid metabolism	Cereals, legumes
Molybdenum	Oxidation reactions	Legumes, meats
Phosphorus	Promote bone and tooth formation, bone maintenance; component of DNA, RNA, ADP, ATP, and TPP for metabolic reactions	Meats, poultry, fish, milk, cheese, legumes, nuts
Potassium	Maintain osmotic pressure and acid–base balance, transmit nerve impulses	Oranges, dried fruits, bananas, meats, coffee, peanut butter
Sodium	Maintain osmotic pressure and acid–base balance, relax muscles	Salt, cured meats, milk, olives, chips, crackers
Sulfur	A component of thiamin; part of structural proteins in hair, nails, and skin	Meats, milk, cheese, eggs, legumes, nuts
Zinc	Promote protein metabolism, transfer of carbon dioxide	Whole-grain cereals, meat, eggs, legumes

Note: ATP = adenosine triphosphate; DNA = deoxyribonucleic acid; RNA = ribonucleic acid; ADP = adenosine diphosphate; TPP = thiamin pyrophosphate

problems. Certainly vitamins are vital to life itself, but they represent only a portion of the nutrients people must eat in order to live, and they do not provide calories.

On the basis of their solubility, vitamins A, D, E, and K are classified as fat soluble and the B vitamins and vitamin C (ascorbic acid) are water soluble. The B vitamins include vitamin B_1 (thiamin), vitamin B_2 (riboflavin), vitamin B_3 (niacin), pantothenic acid, folacin (folic acid), vitamin B_6 (pyridoxine), vitamin B_{12} (cobalamin), and biotin.

Although vitamins are needed only in milligram or even microgram quantities daily, attention must be given to selecting foods containing these important substances and to preparing these foods carefully to retain the vitamin content. Unlike minerals, which tend to be held tightly within foods, vitamins may be leached out into the cooking medium or may undergo chemical changes during preparation, resulting in reduced nutritive value of the food as actually consumed. Throughout this book, comments are given regarding vitamin content of foods and ways of retaining optimal levels compatible with the preparation of high-quality food products.

The various vitamins perform a wide range of functions within the human body. Unless adequate amounts of the individual vitamins are provided in the diet, deficiency conditions will develop. The functions, food sources, and deficiency conditions for the various vitamins are presented in Table 2.3.

TABLE 2.3
VITAMINS, THEIR FUNCTIONS, SOURCES, AND DEFICIENCY CONDITIONS

Vitamin	Functions	Selected Food Sources	Deficiency Condition
Fat Soluble			
Vitamin A	Promotion of night vision, growth, health of eye and skin, resistance to bacterial infections	Liver, egg yolk, milk, sweet potatoes, carrots, greens	Night blindness, xerophthalmia, Bitot's spots, poor growth
Vitamin D	An aid in absorbing calcium and phosphorus	Vitamin-D fortified milk, eggs, cheese	Rickets, osteomalacia
Vitamin E	Spare vitamins A and C (prevent oxidation)	Vegetable oils, greens	
Vitamin K	Formation of prothrombin and proconvertin for blood clotting	Greens, liver, egg yolks	Hemorrhage
Water Soluble			
Thiamin	Release of energy (in TPP), form ribose for DNA and RNA synthesis	Meats, whole-grain and enriched cereals	Beriberi
Riboflavin	Release of energy (in FMN and FAD), convert tryptophan to niacin	Milk, green vegetables, fish, meat	Ariboflavinosis
Niacin	Release of energy (as part of NAD and NADP), fatty acid synthesis	Meat, poultry, fish, peanut butter, cereals	Pellagra
Pantothenic acid	Part of coenzyme A (to metabolize fatty acids), form hemoglobin and steroids	Whole-grain cereals, organ meats	Fatigue, lack of antibodies
Folacin	Transfer single-carbon units, make amino acids and other compounds	Greens, mushrooms, vegetables, fruits	Macrocytic anemia
Vitamin B_6	Transaminate and deaminate amino acids, convert tryptophan to niacin	Meats, whole-grain cereals, lima beans, potatoes	
Vitamin B_{12}	Aid in maturing red blood cells, energy for central nervous system, convert folacin to active form	Animal foods	Pernicious anemia
Biotin	Release energy, deaminate amino acids	Egg yolks, milk, cereals, nuts	
Vitamin C	Form connective tissue, absorption of calcium, strengthen capillaries	Citrus fruits, tropical fruits, tomatoes, cabbage	Scurvy

Note: TPP = thiamin pyrophosphate; DNA = deoxyribonucleic acid; RNA = ribonucleic acid; FMN = flavin mononucleotide; FAD = flavin adenine dinucleotide; NAD = nicotinamide dinucleotide; NADP = the phosphate form of NAD.

dietary reference intakes (DRIs) Recommended intake of nutrients needed by most healthy people on a daily basis to maintain healthy bodies.

http://fnic.nal.usda.gov/ nal_display/index.php?info_ center=4&tax_level=3&tax_ subject=256&topic_ id=1342&level3_id=5140

—Site for the DRI tables.

dietary guidelines for Americans, 2010 USDHHS and USDA dietary recommendations, 2010.

http://www.cnpp. usda.gov/Publications/ DietaryGuidelines/2010/ PolicyDoc/TOC.pdf

—Booklet on the 2010 dietary guidelines.

Dietary Reference Intakes

Complete understanding of nutrition and the body's use of nutrients has not yet been achieved, but much is known to help guide people in their quest for good health through wise food selection. To aid dietitians and other health professionals who work with groups to plan effectively for good nutrition, the Food and Nutrition Board of the Institute of Medicine, National Academy of Sciences, has developed **Dietary Reference Intakes**, often termed simply the DRIs for the macronutrients, vitamins, elements (minerals), and energy. The DRI values are reviewed by the Food and Nutrition Board at intervals of approximately five years, and adjustments are made in relation to the most recent research findings about the various nutrients.

ACHIEVING GOOD NUTRITION

Dietary Guidelines for Americans, 2010

Every five years the U.S. Department of Health and Human Services (USDHHS) and the U.S. Department of Agriculture (USDA) publish **Dietary Guidelines for Americans**, which presents recommendations for healthy eating based on current research in nutrition.

The most recent edition, *Dietary Guidelines for Americans,* 2010, identified two major objectives of importance for using nutrition as a means of achieving good health for a lifetime. These are

- Maintain calorie balance over time to achieve and sustain a healthy weight.
- Focus on consuming nutrient-dense foods and beverages.

Under each of these are recommendations for achieving them. Food choices, food safety, and physical activity are highlighted as the areas for planning and modifying behavior as needed to achieve optimum health through good nutrition throughout all stages of life.

Food Choices. The following are the guidelines for choosing nutrient-dense foods to provide the necessary nutrients within the calorie level that leads toward and maintains a healthful weight:

- Increase vegetable and fruit intake, focusing on a variety of vegetables, particularly red and orange ones, beans, and peas.
- At least half of grain choices should be whole grains.
- Select fat-free or low-fat milk and milk products (3 glasses or equivalent daily)
- Vary protein choices and emphasize seafood (8 ounces weekly), poultry, and soy within the recommended quantity.
- Keep fat intake low, minimizing solid (< 10 percent of calories) and *trans* fats and substituting them with oil where possible.
- Choose foods that are good sources of potassium, dietary fiber, calcium, and vitamin D and try to limit sodium intake (< 1,500 mg to 2,300 mg, depending on age) and cholesterol (< 300 mg per day).
- If consumed (and only by adults of legal drinking age), limit alcohol to one drink for a woman or two for a man.
- Limit sugar-sweetened and fruit beverages and foods with added sugar.
- Remember that undercooked animal foods and unpasteurized dairy products and juices pose a high risk for food-borne illnesses and should be avoided.

Specific recommendations for special groups are identified.

1. Women capable of becoming pregnant should choose foods with heme iron (red meats) as well as other foods rich in iron. They also should include rich sources of vitamin C and folate (400 μg from fortified foods or supplement).

2. Pregnant or lactating women should eat 8–12 ounces of seafood per week, but limit intake of white (albacore) tuna to 6 ounces weekly and avoid shark, tile fish, swordfish, and king mackerel. Pregnant women should take an iron supplement if recommended by a health care professional.

3. People of age 50 and older should select food sources fortified with vitamin B_{12} or take a supplement.

Food Safety. Food safety is an area of importance when considering food and its role in health. The basic principles identified in the *Dietary Guidelines* are (1) clean, (2) separate, (3) cook, and (4) chill. These issues are discussed in detail in Chapter 3. It is appropriate here to point out that these basic principles are included in the guidelines.

Physical Activity. Recommendations for physical activity are different for people of different ages. Below age 6, the suggestion is active play several times a day. From age 6 through adolescence, children should include 60 minutes of physical activity in each day's schedule, although this may occur in short bursts. The guidelines recommend that adults spend at least 2 1/2 hours weekly in physical activities of moderate intensity or at least 75 minutes weekly in vigorous aerobic activity (at least 10 minutes each time and spread through the week). Some adults will need five hours or more weekly as part of their program to achieve and maintain a healthy body weight.

Applying the 2010 Dietary Guidelines. Food plans for individuals need to be developed in relation to their current weight status so that calorie and activity levels can be coordinated with the objective of achieving and maintaining a healthy weight. Body mass index (BMI) is a useful measure in determining the appropriateness of body weight (Table 2.4). BMI calculations can be done easily by simply entering height and weight on the calculator at http://www.nhlbisupport.com/bmi/.

The calories needed for body maintenance (and growth for children) and activity are a key part of planning a diet that promotes good health. For people of a healthy weight, the calories listed in the category for age, weight, and activity level in Table 2.5 indicate the appropriate value to use in planning the total daily food intake. Persons needing to lose or gain weight will need to adjust the value, remembering that a deficit of 500 calories per day (3,500 per week) is needed to lose a pound of fat. The reverse is true for those who are trying to gain; they need a surplus of 500 calories daily. Patience and persistence are needed when eating to adjust weight because the changes often require many weeks and even months. Gradual change is recommended so that eating habits can be modified permanently to avoid reverting to an unhealthful weight.

The dietary guidelines include a comparison of eating patterns: the usual U.S. intake, the Mediterranean, DASH (Dietary Approach to Stop Hypertension), and USDA

http://www.nutrition.gov/nal_display/index.php?info_center=11&tax_level=1
—Convenient website to access much government information on food and nutrition.

http://www.hc-sc.gc.ca/fn-an/food-guide-aliment/index-eng.php
—Canadian food guide.

TABLE 2.4
CATEGORY OF BODY WEIGHT AS BODY MASS INDEX (BMI)[a]

Category	Children and Adolescents (BMI for age) (Percentile range)	Adults (BMI)
Underweight	Less than the 5th percentile	Less than $18.5\ kg/m^2$
Healthy weight	5th percentile to less than the 85th percentile	$18.5–24.9\ kg/m^2$
Overweight	85th percentile to less than the 95th percentile	$25.0–29.9\ kg/m^2$
Obese	Equal to or greater than the 95th percentile	$30.0\ kg/m^2$ or greater

Source: National Heart, Lung and Blood Institute.
[a]Adult BMI can be calculated at http://www.nhlbisupport.com/bmi/. A child and adolescent BMI calculator is available at http://apps.nccd.cdc.gov/dnpabmi/. 25. Growth charts are available at http://www.cdc.gov/growthcharts.

TABLE 2.5

ESTIMATED CALORIE NEEDS BY AGE, GENDER, AND ACTIVITY LEVEL[a]

Gender/Activity Level[b]	Male/ sedentary	Male/ moderately active	Male/active	Female[c]/ sedentary	Female[c]/ moderately active	Female[c]/active
Age (years)						
2	1,000	1,000	1,000	1,000	1,000	1,000
3	1,200	1,400	1,400	1,000	1,200	1,400
4	1,200	1,400	1,600	1,200	1,400	1,400
5	1,200	1,400	1,600	1,200	1,400	1,600
6	1,400	1,600	1,800	1,200	1,400	1,600
7	1,400	1,600	1,800	1,200	1,600	1,800
8	1,400	1,600	2,000	1,400	1,600	1,800
9	1,600	1,800	2,000	1,400	1,600	1,800
10	1,600	1,800	2,200	1,400	1,800	2,000
11	1,800	2,000	2,200	1,600	1,800	2,000
12	1,800	2,200	2,400	1,600	2,000	2,200
13	2,000	2,200	2,600	1,600	2,000	2,200
14	2,000	2,400	2,800	1,800	2,000	2,400
15	2,200	2,600	3,000	1,800	2,000	2,400
16	2,400	2,800	3,200	1,800	2,000	2,400
17	2,400	2,800	3,200	1,800	2,000	2,400
18	2,400	2,800	3,200	1,800	2,000	2,400
19–20	2,600	2,800	3,000	2,000	2,200	2,400
21–25	2,400	2,800	3,000	2,000	2,200	2,400
26–30	2,400	2,600	3,000	1,800	2,000	2,400
31–35	2,400	2,600	3,000	1,800	2,000	2,200
36–40	2,400	2,600	2,800	1,800	2,000	2,200
41–45	2,200	2,600	2,800	1,800	2,000	2,200
46–50	2,200	2,400	2,800	1,800	2,000	2,200
51–55	2,200	2,400	2,800	1,600	1,800	2,200
56–60	2,200	2,400	2,600	1,600	1,800	2,200
61–65	2,000	2,400	2,600	1,600	1,800	2,000
66–70	2,000	2,200	2,600	1,600	1,800	2,000
71–75	2,000	2,200	2,600	1,600	1,800	2,000
76+	2,000	2,200	2,400	1,600	1,800	2,000

Source: National Academies Press.

[a]Based on Estimated Energy Requirements (EER) equations, using reference heights (average) and reference weights (healthy) for each age–gender group. For children and adolescents, reference height and weight vary. For adults, the reference man is 5 feet 10 inches tall and weighs 154 pounds. The reference woman is 5 feet 4 inches tall and weighs 126 pounds. EER equations are from the Institute of Medicine. Dietary Reference Intakes for Energy, Carbohydrate, Fiber, Fat, Fatty Acids, Cholesterol, Protein, and Amino Acids. Washington, DC: The National Academies Press, 2002.

[b]Sedentary means a lifestyle that includes only the light physical activity associated with typical day-to-day life. Moderately active means a lifestyle that includes physical activity equivalent to walking about 1.5–3 miles per day at 3–4 miles per hour, in addition to the light physical activity associated with typical day-to-day life. Active means a lifestyle that includes physical activity equivalent to walking more than 3 miles per day at 3–4 miles per hour, in addition to the light physical activity associated with typical day-to-day life.

[c]Estimates for females do not include women who are pregnant or breastfeeding.

Food Pattern (Table 2.6). They also have information for lacto-ovo and vegan vegetarian diets (Table 2.7). For vegans, the dairy group includes calcium-fortified beverages and foods commonly used as substitutes for milk and milk products. These vegetarian variations represent healthy eating patterns, but rely on fortified foods for some nutrients. In the vegan patterns especially, fortified foods provide much of the calcium and vitamin B_{12},

TABLE 2.6
EATING PATTERN COMPARISON: U.S. USUAL INTAKE, MEDITERRANEAN, DASH, USDA FOOD PATTERN
INTAKE AT OR ADJUSTED TO A 2,000 CALORIE INTAKE

Pattern	Usual U.S. Intake Adults[a]	Mediterranean Patterns[b] Greece (G) Spain (S)	DASH[c]	USDA Food Pattern
Food Groups				
Vegetables: total (c)	1.6	1.2 (S)–4.1 (G)	2.1	2.5
Dark-green (c)	0.1	n.d.[c]	n.d.	0.2
Beans and peas (c)	0.1	<0.1 (G)–0.4 (S)	See protein foods	0.2
Red and orange (c)	0.4	n.d.	n.d.	0.8
Other (c)	0.5	n.d.	n.d.	0.6
Starchy (c)	0.5	n.d.–0.6 (G)	n.d.	0.7
Fruit and juices (c)	1.0	1.4 (S)–2.5 (G) (including nuts)	2.5	2.0
Grains: total (oz)	6.4	2.0 (S)–5.4 (G)	7.3	6.0
Whole grains (oz)	0.6	n.d.	3.9	>—3.0
Milk and milk products (dairy products) (c)	1.5	1.0 (G)–2.1 (S)	2.6	3.0
Protein foods				
Meat (oz)	2.5	3.5 (G)–3.6 (S) (including poultry)	1.4	1.8
Poultry (oz)	1.2	n.d.	1.7	1.5
Eggs (oz)	0.4	n.d.–1.9 (S)	n.d.	0.4
Fish/seafood (oz)	0.5	0.8 (G)–2.4 (S)	1.4	1.2
Beans and peas (oz)	See vegetables	See vegetables	0.4 (0.1 c)	See vegetables
Nuts, seeds, and soy products (oz)	0.5	See fruits	0.9	0.6
Oils (g)	18	19 (S)–40 (G)	25	27
Solid fats (g)	43	n.d.	n.d.	16[d]
Added sugars (g)	79	n.d.–24 (G)	12	32[d]
Alcohol (g)	9.9	7.1 (S)–7.9 (G)	n.d.	n.d.[e]

Source: United States Department of Agriculture.

[a]1 day mean intakes for adult males and females, adjusted to 2,000 calories and averaged.

[b]See the DGAC (Dietary Guidelines Advisory Committee) report for additional information and references at www.dietaryguidelines.gov.

[c]n.d. = Not determined.

[d]Amounts of solid fats and added sugars are examples only of how calories from solid fats and added sugars in the USDA Food Patterns could be divided.

[e]In the USDA Food Patterns, some of the calories assigned to limits for solid fats and added sugars may be used for alcohol consumption instead.

and either fortified foods or supplements should be selected to provide adequate intake of these nutrients.

USDA Food Patterns and DASH incorporate the 2010 *Dietary Guidelines* and provide a sound basis for planning meals and snacks. The Mediterranean diet follows a similar healthful pattern.

http://www.oldwayspt.org/mediterraneandiet
—Information on the Mediterranean diet.

MyPlate

The U.S. Departments of Health and Human Services and of Agriculture developed **MyPlate**, a visual to accompany the *Dietary Guidelines for Americans, 2010* (Figure 2.4). It is designed as a personal dietary aid and features a plate divided into four parts (red for fruits, green for vegetables, orange for grains, and purple for protein) and a blue circle for dairy on the side.

MyPlate Visual representing the relative amounts of foods from each of the five food groups that should be eaten daily.

TABLE 2.7
AVERAGE DAILY AMOUNTS IN THE PROTEIN FOODS GROUP IN THE USDA FOOD PLAN AT THE 2,000 CALORIE LEVEL AND ITS VEGETARIAN ADAPTATIONS

Food Category	USDA Food Pattern	Lacto-Ovo Adaptation	Vegan Adaptation
Meats (e.g., beef, pork, lamb)	1.8 oz-eq[a]	0 oz-eq	0 oz-eq
Poultry (e.g., chicken, turkey)	1.5 oz-eq	0 oz-eq	0 oz-eq
Seafood	1.2 oz-eq	0 oz-eq	0 oz-eq
Eggs	0.4 oz-eq	0.6 oz-eq	0 oz-eq
Beans and peas[b]	N/A	1.4 oz-eq	1.9 oz-eq
Processed soy products	<0.1 oz-eq	1.6 oz-eq	1.4 oz-eq
Nuts and seeds[c]	0.5 oz-eq	1.9 oz-eq	2.2 oz-eq
Total per day	**5.5 oz-eq**	**5.5 oz-eq**	**5.5 oz-eq**

Source: United States Department of Agriculture.

[a]Amounts shown in ounce-equivalents (oz-eq) per day. These are average recommended amounts to consume over time.

[b]Beans and peas are included in the USDA Food Patterns as a vegetable subgroup rather than in the protein foods group. Amounts shown here in the vegetarian patterns are additional beans and peas, in ounce-equivalents. One ounce-equivalent of beans and peas is 1/4 cup, cooked. These amounts do not include about 1 1/2 cups per week of beans and peas recommended as a vegetable in all of the 2,000 calorie patterns.

[c]Each ounce-equivalent of nuts is 1/2 ounce of nuts, so on a weekly basis, the 2,000 calorie patterns contain from 2 ounces to 8 ounces of total nuts.

http://www.choosemyplate.gov

—MyPlate information in depth, including individual food planning and tracking individual eating progress.

Fruits and vegetables cover half the plate, with vegetables covering a little larger part than fruits. Grains (at least half should be whole grain) and protein foods occupy the other half; the space for protein is noticeably less than for grains.

Recommendations accompanying MyPlate emphasize:

- Enjoying food, but eating less.
- Switching to fat-free or low-fat (1 percent) milk.
- Choosing foods containing less sodium.
- Drinking water instead of sugary drinks.

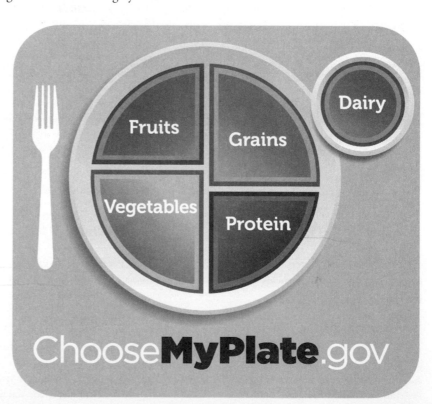

Figure 2.4
MyPlate is the graphic developed to illustrate the diet recommended for good health. Courtesy of the U.S. Department of Agriculture.

Buying Good Nutrition

Most people need to buy most or all of their food and many of the decisions are made in the grocery store. Ideally, well-planned menus and an accurate shopping list provide the basis of shopping decision. However, such preparations often are not done, and impulse buying may dominate food purchases. When this occurs, some nutrient-dense foods (milk, for example) may be forgotten, and high-calorie, low-nutrient snack items (soft drinks are just one popular example) may find their way into the shopping basket. Since the food that is carried home is the food that makes up much of the food eaten that week, these shopping decisions definitely shape the nutrient intake of the family.

Nutrition Labeling.   The Food and Drug Administration (FDA) has responsibility for **nutrition labeling**, a system designed to inform shoppers about the nutrient content of foods. Regulations for nutrition labeling are very specific and are revised if deemed necessary. The most recent revision, in 2006, was the addition of information about the level of *trans* fats. Consideration currently is being given to possible designation of foods that are gluten free, information that is sought by people needing to avoid eating foods containing gluten because of their allergic response to it. Such labeling provides valuable insights into the nutritional adequacy of menus if shoppers study the labels (Figure 2.5).

nutrition labeling   Label on packaged foods indicating the caloric and nutritive content of a serving of the item according to specific federal guidelines.

http://www.nytimes.com/2011/01/25/business/25label.html?_r=1&emc=eta1

—Label for front of package developed by Grocery Manufacturers Association and the Food Marketing Institute, a trade group that represents retailers.

http://www.dailyfinance.com/2011/01/24/usdas-new-green-label-can-you-trust-it/

—Critique of green labeling.

http://www.efitnessnow.com/news/2011/01/25/new-nutrition-facts-label-unveiled/

—Introduction of new Nutrition Facts label.

Nutrition Facts

Serving Size 3 oz
(84g/about ½ stalk)
Servings Per Container about 2.5

Amount Per Serving	
Calories 30	Calories from Fat 0

	% Daily Value*
Total Fat 0g	**0%**
Saturated Fat 0g	**0%**
Cholesterol 0mg	**0%**
Sodium 20mg	**1%**
Total Carbohydrate 5g	**2%**
Dietary Fiber 3g	**11%**
Soluble Fiber 1g	
Sugars 0g	
Protein 3g	

Vitamin A 25%	•	Vitamin C 110%
Calcium 4%	•	Iron 4%

* Percent Daily Values are based on a 2,000 calorie diet. Your daily values may be higher or lower depending on your calorie needs:

	Calories:	2,000	2,500
Total Fat	Less than	65g	80g
Sat Fat	Less than	20g	25g
Cholesterol	Less than	300mg	300mg
Sodium	Less than	2,400mg	2,400mg
Total Carbohydrate		300g	375g
Dietary Fiber		25g	30g

Figure 2.5

Nutrition Facts label. Courtesy of the U.S. Department of Agriculture.

Retaining Nutrients in Food

Nutrients, particularly vitamins, may be lost during food preparation. Fortunately, these losses can be kept to a minimum if certain precautions are observed.

Water Solubility.   Some nutrients, notably the water-soluble vitamins, may be dissolved into the surrounding cooking water during preparation. This is not a problem if all of the cooking liquid is to be consumed with the food, as would be the case in a soup, but it does represent a problem in such items as boiled vegetables.

Loss of water-soluble nutrients can be minimized by not soaking foods in water. By using as little cooking water as is consistent with producing a palatable result, losses during cooking can be kept low. Another good practice is to keep cooking times as short as possible so that the time for leaching the water-soluble vitamins from foods will be brief.

Cut surfaces increase solubility losses. If foods can be pared and/or cut into the desired pieces after cooking, the vitamin content can be kept higher than is the case if considerable cut surface area is exposed throughout the period of boiling.

Heating.   Intense heat may cause proteins to be utilized less well by the body than is the case when mild cooking temperatures are used. This is particularly true of excessively high temperatures used in some deep-fat frying or in some instances of baking. The length of time for heating is also of concern, not only for proteins in foods but also for vitamins, particularly some of the B vitamins, such as thiamin. As much as is consistent with palatability, foods should be cooked at moderate temperatures for a short time. Microwave heating can help to retain nutrients because it shortens cooking time, but this method of heating may not produce the characteristics desired in some food products.

Oxidation.   Certain nutrients, particularly some of the vitamins (vitamin C, vitamin A, thiamin, riboflavin, vitamin B_6, and folacin) and the polyunsaturated fatty acids, may be unable to perform their usual roles in the body because of oxidation. Such reactions occur when cut surfaces are exposed to air. Paring and cutting foods (e.g., potatoes) close to the time they are to be cooked and/or served can reduce oxidative losses. The practice of dipping pieces of cut fruit in some acidic fruit juice is an effective means of preventing air from oxidizing the vitamin C or other vitamins in foods.

Light.   A few nutrients are sensitive to light and will lose their vitamin activity when exposed to light for a period of time. Riboflavin is the nutrient that is most sensitive to light. This B vitamin, which is particularly abundant in milk, is reduced significantly in its activity if milk is allowed to sit in sunlight in clear glass containers, which explains why milk is packaged in opaque containers. Although also light-sensitive, vitamins E, K, and B_6 are much more stable to light than is riboflavin.

pH.   The pH—that is, whether acidic or alkaline—of the medium in which a food is placed will have an effect on the nutritive value of the food. Most vitamins (particularly thiamin) are quite stable in acids, but they are unstable in an alkaline medium, which occurs if baking soda is added or if extremely hard water is used.

SUMMARY

Food quality is a term that broadly defines all aspects of a food, including the original ingredients, the sanitary handling of the food, and its preparation and service. To obtain food of an acceptable quality, people may select from a variety of approaches to suit their lifestyles. Some may elect to prepare foods from the basic ingredients because of the creative aspects of preparation or because of the desire to avoid food additives. Others may prefer to use convenience foods and do a minimum of preparation, while still others may eat away from home.

Regardless of the style of food selected, the ultimate goal is to eat the nutrients needed to achieve and maintain optimal health. These nutrients include the energy nutrients—carbohydrates, fats (lipids), and proteins—which are important for forming tissues and many other compounds in the body as well as providing energy. Minerals are needed to help form the body's structure and many compounds within the body. They also help to maintain the normal balance of acids and bases in the body and to attain water balance in various bodily components. Even the transmission of nerve impulses requires the presence of minerals. The last category of nutrients is the vitamins, including the fat-soluble vitamins (vitamins A, D, E, and K) and the water-soluble B vitamins (thiamin, riboflavin, niacin, pantothenic acid, folacin, vitamin B_6, vitamin B_{12}, and biotin) and vitamin C.

The Dietary Reference Intakes, the amounts of the essential nutrients that are needed by people of various ages, are specified in the Food and Nutrition Board of the Institute of Medicine, National Academy of Sciences, and are used by dietitians and other health professionals in their roles of planning, feeding, and counseling about food and diets. *Dietary Guidelines for Americans, 2010*, presents extensive information for helping individuals select a diet that will afford the necessary amounts of these various nutrients. MyPlate is a visual illustrating how to implement these guidelines into daily eating. People can develop their own personal plan that includes appropriate servings of milk and dairy products, meats and meat alternatives, fruits, vegetables, and breads and cereals. Some help in food selection is available by using nutrition labeling. This gives considerable information about the nutrients in many canned and packaged items.

To retain the nutrients in foods that are purchased, careful preparation needs to be done to avoid extensive losses, particularly losses of vitamins. Nutrient losses can be minimized by keeping cooking times short and at moderate temperatures and avoiding excessive contact with water, oxygen, light, and alkali.

STUDY QUESTIONS

1. Keep a record of all of the food you eat for three days. Compare your food intake with the recommendations for MyPlate. Identify the groups where your intake was adequate and those where you did not meet the recommendation.

2. What suggestions can you make to yourself to improve your usual nutrient intake?

3. Go to the grocery store and read nutrition labeling on some canned products, some cereals, breads, and frozen foods. What information did you find to help you in making wise food choices?

4. What are four ways to reduce nutrient losses when you are preparing fruits and vegetables?

5. Why is nutrition an important subject to consider when studying food preparation?

SELECTED REFERENCES

Anonymous. July 19, 1990. Food labeling; reference daily intakes and daily reference values; mandatory status of nutrition labeling and nutrient content revision; serving sizes; proposed rules. *Federal Register 55*(130): 29476–29533.

Berry, D. 2010. Diet food by any other name. *Food Product Design 20*(11): 18.

Brandt, M. B., et al. 2010. Tracking label claims. *Food Technol. 64*(2): 34.

Committee on Diet and Health. 1989. *Diet and Health*. Food and Nutrition Board. National Research Council, National Academy of Sciences. National Academy Press. Washington, DC.

Dietary Guidelines Advisory Committee. 2011. *Dietary Guidelines for Americans, 2010*. 3rd ed. Department of Agriculture and Department of Health and Human Services. Washington, DC.

Flegal, K. M., et al. 2010. Prevalence and trends in obesity among U.S. adults, 1999–2008. *JAMA 303*(3): 235–241.

Harris, M., et al. 2009. Communicating the net benefits of seafood consumption. *Food Technol. 63*(11): 38.

Hazen, C. 2010. Reducing sodium: Maintaining flavor and functionality. *Food Product Design 20*(7): 84.

Hazen, C. 2010. Baking sans *trans*. *Food Product Design 20*(8): 32.

Health and Human Services Department. 2005. *A Healthier You: Based on the Dietary Guidelines for Americans*. U.S. Government Printing Office. Washington, DC.

Kelly, F. 2011. Being upfront with front-of-pack labeling. *Food Technol. 65*(1): 41.

McWilliams, M. 2008. *Fundamentals of Meal Management*. 5th ed. Prentice Hall. Upper Saddle River, NJ.

McWilliams, M. 2011. *Food Around the World*. 3rd ed. Prentice Hall. New York.

Mermelstein, N. H. 2009. Analyzing for mercury in food. *Food Technol. 63*(9): 76.

Nachay, K. 2008. Combating obesity. *Food Technol. 62*(2): 24.

Newsome, R. 2010. Feeding the future. *Food Technol. 64*(7): 49.

Nord, M., et al. 2010. *Household Food Security in the United States, 2009*. Washington, DC: U.S. Department of Agriculture, Economic Research Service. 2010 Nov. Economic Research Report No. ERR-108.

Pleis, J. R., et al. 2009. Summary health statistics for U.S. adults: National Health Interview Survey, 2008. *Vital Health Stat. 10*(242): 1–157.

Remig, V., et al. 2010. *Trans* fats in America: Review of their use, consumption, health implications, and regulation. *J. Amer. Dietet. Assoc. 110*(4): 585.

Spano, M. 2010. Heart health and fats. *Food Product Design 20*(3): 22.

Spano, M. 2010. The skinny on fiber and weight management. *Food Product Design 20*(9): 24.

Spano, M. 2011. Plant-based proteins. *Food Product Design 21*(2): 20.

Stewart, H., et al. 2006. *Let's Eat Out: Americans Weigh Taste, Convenience, and Nutrition*. U.S. Department of Agriculture, Economic Research Service, Economic Information Bulletin No. 19.

Swientek, B. 2008. Importance of food safety. *Food Technol. 62*(5): 109.

Troiano, R. P., et al. 2008. Physical activity in the United States measured by accelerometer. *Med. Sci. Sports Exerc. 40*(1): 181–188.

Whitney, E. N., and S. R. Rolfes. 2004. *Understanding Nutrition*. 10th ed. Wadsworth. Belmont, CA.

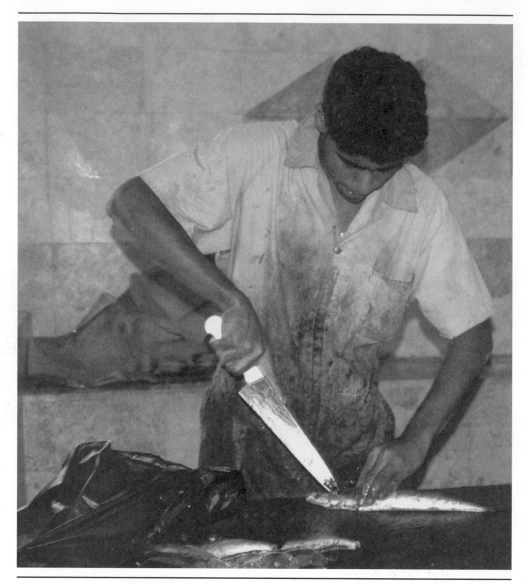

A fish market on the Arabian Peninsula presents the perfect storm for food-borne illness: a hot day, lack of refrigeration, a worker with dirty clothes and hands, filthy counter and floor, and lack of water for keeping surfaces clean. Courtesy of Plycon Press.

3
Food Safety

Chapter Contents

Key Concepts

1. Food safety requires careful temperature control of foods from farm to table.

2. Enforcement of high standards of sanitation for all food handlers is needed in all environments where food is being stored, prepared, and served.

3. Food-borne illnesses, ranging from causing physical discomfort to death, can be caused by various bacteria, viruses, molds, parasites, and chemicals that may be found in some foods that have not been refrigerated properly and handled safely.

4. The FDA regulates additives that may be incorporated in food products for a variety of reasons, for example, to improve nutritional value, enhance such sensory characteristics as flavor, and for other reasons specified by law.

5. Several federal agencies share responsibility for the safety of the nation's food supply.

INTRODUCTION

Food is not only vital to human survival but also is used by certain microorganisms (e.g., *Escherichia coli, Clostridium botulinum*) and parasites for their sustenance and reproduction. When those that are dangerous to people find their way into foods, the potential for food-borne illnesses begins. Harmful and infective agents may be introduced during any of the following steps:

- Growing
- Harvesting
- Marketing (including transportation and storage)
- Storing and preparing (in the home or in commercial operations)

Food usually reaches consumers via restaurants, fast-food outlets, and supermarkets and other retail outlets after it has traveled an extended route from farm to dining table, and much can happen somewhere along the way. In 2010, over 500 million eggs were recalled after more than 1,500 people became ill when they ate undercooked eggs infected with *Salmonella* (ultimately traced to two egg producers in Iowa). Another outbreak that year (affecting about 89 people in a total of 15 states and the District of Columbia) was traced to raw alfalfa sprouts contaminated with *Salmonella*.

These are but two of numerous cases of food-borne illnesses. In fact, 48 million cases are estimated to occur in the United States annually, but the causes of only about a fifth of these are determined. In 2010, norovirus apparently caused 5.5 million cases; various types of bacteria were responsible for 3.9 million cases, among which were non-typhoidal *Salmonella* spp. (more than a million illnesses and 378 deaths), *Clostridium perfringens* and

http://www.safe-poultry.com/preventionandcontrol.asp
—Recommendations for controlling *Salmonella* in poultry.

http://www.cdc.gov/eid/content/17/1/7-T2.htm
—CDC 2010 data on cases of food-borne illness.

Campylobacter spp., *Listeria* (1,591 illnesses, with 255 deaths), and forms of *E. coli* (more than 175,000 illnesses and 20 deaths). Hospital admissions included patients with non-typhoidal *Salmonella* spp. (35 percent), norovirus (26 percent), *Campylobacter* spp. (15 percent), and *Toxoplasma gondii* (8 percent). Of these cases, those resulting in death (in descending order) were non-typhoidal *Salmonella* spp., *T. gondii, Listeria monocytogenes,* and norovirus.

Serious outbreaks are not just a recent occurrence. The 1993 outbreak of illness caused by viable *E. coli* O157:H7 in hamburgers sold at several outlets of a fast-food chain focused national attention on the potentially fatal outcome if microorganisms are allowed to flourish in a food that is consumed without adequate heat treatment to kill the pathogens. Since then numerous outbreaks have been traced to environmental contamination of field crops, processing plants, and food service on cruise ships and in commercial facilities.

In 2006, spinach contaminated with *E. coli* O157:H7 sickened more than 200 people and caused three deaths. The origin of this outbreak was traced to the spinach fields where the offending bacteria were found in fecal material from feral pigs or other wildlife in the area (Figure 3.1). In another outbreak of food-borne illness, unpasteurized fruit juices containing *E. coli* O157:H7 resulted in at least 49 identified infections and one death. This happened despite the fact that similar problems were identified in unpasteurized fruit juices several years earlier.

A major recall in July 2007 resulted when cases of botulism were traced to canned meat products that had not been heated adequately to kill spores of *C. botulinum.* Other prominent cases include a hepatitis A outbreak caused when strawberries harvested in fields lacking adequate toilet facilities for workers were frozen and ultimately served in school lunch programs in Michigan and a few other states. Increasingly, such problems are being detected in our food supply because of the large amounts of fresh produce being imported from around the world. Food safety is becoming an international problem. Shellfish from waters contaminated with human waste have also been the source of such food-borne infections as hepatitis A. In major outbreaks, newspapers, radio, television, and Internet news stories are important in alerting people when recalls are made.

The frequency of food recalls has resulted in the 2011 Food Safety Modernization Act (FSMA). This legislation, which is designed to give the FDA greater enforcement powers, has three major thrusts:

- Increased frequency of inspections
- Required certification by an accredited third-party auditor for imported foods and facilities
- Establishing a product-tracing system that allows the agency to effectively track and trace foods, particularly those on the list of high-risk foods.

http://www.fda.gov/ NewsEvents/Newsroom/ PressAnnouncements/ 2007/ucm108873.htm

—FDA summary of the 2006 outbreak from contaminated raw spinach.

http://www.ift.org/ food-technology/ newsletters/ift-weekly- newsletter/2011/ january/011011.aspx

—Summary of Food Safety Modernization Act.

Figure 3.1
Geneticist Michael Cooley collects a sediment sample to test for *E. coli* O157:H7. The pathogen was found near fields implicated in the 2006 outbreak of *E. coli* O157:H7 on baby spinach.
Courtesy of Agricultural Research Service.

POTENTIAL MICROORGANISMS IN FOODS

Types of Microorganisms

Bacteria, molds, parasites, and viruses are types of microorganisms that can cause food spoilage and/or food-borne illnesses. The food substrates each of these types prefers vary from one to another. Consequently, the care of food during storage and preparation varies with the type of food and its likely contaminants.

Bacteria are the type of microorganism most commonly causing food-borne illnesses. These microscopic organisms are single-celled and vary in shape, being possibly filament-like, rod-shaped, round, or spiral. When live bacterial cells are consumed, they may create symptoms ranging from general discomfort to nausea, vomiting, and even death. Although many bacteria grow well in a wide range of foods, sugar and salt concentrations that create an unfavorable osmotic pressure can destroy bacteria by dehydration.

Classification of bacteria may be done on the basis of adaptability to oxygen requirements or temperature levels. On the former basis, bacteria are **aerobic** or **anaerobic**, depending on their need for oxygen for survival. Aerobic bacteria will die if they lack an adequate supply of oxygen. Conversely, anaerobic bacteria flourish in an oxygen-free system. Bacteria that are able to reproduce rapidly at temperatures well above room temperature are classified as **thermophilic** (heat loving), and those thriving at cold temperatures are **cryophilic** (cold loving). Clearly, there are some bacteria capable of adapting to many of the conditions employed in storing foods.

Molds are usually multicellular and often form a filament topped by a head with spores that scatter when food containing a colony of mold is moved. Molds can be seen sometimes on cheeses and some other foods, such as loaves of breads made without preservatives and stored at room temperature. The moisture level maintained in a tightly wrapped loaf of bread is just right for molds to flourish. However, molds can remain viable even if a food has been stored at moisture levels as low as 13 percent, a characteristic that makes molds the most troublesome of the microorganisms to control in the storage of dried foods.

The visibility of molds on foods helps to avoid the problem of food poisoning from them. However, a few molds produce **mycotoxins** that are poisonous. Perhaps the most familiar example is **aflatoxin**, the mycotoxin sometimes found in stored moldy peanuts, a problem particularly in some parts of Africa.

Viruses that can be food- and water-borne are rather small, spherical viruses that contain single-strand DNA (deoxyribonucleic acid) or RNA (ribonucleic acid). The two that have been particularly prominent problems in foods are hepatitis A and noroviruses. The virus particle is inactive in a food until ingested by a receptive host. Replication of the virus occurs in the host's cells, not in the food, but viruses can survive in foods for very long times. Contamination of food by these viruses can be from fecal origin or from vomit. Control of viral food-borne illness requires elimination of any possible contamination from fecal matter or vomit.

AGRICULTURAL INSIGHT
MAD COW DISEASE

Examples of potential food hazards during production have received worldwide press coverage and generated considerable efforts to minimize identified risks in the future. For example, **mad cow disease** (actually named bovine spongiform encephalopathy, or BSE), a fatal disease in cattle, has been linked to new variant **Creutzfeldt–Jakob disease (CJD)** in humans. This is classified as a **prion** disease; a prion is an abnormal agent characterized by abnormal folding of prion proteins in the brain and if transmitted results in a fatal condition in the host (Figure 3.2).

Outbreaks of mad cow disease have resulted in huge economic losses to cattle farmers in Britain and several other countries. Infected herds had to be destroyed in

(Continued)

---

bacteria Round, rod-shaped, or spiral single-celled microorganisms in soil, water, or organic matter.

aerobic Requiring air for survival.

anaerobic Living without air.

thermophilic Thriving in warm temperatures.

cryophilic Cold loving

molds Filamentous, often wooly fungi that can thrive on damp surfaces, such as cheeses.

mycotoxins Toxic substances produced by some molds.

aflatoxin Mycotoxin produced by molds (*Aspergillus flavus* or *Aspergillus parasiticus*) in some food crops, for example, peanuts grown in mold-contaminated soil or stored in a damp place.

virus Submicroscopic molecules composed of genetic material surrounded by a protein coat; some can cause diseases in their host.

mad cow disease Fatal disease of the central nervous system sometimes occurring in cows caused by eating feed containing infected meat and bone meal; another name for bovine spongiform encephalopathy (BSE).

Creutzfeldt–Jakob disease Fatal brain disease in humans that can be contracted by eating beef from cattle with mad cow disease.

prion Abnormal agent that is transmitted to cause a fatal condition characterized by abnormal folding of prion proteins in the brain, as in BSE.

http://www.cdc.gov/
ncidod/dvrd/prions/
—Information on prion
diseases, including BSE.

http://www.fda.gov/Anim
alVeterinary/Resourcesfor
You/AnimalHealthLiteracy/
ucm136222.htm
—FDA site for BSE
information.

(Continued)

1986 and subsequent years to prevent continuing spread of the disease to animals throughout the world. The infection originally spread through sale of animal feed containing animal tissue from infected sheep whose BSE did not produce immediate symptoms. International efforts are being made to prevent the spread of the disease by regulating the sources of cattle feed. The United States has been able to mostly avoid contamination by BSE due to a ban on feeding scrapie-infected tissue as far back as 1932 and the important ruminant feed ban that has been in effect since 1997. Additionally the United States has been proactive in putting up necessary firewalls to protect the U.S. food supply and its exports.

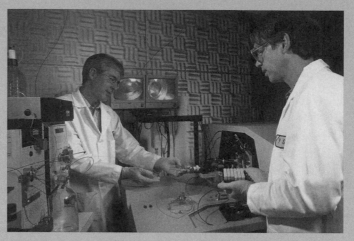

Figure 3.2
Chemist Chris Silva (left) and research leader J. Mark Carter load samples to characterize BSE prions with unprecedented precision using nanospray liquid chromatography coupled to mass spectroscopy. Courtesy of Agricultural Research Service.

FOOD-BORNE ILLNESSES

Not surprisingly, the food that is so helpful in supporting life and growth for humans also can be just what microorganisms need to flourish. Therefore, basic knowledge of food microbiology needs to be applied when preparing and serving food to ensure that the products you prepare will be safe to eat.

Bacterial Poisoning

http://www.cdc.gov/
foodsafety/diseases/
—Centers for Disease
Control site information
about food-borne illnesses.

http://www.cdc.gov/
foodsafety
—Food-borne illnesses and
food safety information.

When present in food, several different microorganisms classified as bacteria are capable of causing illness among people. Among the comparatively common bacteria capable of causing illness when they are eaten are strains of *Salmonellae, Streptococci, Clostridia,* and *Staphylococci.* Illnesses resulting from eating food contaminated with *Salmonella* species or *C. perfringens* are classified as food infections. *Salmonella* and other food-borne bacterial poisonings are identified in Table 3.1.

Illnesses caused by eating foods containing the toxins produced by *Staphylococcus aureus* and *C. botulinum* are classified as food intoxication. To persons afflicted with the very unpleasant symptoms triggered either directly by the bacteria or by the toxin produced by some, this distinction is of little concern. The main focus of the victim in the throes of an episode is more likely to be the temporary conflict between wishing to live or wishing to die.

TABLE 3.1
SOME FOOD-BORNE ILLNESSES FROM BACTERIA

Name of Illness	What Causes It	Symptoms	Characteristics of Illness	Control Measures
Salmonellosis	Salmonellae. Bacteria widespread in nature that live and grow in intestinal tracts of human beings and animals. About 1,200 species are known; one species causes typhoid fever. Bacteria grow and multiply at temperatures between 44° and 115°F (6–46°C).	Severe headache, followed by vomiting, diarrhea, abdominal cramps, and fever. Infants, elderly, and persons with low resistance are most susceptible. Severe infections cause high fever and may even cause death.	Transmitted by eating contaminated food or by contact with infected persons or carriers of the infection. Also transmitted by insects, rodents, and pets. Onset: usually within 12–36 hours. Duration: usually 2–7 days.	Salmonellae in food are destroyed by heating the food to a temperature of 140°F (60°C) and holding for 10 minutes or to higher temperatures for less time. Refrigeration at 45°F (7°C) inhibits the increase of Salmonellae, but they remain alive in the refrigerator or freezer and even in dried foods.
Perfringens poisoning	Clostridium perfringens. Spore-forming bacteria that grow in the absence of oxygen. Spores can withstand temperatures usually reached in cooking most foods. Surviving bacteria continue to grow in meats, gravies, and meat dishes held without proper refrigeration.	Nausea without vomiting, diarrhea, acute inflammation of stomach and intestines.	Transmitted by eating food contaminated with abnormally large numbers of bacteria. Onset: usually within 8–20 hours. Duration: may persist for 24 hours.	To control growth of surviving bacteria on cooked meats that are to be eaten later, cool meats rapidly and refrigerate promptly at 40°F (5°C) or below.
Staphylococcal poisoning (frequently called staph)	Staphylococcus aureus. Bacteria fairly resistant to heat. Bacteria growing in food produce a toxin that is extremely resistant to heat. Bacteria grow profusely with production of toxin at temperature between 44° and 115°F (6–46°C).	Vomiting, diarrhea, prostration, abdominal cramps. Generally mild and often attributed to other causes.	Transmitted by food handlers who carry the bacteria and by eating the food containing the toxin. Onset: usually within 3–8 hours. Duration: 1–2 days.	Growth of bacteria that produce toxin is inhibited by keeping hot foods above 140°F (60°C). Toxin is destroyed by boiling for several hours or heating the food in pressure cooker at 240°F (116°C) for 30 minutes. (Continued)

TABLE 3.1 (Continued)

Name of Illness	What Causes It	Symptoms	Characteristics of Illness	Control Measures
Botulism	*Clostridium botulinum.* Spore-forming organisms that grow and produce toxin in the absence of oxygen, such as in a sealed container. The bacteria can produce a toxin in low-acid foods that have been held in the refrigerator for two weeks or longer. Spores are extremely heat resistant. Spores are harmless, but the toxin is a deadly poison.	Double vision, inability to swallow, speech difficulty, progressive respiratory paralysis. Fatality rate is high, in the United States about 65 percent.	Transmitted by eating food containing the toxin. *Onset:* usually within 12–36 hours. *Duration:* 3–6 days.	Bacterial spores in food are destroyed by high temperatures obtained only in a pressure canner. More than 6 hours is needed to kill the spores at boiling temperatures (212°F or 100°C). The toxin is destroyed by boiling for 10–20 minutes; time required depends on kind of food.
Listeriosis	*Listeria monocytogenes.* Bacteria widespread in nature, particularly in animals. Multiplies slowly in cold to below freezing.	Fever, nausea, vomiting, diarrhea, fatigue; severe cases include meningitis, septicemia, endocarditis.	Transmitted by eating under-heated animal foods containing *L. monocytogenes.* *Onset:* 12 hours. *Duration:* 5–10 days.	Avoid unpasteurized milk and soft cheese made from unpasteurized milk. Heat meats and fish to at least 160°F (71°C).
Campylobacter infection	*Campylobacter.* Found commonly in intestinal tract of pigs, poultry, and cattle. Easily killed by heat.	Fever, headache, muscle pain, diarrhea, nausea, stomach pain.	Transmitted by drinking untreated water or raw milk or by eating undercooked poultry or meat.	Don't drink untreated water or unpasteurized milk. Avoid cross contamination after handling raw poultry and meat. Heat poultry and meat to at least 160°F (71°C).
Traveler's diarrhea	May be caused by a wide variety of microorganisms, including bacteria such as enterotoxigenic *E. coli* and enteropathogenic *E. coli*, amoebae, and viruses.	Vomiting, diarrhea.	Transmitted by eating contaminated raw or undercooked foods. *Onset:* 8–44 hours. *Duration:* 24–30 hours.	Tight sanitation control. Adequate refrigeration of meat and poultry. Pasteurization of juices. Heat ground meats to at least 160°F (71°C) and other meats to at least 145°F (63°C). Heat poultry to at least 170°F (77°C).
Yersiniosis	*Yersinia enterocolitica*	Diarrhea, joint pain.	Transmitted by eating undercooked pork or raw milk. *Onset:* 4–7 days. *Duration:* 3 weeks or longer.	Cook pork to 170°F (77°C); pasteurize milk.

Salmonellosis *Salmonella* is a type of bacterium (Figure 3.3) capable of causing the gastrointestinal illness called **salmonellosis**. (The nomenclature recognizes the research of D. E. Salmon in 1885.) The symptoms of salmonellosis develop between 6 and 72 hours after eating the infected food, with 12 hours being the customary incubation period prior to evidence of symptoms. Evidence of salmonella infection includes abdominal cramps, fever, nausea, and diarrhea. Susceptibility to developing salmonellosis varies from one individual to another, but infants and people who already are sick are likely candidates. However, even healthy adults can develop salmonellosis if they eat a food with a high count of viable *Salmonella*. The increasing numbers of cases of salmonellosis being diagnosed may be the result of more problems with food sanitation, or it may simply mean that diagnosis is being done with increased accuracy, resulting in identification of the cause of the problem rather than the vague description of "something he ate."

Salmonellae are found commonly in protein foods such as pork, poultry, and eggs. To prevent serious episodes of intoxication by *Salmonellae*, keep foods containing these items at refrigerator temperatures or above the danger zone (above 140°F (60°C)) and minimize storage in the danger zone (40° to 140°F (5° to 60°C)). Frozen storage does not kill all *Salmonellae* in a food; even a storage period of six months at 0°F (–18°C) still is not sufficient to kill all *Salmonellae*. To ensure safety from *Salmonellae* infection, heat foods that might contain these bacteria to at least 140°F (60°C) and hold for 10 minutes, or use a somewhat higher temperature for a shorter period.

Yersiniosis *Yersinia enterocolitica* in raw milk or pork can cause yersiniosis, a bacterial illness that may last three weeks or longer. These bacteria are related to *Yersinia pestis*, which caused the historically important bubonic plague. This problem can be avoided by pasteurizing milk and cooking pork adequately.

Perfringens Poisoning **Perfringens poisoning** is the result of the presence of an anaerobic bacterium, ***Clostridium perfringens***. This bacteria is found in meats and meat dishes, and it can form spores that are extremely resistant to heat. The obvious means of protecting against

Salmonella Type of bacteria capable of causing severe gastrointestinal upset when ingested in large quantities in a food.

salmonellosis Food-borne illness characterized by fever, nausea, abdominal cramps, and diarrhea caused by eating food contaminated with viable *Salmonella*.

Yersinia enterocolitica Bacteria sometimes found in raw and undercooked pork and raw milk, which cause yersiniosis.

Perfringens poisoning Food-borne illness caused by eating food containing viable *C. perfringens*.

Clostridium perfringens Anaerobic, spore-forming bacteria that multiply readily at room temperature; ingestion can result in perfringens poisoning.

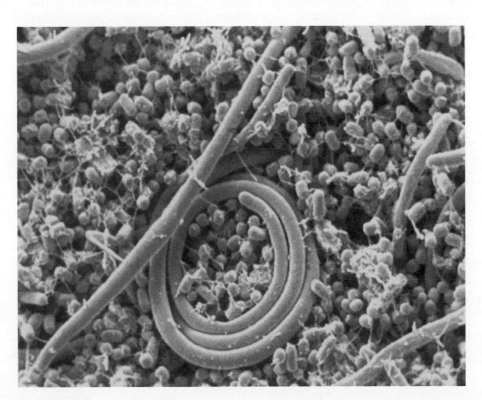

Figure 3.3
Salmonella enteritidis, a strain of *Salmonella* that can cause salmonellosis. Courtesy of Agricultural Research Service.

this type of food contamination is to avoid infecting the meat and to prevent rapid reproduction and increase in population. By avoiding storage at room temperature, this hazard can be reduced.

Meats and meat-containing dishes should be served soon after they are prepared, or held for service at 140°F (60°C), and leftovers should be refrigerated promptly, not being allowed to sit on the kitchen counter for hours while cooling. Careful temperature control minimizes the reproductive capacity of these bacteria and is very important because of the strong resistance to heat exhibited by the spores when they have formed. The usual practice of simply heating foods to a temperature of 165°F (74°C) or more is not effective in killing *C. perfringens*. Avoidance of growth is the key to reducing the possibility of contracting perfringens poisoning.

Nausea is a key symptom of perfringens poisoning. Vomiting does not occur, but there is a general feeling of discomfort due to irritation of both the stomach and the intestines.

toxin Poisonous substance produced by metabolic reactions; *S. aureus* and *C. botulinum* are the bacteria most commonly responsible for food poisoning from toxins.

Staphylococcal Infection   Staphylococcal **toxin** infections (also referred to as *staph*) from food are common. This is due primarily to the ease with which infected food handlers transmit *staphylococci*. The signs prominently displayed in restrooms cautioning people to be sure to wash their hands well with soap are a public effort to help eliminate staph infections. The infection is evidenced by vomiting, diarrhea, and stomach cramps and is due to eating food containing the toxin produced by *Staphylococcus aureus*. This strain of bacteria reproduces with vigor in the danger zone between 44°F (6°C) and 115°F (46°C), resulting in a dangerous level of toxin in a matter of hours. Symptoms are evident within three to eight hours after ingestion and last for a day or two (although to the victim, it seems more like an eternity).

INDUSTRY INSIGHT
TSP

Salmonella contamination of poultry has grabbed public attention because of the widespread potential for causing salmonellosis. Many ideas have been pursued to try to reduce the problem. In 1992, the Food and Drug Administration authorized the use of trisodium phosphate (TSP) in a special process to reduce *Salmonella* counts. Processors adjust the pH of the subsequent rinse by adding some acid to compensate for the alkaline pH created by the TSP.

Tests have shown that application of TSP to chickens following emergence from the chill tank can reduce *Salmonella* levels to less than 5 percent (compared with levels as high as 40 percent in untreated chickens). TSP is providing one means of reducing the risk of salmonellosis. Due to environmental concerns, the poultry and chemical industries are constantly designing alternative treatments that can reduce pathogenic microorganisms like *Campylobacter* and *Salmonella*. These include the use of oxidizing agents such as ozone and acid compounds like organic acids.

As an added means of assuring that poultry is safe to eat, consumers are also receiving information about safe handling in the home. Presently, the U.S. Department of Agriculture (USDA) is requiring labels on poultry and meats telling consumers basic information for safe handling (Figure 3.4).

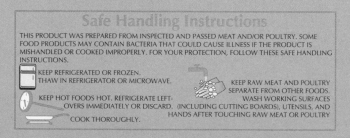

Figure 3.4
Safe handling instructions are placed on packages of meat and other foods that may present a risk of bacterial infection if not handled suitably. Courtesy of U.S. Department of Agriculture.

SCIENCE NOTE
PH, TEMPERATURE, AND OSMOSIS

Microorganisms can cause food-borne illnesses when they are alive and present in significant quantities capable of overcoming the body's defenses. Food safety can be achieved by killing any microorganisms that might be present. One technique used is to lower the pH of the medium by adding acid to the point where microorganisms cannot grow. This technique is used in making pickles.

Heat is a particularly effective means of killing microorganisms. Canning is a preservation technique that works because the very high temperatures used are sufficient to kill all of the microorganisms that might be present. Heat and acidity interact in the canning of fruits. The comparatively high acidity (low pH) of fruits makes it possible to can them safely by boiling the cans or jars for a prescribed, acceptably brief time without added pressure. However, vegetables are not very acidic, so they need to be processed at a temperature hotter than 212°F (100°C). By using a pressure canner, the necessary temperature can be reached and the vegetables are preserved safely.

Jams and jellies are a means of preserving fruit by adding a large amount of sugar. The concentration of sugar outside the cell walls is far greater than that inside the cell walls of microorganisms. The result is that osmotic pressure develops and draws out the water in the cells of the microorganism, effectively killing any that might be present.

Staphylococcal poisoning is thought to be a major cause of diagnosed cases of food poisoning in the United States, despite the frequent warnings issued on the safe handling of food. The foods that are particularly vulnerable to invasion and production of staphylococcal toxin include baked ham, creamed foods, poultry, cream pies, and milk and cheese products of all types. These types of foods require particularly careful attention to adequate refrigeration or to control of temperatures above 140°F (60°C) to retard growth of staph and development of the toxin.

The toxin, once formed, is very resistant to heat, requiring boiling for several hours or cooking under pressure at 15 pounds per square inch (psi) for 30 minutes to render the toxin harmless to humans. Such extreme treatment decreases food quality; clearly, prevention of toxin formation is the important measure in preventing staphylococcal poisoning.

Vibrio cholerae is another toxin-forming bacterium, and this one is a significant health hazard in parts of the world where food and water supplies are contaminated with fecal matter. Cholera, the illness caused by *Vibrio cholerae*, results in severe diarrhea and dehydration. Death results quickly unless effective rehydration is done very promptly. Two other important *Vibrio* species are *V. vulnificus* and *V. parahaemolytica*. These are both possible contaminants of raw seafood and can cause serious illness and death. *V. vulnificus* has a very high mortality rate compared to other bacteria.

Botulism   The other familiar type of bacterial poisoning from a toxin is **botulism**, a type of food poisoning that frequently may be fatal (Figure 3.5). The cause is ingestion of the toxin produced by any of several strains of ***Clostridium botulinum***. The problem originates when foods contaminated with *C. botulinum* are not heat processed adequately to kill the spores prior to anaerobic storage for a period of time.

Because these bacteria can survive nicely in an oxygen-free environment, some canned products may be subject to toxin production. The very heat-resistant spores of *C. botulinum* may not have been killed during the canning process. The problem is found most commonly in canned, low-acid foods such as vegetables and meats, poultry, or fish. Fruits, because of their acidity, are not receptive to the survival of *C. botulinum,* and an adequate heat treatment during canning is not difficult to accomplish.

Ingestion of the toxin is not always fatal, but it often is; the approximate statistic is that two out of three people who are infected will die. The toxin is so potent that a mere 0.35 micrograms of it will kill an adult.

The symptoms of botulism generally are related to the functioning of the nervous system, with the most severe reactions occurring in the respiratory system. Death, if it occurs, is caused ultimately by paralysis of the respiratory muscles. The initial symptoms are observed 12–36

Staphylococcal poisoning
Food poisoning due to ingestion of enterotoxin produced by *S. aureus*; violent disturbances of gastrointestinal tract for one or two days and occurring usually within eight hours of ingestion.

Vibrio cholerae   Bacterium sometimes found in foods and water with fecal contamination; causes cholera.

botulism   Food poisoning caused by eating the toxin produced by *C. botulinum*; human infection is most commonly associated with types A, B, or E.

Clostridium botulinum
Type of bacteria producing a toxin that is highly poisonous and frequently fatal to humans when consumed.

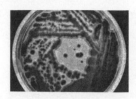

Figure 3.5
Culture of *Clostridium botulinum* type B. Its toxin can be found in canned meats and vegetables if they are not processed to a high enough temperature for a sufficient time.
Courtesy of U.S. Department of Agriculture.

hours after ingestion of the food containing the toxin. If a patient survives until the ninth day, the prognosis for recovery is good, although the recuperative process may be quite slow.

Occasional instances of botulism result from home-canned foods that have been processed inadequately, with the result that some spores of *C. botulinum* survive and the toxin is generated within the can. Although similar problems can occur in commercial canning, standards of quality control generally are far in excess to ensure avoiding this potential risk. Even so, an occasional scare does develop. Such episodes are publicized extensively in the media, and potentially hazardous items (cans from the problem lot) are recalled and removed from all markets.

To avoid problems, home-canned vegetables, meat, poultry, and fish should be boiled actively for 15 minutes prior to even tasting them. This is not necessary with fruits, because their acid generally is sufficient to discourage *C. botulinum* growth.

An important requisite for home canning any vegetables, fish, poultry, or meat is a pressure canner, for this is the only way that the food can be brought to a temperature high enough to ensure inactivation of the spores. In a pressure canner, the temperature will reach 240°F (116°C) if the food is processed at a pressure of 15 psi, which allows adequate heat processing for safety within a reasonable period of time.

People processing these low-acid foods must maintain pressure at the appropriate 15 psi throughout the required processing time. The safe processing period ordinarily is at least 25 minutes at 15 psi, but the number and size of containers being processed will influence the recommendation. Since the time–temperature relationships are so critical to achieving safety in canned vegetables and meats, careful timing is essential for the number of minutes indicated at the correct pressure in a pressure canner.

Listeria monocytogenes
Type of bacteria that can cause listeriosis; sometimes found in unpasteurized milk.

listeriosis Potentially very serious food-borne illness caused by ingesting viable *L. monocytogenes*.

Listeriosis   *Listeria monocytogenes* can cause humans to develop **listeriosis** in 12 hours to 6 weeks after eating food contaminated with this type of bacteria. The symptoms are described in Table 3.1 on page 33. Actually, *L. monocytogenes* can be found widely in farm animals and rural environs, which means that careful sanitation is important in preventing the bacteria from entering the food supply.

Prevention or avoidance of contamination is especially important because *L. monocytogenes* can survive and multiply at refrigerator temperatures; heat, acid, and salt also are of limited effectiveness in preventing multiplication and/or in killing the bacteria. Contamination needs to be avoided by

1. using only pasteurized milk and dairy products;
2. keeping raw foods separate from cooked foods until very close to serving time;
3. keeping all cutting boards and other items that contact food meticulously clean;
4. washing all raw foods before eating;
5. maintaining foods below 40°F (5°C) or above 140°F (60°C); and
6. cooking poultry to 180°F (82°C) and other meats and fish to 160°F (71°C).

Campylobacter jejuni
Type of bacteria sometimes found in poultry and meats.

Campylobacter Infection   *Campylobacter* bacteria can be found in the intestinal tract of meat animals and poultry, which can mean that they might be found in some meats. ***Campylobacter jejuni*** contamination in water, unpasteurized milk, and raw and undercooked meats has caused illness and some deaths. However, heating all meats and poultry to at least 160°F (71°C) will destroy any *Campylobacter* that might be present. Untreated water and unpasteurized milk are other potential sources of contamination, but pasteurization or boiling will assure safety from *Campylobacter*.

escherichia coli (E. coli)
Group of bacteria often found as the cause of food-borne illnesses.

Escherichia coli   Depending upon the specific type of ***Escherichia coli*** ingested, infections caused by *E. coli* (Figure 3.6) may be classified as enteroinvasive, enterotoxigenic, or enterohemorrhagic. The most common type is enterotoxigenic, often called traveler's diarrhea, which usually strikes between 8 and 44 hours after eating *E. coli* and lasts about 24–30 hours. There usually is an outpouring of fluid in the form of diarrhea and possible vomiting, which leads to dehydration, but does not invade the epithelial tissue of the small intestine.

In contrast, *E. coli* O157:H7 is classified as enterohemorrhagic; it is manifested by bloody diarrhea and may lead to renal failure due to this organism's ability to produce virulent toxins in the host. The cause of *E. coli* O157:H7 infections is linked to eating undercooked meat, raw milk, unpasteurized juices, and contaminated leafy greens. This type of infection has received great media attention since the first outbreak in 1993, which was traced to a fast-food operation and that had tragically fatal consequences.

Shigella Fecal contamination is usually the source of **Shigella boydii**, a type of bacteria that can cause shigellosis and bacillary dysentery. By using chlorinated water and practicing good sanitation standards when handling food, food workers can prevent this food-borne illness.

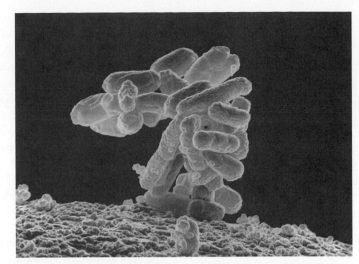

Viral Poisoning

Food-borne viruses have become a growing concern, including hepatitis A virus, which causes a highly infectious disease that affects the liver. Hepatitis A virus is most often associated with contaminated food handlers, which reinforces the great need for good hygiene and hand-washing practices. Virus particles may be shed in the feces of contaminated persons for 1–3 weeks without the person knowing he or she is sick. This can potentially lead to the infection of many people.

Another food-borne virus was identified on some cruise ships carrying large numbers of passengers who had severe symptoms that involved the gastrointestinal tract. These outbreaks and subsequent ones have been traced to **noroviruses** on the ships. Outbreaks of norovirus are not confined only to cruise ships; group feeding situations have also suffered from norovirus contamination. Norovirus can be associated with any food that is handled or processed, but fortunately the illness usually runs its course within 48 hours.

These viruses may be found in tainted water or may be spread by infected food handlers. This problem underscores the importance of food handlers practicing such significant sanitary measures as washing hands thoroughly in hot, soapy water before handling food and after using the bathroom.

Parasites

Sometimes foods are contaminated with small living organisms, occasionally in the egg or larval stages. If consumed in a viable state, these organisms (called **parasites**) may remain in the body and proceed through the reproductive and total life phases, relying on a parasitic relationship with the host. Such foreign organisms can pose serious health hazards.

Figure 3.6
Low-temperature electron micrograph of a cluster of *E. coli* bacteria. Each individual bacterium is oblong shaped. Courtesy of Agricultural Research Service.

Shigella boydii Bacteria spread by fecal contamination in water or food.

noroviruses Virus that can cause hepatitis A, spread easily through contaminated water and by infected unsanitary food handlers who fail to wash their hands adequately in hot, soapy water.

parasite Organism living within another organism and deriving its sustenance from the host; worms, such as *Trichinella spiralis*, can cause weight loss and other health problems in people.

CULTURAL ACCENT
SOY SAUCE

Oriental cultures have been highly creative in developing food products from soybeans. One of the most ubiquitous of these products is soy sauce. Although many different versions of soy sauce exist, the basic preparation involves cooking, salting, and fermenting soybeans and aging this brew for an extended period (sometimes two years or longer). The initial cooking kills microorganisms, and the high salt content effectively creates osmotic pressure that prevents growth of microorganisms during the storage period.

Making soy sauce is a very effective means of obtaining a food product from soybeans that can be used safely for a few years. The other side of the coin is that the extremely high sodium content fosters high blood pressure in susceptible people.

Figure 3.7
Trichinella spiralis
larva encapsulated in
muscle. Courtesy of U.S.
Department of Agriculture.

trichinosis Illness caused
by eating viable *T. spiralis,*
a parasite sometimes
contained in undercooked
pork.

Trichinella spiralis
Parasite sometimes found
in pork; causes trichinosis
in humans.

Cyclospora cayetanensis
Protozoan (type of parasite)
that can cause cyclosporiasis
when consumed.

cyclosporiasis Food-borne
illness caused by eating
produce contaminated with
C. cayetanensis.

shellfish poisoning
Life-threatening
poisoning from saxitoxin
produced in shellfish
feeding on *Gonyaulax
catanella;* characterized
by loss of strength and
respiratory failure.

saxitoxin Neurotoxin
from *G. catanella* that
accumulates in shellfish
during conditions of red
tide; causes shellfish
poisoning and can be fatal.

Trichinosis is the most familiar parasitic disease in this country. The problem stems from eating meat, notably pork, that contains larvae of **Trichinella spiralis**. The presence of these larvae is fairly rare today, but the feeding of uncooked garbage to pigs (the most likely source of parasitic contamination) still occurs occasionally.

Since the potential exists for pork to be contaminated with *T. spiralis* (Figure 3.7) and since there is no way of detecting it by governmental inspection, appropriate cooking precautions need to be taken to kill any parasites that might be present. The heating of pork to an internal temperature of 170°F (77°C) is the recommended way of ensuring against eating viable trichinae. Actually, the parasites are killed when the internal temperature of a cut of pork reaches at least 140°F (60°C), but the higher temperature (160°F or 71°C) is recommended to ensure a suitable margin of safety without impairing the palatability of the meat. A meat thermometer is a convenient tool for measuring the degree of doneness in the center of the cut. Another means of killing trichinae is by freezing at 0°F (−18°C) for a minimum of one day or at 5°F (−15°C) for at least 20 days.

Although rarely fatal, trichinosis can be debilitating over an extended period. The larvae first are confined to the intestinal region, but they soon mature and produce larvae within the host before they die. Ultimately, the trichinae invade the muscular areas of the body only to become encapsulated in cyst-like formations that may be viable as long as 10 years in the host. Symptoms in severe infestations may include diarrhea, nausea, and vomiting, but such reactions are intermittent. Over a period of weeks, recurring fever and muscular pains accompany the migration of larvae within the body. Treatment with thibenzole aids in controlling the course of the illness.

Parasitic invasions are not limited to *T. spiralis*. Other worms may be introduced from a variety of sources, but the most common route is via the water supply. Filtering of water is necessary when the water supply is unsafe. Potable water also should be used to wash all fresh fruits and vegetables carefully to help avoid possible parasites. The other source of contamination may be food handlers who are careless about keeping their hands and their working areas in the kitchen clean.

Cyclospora cayetanensis is a protozoa (a different type of parasite) that garnered attention in 1995 and 1996 when outbreaks of **cyclosporiasis** occurred in the United States. Both of these were traced to imported produce that was contaminated with *C. cayetanensis*. Additional outbreaks have also been occurring, and these also have been traced to fresh produce that carried it. Contamination often may occur when produce is harvested in fields where toilets are not available for field-workers. International efforts are being focused on standards that need to be maintained if food is to be imported into other countries.

The symptoms of cyclosporiasis generally are fairly mild and begin about a week after consumption of the contaminated food. It is possible for protozoa to survive freezing for a period of time. Careful washing of all fresh produce is recommended to avoid this problem; however, this type of contamination is not at all common in the United States at the present time.

Contaminants in Fish

Possible problems with environmental contaminants are certainly not a phenomenon of the past couple of decades. The maxim to eat oysters only in months with an *r* in their names emerged long before the current concern over detrimental changes in the environment, apparently because some people eating oysters in the summer months became ill. This illness, called **shellfish poisoning**, was and still is transmitted through scallops, clams, and mussels, as well as oysters, at certain times of the year.

During the summer months and early fall, a one-celled organism, *Gonyaulax catanella,* is an abundant food for shellfish. In extremely large concentrations, this organism actually causes the fluorescence and reddish coloring of ocean water known familiarly as red tide. However, somewhat lesser concentrations (insufficient to cause red tide) still have the potential for causing shellfish poisoning when contaminated oysters or other shellfish are eaten.

The substance secreted by *G. catanella* that actually causes the poisoning is saxitoxin, which is toxic enough to kill people but is not poisonous to the shellfish host. **Saxitoxin** accumulates in the digestive gland of the shellfish and may increase within a matter of three or four days from levels barely detectable to lethal.

If a shellfish containing saxitoxin is eaten, the poison acts with startling rapidity, for death can ensue in as little as two hours after ingestion. Symptoms begin with a loss of strength in the extremities and the neck, followed by failure of the respiratory system. The quantity of poison ingested is a factor in determining whether or not the patient will survive. If the shellfish has been fried in oil and eaten as part of a large meal, the toxic effects will be less than in other circumstances. Artificial respiration is an important aid in treating cases involving the respiratory system.

The most obvious means of avoiding this poisoning is to avoid shellfish from uncontrolled areas during times of possible problems. The risk can also be reduced by holding shellfish in clear water for a period of time to provide the opportunity for the shellfish to eliminate some of the poison. Oysters dissipate the saxitoxin relatively quickly, mussels are rather slow in eliminating saxitoxin, while butter clams are extremely slow.

The potential for shellfish poisoning can be reduced still further after the holding period in clear water by frying the shellfish meat or using steam or boiling water to help destroy the potency of the saxitoxin. Very high cooking temperatures and plenty of water to leach out the toxin are two effective methods to help reduce potential risk of shellfish poisoning.

Commercial fish canneries heat shellfish in steam to reduce greatly the amount of poison that might be present. Chemical tests provide yet another check against the toxin. In addition, the commercial harvesting of clams and mussels is done under the control of the government to reduce the hazard further.

Although shellfish poisoning is particularly dramatic, both ocean and freshwater fish are subject to other possible environmental hazards. Contaminated waters can cause contaminated fish. The presence of mercury, the result of uncontrolled effluents from factories into local waters, has been responsible for episodes of mercury poisoning from fish (swordfish, for example) and other seafood, such as some oysters harvested off the coast of Japan. Protests about such contamination and improved monitoring have helped to reduce the problem.

Fish are extremely susceptible to spoilage during marketing because the enzyme systems in fish are active at somewhat lower temperatures than are optimal for land animals, which makes appropriate handling imperative. Icing of fish helps to keep the temperature low enough to retard spoilage. Special attention is needed in handling oysters or other fish that might be consumed raw and in storing shrimp, for they may be eaten whole, digestive tract and all. Even with such precautions, fish will spoil quickly, necessitating either consumption within a day or two or else prompt processing (freezing, canning, or drying).

http://www.fda.gov/ Food/FoodSafety/ FoodborneIllness/ FoodborneIllnessFood bornePathogensNatural Toxins/BadBugBook/ default.htm

Bad Bug Book— information about disease-causing microorganisms that might be in food.

SOURCES AND CONTROL OF MICROORGANISMS

Many varieties of bacteria, yeasts, and molds may appear in foods being marketed to consumers. These microorganisms are present as a result of numerous possibilities: the soil in which plant foods are grown may contain microorganisms; crops may be fertilized with natural fertilizers containing viable microorganisms; the storage containers of trucks or other conveyances may have microorganisms remaining from previous loads; even the air may transport microorganisms into the food supply. These are not the only possible sources of contamination; people handling food from field to market are yet another significant source of contamination. In short, there is little possibility that a food will not encounter some form of microorganism at some point before it reaches the consumer.

Fortunately, consumers can protect themselves from food-borne microorganisms by paying attention to the way in which they handle and prepare food. Thorough washing of fresh produce before storage and before preparation removes many of the microorganisms clinging to these items.

Similarly, thorough washing of hands with soap and water before handling food is an effective way of reducing the contamination by food handlers. To minimize contamination, people handling food should not have colds, flu, or other contagious diseases, such as tuberculosis.

Adequate temperature control of protein-containing foods is essential to retard the growth of microorganisms in milk, egg products, meats, fish, poultry, gelatin, and other foods of this type. By keeping these foods in the temperature range below 40°F (4.4°C) and above 140°F (60°C), the reproduction of many microorganisms will be kept to an absolute minimum, which is vital to food safety (Figure 3.8).

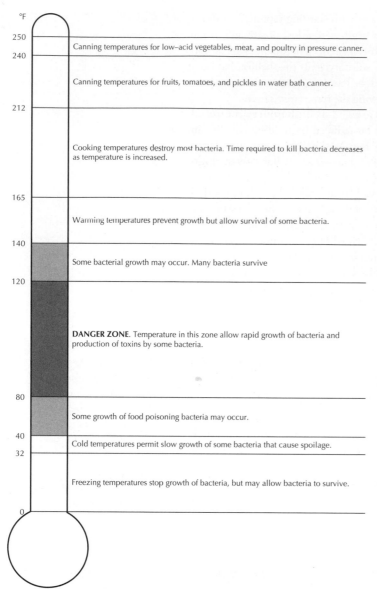

°F

250
240 ── Canning temperatures for low-acid vegetables, meat, and poultry in pressure canner.

── Canning temperatures for fruits, tomatoes, and pickles in water bath canner.

212

── Cooking temperatures destroy most bacteria. Time required to kill bacteria decreases as temperature is increased.

165

── Warming temperatures prevent growth but allow survival of some bacteria.

140
── Some bacterial growth may occur. Many bacteria survive

120

── **DANGER ZONE**. Temperature in this zone allow rapid growth of bacteria and production of toxins by some bacteria.

80
── Some growth of food poisoning bacteria may occur.

40
── Cold temperatures permit slow growth of some bacteria that cause spoilage.
32

── Freezing temperatures stop growth of bacteria, but may allow bacteria to survive.

0

Figure 3.8
Temperatures relative to controlling bacterial growth in food. Courtesy of Plycon Press.

High temperatures are important to kill viable microorganisms present in foods before they are eaten. For instance, pasteurizing milk or cooking pork to a uniform interior temperature of 170°F (76.7°C) will ensure that these foods are perfectly safe to eat, even though they may have contained microorganisms before being heated.

Although foods have been heated enough to kill microorganisms in them, careful attention to temperature control still is essential for assuring safety of protein-containing foods. These types of food may be contaminated again by food handlers or other agents, and the new microorganisms will flourish unless the food is stored at refrigerator or steam table temperatures— that is, below 40°F (5°C) or above 140°F (60°C).

WHY THE CONCERN?

Microbiological contamination is a concern throughout the world, for contamination results in both economic and human losses. Considerable loss of food occurs due to spoilage, either before reaching the consumer or while being stored by the consumer. Spoilage at any time represents an economic loss, whether to the farmer, the middlemen in the marketing chain, the retailer, or the consumer. Losses incurred prior to sale to the consumer ultimately will be reflected in increased costs to the purchaser at the point of sale. Unfortunately, losses do not stop there. Foods stored at home also are susceptible to spoilage by microorganisms. For instance, if some potatoes spoil while being held in a bag, they are thrown away, clearly adding to the cost of food.

With the worldwide concern about adequate supplies, food spoilage translates dramatically into human terms. For instance, grain that ferments before distribution represents a tragic loss to those needing the food simply for survival. And when food is scarce, even contaminated food may be eaten, causing serious health problems, as sometimes is the case when moldy peanuts are distributed for consumption. Although not always life threatening, a food-borne illness will certainly make people wish to avoid a recurrence of the discomfort. Such episodes represent not only an unpleasant period for the person afflicted but also an economic loss because of work time lost during the illness. No good figures are available to tell accurately the cost of food-borne illnesses, but the problem is all too common, particularly when most episodes could be avoided with improved food handling practices.

ADDRESSING THE PROBLEM

The food industry can take steps to avoid the initial contamination and also to remove or kill microorganisms and other viable invaders before moving the food into the marketing chain. Food safety is dependent upon what is allowed to enter a particular food and the treatment it receives until it is consumed. At home and in food service operations, people need to maintain sanitary kitchens, discard food that obviously is contaminated, wash fresh produce and meats, avoid cross contamination of surfaces, maintain correct temperature controls, and practice good personal hygiene. Anyone handling and/or preparing food needs to be aware of the hazards that it can harbor and should always follow safe sanitary practices and temperature controls.

If living microorganisms, insects, and/or parasites are present in foods that can support their lives, they will multiply until they are removed from the food by washing or are killed

INDUSTRY INSIGHT
HACCP

Although a system was designed in the 1960s to aid in assuring that food reaching the public is safe, it was only in the 1990s that the food industry moved aggressively to implement its use. **Hazard Analysis and Critical Control Points (HACCP)**, the system with a cumbersome name, is being utilized today by the food industry and food service operations, such as hospitals. In fact, worldwide interest is developing as increasing globalization of the food supply is occurring.

Government agencies involved in monitoring and regulating the safety standards of the American food supplies (notably the Food and Drug Administration and the Food Safety and Inspection Service, FSIS) base their programs on HACCP. In 1996, the Food Safety and Inspection Service of the U.S. Department of Agriculture issued its Pathogen Reduction and HACCP Final Rule, which required meat and poultry processing plants to establish and utilize HACCP plans that assure compliance with required standards for safe products continually.

Hazard Analysis and Critical Control Points is a seven-point system that is developed by each food company to create a food safety program that uniquely fits the particular company. Each company's plan for HACCP is to include

1. Analysis of hazards that may occur and ways of preventing occurrence of the hazards.
2. Identification of critical control points where identified hazards can be prevented or reduced.
3. Establishment of preventive measures with critical limits (specific temperature and time limits, for example) at each critical control point.
4. Establishment of a monitoring system at each critical control point.
5. Plans for corrective action if monitoring indicates failure to meet a critical limit at any critical point.
6. Establishment of a record-keeping system that documents all of the above actions.
7. Establishment of verification of the HACCP plan to be sure the plan is effective.

HACCP is utilized in the food industry to help reduce pathogens in foods and enhance food safety, but some outbreaks of food-borne illnesses still occur.

---

by such destructive conditions as adequate high heat, irradiation, or dehydration. Five microorganisms have been identified by the Centers for Disease Control as having high infectivity via food contaminated by infected food handlers: norovirus, *Salmonella typhi*, enterohemorrhagic or *Shiga* toxin-producing *E. coli, Shigella* spp., and hepatitis A virus.

The Food and Drug Administration (FDA) and the Centers for Disease Control and Prevention (CDC) of the U.S. Department of Health and Human Services (HHS) and the Food Safety and Inspection Service of the U.S. Department of Agriculture (USDA) jointly publish and frequently revise the ***Food Code,*** a document intended as a model code and reference for state, city, county, and tribal agencies to apply to regulate food safety in restaurants, retail food stores, vending operations, and food-service operations in institutions such as schools, hospitals, nursing homes, and child-care centers (Figure 3.9).

In *Food Code 2009,* the five key areas identified where food safety may be impacted are:

- Improper holding temperatures,
- Inadequate cooking, such as undercooking raw shell eggs,
- Contaminated equipment,
- Food from unsafe sources, and
- Poor personal hygiene

These problems need to be addressed at all levels to help reduce the incidence of food-borne illness nationally and around the world. Several federal agencies have the responsibility and authority to establish and enforce preventive measures that can be taken all along the food chain. The Food Safety Modernization Act was passed in 2011 and is intended to ensure the U.S. food supply is safe by shifting the focus of federal regulators from responding to contamination to preventing it.

The Food and Drug Administration in the Department of Health and Human Services has particularly broad responsibilities for a safe food supply. Labeling requirements for the majority of foods (not meat, poultry, or fish), regulation of food additives, and inspection of many food plants are under the jurisdiction of the Food and Drug Administration. Programs focusing on consumer education about food safety also are found in its domain. The Centers for Disease Control (home of the Food Safety Office), another powerful agency in the Department of Health and Human Services, focuses on food-borne illnesses.

Hazard Analysis and Critical Control Points (HACCP) Seven-point system developed by each food company to create its own food safety program.

food code Code issued jointly by FDA, CDC, and FSIS that guides government agencies overseeing safety in food service operations.

http://www.fda.gov
—Food and Drug Administration website.

http://www.fda.gov/ Food/FoodSafety/ RetailFoodProtection/ FoodCode/FoodCode2009/
—Text of *Food Code 2009.*

http://www.fda.gov/Food/ FoodSafety/fsma/default. htm
—FDA Food Safety Modernization Act (FSMA)

Figure 3.9
Galleys on cruise ships are just one of the settings in which the guidelines in the *Food Code* and HACCP are applied to help assure safe food for diners. Courtesy of Plycon Press.

Fight Bac®   FDA's food safety education program based on four points: clean; separate; cook; and chill.

http://www.fightbac.org/ safe-food-handling

—Information on FDA's Fight Bac program.

Inspection of meat and poultry are the domain of the Food Safety and Inspection Service under the Department of Agriculture. Other agencies in the same department include the Agricultural Marketing Service and the Agricultural Research Service. The National Marine Fisheries Service is housed in the Department of Commerce. Inspection and safety of seafood and freshwater fish are the responsibilities of this agency. Many states and counties have similar agencies overseeing food safety and presenting food safety information to food companies, retailers, food service operations, and consumers.

Some additives which are components of many commercial food products can be used to help maintain the safety of the food, while others are added for diverse reasons that are outlined later in this chapter. The discussion of additives is included because of the preservative benefits of specific ones and because of the quality benefits contributed by others.

Even when food is safe from harmful levels of microorganisms when brought into the kitchen, the potential for food-borne illnesses still exists. Whether in a commercial food establishment or in the home, standards of hygiene need to be maintained in all aspects of food preparation. It is important to remember that cross contamination, time–temperature abuse, and poor personal hygiene are major causes of food-borne illnesses. The FDA developed **Fight Bac**® as its food safety education program for businesses and consumers. Its four-point message is:

- Clean: Wash hands and surfaces often.
- Separate: Don't cross contaminate.
- Cook: Cook to proper temperature.
- Chill: Refrigerate promptly.

There are four key areas to check when monitoring safety in food handling: (1) personal hygiene of the food handler, (2) kitchen sanitation, (3) cooking temperatures, and (4) storage conditions and practices.

Food Handler Hygiene

Habits that may prevent transport of microorganisms from the food handler to the food are vital to maintaining high standards of sanitation. As a starting point, all people handling food should be sure to wash their hands thoroughly with soap and hot water before beginning preparation and again at any time that the hands are used to touch hair or blow the nose. Any restroom stop should end with a thorough hand washing with hot water and soap before returning to the kitchen or laboratory. Disposable gloves are to be worn in commercial kitchens after washing hands and before handing food. In addition, personal habits, such as licking fingers or playing with a lock of hair, need to be recognized and eliminated.

Although tasting is necessary to be sure that seasonings are right, only clean utensils should be used. Tasting utensils should be used only once. Otherwise, the taster's saliva will contaminate the food.

Kitchen Sanitation

Clean food can only be prepared in a clean kitchen. All dishes need to be scrubbed thoroughly, washed in soap or detergent and hot water, and rinsed thoroughly in very hot water. Both the heat of the water and the sanitizing afforded by the detergent and a good rinsing are valuable in killing microorganisms that might otherwise remain and contaminate food subsequently.

To avoid cross contamination, all surfaces in the food preparation area should be washed carefully with soap and water after each use, with particular attention being given to such difficult areas as the rim around the sink and grouting between tiles. This also includes the top of the range.

Cutting boards require special attention, for they can easily be a source of cross contamination, particularly for foods that are going to be served without additional heating after being cut on the cutting board. Cutting boards made of plastic can be washed in the dishwasher to keep them sanitary. Wooden cutting boards need to be scrubbed vigorously with soap and hot water or chlorine solution and then rinsed thoroughly to be certain to eliminate microorganisms that might tend to collect in the cuts in the surface.

Cooking Temperatures

Proper temperature control is particularly important when cooking meats, poultry, fish, and eggs and when reheating leftovers. A clean thermometer should be used to check the temperature in the thickest part of the food to be sure these foods have been heated adequately. Fight Bac temperature recommendations for food safety are listed in Table 3.2. If serving is delayed after cooking, the holding temperature needs to be 140°F or hotter.

http://www.temperatures. com/food.html
—Information on various types of food thermometers.

http://www.fsis.usda.gov/ Fact_Sheets/Use_a_Food_ Thermometer/index.asp
—Guide to using food thermometers.

http://www.fsis.usda.gov/ Fact_Sheets/Safe_Food_ Handling_Fact_Sheets/ index.asp
—Fact sheets for safe food handling of various types of foods.

TABLE 3.2
FINAL COOKING TEMPERATURES

Food	Temperature
Ground meats and mixtures	160°F
Ground poultry	165°F
Beef, veal, lamb	
Medium rare	145°F
Medium	160°F
Well done	170°F
Pork (fresh)	
Medium	160°F
Well done	170°F
Ham	
Fresh (raw)	160°F
Precooked (reheating)	140°F
Poultry	
Whole and parts	165°F
Stuffing (alone or in bird)	165°F
Seafood	
Finfish	145°F or flesh is opaque and separates easily with a fork
Shrimp, lobsters, crabs	Flesh pearly and opaque
Clams, oysters, mussels	Shells open during cooking
Eggs and egg dishes	
Eggs	Cook until yolk and white are firm
Egg dishes	160°F
Leftovers and casseroles	165°F
Reheating sauces, soups, gravies	Bring to a boil

Source: Recommended in Fight Bac®
Note: Be sure there are no cold spots in microwaved foods; rotate and stir frequently.

Storage Conditions and Practices

Because of the tremendous impact of temperature on the survival and growth of microorganisms, careful attention to food temperatures is of great importance in assuring the safety of protein-rich foods. Refrigerators should be monitored to be certain that they are maintaining a temperature no higher than 40°F (5°C), the range needed to retard reproduction and growth of most microorganisms that might be present. Cold foods should be kept refrigerated, removing them from the refrigerator only for efficient preparation and service. Extended time standing at room temperature should be avoided.

The Food Safety and Inspection Service (FSIS) of the U.S. Department of Agriculture, the U.S. Food and Drug Administration (FDA), and the Centers for Disease Control and Prevention (CDC) are coordinating many of their food safety work and have released recommendations for refrigerated and frozen storage of eggs and egg products (Table 3.3).

After preparation, protein-containing foods that are to be served cold should be chilled until serving time because some microorganisms, such as *Salmonella,* can thrive in them if they are present. For example, meringue and custard pies contain eggs that may not have been adequately heat treated; therefore, they should be refrigerated when the pan has cooled sufficiently to be held comfortably in the hand. Cakes with cream fillings (milk and/or egg proteins) need to be refrigerated as soon as the icing has been added. Egg salad, tuna salad, and other protein-rich salads should be kept refrigerated at all times except when being served. Their abundance of cut surfaces makes them prime targets for microorganisms. Federal recommendations for refrigerated storage limits for safety and frozen storage for quality are summarized in Table 3.4.

Leftovers need to be cared for promptly after the meal. Hot foods should be cooled as quickly as possible to the point where they can be placed in the refrigerator without temporarily raising the temperature of the refrigerator above 45°F (7°C). The refrigerator will be able to return quickly to its desired cooler temperature while also completing the rapid chilling of the leftover. Stripping the meat from the bones of turkeys and scooping the dressing from the cavity will ensure that this bulky and potentially hazardous type of leftover can be cooled and refrigerated very quickly after roasting and serving.

http://www.foodsafety.gov/keep/emergency/index.html

Guidelines for dealing with food in and after emergencies and power outages.

TABLE 3.3
RECOMMENDATIONS FOR REFRIGERATED AND FROZEN STORAGE OF EGGS AND EGG PRODUCTS

Product	Refrigerator	Freezer
Raw eggs in shell	3–5 weeks	Do not freeze. Instead, beat yolks and whites together; then freeze.
Raw egg whites	2–4 days	12 months
Raw egg yolks	2–4 days	Yolks do not freeze well.
Raw egg accidentally frozen in shell	Use immediately after thawing.	Keep frozen; then refrigerate to thaw.
Hard-cooked eggs	1 week	Do not freeze.
Egg substitutes, liquid (Unopened)	10 days	12 months
Egg substitutes, liquid (Opened)	3 days	Do not freeze.
Egg substitutes, frozen (Unopened)	After thawing, 7 days or refer to "Use-By" date.	12 months
Egg substitutes, frozen (Opened)	After thawing, 3 days or refer to "Use-By" date.	Do not freeze.
Casseroles with eggs	3–4 days	After baking, 2–3 months.
Eggnog (Commercial)	3–5 days	6 months
Eggnog (Homemade)	2–4 days	Do not freeze.
Pies (Pumpkin or pecan)	3–4 days	After baking, 1–2 months.
Pies (Custard and chiffon)	3–4 days	Do not freeze.
Quiche with filling	3–4 days	After baking, 1–2 months.

TABLE 3.4
FEDERAL RECOMMENDATIONS FOR REFRIGERATED STORAGE LIMITS FOR SAFETY AND FROZEN STORAGE FOR QUALITY

Category	Food	Refrigerator (40°F or below)	Freezer (0°F or below)
Salads	Egg, chicken, ham, tuna and macaroni salads	3–5 days	Does not freeze well
Hot dogs	Opened package	1 week	1–2 months
	Unopened package	2 weeks	1–2 months
Luncheon meat	Opened package or deli sliced	3–5 days	1–2 months
	Unopened package	2 weeks	1–2 months
Bacon and sausage	Bacon	7 days	1 month
	Sausage, raw—from chicken, turkey, pork, beef	1–2 days	1–2 months
Hamburger and other ground meats	Hamburger, ground beef, turkey, veal, pork, lamb, and mixtures of them	1–2 days	3–4 months
Fresh beef, veal, lamb and pork	Steaks	3–5 days	6–12 months
	Chops	3–5 days	4–6 months
	Roasts	3–5 days	4–12 months
Fresh poultry	Chicken or turkey, whole	1–2 days	1 year
	Chicken or turkey, pieces	1–2 days	9 months
Soups and stews	Vegetable or meat added	3–4 days	2–3 months
Leftovers	Cooked meat or poultry	3–4 days	2–6 months
	Chicken nuggets or patties	3–4 days	1–3 months
	Pizza	3–4 days	1–2 months

Source: U.S. Department of Health and Human Services.

CONTROL OF FOOD WASTE

Short Term

Many foods can be moved through the marketing chain and consumed in the home without spoiling if attention is given to safe handling during this comparatively short interval of time. One of the keys to successful control of food waste is careful handling of fresh foods at all stages.

Fresh produce contains enzymes that are capable of catalyzing chemical changes in fresh fruits and vegetables that shorten the length of time these foods can be held in the marketing process. If bruising can be avoided, enzymatic changes will not occur as readily as they do in bruised tissues of fruits and vegetables. A particularly important means of controlling enzyme-catalyzed spoilage is to chill most fresh produce as soon as it is harvested and to continue to keep it at refrigerator temperatures during all phases of marketing and storage. Such treatment also helps to keep growth of microorganisms to a minimum.

In addition to controlling temperatures when handling fresh produce, control of the atmosphere is important. Some moisture is needed in the air to prevent dehydration during storage, but too much moisture can encourage growth of molds. Some commercial storage units have controlled atmospheres, with the levels of both carbon dioxide and moisture being regulated carefully. Sometimes other gases, such as ethylene gas, may be introduced at controlled levels to help achieve optimal quality of bananas and other fresh produce. Related to the control of gases and moisture is the need for some circulation of air among the stored foods.

In the home, hydrator drawers need to be kept clean in refrigerators to avoid contaminating newly purchased produce with microorganisms remaining from previous produce.

A cool, dry area is needed for storage of such items as potatoes and winter squash. These items should be checked regularly to be sure that no spoiling vegetables are being held to contaminate the remainder of the lot. In addition, purchase of all fresh produce (whether intended for storage in the refrigerator or at cool room temperature), all protein-rich foods (meats, milk, and similar foods), and cereal products (including flour and pastas) should be planned to avoid long storage periods. Purchase of just the amounts that will be used before they spoil can be the key to preventing food spoilage.

Some foods, particularly the cereal grains, are attractive to mice and other rodents. To avoid food waste of this nature, rodents and insects must be eliminated from storage areas. Cool storage temperatures extend the shelf life of flour and other cereal products because hatching of insect eggs that may be present is delayed.

To avoid possible accidental poisoning, pesticides and other harmful chemicals should not be kept in the vicinity of food. Another important precaution is to be sure that any toxic compounds are labeled clearly and stored in cupboards away from the food preparation areas.

Long Term

Many foods are now available virtually all year long in one form or another, but some foods that are intended for extended storage will require special processing to avoid spoilage. The methods commonly used for making foods resistant to spoilage during long-term storage include canning, freezing, preserving with sugar, pickling, and drying. The mechanisms of destroying the microorganisms in foods differ for these various methods (Chapter 19).

ADDITIVES

Societal changes have altered lifestyles, including food habits. People consume a considerable amount of food that is prepared in factories and food-processing facilities and then shipped to consumer retail outlets. Preparation of complex food mixtures in industrial quantities entails many technical problems not encountered in a family's kitchen, and the extended route to the dinner table further compounds the problems that food technologists must solve. Food additives often can solve technical difficulties and/or enhance the palatability and quality of commercial food products. It also is essential that these additives be safe to eat.

What Are Additives?

Additives are substances added either by intent or by accident into foods. The former are termed intentional additives, and the latter are incidental or accidental additives. The incidental additives are the result of carelessness in food processing or preparation and are to be avoided. This section of the chapter examines intentional additives. These substances are regulated by the **Food and Drug Administration (FDA)** in the Department of Health and Human Services. The FDA's legal authority stems from the **Food Additives Amendment of 1958** and the Food, Drug, and Cosmetic Act of 1938.

Hundreds of substances are potential ingredients in food products today; many have been in use for a very long time, in fact, well before the Food Additives Amendment of 1958. The amendment called for a review of the safety of the various additives in use at that time or being proposed for use in the future. To approach this assignment, the FDA appointed a group of experts to identify the additives it considered to be safe, based on previous use in foods for many years. The result of the work of this group was the **GRAS list**, a list of over 680 additives that were "Generally Recognized as Safe." Substances on the GRAS list were permitted while vast series of tests were conducted over a period of years to prove that the various additives actually are safe for humans. The GRAS list continues to be monitored today, and substances occasionally are added as they are identified and tested.

---

http://www.fda.gov/ AboutFDA/WhatWeDo/ History/FOrgsHistory/ CFSAN/ucm083863.htm

—Brief history of FDA oversight of food safety.

http://www.fsis.usda.gov/ factsheets/Additives_in_ Meat_&_Poultry_Products/ index.asp

—Overview of food additives amendment.

additives Substances added by intent or by accident into foods.

Food and Drug Administration (FDA) The federal agency regulating food additives.

Food Additives Amendment of 1958 Amendment to the Food, Drug, and Cosmetic Act of 1938; regulates food additive usage.

http://www.fda.gov/Food/ FoodIngredientsPackaging/ GenerallyRecognizedas SafeGRAS/default.htm

—Overview of GRAS list.

GRAS list List of over 680 additives considered safe and legal to use.

Work to test the safety of the various additives, particularly to identify any potential **carcinogens**, has been proceeding in laboratories across the country. If an additive is found to cause cancer at any level (regardless of whether or not that level would be consumed by a person), the **Delaney clause** of the Food Additives Amendment requires that the additive not be permitted. This clause has been challenged on rare occasions where benefits of a substance far exceed risks, such as in the case of saccharin.

Why Are Additives Used?

A very general answer to the question of using additives is that additives improve food quality. Actually, this answer barely skims the surface, for various additives may enhance products in different ways. Specific reasons for their use may include one or more of the following:

1. Extend shelf life.
2. Improve nutritive value.
3. Improve color.
4. Improve flavor.
5. Improve texture.
6. Control pH.
7. Leaven.
8. Bleach and mature.
9. Facilitate food preparation.

Extending shelf life can mean savings in money and in food. Risks of food-borne illnesses can be reduced by the use of some additives. Similarly, substances are added to influence consumer food choices by enhancing the sensory appeal of foods, increasing nutrient value, or providing some other function valued by consumers.

Although some people prefer to avoid food additives by preparing almost all their foods from the basic ingredients, many prefer to buy at least some items that contain additives in their formulations. These consumers may be attracted by the nutritive merits, convenience, and time saving, or by such quality characteristics as color, texture, and flavor. Regardless of the reasons a consumer cites, the decision to buy an item containing food additives is evidence that many people feel that the benefits clearly outweigh any possible risk associated with the use of additives.

How Are Additives Categorized?

Since additives can do so many things, it is not surprising that they are classified according to their specific qualities. The *Federal Register* 39(185): 34175 (1974) classifies additives according to technical functions:

1. Anticaking agents (free-flowing agents).
2. Antimicrobial agents.
3. Antioxidants (prevent oxidation of fats and nutrients).
4. Colors, coloring adjuncts (including color stabilizers, color fixatives, color-retentive agents, etc.).
5. Curing and pickling agents.
6. Dough strengtheners.
7. Drying agents.
8. Emulsifiers, emulsifier salts.
9. Enzymes.
10. Flavor enhancers.
11. Firming agents.
12. Flavoring agents, adjuvants.
13. Flour-treating agents (including bleaching and maturing agents).
14. Formulation aids (including carriers, binders, fillers, plasticizers, film-formers, etc.).
15. Fumigants.

carcinogen Substance that is capable of causing cancer.

Delaney Clause Clause in the Food Additives Amendment mandating that additives shown to cause cancer at any level must be removed from the marketplace.

16. Humectants (moisture-retention agents), anti-dusting agents.
17. Leavening agents.
18. Lubricants, release agents.
19. Non-nutritive sweeteners.
20. Nutrient supplements.
21. Nutritive sweeteners.
22. Oxidizing and reducing agents.
23. pH control agents (including buffers, acids, alkalis, neutralizing agents).
24. Processing aids (including clarifying agents, clouding agents, catalysts, flocculants, filter aids, etc.).
25. Propellants (aerating agents), gases.
26. Sequestrants (binding of metal ions).
27. Solvents, vehicles.
28. Stabilizers, thickeners (including suspending and bodying agents, setting agents, gelling agents, bulking agents, etc.).
29. Surface-active agents (other than emulsifiers, including solubilizing agents, dispersants, detergents, wetting agents, rehydration enhancers, whipping agents, foaming agents, defoaming agents, etc.).
30. Surface-finishing agents (including glazes, polishes, waxes, protective coatings).
31. Synergists (enhancers of other additives).
32. Texturizers.

This extensive list outlines many specific roles of the various types of additives in modifying food products to make them successful commercially, both from the perspective of quality maintenance throughout marketing and the quality characteristics the consumer is presumed to desire. Manufacturers use many of the additives to give their products increased consumer appeal.

The importance of such an obvious characteristic as food color has a tremendous impact on consumer acceptance. For example, additives are added to color margarines so they resemble butter; clearly, a white spread on bread lacks appeal. Similarly, people tend to pick the cherry pie with the cherry-red filling rather than the subdued canned cherry color. Illustrations of this type can be found throughout the food marketplace. Manufacturers use additives to enhance the appeal of a food because consumers respond by buying the modified food products. However, they cannot use additives to mask poor quality.

Federal regulations aid consumers by requiring that additives be listed in the ingredient label on each package. **Ingredient labeling** lists all ingredients in decreasing order of the amount (by weight) in the product. Since most additives are used in comparatively small quantities, they often are toward the end of the label. The chemical name of an ingredient or additive is not terribly informative to the average consumer, so many food processors now are providing a very brief explanation of the reason for the various additives listed on the label. This is being done to help relieve consumer anxiety about additives.

There are so many different additives listed that it is not reasonable to expect people to recognize the reasons for their inclusion in a food. However, it is useful at times to be able to identify the reason for using a particular additive. Appendix B provides information about some of the additives used commonly in the American food supply.

ingredient labeling
Mandatory listing of all ingredients (in descending order by weight) on package labels.

Incidental Contaminants

The additives identified in the preceding section—intentional additives—are used in formulating the food for a specific purpose. These substances are legal when used according to the regulations mandated through the FDA. The other type of additives—incidental (accidental) contaminants—is not desirable and should not be found in foods; for example, a stem from a pea plant or a rodent hair. Fortunately, the heat treatment utilized in canning foods makes these contaminants safe, if not very pleasing. In addition, such items usually are readily apparent to anyone preparing the food, and they can be removed without harm.

Insect infestations, particularly of grain products, represent a range of **incidental contaminants** that might be introduced to the food during storage. Detection presents some difficulties, although considerable effort has been expended to attempt to develop good tests for insects. Visual observation tests are only moderately successful, because the eggs of insects may be buried within kernels. A staining technique aids detection by staining the plugs covering the holes where insects have laid eggs. Other useful tests include flotation tests, density differences, and X-ray radiography.

Insects create problems in the various stages from larva, to pupa, and the adult stage, as well as in the egg phase. For example, some beetles have been found to shed more than 10 skins. Beetles and cockroaches are highly visible; mites are so small that they are very difficult to see in grains. However, it is clear that when any type of insect invades a food, other insects are likely to follow.

Serious economic losses can be the result of insect invasions into foods. Entire boxcars full of grain may be declared unfit for human use. The original contamination can be controlled somewhat by not storing infested grains and by thoroughly cleaning any storage area before introducing fresh grain. Storage in a cool, dry environment retards the life cycle and reproduction of many of the pests. The presence of these uninvited guests is not limited to granaries and warehouses; insects may hatch while grain products are stored in the home. Storage in metal or glass containers helps to prevent insect infestation into uncontaminated foods.

Rodent control is another important line of defense in protecting food from incidental contaminants. Well-constructed warehouses and granaries represent a good line of defense, but careful monitoring and elimination of any rodents in the vicinity must be maintained to avoid this source of contamination.

Natural Toxicants

The additives used in producing foods commercially are tested for their safety. However, no such testing occurs as nature synthesizes foods. For the most part, the foods normally eaten are quite free of harmful substances. Nevertheless, some compounds tend to block utilization of nutrients; certain others have physiological effects, particularly in sensitive people. A listing of some of the toxicants found in foods is given in Table 3.5.

incidental contaminants
Any substance that accidentally is contained in a food product.

http://www.ansci.cornell. edu/plants/toxicagents/ vicine.html#poison

—Discussion of the effect of fava bean pollen or ingestion of beans on people of Mediterranean heritage lacking the enzyme glucose-6-phosphate dehydrogenase (G6PD) in their red blood cells.

TABLE 3.5
SOME NATURAL TOXICANTS FOUND IN FOODS

Toxicant	Food Source	Characteristics
Unidentified	Fava beans	Hemolysis, vomiting, dizziness, prostration
Aflatoxin	Moldy peanuts contaminated with A. *flavus*	Liver damage; chronic consumption may lead to cancer
Ergot	Moldy rye	Severe muscle contraction, serious to fatal nervous system involvement
Antitrypsin	Legumes (raw)	Blocks protein digestion; inactivated by heat
Goitrogen	Cabbage	Blocks thyroxin synthesis
Phytin	Cereals	Restricts absorption of calcium and iron
Solanine	Sun-burned potatoes	Vomiting and diarrhea
Oxalic acid	Rhubarb, spinach	Restricts calcium absorption
Caffeine	Coffee	Possible carcinogen and teratogen
Benzopyrene	Charcoal-broiled meats	Carcinogen
Nitrates and nitrites	Cured meats, some vegetables	Potential carcinogen
Gossypol	Cottonseed	Toxic to animals
Cyanogens (amygdalin)	Almonds, peach and apricot pits	Headache, heart palpitations, weakness; can be fatal

SUMMARY

Food safety is a vital concern of all consumers, whether the food being eaten is prepared from basic ingredients in the home or produced in factories or large food-service facilities. A key part of maintaining safe food is to control contamination by microorganisms (bacteria, viruses, and molds), as well as parasites, which can cause food-borne illnesses.

Salmonellosis, perfringens poisoning, listeriosis, and infections from pathogenic *E. coli* and *Campylobacter* are familiar examples of food-borne illnesses caused by bacteria. The toxins produced by *Staphylococci* and by *C. botulinum* are other causes of illness. Botulism is particularly serious because of its potential for being fatal.

Viruses cause other food-borne illnesses—for example, hepatitis A, caused by noroviruses, and cyclosporiasis, caused by the protozoan parasite *C. cayetanensis*. Parasites are another potential cause of human illnesses. Trichinosis, usually traced to pork containing viable *Trichinella spiralis* parasites, can be prevented by cooking pork to a uniform internal temperature of 160°F (71°C). Shellfish poisoning is a particular problem in the summer months if conditions allow *G. catanella*, a type of algae, to multiply rapidly and develop high levels of saxitoxin.

Control of these types of food-borne illnesses can be effected by careful use of HACCP and by controlling temperatures of food at all times, including cooking, holding, serving, processing, and storage. The danger zone for reproduction of many microorganisms is between 40°F (5°C) and 140°F (60°C), necessitating refrigerated storage or cooking and holding so that protein-rich foods are kept at temperatures above or below the danger zone.

High standards of sanitation in maintaining the kitchen and among people handling food are important to keep contamination from microorganisms and parasites to a minimum. Thorough washing of fresh produce with safe water is an important means of helping to avoid food-borne illnesses. Food handlers need to wash hands frequently with soap and warm water and avoid touching their faces. Cross contamination can be avoided by keeping surfaces and cutting boards washed adequately with soap and water before other foods are placed on them. Gloves can provide additional protection in food-service operations.

Food can be kept safe for later consumption by a variety of preserving methods, including canning, freezing, drying, and preserving with sugar. Vegetables and meats need to be canned in a pressure canner to reach the high temperature needed for killing the spores of *C. botulinum* that might be present and flourish in these low-acid foods. Water-bath canning is adequate for fruits. Freezing is a successful and simple technique for preserving food if frozen storage is available. Drying is the oldest of the preserving methods and is useful, despite the significant changes it causes in color and texture.

Food additives, monitored by the FDA, are of two types: incidental and intentional. Intentional additives are used to extend the shelf life of foods, to improve nutritive value, and to enhance food quality. Many additives were originally placed on the GRAS list and have subsequently been tested for safety. The FDA must approve all new substances being proposed as additives before they can be included in foods. Incidental (accidental) contaminants, notably insect and rodent contaminants, need to be kept to an absolute minimum through careful storage and monitoring techniques.

Some natural toxicants are found in foods. The severity of natural toxicity ranges from the possibly fatal result of consuming cyanogens in almonds and the pits of apricots and peaches to a minor influence in restricting mineral absorption.

STUDY QUESTIONS

1. What types of food poisoning may result from poor handling of food during processing or in the home?
2. What are some precautions that can be taken to reduce the possibility of contracting a food-borne illness?
3. What foods are the probable sources of the various types of food-borne illnesses?
4. What type of poisoning may result from eating improperly processed home-canned vegetables or meats? How may this hazard be controlled?
5. What is HACCP? Explain the significance of HACCP in the food industry.
6. Where can you find information about the additives in a food? Select a specific processed food and explain why each is used in the formulation.
7. What federal agency enforces the Food, Drug, and Cosmetic Act and the Food Additives Amendment?
8. Explain why five different additives are commonly used.
9. Identify five sources of natural toxicants.

SELECTED REFERENCES

Anonymous. 1996. Bovine spongiform encephalopathy. USDA Animal and Plant Health Inspection Service. Washington, DC. March.

Berry, D. 2010. Pathogen protection. *Food Product Design* 20(11): 33.

Bibek, R., and A. Bhunia. 2007. *Fundamental Food Microbiology*. 4th ed. CRC Press. Boca Raton, FL.

Cromeans, T. L. 1997. Understanding and preventing virus transmission via foods. *Food Technol.* 51(4): 20.

Duxbury, D. 2004. Keeping tabs on *Listeria*. *Food Technol.* 58(7): 74.

Esquivel, T. 2010. Egg safety. *Food Product Design* 20(10): 14.

Fan, X., et al. 2009. *Microbial Safety of Fresh Produce*. Wiley-Blackwell & IFT Press. Ames, IA.

Floyd, B. 2005. Increasing Listeria awareness. *Food Product Design 15*(2): 93.

Gillette, M. 2009. Important steps to improve tracing in food systems. *Food Technol. 63*(11): 11.

Hall, P. A. 2011. What does FSMA mean for you? *Food Product Design 27*(3): 16.

Jay, J., et al. 2006. *Modern Food Microbiology*. 2nd ed. Springer. New York.

Liu, D. 2009. *Molecular Detection of Foodborne Pathogens*. CRC Press. Boca Raton, FL.

Looney, J. W., P. G. Crandall, and A. K. Poole. 2001. The matrix of food safety regulations. *Food Technol. 55*(4): 60–76.

McEntire, J. C. 2004. IFT issues update on foodborne pathogens. *Food Technol. 58*(7): 20.

McLellan, M. R., and D. F. Splittstoesser. 1996. Reducing risk of *E. coli* in apple cider. *Food Technol. 50*(12): 174.

McWilliams, M. 2011. *Foods: Experimental Perspectives*. 7th ed. Prentice Hall. Upper Saddle River, NJ.

Mermelstein, N. H. 2009. Analyzing for microbial contaminants. *Food Technol. 63*(10): 68.

Mermelstein, N. H. 2010. Targeting non-O157 *E. coli* serotypes. *Food Technol. 64*(10): 85.

Miller, H. I. 2009. Can biotechnology prevent foodborne illness? *Food Technol. 63*(12): 104.

Murphy, P. A., et al. 2006. Food mycotoxins: An update. *J. Food Science 71*: R51.

Newsome, R. 2006. Understanding mycotoxins. *Food Technol. 60*(6): 50.

Pommerville, J. C. 2007. *Alcamo's Fundamentals of Microbiology*. 8th ed. Jones and Bartlett. Sudbury, MA.

Pszczola, D. E. 2002. Antimicrobials: Setting up additional hurdles to ensure food safety. *Food Technol. 56*(6): 99–107.

Sachs, S., and K. Hulebak. 2002. A dialogue on pathogen reduction. *Food Technol. 56*(9): 55.

Scallan, E., et al. 2011. Foodborne illness acquired in the United States—major pathogens. *Emerging Infectious Diseases* [serial on the Internet]. 2011 January [*date cited*]. http://www.cdc.gov/EID/content/17/1/7.htm

Schauwecker, A. 2005. To preserve and protect. *Food Product Design 15*(3): 67.

Sloan, A. E. 2010. Consumers are confused, concerned about food safety. *Food Technol. 64*(3): 17.

Smith, R. L., et al. 2005. GRAS flavoring substances. *Food Technol. 59*(81): 24.

Sneed, J., and C. H. Strohbehn. 2008. Trends impacting food safety in retail foodservice: Implications for dietetics practice. *J. Am. Dietet. Assoc. 108*(7): 1170.

Spano, M. 2011. Food colors and ADHD. *Food Product Design 21*(1): 26.

Spittler, L. 2010. Keeping foods safe: How imported foods get to our tables. *ADA Times 8*(1): 5.

Stevens, H. C., and L. O. Nabors. 2009. Microbial food cultures: A regulatory update. *Food Technol. 63*(3): 36.

Swientek, B. 2006. Global challenges to food safety. *Food Technol. 60*(5): 123.

Swientek, B. 2008. Ensuring food safety and quality. *Food Technol. 52*(8): 105.

Teixeira, A., et al. 2006. Keeping botulism out of canned foods. *Food Technol. 60*(2): 84.

Tortora, G. J., et al. 2006. *Microbiology: An Introduction*. 9th ed. Benjamin Cummings. San Francisco, CA.

Von Eschenbach, A. C. 2007. FDA's new approach to food protection. *Food Technol. 61*(12): 116.

Section Two
Food Preparation

High-quality cutlery and pans are important components for efficient, successful food preparation.
Courtesy of Plycon Press.

4

Factors in Food Preparation

Key Concepts

1. Knowledge of basic kitchen equipment used in preparing and cooking is essential for people to be successful in preparing foods.

2. Temperatures involved in food preparation range from below freezing to those reached in boiling, baking, and frying; temperatures and time need to be controlled accurately.

3. In food preparation, heat may be transferred by conduction, convection, and radiation.

BASIC EQUIPMENT

Food preparation can be done efficiently and safely when appropriate equipment is available. Measuring equipment, mixing bowls, a mixer, assorted utensils, cutlery, thermometers, pots, pans, and baking dishes are among the basic items needed for success in the kitchen. This section reviews many of the basic items needed in commercial and home kitchens.

Individuals doubtless would add more items to this list to accommodate their preferred techniques for preparing favorite dishes. Cookware stores are packed with numerous items to meet individual needs. Many of these items are convenient to own but are not necessary for basic food preparation. The principles involved in heating foods are explained in this chapter to clarify how heating alters food.

www.cooking.com/
products/buyingGuides.asp
—Tips on selecting equipment.

Preparation Equipment

Successful preparation of recipes begins with accurate measurement of ingredients. Cookbooks list the amount of each ingredient based on standard measuring techniques using standardized measuring equipment (Figure 4.1). The equipment needed includes a set of graduated measuring cups (1 cup, 1/2 cup, 1/3 cup, and 1/4 cup measures) for measuring dry ingredients, a 1-cup glass measuring cup with measurements indicated on the sides and a pouring spout for measuring liquids, and a set of graduated measuring spoons (1 tablespoon, 1 teaspoon, 1/2 teaspoon, and 1/4 teaspoon). Use of these items is discussed in Appendix A.

A set of mixing bowls of different sizes that nest together is needed for mixing ingredients. Some recipes require at least two mixing bowls during preparation, and often more than one recipe may be in progress at the same time. Considerable time can be lost if it is necessary to keep shifting food and washing

Figure 4.1
Liquids are measured in a glass measuring cup; other ingredients are measured in graduated measuring cups and spoons. Courtesy of Plycon Press.

www.kitchenkapers.com

—Suggestions on selecting cutlery and other chef's equipment.

www.catra.org/pages/products/sharpening/careof.htm

—Care of cutlery and flatware.

double boiler Two-part pan and lid designed to hold water in the bottom pan and the food in the top; its French name is *bain-marie*.

bowls to make the next mixture. These bowls can be made of metal, glass, or ceramic.

An electric mixer is a convenience and saves energy. A mixer on a stand is more powerful than handheld mixers and frees the hands for adding ingredients. These mixers can be released from the stand and operated while being held by hand.

Basic utensils (Figure 4.2) needed include a two-tined cooking fork, a large slotted spoon, a large mixing spoon, assorted wooden spoons, tongs, kitchen shears, a narrow spatula, a wide spatula, a grater, a wire whisk and/or a rotary eggbeater, a vegetable peeler, and a potato masher. A can opener is essential, and a jar opener is very useful.

A cooking thermometer is an essential piece of equipment that should be used habitually while cooking meats and all other protein-rich foods or casseroles containing eggs, milk, and all types of flesh foods. Safety of protein foods is dependent on heating them to a temperature high enough to kill harmful microorganisms that might be present (see Chapter 3).

Essential pieces of cutlery include a paring knife, French or chef's knife, slicing knife, and butcher knife. There are many special knives that are convenient to add when possible (Figure 4.3). Knives of high-quality construction with blades of forged steel and that are well balanced are invaluable and can be used for many years. To keep these knives sharp, a sharpening device is needed.

Cooking Equipment

Pots and pans are essential for heating many foods (Figure 4.5). Pots have straight sides, a handle on both sides, a lid, and are often rather deep. They are convenient for heating fairly large quantities that do not require much stirring. Pans are rather shallow and usually have only one moderately long handle and a lid. Their dimensions make them convenient to use when frequent or continuous stirring will be done.

Pots and pans are available in different sizes. Selection should be consistent with the quantity of food that usually will be cooked in them. A range of pan sizes is convenient. A **double boiler** (*bain-marie*) is useful because it can be assembled for cooking custards and other delicate dishes, or it can be used as two separate pans.

Frying pans usually have sides with a bit of a slope, which makes it easy to push a spatula under the food being fried. It is convenient to have frying pans of more than one size; the amount of food should fit into the frying pan and still leave a little space for turning or stirring the food.

Figure 4.2
Basic utensils include (left to right) spatula (wide and narrow), two-tined cooking fork, slotted spoon, wooden spoon, wire whisks, rotary eggbeater, masher, and tongs. Courtesy of Plycon Press.

Figure 4.3
Examples of cutlery include (left to right) slicing (serrated blade), cleaver, medium and large French chef, and paring knives. Courtesy of Plycon Press.

INDUSTRY INSIGHT
CUTLERY

Professional chefs consider their cutlery to be extremely important, and they select each knife with care. The blades selected usually are carbon steel or high-carbon stainless steel, an alloy that maintains its appearance because of the stainless steel while also having the desired sharpening characteristics provided by the carbon steel. The tang, or end, of the blade on a knife a chef selects extends the entire length of the handle and is flanked on both sides by the handle, which is attached very firmly (Figure 4.4). These knives should be washed by hand immediately after being used. They are not washed in dishwashers. Blades can be damaged too easily by the detergent, heat, and bumping against other utensils.

Knife sharpening is done using a whetstone dampened with water. A whetstone may have three surfaces ranging in texture from the coarsest to the finest. A blade is sharpened effectively by placing the heel of the blade on the coarsest surface at a 20° angle and pushing the knife away along the stone while maintaining pressure on the blade. The action resembles trying to slice a thin slice off the whetstone while pushing down and away from you. This is done on both sides of the blade. This procedure is then repeated with the intermediate texture using the same motion on both sides of the blade. Finally, the same strokes are used on the side of the whetstone with the finest texture.

The edge of a blade needs to be sharp and straight. This can be achieved using a steel, which is a roughened steel rod held in the left hand while being used. The knife is held in the right hand, and the blade is held against the lower end of the steel at a 20° angle and pushed away along the length of the steel. This procedure is repeated on both sides of the blade until the blade is straight and sharp. Professional chefs are meticulous in the care, sharpening, and handling of knives.

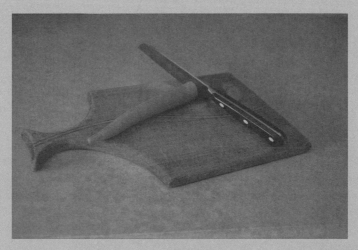

Figure 4.4
High-quality knives feature a fine steel blade with a tang extending down the length of the handle and firmly attached. Courtesy of Plycon Press.

Figure 4.5
Sauce pan and frying pans (front, left to right) and Dutch oven and large double boiler (rear, left to right) and lids are some of the pans needed. Courtesy of Plycon Press.

Uniform heating of the bottom of a frying pan or a pan is crucial to success in cooking food. Pans that are fairly heavy and thick are convenient to use because they will not dent or warp easily, especially if they are made with aluminum or with a core of a metal that conducts heat rapidly and evenly. Cast-iron frying pans heat very evenly and retain the heat, but they are heavy and also are susceptible to rusting unless they are carefully maintained. Several pans of a durable weight with good heat conductivity are available today. These pans are usually suitable, but they are expensive choices. However, high-quality pans of thick metal and with good heating properties are sufficiently durable to justify the expense.

Frying pans become extremely hot when they are used for frying, so they should not be placed directly on countertops or other surfaces that are damaged by temperatures hotter than boiling water. To avoid warping, hot frying pans should be allowed to cool considerably before water is put into them.

Individual needs for baking equipment are dictated by the types of foods that will be prepared. Baking equipment

CULTURAL ACCENT
WOKS TO OMELET PANS

For centuries, the Chinese have been using the wok as an essential piece of equipment for preparing their stir-fry recipes. The rounded bottom and sloping sides of a wok allow food to be shifted upward in the pan while other portions migrate toward the bottom where the heat is most intense. Quick, deft stirring or flipping prevents food from burning while cooking proceeds quickly. A lid that fits over the wok traps steam inside to help cook foods through; only minimal stirring is done to prevent burning and cook the food uniformly if a lid is being used (Figure 4.6).

Although woks originally were always rounded on the bottom, some are designed today with a small flat area

that helps keep the wok upright if placed on a flat surface. A traditional wok may have a heat-resistant circle on which it can be placed to remain upright. Electric woks are also available; these are supported on legs above the electrical element.

Other cultures also have unique pans for preparing special foods. In French cuisine, one of the familiar dishes is the omelet. Special omelet pans are available to help in cooking them. For preparing French omelets, an omelet pan designed with sloping sides makes flipping or folding easy.

Figure 4.6
Using a spatula made from part of a coconut shell, a chef in Bangkok stirs a sauce he is preparing in a brass wok. Courtesy of Plycon Press.

is designed for specific types of food preparation (Figure 4.7). For example, soufflé dishes are important for baking soufflés, and popover pans are designed specifically for baking popovers. Muffin pans are made with depressions about half as deep as those in popover pans, and they are available in various sizes, ranging from mini to large. The right equipment is essential to making successful products.

Cake pans are available in various sizes and in circular or rectangular shapes. They have straight sides about 2 inches high. These can be used for a range of casserole dishes and other products, as well as for baking cakes. Tube pans and bundt pans, with their high walls and center tube, are designed for baking angel food, chiffon, and sponge cakes. A two-piece tube pan is designed with a removable bottom, making it easy to remove the baked cake.

Cookie sheets are designed simply as flat sheets without sides, and they are suitable for a variety of baked goods, including cookies, some yeast breads, biscuits, and pizza. Jelly-roll pans are the size of cookie sheets, but their shallow sides make them functional for baking jelly rolls, as well as the items that can be baked on cookie sheets.

Pie pans are available in varying sizes, ranging from individual to 9 inches. They are designed with sloping sides for easy serving of slices and with a broad lip so that a decorative edging can be made all around the edge of the crust (Figure 4.8).

Figure 4.7
Specialized baking pans include (clockwise from top) muffin pan, two-piece angel food cake pan, Pyrex loaf pan, soufflé dish, and cast-iron popover pan. Courtesy of Plycon Press.

MEASURING INGREDIENTS

Replication of prepared dishes is an important characteristic of quality food preparation, and it can only be achieved through clear recipes and controlled amounts of all the ingredients to be used. To achieve these accurate and reproducible measurements, U.S. food-research laboratories and commercial kitchens, as well as food preparers in Europe, commonly weigh ingredients. However, home cooks in the United States generally use volumetric measures. Volumetric measuring is done using a glass measuring cup for liquids, graduated measuring cups for fats and dry ingredients, and measuring spoons for smaller quantities.

Dry Ingredients

Depending upon the amount to be measured, dry ingredients are measured either in graduated measuring cups (ordinarily a set consisting of 1/4 cup, 1/3 cup, 1/2 cup, and 1 cup) or in graduated measuring spoons (usually 1/4 teaspoon, 1/2 teaspoon, 1 teaspoon, and 1 tablespoon). The measuring spoons are used only to measure quantities less than 1/4 cup.

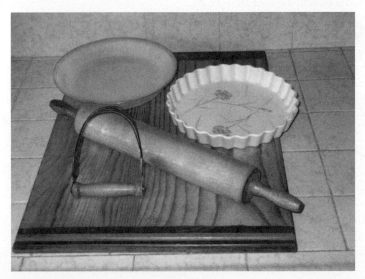

Figure 4.8
Sloping sides and a lip distinguish a pie pan (left rear) from a quiche pan (right rear). Pastry blender and rolling pin are used in making pastry. Courtesy of Plycon Press.

TABLE 4.1
VOLUMETRIC EQUIVALENT MEASURES

Measure	Equivalent
1 Tablespoon (T)	3 teaspoons (tsp)
2 T	1 fluid ounce (fl oz)
4 T	1/4 cup (c)
5 1/3 T	1/3 c
8 T	1/2 c
16 T	1 c
8 fl oz	1 c
2 c	1 pint (pt)
4 c	1 quart (qt)
4 qt	1 gallon (gal)

Measuring is done by stirring or sifting and then spooning the dry ingredient into the appropriate measuring cup(s) until the cup is overflowing. Then the straight edge of a spatula is scraped across to level the measure. For accuracy, the minimum number of measurements is done (e.g., 1 cup is measured more accurately by using the 1 cup measure one time rather than filling the 1/2 cup measure two times).

Only full measures should be used. For example, measuring 3/4 cup of sugar would require filling the 1/2 cup and the 1/4 cup measures. Similarly, 1 1/2 tablespoon would be done by using the 1 teaspoon and the 1/2 teaspoon measures. To know what measures to use in the various cases, it is necessary to know certain equivalent measures. Those commonly needed in home food preparation are provided in Table 4.1.

Dry ingredients often pack down in the package or form lumps. To avoid discrepancies resulting from close packing, these ingredients should be stirred to eliminate lumps and consequent excesses in measurements. This is particularly important when measuring cornstarch, which tends to pack considerably during shipping and storage.

Flour is another dry ingredient that has a tendency to pack, which can lead to significant variations in the amounts measured. To eliminate this problem, recipes are developed based on the practice of sifting flour one time and then lightly spooning it into the measuring cup, being careful not to tap the cup or otherwise cause the flour to pack. This technique results in a measured cup of all-purpose flour weighing between 92 and 120 grams, while measuring without sifting may result in a cup weighing as much as 150 grams. Obviously, such variation would cause wide variation in a product from one time to the next.

Different types of sugar require somewhat different measuring techniques. Granulated sugar only needs to be stirred to eliminate any lumps before being measured like any other dry ingredient. Powdered sugar, like flour, tends to pack; sifting prior to measuring is necessary to lighten it and eliminate lumps. Brown sugar needs to be stirred to eliminate any lumps before being pressed gently, but firmly, into the appropriate graduated measuring cup(s). It should be packed just firm enough so that the sugar will hold the shape of the cup when the cup is inverted to remove the sugar.

Fats and Oils

Shortening, margarine, and butter often are available in rectangular bars equivalent to 1/2 cup or 8 tablespoons. Each bar is in a wrapper marked in eight 1-tablespoon measures along its length. Such fats can be measured by cutting vertically at the correct mark. Other solid fats are measured by pressing them firmly into the appropriate graduated measuring cup and then leveling with a spatula. Care must be taken to be sure that there are no air pockets remaining when the fat has been packed in.

Some people use the water displacement method for measuring solid fats, but this method is inaccurate because the measurement includes the water clinging to the fat. The water acquired by this method is a particular problem when making pastry. To use this method, however, water is placed in a clear glass measuring cup to equal the difference between the desired amount of fat and 1 cup (e.g., to measure 1/3 cup fat, 2/3 cup water is placed in the measuring cup before the fat is pressed in). Then the fat is pressed into the cup until the water level rises to the 1-cup mark. It is essential that the fat be pressed below the surface of the water when measuring by this method to achieve any degree of accuracy. The water is drained from the fat in the cup before the fat is removed and added to the other ingredients.

Oils are measured by pouring into a glass measuring cup until the bottom of the meniscus (the curved upper surface of liquid) of the oil reaches the desired marker on the cup. The cup should be placed on the counter and the measure taken by bending over to look across rather than down on the surface.

Liquids

Liquids are measured easily in a standard glass measuring cup placed on a level surface. Accurate readings require bending over until the eye is at the same height as the cup and then pouring in liquid until the bottom of the meniscus reaches the desired level. The glass measuring cup works well with liquids because there is no need to do any mechanical leveling. The glass cup itself also has the advantage of extending a bit above the 1-cup mark, which makes it possible to carry the measured liquid without spilling it.

SAFETY IN THE KITCHEN

The kitchen can be a dangerous place, but awareness of potential hazards leads to the formation of habits that promote safety. Spills on the floor are dangerous because of the likelihood of slipping on them. They need to be cleaned up immediately to eliminate the hazard. To avoid tripping in the kitchen, nothing should be on the floor. If a mat or rug is used, the backing should be slip-proof, and the edges need to be flat.

Electrical appliances should be checked to be sure they are in the "off" position before they are plugged in. Nothing except food should be inserted into electrical appliances when they are operating. Fingers and spatulas can easily be caught in mixers while the blades are rotating. Hair needs to be confined not only for sanitary reasons but also to keep it from accidentally getting caught in appliances.

Knives are an obvious hazard. Always hold a knife by the handle; the blade should be pointed at the floor when a knife is carried. If it is laid on the counter, the handle should be placed so that it is more convenient to reach than the blade. When cutting with a knife, cut away from, not toward you. Be sure that all fingers are away from the blade when cutting or slicing.

Burns can occur unless precautions are taken to avoid them. Hot pads should be used when handling hot pans. The hot pads need to be placed where they can be reached easily when handling baking pans or other items being baked in the oven, as well as when cooking on the range top (Figure 4.9). Hot pads need to be flexible enough to grasp pans securely and thick enough to provide good protection for the hands. Towels are dangerous to use as hot pads because they are so big that they may accidentally be held where they catch fire. When hot pans are removed from the oven, it is wise to leave a hot pad beside the pan as a reminder that the pan is too hot to touch without protection.

Handles of pans need to be placed so that they are convenient to grasp but not protruding over the edge of the range or over other burners. If they are arranged in this manner, the

http://www.homesafety
council.org/SafetyGuide/
sg_cooking_w001.asp
—Tips on safety in the
kitchen.

http://www.cdc.gov/
HealthyHomes/ByRoom/
kitchen.html
—CDC Information on
kitchen safety.

Figure 4.9
Hot pads conveniently placed next to the oven, but away from the burners on a range, are needed to avoid burns when baking.
Courtesy of Plycon Press.

Figure 4.10
To avoid burns, pan handles need to be pointed toward the edge of the range and never extend over the front edge or other burners.
Courtesy of Plycon Press.

pans will not be knocked off the range onto the floor and the handles will not be heated if the neighboring heating element is turned on (Figure 4.10).

Personal habits that are important for assuring food safety are discussed in Chapter 3. Sanitation in the kitchen is an essential component of food safety, and food handlers must always practice personal habits that assure food safety. Careful monitoring of temperatures reached in cooking and attention to proper handling and storage conditions also are essential to assuring that food is safe to eat.

TEMPERATURES IN FOOD PREPARATION

Temperatures involved in food preparation range from below freezing to extremely high temperatures in baking and in frying. The factors that influence the temperatures for boiling and freezing are examined next. Finally, this chapter concludes with a look at the various mechanisms by which heat is transmitted through foods.

Expressions such as "freezing cold" and "boiling hot" are used frequently in conversation to describe temperature extremes, but in food preparation, the range of temperatures actually is considerably greater than the implied range of 32°F (0°C) to 212°F (100°C). When dealing only with pure water, these two temperatures represent the range of extremes. However, food preparation involves using an array of foods and food mixtures and also different means of heating. As a result, temperatures in food and cooking equipment may range from about 0°F (–18°C) to 425°F (220°C) or even 450°F (232°C).

Freezing Temperatures

Water is a key component of many foods—not only of sauces and soups but also of such foods as gelatins and ice creams that do not flow. Because of this abundance of water in foods, the temperature at which foods freeze often is quite close to the freezing temperature of water. The transition of water from its liquid state into ice is essential in making ice cream and certainly is an important textural determinant in frozen fruits, vegetables, meats, and other frozen foods.

Freezing is the transition of a liquid into a solid, and the freezing point is the temperature at which this happens. This process of solidification results in a heat loss of 80 kilocalories per gram of water converted to ice, referred to as the **heat of solidification**. The converse occurs (80 kilocalories per gram are absorbed) when ice is changed back into liquid. This is the reason water feels so cold when ice melts.

The temperature at which freezing occurs influences the preparation and the quality of frozen foods. While such a statement may sound simplistic—for everyone has learned since childhood that water freezes at 32°F (0°C)—the fact is that substances dissolved in water will alter the temperature at which a solution freezes. In practical terms, this means that sugars and soluble salts, such as table salt, dissolve in water and modify the freezing point.

heat of solidification
Heat given off when water is transformed into ice; 80 kilocalories per gram of water.

Sugar in solution depresses the temperature at which the freezing of the solution occurs; the freezing point drops 3.35 F° (1.86 C°) for each gram molecular weight of sugar per liter. Consequently, an ice cream made with a large quantity of sugar will take a long time to freeze because it has to be cooled to a lower temperature for freezing to occur than would be required to freeze a less sweet ice cream. The high sugar content also means that the ice cream will melt more rapidly than will a product with less sugar. Thus, this sweet ice cream will be somewhat difficult to serve.

The fact that salt ionizes results in an even greater drop in the freezing point of salt solutions than of comparable sugar solutions. Although salt solutions are unpalatable at concentrations sufficient to have a significant effect on freezing points, this property of salt is utilized advantageously in making ice cream in an ice cream freezer. The ice cream mixture is placed in a container, which then is agitated and chilled in a mixture of salt and ice until the ice cream is frozen. The ice cream freezes much faster in the salt/ice mixture because the salt lowers the temperature of the ice mixture below the temperature of ice alone. The reduced time for freezing means that the freezer needs to be agitated a shorter time, and energy is saved. An additional benefit is that rapid freezing produces smaller ice crystals, resulting in an ice cream with a smoother texture.

Intermediate Temperatures

Some foods (a notable example being stirred custard) are particularly sensitive to temperatures during cooking. A controlled, fairly low heat is important to achieving the desired thickening without overheating and damaging the protein in custards and several other protein-containing foods.

Double boilers are designed specifically to avoid letting heat-sensitive items heat too quickly and boil. Water placed in the lower container is heated to produce steam all around the upper container where the food is being heated. This arrangement makes it impossible to bring the mixture in the upper container to a boil and helps to ensure gentle enough heating for heat-sensitive foods. Many ranges are equipped with a simmer setting to permit comparable rates of heating without requiring a double boiler.

Descriptive words are used to indicate the desired temperature in working with such foods as yeast or milk, which require careful temperature control for success. The coolest of these temperatures is **lukewarm**, or a temperature of about 100°F (40°C), a little above body temperature. **Scalding** temperatures are used to prepare milk for use in bread making, for loosening skins on tomatoes, and for a few other procedures. Scalding water (about 150°F or 65°C) can be characterized as having large bubbles collecting on the sides and bottom of the pan, but with little movement. Between 180°F (82°C) and 211°F (99°C) is the range designated as **simmering**. Water held in this temperature range will have large bubbles forming and rising almost to, but not breaking the surface of the water.

Many foods are stored and/or prepared at temperatures that lie between the freezing and boiling points of water. Protein-containing foods have the potential for causing food poisoning if they are held at temperatures promoting the growth of microorganisms. Storage just above freezing to a maximum of 40°F (0°C to 5°C) in the refrigerator is important to slow the reproduction of microorganisms and to also control spoilage in other foods. Protein-containing foods being held for delayed service need to be maintained at temperatures outside the danger zone (preferably at 140°F) to avoid food poisoning. Careful control of the temperature of foods is critical to maintaining both food safety and food quality (Chapter 3).

Boiling Temperatures

Boiling is extremely active agitation of a liquid, at which time some of the liquid changes to the vapor state. This occurs when the **vapor pressure** (pressure in a liquid to escape) of a liquid just exceeds **atmospheric pressure** (downward pressure on the liquid). The temperature at which boiling occurs is the boiling point, which is 212°F (100°C) for water at sea level. Interestingly, pure water at sea level will remain at 212°F (100°C) regardless of how fast the water is boiling. The heat can be turned higher, and the water will boil more rapidly than before, but the temperature will remain constant.

lukewarm Approximately body temperature; about 100°F (40°C).

scalding Temperature used to loosen fruit skins and perform other similar functions; about 150°F (65°C).

simmering Range of temperatures between 180°F (82°C) and 211°F (99°C); bubbles form and rise, but rarely break the surface; more gentle heat treatment than boiling.

boiling Active agitation of liquid and transition of some liquid to the vapor state; occurs when vapor pressure just exceeds atmospheric pressure.

vapor pressure Pressure within a liquid for individual molecules to escape from the liquid; varies with the temperature of the liquid and with dissolved substances.

atmospheric pressure Pressure of the atmosphere pressing downward on the surface of a liquid; varies with elevation.

The fact that fish do not freeze while living in the icy waters of the Arctic and Antarctic oceans has piqued the curiosity of food researchers since the middle of the 20th century. Considerable research has led to the isolation of a family of glycoproteins called antifreeze glycoprotein (AFGP), which is credited with keeping these fish from freezing to death by lowering the freezing point of their tissues dramatically. Two Antarctic fish, *Trematomus borchgrevinki* and *Dissostichus mawsoni*, and a northern fish, *Boreogadus saida*, produce glycoproteins.

Possible applications for AFGPs in food products are being explored now. AFGPs not only lower the freezing point but they also retard recrystallization, which helps to block the growth of large ice crystals. Because of these favorable qualities in determining ice crystal size, AFGPs might be useful as an additive in ice cream bars to help prevent the growth of large ice crystals; small ice crystals contribute to the smooth texture.

http://meetings.aps. org/Meeting/MAR07/ Event/58977

—Abstract of a paper presenting research on the effects of antifreeze glycoproteins on freezing temperatures.

heat of vaporization
Energy required to convert boiling water into steam; 540 kilocalories per gram of water.

To change water from the liquid state into the gaseous state (steam) requires input of a considerable amount of energy, called the heat of vaporization. In fact, to convert a gram of boiling water into steam requires 540 kilocalories. **Heat of vaporization** requires almost seven times more energy than is involved in the heat of solidification.

When water is being heated, the temperature will rise quickly until the boiling point is reached, but there will be a lag before boiling actually begins because of the tremendous heat input needed to supply the energy needed for vaporization (steam) to occur. The situation is reversed when steam condenses into water, as occurs when steam comes in contact with skin. The serious burns resulting from contact with steam reflect the fact that 540 kilocalories are given off onto the skin when steam is converted back into water. This is one of the reasons to be careful to avoid contact with steam.

Atmospheric Pressure   The pressure being exerted downward upon a pan of water (atmospheric pressure) must be overcome before boiling can occur. Clearly, this pressure has an instrumental role to play in determining the temperature at which boiling will happen. Altitude modifies atmospheric pressure; in the mountains there is less atmosphere above the surface of the ground than there is at sea level. Consequently, atmospheric pressure is lower at high elevations than at low ones. This means that boiling will take place more easily at a high elevation than at sea level; in other words, the temperature at boiling is lower on a high mountain than it is at the ocean. In fact, the boiling temperature of water drops 1°F for each 500 feet of gain in elevation (1°C for each 960 feet of gain).People who live at an elevation of 8,000 feet boil vegetables at a temperature of 196°F (91°C) in contrast to a temperature of 212°F (100°C) at the ocean. This is why vegetables or other foods cooked in boiling water in the mountains require a longer time to become tender than they do at lower elevations. A remarkable illustration of this drop in the temperature of boiling is noted in people's accounts of expeditions on Mt. Everest, where the extremely high elevations and the consequently low atmospheric pressure cause such a decrease in the boiling temperature of water that it is possible to reach directly into a pot of boiling water.

A partial vacuum can be created in special equipment to modify the effect of atmospheric pressure. Sometimes this is done in food processing to reduce the temperature of boiling so much that water can be evaporated without causing a cooked flavor to develop. This is desirable when making orange juice concentrate. In processing the concentrate, a partial vacuum reduces the atmospheric pressure above the orange juice, causing the original orange juice to boil at a cool temperature. This technique promotes the evaporation of water, yet avoids actually "cooking" the orange juice.

Pressure saucepans and pressure canners artificially increase atmospheric pressure, resulting in a higher temperature for boiling, which shortens cooking times. Commonly, 15 pounds of pressure will be generated within this very tight system, and this raises the cooking temperature to about 240°F (116°C). The elevated temperature significantly shortens the cooking time needed to tenderize a food (Figure 4.11). Commercially pressurized equipment accomplishes this same increase in temperature of the cooking medium.

Vapor Pressure The temperature of the water influences the vapor pressure, or the energy of water molecules trying to escape the liquid system. At room temperature, vapor pressure is quite low, but it increases rather rapidly as water temperature rises toward the boiling point. With adequate heat, vapor pressure will just exceed atmospheric pressure, and some of the water molecules will begin to escape into the air above the pan. Substances that form a true solution in water reduce the vapor pressure of the solution. For boiling to take place, additional heat must be supplied to raise the vapor pressure to the point at which vapor pressure just exceeds atmospheric pressure. The net result of the addition of a solute to water is to raise the boiling point. The greater the concentration of solute, the higher is the temperature of the boiling solution.

This effect is utilized in the preparation of candies, which are boiled to specified final temperatures. For example, fudge usually is cooked to 234°F (112°C), a temperature well above the 212°F temperature of boiling water. Several minutes of active boiling is required before the thermometer will finally reach the desired temperature because it is necessary to evaporate much of the liquid to concentrate the sugar sufficiently. It is this high concentration that successfully reduces the vapor pressure of the solution sufficiently to cause boiling to occur at 234°F (or even higher in some other candies with still greater concentrations). Thus, the temperature is a reliable indicator that boiling sugar solution has reached the desired point. This subject is discussed in some detail in Chapter 9.

The molecules of sugar, as pointed out, are small enough to go into solution. Molecules smaller than 1 millimicron are able to form true solutions and reduce vapor pressure. Salt (sodium chloride) ionizes when it is placed in water, resulting in the formation of two ions (sodium and chloride) from a single molecule of salt. As a consequence, salt has twice as great an effect on vapor pressure as sugar. However, the unpalatable quality of a salty solution makes this effect of little practical use in cookery.

Many substances in foods are much larger than a millimicron. Proteins, for example, are large molecules that are unable to go into solution but form a **colloidal dispersion**. Therefore, they have no appreciable effect on the boiling point. Gelatin, starch, gums, cornmeal, and countless other food items can be added to boiling water in varying concentrations, but they will not cause a measurable change in the boiling point because they form **coarse suspensions**, not true solutions.

Figure 4.11
A cook near Lake Titicaca in Peru adds the pressure gauge to her pressure cooker to build pressure and help speed the cooking of the vegetables she is preparing in the Andes Mountains at an elevation of 12,500 feet. Courtesy of Plycon Press.

colloidal dispersion
System containing protein or other molecules or particles between 1 and 100 millimicrons in size dispersed in a continuous phase, in this case in water.

coarse suspension
Dispersion of particles larger than colloidal size mixed in water or other liquid.

Frying Temperatures

With the exception of sugar solutions, cookery in boiling water is done at 212°F (100°C) or less unless a pressurized system is used. However, much higher temperatures can be utilized when fat is the cooking medium, because fat does not boil even when the temperature rises as high as 475°F (246°C). Fat can be maintained at around 375°F (190°C), a desirable temperature for frying. Such hot fat means that foods will reach their desired degree of doneness quite quickly in comparison with the length of time that would be needed if they were to be boiled in water at 212°F (100°C). After all, boiling water is more than 150 F° (83 C°) cooler than the fat used in frying.

The temperatures utilized in the preparation and storage of food generally span a range over almost 500 F° (about 280 C°). People working in food preparation and management need to know what temperatures are appropriate and how to control them. An overview of the various temperatures and their applications is illustrated in Figure 4.12.

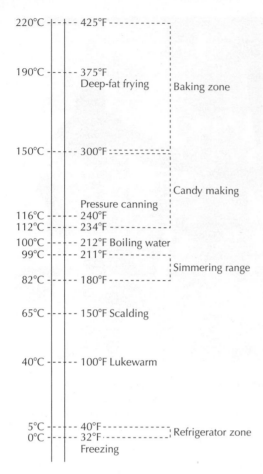

220°C ----- 425°F ---------------------

190°C ----- 375°F
              Deep-fat frying   Baking zone

150°C ----- 300°F

                                      Candy making

              Pressure canning
116°C ----- 240°F
112°C ----- 234°F ---------------------
100°C ----- 212°F Boiling water
99°C ----- 211°F
                                      Simmering range
82°C ----- 180°F

65°C ----- 150°F Scalding

40°C ----- 100°F Lukewarm

5°C ----- 40°F
                                      Refrigerator zone
0°C ----- 32°F
              Freezing

Figure 4.12
Temperatures in food preparation. Courtesy of
Plycon Press.

Such high temperatures highlight the need for being safety conscious in preparing foods. Burns occur all too easily when people fail to appreciate the extremely high temperatures of boiling candies or of the fat being used in deep-fat frying. In fact, kitchen counters with vinyl or formica tops can be damaged simply by placing a pan with a boiling candy solution or hot fat on them.

A related danger exists when water is added to caramelizing sugar or to hot fat. The extreme temperature difference between a caramelizing sugar or hot fat and cold water causes excessive splattering, which may result in burns on the hands, arms, or face—wherever the splatters reach the skin. To reduce splattering, water should be boiling when it is added to caramelizing sugar, and potato slices for French-frying should be blotted as dry as possible with paper towels before being added to the fat.

THERMOMETERS

To help ensure good temperature control in food preparation and handling, appropriate thermometers are used: generally, a candy thermometer, a deep-fat frying thermometer, and a meat thermometer (Figure 4.13). The thermometer for candy making will need to have an upper limit of approximately 325°F (163°C) to allow a margin of safety above the probable high of 300°F (149°C) needed for some candies. The deep-fat frying thermometer will have an upper limit of at least 500°F (260°C). A meat thermometer will register up to about 185°F (85°C) and should have a short sensing rod to accommodate to roasting in the oven. A pocket thermometer is convenient, but its plastic cover will melt if used in the oven.

Appliances occasionally may fail to maintain their thermostatic control. A refrigerator thermometer and an oven thermometer are useful checks on appliances to be sure that food is being held at safe temperatures. Food-service professionals in industry find thermometers invaluable in ensuring that foods on the steam table are being held at a high enough temperature and that refrigerated items are being stored at safe temperatures.

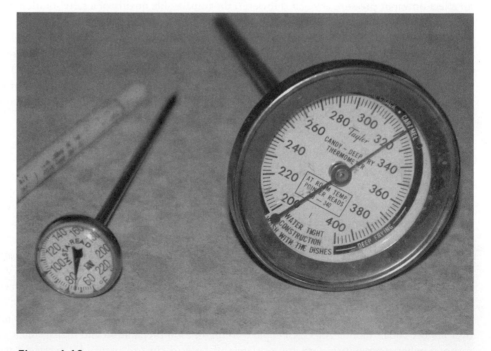

Figure 4.13
Instant-read thermometer (left) measures temperatures to 220°F; candy-making and deep-fat frying thermometers measure much higher temperatures. Courtesy of Plycon Press.

PRINCIPLES OF HEATING FOODS

Conduction

Heat can be transferred by **conduction**; that is, heat is transferred directly from one molecule to another. In cooking, heat is transferred by conduction from the metal of an electrical coil on a range directly to the metal of the pan in which a food is being heated. This method of heat transfer works slowly, but it is fairly successful when good conductors are used. Aluminum pans, for example, provide quite uniform heating if they are thick. In contrast, stainless steel conducts heat unevenly, causing some pans made with this metal to develop some spots that are too hot, while others may be too cool.

Convection

When water, oil or other fat, or air is heated, currents begin to develop within the system and aid in moving the heat throughout the food. This circulation of heated liquids or air is a process called **convection**. The convection oven is based on this principle. By forcing the circulation of heated air currents in this type of oven, foods will be heated and baked significantly more quickly than they will be when circulation of heated air is limited.

All ovens maintain some circulation of heated air during operation, but the amount of movement in a regular oven is quite low. If conventional ovens are loaded so that baking pans extend to the sides, front, or back of the oven, the normal flow pattern of the hot air currents will be obstructed, and uneven baking results. It is important to avoid placing one pan directly beneath another or to prevent loading an oven with pans being jammed right against each other and against the oven walls if even baking and browning are to be achieved in a conventional oven. However, pans can be placed beneath other pans in a convection oven satisfactorily because of the effective circulation of hot air. Convection currents are the key to successful baking in both convection and conventional ovens.

Convection is also a significant part of the heating process when foods are being heated on the range. The pan holding the food will be heated by conduction, but the heat begins to move through the food itself with the aid of warming currents of water or other liquid. Stirring is an added aid in helping to distribute the heat uniformly through the food.

Radiation

Radiation is the direct transfer of energy from the energy source to the food. Broiling is a familiar example of this type of heating. The energy involved in radiation from broiling is in the infrared range (somewhat longer waves than are in the range of visible light).

http://hyperphysics. phy-astr.gsu.edu/hbase/ thermo/heatra.
—Information on types of heat transfer.

conduction Transfer of heat from one molecule to the next.

convection Transfer of heat throughout a system by movement of currents of heated air, water, or other liquid.

radiation Transfer of energy directly from the source to the food being heated.

SCIENCE NOTE
HEATING BY MICROWAVES

Food in a microwave oven is heated by radiation. Microwave energy penetrates directly into the food to produce heat. Microwaves are a form of electromagnetic radiation, the waves being generated by a magnetron vacuum tube that converts electrical energy received by an amplifier into microwave radiation. The Federal Communications Commission has assigned two frequencies, 915 and 2,450 MHz, for radiation in microwave ovens. Both these frequencies are above the visible light range. The 2,450 MHz frequency has a shorter wavelength than the signal at 915 MHz; hence, it does not penetrate as deeply into the food mass as does the longer wavelength at 915 MHz.

Microwaves generate heat in food because of the electrical nature of water molecules. Water is a dipolar molecule: One portion of a water molecule carries a positive electrical charge, while the other part carries a negative charge. The microwave energy penetrating the food is characterized by its very rapid alternating of electrical charge. This constant change causes the water molecules to vibrate very actively, and the resulting vibration generates heat.

Unlike other forms of cookery, this energy is generated within the food rather than traveling from the surface toward the interior. Once the food begins to heat because of the dipolar nature of the food in relation to the microwave energy, conduction also occurs, helping to equalize the temperature throughout the food. The standing time recommended in many microwave oven recipes acknowledges the importance of allowing conduction to contribute to the overall cookery mode.

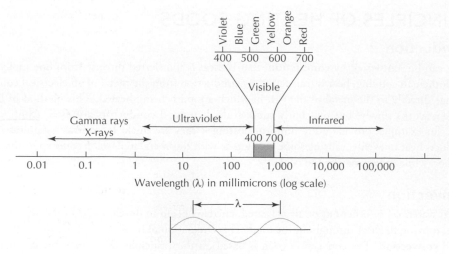

Figure 4.14

Frequencies assigned to microwave ovens (915 and 2,450 MHz) are above visible light.

Courtesy of Plycon Press.

http://www.colorado.edu/
physics/2000/microwaves/
index.html
—Interactive site explaining
heating by microwaves.

http://www.fda.gov/
Radiation- Emitting
Products/ResourcesforYou
RadiationEmittingProducts/
Consumers/ucm142616.htm
—Information on cooking
food safely using
microwave ovens.

microwave oven   Special
type of oven that is able to
heat food by sending waves
of 915 or 2,450 MHz from
a magnetron tube directly
into foods, where water
and/or fat molecules vibrate
and heat foods.

magnetron tube   Tube
generating microwaves in a
microwave oven.

microwave   Form of
electromagnetic energy;
915 and 2,450 MHz are the
assigned frequencies for
microwave ovens.

Although these are distinctly different types of heating, most foods are heated by a combination of at least two of these cooking techniques. For instance, a broiled steak will be heated by conduction as well as by radiation. A soup being heated in a pan will be heated by conduction and convection.

Microwave ovens also utilize the infrared frequency range (Figure 4.14) for a unique way of heating foods. In microwave ovens, a **magnetron tube** is used to generate waves of frequency above the length of visible light, specifically either 915 or 2,450 megahertz (MHz). These waves, called **microwaves**, penetrate as much as an inch into a food, causing rapid vibrations of individual molecules of water or fat. It is these vibrations that cause the food to begin to heat rapidly.

For food to be heated by microwave energy, there must be some water or fat present, although a large quantity is not essential to success. Fat becomes very hot even more quickly than water does in a food being heated by microwaves. Thus, butter or other fats can be melted very quickly in a microwave oven. Similarly, meats tend to be overheated quickly by microwave cookery unless the slices are relatively thin and the progress of the microwaves into the meat is monitored with extreme care.

Microwave ovens must be operated only when water or food has been placed in them, for the microwaves introduced into the cavity must have a substance to absorb them. Otherwise, the waves will be bounced right back toward the magnetron tube, causing irreparable damage to the tube. An empty pan or dish will not absorb the microwaves any better than the empty cavity. Even if food is present, microwaves will arc back toward the magnetron if metal is placed within the unit. Consequently, water or food must always be in a microwave oven before it is turned on or operated. Also, metal should not be placed in a microwave oven because it will cause arcing.

SUMMARY

Food preparation is done most successfully when the appropriate equipment is available. Basic preparation equipment includes measuring cups and spoons, mixing bowls, an electric mixer, a variety of utensils, a cooking thermometer, and a variety of cutlery. A set of pans, a large pot, frying pans, and appropriate baking pans are necessary for cooking and baking.

Accurate measurements are essential for preparing recipes successfully. Dry ingredients are measured volumetrically using graduated measuring cups or spoons. Liquids are measured in clear glass measuring cups.

The risk of a fall in the kitchen can be reduced if spills are wiped up as soon as they happen. Any mats or rugs in the kitchen should lie flat and have a backing that prevents slipping. Care needs to be exercised when plugging in or using electrical appliances. Food should be cut by pushing the knife blade away from the body. Burns can be prevented when handling hot pans by using hot pads (not towels). Safety of the food is dependent upon the sanitation practices of food handlers and on proper temperature control.

Freezing and boiling temperatures are influenced by the presence of sugar. Sugar dissolves and lowers the freezing point of ice creams and other foods high in sugar. Sugar solutions boil at elevated temperatures because sugar lowers vapor pressure. Although salt also alters boiling temperatures, it is used in such small amounts that the effect is insignificant in food preparation.

Heat control is important in food preparation and storage. Moderate heats include lukewarm, scalding, and simmering. These can be achieved by use of a double boiler or a very low heat setting on a range.

High elevations and/or partial vacuums will cause water to boil at a lower temperature than normal. The converse is provided by pressure saucepans or pressure cookers, which reach elevated temperatures, thus reducing cooking times. Deep-fat frying is another technique that provides fast cooking because temperatures in fat can be about 375°F (190°C) or even a bit hotter.

Food may be heated by conduction, convection, radiation, or a combination of these methods. Radiation is quite fast, resulting in reduction of cooking time compared with either convection or conventional ovens; microwaves cause water and fat molecules within a food to vibrate rapidly, resulting in heat generation and rapid heating of food from within.

STUDY QUESTIONS

1. Describe the way to measure flour and explain the rationale for the technique.
2. What is the best way to measure 3/4 cup of rice volumetrically?
3. What is the most accurate way of measuring (a) 3 teaspoons of baking powder, (b) 5 1/3 tablespoons of sugar?
4. What is the recommended method for measuring 1/2 cup of shortening? Describe a second method sometimes used to measure solid fats in the home. Why is this method less desirable than the first?
5. Why does the temperature rise when a sugar solution is boiled actively for several minutes?
6. How can atmospheric pressure be modified? What influence does atmospheric pressure have on the boiling point of water?
7. Describe the ways in which heat is transferred into foods.

SELECTED REFERENCES

Ben, R. N. 2001. Antifreeze glycoproteins: Preventing the growth of ice. *ChemBioChem. 2*: 161.

Bertrand, K. 2005. Microwavable foods satisfy need for speed and palatability. *Food Technol. 59*(1): 30.

Burcham, T. S., et al. 1986. A kinetic description of antifreeze glycoprotein activity. *J. Biol. Chem. 261*(14): 6390.

Cheng, C. C., et al. 2003. Functional antifreeze glycoprotein genes in temperate-water New Zealand nototheniid fish infer an Antarctic evolutionary origin. *Mol. Biol. Evol. 20*(11): 1897.

Clark, J. P. 2006. High-pressure processing research continues. *Food Technol. 60*(2): 63.

Clark, J. P. 2007. High pressure effects on foods. *Food Technol. 61*(2): 69.

Clark, J. P. 2009. Getting to the heart of heat transfer. *Food Technol. 63*(9): 82.

Datta, A. K., et al. 2005. Microwave combination heating. *Food Technol. 59*(1): 36.

Feeney, R. E., and Y. Yeh. 1993. Antifreeze proteins: Properties, mechanisms of action, and possible applications. *Food Technol. 47*: 82.

Feeney, R. E., and Y. Yeh. 1998. Antifreeze proteins: Current status and possible food uses. *Trends Food Sci. Technol. 9*(3): 102.

Feeney, R. E., and Y. Yeh. 2000. Future food ingredients: antifreeze proteins. *Prepared Foods.*

Harding, M. M., et al. 2003. 'Antifreeze' glycoproteins from polar fish. *Eur. J. Biochem. 270*(7): 1381.

McWilliams, M. 2008. *Illustrated Guide to Food Preparation.* 10th ed. Prentice Hall. Upper Saddle River, NJ.

McWilliams, M. 2012. *Foods: Experimental Perspectives.* 7th ed. Prentice Hall. Upper Saddle River, NJ.

Mudgett, R. E. 1986. Microwave properties and heating characteristics of foods. *Food Technol. 40*(6): 84.

Tharp, B., and S. Young. 2003. Tharp and Young on ice cream. *Food Products. Nov. 21.*

Wilson, E. 2004. How Arctic fish avoid freezing. *Chem. Eng. News 82*(7): 13.

Farmers' markets provide an array of high-quality vegetables fresh from the fields. Courtesy of Plycon Press.

5
Vegetables

Chapter Contents

Key Concepts

1. Vegetables are important in meals to provide not only an array of minerals and vitamins but also color, flavor, and textural contrasts.

2. Various parts of plants are eaten as vegetables, either raw or cooked (e.g., boiled, steamed, roasted, or fried).

3. Careful selection and handling of fresh, frozen, and canned vegetables are necessary to procure the desired quality.

4. Preparation of vegetables should be done to optimize sensory qualities (color, aroma, flavor, and texture) and to retain nutrients.

Vegetables contribute color and nutrients to meals. They contain fiber and **phytochemicals** such as beta-carotene and lycopene that may play protective roles in reducing the risk of such potential health problems as cancer and heart disease (Figure 5.1). Vegetables are not only rich sources of these important compounds, but they also contain significant amounts of other vitamins and minerals. Add to this health note the fact that vegetables generally are quite low in calories, and it is little wonder that they are popular.

Vegetables have the potential for adding wonderful colors, textures, and intriguing flavors to a meal. Imagine how drab the main course of a meal would be if the bright red of a tomato, the striking orange of carrots, the intense green of broccoli, the pearly white of cauliflower, or some other color accent were absent. Slightly crisp cooked green beans, fluffy mashed potatoes, or the crunch of a celery strip add essential textural interest to a meal. And what would many meals be without the flavor lift of an onion, sweet corn, or green pepper?

High-quality preparation of vegetables may seem to be a challenge at first, but they can be truly beautiful to look at and appealing to eat if prepared well. Unfortunately, they also can be ruined by poor cooking techniques. Mastery of vegetable cookery is an essential aspect of the study of foods. Exciting color, flavor, and textural contrast can be added to a meal when vegetables are selected and prepared with imagination and skill.

phytochemicals
Substances contained in plants that provide some protection against heart disease and certain cancers.

73

Figure 5.1
Tomatoes are rich
sources of nutrients (e.g.,
vitamin C) and lycopene,
a phytochemical with
potential health benefits.
Courtesy of Plycon Press.

CLASSIFICATION

Today, people still debate whether some plant foods should be classified as vegetables. The argument involves foods such as tomatoes and pumpkins that are viewed by some as fruits and by others as vegetables. The confusion can, however, be resolved in good order by using the following definition of a vegetable: a plant, usually herbaceous (with little or no woody tissue), containing an edible portion that is suitably served with the main course of a meal. Corn, beans, and most other vegetables are from plants that wither after the growing season, a characteristic common to herbaceous plants. The limited sweetness of most vegetables suits these foods to the main course rather than to dessert. Thus, this definition helps to classify tomatoes as vegetables, even though they are the fruit of the plant on which they grow.

Almost all parts of plants can be used as vegetables, but specific portions of the various plants are selected for use in meals. It is on the basis of the part of the plant that is eaten that vegetables are classified. For example, although the tender green tops of onions may be used, the bulb is the main portion eaten, so onions are classified as bulbs. The roots of carrots are the portion considered to be a vegetable, while tubers, leaves and stems, fruits, and seeds of various other plants are also viewed as vegetables (Figure 5.2). Table 5.1 illustrates the classification for many of the common vegetables.

Figure 5.2
This market offers many
examples of vegetables of
all types: bulbs (onions), root
(beets and carrots), tubers
(potatoes), leaves/stems
(lettuce), fruits (eggplant),
and seeds (corn). Courtesy of
Plycon Press.

TABLE 5.1
CLASSIFICATION OF VEGETABLES

Bulb	Root	Tubers[a]	Leaves/Stems	Fruits	Seeds
Garlic	Beets	White potatoes	Broccoli	Tomatoes	Legumes[b]
Leeks	Carrots	Sweet potatoes	Brussels sprouts	Eggplant	lima beans
Onions	Radishes	Jerusalem artichoke	Celery	Peppers	kidney beans
Shallots	Parsnips	Jicama	Cabbage	Okra	red beans
	Rutabagas		Chinese cabbage	Squash, summer and winter	navy beans
	Turnips		Endive		pinto beans
	Daikon		Parsley	Cucumbers	chickpeas
	Celeriac (celery root)		Cilantro	Chinese snow peas	black-eyed peas
			Leaf lettuce	Artichokes	split peas
			Head lettuce	Green beans	black beans
			Kale	Wax beans	
			Kohlrabi		

[a]Enlarged, edible fleshy stems growing under the ground.

[b]Seeds from the Leguminosae family, a family of plant unique for the ability to fix nitrogen into the soil, thus enriching the soil.

SURVEY OF VEGETABLES

One of the pleasures of vegetables is their great variety. With the excellent transportation and storage facilities now available for marketing vegetables, it no longer is necessary to restrict menus to corn, peas, beans, and carrots. The array in some markets may be almost puzzling; the paragraphs that follow will help to identify many different vegetables and highlight their storage and preparation.

Anise, also called sweet fennel, is unique among vegetables because of its flavor; in fact, it can be described as licorice-flavored celery. The bulb can be eaten raw or may be cut up and cooked by boiling, steaming, or braising. Storage following purchase should be in the hydrator drawer of the refrigerator.

Globe (or French) artichokes, the artichoke type found commonly in U.S. markets, are actually the flower of a thistle-like plant (Figure 5.3). The globe artichoke has an edible portion at the base of each leaf and under the choke (fuzzy portion), called the heart.

www.friedas.com

—Current information regarding a variety of unusual fruits and vegetables.

http://www.ams.usda.gov/AMSv1.0/fv

—Federal fruit and vegetable programs.

Figure 5.3
Globe artichokes are a type of thistle grown around the Mediterranean and also near Monterey, California, where the climate is similar.
Courtesy of Plycon Press.

Figure 5.4
Cross sections of artichokes reveal the edible heart, the white solid area at the base of the petals and between the purplish choke and the fibrous stem. Courtesy of Plycon Press.

www.artichokes.com

—Information on raising, harvesting, and preparing artichokes.

www.asparagus.org

—Website of the Michigan Asparagus Advisory Board.

These beautiful vegetables are deceptive in terms of quantity because of their limited amount of edible pulp in relation to fibrous petals and choke (Figure 5.4). However, the ceremony of dipping the base of each petal into a sauce of some type and then delicately scraping the pulp from the petal with the front teeth gives any meal a festive appeal. Globe artichokes can be stored in the refrigerator for a few days in a plastic container or in the hydrator drawer. After being boiled, steamed, or baked, globe artichokes may be served hot or cold.

Jerusalem artichokes, sometimes called sunchokes, are quite different and for this reason are classified as a tuber. Despite their name, Jerusalem artichokes are thought to be natives of North America. Their use ranges from raw slices in salads and garnishes to serving as a boiled or broiled alternative to potatoes.

Asparagus, whether green or the highly prized white, traditionally is available fresh for only a very brief period in the spring, and even then, its price is often high. For best results, storage time should be kept short, in the hydrator drawer in the refrigerator. Boiling, steaming, and stir-frying are all excellent techniques for preparing asparagus. Sometimes cooked asparagus is chilled before serving and used in salads.

Fresh beans often available in the market include green or snap beans, wax beans, lima beans, and fava beans (a bean similar to lima beans). Refrigerator storage should be limited to about three days, in a closed plastic bag or the hydrator drawer. Boiling, stir-frying, and steaming are suitable cookery methods.

Dried beans include an array of varieties: red, kidney, navy, pinto, black, pink, white, garbanzo, and lima. Unlike the other vegetables discussed here, dried beans can be stored at room temperature for several months as long as they are in their dried state. A tightly closed bag is recommended for storage in a damp climate. An extended soaking and/or cooking period rehydrates and tenderizes dried beans.

Beets are prized (or cursed when spilled) as a vegetable dye because of their deep red color. When harvested quite young, the greens are excellent when they are either steamed or boiled. Preparation usually involves boiling, followed by peeling and slicing. Sweet-and-sour sauces, such as the sauce used in Harvard beets, are used sometimes to heighten the flavor interest. Beet pickles are another popular means of preparing this vegetable.

Broccoli is a popular choice when people are seeking ways to raise the nutrient content of a meal. Not only is it nourishing, but it also is attractive on the plate, with its combination of little flowers and the stem of the plant. Optimal quality is obtained when the flowers are deep bluish-green; yellowing is an indication of aging. Boiling and steaming are the most frequent preparation methods, but sometimes broccoli is deep-fat fried or stir-fried. Prior to cooking, storage needs to be in a hydrator drawer or tightly covered container to avoid moisture loss.

Brussels sprouts, "little cabbages," can add the appeal of line, color, and flavor in a meal when properly prepared (Figure 5.5). Each sprout should be a tight, small head with no trace of yellowing on the green leaves. A comparatively short storage period in the hydrator drawer of the refrigerator will be possible without losing quality significantly.

Cabbage is a rather short word that includes an intriguing range of vegetables. The common green cabbage is known to most markets and is particularly valuable as a source of vitamin C when eaten in quantity. Heads should be firm, with a good green color and smooth leaves. A similar description can be made for red cabbage, with the exception of the color, which should be a deep purplish-red. Savoy cabbage is a close relative of green cabbage, but the leaves are characterized as being deeply crinkled. Chinese cabbage (also called Napa) is quite different in appearance, having a wide and prominent central rib in each leaf and an overall shape of an elongated head. Since all of these are susceptible to loss of moisture from their leaves and consequent loss of crispness, careful hydrator storage is necessary. These various forms of cabbage are served either raw in salads or cooked, usually by boiling.

Carrots have lacy tops that suggest the fact that they belong to the parsley family; other relatives of this varied group include celery and parsnips. The bright orange color and delicate flavor of high-quality carrots have made them a favorite vegetable, either raw or cooked.

Figure 5.5
Brussels sprouts grown tightly packed on a tall stalk present a striking appearance for a cooking adventure. *Courtesy of Plycon Press.*

One of their virtues is their comparatively low cost and availability throughout the year. When stored without their tops, carrots can be kept in a hydrator drawer or plastic bag for many days. Carrots are remarkably versatile and can be used raw as carrot curls or sticks or shredded in a salad with raisins; boiled or steamed and served plain or with sauces; and even grated and used in carrot cake.

Cauliflower should be a white, compact head, free of dark blemishes or spots. Its cabbage-like flavor indicates its relationship to cabbage. Some people use small flowerets raw for dipping or in vegetable salads. In addition, the head may be cooked whole by boiling, or individual flowerets may be broken off and boiled or steamed.

Celery is one of the stem vegetables particularly popular in its raw form. Pascal is the variety generally preferred because of its reduced stringiness and mild flavor.

Celeriac is a relative of celery. However, it is the bulb-like root that is used for the vegetable (Figure 5.6). Its large cross section requires thorough cooking to tenderize it, a problem that can be minimized by cutting the root into cubes before cooking. The gnarled skin of celeriac should be removed.

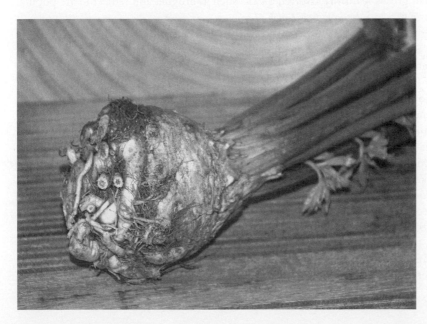

Figure 5.6
Celeriac (celery root) is peeled and cooked before being served as a root vegetable. *Courtesy of Plycon Press.*

Figure 5.7
Daikon (the large and long white Japanese radishes seen in the back green bin toward the right of this stall in Kyoto) are also available in many American markets.
Courtesy of Plycon Press.

Sweet corn, quite a different product from the field corn used to feed cattle, is a highlight of summer when served boiled or steamed on the cob. Occasionally, it is roasted in a tight foil wrap. Enthusiasts often have a pot of water boiling before rushing corn from its place on the cornstalk to the pot for a brief boiling before eating. This ceremony reflects the rapid reduction in sugar content that happens after picking.

Daikon, also called the Japanese radish (Figure 5.7), is often available to satisfy the demand for it generated by Asians living in the United States. It may be as much as 18 inches long. Use of daikon can be similar to the use of white radishes when washed and peeled. It provides a flavor highlight and crispness of texture that is particularly appealing in raw vegetable salads.

Eggplant, originally found in India and China, now is a particularly popular vegetable for Middle Eastern meals. The deep purple, glossy skin of the eggplant is unique among vegetables. Size varies, but often eggplants will be as big as 6 inches in diameter. For best results, eggplant should be held only briefly in the refrigerator before cooking. Sautéed slices or baked eggplant are particularly popular ways of preparing this vegetable.

Greens may be either salad greens served raw or cooked greens. Although spinach is used both ways, most greens are used only as the raw or as the cooked version. Those used for cooking include kale, turnip greens, beet greens, mustard greens, and collards. During cooking, these greens will wilt drastically as water departs from the leaves, and the fragile cell walls collapse. For optimal quality, greens should be stored in the hydrator drawer of the refrigerator for only a day or two and then should be cooked just until they are wilted.

Greens salads are extremely popular, but their quality and interest are influenced by the careful selection and proper storage of the greens. Considerable interest can be added to salads by selecting different types of lettuce to provide variety of color and texture. For instance, butterhead (Boston and Bibb) lettuces, with their moderate, slightly yellow-green color and almost oily, undulating leaves, are excellent for liners under other salads as well as for use in green salads. Bibb lettuce sometimes is known as "limestone" lettuce. Endive, a green with long, thin, curly leaves, has a scratchy texture, while escarole is somewhat less abrasive in the mouth and throat. Leaf lettuces afford yet another choice when looking for good salad greens. Some leaf lettuce is bronze or red in color. Prepackaged mixtures of salad greens featuring assorted greens such as arugula and radicchio are popular for their convenience and variety.

Jicama is a vegetable introduced to the United States from Mexico. Its skin must be pared before it is used—raw or boiled. Its most popular uses currently are in the raw state, as sticks for dips and as cubes in raw vegetable salads. Raw jicama often is garnished with a bit of chili powder.

Mushrooms are highly prized as a complement to steaks, in sauces and gravies, and as a vegetable ingredient. Commercial production of this delicacy requires careful control of humidity, temperature, and ventilation, as well as rich mulch and dark growing conditions, but the excellent financial returns have caused a healthy industry in mushroom growing. In addition to the familiar cup and button mushrooms, some markets also feature cremini, shiitake, morel, chanterelles, enoki, portabello, and oyster mushrooms (Figure 5.8). Refrigerator storage is the recommended way of storing mushrooms, but even this method should be limited to only a few days.

Some people like to go mushroom gathering in the woods, an idyllic pastime. Unfortunately, many varieties are highly toxic, a fact that has caused fatalities.

Okra, Creole cookery, and gumbo are inseparable. The comparatively small pods of okra contain a slippery exudate that can be minimized by drying the pods thoroughly before cutting

Figure 5.8
Cremini and oyster mushrooms are among the choices available when buying mushrooms in this market. Courtesy of Plycon Press.

them. Most often, okra is used as a sliced vegetable in soups and gumbos, but it also can be dipped in batter and fried.

Onions and their relatives are valued for their unique flavor contributions to foods, both from the bulbs themselves and also, frequently, from the green tops. The choices range from large, dry Spanish onions to tiny scallions and chives. The globe-shaped or flat-topped dry onions are useful in heightening flavors of many different foods. Red onions, because of their attractive appearance and pleasing flavor, are useful ingredients in salads. Shallots (onion-like bulbs) are yet another possibility for flavoring. Boiling onions, small dry onions about an inch in diameter, are popular for skewering on kabobs and for the primary ingredient in creamed onions. All types of dry onions should be stored in a cool, dry place to delay root growth and possible decay.

Green onions are onions that are harvested before the bulb develops fully. Scallions, another member of this cluster of edible and flavorful group from the lily family, ordinarily are harvested when the shoots are well developed but the bulb has not formed. Chives have become a familiar sight in gourmets' kitchens where they provide an attractive touch of green and a continuing supply of flavorful shoots for garnishes. Leeks are the hardiest of the green onion-like foods. They have a somewhat flat, thick edible stalk noted for its onion flavor. For optimum quality, these various types of green onions, with the exception of chives planted in pots, need to be refrigerated in the hydrator drawer and used within a matter of days.

Peas, like sweet corn, are sweetest when they can go directly from the vine to the pot. Delays result in a gradual change from sugar to starch. The maturity of the pea also influences the development of starch, with mature peas being less sweet and starchier in flavor than new peas. Storage of peas should be in the pod and in the hydrator drawer of the refrigerator.

The **Chinese** or **snow pea** is a strain of pea that has been gaining rapidly in popularity recently in this country. This delicate pea is cooked and consumed pod and all, with only the tips of the pods being broken off before cooking. The bright color and crispness of the pod add both textural interest and eye appeal to many Oriental and other dishes. Another pea also eaten in its pod is the sugar pea. These are popular cooked in stir-fries or raw in salads.

Although not used in large quantities in the typical American diet, dried peas should be noted. Split peas are one type of legume that can be stored for a comparatively long period in a dry storage area. Their most popular use is in making split pea soup, usually flavored with a ham bone.

The word *pepper* seems to mean "hot" to people, yet **sweet peppers** are anything but that. Red, yellow, orange, and green sweet bell peppers are the source of pleasing color accents and

www.onions-usa.org
—Information on onions.

intriguing flavors. Sometimes the top is cut off, the seeds are removed, and then the remaining whole pepper shell is parboiled in preparation for stuffing and baking. Often, bell peppers are diced or sliced and are used raw in salads or as ingredients in casseroles.

Other types of peppers also find their way to the table in different ways. For instance, paprika (Figure 5.9), one of the most common of the spices, is prepared for market by drying and grinding paprikas (sweet red peppers).

Potatoes form the backbone of diets in some areas of the world. In fact, the spread of this native South American food to Europe created such shifts in diet patterns that the Irish suffered an extremely serious famine in the mid-19th century when the potato crop failed.

Potatoes occupy a unique place among vegetables because of their excellent keeping qualities when stored properly and their remarkable versatility in preparation. There even are whole cookbooks devoted to ways to prepare potatoes. Although potatoes are found in markets throughout the year all across the country, the specific varieties available in different regions vary according to the types that will grow best in the local climate. The basic types of potatoes are

1. Round white,
2. Russet,
3. Round red, and
4. Long white.

Figure 5.9
Paprikas, virtually the Hungarian national vegetable, are drying in the sun awaiting their chance to add a lively burst of color and flavor to a meal. Courtesy of Plycon Press.

The storage temperature will influence the starch and sugar content of potatoes. The recommended temperature is about 60°F, or somewhat cooler than the average room. At this temperature, the sugar/starch levels in potatoes remain approximately the same as they were when the potatoes entered storage. However, when temperatures dip to around 45°F, sugar begins to accumulate, and starch levels drop; these changes are detrimental to optimal quality when cooked.

Sweet potatoes are available in markets throughout the year, with the choice generally being between those with a light-colored skin and a somewhat dry interior and the deeper-colored moist variety. Members of this latter variety often are called yams, even though they are not actually yams. True yams are not available in the markets in this country. Whether selecting the broad, bulky sweet potatoes with their tapered ends or "yams," the ends need to be dry and free from any hint of rot. Otherwise, they will not keep well even in cool, dry storage.

Red radishes are popular as a garnish or sliced in salads. The ability of the radish to fan out or to unfold when thin cuts are made in the vegetable is extremely useful when preparing garnishes to beautify a dinner plate or salad. White radishes, although lacking the bright color of the red radish, are extremely pleasing flavor accents when sliced into salads or simply eaten raw.

Rutabagas can be held in cool storage over the winter months. When coated with wax, this vegetable can be held for an extended period, but the wax needs to be peeled from rutabagas before they are boiled. After boiling, this yellow-fleshed vegetable often is mashed.

Summer squash are noted for their intriguing shapes, subtle flavors, and high water content. These squash can be kept in refrigerated storage only a few days before losing quality.

Zucchini is perhaps the best known of the summer squashes; it may be used raw in sticks for dips or in salads and also cooked in a variety of ways. Other summer squashes include yellow crookneck, pattypan or scallop, and cocozelle.

The hard-shell **winter squash**, in sharp contrast to the softer-skinned summer varieties, can be held in cool, dry storage (but not in the refrigerator) for several months. The hard shell and relatively low moisture content of winter squashes necessitate thorough cooking, often by baking, to make them highly palatable. Familiar winter squashes include Hubbard, table queen (acorn), buttercup, butternut, Turk's turban, spaghetti, and banana (Figure 5.10).

Even though they are the fruit of the plant, **tomatoes** are classified as a vegetable because they are often served in the main part of a meal. The versatility of the tomato (as a raw vegetable simply sliced as a component of vegetable salads or cooked in many ways, including in sauces and casseroles) makes this one of the most popular and widely accepted vegetables. Considerable research effort has been expended to develop tomato varieties suited for specific purposes and with the desired growing characteristics. For example, the elongated tomato was developed to fulfill the needs of commercial canners. The cherry tomato has found its niche in the hearts of salad lovers. Roma tomatoes, because of their bright red color and excellent cooking properties, have gained prominence in many recipes.

Turnips have gained in status with the institution of salad bars in U.S. restaurants and fast-food franchises. The turnip's white, crisp character adds interest to salads, either in grated form or in julienne strips. This vegetable is also physically strong enough to be used with dips. Of course, turnips can also be cooked. When fresh, the tops of turnips are excellent for boiling or steaming and serving as greens.

This is far from an exhaustive list of vegetables that might be available fresh, frozen, or canned in the market. The broadening interest in other cuisines doubtless will increase the availability of cilantro, bok choy, gobo, jicama, and other vegetables popular with the various ethnic groups in this country.

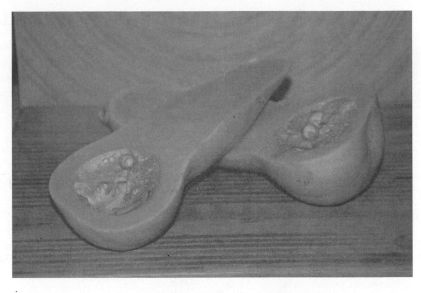

Figure 5.10
Butternut squash is a winter squash with the typical hard skin. Courtesy of Plycon Press.

INDUSTRY INSIGHT
BIOTECHNOLOGY

Biotechnology applied to developing new varieties of vegetables is an exciting and very active area of research at present. Development of plant foods with modified characteristics can be accomplished through genetic engineering and crossbreeding of carefully selected plants. By selective breeding, tomato varieties with less acid (a pH higher than the average of 4.5) were developed in the mid-1970s. Palatability and cooking characteristics were improved, but less acidic tomatoes presented a possible health risk in processed tomatoes because of the difficulty in killing *Clostridium botulinum* spores that might be present.

Another possible benefit of biotechnological research on plants may be reduced use of insecticides and pesticides. Concerns over the potential hazards created by these chemicals have sparked efforts to develop plant varieties that are resistant to insects due to the natural pesticide(s) they contain.

The possibility of creating plants that could serve as "edible vaccines" is even being explored. Among the ideas being pursued are alfalfa that can prevent cholera, a banana to prevent heptatitis B, and a potato to prevent gastroenteritis. Creation of edible vaccines is a complex process that begins by isolating the antigen from the toxin that is to be blocked. The genetic sequence of the antigen is cut out, and the antigen genes are injected into cells of the organism that causes crown gall disease. The plant being developed is infected with the crown gall disease, which transfers the altered genes into the plant.

Cells from this modified plant then are cultured to regenerate the desired plant, complete with its antigen. Consumption of such plants in adequate quantities is expected to provide immunity without the need for human inoculation. However, much remains to be learned before such a technique becomes viable as a means of preventive health care.

ASPECTS OF PALATABILITY

Clearly, the category dubbed vegetables includes a very large range of foods, some of which are very popular and others which may only be eaten because they are "good for health." Texture (mouthfeel), color, and flavor comprise the key to acceptance. Individuals likely will have different preferences, but these characteristics play major roles in their choices.

Texture and Structure

Vegetables vary somewhat in their structure from one type to another, but generally they have an outer covering (dermal tissue), a transport system (vascular system), and pulp, which is composed primarily of **parenchyma cells**. The parenchyma cells have permeable walls to permit some substances to pass back and forth. Some rigidity is provided by the presence of **cellulose**, with additional strength being the result of **pectic substances** and **hemicelluloses** serving as connecting links between cells. These various substances are types of carbohydrates. These contribute to the texture perceived in the mouth when a vegetable is eaten.

Flavor

Flavoring substances also are vital to the appeal of vegetables. The organic acids in vegetables certainly heighten the interest of the various flavors; some sulfur-containing compounds contribute to the unique flavor overtones found in onions and members of the cabbage family. Carrots and sweet corn are among the vegetables that gain part of their popularity to the sweet taste contributed by sugar, particularly when they are barely mature. Potatoes exemplify the effect of starch on flavor.

parenchyma cell Type of cell comprising most of the pulp of a vegetable or fruit.

cellulose Complex carbohydrate made up of glucose, but not digested by people.

pectic substances Complex carbohydrates acting as cementing substances between cells; sequence of change during ripening is protopectin to pectin to pectic acid.

hemicelluloses Complex carbohydrates made up of several different sugars and sugar derivatives.

SCIENCE NOTE
STRUCTURE OF PLANT FOODS

The strong, thick nature of the dermal layer is evident when fruits or vegetables are peeled. This protective layer has a high concentration of cellulose in the cell walls. Cellulose, like other structural carbohydrates, is not digested and absorbed for energy by people. This seems surprising when its content of only glucose units is known, for that is the same building material found in starch. However, the glucose units in cellulose are linked together differently from the linkage found in starch. The cellulose linkage is termed a 1,4-β glucosidic linkage, whereas that in starch is a 1,4-α glucosidic linkage. These two types of linkages are shown below. Note that the only difference is found on the carbon labeled 1. The union on the fourth carbon of the next glucose unit is the same in both cellulose and starch.

1,4-α—Glucosidic linkage

Starch fragment

Hemicelluloses also are important components of cell walls in fruits and vegetables. These compounds are more difficult to define than cellulose because hemicelluloses contain a variety of different sugar-related products. These include derivatives of some sugars with five carbons (arabinose and xylose) as well as galactose and mannose, each of which contains six carbons. The pectic substances, discussed in detail in Chapter 19, are made up of galacturonic acid units. These units are derivatives of galactose and undergo chemical changes during ripening of fruits. Unlike hemicelluloses, pectic substances are found between cells, where they act as substances to cement cells together rather than as parts of the cell wall.

Parenchyma cells constitute the bulk of the edible portion of fruits and vegetables. Their structure, therefore,

1,4 β Glucosidic linkage

Cellulose fragment

is of special interest. Within the parenchyma cell, as can be seen in Figure 5.11, there are special structures, the **plastids**, within the **cytoplasm**. The various types of plastids perform specific, unique functions and provide diverse characteristics to specific vegetables. For instance, in green vegetables chlorophyll is formed in a special plastid called a **chloroplast**. Chloroplasts are in the cytoplasm layer just inside the cell. The orange pigments in vegetables are found in other plastids called **chromoplasts**, which also are in the cytoplasm just next to the cell wall. Starch is found in still other plastids called **leucoplasts**.

A large portion of each of the parenchyma cells is occupied by the **vacuole**. The vacuole is of particular interest because this is the region where the fluid of the cell is concentrated and where such important flavor constituents as sugars, acids, and salts are found. This is also the location of the flavonoid (white or bluish to reddish-purple) pigments. When a vegetable is

cut or peeled, many parenchyma cells are opened, allowing considerable loss of pigments and other compounds found in the vacuole.

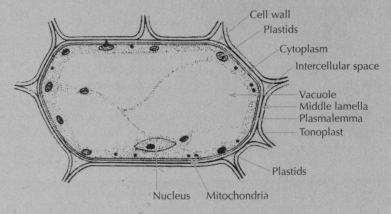

Figure 5.11
Diagram of a parenchyma cell. Courtesy of Plycon Press.

Color

The eye has a tremendous influence over the acceptance of vegetables, and color is a key aspect of their visual appeal. There are three principal pigment categories (Table 5.2), with each of these categories having subgroups within them. **Chlorophylls**, the predominant pigments in green vegetables, are formed in chloroplasts (a type of plastid in parenchyma cells).

TABLE 5.2
COMMON VEGETABLE PIGMENTS

Pigment	Color	Vegetable
Chlorophylls		
Chlorophyll a	Intense blue-green	Broccoli, lettuce, spinach, peas, green beans
Chlorophyll b	Yellow-green	
Pheophytin a	Pale green-gray	Green vegetables cooked more than 7 minutes
Pheophytin b	Olive green	
Carotenoids		
Carotenes		
Alpha-carotene	Yellow-orange	Winter squash, carrots, sweet potatoes, rutabagas
Beta-carotene	Red-orange	
Lycopene	Red	Tomatoes, watermelon
Xanthophylls		
Cryptoxanthin	Yellow	Sweet corn
Lutein	Orange	Spinach
Flavonoids		
Anthocyanins	Red, purple, blue	Red cabbage
Anthoxanthins	White	Cauliflower, white onions, turnips

cytoplasm Viscous layer just inside the cell wall of the parenchyma cell; contains plastids.

chloroplasts Plastids containing chlorophyll in parenchyma cells.

chromoplasts Plastids containing carotenoids (orange pigments) in parenchyma cells.

leucoplasts Plastids serving as the site for formation and storage of starch in parenchyma cells.

vacuole Largest region of the parenchyma cell; the portion encircled by the cytoplasm.

chlorophylls Green, magnesium-containing pigments formed in chloroplasts in fruits and vegetables.

flavonoids Class of pigments contributing white and red to blue colors in fruits and vegetables; two main divisions are anthoxanthins and anthocyanins.

anthoxanthins Group of flavonoids providing the white or creamy colors in fruits and vegetables.

anthocyanins Group of flavonoids providing the reddish to bluish hues of fruits and vegetables.

The orange-colored vegetables, such as sweet potatoes, carrots, and rutabagas, contain carotenes. This pigment group not only provides the attractive color of these vegetables but several of the carotenoid pigments also are nutritionally important as precursors of vitamin A. Beta-carotene is a particularly important form from the perspective of nutrition.

Vegetables that are white, blue, purple, and purplish-red contain the third group of pigments, the **flavonoids**, which are in the vacuole of parenchyma cells. Some flavonoids provide the white pigment, as seen in cauliflower. This flavonoid belongs to a group called the **anthoxanthins**. Dramatic deep reds, purples, and blues are contributed by the flavonoid group known as the **anthocyanins**.

This discussion is something of an oversimplification, for a blend of pigments commonly occurs in vegetables, with one of the pigments predominating over the others. This blending is the reason for the range of colors observed.

SCIENCE NOTE
PIGMENTS

Chlorophyll pigments (chlorophyll a and chlorophyll b) are susceptible to changes in their chemical structure during cooking. In the raw vegetable, these two structures differ only in the functional group attached to one of the rings in the structure. Actually, the structure of chlorophyll resembles that of heme (in hemoglobin), except that the metal complexed in chlorophyll is magnesium rather than the iron atom found in heme. In chlorophyll a, a methyl group (—CH_3) is the functional group, resulting in the fairly intense blue-green pigment color seen in the blue-green buds on broccoli. The aldehyde (—CHO) group in chlorophyll b imparts a rather yellow-green hue to green vegetables.

When chlorophyll-containing vegetables are cooked for at least five minutes, magnesium ions are released from some of the molecules of chlorophyll and are replaced by hydrogen. This reaction results in the formation of pheophytin a from chlorophyll a or pheophytin b from chlorophyll b. Pheophytin a causes the color to be a greenish-gray; pheophytin b is a distinctive olive drab. The combination of these two types of pheophytin yields the familiar, and rather dull, olive-green color characteristic of canned green vegetables.

The carotenoid pigments are highly unsaturated, as can be seen in the accompanying structure. These conjugated (alternating double and single bonds) double bonds account for the bright pigments of the carotenoid compounds.

Beta-carotene is but one example of the carotenes, all of which contribute color to vegetables. When this particular carotenoid (β-carotene) is split in the body, it yields vitamin A. The structures of the various carotenes are quite similar, varying only slightly in one of the rings at the end of the carbon chain. Lycopene (the red pigment in tomatoes) has no rings. The carotenes are quite stable pigments.

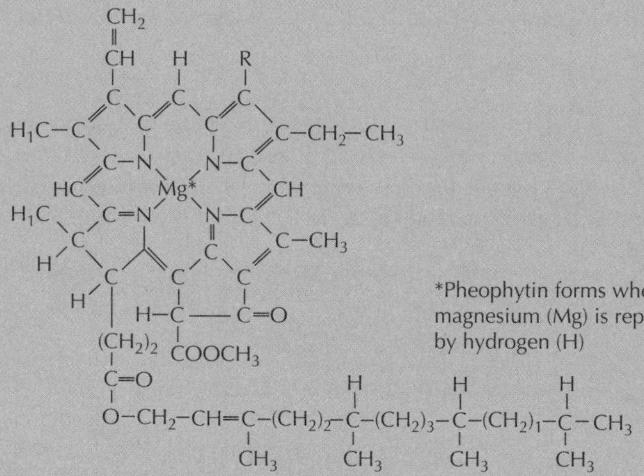

*Pheophytin forms when magnesium (Mg) is replaced by hydrogen (H)

Chlorophyll

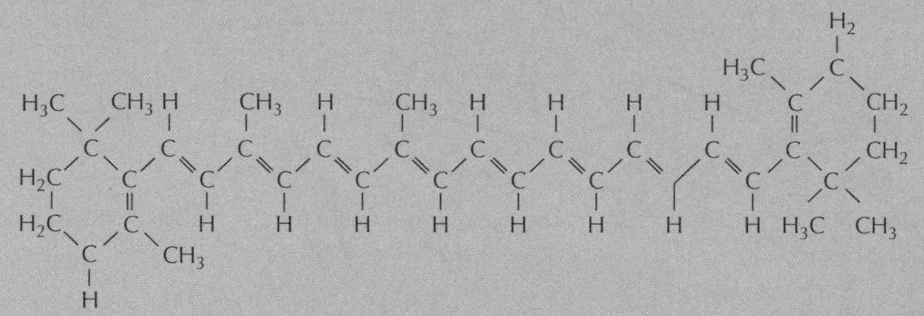

β–Carotene

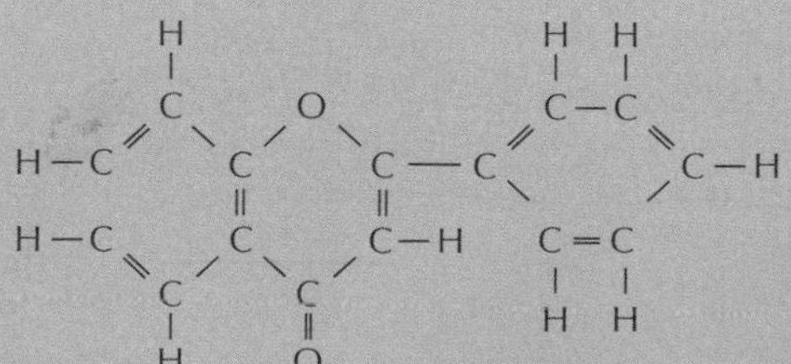

Flavone

Xanthophylls are carotenoid pigments that are very similar to the carotenes, the exception being that xanthophylls have some oxygen (in the form of —OH or hydroxyl groups), while the carotenes lack this element. Examples of xanthophylls are the cryptoxanthin in corn and lutein, an orange compound in spinach (but masked by chlorophyll).

Unlike the chlorophylls and carotenoids, which are contained in plastids, the flavonoids are in the vacuole of parenchyma cells, which causes these pigments to be released into the cooking water when vegetables containing them are cut or peeled. The various flavonoids are derivatives of the parent compound, flavone. Anthoxanthins are the white or colorless pigments in vegetables, such as cauliflower. The three-carbon unit in the middle of the structure of anthoxanthins includes a carbonyl (C=O); the reddish, purple, or blue colors of anthocyanins are the result of a somewhat different structure, for they lack this carbonyl as shown in the structure.

Shifts in the pigment color of the anthocyanins occur as a result of the number of hydroxyl (—OH) groups on the molecule. An increase in hydroxyl groups shifts the pigment from a reddish color toward a more bluish hue. The color shifts toward red in acid and toward blue in alkaline media, paralleling the change of color observed with litmus paper.

Metal ions (notably iron, tin, and aluminum) complex with flavonoids if they come in contact. These complexes

Flavonal (an *anthoxanthin*)
*Carbonyl of anthoxanthins is replaced with hydrogen in anthocyanins.

Cyanidin (an *anthocyanin*)

result in unattractive hues of blue, ranging from slate blue to a greenish-blue. Such colors are not appealing in foods and should be avoided by removing metal sources of contamination.

NUTRIENT CONTENT

For optimal health, five or more servings of fruits and vegetables are recommended. Their relatively large amounts of vitamins, minerals, and phytochemicals (Figure 5.12) are available with limited calories because of their minimal fat and large amount of water, which is particularly good news for people attempting to limit their caloric intake. In fact, green beans, cabbage, broccoli, asparagus, and many other vegetables are more than 90 percent water. Few vegetables other than legumes have less than 80 percent water.

http://www.fruitsand veggiesmatter.gov/
—General nutrition information on vegetables.

Figure 5.12
Vitamins, minerals, and phytochemicals (including some carotenoids and flavonoids) are available in abundance in fresh produce.
Courtesy of Plycon Press.

TABLE 5.3
APPROXIMATE COMPOSITION OF SELECTED VEGETABLES (1 CUP)

Vegetable	Calories	Protein (g)	Fat (g)	Total Carbohydrate (g)	Water (%)
Asparagus, cooked	40	4	Trace	8	92
Beans, green (cooked)	44	2	Trace	10	89
Beets, cooked	74	3	Trace	17	87
Broccoli, cooked	54	4	1	17	91
Brussels sprouts, cooked	56	4	1	11	87
Cabbage, raw	22	1	Trace	10	92
Cauliflower, cooked	28	2	1	5	93
Corn, sweet, cooked	143	5	2	31	79
Lettuce, raw	8	1	Trace	11	96
Peas, cooked	134	5	Trace	25	89
Spinach, cooked	43	5	Trace	7	91
Squash, summer, cooked	36	2	1	8	94
Sweet potatoes, baked	180	4	Trace	41	72
Tomatoes, raw	32	2	Trace	7	94

Source: Compiled from Nutritive values of the edible part of foods. *Home and Garden Bulletin No. 72.* U.S. Dept. Agriculture. Washington, DC, 2002 and U.S. Department of Agriculture, Agricultural Research Service. 2010. USDA National Nutrient Database for Standard Reference, Release 23. Nutrient Data Laboratory Home Page.

http://www.ars.usda.gov/
ba/bhnrc/ndl

—USDA nutrient database.

www.nal.usda.gov/fnic/food
comp/Data/HG72/hg72_
2002.pdf

—Home and Garden Bulletin
72 on nutritive content.

http://www.nal.usda.gov/fni
c/foodcomp/search/

—Access to entries for
nutritional composition
of specific foods in USDA
database.

Carbohydrate content varies, in both form and amount. Some of the sugar that may be present in some immature vegetables will gradually change to starch as they mature. Starch levels in white potatoes are around 15 percent and 25 percent for sweet potatoes, while cooked legumes average around 20 percent starch. In contrast, the carbohydrate level in cabbage is only about 5 percent (Table 5.3), and that is largely sugar rather than starch. The carbohydrate levels of most vegetables range between these figures, but tend toward 10 percent or less.

In addition to starch and sugars, which are digestible carbohydrates, vegetables gain much of their structure from indigestible pectic substances, hemicelluloses, and cellulose, all of which have been described briefly. The most durable of the structural components actually is not a carbohydrate; it is a woody substance called lignin and is used in the body only as roughage.

Protein and fat levels generally are very low in vegetables, thus partly accounting for the low energy value of most vegetables. The exceptions to this statement are the legumes, which are very useful sources of incomplete protein at a comparatively low cost. The protein content of cooked legumes averages approximately 8 percent—well below the protein content of meats, but much higher than the content of other vegetables and fruits. This amount of protein influences the cookery techniques needed for optimal quality.

Minerals and vitamins are found in widely varying amounts (Table 5.4) in the different vegetables, with some vegetables being notable in their content of specific nutrients. For example, the provitamin A content of dark green, leafy vegetables and orange vegetables is noteworthy, accounting for the recommendation of one of these vegetables at least every other day to ensure sufficient vitamin A is in the diet. Thiamin is relatively high in legumes, while folacin is found in excellent amounts in the leafy vegetables, and vitamin C plus other B vitamins are in other vegetables. Calcium and magnesium are found in useful amounts, too.

TABLE 5.4
VITAMIN AND MINERAL CONTENT OF SELECTED VEGETABLES (1 CUP)

Vegetable	Calcium (mg)	Iron (mg)	Vitamin A (IU)	Thiamin (mg)	Riboflavin (mg)	Niacin (mg)	Ascorbic Acid (mg)
Asparagus,							
cooked	42	1.6	970	0.18	0.25	1.9	14
canned	39	4.4	1,285	0.15	0.24	2.3	45
Beans, lima, cooked	37	2.3	323	0.13	0.10	1.8	22
Beans, green, cooked	55	1.6	833	0.09	0.12	0.8	12
Beans, wax							
cooked	58	1.6	101	0.09	0.12	0.8	12
canned	35	1.2	142	0.02	0.08	0.3	6
Beets, cooked	27	1.3	60	0.05	0.07	0.6	6
Beet greens, cooked	164	2.7	7,344	0.17	0.42	0.7	36
Broccoli, cooked	62	1.0	2,414	0.09	0.18	0.9	101
Brussels sprouts, cooked	56	1.9	1,122	0.17	0.12	0.9	97
Cabbage							
raw	37	0.4	93	0.04	0.03	0.2	32
cooked	47	0.3	198	0.09	0.08	0.4	30
Carrots, cooked	48	1.0	38,304	0.05	0.09	0.8	4
Cauliflower, cooked	20	0.4	27	0.05	0.06	0.5	55
Corn, sweet, cooked	4	0.5	392	0.17	0.06	1.2	8
Lettuce, raw (1 head)	110	2.7	1,779	0.25	0.16	1.0	21
Peas, cooked	67	3.2	282	0.20	0.12	0.9	72
Potato, baked	8	0.5	0	0.22	0.07	3.3	26
Spinach, cooked	245	6.4	14,742	0.17	0.42	0.9	38
Squash, cooked							
summer	49	0.6	517	0.08	0.07	0.8	10
winter	46	1.4	10,701	0.12	0.09	1.1	12
Tomatoes (1 raw)	9	0.8	1,499	0.11	0.09	1.1	34

Source: Compiled from Nutritive values of the edible part of foods. *Home and Garden Bulletin No. 72.* U.S. Dept. Agriculture. Washington, DC, 2002 and U.S. Department of Agriculture, Agricultural Research Service. 2010. USDA National Nutrient Database for Standard Reference, Release 23. Nutrient Data Laboratory Home Page.

HARVESTING AND MARKETING

The high quality of vegetables in the food supply today is something that is expected. Modern farming techniques, including use of fertilizers and pesticides, are used to produce crops that are high both in quantity and quality. Attention also is directed to avoiding contamination of field crops due to fecal matter from wild animals, runoff from livestock in neighboring fields, or farmworkers.

The need for care and attention continues into harvesting and marketing operations to help retain maximum nutrient content and palatability. From the moment vegetables are harvested, proper temperature and moisture controls are necessary, for metabolic processes continue in the harvested food. Control of these chemical changes is essential to the retention of vitamins and to overall palatability of produce.

When fresh vegetables are crated, the temperature in the crates slowly begins to rise, even though they generally have an open design. This is the consequence of the respiration that is continuing after harvest. For instance, the temperature in a crate of spinach has been measured to rise as high as 100°F, causing a soft rot to develop rapidly. Although leafy greens have a faster respiration rate than do other types of vegetables, increasing temperatures in crates of all types of vegetables still reduce quality. Vegetables can be packed loosely in crates, preferably along with some crushed ice, to reduce this problem.

The next step is rapid transport to the processing plant if vegetables are to be canned or frozen. The shorter the time and the better the temperature is controlled between harvesting and processing, the higher the nutrient value and the palatability of the processed vegetables.

If vegetables are to enter the retail market as fresh produce, proper temperature control must be maintained from harvest until they are cooked and consumed in the home. Ordinarily, they are loaded efficiently into refrigerated trucks or refrigerated railroad cars for transport to wholesale and, ultimately, retail markets. These special trucks or railroad cars work in opposite fashion at different seasons of the year, chilling the vegetables in the summer and keeping them from freezing with the assistance of heaters in the winter.

By paying careful attention to the circulation of air, maintenance of a desirable level of humidity, and control of temperature during transport in refrigerated cars, vegetables can be shipped clear across the country and arrive on the opposite coast in excellent condition. In fact, when vegetables shipped in refrigerated storage across the continent are compared with those grown locally and marketed without chilling, the refrigerated and transported produce may be of higher quality than that from local fields.

Local marketing arrangements are important if the consumer is to be able to purchase high-quality produce (Figure 5.13). Refrigerated transport from wholesale markets or warehouses to retail outlets is essential. Within the market, the retailer must have adequate refrigerated storage to maintain quality of produce awaiting display for purchase. Retail markets doing a high volume of business have the advantage of rapid turnover of produce, which is important in maintaining quality and nutritive value.

Market orders, established as a result of the Agricultural Marketing Agreement Act of 1937, are an important part of the marketing procedures. This legislation enables the U.S. Department of Agriculture to draw up and enforce marketing agreements via boards to regulate quality, quantity, standardization of packs, research and development projects, specification of unfair trade practices, required filing of selling prices, and collection of marketing information for the producers of the commodity specific to the marketing order. Such boards have had considerable impact over the years in influencing the development of markets for their products and promoting improvements intended to benefit producers and consumers alike.

market order   Regulations for the marketing of specific food products under the guidance of a board authorized by the U.S. Department of Agriculture.

Figure 5.13
Shoppers sometimes buy their fresh produce at farmers' markets featuring locally grown vegetables and fruits. Courtesy of Plycon Press.

SELECTION

Selection of specific vegetables for a meal begins with the decision to buy them fresh, frozen, canned, or, in some cases, dried. Individual preference may influence this decision, but price and availability also play key roles in the choice. When a vegetable is in season, the quality is high and the price usually will be competitively low, making purchase of the fresh form often the best choice. However, the convenience of preparing frozen or canned vegetables may motivate people to select one of these forms even when the fresh food is comparatively inexpensive and of high quality.

Fresh Vegetables

The eye is an excellent guide to selecting fresh produce, although wholesalers may use grading as an aid at that point in the marketing process. The quality of fresh vegetables is influenced by the season of the year and the handling during the marketing process, with the peak harvest period ordinarily providing a particular vegetable of the highest quality.

Grade standards have been established for many vegetables under the authority of the Agricultural Marketing Act of 1946. This optional grading, under the Agricultural Marketing Service of the U.S. Department of Agriculture, is useful in the wholesale phase of marketing. However, it is not ordinarily visible to consumers directly. Typically two grade designations are used for a particular type of vegetable, although four grade designations can theoretically be used.

Today consumers may find some produce labeled with an **organic seal** (Figure 5.14). The Agricultural Marketing Service of the U.S. Department of Agriculture is responsible for administering the Organic Food Production Act of 1990 and for use of the USDA Organic seal. This seal means that the produce has been raised and marketed without pesticides, petroleum- or sewage sludge-based fertilizers, bioengineering, or ionizing radiation. However, the nutritive value of such produce is comparable to other produce raised according to standard farming practices.

Consumers usually rely on their own knowledge and experience in selecting fresh vegetables to meet their own personal standards. Such characteristics as crispness, color, and freedom from blemishes are characteristics that frequently can be used by consumers in making wise selections in the produce department. Some suggested guides for selected fresh vegetables are presented in Table 5.5.

Figure 5.14
USDA's Organic Seal can only be used when produce is grown according to legal specifications. Courtesy of U.S. Department of Agriculture.

organic seal   Seal used to designate food that meets the standards required by the National Organic Program.

http://www.ams.usda.gov/ AMSv1.0/standards
—Federal produce grading standards.

http://www.ams.usda.gov/ AMSv1.0/NOP
—Overview of National Organic Program.

http://www.nal.usda.gov/ afsic/pubs/ofp/ofp.shtml
—Overview of requirements for organic production.

www.earthboundfarm.com
—Organic farming information.

TABLE 5.5
GUIDE TO SELECTION OF FRESH VEGETABLES

Vegetable	Criteria
Artichoke	Plump, firm, heavy in comparison with size; green petals with absence of brown discoloration
Asparagus	Good green color extending down much of stalk; closed and compact tips; crisp and tender stalk
Beans (green and wax)	Bright color for variety; pods firm and crisp rather than flabby
Beets	Fresh-looking tops if still attached; surface that is smooth and deep red, firm and round with slim taproot
Broccoli	Dark green to bluish bud clusters with no trace of yellow; smooth stalks of moderate size with no traces of spoilage
Brussels sprouts	Fresh green color void of yellow leaves; tight outer leaves free of injury; tight heads
Cabbage	Firm head; fresh color in outer leaves, crisp leaves
Carrots	Crisp rather than flabby; good orange color free from sunburned green at top

(Continued)

TABLE 5.5 (Continued)

Vegetable	Criteria
Cauliflower	Uniform creamy white color with no trace of dark discoloration; solid and compact head; fresh leaves, if attached
Celery	Crisp stalks with a solid feel; glossy surface on stalk; crisp leaves; no discoloration on inside surface of large outer stalks
Corn	Ear well covered with plump young kernels; fresh husks that are green and unwilted; silks free of decay
Cucumbers	Firm, moderate size; green color all over
Eggplant	Smooth and firm with deep purple skin free of blemishes
Greens	Crisp appearance with good green color typical of the type of green; free from rust and other blemishes; no wilted or decaying areas
Lettuce	Crisp quality to leaves, with butter lettuces being somewhat less crisp, but still succulent; free of decay; good color for the variety
Mushrooms	Caps closed around the stem; surface of cap light-colored and gills (if showing under cap) should be light rather than dark; smooth and firm cap with no suggestion of drying out
Okra	Pods tender enough to bend under some pressure; less than 4 1/2 inches long; fresh green color; no blemishes
Onions, dry	Firm and dry with small necks; no decay
Onions, green	Crisp, bright green tops; free from decay
Parsnips	Smooth and firm; small to medium size; free from blemishes
Peas	Crisp pods with fresh green color; pods full but not bulging
Peppers	Firm, deep color; no trace of flabbiness or decay
Potatoes	Firm; free from sunburned green areas; no decay; skin intact and free from blemishes
Radishes	Medium size; firm and plump; fresh red color
Squash	Well developed with no soft areas, firm; summer squash has glossy and tender skin; winter squash has tough, hard skin
Sweet potatoes	Firm, no signs of decay at ends; good color
Tomatoes	Smooth; good color for stage of ripeness; firm if not fully ripe; free from blemishes
Turnips and rutabagas	Firm and smooth; free of blemishes

waxy potatoes Potatoes with a high content of sugar and low amount of starch; best suited for boiling and other preparations where shape is important.

non-waxy potatoes Potatoes with a low sugar content and high starch level; best suited for baking, mashing, and frying.

Wise selection depends not only on quality of the item selected but also sometimes on the variety. For instance, a choice might need to be made between buying large beefsteak tomatoes or cherry tomatoes for making a salad. Onions are yet another type of vegetable requiring some decision between varieties. When a recipe calls for pea pods, the variety to choose is the Chinese or snow pea, with its tender, flat pods. Regular garden peas have a pod that is too tough to provide the delicate crispness desired.

Selection of the variety of potatoes to buy should be based on the intended preparation, because cooking characteristics vary. Some potatoes, termed **waxy potatoes**, are relatively high in sugar and low in starch. The opposite type, non-waxy (mealy), have high starch content and are low in sugar. Waxy potatoes have a low specific gravity, which causes them to float in water (Figure 5.15). Conversely, **non-waxy potatoes** have a high specific gravity; they will sink to the bottom of a solution containing 11 parts of water to 1 part salt.

Non-waxy potatoes will tend to slough off and to lose their shape during boiling, while waxy potatoes hold their shape well during boiling (Figure 5.16). This is not surprising, for the high starch content of the non-waxy potatoes means that there will be considerable swelling of the cells when non-waxy ones are boiled due to gelatinization or swelling of the starch in these potatoes. These characteristics make non-waxy potatoes excellent for mashing and baking. In contrast, waxy potatoes, with their low starch and comparatively high sugar content, retain their shape, making them well suited to preparations such as potato salad, where shape of the pieces is important.

Fried potatoes, particularly French fries, are a popular way of preparing potatoes. Here again, the type of potato selected will influence the quality of the finished product. As predicted, waxy potatoes (such as the Red Pontiac) will not perform well when fried, because the high sugar content causes them to brown quite quickly or even to burn before the interior of the piece is cooked. Non-waxy potatoes, however, with their low sugar content, brown rather slowly, thus allowing time for the heat to cook the interior of the piece before the exterior becomes too dark. The familiar example of non-waxy potatoes is the Russet Burbank. Its long, flat shape is excellent for making the long slices desired in French fries.

It is desirable to buy the right variety of potato for the intended use, but people who use potatoes infrequently may find the purchase of a single type is appropriate. In such instances, an all-purpose potato, such as the White Rose, may be selected. The products prepared may not be quite as good as they would be if the correct type of potato had been used, yet the quality is satisfactory for any type of preparation (boiling, mashing, or even frying). Although the White Rose often will not make mashed potatoes as light and fluffy as those from Russet Burbank, the White Rose is comparatively excellent when contrasted with the rather dark, somewhat gummy character of mashed potatoes made with Red Pontiac.

Figure 5.15
Potatoes with low specific gravity float in 1:11 salt water brine and retain shape well when boiled, which are characteristics of waxy potatoes. "Sinkers" are non-waxy potatoes that slough off when boiled.
Courtesy of Plycon Press.

Canned and Frozen Vegetables

Canned vegetables are a mainstay in the menu plans of some people. They have the advantages of being convenient to store and quick and easy to serve because they are cooked fully during canning. Since canned vegetables can be stored for many months at room temperature, they can be bought when on sale and held for later use without a significant loss in quality. No special equipment is needed to prepare commercially canned vegetables. In fact, salads often include canned vegetables that have simply been drained before being incorporated into the salad. Of course, canned vegetables can be used in many different recipes, even ones involving complex preparation steps.

One limitation of canned vegetables is the soft texture due to the rigorous heat treatment involved in safe processing of canned vegetables. The other limitation in canned vegetables is the color of green vegetables. Again, the intense and extended heat treatment required to prevent the possibility of botulism in canned vegetables always changes the bright color of fresh green vegetables into the familiar olive drab observed in canned green beans and spinach.

Frozen vegetables have gained an important segment of the vegetable market as a result of some creative marketing as well as inherently pleasing quality. The bright green color of frozen peas and beans is a real plus for these and other frozen green vegetables. Although frozen vegetables do require a bit of cooking before they are ready to serve, the time actually is very short, particularly when the vegetables are being heated in a microwave oven. This gives them a real advantage over fresh vegetables, which require some time to prepare for cooking and then a cooking period

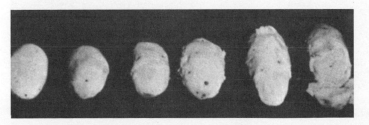

Figure 5.16
Waxy potatoes (left) have low specific gravity and hold shape when boiled; as specific gravity rises (toward right) potatoes are non-waxy and slough off. Courtesy of Plycon Press.

usually at least six minutes long. To enhance sales, manufacturers have created some unusual vegetable combinations, several with sauces to add a gourmet touch to the frozen food section. Although comparatively expensive, these frozen vegetable products have been well accepted.

A disadvantage of frozen vegetables is the requirement for freezer space. The freezer compartment in most refrigerators is adequate to accommodate the amount of frozen vegetables many families might wish to store for a week or longer. People who have a freezer can purchase frozen vegetables when special sales occur and store them for use perhaps as long as six months later.

Grading standards for quality have been established by the U.S. Department of Agriculture, the same agency that is responsible for monitoring enforcement of these regulations. The three grades for canned and frozen vegetables are U.S. Grade A or Fancy, U.S. Grade B or Extra Standard, and U.S. Grade C or Standard. To use these federal grades, packers must have a federal inspector from the U.S. Department of Agriculture present constantly. These inspectors monitor to be sure that the grade specifications are being satisfied. For U.S. Grade A, vegetables must be of top quality and have the appropriate color, have a high degree of tenderness, and be free of blemishes. U.S. Grade B is characterized as being slightly more mature than U.S. Grade A and less carefully selected for color and tenderness. Vegetables in U.S. Grade C are lacking in uniformity and have poorer color and flavor. This lowest grade is perfectly adequate for use in casseroles and soups and can save consumers money.

Packers are not required to use the federal grades. They can use their own grade designations or even designate their grades as *Grade A* or *Fancy* if they choose. Unless the product is designated as *U.S. Grade A, B*, or *C*, a federal inspector is not required to supervise the grading process. Consumers often use the brand name as the guide to quality rather than reading the grade designation. By noting quality and uniformity available in different brands, it is possible to make purchasing decisions that integrate quality and price to meet specific needs.

The suggested serving size for cooked vegetables is half a cup. To ensure that enough vegetable is being purchased to provide the appropriate number of servings, it is helpful to have a guide to estimated yields of fresh, frozen, and canned vegetables. The number of servings for common market units of vegetables is provided in Table 5.6.

TABLE 5.6
ESTIMATED SERVINGS OF FRESH, FROZEN, AND CANNED VEGETABLES

Vegetable	Estimated Servings from		
	Fresh (1 lb)	Frozen (10 oz)	Canned (1 lb)
Asparagus	4	2 1/2	2–3
Beans, green or wax	5	3–4	3–4
Beans, lima	2 (in pods)	3–4	3–4
Beets	4	—	3–4
Broccoli	3–4	3	—
Brussels sprouts	5	3–4	—
Cabbage	4	3–4	—
Carrots	4	3–4	3–4
Cauliflower	3	3	—
Corn	1 per ear	3–4	3–4
Peas	2 (in pods)	3–4	3–4
Potatoes	3–4	3–4	3–4
Spinach	4	2–3	2–3
Tomatoes	4	—	4

Source: Adapted from *Handbook of Food Preparation*. American Home Economics Association, Washington, DC, 8th ed., 1980; Peterkin, B., and C. Cromwell. Money's worth in foods, *Home and Garden Bulletin No. 183*, Ag. Res. Serv., USDA, Washington, DC, 1977; Thompson, E. R. How to buy canned and frozen vegetables, *Consumer Marketing Service Bulletin, No. 167*, Washington, DC, 1969.

STORAGE

Fresh vegetables, with a few exceptions, should be stored in the refrigerator. Since refrigerator space often is limited, trimming of the tops of radishes and carrots, as well as the removal of leaves around a head of cauliflower and other inedible portions, may be done before storing produce. The cool air of the refrigerator will slow respiration and help to delay deteriorative changes, but the dryness of the air causes serious loss of moisture unless storage is in the closed hydrator drawers or in sealed plastic bags.

Although all vegetables rely on their moisture content for part of their crisp texture, moisture is particularly important for succulents, such as the various greens. The combination of the cool air (which will be saturated with only limited loss of moisture from the leaves) and the small amount of air surrounding greens in the hydrator drawer or plastic bag is the best possible way to help keep the cells in the leaves of the greens filled with their normal amount of water. Many other fresh vegetables, such as sweet corn, broccoli, and peas, also will maintain quality best by storage in the hydrator drawers.

The chief exceptions to the rule of storing fresh vegetables in the refrigerator hydrator drawers are potatoes, winter squash, Spanish and other dry onions, dry legumes, and other dried foods. All of these types of vegetables should be stored in a dark, dry, and somewhat cool place with some air circulation (Figure 5.17). As mentioned earlier, the temperature control for potatoes is of particular importance because of the potential for shifts in the type of carbohydrate in the stored potatoes. About 60°F (15.6°C) is considered optimal. Low temperatures cause an accumulation of sugar, and warmer temperatures raise the level of starch.

Figure 5.17
Red onions, garlic, Spanish onions, shallots, and boiling onions (left to right) are best stored in a cool, dark, and dry place. Courtesy of Plycon Press.

VEGETABLES IN MENU PLANNING

Vegetables have the potential for being the highlight of the meal when they are chosen carefully and prepared with skill. The attractive colors, distinctive shapes, and assorted flavors can be utilized to add just the right touch to a menu that might otherwise be a bit dull. Selection of the vegetable and the way it will be prepared should be based on color, texture, shape, and flavor of the vegetable in relation to the other foods being served. For instance, confetti corn (sweet corn with diced green pepper and pimiento) adds color and flavor excitement to a meal of white fish and rice pilaf. The bright color and delicate flavor of a broiled tomato accents a dinner featuring baked halibut. Mashed potatoes provide a pleasing textural contrast when served with slightly crisp, buttered, boiled carrots as the vegetables in a meal. Some vegetables can be cut into different shapes to give the desired line to a plate. For instance, carrots can be cut into slices or into matchsticks or even left whole, depending upon the other foods being included in the meal.

INGREDIENT HIGHLIGHT
BROCCOLINI

The focus on eating more vegetables and fruits is stimulating research to develop vegetables that will capture the attention of the dining public. Broccolini (also called asparation) is a hybrid of broccoli and Chinese kale that was created by Sakata Seed Co. (Figure 5.18). Sometimes this vegetable is simply named baby broccoli.

Broccolini is a rather delicate vegetable to grow. Extremes in temperature can seriously affect the crop; irrigation also requires careful regulation. With proper controls, harvesting can be done throughout the year. However, this is a vegetable that is expensive to produce because it is fairly labor intensive; this helps to explain its comparatively high cost in markets. *(Continued)*

(Continued)

Figure 5.18
Broccolini (a hybrid of broccoli and Chinese kale) sometimes is called asparation because its flavor is reminiscent of asparagus. Courtesy of Plycon Press.

The slim stalks of broccolini are topped by quite delicate flowerets resembling broccoli. These tender stalks help to make broccolini popular. Tenderizing happens simply by blanching the vegetable in boiling water for a minute or two, which serves also to develop a bright green color. The flavor has overtones of asparagus, which helps to explain why this vegetable sometimes is called asparation.

FACTORS IN VEGETABLE COOKERY

Nutrient Retention

Vegetables have a well-deserved reputation as being good sources of nutrients, but the truth is that the way in which vegetables are prepared can have a definite influence on their actual nutritive value. Even more important than the nutrient content in a vegetable is its palatability and general appeal. A vegetable can be a good source of nutrients, but they will not be available to the body if the vegetable is not eaten. Preparation for maximum palatability is clearly an important factor in the nutrient contribution of vegetables.

Efficient transport of vegetables through the marketing process to the table is essential to maintaining maximum vitamin content. They are at risk during the marketing period. Vitamins A and C (ascorbic acid) undergo oxidative losses most easily. Keeping cut surfaces to a minimum during preparation reduces oxidation and maximizes the levels of both vitamins.

The length of time vegetables are cooked will influence nutrient retention, and so will the method used in cooking. Stir-frying is a method that helps to conserve nutrients because it is rapid and is done with little or no added water. The iron content of green beans is increased very slightly if they are stir-fried in a stainless steel pan.

Due to their solubility in water, the B vitamins and vitamin C are lost to an extent when vegetables are boiled; these losses are accelerated if the water is alkaline. However, their loss is minimized if the cooking water is boiling when vegetables are added because the cooking time is reduced. The sudden, intense heat halts enzyme action and expels some oxygen, which

TABLE 5.7
PROPERTIES OF VITAMINS IMPORTANT IN FOOD PREPARATION

		Sensitivity to			
				Heat in Presence of	
Vitamin	Solubility in Water	Oxygen	Light	Acid	Alkali
Vitamin A	No	Sensitive	Sensitive	Stable	Stable
Thiamin	Yes	Stable	Stable	Sensitive	Sensitive
Riboflavin	Yes	Stable	Sensitive	Stable	Sensitive
Niacin	Yes	Stable	Stable	Stable	Stable
Ascorbic acid	Yes	Sensitive	Sensitive	Sensitive	Sensitive
Vitamin D	No	Stable	Stable	Stable	Stable

intensifies the color. Soda should not be added to the cooking water because this is particularly destructive to thiamin, a B vitamin (Table 5.7).

Microwave cookery is one technique for helping to keep vitamin losses to a minimum. The extremely small amount of water used is helpful in retaining the water-soluble vitamins. Additionally, the cooking time is relatively short in microwave cookery. Stir-frying is another technique involving almost no water. Despite the numerous cut surfaces that promote vitamin losses, this method conserves vitamins because of the very short cooking time required to tenderize the thin slices. Steaming is another method effective in conserving nutrients. A pressure saucepan provides yet another alternative for cooking vegetables. This causes some increase in vitamin loss despite the short cooking time because the cooking temperature is higher than that of boiling water.

Texture

Denaturation of protein, gelatinization of starch, and softening of the cellulose and other structural elements are changes taking place when vegetables are cooked. These physical changes result in distinct changes in texture, with the final effect being determined by how long the vegetable is cooked. The increasing tenderness that occurs during cooking is due primarily to softening of cellulose and conversion of some of the cementing pectic substances into more soluble pectic compounds. When these changes have proceeded to suit individual taste, the palatability of some vegetables is enhanced.

The acidity or alkalinity (pH) of the cooking water will have a definite influence on the softening occurring during boiling of a vegetable. The texture quickly becomes mushy and the shape blurs if soda is added to make the water alkaline. This change is detrimental to palatability (as well as being harmful to thiamin retention). Ordinarily, soda is not added when cooking vegetables because of the detrimental effects. However, the softening of dried beans can be speeded significantly by adding a maximum of 1/8 teaspoon of soda per cup of beans; even this small amount causes the beans to be slightly lower in thiamin than they would be if no alkali were added to the soaking and/or cooking water.

If lemon juice or other acid is added to the water used for boiling a vegetable, the effect on texture will be just the opposite of the effect of alkali. In fact, the vegetable will be extremely resistant to softening over an extended boiling period if water is acidified. This effect is particularly important to remember, for some vegetable recipes involve the use of acid. For example, in the preparation of Harvard beets, first the beets are boiled in water to soften them. When tender, the sliced beets are combined with a vinegar (acidic) sauce and heated to serving temperature. Unless the beets are tender before they are combined with the sauce, the slices will be too crisp to enjoy. Similarly when lemon butter sauce is to be combined with boiled carrots or other boiled vegetable, the vegetable must be cooked until the desired degree of tenderness is achieved before the acidic lemon juice is added.

Calcium ions are often found in hard water, and these ions can combine with pectic substances to form insoluble salts in the vegetables. The apparent result is a hard vegetable that is extremely resistant to softening during cooking. This is a particular problem when dried beans are being cooked. However, food processors use this ion to advantage when processing tomatoes. By the addition of a calcium salt (usually calcium chloride), tomatoes can be kept in their original round form instead of becoming mushy and indistinct.

Molasses is an acidic food ingredient that has a fair amount of calcium ions. When baked beans are being prepared with molasses in the sauce, it is imperative that the beans be softened to the desired degree of tenderness before the flavorful, molasses-containing sauce is added and baked with the beans. If the sauce is added too soon, the beans will not become tender.

Color

The problem in vegetable preparation is to optimize color by proper cooking techniques, being sure that the cooking medium and the cooking time are controlled to give the desired results. The specific techniques that are appropriate differ with the pigments predominating in the various vegetables.

Pigments sometimes change color or hue when a vegetable is cooked, and the results range from pleasing to distinctly unpalatable. Because of this potential for detrimental changes, pigments require special consideration when planning cooking methods. Initially, the original color intensifies when vegetables are plunged into boiling water. This drastic change in temperature apparently causes expulsion of the small amount of air between the cells, making pigments (particularly chlorophyll) appear even brighter than before heating. This abrupt start to heating vegetables has the added advantage of keeping cooking times as short as possible, which helps to avoid converting chlorophyll to pheophytin and also aids in retaining nutrients.

The acidity or alkalinity of the water in which vegetables are being boiled will modify the colors of all pigments except the carotenoids. Vegetables containing chlorophyll will gradually take on an olive-drab color while they are cooking if the water is acidic (or if the cooking period exceeds about five to seven minutes). However, a slightly alkaline medium promotes retention of chlorophyll, as pointed out in Table 5.8.

Flavonoids, both anthoxanthins and anthocyanins, retain a desirable color in a slightly acidic medium, while alkali will cause poor color. For instance, the white of cauliflower in a barely acidic medium is considered desirable, but yellowish cauliflower, the result of alkali, is not acceptable. The color change from the rather pinkish-red seen in red cabbage cooked in a mild acid to the bluish color of a barely alkaline medium can cause complete rejection of that vegetable simply because of the change in the anthocyanin pigment with increasing alkalinity.

Vegetable cells naturally contain some mild organic acids, but these acids may be released into the cooking medium, causing pigment changes to begin to develop. In the case of chlorophyll, the change will be toward an olive green, a transition that should be avoided if possible. If green

---

TABLE 5.8
COLOR REACTIONS OF VEGETABLE PIGMENTS

Pigment	Example	Color in Acid	Color in Alkali	Color Reaction to Metals
Chlorophyll	Broccoli	Olive green[a]	Bright green[b]	Copper, iron: bright green
Carotenoids	Carrots	Orange	Orange	
Flavonoids				
Anthoxanthins	Cauliflower	Colorless, white	Yellow	Aluminum: yellow
				Iron: brown
Anthocyanins	Red cabbage	Red	Blue to green	Iron: blue
				Tin: purple

[a]Pheophytin.
[b]Chlorophyllin.

vegetables are boiled in an uncovered pan, the volatile organic acids will escape from the cooking medium, thus maintaining the water close to neutral. The desired chlorophyll pigment will be maintained by keeping the lid on only until the water returns to boiling after the vegetable has been added and keeping the cooking time short.

The technique for boiling the flavonoid-containing vegetables is the reverse of that for those containing chlorophyll. Both the anthocyanin and anthoxanthin pigments are considered to be more desirable in an acidic than in an alkaline medium. Thus, using a lid on the pan retains the volatile organic acids and protects the pigments.

The pH of the water when boiling vegetables pigmented with carotenoids has little effect on their color. From the perspective of color, there is no compelling reason either for using or not using a lid on carotenoid-pigmented vegetables.

Flavor

Although color will have a very strong influence on the acceptance of vegetables, other sensory qualities of vegetables also play a role. Flavor and the related characteristic, aroma, are key aspects of palatability. The aroma of onions cooking may be tempting to many, but the strong odor of cabbage boiling may completely repel others. Aromas are important because they contribute to the perceived flavor of a food, too. Vegetables with a strong aroma will also have a strong flavor and may be rejected on that basis.

To help promote a desirable flavor, it is advisable to cover a pan when a mild-flavored vegetable is being prepared. Conversely, do not use a cover when a strong-flavored vegetable is being boiled so that the volatile flavoring compounds can escape from the product. Remember, any odor escaping into the air is simply that much less odorant remaining to strengthen the flavor of the finished product.

Anyone who has ever sampled the cooking water from boiled cabbage is well aware of the solubility of some of the flavoring components. By using enough water to cover strong-flavored vegetables with an excess of about 1/4 inch of water, the flavoring components will be diluted by the leaching action of the cooking medium. This small excess will help to weaken the strong flavors of the various members of the cabbage family, thus promoting palatability. When mild-flavored vegetables are being prepared, however, using just enough water to barely boil over the vegetable will assure uniform boiling of the vegetable with a minimum influence on losing flavoring compounds into the cooking water.

The length of cooking time has a distinct influence on the flavors of certain key vegetables. The onion family, with its intense, sulfur-containing flavoring components, will grow increasingly mild with continued heating. This is because some of the key flavoring compounds (including propionaldehyde, hydrogen sulfide, and sulfur dioxide) are volatile and lost from the vegetable. While a certain reduction in quantity of these intense substances is helpful, excessive loss leads to uninteresting flavors. The desired compromise can be achieved by cooking onions for a moderate length of time without a cover.

In contrast to onions, the cabbage-like vegetables develop intense flavors with extended cooking. Raw cabbage contains **sinigrin**, a glycoside found in various members of this family (Figure 5.19). In the presence of water and heat, sinigrin is converted to allyl isothiocyanate and ultimately to hydrogen sulfide, a strong and unpleasant-smelling compound. The longer the cooking time, the greater is the production of hydrogen sulfide. By keeping cooking time short for members of the cabbage family, palatability will be increased significantly.

For optimum flavor of cooked vegetables, you will need to decide (1) whether to use a lid or not, (2) how much water is needed, and (3) how long the cooking period should be. Appropriate decisions with regard to these three variables will yield significant dividends in the preparation of highly pleasing cooked vegetables.

sinigrin Compound in the cabbage family that ultimately is converted to hydrogen sulfide, causing an unpleasant flavor.

Figure 5.19
Raw cabbage (right) contains sinigrin, a glycoside that is converted to hydrogen sulfide when cabbage is boiled (left).
Courtesy of Plycon Press.

PREPARATION PROCEDURES FOR FRESH VEGETABLES

Preliminary Steps

For all fresh vegetables, careful washing is essential. Many vegetables are cleansed well by washing them directly under a stream of cold, running water, using a vegetable brush or plastic scouring pad for scrubbing potatoes or other vegetables with stubborn dirt clinging to them. The quickest and most efficient way of cleaning mud from the veins and convolutions of greens is to fill a clean sink with cold water and then slosh the leaves up and down vigorously to remove the dirt. Drain the water from the sink, being sure to rinse the dirty sediment down the drain. Then refill the sink with fresh, cold water. Repeat the vigorous sloshing action and draining until the water remains clean and sediment no longer collects in the bottom of the sink as the rinse water is drained.

Following washing, careful inspection of fresh produce to remove all blemishes provides an important quality control check. At this point, any necessary trimming, paring, and cutting should be done judiciously. For example, corn on the cob is prepared by removing the husks and also the fine corn silks caught in the rows between kernels. Similarly, green beans are trimmed at both ends to eliminate the very tough cellulosic areas sealing off the ends of the pods. Practically all fresh vegetables will need some judicious trimming to eliminate woody stalks, heavy, tough leaves, or other features that are not appropriate for human consumption.

Not all vegetables require extensive trimming prior to cooking. For instance, cabbage wedges should be cut so that enough of the core remains with each piece to ensure that the wedge will remain intact during boiling. Beets are left whole, with the root still attached and at least an inch of the stem remaining. These precautions help to avoid damaging any of the cells holding the anthocyanin pigments.

Paring can be done to remove the skins of potatoes, carrots, and a few other vegetables. Use of a vegetable peeler helps to keep trimming losses to a minimum, although a paring knife also is a convenient way of removing skins. To reduce oxidative losses of vitamins and also to avoid possible discoloration, paring should be done right before cooking the vegetable.

Discoloration in some potatoes is caused by enzyme action causing formation of a pigment called melanin from the amino acid tyrosine. This color change progresses through a brownish pink finally to a gray color. If potatoes have to stand after paring, discoloration can be minimized by placing them in a bowl of water to cover the entire surface and prevent oxygen from reaching the potatoes.

Many vegetables are cut into various shapes and pieces prior to being cooked. This permits them to enhance the line and design of the menu. Cooking time is also reduced.

Boiling

Probably the most common way of preparing cooked vegetables is by boiling them. Most fresh vegetables can be tenderized by boiling in water, with or without a lid, depending on color and flavor considerations. In preparation for boiling vegetables, enough water should be brought to boil in a covered pan to barely cover the vegetable (or to exceed this depth by about 1/4 inch for strong-flavored vegetables). The cleaned and cut or whole fresh vegetables then are added to the boiling water, with the lid being replaced or removed, depending upon the specific vegetable. Boiling is continued just until the vegetables can be cut conveniently with a fork, but are not mushy. Guidelines for boiling selected vegetables appear in Table 5.9.

Steaming

Steaming requires a rack to hold vegetables in the steam above the water boiling in a pan. Many variations of steamers and steamer baskets are on the market today. Steamed vegetables generally retain their water-soluble nutrients because they are not directly in water. The time required for steaming is longer than the time for boiling if home-style steamers are used. Commercially, pressurized steamers are fairly common. The elevated temperature of steam under pressure makes it possible to steam vegetables to the desired stage of doneness more quickly than boiling.

TABLE 5.9
SUGGESTED TECHNIQUES FOR BOILING SELECTED FRESH VEGETABLES

Vegetable	Use of Cover	Reason to Cover or Uncover	Amount of Water	Size of Piece	Boiling Time (min)[a]
Artichoke, globe	Covered[b]	Steam needed	3/4 in.	Whole	35–45
Asparagus	Uncovered	Green color	Small[c]	Stalks	4–7
Beans, green	Uncovered	Green color	Small	Whole	5–7
Beets	Covered	Mild flavor	Small	Whole	30
Broccoli	Uncovered	Green color, strong flavor	—[d]	Split stalk	4–6
Cabbage, green	Uncovered	Green color, strong flavor	Large[e]	Wedge	4–6
Cabbage, red	Uncovered	Strong flavor	Large	Wedge	4–6
Carrots	Covered	Mild flavor	Small	Small, whole	5–8
Cauliflower	Uncovered	Strong flavor	Large	Whole flower	12–15
				flowerets	6–8
Corn	Covered	Mild flavor	Small	Kernels	4–6
Corn on the cob	Covered	Mild flavor	To cover	Whole	4–7
Onions	Uncovered	Strong flavor	Large	Whole	12–17
Parsnips	Uncovered	Strong flavor	Large	Whole	20–40
Peas	Uncovered	Green color	Small	Whole	5–7
Potatoes	Covered	Mild flavor	Small	Whole	15–20
Spinach	Covered to wilt, then uncovered	Green color	Clings to leaves	Leaves	3–5
Sweet potatoes	Covered	Mild flavor	Small	Whole	15–20
Tomatoes	Covered	Mild flavor	None	Whole	7–15

[a]Variation in cooking times depends on size and maturity of vegetables, as well as personal preference.

[b]Chlorophyll turns olive green with or without a cover because of the long cooking time needed for artichokes, so cover is used to trap steam in the pan to aid in retaining the flavor.

[c]Just enough water is used to bubble to the top of the vegetable when the water is boiling gently.

[d]Water to within 1/4 in. of flowers if broccoli is standing upright in water.

[e]Enough water is used to provide an extra 1/4 in. of water over the vegetable.

Some green vegetables may be less palatable when steamed than when boiled because steaming requires a cover, which may result in an olive green color. Strong flavors may be intensified by steaming because the lid traps volatile flavoring components; in addition, there is limited loss of soluble substances into the steam, as contrasted with the probable escape of these flavors into the water when vegetables are boiled.

Mild-flavored, sweet vegetables are well suited to steaming, which develops a tender, yet slightly crisp texture while retaining a desirable flavor. Table 5.10 outlines some appropriate preparation techniques for many vegetables.

Simmering

The high protein content and low moisture level in dried legumes necessitate special preparation techniques for these nutritious vegetables. Rehydration is necessary, and this is a fairly slow process compared with the preparation of fresh vegetables. To promote the rehydration and softening of legumes, a soaking period (use of 1/8 tsp soda being optional) is the first preparation step. Either an overnight soaking period or a two-minute boiling period followed by an hour of soaking in the same water can be used equally well to shorten the simmering time needed to tenderize the beans. The exceptions to this soaking period are lentils and split peas, for they will become tender when simply simmered for about an hour or less.

TABLE 5.10
SUGGESTED METHODS FOR PREPARING VARIOUS VEGETABLES

Vegetable	Boiled	Steamed	Broiled	Baked	Fried	Stir-fried
Artichoke, globe	X	X				
Asparagus	X	X				X
Beans, string	X	X				X
Beans, dried lima		Simmered		X		
Beans, fresh lima	X	X				
Beets	X	X		X		
Broccoli	X	X			X	X
Brussels sprouts	X	X				
Cabbage, green	X	X				X
Cabbage, red	X	X				X
Carrots	X	X		X		X
Cauliflower	X	X			X	X
Celery	X					X
Corn	X	X		X		
Eggplant				X	X	
Mushrooms			X		X	X
Okra	X				X	
Onions	X	X	X	X	X	X
Parsnips	X	X		X	X	
Peas	X	X				
Potatoes	X	X		X	X	
Spinach	X	X				X
Squash, acorn				X		
Squash, summer	X	X			X	X
Sweet potatoes	X	X		X	X	
Tomatoes	X	X	X	X	X	
Zucchini	X	X			X	X

Ordinarily legumes are simmered in the water used to soak them so that the water-soluble B vitamins leaching into the soaking water will be retained with the cooked beans. The recommended amount of water for soaking is a maximum of three cups per cup of dried beans. The anticipated final yield of cooked beans from a cup of the original beans is about two to three cups after the simmering period of 90 minutes or more. At this point, the starch in the legumes will have gelatinized, causing the beans to swell significantly. The comparatively mild heat treatment will denature the protein, tenderize the cellulose and pectic substances, and eliminate possible toxic substances, as well as deactivate a trypsin inhibitor. The net result of these changes is that simmered legumes are palatable and comparatively inexpensive sources of protein that can be utilized fairly well by the body, particularly when cereals (rice, for example) or nuts are served with them.

If pectic substances in legumes are precipitated by calcium, tenderizing is difficult. Usually, the phytic acid found in legumes is able to bind calcium ions to prevent combination with pectic substances and formation of insoluble pectinates. The difficulty in softening legumes is compounded if molasses is added before adequate softness has been achieved by simmering. This problem is the result of the action between the calcium ions and acid in the molasses. Hard water causes a similar problem due to calcium salts. When preparing baked beans, the beans need to be tender before the molasses-containing sauce is added. Acids, such as tomatoes, also should not be added before legumes are softened by simmering because of the retarding effect that all acids will have on the softening of the pectic substances and cellulose.

Broiling

Broiling is a direct heat method of preparing tender vegetables quickly. Tomatoes (cut in half) and stuffed mushroom caps are two vegetables that can be broiled successfully. A few other vegetables, such as boiling onions, are excellent when broiled if they have been parboiled first. Parboiling almost to the point of tenderness prior to broiling ensures that the center of the vegetable will be appropriately tender by the time the exterior becomes a pleasing, golden brown color.

Baking or Oven Roasting

Baking and oven roasting are essentially the same dry heat method of heating food. However, the usual preparation for baking is slightly different from oven roasting. Baked potatoes have long been practically a national institution, but other vegetables, for instance winter squash and eggplant, also are suitable for baking because their skins protect them from drying excessively while baking. Preparation is simple—scrub thoroughly and bake until tender. Roasting ears of corn are also well suited to baking. Many other vegetables, with the exception of green vegetables, can be baked satisfactorily if they are placed in a covered casserole to help keep them moist.

Temperatures for baking vegetables may range anywhere from 300° to 425°F (149°C to 218°C), depending upon the other items that may be in the oven at the same time. Energy conservation suggests that baking vegetables when some other menu item also is being baked is good use of resources. Toaster ovens are useful for baking vegetables when they are the only item to be baked.

Oven-roasted vegetable medleys are colorful and healthy menu items. Sweet peppers of various colors, small new potatoes, carrots, eggplant slices, or other vegetables cut into smaller (≈1 in.) pieces are suitable for roasting. Parboiling of whole onions or other large pieces may be done to shorten the roasting time. After they have been brushed or sprayed with olive or other oil and any desired seasonings, the vegetables are roasted at 400°F (204°C) or hotter and are stirred occasionally while roasting about an hour or until tender. If necessary, vegetables can be removed from the pan as they become tender and are pleasingly browned.

Frying

French-fried potatoes and onion rings are popular menu items despite the advice that Americans should eat less fat. The techniques used in frying vegetables can be geared toward keeping the fat level of such items as low as possible when they are being prepared. The fat for deep-fat frying should be at about 375°F (190.5°C) before the vegetables are placed in the fat. This temperature is hot enough for rather fast cooking of the vegetable, but not so hot that the vegetable burns on the exterior before it is soft in the center. With cooler temperatures, the vegetable will absorb increasing amounts of oil as the cooking time is extended.

By placing small amounts of raw vegetable into the frying oil, the temperature of the fat will drop only slightly from the desired frying heat. Careful draining of the fried food and blotting on paper towels before serving are also important ways of helping to keep the fat content of deep-fat fried foods comparatively low.

Vegetables to be fried sometimes are dipped in a batter prior to frying, and sometimes they are blotted rather dry with paper towels and then dropped carefully into the hot fat. French-fried potatoes are always fried without batter, while dipping in batter before frying enhances onion rings and such familiar Japanese tempura morsels as sliced sweet potatoes, carrots, and green beans.

Shallow-fat frying of vegetables is done to a limited extent. Potatoes often are prepared in this way, with cottage fries and hash browns being two of the very popular recipes. Since the fat level is too shallow to check with a thermometer, the rule is to keep the fat from getting so hot that it smokes.

Figure 5.20
Green beans and bean sprouts are the first of the ingredients being stir-fried in a Thai recipe. Courtesy of Plycon Press.

wok Metallic, bowl-shaped pan developed in Asia for stir-frying.

Stir-Frying or Panning

Stir-frying or panning, utilizing either a **wok** or a frying pan, is a method of vegetable cookery borrowed from Oriental cuisines (Figure 5.20). A wok relies on intense heat at the bottom of the bowl to cook thin slices of the vegetable very quickly in a small amount of oil. As soon as the vegetable slices brown slightly, they are pushed up the side, where heat conduction will keep finished portions warm while other slices are being fried in the bottom.

One of the delights of stir-frying is that vegetables, despite their thin slices, maintain just a suggestion of crispness. Another plus for this method of vegetable cookery is its speed. This not only saves preparation time but also helps to retain nutrients. The combination of the very short preparation time and the limited contact with water results in good retention of vitamin C and other water-soluble nutrients in spite of the large surface area exposed by the thin slices. Other advantages of stir-frying are the fresh and vibrant green color maintained in chlorophyll-containing vegetables and the fresh flavors.

Although many vegetables will become sufficiently tender just with the heating that occurs while the slices are being browned slightly, some require additional time to achieve the desired texture. With extended frying in the intense heat of the wok, thick pieces may become too dark or even burn before the slices are done and the texture is sufficiently tender. In preparing vege s that tenderize slowly, stir-frying is initiated as usual (i.e., with a small amount of salad oil, butter, or margarine in the bottom of the wok). However, the wok may be covered with a lid whenever stirring is not being done, and just a little water added to form steam to help tenderize the slices.

Other Techniques

Microwaving   Microwave ovens offer yet another means of preparing vegetables comparatively quickly. One of the advantages of a microwave oven is the rapid cooking that can happen if only small quantities are being prepared. Although cookery methods in the microwave oven frequently include adding a small amount of liquid and covering the vegetable with a paper towel or other suitable protection to trap moisture, the retention of the water-soluble vitamins (even the elusive vitamin C and the B vitamins) is good.

The texture of fresh vegetables that have been prepared in a microwave oven is often a bit more tenacious and chewy than is true of similar vegetables that have been boiled. Some people find that this texture is undesirable. Others find the excellent color and flavor provide sufficient compensation. Microwaving results in uneven cooking of various parts of the vegetable. This can be offset to a degree by rotating or stirring once or twice during the cooking period if the vegetables are in slices or pieces. Even then, the loss of water from parenchyma cells will be greater in these vegetables than in boiled counterparts; this loss explains, in part, the difference in texture resulting from these two cookery methods.

Pressure Cooking   Some time can be saved in cooking some vegetables by using a pressure saucepan, but the greatest savings are gained with vegetables requiring 20 minutes or more to become appropriately tender. The use of a pressure saucepan is particularly helpful at high altitudes where reduced temperature of boiling water at atmospheric pressure causes considerable delay in tenderizing vegetables.

petcock Small opening in the cover of a pressure saucepan to let steam escape and on which the pressure gauge is placed.

A small amount of water is placed in a pressure saucepan along with the washed and trimmed vegetables. The cover is secured, and the pan is heated, keeping the **petcock** open. When steam begins to come continuously through the open petcock, the pressure gauge (15 pounds) is put in position and full heat is continued until the gauge begins to jiggle. This indicates the correct pressure has been reached, and the timing of the cooking begins. The heat is adjusted lower until the gauge jiggles about three times per minute. Since the pressure is creating

---

JUDGING POINTS
COOKED FRESH VEGETABLES

- Attractively cut
- Pleasing, bright color
- Texture tender enough to be cut, but not soft (puréed or mashed should be very soft)
- Flavor delicate, yet characteristic of the vegetable

---

a very high temperature, timing must be done carefully, for an error of 30 seconds can cause a significant variation from the desired result in tenderizing the vegetable.

As soon as the desired time has elapsed, the pressure saucepan is removed from the heat and is held under cool running water briefly to reduce the pressure inside before the pressure gauge is removed and the lid opened. Strong-flavored and green vegetables are suited less well to pressure sauccpan cookery than are other vegetables, but many can be cooked successfully this way.

PREPARING CANNED AND FROZEN VEGETABLES

Canned Vegetables

Preparation of vegetables canned commercially is as simple as opening the can and heating them to serving temperature in their own juice, or draining and using them cold in salads. The canning process has cooked the vegetables completely. Reheating vegetables in a microwave oven is done in a glass dish, with only enough of the liquid added to provide the juice desired in serving (often only the liquid clinging to the vegetable as it is spooned from the can). No cover is required for this brief period of microwaving unless a sauce, such as that on creamed corn, is being heated with the vegetable.

Home-canned vegetables present the potential hazard of being a source of the toxin produced by *C. botulinum*. Since this toxin can be fatal in even extremely small amounts, home-canned vegetables should be boiled actively for at least 15 minutes before they are even tasted. To use home-canned vegetables without following this precaution is to take a risk that could result in death (Chapter 19). The sole exception to the rule of boiling for 15 minutes is tomatoes, for they are usually acidic enough that they do not favor growth of *C. botulinum* spores.

Frozen Vegetables

Frozen vegetables have been **blanched** before freezing to inactivate enzymes that might cause oxidative changes during frozen storage. This brief cooking period is enough to begin to soften the cell walls and shorten the subsequent cooking period required when the frozen vegetable ultimately is cooked. Usually, the block of frozen vegetable is placed in a small amount of boiling water (ordinarily about half a cup of water for a 10-ounce portion of vegetable) and is boiled just until the vegetable is tender. Some frozen vegetables are packaged in bags designed to remain sealed until after cooking. These should be prepared according to the directions on the package.

A lid can be used to help trap the steam for melting the upper portion of the frozen block. Even green vegetables can be cooked from their frozen state to their serving temperature with the pan covered because the oxidative enzymes that promote pheophytin formation have been inactivated by the prior blanching period. In addition, the very short boiling period is unlikely to result in pheophytin being formed from chlorophyll.

Microwaving works particularly well for preparing frozen vegetables. As the frozen block softens during the heating process, the vegetables should be stirred to promote even heating. The texture of frozen vegetables heated in a microwave oven is close to those that are boiled, because the changes in the cell walls resulting from the blanching period and the formation of ice crystals during freezing usually result in adequate tenderizing, even with a fairly brief cooking period in the microwave oven.

blanching Boiling or steaming for a brief period to inactivate enzymes prior to freezing.

Figure 5.21
Basil is an herb that can be used as a flavoring or a garnish to add interest to vegetables. Courtesy of Plycon Press.

ADDING INTEREST

Even when vegetables have been prepared perfectly, they may seem monotonous if only a narrow range of vegetables is prepared, particularly if only one or two preparation techniques are being used. The use of sauces, seasonings, and spices can add considerable appeal to the vegetables in meals. Sauces that are appropriate for vegetables include lemon butter, hollandaise, béchamel, and mornay, as well as sweet-sour sauces. Imaginative use of herbs is another way of accenting vegetables. Basil (Figure 5.21), dill, marjoram, mint, oregano, chopped parsley, chopped chives, rosemary, sage, savory, tarragon (very sparingly), and thyme are some of the popular herbs for vegetables.

Attractive and appetizing service of vegetables is important to acceptance. Careful draining before serving is essential if a sauce is going to be added or if the vegetable will be served directly on the main dinner plate. Herbs may be stirred into the drained vegetable, along with the margarine or butter, before serving. A squeeze of lemon juice stirred into the vegetable is another way of adding a subtle flavor accent.

SUMMARY

Vegetables often are classified according to the part of the plant that is used as food, the resulting classifications being bulbs, roots, tubers, leaves and stems, fruits, and seeds. Vegetables have an outer covering, a vascular transport system, and pulp, which is composed mostly of parenchyma cells. The structural components of vegetables are primarily cellulose, hemicelluloses, and the pectic substances. Within the parenchyma cells, starch is formed and stored in the plastids called leucoplasts, carotenoid pigments in the chromoplasts, chlorophylls in the chloroplasts, and flavonoid pigments, plus sugars, acids, and salts, in the large portion of the cell, called the vacuole.

Vegetables are valuable sources of nutrients when they are prepared and served in tempting ways. Among the nutrients contained in vegetables are many of the vitamins (particularly provitamin A in the dark green, leafy, and yellow vegetables) and minerals. A few are also excellent sources of starch. An important contribution of vegetables in the diet is their fiber, which is useful in promoting intestinal motility.

Throughout the year, a wide range of fresh vegetables can be obtained in large supermarkets. Many of these should be stored in the refrigerator, carefully wrapped to protect against moisture loss in the home. A few, potatoes being a notable example, should be stored about 10°F (6°C) below room temperature to promote optimum quality retention. At 60°F (15.6°C), starch content of non-waxy potatoes remains high, thus promoting their excellent performance for mashing, baking, and frying. Waxy potatoes held at this temperature will retain adequate amounts of sugar, yet starch content will be controlled to enable them to be used for their best preparation modes, for boiling and in salads and casseroles.

Considerable nutrients and palatability can be lost if care is not exercised in the handling of vegetables from the farm to the market and, ultimately, the family table. Temperature control is vital to nutrient retention and the avoidance of spoilage. Control of the moisture level in the surrounding environment during storage also is important. The eye can be a good guide to the selection of vegetables of high quality and nutrient value.

Cookery techniques should be designed to optimize color, flavor, total palatability, and nutrient content. This is a large order, but appropriate decisions regarding the amount of water to use in boiling, the use of a lid, and length of cooking can be made. Green vegetables will retain their chlorophyll rather than form pheophytin if the cooking time is kept short and a lid is not used. A tiny bit of acid helps to retain the desired color in the flavonoids (anthoxanthins and anthocyanins), but adding much acid will cause vegetables to remain hard. Using a lid on a boiling vegetable helps to hold in the natural organic acids. A minimum amount of water to just boil over a fresh vegetable and the use of a lid will promote optimum flavor in a mild-flavored vegetable, whereas uncovering a strong-flavored vegetable like cabbage helps to increase palatability by weakening the flavor. If either color or flavor is improved without the lid, the cover should be left off for maximum palatability.

In addition to boiling, vegetables can be prepared by steaming. Legumes are simmered because they take a long time to soften. Broiling, baking, frying, and stir-frying are other techniques suited to preparing some vegetables. Microwave cookery of vegetables, particularly of canned and frozen vegetables, is yet another quick technique. A pressure saucepan is a time saver in cooking vegetables that require at least 20 minutes to soften appropriately; it is of particular merit when cooking vegetables in the mountains.

STUDY QUESTIONS

1. Compare the cost and palatability of the following vegetables in their fresh, frozen, and canned forms: corn, peas, string beans, carrots, and potatoes. Which products represent (a) the most economical choices and (b) the greatest palatability?

2. Make a list of the various gourmet vegetables in the frozen food section. What types of sauces or special ingredients are incorporated in these items? How does the cost compare with the cost of the plain frozen vegetables?

3. What are some vegetables that are examples of each of the pigment categories? What color changes may be anticipated in each in the presence of acids and alkalis? How can cookery technique influence the color of cooked vegetables?

4. Describe the techniques involved in cooking vegetables by each of the following methods: boiling, steaming, broiling, baking, frying, stir-frying, microwaving, and pressure cooking. Name at least one vegetable suitable for each method.

5. Explain the use of a lid and the amount of water to be used in boiling each of the following fresh vegetables: corn, broccoli, onions, red cabbage, Brussels sprouts, spinach, cauliflower, beets, carrots. Explain why you chose each.

SELECTED REFERENCES

Backas, N. 2009. Eat your veggies. *Food Product Design* 19 (10): 44.

Camp, D. B., et al. 2010. Paradox of organic ingredients. *Food Technol.* 64(11): 20.

Cannon, R. 2008. Organic vs. natural. *Food Product Design* 18(8): 26.

Clemens, R. A. 2001. Redefining fiber. *Food Technol.* 55(2): 100.

Fan, X., et al. 2009. *Microbial Safety of Fresh Produce.* Wiley-Blackwell. New York.

Gerdes, S. 2004. Perusing the food-color palette. *Food Product Design* 14(9): 94.

Getz, J. G., et al. 2010. Nutrigenomics and public health. *Food Technol.* 64(2): 28.

Hoover, D. B. 1997. Minimally processed fruits and vegetables: Reducing microbial load by nonthermal physical treatments. *Food Technol.* 51(6): 66.

Johnston, C. S., and D. L. Bowling. 2002. Stability of ascorbic acid in commercially available orange juices. *J. Am. Dietet. Assoc.* 102(4): 525.

Kuntz, L. A. 2010. Beta-carotene's bonanza. *Food Product Design* 20(2): 16.

Luff, S. 2002. Phytochemical revolution. *Food Product Design: Functional Foods Annual* Sept.: 77.

Luff, S. 2005. Organic identity preservation. *Food Product Design* 15(7): 107.

Massengale, R. D. 2010. Biotechnology: Going beyond GMOs. *Food Technol.* 64(10): 30.

McCullum, C. 2000. Food biotechnology in the new millennium: Promises, realities, and challenges. *J. Am. Dietet. Assoc.* 100(11): 1311.

McWilliams, M. 2012. *Foods: Experimental Perspectives.* 7th ed. Prentice Hall. Upper Saddle River, NJ.

Miraglio, A. M. 2006. Beyond lycopene. *Food Product Design.* 15(10): 77.

Montecalvo, J. 2001. The National Organic Program: An opportunity for industry. *J. Food Technol.* 55(6): 26.

Newman, V. S., et al. 2002. Amount of raw vegetables and fruits needed to yield 1 c juice. *J. Am. Dietet. Assoc.* 102(7): 975.

Palmer, S. 2009. Coloring the anthocyanin age. *Food Product Design* 19(3): 26.

Park, J., and H. C. Brittin. 1997. Increased iron content of food due to stainless steel cookware. *J. Amer. Dietetic Assoc.* 97(6): 659.

Pszczola, D. E. 2007. Emerging ingredients: Good as gold. *Food Technol.* 61(7): 63.

Stables, G. J., et al. 2002. Changes in vegetable and fruit consumption and awareness among U.S. adults: Results of the 1991 and 1997 5-a-Day for Better Health Program surveys. *J. Am. Dietet. Assoc.* 102(6): 809.

Turner, R. Elaine. 2002. Organic standards. *Food Technol.* 56(6): 24.

Van Duyn, M. A. S., and E. Pivonka. 2000. Overview of the health benefits of fruit and vegetable consumption for the dietetics professional: Selected literature. *J. Am. Dietet. Assoc.* 100(12): 1511.

Winter, C. K. 2006. Organic foods. *Food Technol.* 60(10): 44.

Asian pears are classified as pomes. Courtesy of Plycon Press.

6

Fruits

Chapter Contents

Key Concepts

1. Fruits generally are more delicate and perishable than vegetables.

2. The varied types of fruits (berries, citrus, drupes, grapes, melons, pomes, and tropical and subtropical) provide not only good sources of vitamins and minerals but also a broad spectrum of colors, flavors, and textures.

3. Careful selection and storage of fruits will provide optimum quality of fresh, frozen, canned, and dried fruits.

4. Control of osmotic pressure is important when preparing fruits with fragile cells.

Fruits—fresh, frozen, canned, or dried—are favorite foods for many people. They are popular at all meals of the day and as snack foods, too, for they are often eaten raw and require little preparation except washing. Fruits have flavors tinged with sweetness and textures ranging from crisp to very soft to brighten any meal or snack. In contrast, vegetables require some skill and imagination to bring them to the table as a meal highlight. The challenge with fruits is to select those of high quality and then store them appropriately until they are prepared for simple or elegant service.

The array of fruits available to today's consumers throughout the year would have amazed even royalty 50 years ago, for wealth alone could not have bought items considered standard fare today. The secret of this difference is a combination of significant changes in shipping and marketing practices, plus agricultural innovations (Figure 6.1).

Summer is still the height of the fruit season, but even in winter the choices extend far beyond the traditional oranges, grapefruit, and apples of yesteryear. Not only are many fruits available, but choices must also be made among the fresh, frozen, canned, and dried fruits in the market. This chapter considers the fascinating array of fruits, their selection, nutritive value, care, and preparation.

CLASSIFICATION

Fruits are defined as being the edible, more or less succulent products of a tree or plant and consist of ripened seeds and adjacent tissues. Although a few fruits actually will end up classified as vegetables because of their use in the main course of a meal (tomatoes, for example), the majority will be used for salads, desserts,

Figure 6.1
Fruits in markets today often have traveled thousands of miles and yet are in excellent condition to broaden the spectrum of food choices. Courtesy of Plycon Press.

or as a flavor accent in combination with a savory because of their naturally sweet flavor. Some order can be made out of the many fruits by classifying them into groups or families on the basis of shape, cell structure, type of seed, or natural habitat. Commonly, fruits are categorized according to the following groups: berries, citrus, drupes, grapes, melons, pomes, and tropical and subtropical.

Berries

Berries typically are small fruits with a fragile, easily damaged cell structure. These fruits rely heavily on a high content of water within the cells to give the juicy plumpness associated with them. This high water content accompanied by thin cell walls causes berries to lose their notably juicy and slightly firm character if they are frozen and thawed; the sharp ice crystals that form during freezing rupture cell walls and release the juice. Familiar members of the berry group include blackberries, blueberries, boysenberries, red and black raspberries, youngberries, cranberries, gooseberries, huckleberries, and strawberries. Less familiar berries that can be found occasionally are lingonberries (Figure 6.2), cloudberries (natives of the Arctic Circle), and dewberries.

As a group, berries often are used fresh as desserts, served simply in a bowl, or made into baked products, such as a fresh berry pie or other types of bakery goods. They also can be made into gourmet pies by preparing a glaze into which the fresh berries are stirred in preparation for filling a baked piecrust.

Raspberries, blueberries, and strawberries have a wide sale in the frozen food market. Blueberries are even marketed in blueberry muffin mixes. Pancakes and waffles become festive when they are topped with berries in the form of fresh fruit, syrups, or even jams and jellies. Cranberries earn their special place by being available in the fall when many other fruits have faded. They are unique among the berries in their diverse forms in cranberry sauce, jelly, and juice.

Citrus

Citrus fruits, including oranges, grapefruit, lemons, tangerines, limes, and temple oranges are a rich source of vitamin C. Nutritionists recommend serving a citrus fruit daily. The inability of the body to store vitamin C efficiently has been a boon to the citrus industry, for oranges and other citrus fruits are year-round crops and a comparatively inexpensive source of this essential, but somewhat elusive, vitamin. The menu need not be limited to these citrus sources of vitamin C. Kumquats and citron are eaten only rarely, yet they also can provide this vitamin.

The two common types of orange in U.S. markets are Valencias and navels. Valencia oranges, preferred for juice, can be distinguished from navel oranges by examining the bottom of the orange. The bottom of the Valencia is smooth, whereas the bottom of the navel has a formation that is the beginning of an orange within an orange. Navels peel more easily than do the Valencias, are seedless, and slice readily; these attributes make navel oranges particularly popular for eating.

The popularity of oranges extends far beyond their role as a provider of vitamin C. The delightful flavor of oranges lends a pleasing accent to other foods; the bright color is yet another asset. Commercially, the production of orange juice to be marketed fresh (single-strength), canned, or as frozen concentrate is a big business, for this is a convenience food that is a welcomed time saver in many U.S. homes. Also of interest is the fact that the

Figure 6.2
Lingonberries are too fragile to ship from Scandinavia, so they often are made into jam for distant markets. Courtesy of Plycon Press.

white (albedo) portion of the skins of citrus fruits is a major source of pectin, which is used in manufacturing jams and jellies.

The tangerine, another type of citrus, has the shape of a slightly flattened orange. Its particular virtue is the loosely fitting skin, which can be peeled off with almost no effort; on the other hand, the sections of flesh contain a number of seeds that have to be removed. Mandarin oranges, actually a type of tangerine, are utilized in the canned form frequently as a salad and dessert ingredient (Figure 6.3). A close relative is the tangelo, which is a hybrid between a grapefruit and a tangerine. Temple oranges are another result of breeding experiments by botanists. This very pleasing citrus fruit has the juiciness of oranges and the easy peeling of tangerines.

Grapefruit, the largest of the citrus fruits, is enjoyed not only in the United States but also from South Africa to Israel. The flesh may be either white or pink. Although grapefruit frequently are eaten simply cut in half, they are excellent also when broiled, perhaps topped with a bit of brown sugar and served hot. Southeast Asia is the source of the pomelo, a very large citrus that looks like a giant grapefruit with an excessively thick skin; its taste is less tart than grapefruit (Figure 6.4).

Lemons are a particular boon to people who are trying to follow weight-reduction diets because a squeeze of lemon juice or a bit of grated lemon rind can add an exciting flavor accent to many different foods without adding enough calories to mention. For instance, a touch of lemon on a green salad can replace a high-calorie salad dressing and give a pleasing flavor. Lemons can also be used in high-calorie preparations such as lemonade and lemon meringue pies, as well as in other desserts that rely on large quantities of sugar to compensate for the tartness of the lemon juice.

Two other citrus fruits are kumquats and citron. Kumquats, originally from China, now are grown in Florida and California. The fruit is only about an inch long and, because of its size, makes an attractive garnish when used raw, preserved, or candied. Citron, a fruit from the hot deserts of the Middle East and now grown in California and Florida, resembles a large avocado with a very thick peel. Citron is valued for its edible peel, which ordinarily is candied and used in fruit cakes and some holiday cookies.

Figure 6.3
Mandarin oranges have a skin that peels easily and sections that separate readily, characteristics that make them an ideal snack.
Courtesy of Plycon Press.

http://www.hort.purdue. edu/newcrop/morton/ mandarin_orange.html
—Information on mandarin oranges.

INDUSTRY INSIGHT
PRODUCTS AND BY-PRODUCTS

The food industry, of necessity, must focus attention not only on the principal product being prepared but also on potentially marketable by-products that might otherwise be discarded without generating income and actually cost money for disposal. Examples of successful ones from the citrus industry are numerous, including limonene for use in producing resins and soaps, as well as potential use in food flavorings; cold-pressed oils for flavoring juices, other beverages, and candies; essences to enhance juice flavors; pectin, a complex carbohydrate thickening agent; and molasses and dried pulp for animal feed.

Microbiological contamination of citrus products has to be monitored carefully and controlled to avoid possible health problems because the juice products, in particular, are very supportive of the growth of microorganisms that thrive in cool, moist, and acidic environments. (The typical acidity of orange juice falls within the range of pH 3–4.) Consumers have been quick to accept single-strength (also called ready-to-serve or RTS) orange juice because of the freshness and quality. However, freshly squeezed juice has a limited shelf life unless extremely careful sanitary controls are exercised and temperature is controlled during production and marketing. Light pasteurization, which entails holding a liquid at 185–203°F (85–95°C) for 15–60 seconds, is a suitable means of helping to control microbiological growth during storage of RTS orange juice. Although this mild heat treatment alters the volatile flavoring compounds contained in the juice, the effect is quite minimal—certainly far less than the changes found in juice reconstituted from frozen concentrate.

Figure 6.4
Pomelo is a citrus that looks like a giant grapefruit with an extremely thick rind and a sweeter taste. Courtesy of Plycon Press.

drupe Fruit with a single seed surrounded by edible pulp.

muskmelon One of two general subdivisions of melons; includes cantaloupe, honeydew, and other melons characterized by having a thick pulp surrounding a large central cavity full of small seeds.

Figure 6.5
Dates hanging in clusters from a date palm tree in Oman; they are classified as drupes because of the thick flesh surrounding a single seed. Courtesy of Plycon Press.

Drupes

Drupes are fruits that have a single large seed surrounded by edible pulp. Apricots, cherries, peaches, plums, and prunes are familiar drupes. These fruits are popular in many forms—fresh, frozen, canned, in jams and jellies, and sometimes even dried. A showy example of a drupe is the maraschino cherry, which is made by bleaching sweet cherries with sulfur dioxide and then adding food coloring. Prunes, apricots, and peaches are popular dried; apricots and peaches usually are sulfured to retain their familiar orange color.

Somewhat less common examples are mangoes and dates (Figure 6.5). Dates, formerly an exotic fruit from distant oases overseas, now are grown commercially in California. The three stages of ripening (*khalal,* developing of a yellow or red color; *rutab,* softening; and *tamar,* time for curing the fruit) culminate in the curing of dates high in sugar content. Their sweetness makes them popular in baked products, salads, and confections as well as in milk drinks.

Grapes

Grapes are an important fruit crop in many parts of the world, valued both for the fruit itself and for the wine that can be made from certain varieties. Table grapes are available in such varieties as Thompson seedless, Flame Tokay, Emperor, Muscat, Malaga, and Concord. These stem from two basic types—the American grape with its round shape and the European grape, typified by an oval outline. The familiar blue Concord grape is an example of an American grape, and the Thompson seedless is classified as European.

Concord grapes are eaten fresh in season, but they also are the basis of many commercial products, including grape jelly, jam, conserves, juice, and frozen grape juice concentrate. Other grapes are used to make commercial products. Thompson seedless grapes are canned in fruit cocktail and are made into raisins by sun drying. Muscat grapes and currants are other popular dried products.

Melons

Melons, unlike most other fruits, generally are restricted to use as the fresh fruit. Preservation methods cause undesirable textural changes, with the exception of watermelon pickles. Even freezing presents problems; freezing damages the delicate cell structure, resulting in a slippery and slightly unpleasant texture when thawed.

Fortunately, melons can be grown over a rather wide geographic area from north to south, so the growing season for melons is fairly long. For instance, melons grown in the Imperial Valley of southern California are shipped to markets from the middle of May until early July, at which time northern California takes over the market, only to relinquish it again to the Imperial Valley for a fall crop.

The two general categories in the melon group are watermelons and muskmelons (Figure 6.6). **Muskmelons**, with their central cavity filled with seeds and thick, colorful pulp under a thin outer skin, are subdivided into several familiar varieties: cantaloupe, honeydew, Persian, casaba, honey ball, and Crenshaw.

Persian melons, noted for their thick, orange-colored flesh, are closely related to cantaloupe, while casaba has a soft flesh and creamy color. Persian and casaba melons were crossed to produce Crenshaw, a variety with a rich flavor

Figure 6.6
Watermelons are a type of melon that is enjoyed not only in Kenya but also in the United States and many other countries around the world.
Courtesy of Plycon Press.

and lovely salmon color. Both casaba and Crenshaw melons have excellent marketing characteristics, for they are best if picked green and ripened off the vine, which makes shipping comparatively easy. Cantaloupe and Persian melons present shipping problems; they are best when allowed to ripen on the vine. Honeydew melons provide a distinct contrast to other melons because of the very sweet flavor and delicate green color. Occasionally, honeyball melons are seen in markets. They have an exterior resembling honeydew, while the interior is similar to a mild-flavored cantaloupe.

Pomes

Pomes are fruits from the botanical family Malaceae, which is characterized by a central core containing five encapsulated seeds surrounded by a thick and fleshy edible layer. This core structure is characteristic of all of the fruits classified as pomes (Figure 6.7). Familiar pomes are apples, pears, and quince. Apples are particularly common in the American diet, due to their great versatility and their excellent keeping qualities. Commercially, apples are processed into juice, vinegar, jelly, apple butter, applesauce, and pie fillings. They may also be dried in slices or used in frozen pie fillings. In the home, baked apples, apple pie, fruit salads, and apple fritters are just some of the ways in which apples are incorporated into the diet.

Pears can be used in many recipes interchangeably with apples. For instance, pears can be used in fruit salads and in making a pear pie. The greater juiciness of pears makes it necessary to make some adjustments in some products, such as quick breads where liquid levels are particularly important. Bartlett pears are a rich yellow color when ripe; d'Anjou pears are still green in color but yield slightly to pressure when ripe; Bosc pears have a brown network on the skin, called russeting, which makes them appear rather brown when ready to use.

www.rainierfruit.com/consumers/wax.html
—Information about apples, cherries, and pears.

pome   Fruit with a central core containing five seeds surrounded by thick, edible pulp; apples, quince, and pear are examples.

Figure 6.7
An apple is classified as a pome because it contains five seeds encapsulated within the core. Courtesy of Plycon Press.

www.itfnet.org

—International Tropical Fruit
Network website; overview
of many tropical fruit crops.

http://www.friedas.com/
index.cfm?show=products_
category&side=products&
category=Fresh%20
Specialty%20Fruits

—Information on tropical
and other unusual fruits.

re-greening Reversal of
color to green on some
ripe oranges if chlorophyll
becomes dominant over
carotenoids.

Figure 6.8
A shopper pauses to buy
papayas (left) and mangoes
(right) in this tropical
farmers' market. Courtesy of
Plycon Press.

Tropical and Subtropical Fruits

Tropical and subtropical fruits usually are available throughout the year because of today's excellent transportation facilities. Although they may have to be shipped from distant ports, they still can serve as alternative sources of vitamin C in the diet. They also are important because of the interest they can add to menus.

Among the popular tropical and subtropical fruits are avocados, pineapples, papayas, mangos, bananas, figs, dates, and pomegranates. The avocado is unique among fruits because of its comparatively high fat content (about 13 percent) in contrast to other fruits having negligible levels of fat. Gros Michel is the variety of banana commonly used for eating and in salads and various baked products. Caribbean recipes call for another type of banana, the plantain, a starchy banana suitable for frying and baking, but not ordinarily consumed raw.

Figs were popular in the Mediterranean countries many centuries ago, but in the United States today they are best known as canned kadota figs or as the filling in Fig Newton® cookies. Now they are grown in California and can be shipped fresh from the tree in late summer. Although fresh figs have limited availability because they are quite perishable, dried figs (the usual form) can be purchased all year.

Pineapple, found originally in Central America, now is available on a large scale from Hawaii, with Puerto Rico and Florida also adding to the supply. In Hawaii, pineapple production and processing still represent a key industry, despite the fact that real-estate ventures are beginning to crowd out some of the land once devoted to raising this key tropical fruit. Nevertheless, a large volume of pineapple, in the form of juice, spears, rings, crushed, and chunks, is shipped regularly to the mainland.

Another important tropical fruit exported from Hawaii to the mainland and also from other tropical lands is the papaya (Figure 6.8). The delicate flavor and lovely orange color make this fruit a welcome addition to fruit salads or poultry salads; papayas are excellent when served alone, sometimes heightened by a squeeze of lime or lemon juice. Surprisingly, even the seeds of papayas can be used as food, for they can be ground and used in salad dressing. The papaya is a source of the enzyme papain, used in tenderizing less tender cuts of meat.

Pomegranates are unique fruits, for they are valued for the edible seeds, which contain a comparatively large amount of a flavorful, red juice (Figure 6.9). The juice may be extracted from the seeds to make grenadine and fruit juice combinations. In the home, the seeds are prized as an attractive red color accent in fruit salads.

PIGMENTS

The pigments found in fruits are classified in the same categories discussed in Chapter 5. As is true in vegetables, fruits contain a blending of pigments (some of which are considered to be phytochemicals potentially useful in protecting against certain chronic diseases). Oranges afford an excellent illustration of this. The rind (flavedo) of most oranges shows just a bit of chlorophyll in addition to the characteristic carotenoid pigments that gave this fruit its name. Oranges are susceptible to a process called **re-greening**, in which the chlorophyll may begin to dominate the carotenoids, often causing consumers to think (erroneously) that the re-greened oranges are not yet ripe. Other pigments also are found in oranges. The white area (albedo) just under the flavedo contains anthoxanthin pigments, while blood oranges contain anthocyanins in the pulp of the fruit.

Figure 6.9
Pomegranates, a subtropical fruit, are gaining in popularity because of their pretty reddish color and the anthocyanin and other phytochemicals in the juice from the seeds. Courtesy of Plycon Press.

Very few vegetables provide examples of anthocyanins, but fruits illustrate the range of anthocyanins clearly. Delphinidin is a blue anthocyanin found in Concord grapes; other fruits run the gamut of potential colors in the anthocyanin group, from the blue of the Concord grape through purples to a bright red. Examples of these pigments are found in Table 6.1.

Although color changes during cooking are not generally a problem in fruit cookery, there is considerable potential for problems when fruits containing anthocyanins are combined. The addition of an acidic juice such as lemon juice to an anthocyanin-containing fruit juice will heighten the red, which is usually acceptable. However, the juices containing anthocyanins may become blue when they come in contact with hard water or are otherwise brought to an alkaline reaction. The pigments in strawberries and cranberries are quite stable, which makes them useful as ingredients when a red color needs to be maintained in a fruit juice mixture.

Flavonoids (both anthocyanins and anthoxanthins) are capable of complexing readily with metal ions, causing undesirable color changes. Thus, fruits containing these pigments should be kept away from aluminum, iron, or tin.

COMPOSITION OF FRUITS

Most fruits have high water content, ranging between 80 and 90 percent, with watermelons and muskmelons at the upper end (about 92 percent moisture level). Even dried fruits are about 25 percent water. The carbohydrate levels in fresh fruits range generally from about 3 to 14 percent. Protein and fat are notably low in fruits (except the avocado). Table 6.2 provides information on the composition of some familiar fruits.

TABLE 6.1
ANTHOCYANIN PIGMENTS IN FRUITS

Anthocyanin Compound	Color	Examples in Fruit
Delphinidin	Blue	Concord grape
Cyanidins	Purple to deep red	Bing cherries, sour cherries, blueberries, raspberries, boysenberries
Pelargonidin	Red	Strawberries, red raspberries

TABLE 6.2
AVERAGE VALUES OBTAINED IN THE ANALYSIS OF SELECTED FRUITS[a]

Fruit	Water (%)	Calories	Carbohydrate (g)	Vitamin A Value (IU)	Ascorbic Acid (mg)
Apples, 1 medium	84	81	21	73	8
Apricots, 3	86	17	55	3173	8
Avocado, 1/2 of 10 oz	73	50	2	174	2
Banana, 1 medium	74	109	28	96	11
Cantaloupe, 1c cubed	90	56	13	5158	68
Grapefruit, 1/2 medium	91	37	9	319	47
Navel orange, 1 large	87	62	15	269	70
Peach, 1 medium	88	42	11	524	6
Pear, 3" × 2 1/2"	84	98	25	33	7
Pineapple, 1c diced	87	76	19	36	24
Strawberries, 1c	92	50	12	45	94
Watermelon, 4" × 8" slice	92	92	21	1047	27

Source: United States Department of Agriculture.
[a]All values are for the raw fruits.

http://www.nal.usda.gov/
fnic/foodcomp/Data/HG72/
hg72_2002.pdf
—Home and Garden
Bulletin 72

The type of carbohydrate found in individual fruits varies with the maturity of the fruit (Figure 6.10), but the total amount of carbohydrate remains relatively constant as the fruit develops from the green to mature state. Starch content, high in immature fruits, usually declines as ripening occurs, whereas the sugar level rises. This relationship in these two forms of carbohydrate reflects the gradual transition of starch into sugar with maturation, a change that can be detected in the sweet flavor of ripened fruits. Actually, there is a remarkable range in the sugar levels found in ripe fruits, from only about 1 percent for avocados to about 61 percent in dates. The types of sugars include fructose, invert sugar (an equal combination of glucose and fructose), sucrose, and glucose, all of which add a sweet taste to the fruits in which they are found.

Much of the structural material of fruits is other indigestible carbohydrates, commonly referred to as fiber or roughage. These structural components, so important to texture, occur in differing proportions in the various fruits.

Cellulose is one of the key constituents (Chapter 5), particularly in the dermal cells forming the protective skin in fruits. The vascular (those carrying food and water to the parenchyma cells) also contain cellulose in their cell walls. The parenchyma cells are the type of cell comprising most of the edible pulp in fruits, and these also have some cellulose in their walls.

In addition to cellulose, hemicelluloses add to the strength of cell walls, particularly in the parenchyma cells. The pectic substances are complex carbohydrates that help to cement the individual cells together in fruits. Changes in pectic substances are responsible in large measure for the change observed in the hard texture of green fruit to the mushiness of very ripe fruit.

Other important constituents in fruits are enzymes and organic acids. The enzymes are of interest because they are responsible for effecting changes in fruits during the ripening process, including softening of the fruit and development of sugar, as well as other flavor components of the ripened fruit. Unfortunately, sometimes enzyme action causes browning on the cut surfaces. Organic acids are of importance both because of contributions to flavor and to the role they play in preservation techniques, specifically in canning and in making jams and jellies (Chapter 19).

Figure 6.10
The blossom at the end and small bananas can be seen forming on the stalk projecting left from the banana tree (in front of the date palm tree at an oasis in Oman); starch in the bananas will gradually change to sugars as the fruit matures. Courtesy of Plycon Press.

NUTRITIVE VALUE

People have long been aware that fruits are important sources of nutrients, even though the specific nutrients in individual fruits may have remained a mystery to them. The actual contributions of the various fruits include a range of nutrients, but fruits, as a group, are important nutritionally primarily for their contributions of vitamins A and C, supplemental contributions of calcium and other minerals and vitamins, as well as their excellent fiber content. Fruits also are a good source of energy because of the sugar they provide in the diet.

As can be seen in Table 6.2, some of the yellow fruits (apricots, peaches, and cantaloupe, for example) are potential sources of vitamin A because they contain carotenes, which can be converted to vitamin A in the body. Several other fruits are outstanding sources of ascorbic acid or vitamin C, and most fruits contain at least some of this vitamin. Citrus fruits are abundant year round and are rich sources of vitamin C, while many of the tropical and subtropical fruits and also berries afford other outstanding sources of this vitamin.

Fruits also contribute to the day's total intake of minerals. Dried fruits are relatively good sources of iron. Some calcium is contained in oranges, with other fruits contributing minor amounts. Although oranges are useful in supplementing the calcium from milk, their level is inadequate as the primary source of this key mineral. However, commercially processed orange juice can be purchased with added calcium and vitamin D to approximate the levels of these in milk.

The need for fiber to help promote motility of the digestive tract is extremely important from the standpoint of good health, even though the fiber is not actually absorbed into the body and used in the ways that nutrients are. Therefore, fruits are important foods in the diet, for they provide excellent amounts of cellulose, hemicelluloses, and pectic substances, all of which are components of fiber.

MARKETING ASPECTS

www.cffausa.org/us_con_index.htm

—Chilean fruit crops information.

Since fruits often are produced far from the markets where they will be purchased by consumers (Table 6.3), shipping must be done quickly and economically to bring products to stores while they are still of excellent quality and high in nutrients. To do this, refrigerated trucks and freight cars are utilized. Control of humidity within vehicles and storage areas is vital, for too much moisture favors mold formation and too little causes dehydration and shriveling.

Deterioration during storage and shipping of fruits also can be retarded by controlling the carbon dioxide level in the storage area, for carbon dioxide gas inhibits yeast and mold growth as well as retards the ripening process. Unfortunately, too much carbon dioxide promotes the formation of alcohol in apples and pears. Use of carbon dioxide in storing fruits is not limited to commercial operations. Plastic containers specially designed with a tight cover and small openings to permit some entry of oxygen and to regulate moisture level are available for home use to aid consumers in controlling the ripening of immature fruits. In these containers, the carbon dioxide is produced by the fruits themselves and is trapped in the closed container, a system that functions rather efficiently.

Apples and citrus are particularly good fruits for long-term storage, due in part to their excellent dermal layer. Most other fruits have to move through the marketing chain comparatively rapidly after harvest, which results in close to a glut, with low prices at some times and only "greenhouse" or imported products at high prices during the remainder of the year.

Grapes are an especially perishable commodity because of their tendency to promote mold growth during shipping and storage. The use of sulfur dioxide gas in the storage environment is an aid in reducing problems due to mold.

Bananas and avocados are fruits that will continue to ripen after they have been harvested. This allows them to be picked green and shipped while they are still quite firm, thus reducing the damage incurred during shipping. On the other hand, pineapple, citrus fruits, and some melons (cantaloupe and Persian melons) fail to develop their full flavor potential when picked before becoming ripe.

Ethylene gas is a valuable adjunct to the marketing of some fruits because of its ability to promote ripening and the resultant color changes in fruits. Chlorophyll can be decomposed to

TABLE 6.3
AVAILABILITY OF FRUITS FROM CHILE

Fruit	Jan	Feb	March	April	May	June	July	Aug	Sept	Oct	Nov	Dec
Apples		X	X	X	X	X	X					
Blueberries	X	X	X	X							X	X
Cherries	X										X	X
Grapes	X	X	X	X	X						X	X
Kiwifruit			X	X	X	X	X	X	X		X	
Peaches	X	X	X								X	X
Nectarines	X	X	X								X	X
Pears	X	X	X	X	X	X	X					X
Plums	X	X	X	X								
Avocados	X								X	X	X	X
Clementines					X	X	X					
Raspberries	X	X	X	X	X					X	X	

reveal the desired carotenoid pigments in oranges when ethylene gas is present in the storage atmosphere. Although the flavor is not changed in these oranges, the enhanced color makes them very marketable. Oranges, bananas, and a few other fruits are ripened in storage by the use of ethylene gas.

Selection of fruit is based to a large extent on the visual message provided by the color and appearance. Since 1922, citrus fruits have been waxed to enhance their appearance. Carnauba wax (from palm fronds) is applied in an extremely thin film to apples, peaches, cantaloupe, and some other fresh produce in such a small amount that a gallon of the wax will coat 5 tons of apples! In the case of oranges, about six drops are applied to each orange, then buffed with brushes to add to the eye appeal. This wax also serves as a protective coating to reduce moisture loss and resultant shriveling and as a shield against decay. Thus, a wax coating helps to extend the period when quality of the fruit will be high.

SELECTION

Fresh Fruits

Select those that are an appropriate size for the intended use when buying fresh fruits. Be sure they are fresh and plump, free of bruises and blemishes, and at the desired degree of ripeness. Freshness can be seen visually by looking for plump, rather than limp, fruits. If at all possible, avoid blemishes and bruises, for these are the areas in which spoilage begins during storage.

When fruits are available in more than one size, the larger size almost invariably will be appreciably higher in price than the smaller one. If the fruit is to be displayed in an arrangement or to be served whole or as a garnish, the large size may be worth the price, but the small size might be used very satisfactorily in recipes at a significant saving.

Fruits often are graded according to federal grading standards, although consumers usually do not see the designation. The Agricultural Marketing Service of the U.S. Department of Agriculture is the agency charged with grading standards for fruits. At the wholesale level, grade is an important determinant of price, which ultimately is passed on to consumers. The federal grades established by the Agricultural Marketing Service are as follows:

U.S. Fancy Premium produce

U.S. No. 1 Chief trading grade

U.S. No. 2 Intermediate quality range

U.S. No. 3 Lowest commercially useful grade

Often only two of these grades may be used for a specific fruit. Any fruit undergoing federal grading will have its container marked with an official USDA grade shield or a label stating "Packed Under Continuous Inspection of the U.S. Department of Agriculture" or else "Packed by _____ Under the Continuous Federal-State Inspection."

Grade designations of fresh fruit are usually not displayed at the site of purchase, but consumers can make wise decisions by examining the fruit. Table 6.4 provides some information regarding factors to note when making selections in the market. By making mental notes regarding the quality of fruits selected, shoppers can gradually build up an ability to select wisely.

Sometimes choices must be made between varieties as well as within varieties of a fruit. Choice of the right variety depends upon the intended end use for the fruit. For example, Bing cherries and sour (pie) cherries may be available at the same time. The Bing cherries will give particularly good results in salads or simply for eating, while sour cherries are excellent for making cherry pie.

Several varieties of tangerines may also be on the market at the same time. If intended for a child's school lunch, the few seeds and easy peeling typical of Satsuma mandarins would make this a good choice, while the difficulty of peeling the Orlando tangelo and removing its many seeds would be a poor one. Of the tangerines, the Dancy is the variety found most commonly; its easy peeling and tart flavor help to compensate for the annoyance of removing so many seeds.

http://www.ams.usda.gov/ AMSv1.0/ams.fetch TemplateData.do?template= TemplateN&page=Fresh MarketFruitStandards
—Grading standards for fresh fruits.

www.hort.purdue.edu/ fruitveg/nutrition_labels.pdf
—Federal guidelines on labeling fresh fruits.

www.rules.utah.gov/ publicat/code/r068/ r068-004.htm
—Grading regulations for fresh fruits and vegetables in Utah.

TABLE 6.4
A GUIDE TO THE SELECTION OF FRESH FRUITS

Fruit	Desirable Qualities	Characteristics to Avoid
Apples	Firm; crisp; good color for the variety of apple	Overripe; soft and mealy; bruises
Apricots	Uniform, golden color; plump; juicy; barely soft	Soft or mushy; hard; pale yellow or green color
Avocados	Firm; bright color; free from bruises	Bruises; discolored skin
Blueberries	Dark blue with silver bloom; plump; firm; uniform size	Bruises; discolored skin
Cherries	Dark color in sweet cherries; bright red in pie cherries; glossy; plump	Shriveling; dull appearance; soft, leaking juice; mold
Cranberries	Plump and firm; lustrous; red color	Soft and spongy; leaking
Grapefruit	Firm; well shaped; heavy for size; thin skin indicates juiciness	Soft and discolored areas; mold
Grapes	Plump; yellowish cast for white or green grapes; red color predominating for red grapes; stems green and pliable	Soft, wrinkled; bleached area around stem; leaking
Lemons	Rich yellow color (pale or greenish yellow for higher acid content); firm; heavy	Hard or shriveling; soft spots; mold; dark yellow
Limes	Glossy skin; heavy	Dry skin; decay
Melons		
Cantaloupe	Smooth area where stem grew; bold netting; yellowish cast to skin	Soft rind; bruises
Casaba	Yellow rind; slight softening at blossom end	Decayed spots
Cranshaw	Deep golden rind; very slight softening of rind; good aroma	Decayed spots
Honeydew	Faint odor; yellow to creamy rind; slight softening at blossom end	Greenish-white rind; hard and smooth skin
Persian	Same as cantaloupe	Same as cantaloupe
Watermelon	Slightly dull rind; creamy color on the underside	Cracks; dull rind
Nectarines	Slight softening; rich color; plump	Hard or shriveled; soft
Oranges	Firm and heavy; bright, fresh skin either orange or green tint	Light weight; dull skin; mold
Peaches	Slightly soft; yellow color between the red areas	Very firm, hard; green ground color; very soft; decay
Pears	Firm, but beginning to soften; good color for variety (Barlett, yellow; d'Anjou or Comice, light green to yellow green; Bosc, greenish-yellow with skin russeting; Winter Nellis, medium to light green)	Weakening around the stem; shriveled; spots
Pineapples	Good pineapple odor; green to yellow color; spike leaves easily removed; heavy for size	Bruises; poor odor; sunken or slightly pointed pips
Plums	Good color for variety; fairly firm	Hard or shriveled; poor color; leaking
Raspberries	Good color for kind; plump; clean; no caps	Mold; leaking
Strawberries	Good red color; lustrous; clean; cap stem attached	Mold; leaking; large seeds
Tangerines	Bright lustrous skin	Mold; soft spots

INGREDIENT HIGHLIGHT
GRĀPPLE®

Researchers have infused Fuji apples with grape flavoring and a bit of water to create a unique apple designated as a Grāpple (pronounced with a long a, as in grape, and a nod to the apple with the end of the name). The grape aspect is featured because the grape flavor of the apple is what makes eating a Grāpple a unique experience (Figure 6.11). Its nutritional value is comparable to Fuji apples, and its availability is the same.

Creation of the Grāpple is done using a patented process. This unique approach to creating a new fruit for the market contrasts with fruits resulting from crossing two different fruits or with genetic modification. Luther Burbank (1849–1926) conducted countless breeding experiments on many plants at his experimental farm in Santa Rosa, California, and is credited with developing numerous varieties of various fruits. To identify just a part of his fruit varieties, he created a remarkable 113 varieties of plums and prunes, 10 apples, 8 peaches, 5 nectarines, and 16 blackberries, plus several other kinds of fruits.

Figure 6.11
Fuji apples infused with grape flavor are marketed as Grāpple®. Courtesy of Plycon Press.

Varieties of apples in the market vary greatly from one part of the country to another, and new ones continue to be developed by researchers. Some are particularly well suited to eating raw and in salads, while others may be used to good advantage in such cooked preparations as sauce, coddling or poaching, baking, and in pies or other baked products. Table 6.5 provides a partial guide to the use of various apples in food preparation.

The seasonal nature of many fruits limits their use in the fresh form to a rather short time period (Figure 6.12). Knowledge of the usual times when each of the fruits may be expected to be available is an aid in menu planning. Generally, the quality of fruits will be the best and the price will be lowest when the fresh fruit is at the height of its season. At such times, generous use of fresh fruits can add considerable interest as well as nutrients to the diet. Of course, many fruits can be obtained frozen, canned, or dried at any time of the year.

www.grāpplefruits.com

—Information about Grāpple®, a grape-flavored Fuji apple.

Canned and Frozen Fruits

The Agricultural Marketing Service of the U.S. Department of Agriculture is responsible for the federal standards used for grading frozen and canned fruits. The top grade, U.S. Grade A or

TABLE 6.5
SUGGESTED USES FOR SELECTED VARIETIES OF APPLES[a]

Variety	Fresh and Salads	Pie	Sauce and Coddling	Baking
Delicious				
Red	Excellent			
Golden	Excellent	Excellent	Good	Good
Fuji	Excellent	Good	Good	Good
Gala	Excellent	Good	Good	Good
Granny Smith	Good	Excellent	Excellent	Good
Gravenstein	Good	Good	Good	Good
Jonathan	Good	Good	Excellent	Good
McIntosh	Excellent	Excellent	Good	
Newtown Pippin	Good	Excellent	Good	Good
Northern Spy				Good
Rhode Island Greening		Excellent	Excellent	Good
Rome Beauty	Good	Good	Excellent	Excellent
Stayman	Good	Good	Good	Good
Wealthy	Good	Good	Good	
Winesap	Excellent	Good	Excellent	Good
Yellow		Excellent	Good	

[a]No recommendation indicates the variety is not well suited to that use.

Figure 6.12
Cherries are ready for picking in early summer.
Courtesy of Brian Jung.

Fancy, is characterized by fruit of excellent color, uniform size, optimum ripeness, and few or no blemishes. When canned or frozen fruits are being used in fruit plates, as a baked or broiled accompaniment to an entrée, or served alone as a simple dessert, this grade is the best choice and will provide optimum eye appeal. U.S. Grade B or Choice is used to designate fruit that is somewhat less perfect than this grade, but certainly fine for use in molded gelatin products and in fruit mixtures where perfect, large pieces are not needed. The lowest grade available to consumers is U.S. Grade C or Standard; such fruits are wholesome and nourishing, but they will have uneven pieces and occasional blemishes. These are well suited to making sauces, jams, cobblers, or other products where individual pieces are not of great importance.

Consumers are aided in picking frozen and canned fruits because of labeling requirements. This is fortunate, for the packages usually obstruct the view of the fruit inside, which makes grading or other labeling information essential. Required information includes the following:

1. Common or usual name of the fruit.
2. Form (whole, slices, halves, pitted) if not visible in the container.
3. Variety or color, in the case of some fruits.
4. Syrups, sugar, or liquid used in packing. Canned fruits may be packed in syrups of varying viscosities (extra heavy, heavy, light, extra light) or simply in a water pack. Frozen fruits usually are packed in sugar.

5. Net weight of contents in ounces (also in pounds and ounces or pounds and fractions of pounds for containers between 1 and 4 pounds).

6. Ingredients, including spices, flavoring, coloring, and any other additives.

7. Any special type of treatment.

8. Packer's or distributor's name and place of business.

Nutrition labeling is another feature that must conform to federal requirements for such labels. The Food and Drug Administration monitors nutrition labeling. If the fruit has been canned or frozen under continuous inspection by the U.S. Department of Agriculture, the USDA grade shield can be printed on the label.

Gradually, definitions are established for processed fruit products. For instance, various orange juice products have been defined by the U.S. Department of Agriculture as follows:

Orange juice drink blend	Product containing 70–95% orange juice
Orange juice drink	Product containing 35–70% orange juice
Orange drink	Beverage containing 10–35% orange juice
Orange-flavored drink	Beverage containing more than 0% but less than 10% orange juice

CULTURAL ACCENT
FRUITS FROM AFAR

Various tropical fruits are found in many markets today, adding greatly to the dining adventures available. Of course, bananas and pineapples have become commonplace on menus; several others are beginning to gain favor with diners. Cherimoya is a tropical fruit with a medium green, rather intriguing exterior that bears a very slight resemblance to an artichoke (Figure 6.13). The similarity ends there, for the interior has a number of large dark seeds embedded in a smooth, soft flesh that has a slightly sweet, mild flavor. Mexico is the source of many of the cherimoyas sold in this country, but California also grows and markets some.

Carambola, often called starfruit because of its sculpted shape (Figure 6.14), is an intriguing tropical fruit originally from Sri Lanka. It is oblong and has a waxy yellow skin with deep ridges terminating at its end. The texture of carambola is rather crisp, and the flavor is mild and slightly sweet. Cross-sectional slices are in the shape of a star, the points being formed by the ridges of the fruit. These yellow stars make attractive garnishes. This fruit rewards the eye more than the palate of the diner.

Breadfruit is best known to many because of its famous trip from the Philippines in *Mutiny on the Bounty*. Apparently the Spanish deserve credit for bringing this tree

Figure 6.13
Cherimoyas (center front) are surrounded by kiwi, plums, and tangerines.
Courtesy of Plycon Press.

(Continued)

(Continued)

crop to Central America and the West Indies after they encountered it in the Philippines. This large fruit sometimes grows to 18 inches long, a size appropriate to a tree that may be as tall as 85 feet. When still green, the interior is fibrous, white, and quite starchy. It softens a bit and begins to develop a slightly sweet taste as it matures, and the flesh changes to a yellowish color. Breadfruit is a familiar food in the Caribbean.

Dragon fruit, the red fruit of a cactus, has such a dramatic appearance with its scales that it is even used in floral arrangements (Figure 6.15). When it is cut in half, it is evident that the brightly colored skin is fairly thin and encloses a rather mushy pulp containing countless small, edible seeds. The flavor is delicate and reminiscent of

kiwifruit. It is popular in Vietnam and other countries in Southeast Asia, and it is now beginning to enter markets in the United States.

Durian is a rather round, large fruit (about 12 inches long) that is covered with sharp spines all over its rough surface. This fruit is the butt of many jokes because it exudes an aroma reminiscent of rotting cheese when it is cut open. Despite its hostile exterior and the stench, durian is enjoyed throughout Southeast Asia because of its sweet flesh and balsamic aftertaste.

Similarly, jackfruit is a huge fruit (commonly weighing between 10 and 60 pounds) that has a dreadful, rotting smell. Its redeeming feature is the flavor of the pulp, combining overtones of banana and pineapple.

Figure 6.14
Starfruit is appealing to the eye because of its appearance, but its flavor and texture do not live up to the promise. Courtesy of Plycon Press.

Figure 6.15
Dragon fruit has a thin red skin and white flesh surrounding numerous small seeds. Courtesy of Plycon Press.

Since the various definitions provide a wide range in quantity of orange juice, the label must indicate to the nearest 5 percent the percentage of juice actually included in the beverage.

Dried Fruits

Since federal grading standards are rarely applied to dried fruits, selection must usually be based on prior experience and color if the fruit can be seen through the packaging material. Fruits should be firm, yet pliable. Regardless of the type of dried fruit, prices in the market parallel size of the fruit, with prices increasing as the fruits progress through small, medium, large, and extra large.

Dried apples usually have a creamy color, which has been retained through the use of a dip in acidic fruit juice or ascorbic acid prior to drying. Similarly, dried pears are treated to help retain the desired, somewhat yellow color.

Figure 6.16
Date palm groves in the United Arab Emirates and other hot desert countries ordinarily have a system for irrigating the trees as needed. Courtesy of Plycon Press.

http://www.fao.org/ docrep/006/y4360e/ y4360e00.htm
—FAO report on dates and date palms around the world.

http://www.palmwonders. com/content/about-dates/
—Background about dates and date palms in the Arabian Peninsula.

Apricots, peaches, and golden seedless raisins ordinarily are exposed to sulfur dioxide fumes while drying so that the desired orange color will not give way to a drab brown. Raisins, prunes, and currants become a deep brown when they are being dried.

Most of the world's dates are grown in hot desert regions in the Middle East and North Africa, but some varieties are also produced in the California desert (Figure 6.16). Some are sold fresh, but many are dried for the retail market.

Sun drying has been the method for preserving certain fruits for thousands of years, but newer methods have evolved and now include freeze-drying, dehydration, and vacuum drying. The moisture levels, regardless of the technique used, are brought to below 25 percent. The exception to this practice is in the case of prunes, some of which are marketed in special packages that inhibit mold development even though the moisture level is above 25 percent. This comparatively high moisture level results in prunes that are soft and pliable, having the advantage of being easily rehydrated by stewing.

STORAGE IN THE HOME

The length of time fruits can be stored successfully in the home depends on the type of fruit and the condition when purchased. When fruits are ripe at the time they are purchased, they need to be consumed as soon as possible and stored at the appropriate temperature, usually in the refrigerator, until served.

Berries of all types are particularly susceptible to spoilage, necessitating a short storage period. Because of their fragile nature and their problems with mold formation, berries should be sorted before they are stored to be sure that any spoiling berries are removed. If this is not done, the spoiled areas will spread quickly throughout the container. Since high moisture promotes molding, berries are not washed when being prepared for storage; instead, they are washed when being prepared and served. Other fruits only need to be inspected before being stored if they were not checked when being selected at the market.

Some tropical and subtropical fruits retain their quality better if they are stored at a cool room temperature rather than refrigerated. Bananas, pineapples, and melons are best held at room temperature unless they are fully ripe. Then they need to be refrigerated to retard the ripening process. However, banana skins will develop a startling brown color at refrigerator temperatures. Citrus fruits ideally are stored just above the temperature in the refrigerator, a difficult condition to provide in most homes. Consequently, refrigerator storage often may be necessary.

Peaches, plums, pears, apricots, and similar fruits frequently are rather green when purchased at the store. These should be kept at room temperature until they achieve the desired degree of ripening. Then, they should be refrigerated and served rather soon.

If fruits are likely to be eaten without being washed after they are taken from the refrigerator, the fruit should be washed and wiped dry before being placed in the refrigerator. Exceptions to this recommendation are berries, cherries, and grapes, for these are fruits that tend to mold even during refrigerator storage if their moisture content is high.

Fresh fruits in the refrigerator should be in the hydrator drawers where the small volume of cold air limits the moisture loss and helps to retain high quality. Dried fruits, because they should have low moisture content, can be stored in sealed plastic bags or unopened packages in a cupboard. Unopened canned fruits retain their nutrient levels best if stored in a dark, cool cabinet for less than a year.

PREPARATION

Raw Fruits

Preparation of fresh fruits often is as simple as washing the fruit and serving it raw (whole or sliced) or in salads or as a dessert (Figure 6.17). Both appearance and nutritive value need to be kept in mind when preparing raw fruits. In particular, attention should be directed to retaining vitamin C, which is easily oxidized or dissolved in water. Fortunately, the acidic nature of most fruits is helpful in retaining vitamin C. The key problems to remember in trying to keep vitamin C levels high are the possibility of oxidation by exposing cut surfaces to air and loss by placing in water for soaking. Fruits that are good sources of vitamin C should be prepared as close to serving time as possible and by coating cut surfaces with a solution of ascorbic acid or an acidic fruit juice (lemon, orange, or pineapple works well). These same practices will help to retain vitamin A levels, too.

Fruits have tremendous potential for beautifying a meal when served and arranged artistically. Attractive slices of fruit arranged in a pleasing style may be slightly less nourishing than uncut fruit, but the appealing appearance may tempt people to eat more of it than they would otherwise, with the result that more nutrients actually are consumed. For example, an orange that has been sliced and arranged carefully on a plate is more approachable than is an unpeeled orange. Melon balls, pineapple chunks, ellipses of bananas, and peach slices are some of the variety of shapes available when fruits are cut creatively. The design element of line can be very important when arranging fruits. The beauty that can be created more than compensates for the extra time required to arrange fruits attractively.

Browning of cut surfaces can be a problem in certain raw fruits, such as apples, avocados, peaches, and bananas. This color change is caused by action of oxidative enzymes, especially phenol oxidase, on catechin, leucoanthocyanins, and some other flavonoid compounds. Since this change requires oxygen, the enzyme cannot cause this oxidative change unless the fruit has been cut to expose the cut surfaces to air. The key to avoiding this problem is to block air from the surface. This can be done by dipping the cut fruit into an acidic fruit juice or by sprinkling some granulated sugar on the surface and stirring to spread the sugar uniformly. The sugar draws some water from the cut cells to make a sugar solution on the surface, thus effectively blocking air from the fruit itself. A solution of ascorbic acid is yet another means of preventing browning, in this case by providing ascorbic acid to interact with oxygen and protect the pigments. Browning problems can be reduced by chilling fruit in the refrigerator from the time that it is cut until it is served.

Figure 6.17
Melons prepared by peeling and slicing into attractive pieces are a nourishing dessert with particular appeal to people watching calories. Courtesy of Plycon Press.

Simmered Fruits

Fruits can be heated gently in water to tenderize them. When fruits are heated in water just below boiling, the process is called poaching, simmering, or stewing. **Poaching** softens the cellulose and other fibrous tissue, modifies the flavor, and halts enzymatic browning. Usually, a limited amount of water is heated to just below boiling in a covered pan containing the fruit. By controlling the heat at simmering, agitation from active boiling is avoided, and the shape of the fruit is retained rather well. Retention of the delicate flavors of fruits is aided by keeping the cover on throughout the simmering period, thus reducing loss of volatile flavoring components.

Apples, pears, and peaches are well suited to simmering without losing their shape. Cranberries and rhubarb also are simmered to make sauces, but their structures are broken, and their shapes become quite blurred during cooking.

Dried fruits frequently are simmered to tenderize and rehydrate them before being served or used in other recipes. Dried plums (also called prunes) and other dried fruits are ready when they can be cut with ease. The actual simmering time required depends on the amount of soaking done prior to simmering, the size of the pieces of fruit, and the amount of cut surface exposed. By soaking dried fruit in warm water for an hour before simmering is begun, the simmering time is shortened. Dried fruits with cut surfaces rehydrate more quickly than do whole fruits because the cut cells provide easy entry into the fruit.

poaching Simmering in water or other liquid just below boiling until food is tender.

SCIENCE NOTE
OSMOTIC PRESSURE

Fruits have cells with walls that are semipermeable membranes; that is, water can pass in and out of the cells, but the wall blocks other substances. Equilibrium exists when the concentration of solute is the same on both sides of the cell membrane. However, a change in the concentration of the solute in the solvent outside the cells can cause water to move in or out of the cell, depending on the external concentration. The pressure that builds up to attempt to equalize the concentrations is termed **osmotic pressure.**

Fruits naturally contain sugars dissolved in the water inside the cells. If apples or other fruits are placed in water and simmered, water will begin to move into the cells in an attempt to dilute the sugar present in the cells. The osmotic pressure created in this circumstance can cause so much water to go into the cells that some of the walls will rupture, creating a mushy texture. This is desirable in making a puréed product. This is the reason that sugar is added to taste only after the desired mushy texture has been achieved when making applesauce. The rehydration of dried fruits is also promoted by simmering them in water without adding sugar.

The reverse may also occur with **coddling** fruits, or simmering of fruits in a sugar syrup. The aim is to have just enough sugar in the cooking syrup to approximate the level in the cells. Then water will pass into and out of the cells in equilibrium; it will not build up in excess in the cells. A very slightly lower level of sugar in the cooking syrup will cause a small amount of water to be drawn into the cells of the coddled fruit, giving just a suggestion of plumpness. With prolonged use of the sugar syrup, the loss of water will begin to raise the relative concentration of sugar, and water may start to move from the fruit into the syrup to attempt to equalize the two solutions. When this happens, the fruit being coddled will start to look wizened due to loss of water from the cells. By simply adding a bit of water to the sugar syrup, water can once again be moved back into the fruit cells.

The coating of berries or other fruit with some dry sugar has a dehydrating effect on the fruit. Again, osmotic pressure develops because the high external concentration of sugar draws water out of cells. Evidence of this is seen when strawberries are allowed to sit for a while after sugar has been added. Juice from the berries will begin to collect in the bottom of the bowl, and the berries will begin to droop. Thus, berries should be sweetened just before they are served.

osmotic pressure Pressure exerted to move water in or out of cells to equalize the concentration of solute in the cell and in the surrounding medium.

coddling Simmering fruit in a sugar syrup.

Other Preparation Procedures

A few fruits, notably apples and pears, are well suited to baking, their skins serving as an adequate protection against drying. A considerable amount of pressure can build up in these fruits because of the conversion of some of the juice to steam during baking. To avoid a possible explosion of the fruit, a narrow strip of skin should be peeled around the equator of the fruit. Microwaving rather than baking these fruits saves considerable time. Since browning is not necessary, the lack of browning typical of microwave oven cookery does not present a problem. However, the rapid heating of the fruit is very effective in retaining a good skin color and excellent fresh fruit flavor.

Broiling is a quick way of adding interest to fruits. Grapefruit halves can be broiled, sometimes with a light sprinkling of brown sugar for color and flavor, to make a special breakfast treat or a light dessert after a heavy meal. Canned or fresh peach halves also broil quickly to provide eye-catching garnishes for a meat platter.

Frying is yet another means of preparing fruits. Apple rings can be fried in shallow fat to provide a tasty complement to pork chops. Fruit slices can be dipped in a medium batter and then fried in deep fat at 375°F (190°C) until golden brown and served hot with powdered sugar or syrup.

Fruits are featured in many different recipes for baked products. Some quick breads gain their distinctive flavors from fruits incorporated in their batters. Cranberry, blueberry, orange, date, prune, apple, fig, and lemon muffins are some of the variations possible with a basic muffin recipe. Special breads may be made using various mashed, stewed, canned, frozen, fresh, grated, or candied fruits. Pies may have a sweetened filling made from fresh, canned, or frozen fruits thickened with starch. Grated citrus rinds are excellent flavoring substances for meringue and chiffon pies when care is taken to grate only the flavorful and colorful flavedo of the rind. Cream pies often are made with a layer of various fruits such as bananas, peaches, or strawberries.

Fruits combine well with other foods to make special desserts. For instance, sliced fruits may be served with a cream pudding, in combination with yogurt, with ice cream in sundaes or parfaits, or even in a cheesecake or a cobbler (Figure 6.18). Cherries jubilee, peach melba, fruit tortes, fruit-filled angel food cakes, and fruit soufflés are other examples of the excitement that fruits can bring to a dessert. Of course, fruit-flavored ice creams and sherbets also have become very popular uses of fruits.

Preparation Using Canned and Frozen Fruits

Canned fruits are used frequently in food preparation because of their convenience and availability throughout the year. Many recipes are based on the use of canned fruits, particularly for the preparation of pies and other desserts. For success in preparing these recipes, it is important to drain the fruit well, using only the amount of juice specified in the recipe to avoid too thin a product. Extra juice can be reserved for some other use or discarded.

Figure 6.18
Peach cobbler is particularly delicious made with fresh peaches, but canned ones can be used when the season is over. Courtesy of Plycon Press.

Figure 6.19
Fresh pineapple cannot be used in gelatin recipes because bromelain, a protein-digesting enzyme, will prevent setting of the gel structure. Courtesy of Plycon Press.

When pineapple is an ingredient in gelatin products, it is important to use only canned pineapple, never the fresh or frozen fruit (Figure 6.19). The heat treatment in the canning of pineapple is sufficient to destroy its proteolytic enzyme (bromelain). However, the enzyme is active in fresh or frozen pineapple; the result is a gelatin mixture that simply will not set.

Frozen fruits retain the bright color and bright flavors of their fresh counterparts, but their texture is altered significantly by freezing because the ice crystals break cell walls. If frozen fruits can be served while they still have a few ice crystals, the texture will be more appealing than when the fruit has thawed to the point where the pieces are flabby. If only the pieces of fruit are to be used in a recipe, the thawed juice needs to be drained thoroughly and removed. Otherwise, there will be too much liquid in the recipe.

SUMMARY

The various classifications of fruits include berries, citrus, drupes, grapes, melons, pomes, and tropical and subtropical. Characteristically, fruits are very high in water and contain a moderate amount of carbohydrate, usually in the form of sugars and fiber. In addition to fiber, fruits are rich sources of vitamins A and C and modest amounts of other vitamins and minerals, particularly calcium and iron.

The cell walls in fruits are abundant sources of cellulose, hemicelluloses, and pectic substances, which often occur in the intercellular spaces. Fruits have a dermal layer surrounding their vascular cells and parenchyma cells. The parenchyma cells have chloroplasts, and leucoplasts containing pigments and starch in the cytoplasm. Their large vacuole is the site of the flavonoid pigments, sugars, acids, and many other flavoring substances, as well as water.

Careful control of temperature and atmosphere is necessary during the marketing of fruit because fruits are very susceptible to spoilage. When selecting fresh fruits, avoid those with blemishes and spoiled areas. Each type of fruit has certain desirable qualities to guide consumers in selection, and knowledge of these qualities is important since grade designations are not ordinarily available to consumers. The best variety for the type of preparation being planned should be selected when making choices among apples and other fruits with more than one variety on the market at the same time. Select canned and frozen products by reading labels carefully and also remembering previous experience with particular brands.

In the home, temperature control is required to maintain the fruit at its optimum until it is served. Usually, refrigerator storage is recommended, although a few fruits, such as bananas, should be stored in a cool room.

Preparation of raw fruit requires attention to washing and then cutting and arranging close to serving time to avoid loss of vitamin C and the possible problem of enzymatic browning. Always simmer fruits; boiling should be avoided because of its destructive effect on shape. The level of sugar in the cooking liquid should be appropriate to the type of preparation so that osmotic pressure will help to achieve the desired texture. Baking, broiling, and frying are other cookery techniques appropriate to the preparation of some fruits. Many fruits also can be used in a wide array of baked products, as well as in elegant dessert combinations. Canned and frozen fruits can be used in some recipes satisfactorily if they are drained thoroughly to avoid extra juice. The texture in frozen fruits usually is quite soft and mushy unless they are served while some ice crystals are still present. Canned pineapple can be used satisfactorily in gelatin products, but fresh and frozen pineapple should be avoided because gelatin will not set when these forms are used.

STUDY QUESTIONS

1. Visit a grocery store to see what fresh fruits are available. How does the cost of the fresh fruits compare with their canned and frozen counterparts?

2. How does the cost of reconstituted frozen orange juice concentrate compare with fresh orange juice and with a powdered imitation orange drink?

3. How are the following fruits classified: oranges, avocados, strawberries, kumquats, apricots, plums, apples, nectarines, tangerines, Thompson seedless grapes, cranberries, pears, cantaloupe, quince, pomegranates, currants, Tokay grapes, bananas, and pineapple? When is each of these usually available?

4. How can osmotic pressure be controlled to aid in making applesauce and coddled apples?

5. Why is ascorbic acid added to some fruits?

SELECTED REFERENCES

American Home Economics Association. 2001. *Handbook of Food Preparation*. 10th ed. AHEA. Washington, DC.

Baker, R. A., and R. G. Hergenrather. 1997. Reduction of fluid loss from grapefruit segments with wax micro-emulsion coatings. *J. Food Sci. 62*(4): 789.

Barrett, D. M. 2007. Maximizing nutritional value of fruits and vegetables. *Food Technol. 7*(4): 40.

Braddock, R. J., and K. R. Cadwallader. 1992. Citrus by-products manufactured for food use. *Food Technol. 46*(2): 105.

Camp, D. B., et al. 2010. Paradox of organic ingredients. *Food Technol. 64*(11): 20.

Clark, J. P. 2010. Considerations on drying. *Food Technol. 64*(3): 70.

Clark, J. P. 2010. Focus on freezing. *Food Technol. 64*(11): 70.

Decker, K. J. 2008. Fruit and nut snacks for the 21st century. *Food Product Design 18*(9): 34.

Decker, K. J. 2010. Time is ripe: Making sense of fruit flavors. *Food Product Design 20*(11): 26.

Duan, J., et al. 2010. Effect of edible coatings on the quality of fresh blueberries (Duke and Elliott) under commercial storage conditions. *Postharvest Biol. Tec.*, doi:10.1016/j.postharvbio.2010.08.006.

Fan, X., et al. 2009. *Microbial Safety of Fresh Produce*. Wiley-Blackwell. New York.

Foster, R. J. 2004. Fruit's plentiful phytochemicals. *Food Product Design. Functional Foods Annual* Sept.: 75.

Foster, R. J. 2010. Naturally colorful. *Food Product Design 20*(4 supplement): 3.

Harding, T. B., and L. R. Davis. 2005. Organic foods manufacturing and marketing. *Food Technol. 59*(1): 41.

Kenyon, N. 1997. Cultivated blueberries: Good-for-you blue food. *Nutr. Today 32*(3): 122.

Kuntz, L. A. 2010. Beta-carotene's bonanza. *Food Product Design 20*(2): 16.

Lila, M. A., and J. Raskin. 2005. Health-related interactions of phytochemicals. *J. Food Sci. 70*(1): R20.

Luff, S. 2005. Organic identity preservation. *Food Product Design 15*(7): 107.

Massengale, R. D. 2010. Biotechnology: Going beyond GMOs. *Food Technol. 64*(10): 30.

McWilliams, M. 2012. *Foods: Experimental Perspectives*. 7th ed. Prentice Hall. Upper Saddle River, NJ.

Mermelstein, N. H. 2010. Combating citrus disease. *Food Technol. 64*(3): 66.

Montez, J. K., and K. Eschbach. 2008. Country of birth and language are uniquely associated with intakes of fat, fiber, and fruits and vegetables among Mexican-American women in the United States. *J. Am. Dietet. Assoc. 108*(3): 473.

Ohr, L. M. 2009. Functional fruit baskets. *Food Technol. 63*(4): 75.

Palmer, S. 2009. Resveratrol to the rescue? *Food Product 19*(4): 28.

Palmer, S. 2009. Fabulous fruit fibers. *Food Product Design 19*(5): 24.

Parish, M. E. 1991. Microbiological concerns in citrus juice processing. *Food Technol. 45*(4): 128.

Rittman, A. 2003. Preserving your fruit options. *Food Product Design 13*(2): 90.

Rojas-Grau, M. A., et al. 2005. Browning inhibition in fresh-cut "Fuji" apple slices by natural anti-browning agents. *J. Food Science 71*(1): S59.

Sapers, G. M. 1993. Browning of foods: Control by sulfites, antioxidants, and other means. *Food Technol. 47*(10): 75.

Sideras, G. M. 2006. Sweet fruit meets savory. *Food Product Design 16*(2): 52.

Sloan, A. E. 2005. Fixated on fruit. *Food Technol. 59*(11): 19.

Spano, M. 2010. Superfruit nutrition. *Food Product Design 20*(12): 16.

Spano, M. 2010. The skinny on fiber and weight management. *Food Product Design 20*(9): 24.

Summers, S. 2004. In the beginning was the apple. *Food Product Design 14*(5): 15.

Sundaresan, K. 2009. New tropical fruit creations. *Food Product Design 19*(10): 52.

Winter, C. K. 2006. Organic foods. *Food Technol. 60* (10): 44.

Potato, mixed bean, and pasta are chilled salads that tempt diners at this buffet. Courtesy of Plycon Press.

7

Salads and Salad Dressings

Key Concepts

1. Salads can provide many nutrients while adding sensory appeal to any part of a meal.

2. Ingredients can be used from any or all of the food groups (fruits and vegetables, dairy, meat, and breads and cereals) to create tempting salads.

3. Proper storage of fresh ingredients (e.g., greens) and careful preparation of salad components, such as pasta and gelatin, are important in creating salads of excellent quality.

4. Dressings for salads usually are emulsions of oil and vinegar, plus optional ingredients to alter viscosity and flavor.

Salads are assuming prominence in meals, due partly to the increasing focus on weight control and the importance of eating more fruits and vegetables to promote health. Menus in commercial venues, from fast-food outlets to fine restaurants, provide clear evidence that salads are becoming as important to Americans as pastas are to the Italians. Their popularity is due to the wide variety that can be created using virtually any foods as ingredients. Creative chefs welcome the opportunity for the originality that salads afford.

Salads can be created to suit any occasion, temperature, or weather condition; only imagination sets limits on what they can be. Variety in the temperatures and texture of a meal can be achieved by serving a salad that complements the other dishes. For example, a hot potato salad provides a warm and hearty touch to a meal; a frozen fruit or gelatin salad brings a cooling touch to the palate when a spicy meal is served. Textures often are crisp in salads, but combinations of ingredients afford a variety of textures even within the salad itself. For example, the use of crisp iceberg lettuce or celery slices in a shrimp salad provides a sharp textural contrast (Figure 7.1). Gelatin salads feel smooth, cold, and slippery in the mouth, presenting quite a contrast to the other textures in a meal.

The spectrum of foods used in salads keeps expanding. A few years ago, alfalfa sprouts and fresh slices of zucchini would rarely have been found in salads,

Figure 7.1
A wedge of iceberg lettuce dons a festive air when shrimp and a Thousand Island dressing are featured in this accompaniment salad. Courtesy of Plycon Press.

yet they are frequent ingredients today. In fact, many vegetables that formerly would always be cooked before serving now are being added to salads in raw, crisp pieces. Similarly, the range of dressings used on salads has increased remarkably.

THE NUTRITIONAL PERSPECTIVE

Specifics regarding the nutritional value of salads cannot be listed because their ingredients are so variable. Frequently, salads are excellent sources of vitamins and minerals. Some—potato and pasta salads, for example—are good sources of carbohydrates, while others containing fish, meat, eggs, or cheese are good sources of protein. If a large amount of dressing is served on it, the salad probably will be high in fat, whereas those with little or no dressing generally provide almost no fat. Fiber is often abundant in salads.

MyPlate (see Chapter 2) is also a useful way of looking at the range of ingredients that may be found in various salads. In fact, ingredients from each of the following food groups often are major components:

- Vegetables—Many vegetables (raw or cooked).
- Fruits—Practically any raw fruits.
- Dairy—Cheeses of many types and sometimes yogurt.
- Protein foods—Beef, pork, ham, chicken, turkey, fish, eggs, legumes, and nuts.
- Grains—whole grain (preferably) and refined cereals and cereal products.

Because of this representative inclusion from all of the food groups, it is perfectly possible to plan a large main-course salad that provides about a third of the day's recommended nutrient intake as well as a desirable amount of fiber.

PLANNING SALADS

Role in the Meal

The plan for a salad begins with deciding on its role in the meal (Table 7.1). Is it to be a bit of interest on the main plate of the meal or an accompaniment salad on a separate plate? Will it be served as an independent course or even as the main course for a luncheon (Figure 7.2)? Is it to serve as the dessert for a meal? All of these are possibilities, depending on the total menu plan.

Once the role in the menu has been identified, certain aspects of planning will be clarified. For example, an appetizer salad ideally will be a conservative size to whet rather than sate appetites; however, a salad for a main course must be much larger and give more **satiety value** (a satisfied feeling). Accompaniment salads can vary in size, depending on the remainder of

www.epicurious.com/tools/fooddictionary

—Dictionary of ingredients.

www.evergreenherbs.com/new_website/Herbs.html

—Brief descriptions of herbs and baby vegetables.

satiety value   Ability to satisfy hunger.

TABLE 7.1
SUMMARY OF ROLES SALADS PLAY IN MEALS

Role	Parameters	Example
Appetizer	Small	Tomato, mozzarella cheese, butter lettuce, dill garnish
Accompaniment	Small to large to fit rest of menu	Orange cartwheel on lettuce
Main course	Large; ingredients from variety of food groups	Mixed greens, grilled chicken, green onions, grated Swiss cheese, croutons
Dessert	Small; somewhat sweet	Frozen fruit salad

Figure 7.2
This pasta salad is generously laden with cubes of roast turkey to augment the protein when it is the main dish of the meal. Courtesy of Plycon Press.

http://www.epicurious.com/ tools/browseresults?type= browse&att=34
—Salad recipes.

http://www.cooks.com/ rec/ch/salads.html
—Recipes and information on salads and salad ingredients.

http://www.wholefoods market.com/recipes/ search-results. php?recipeTypeId=8
—Salad recipes.

http://www.foodsubs.com/ Greensld.html
—Illustrated glossary of salad greens.

http://www.hort.purdue. edu/newcrop/ncnu02/pdf/ ryder.pdf
—History of lettuce and salad greens.

the menu plan. A large dinner will be complemented by a small salad (Figure 7.3), whereas a light entrée requires a somewhat hearty salad. Dessert salads may vary in size depending on the satiety value of the rest of the meal, but they usually provide a sweet ending to the meal. After the role, size, and satiety value have been defined, the specific plans for ingredients and their combination can be made.

Tossed or Composed

Salads, particularly greens salads, can be classified as tossed or composed. As the name suggests, a tossed salad has a jumbled assemblage of its ingredients, which gives a distinctly casual look. The ingredients are mixed together to achieve uniformity of distribution and to coat them with dressing. They often contain one or more kinds of salad greens, as well as many other optional ingredients to give variety to menus.

Composed salads are arranged carefully to give an artistic, somewhat formal appearance (Figure 7.4). An example might be a pear salad, made by placing an appropriately sized lettuce leaf on the salad plate and putting half of a poached pear on it. A small scoop of lemon sherbet in the middle of the pear and a sprig of mint garnish the top of the composition to complete this dessert salad. Another example might be a hearty main dish such as a Cobb salad, with rows of chopped hard-cooked eggs, crumbled crisp bacon, diced salami, diced green pepper, and small cheese cubes, arranged on a bed of mixed greens. A composed appetizer salad could be made by arranging five small cooked shrimp on a small bed of mixed greens with a dash of chili sauce and a lemon twist completing the dish.

Figure 7.3
Caesar salad can be a very pleasing accompaniment to a meal featuring a hearty entrée. Courtesy of Plycon Press.

Arrangement and Shape

All food has the potential for beauty, but salads offer the greatest opportunity to create artistic and tempting arrangements (Figure 7.5). Whether a salad is being plated for individuals or for all of the diners, there are four aspects to consider: (1) appropriate plate or bowl, (2) use of a lettuce cup or other liner, (3) the main body of the salad, and (4) possible use of a garnish to serve as an accent.

Be sure to use a plate or bowl large enough to hold the salad comfortably. If components are arranged so precariously that removal of a single piece appears to be tempting gravity, diners will have trouble approaching the salad with enthusiasm for fear that the whole arrangement may slide right off the plate. For a more artistic look, try to arrange ingredients to give some height to part of the salad. This could simply be avocado slices fanned atop a salad of mixed greens to elevate the center.

A frame of salad greens often adds a unifying component to provide the diner with a truly beautiful and tempting salad. Ingredients should not extend to the edge of the plate or bowl. Greens hanging over the edge of the plate make a salad look poorly prepared and disheveled.

Figure 7.4
Orange slices are garnished with shredded coconut and dried cherries to complete this carefully composed salad. Courtesy of Plycon Press.

Figure 7.5
A green leaf adds a pleasing line to this shredded green papaya salad featuring Thai ingredients. Courtesy of Plycon Press.

Care given to making attractive salads can pay real dividends; a salad with asparagus spears loses its appeal when the stalks are carelessly tossed on a plate. On the other hand, these same spears become a tempting unit when they are aligned neatly as a center of interest for a composed vegetable salad. This same attention should be given whether arranging individual salads or a buffet salad platter. Balance between various parts of the arrangement is necessary, along with a definite center of interest.

Designs in salad arrangements can be orderly, yet abstract. Some people approach salad making with the air of a serious painter. When a pear half and some added decoration are merged to create a rabbit or peach halves are used to make a snowman, children may be delighted, but many adults will not applaud. The anticipated design preferences of the people who will be eating the salad should serve as the guide to the design approach to use.

Color

Salads have the potential of providing a wonderful, bright touch in a meal. By developing an awareness of color and the potential of various ingredients for heightening color interest and harmony, truly beautiful salads can be created. Sometimes the use of color may be understated, as is the case when a mixed greens salad is made by drawing upon the full spectrum of greens, from perhaps the deep green of spinach or romaine, the medium to almost yellow green of butter lettuce, to the rather light green of iceberg lettuce. Red leaf lettuce, radicchio, and endive are just some of the other salad greens available to augment the color palette (Figure 7.6).

Figure 7.6
Coleslaw featuring red and green cabbage is even more colorful with the addition of julienne carrots and chopped green and red peppers. Courtesy of Plycon Press.

A sharp contrast to monochromatic greens is a colorful tossed salad made with not only a variety of greens but also cherry tomatoes, slivers of red cabbage, chopped green onions, various colors of sweet peppers, radish slices, and bits of celery. A Waldorf salad can lack color if the apples are pared, but yellow-skinned Golden Delicious and bright Red Delicious apples cut into cubes sporting their colorful skins and accented by Flame Tokay grapes will brighten any meal.

INGREDIENT HIGHLIGHT
OLIVES

Olives of various types may be available to add interest to different salads. Choices are not limited to the familiar green Spanish olives and black ripe olives. All olives are processed, because they are inedible as they come from the tree. It is the type and length of processing that determines the color, texture, flavor, and appearance of the specific olives in the market.

As the name suggests, green olives are picked before they are fully ripened, but not until they have matured to the desired size. They are held in a lye solution as their first processing step. Next is a series of rinses in water before brining in a salt solution. Fermentation occurs during the two to three months required for the acidity to drop to pH 3.7. The yellow-green color of the green olives is maintained by keeping them immersed in brine to prevent contact with oxygen.

In contrast to green olives, black olives are picked when ripe (Figure 7.7) and are processed in brine without undergoing the lye-treatment used on green olives. These differences cause black olives to be somewhat higher in oil than green olives and to have a softer texture and milder flavor.

When buying green olives, choices available include pitted and stuffed (using pimiento, or sometimes almonds or capers). Manzanilla and Sevillano are varieties of olives often processed and marketed as stuffed green olives, the latter being the larger size. Picholine is a green olive that the French value for its tartness and crisp texture.

Black olives are most commonly marketed simply as ripe olives, pitted or unpitted and sometimes sliced. However, some markets afford a broader range of choices. Kalamata are purplish-black olives used in Greek salads. They have a soft texture and a mild, slightly smoky flavor that may be heightened by using some red wine vinegar. Nicoise olives are the dark ripe olives chosen by the French when making their famous Nicoise salad (Nicoise olives, green beans, tuna, potatoes, and anchovies dressed with a vinaigrette flavored with Dijon mustard).

Figure 7.7
Ripe olives are harvested in Italy, the first step toward making black olives.
Courtesy of June Kalajian Froncillo.

Flavor

The flavors provided by a salad need to combine well and enhance the total flavor impression of a meal. An accompaniment salad with julienne strips of a cheese containing a touch of hot peppers can provide zip to a bland meal; a fruit-filled gelatin salad may be served to offset the saltiness of ham in a dinner.

The ingredients should combine to provide a pleasing impression of the flavor of the salad. A touch of green pepper cut into a coleslaw does wonders in heightening the flavor of the cabbage, whereas the addition of cauliflower pieces is of little value in enhancing the flavor of the salad. Skillful addition of herbs and spices also can add flavor highlights. Celery seed, dill weed, and mustard are but a few of the possibilities in the spice rack. For instance, celery seed and mustard, when augmented with diced fresh onion, add flavor excitement to a potato salad (Figure 7.8).

Texture

A variety of textures within a salad can be very helpful in creating an appealing salad. Crisp and soft textures combine well. The comparatively soft texture of tuna fish or tofu contrasts with textural accents of crispness provided by diced fresh celery and green pepper. The softness of a tomato wedge complements the crispness of the greens in a tossed salad.

The texture of other foods in the meal also needs to be considered when planning a salad. A meal of mashed potatoes, baked fish, and sliced avocado certainly provides a monotonous texture. This menu could be improved by substituting a crisp vegetable salad for the avocado. On the other hand, crisp fried chicken would present a pleasing contrast to the avocado salad. Many different approaches are available; the important point is to consider the texture of both the salad alone and the salad with the rest of the meal.

Figure 7.8
Potato salad gains appeal when mustard, onion, and celery seeds are incorporated.
Courtesy of Plycon Press.

CULTURAL ACCENT
PARSLEY, ITALIAN PARSLEY, OR CILANTRO?

Flavor accents that are characteristic of certain cultures may be added to salads. Examples of this are parsley, Italian parsley, and cilantro. The parsley most familiar to Americans has a curly leaf, a crisp character, and a clean, fresh flavor. Its deep green color and perky appearance have often cast it in the role of a garnish to brighten food presentations. However, other cultures have similar herbs that can be used to inject different flavor notes.

Italian parsley, as the name suggests, is a member of the parsley family, but its leaf is flat and less crisp than parsley (Figure 7.9). Like parsley, the leaves are clustered on short branches. The flavor of this herb appealed to early Greeks, but it was the Romans who used it so much that it became known as Italian parsley. Its slightly peppery flavor

is stronger and less bitter than that of parsley, making it a suitable ingredient in many salads.

Cilantro looks somewhat similar to Italian parsley because of its flat leaf. However, the flat leaves are on fairly long, delicate stems, reflecting that cilantro (also called coriander) is a member of the carrot family. Its heritage explains its unique flavor that is quite different from the parsley family. The flavor is somewhat elusive to describe, but such words as pungent, slightly soapy, and distinctive are applicable. The cultural background of cilantro is found in Asia and Latin America. In fact, another name for cilantro is Chinese parsley. Cilantro is featured as a key flavoring ingredient in many dishes from Mexico, other Latin American countries, and Asian cuisines.

(Continued)

(Continued)

Figure 7.9
Italian parsley, cilantro, and parsley (left to right) contribute individual flavor and texture to salads.
Courtesy of Plycon Press.

TYPES OF SALADS

Fruit Salads

The sweetness of fruit salads makes them an excellent choice when the salad is to serve as a dessert; they also can be used as the main course of a luncheon or as an accompaniment to the main course (Figure 7.10). A large, dramatic platter of fruit can be the salad for a buffet meal. Even for small family dinners, a modest array of fruits can be combined to make a very pleasing salad. By cutting into shapes that can be arranged artistically, individual fruit salads can gain considerable appeal. Any cutting should be done to enhance the appearance of the fruit and accent the natural beauty of its line. When it is cut into quite small, nondescript cubes, much of the visual appeal of the salad is lost, whereas larger, recognizable pieces are attractive and tempting.

Figure 7.10
The sweet blend of flavors from apples, grapes, bananas, dried cherries, celery, and pecans make a Waldorf salad a possibility to serve as an appetizer, accompaniment, or dessert, depending on the rest of the menu. Courtesy of Plycon Press.

The fruits themselves may be the source of interesting ideas for serving a fruit salad. A dessert salad of pineapple cubes, fresh strawberries, and banana slices gains real distinction when presented on a boat made from a quarter of the pineapple, resplendent with some of its green-spiked leaves. Grapefruit can be scooped out to serve as baskets for salads. A watermelon half makes an admirable salad bowl for a fruit salad at a buffet when the interior has been scooped out to make melon balls and the shell has been scalloped or cut into "V"s all around the top edge.

Hot summer days can be made pleasant when fresh fruit plates are the main menu item for the day. A scoop of cottage cheese, some fruit sherbet, a dollop of yogurt, or some cheese can be added to provide even more nutrients, particularly some calcium and (with the exception of the sherbet) protein.

Another approach to using fruits in summer meals is afforded by a frozen fruit salad. These salads usually are made with a base of whipped cream, mayonnaise, sugar, and sometimes cream cheese. Fresh or canned fruits cut into pieces are folded into this mixture and then frozen. Although some added sugar will help to blend the flavor of the whipped cream with the fruit, this is not absolutely necessary. In fact, excessive use of sugar can make a frozen fruit salad difficult to serve on a hot day, because sugar lowers the freezing point of the mixture, causing the salad to soften and even flow quickly at room temperature.

Vegetable Salads

Most vegetables can be ingredients in a salad. Some are used raw; others may be cooked and chilled. Canned vegetables are a convenience for use in salads, for they merely require chilling and draining. Fresh vegetables require more preparation time, but their bright colors and flavors and their varied textures can add appeal to a salad. Ready-to-eat mixtures of salad greens in sealed plastic bags are gaining in popularity because of their quality and convenience.

Artistry can be brought to vegetable salads when color, line, and design are combined to advantage. An important part of creating beauty in vegetable salads is the skillful cutting of vegetables to create julienne strips (Figure 7.11), thin slicing of fresh mushrooms in silhouettes, or creating other pleasing shapes. Tomatoes, carrots, and onions are some of the vegetables that can be cut in many ways to add interest to the design of salads.

The range of colors available in vegetables is broad: the yellow of corn, the stark white of fresh cauliflower, the bright red of tomatoes, the deep purplish-red of red cabbage, and the great variety of shades of green seen in different salad greens illustrate the tremendous impact that color can have in vegetable salads.

Some vegetable salads are good sources of nutrients and fiber but quite low in calories—for example, various types of greens salads if they have only a modest amount of dressing. Mixed greens salads made with two or three types of greens—spinach, Bibb or leaf lettuce, and iceberg lettuce—can be beautiful studies in shades of green, and they are also high in fiber and provide a useful amount of provitamin A, folacin, and some minerals. Although they have these nutritional assets, greens are primarily a source of water and provide minimal amounts of energy—properties that make them high on the list for people seeking to lose weight. In addition to the familiar greens (i.e., raw spinach, Bibb lettuce, and iceberg lettuce), others (such as romaine, Chinese cabbage, arugula, leaf lettuce, red lettuce, watercress, escarole, and endive) can also be used in making interesting salads. Many of these are useful as liners under other salads, too

Flavor accents often are important in adding interest to vegetable salads. The bright flavor of a green onion, including pieces of its fresh green top, is one means of bringing a salad to life. Other times, a marinated vegetable, perhaps artichoke hearts or button mushrooms, can

Figure 7.11
Multiblade shears are efficient for cutting basil leaves into strips and orange rind and parsley into small pieces; the tool on the right is used for creating julienne strips. Courtesy of Plycon Press.

Figure 7.12

Capers, pickled buds from this Mediterranean plant, add a piquant accent to salads and other dishes. A bud growing up from the stem at the lower right is ready to be picked, dried, and pickled. Courtesy of Bill Malcolm.

http://homecooking.about.
com/od/cookingfaqs/f/
faqcapers.htm

—Information about capers.

http://www.foodsafetynews.
com/2010/02/study-finds-
bacteria-in-packaged-
greens/

—Report on illnesses from
packaged greens.

be the highlight. The sparkle afforded by the tartness of capers (Figure 7.12), a beet pickle, or other type of pickle is another way of enhancing flavor.

Vegetables also provide the opportunity for varying texture. Even mixed greens salads can get a lift by combining the sturdiness of romaine with the soft, buttery character of Bibb lettuce. And a kidney bean salad gains excitement by adding diced celery for crispness.

The variety of vegetable salads that can be made is almost limitless. Among the favorites are potato salads. These often are served cold, but hot potato salad, with its piquancy and overtone of bacon and onion, is appropriate during the cold weather months. Cabbage salads, usually called simply coleslaw, are inexpensive and popular types of salads. By combining other ingredients, such as celery seed, grated carrots, pineapple tidbits, diced green peppers, or other

---

INDUSTRY INSIGHT
SAFETY OF FRESH PRODUCE

The outbreak of food-borne illness that dominated the news in late summer of 2006 was ultimately traced to spinach grown in certain fields in California that were the source of *E. coli* O157:H7. As a result of the outbreak and subsequent investigation of its cause, rigorous checkpoints have been established at Earthbound Farms, and other producers of salad greens and other fresh produce are following their lead. Because field crops are exposed to potential contamination from the bacteria in the environment, increasing attention is being directed to monitoring water runoff and streams, as well as the distance between these fields and livestock.

Even with constant monitoring in the fields, there still is the possibility of contamination by dangerous bacteria. Now Earthbound Farms is randomly sampling each 1600 pounds

of greens that are delivered into the warehouse, which is maintained at 34°F. The samples undergo an eight-hour laboratory test before the greens proceed through processing. Samples failing the first test undergo another four hours of testing before their lots are either cleared or destroyed.

Approved greens are trimmed and washed three times in chlorinated water, checked for foreign objects using lasers, and then packaged. These packages are held another 12 hours and tested before finally being released for market if they pass the final test. Although only a very small amount of the fresh produce is contaminated, some harmful bacteria are found occasionally. Thanks to the intensified screening, these lots are destroyed, and the risk from eating fresh, uncooked produce is being reduced.

accents, coleslaw can be individualized to complement other menu items. At the other end of the price range for vegetable salads are those featuring such ingredients as hearts of palm or asparagus spears and pimiento garnish.

Gelatin Salads

Gelatin salads are popular because they can (in fact, should) be prepared a day in advance of a meal and still be of excellent quality. This makes them ideal for holiday meals or other occasions when preparation time is limited. Commonly, flavored gelatins are the base for these salads, for they provide not only the desired flavor but also the color needed to convey the desired image of the salad. Some gelatin salads are made with unflavored gelatin, which is colorless. When preparing tomato aspic, the red of the tomato is sufficient to provide the desired color.

The usual practice is to add some other ingredients to a gelatin salad. Fruits and vegetables of many different types can be selected to complement particular flavored gelatins. Grated carrots, finely diced celery, and grated cabbage are common ingredients. Sometimes mayonnaise or cottage cheese is blended with the gelatin before the gel sets, giving an opaque appearance and a modified flavor to the salad.

High-Protein Salads

When salads are to be the primary portion of a meal, they need to include adequate protein. For instance, a shrimp salad nestled on a bed of half an avocado is a significant, but expensive, source of protein. Other protein-rich foods well suited to use in salads include tuna and other fish, kidney and other beans (except green and wax), hard-cooked or deviled eggs, cheeses of many types, ground ham or other ground meats, and grilled or chilled beef, lamb, chicken, or other poultry. Almost always, these protein-rich foods have been cooked prior to use in salads. The most notable exception to this is the use of a raw egg in a Caesar salad (and that egg should be pasteurized to assure safety).

Garnishes

Garnishes are intended to accent color and flavor in a meal, not to be a main feature (Figure 7.13). To meet this goal, garnishes usually are quite small. They might be a bright orange carrot curl, perhaps a radish rose spreading its red outer petals to reveal its bright white interior, or even a small spoonful of a corn relish with diced pimiento and green pepper. A few crisp cucumber slices, celery curls, rings of green pepper, disks of onion, or hollowed-out dill pickle rings holding thin carrot sticks are just some of the possible garnishes that can serve as a very small salad.

Figure 7.13
A slice of hard-cooked egg and a twist of lemon are examples of simple garnishes that can be added as focal points. Courtesy of Plycon Press.

PRINCIPLES OF PREPARATION

Freshness of salad ingredients is vital to preparing a pleasing salad. In addition, cleanliness of those ingredients must be assured. Quality of ingredients and careful preparation are the cornerstones of salad preparation.

Washing

Greens are likely to have sand or dirt trapped in their convoluted leaves, and this soil must be removed. To begin, run a large amount of water in the sink and slosh the greens in the water to help loosen the sand and soil (Figure 7.14). The greens may need to be subjected to several washings before the water no longer is loaded with sediment from the leaves. Especially dirty produce may need to be washed under running water, leaf by leaf, in addition to the treatment in the sink full of water. Be sure to keep changing the washing water until no more sediment is found.

Fresh mushrooms can add an unplanned texture to salads if they are not cleaned adequately. An individual, gentle scrub is the key to eliminating the soil that sometimes clings so tenaciously. Zucchini is another vegetable with a particularly tight hold on dirt. However, all fresh produce needs to be rubbed while being held under running water to be sure all dirt is dislodged and removed.

Handling of Greens

http://ucanr.org/freepubs/ docs/7215.pdf

Background information on lettuce production.

The key to quality in many salads is the presentation of the greens. The ideal is an attractive, crisp leaf. Proper preparation is essential to achieving this goal, for greens rely on a high concentration of water in their cells to give the desired crispness.

Lettuce cups can be used as liners for individual salads. To obtain leaves free of disfiguring tears, the core of iceberg lettuce needs to be removed, a job done easily with a paring knife (Figure 7.15). When cold water is run forcefully into the resulting cavity, the leaves will begin to separate gradually, making it easy to ease individual leaves from the head.

Plenty of water clings to greens when they have been washed thoroughly. It is important to remove most of the water before putting the greens in a salad. Otherwise, the dressing will be diluted by the moisture and reduce the vibrant flavors. A salad spinner is a quick, easy way of spinning the water from the greens. An alternative is to pat greens dry with an absorbent towel.

Figure 7.14
Spinach and other greens tend to trap sand and dirt in their leaves; Sloshing in fresh water in a sink needs to be repeated until no sediment is evident in the sink. Courtesy of Plycon Press.

SCIENCE NOTE
TURGOR

Any plant with limited fiber in cell walls relies on water within the cells to hold the walls in an extended position. Greens are excellent examples of plants needing a large amount of water inside their cells. The presence of water within the cell exerts pressure against the walls, helping to hold them in an extended position. The greater the amount of water in the cell, the greater is the push against the cell walls. This pressure creates turgor, a state of tension in the walls. Loss of water from cells reduces this tension, the cells begin to collapse, and greens lose their crispness and begin to droop.

Since crispness in greens is so important, storage and preparation techniques must be designed to keep the water level in cells high enough to maintain the desired turgor. One problem is keeping evaporative losses to a minimum. Storage in an environment where the air is saturated with moisture reduces evaporative losses. Lettuce or other greens will contribute moisture to the surrounding environment in an attempt to saturate the air.

Two factors can be controlled to reduce the amount of water required to achieve saturation: the volume of air to be saturated and the temperature of that air. Obviously, a very small volume of air will require less moisture for saturation than will a large volume. By storing greens in a tightly closed, small space, the air will be saturated easily. Evidence of this is seen in the condensation occurring on the ceiling of the hydrator drawers. Perhaps less obvious, but of no lesser importance, is the fact that cold air cannot hold as much moisture as warm air. Consequently, cold air will become saturated with only a small amount of moisture, while warm air will cause a considerable loss of water from greens before becoming saturated.

The desirable circumstance is to store greens in very small areas that are chilled so that the cells will retain moisture and maintain their turgor. However, it is possible to return some moisture to drooping greens by placing the leaves in a damp towel and refrigerating the wrapped leaves until cells become plump with water once again.

Turgor also can be lost after dressings are added to greens. The loss of water from cells is the result of unfavorable osmotic pressure that develops when the greens are in contact with the dressing and its salts for a period of time. Water will be drawn from the cells into the dressing in a vain attempt to equalize the concentration on both sides of the semipermeable cell walls. To minimize this problem, dressing should be applied to tossed, mixed green, or similar salads just before serving.

Refrigerator storage in the hydrator drawer or a tightly covered container for at least half an hour promotes crispness. After this has been done, the leaves can be used whole or broken into pieces the desired size. Tearing, rather than cutting with a knife, is recommended because the jagged edge that results adds eye appeal to the salad.

Figure 7.15
Lettuce cups for salad liners are prepared by cutting out the core and running cold water into the conical hole to spread the leaves a bit. The leaves can be wrapped loosely in paper towels and refrigerated until needed.
Courtesy of Plycon Press.

Assembling a Salad

Dressing may be added to a salad during preparation or on the side so diners can add the amount they wish. If a green salad is to be tossed in the kitchen, dressing ordinarily should be added as close to serving time as possible because the dressing will begin to draw moisture from the greens and cause them to gradually wilt and lose crispness. However, some tossed salads based on pasta, potato, or other starch-rich ingredients are allowed to marinate for several hours after the dressing is added because they will absorb and be flavored throughout by the dressing.

Composed salads may have fluid dressings drizzled lightly over them, but a small dollop of mayonnaise or other thicker dressing may be added in a position that enhances the appearance of the salad. Another option is to place the dressing in a separate container that is served with the salad or passed around the table.

Presentations vary with the salad and the occasion. Individual salad plates frequently are assembled by starting with a lettuce leaf or cup or a bed of greens, leaving a border around the salad on the plate. Individual ingredients in a composed salad are added sequentially to complete a pleasing picture framed by the greens on the plate. A focal point highlighting a particular part of the salad adds interest. A colorful garnish or ingredient in the salad may be useful to create this feature (Figure 7.16).

Preparing Gelatin Salads

The smooth coolness of a gelatin salad contrasts pleasingly with the various ingredients that commonly are molded in it. However, the desired final effect relies on good preparation techniques. If using unflavored gelatin, be sure to hydrate it by soaking it briefly in cold water (1/4 cup water per tablespoon gelatin) as a preliminary step. Its coarse particles take up water less readily than do the finer particles used in flavored gelatins.

A critical part of preparing a gelatin salad is the complete dispersion of the gelatin. A measured amount of boiling liquid, usually water or a fruit juice, is poured over either flavored or hydrated unflavored gelatin to begin the process of dispersion. Slow stirring is needed to facilitate the solution of the gelatin particles, and this should be continued until absolutely no particles can be seen. In particular, stirring needs to be directed toward scraping all gelatin particles from the bottom of the container, where they tend to settle. Unless this is done, an undesirable rubbery layer may form.

When the gelatin has been dissolved completely, the remainder of the liquid specified in the recipe is stirred into the gelatin dispersion. This portion of the liquid may be cold liquid or even ice cubes. The use of ice speeds the cooling of the dispersion and quickly initiates

Figure 7.16
Bright red pomegranate seeds sparkle as the accent of this composed pineapple and cottage cheese salad.
Courtesy of Plycon Press.

formation of the gelatin gel structure. It is necessary to stir while the ice cubes are melting so that the concentration of gelatin is uniform throughout the mixture and the entire dispersion is cooled at the same rate. If stirring is not done, the regions adjacent to the melting ice will begin to set and contribute a lumpy texture in the finished product. With steady stirring throughout the cooling gelatin, gelation will begin to occur rather slowly. The first sign is the development of a syrupy consistency. Any remaining ice should be removed at this point and fruit or other ingredients stirred in until distributed. This mixture then is refrigerated in a bowl or mold until gelled.

Recipes for gelatin salads are based on proportions known to produce the desired consistency, so that the salad can be served easily without softening. Careless measurements of liquid can affect results; too much liquid produces too soft a product, while too little creates a rubbery texture. When canned fruits are not drained thoroughly, their extra liquid weakens the gel structure. If desired, the drained juice can be used in making the gelatin if this juice is treated as part of the liquid in the recipe.

Most fresh fruits can be added to gelatin salads to add texture, flavor, and color. However, fresh or frozen pineapple and fresh papayas and kiwi fruit cannot be used because enzymes in them react with the gelatin proteins. The result is breakdown of the gelatin **gel** and creation of a **sol** that can only be served as a soup.

http://www.kraftbrands. com/knox/
—Recipes using gelatin.

gel Colloidal system in which a solid forms the continuous phase and a liquid is the discontinuous phase.

sol Colloidal system in which the discontinuous phase is a solid and the continuous phase is a liquid.

SCIENCE NOTE
GELATIN GELS

A dispersion of gelatin is a colloidal dispersion, in which gelatin molecules are the solid. If gelatin (the solid) is dispersed uniformly in a liquid, the dispersion is classified as a sol. A sol is a colloidal system in which the solid is dispersed in a liquid; that is, the solid is termed the discontinuous phase and the liquid is the continuous phase. In other words, in a sol, it is possible to get from one gelatin molecule to another only by passing through the liquid in which it is dispersed. This is the colloidal system being formed when gelatin is being dispersed in boiling liquid in preparing a gelatin salad.

When a gelatin sol begins to cool, the gelatin molecules gradually move slower and slower through the liquid. These fibrous molecules begin to bump against each other and occasionally form hydrogen bonds between molecules. The cooler the system gets, the more slowly the protein molecules move, and the greater is the likelihood of hydrogen bonds beginning to hold one gelatin molecule close to another one. Gradually, many molecules are cross-linked by hydrogen bonding into a jumbled network in which water becomes trapped. Finally, the gelatin molecules form a continuous network, and the water is trapped in discontinuous pockets within this network. In short, the colloidal system has undergone a transition from the original sol to a different colloidal system, that of a gel. A gel no longer exhibits the flow properties characteristic of a sol. This makes it possible to mold gelatin and serve it in a defined shape.

The ease with which gelatin molecules can cross-link to each other to establish the gel structure is influenced by the pH of the dispersion. The addition of some acid to help bring the system to a pH of 5 makes it easy for the gel

to form because this is the isoelectric point of gelatin. At this pH, there will be a minimum electrical charge on each molecule. This lack of electrical charge on the surface helps to keep similarly charged molecules from repelling each other. When molecules can get close together, hydrogen bonds are able to form comparatively easily. If the system is acidified (with lemon juice or other edible acid) to a pH lower than 5 or is more alkaline than 5, it still is possible for hydrogen bonds to form between gelatin molecules and establish a gel. However, this occurs more slowly and produces a gel with somewhat less strength than one at a pH of 5.

The amount of gelatin in a product clearly influences the strength of the gel, for there will be fewer molecules to link by hydrogen bonds and form the continuous network when the gelatin concentration is low than when it is high. A low concentration of gelatin forms a weak gel or may even not gel at all. On the other hand, too high a concentration of gelatin gives such a dense network that the gelatin gel is too tough to be enjoyed. A ratio of a tablespoon of unflavored gelatin per cup of liquid produces a good gel.

If sugar is increased in a gelatin recipe, the gel will be more tender than the original product. In fact, a very large increase can even prevent gelation. The effect is attributed to the reduction in the concentration of protein when sugar is increased.

Gels look like solids, but actually they are undergoing continual change during storage. Evidence of this is the difficulty of trying to serve a gelatin product that has been firm for only an hour versus one that has been chilled for six

(Continued)

(Continued)

hours or more. The gelatin will be more resistant to melting and easier to serve after an extended period of chilling. The difference is due to the increasing numbers of hydrogen bonds between gelatin molecules, drawing the structure ever more tightly together and toughening the gel. This, plus the accompanying squeezing out of water, explains the gradual development of a tough, almost rubbery texture during extended storage.

The ability of gelatin molecules to establish a network is dependent on their long molecules being hydrogen-bonded together. If a proteolytic (protein-digesting) enzyme is added to the system, as occurs when fresh pineapple is added, the gelatin molecules will be altered to shorter molecules and will lose the ability to form a gel. Bromelain, the enzyme contained in pineapple, splits the gelatin molecules into shorter units rather quickly, whereas the heat treatment utilized in canning this fruit alters the bromelain molecules, making them incapable of catalyzing the digestive breakdown of gelatin. Papain from papayas and actinidin from kiwi have a similar proteolytic effect.

SERVING SALADS

Salads are particularly appealing when they are served with careful attention to detail. For example, cold salads assume great importance at a meal when served as a separate course, with the chilled salad being arranged attractively on a chilled plate, accompanied by a chilled fork. Plates should be free of splatters or smears.

Gelatin salads often need to be unmolded before serving. This task should be done at least half an hour before serving so that the unmolded gelatin can be chilled again in the refrigerator to firm the outer portion. To remove from the mold, dip the lower part of the mold very briefly into warm water. This can be done easily by filling a sink with warm water to about the depth of the mold. A gentle shake of the mold should be enough to loosen the gelatin. If not, the mold may be returned again briefly to the warm water. When the gelatin shakes loose from the edges of the mold, the service plate is inverted on the mold, and the assembly is turned over quickly to unmold the gelatin directly on the plate (Figure 7.17). The unmolded gelatin is then placed in the refrigerator to reverse the softening and firm the structural design of the molded salad.

Figure 7.17
To unmold a gelatin salad, dip the mold briefly in warm water, shake sideways sharply to loosen, invert a plate over the salad mold and flip them over while holding tightly. The salad will drop to the plate, and then the plate and salad are refrigerated at least briefly to firm the surface of the gelatin. Courtesy of Plycon Press.

SALAD DRESSINGS

Salad dressings are of many different types, but most contain an oil, an acidic liquid, and seasonings. The combination of oil with an aqueous liquid is often an unstable arrangement because oil and water do not blend together naturally. However, under certain conditions, these two types of liquids can be combined to form a colloidal system called an **emulsion**. Salad dressings usually have droplets of oil (the **discontinuous phase**) suspended in water (the **continuous phase**). Since these salad dressings are droplets of oil in water, the type of emulsion is classified as oil-in-water (written simply as o/w). Emulsions also are classified on the basis of their stability or tendency to separate into two distinct layers, with the oil layer floating on the water layer (Figure 7.18).

Temporary Emulsions

Salad dressings that have to be shaken to distribute the ingredients uniformly each time they are used are classified as **temporary emulsions**. French and Italian dressings are familiar examples. The physical act of shaking breaks the oil phase into small droplets, but the droplets coalesce with each other and quickly form an oily layer when allowed to stand even briefly. The only interference keeping one droplet from merging with another is the dry ingredients, such as dry mustard and paprika, which often are part of the seasonings.

The ingredients in temporary emulsions include a flavorful vinegar or another acid ingredient, such as lemon juice, to add flavor interest. The oil used might be olive oil, but often corn, soybean, peanut, safflower, or other oils are selected because of their extended shelf lives and mild flavors. Usually about two to three times as much oil as vinegar is used in making "vinegar-and-oil" dressings (temporary emulsions), resulting in fairly fluid dressings (Figure 7.19).

Semipermanent Emulsion

Semipermanent emulsions tend to remain intact for a few days. The viscosity of these emulsions, about like heavy cream, reduces the ease of oil droplets bumping into each other and coalescing to break the emulsion. Sometimes this increased viscosity is due to a viscous

emulsion Colloidal dispersion of two immiscible liquids, with one type of liquid being dispersed as droplets in the other type of liquid.

discontinuous (dispersed) phase Droplets in an emulsion.

continuous phase Liquid surrounding the suspended droplets in an emulsion.

temporary emulsion Emulsion that separates very quickly into two layers.

Semipermanent emulsion Viscous emulsion containing an emulsifying agent that rarely separates into two layers.

Figure 7.18
Diagram of an oil-in-water (o/w) emulsion. Courtesy of Plycon Press.

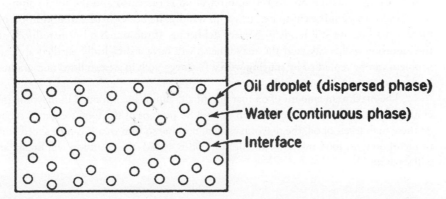
Oil droplet (dispersed phase)
Water (continuous phase)
Interface

Figure 7.19
Balsamic vinegar and olive oil are flavorful basic ingredients for dressing a tossed salad. Courtesy of Plycon Press.

liquid in the recipe, possibly honey, a cooked sugar syrup, an undiluted canned soup base, or a starch-thickened sauce. Commercial dressings of this type (particularly "light" dressings) often contain such stabilizers as gum tragacanth, gum arabic, pectin, or gelatin to increase viscosity and promote stability.

Sweet dressings for fruit salads, herb dressings, and other dressings that pour slowly are semipermanent emulsions. When these dressings do separate, the emulsion can be reformed rather easily by some stirring or shaking.

Permanent Emulsion

permanent emulsion
Viscous emulsion containing an emulsifying agent that rarely separates into two layers.

emulsifying agent
Substance forming a protective coating on the surface of droplets (the interface) in an emulsion.

lecithin Compound in egg yolk that is attracted to both oil and water, making it a very effective emulsifying agent.

http://www.hi-tm.com/
Documents/Mayonnaise.html
—Discussion of mayonnaise and safety issues with egg.

Mayonnaise is the classic example of a **permanent emulsion**. It is an oil-in-water permanent emulsion. The definitely thick character of the dressing restricts the movement of oil droplets throughout the dressing and hinders separation of the oil from the vinegar. In addition to this stabilizing effect, permanent emulsions are stabilized by an **emulsifying agent**, usually egg yolk. An emulsifying agent is capable of forming a protective coating around the spherical surface of each oil droplet, which blocks coalescence, thus preventing oil in one droplet from directly touching the oil in another droplet.

Egg yolk is effective as an emulsifying agent because it contains **lecithin**, a compound attracted to both oil and water. Lecithin aids emulsion formation by forming a thin protective coating around the oil droplets. Lecithin is much more effective as an emulsifying agent than are the various powdered spices because lecithin has chemical functional groups that allow it to cover a large surface area between the two diverse liquids in the emulsion.

Mayonnaise can be made easily by mixing together the seasonings, egg yolk, and part of the vinegar. Then oil is added by drops while beating to help split the oil into small droplets and start forming the emulsion. As the amount of oil is increased and the total volume of mayonnaise begins to be sufficient to be picked up well by the beater blades, the addition of oil can be increased a bit, but still needs to be very deliberate. If too much oil is introduced at any time, the emulsion will break, and the mayonnaise will have a dreadfully curdled appearance. This problem can be remedied by starting with a fresh egg yolk in a clean bowl and gradually beating in the broken emulsion, treating it as oil.

The maximum amount of oil that potentially can be incorporated in mayonnaise before the emulsion breaks is somewhere between 70 and 80 percent of the total weight of the ingredients. At these high levels of oil, the mayonnaise will become so firm that it can be sliced and is too stiff to incorporate in food mixtures. If still more oil is added, the emulsion will break, and fluid oil will separate.

SCIENCE NOTE
"SAFE" MAYONNAISE

Although most eggs are free of bacteria in their interior, about 1 in 10,000 eggs may possibly contain *Salmonella enteritidis* in the yolk. This bacterial contamination, if present, occurs in the chicken while the yolk is forming and is not the result of unsanitary handling following laying of the egg. Strict sanitation measures at facilities where laying flocks are maintained are essential to avoid the production of contaminated eggs.

To assure that mayonnaise does not contain any viable *S. enteritidis*, the safest procedure is to buy pasteurized eggs or pasteurize fresh egg yolk before incorporating it into mayonnaise. The yolk is heated to at least 160°F (71°C) after it has been diluted with liquid (at least two tablespoons liquid per egg yolk. This heated mixture needs to be cooled about four to five minutes before being placed in a blender. Then, the emulsion is formed by very slowly adding the oil to the rapidly whirling yolk mixture in the blender, pausing occasionally to scrape down the splatter on the blender walls. (If egg substitutes or other commercially prepared egg products are used, the yolks will have been pasteurized during their processing and need not be heated again.)

Mayonnaise is somewhat protected against bacterial infections by the presence of lemon juice and/or vinegar. However, the pH needs to be quite acidic (pH 4 or less than pH 4) to assure safety. The possibility that mayonnaise made at home may not be that acidic makes pasteurization (described above) an important step in the home.

Permanent emulsions can be broken not only by adding too much oil but also by freezing or by storage in a very warm place, which will cause oil droplets to coalesce. Although excessive shaking during shipping or handling can be another cause of a broken mayonnaise, this is rarely seen because of the stability of the mayonnaise itself and the excellent present-day control in storing and shipping food products.

Cooked Salad Dressings

Other salad dressings are made with formulations quite different from those just described. In fact, there is a commercial product group marketed as salad dressing and used in many applications in place of the more costly mayonnaise. The Food and Drug Administration's definition of mayonnaise lists specific required ingredients, including a high percentage of oil, whereas salad dressings can have a thickening agent to help give the viscosity normally acquired through the use of a fairly costly salad oil. These salad dressings require only 30 percent oil or more, which reduces their cost and also their calories. Although several different thickening agents can be used, starch is one effective and inexpensive way of producing a cooked salad dressing of the desired viscosity.

Homemade cooked salad dressings usually are thickened by starch and egg protein. Starch mixtures are brought to a boil to ensure maximum thickening and a cooked flavor before the egg is added; then the mixture is heated again above 160°F (71°C) to thicken the proteins and kill any *Salmonella enteritidis* that might be present. The dressing is not boiled or cooked very long after the egg is added to avoid curdling. If homemade dressings contain fruit juices or other acidic liquids, the acid should be added after the starch has been gelatinized. Otherwise, the starch will break down and result in a thin product. Starch cookery and egg cookery principles are discussed in Chapters 10 and 12, respectively.

Varying Salad Dressings

Basic salad dressings can be modified to special dressings by adding appropriate ingredients. For instance, a creamy dressing can be made using sour cream, cream, milk, yogurt, or cream cheese. Exciting flavors can be introduced through the addition of chopped pickles, diced cheeses of many types (including Roquefort), pickle relish, and grated onions, as well as many other types of spices and condiments. Many commercial salad dressing packets are available in the market to provide a skillfully blended assortment of spices for the "do-it-yourself" touch.

http://www.accessdata.fda.gov/scripts/cdrh/cfdocs/cfcfr/CFRSearch.cfm?fr=169.140
—Code of FDA regulations for mayonnaise.

http://www.cdc.gov/salmonella/enteritidis/
—Summary report on 2010 outbreak of *Salmonella enteritidis* infection.

http://blog.thenibble.com/2010/09/09/food-facts-how-to-pasteurize-eggs/
—Suggestion on pasteurizing an egg.

INDUSTRY INSIGHT
DIET SALAD DRESSINGS

Many Americans not only are aware of the health ramifications of fats and oils in the diet but also are seeking food products that provide reduced amounts of fats and/or oils. This strong consumer interest has motivated salad dressing manufacturers to develop and market low-fat and even non-fat versions of some of their dressings. Reduction in oil levels causes a distinct change in the flow properties of salad dressings. Formulations have to be developed that have sufficient viscosity to provide coating of salad ingredients by the dressing and a pleasing mouthfeel.

Various gums commonly are used to contribute the appropriate viscosity when oil is reduced in salad dressings.

Xanthan and cellulose gums are two particularly popular thickeners in low-fat or no-fat dressings. Gums have the advantage of not contributing calories to these diet dressings.

Modified food starch is another approach to creating the desired consistency when oil is reduced. Although not much starch is needed, the calorie content adds to the total calories. Other energy-contributing thickeners sometimes used are sugar, corn syrup, or partially hydrogenated oil. Carbohydrate thickeners (sugars and starch) can produce the desired viscosity while also reducing fat and calories in salad dressings. Partially hydrogenated oil increases viscosity, allowing less oil to be used in the formula.

Evaluating Salad Dressings

The popularity of salads has caused many consumers to turn into "salad dressing gourmets," the people who whip up their own dressings, often using commercial products as aids. Dressings should have a pleasing flavor that enhances the salad ingredients themselves. Such dressings should be thin enough to blend easily with the salad ingredients, yet not so fluid that they drain rapidly to the bottom of the salad. Droplets of oil should not be evident on the surface of permanent emulsions, such as mayonnaise; cooked salad dressings should be free of lumps.

SUMMARY

Salads have the potential for adding virtually all essential nutrients to the diet in many different ways. They can be used in any part of the meal, from appetizer to dessert, with each salad being an artful combination of arrangement and shape, color, flavor, and contrasting textures. Fruits, vegetables, pasta, cereals, gelatin, meats, fish, poultry, eggs, and cheese are all possible ingredients. They may be prepared as a tossed or as a composed salad.

Preparation requires careful washing of fresh produce and proper storage and service to assure that greens exhibit the optimal amount of turgor. Gelatin gels can be made from unflavored or flavored gelatin. With careful preparation and unmolding, these salads add beauty and pleasure to dining. Unmolded gelatins hold their shape well if they are refrigerated briefly following the removal of the mold.

Salad dressings are usually oil-in-water emulsions, with their stability categorized as temporary, semipermanent, or permanent. French and Italian dressings are fluid, have little in the way of emulsifying ingredients, and separate readily, which is why they are termed temporary emulsions. Semipermanent emulsions are considerably more viscous and stable than the temporary emulsions. Permanent emulsions rarely break, although freezing, high temperatures, and considerable shaking can cause even mayonnaise to break. Egg yolk contains lecithin, a particularly effective emulsifying agent, which aids greatly in making mayonnaise a thick, stable permanent emulsion. Yolks in mayonnaise and other dressings need to be pasteurized to kill any *S. enteritidis* that might be present. Some reduced-calorie dressings incorporate gums or other stabilizer so that the oil content can be reduced without affecting viscosity. Others may be thickened using starch or eggs.

Salad dressings should have a fresh flavor that is characteristic of the type of dressing. They should coat the salad ingredients, yet not be too thick to flow.

STUDY QUESTIONS

1. Describe a salad to be served as: (a) the main course of a luncheon, (b) an appetizer, (c) an accompaniment to the main course, and (d) a dessert. Why do you think these salads are appropriate for each application? What characteristics distinguish each type of salad?

2. Find five recipes for salads and classify them as tossed or composed. Explain why you classified each one.

3. Compare the cost of commercial and homemade salad dressings. Be sure to include an estimate of the amount of time and the value of the time required to prepare the product at home. Under what conditions would you make your own dressing? Buy your dressing already prepared?

4. Why should egg yolks be heated when making mayonnaise at home? Describe the process used to heat them.

5. Why does the viscosity of a salad dressing influence the stability of an emulsion?

6. Identify each of the basic categories of salad dressings and name an example. Identify the ingredients in the individual recipes that contribute to the stability of the emulsion.

7. Explain the preparation of a gelatin salad. How is a gelatin gel formed and what happens as it ages?

8. What is the effect of adding fresh pineapple to a gelatin salad? How can this effect be avoided?

9. Compare ingredient labels of comparable regular and low-fat salad dressings. Why are the ingredients different in the two types?

SELECTED REFERENCES

Backas, N. 2009. Eat your veggies. *Food Product Design* *19*(10): 44.

Barrett, D. M. 2007. Maximizing nutritional value of fruits and vegetables. *Food Technol.* *7*(4): 40.

Beckwitt, R., and A. E. Yousef. 2009. Production of shelf-stable ranch dressing using high-pressure processing. *J. Food Sci.* *74*(2): M83–M93.

Berry, D. 2004. Fresh advice on herbs and spices. *Food Product Design* *14*(2): 61.

Berry, D. 2004. Keeping foods fresh. *Food Product Design* *23*(10): 87.

Blumenthal, D. 1990. *Salmonella enteritidis* from the chicken to the egg. *FDA Consumer.* *24*(3): 6.

Bruhn, C. M. 2009. Understanding 'green' consumers. *Food Technol.* *63*(9): 28.

Camp, D. B., et al. 2010. Paradox of organic ingredients. *Food Technol.* *64*(11): 20.

Caranfa, M., and D. Morris. 2009. Putting health on the menu. *Food Technol.* *63*(6): 28.

Condrasky, M. 2008. Building the case for healthy menus. *Food Technol.* *62*(6): 46.

Dev, S. R. S, G. S. V. Raghavan, and Y. Gariepy. 2008. Dielectric properties of egg components and microwave heating for in-shell pasteurization of eggs. *J Food Eng.* *86*(2): 207–214.

Esquivel, T. 2010. Egg safety. *Food Product Design* *20*(10): 14.

Fan, X., et al. 2009. *Microbial Safety of Fresh Produce*. Wiley-Blackwell. New York.

Foster, R. J. 2004. Fruit's plentiful phytochemicals. *Food Product Design. Functional Foods Annual* Sept.: 75.

Gan, R. 2010. Distinctively garlic. *Food Product Design 20*(10): 20.

Gerdes, S. 2004. Perusing the food-color palette. *Food Product Design 14*(9): 94.

Jen, J. J. 1989. *Quality Factors of Fruits and Vegetables—Chemistry and Technology*. ACS Symp. Series 405. Am. Chem. Soc., Washington, DC.

Kuntz, L. A. 2009. Locust bean gum: Good as gold. *Food Product Design 19*(11): 20.

Massengale, R. D. 2010. Biotechnology: Going beyond GMOs. *Food Technol. 64*(10): 30.

McWilliams, M. 2012. *Foods: Experimental Perspectives*. 7th ed. Prentice Hall. Upper Saddle River, NJ.

Mermelstein, N. H. (ed.) 1990. Quality of fruits and vegetables. *Food Technol. 44*(6): 99.

Montez, J. K., and K. Eschbach. 2008. Country of birth and language are uniquely associated with intakes of fat, fiber, and fruits and vegetables among Mexican-American women in the United States. *J. Am. Dietet. Assoc. 108*(3): 473.

Pszczola, D. E. 2010. Pondering the pasta possibilities. *Food Technol. 64*(11): 43.

Sapers, G. M. 1993. Browning of foods: Control by sulfites, antioxidants, and other means. *Food Technol. 47*(10): 75.

Silver, D. 2004. Seasonal ticket. *Food Product Design 14*(4): 75.

Sloan, A. E. 2005. Fixated on fruit. *Food Technol. 59*(11): 19.

Stuhler, G. 2003. Dressing salads with a gourmet touch. *Food Product Design 13*(4): 100.

Summers, S. 2004. In the beginning was the apple. *Food Product Design 14*(5): 15.

Sunflowers growing in a field in South Dakota will eventually produce seeds that will be pressed to release sunflower oil. Courtesy of Agricultural Research Service.

8

Fats and Oils

Key Concepts

1. Knowledge of the chemistry and functionality of edible fats and oils is important when choosing specific products for use in food preparation.

2. Many fats and oils (some familiar and other new products) available in markets have undergone processing steps designed to meet federal requirements and consumer desires for healthful, functional products.

3. The functions of a fat or oil in a food product determine the type of fat or oil to use.

CONTROVERSIAL INGREDIENTS

Among nutritionists and weight-conscious people, fats and oils (collectively identified as **lipids**) are an important diet and health concern because of their relationship to nutritional status and health. Fats and oils are calorie-dense food items, providing nine calories per gram compared with four calories from carbohydrates or proteins. Even alcohol, with its seven calories per gram, is lower in calories than fats and oils. Not only are fats and oils high in calories, but also they often are found in foods containing only a limited amount of water. As a result, many foods rich in fats or oils are concentrated sources of calories.

For optimal health, people need to avoid consuming too much fat (because of the association with overweight and heart disease), particularly saturated fats. In preparing foods, any reduction in fat will reduce the calorie content.

Ideally, fats and oils are selected in recipes to perform specific roles. Knowledge of the properties of the many different types of products available today will make it possible to make optimal choices, resulting in high-quality products without a high level of fat.

lipids Comprehensive term including fats, oils, and some other organic compounds containing carbon and hydrogen and only a very small amount of oxygen.

leaf lard   Fat obtained from the abdominal cavity of hogs; the premium type of lard.

http://www.webexhibits.org/butter/

—History and background information about butter.

http://www.eatwiscon sincheese.com/wisconsin/other_dairy/butter/default.aspx

—Background information and recipes featuring butter.

ghee   Very carefully clarified butter from which the water and milk solids have been removed by heating and filtering; pronounced with a hard g.

TYPES OF FATS AND OILS

Lard

Lard, a fat rendered from hogs, has been used in cooking for centuries wherever hogs were raised for food. **Leaf lard**, considered to be the prime lard, is obtained by rendering the fat from the abdominal cavity around the kidneys. All lard has a slightly distinctive flavor that can be a pleasing addition to the delicate flavor of pastry and other baked products. Its tendency to become rancid, hence strongly flavored, can be retarded significantly simply by storing lard in the refrigerator. Sometimes lard will begin to develop a grainy texture. To alleviate this problem, it can be processed and marketed as rearranged lard.

Butter

The other type of fat from animals is butter. Like lard, butter has been used for centuries as a fat in cooking. However, its popularity today is significantly higher than that of lard, for its attractive yellow color and pleasing flavor make it useful as a table spread as well as a fat for cooking. Milk is churned until the original oil-in-water emulsion in milk breaks and butter, a water-in-oil emulsion, forms. Although a considerable amount of water is removed from butter, the end product still contains about 16 percent, a distinct contrast to lard which has no water.

Butter is graded, with AA being the top grade designated by the U.S. Department of Agriculture standards. Usually butter has a small amount of salt added to it for flavor and to

---

CULTURAL ACCENT
GHEE

Ghee is the primary cooking fat used in India and recipes typical of Indian cuisine (Figure 8.1). This fat is prepared in quantity and often stored for several days or even weeks. It is prepared by heating a pound of butter so that it bubbles vigorously enough to boil off the water in it. This process also causes the milk solids to clump and gradually change color to a golden brown. At this point, the hot fat is cooled a little. Then it is poured carefully through cheesecloth arranged in a strainer just until the browned solids start to empty into the cheesecloth. The solids remaining in the pan and the cheesecloth are discarded. Only the very clear, golden ghee remains for use. It should be kept in a closed container for subsequent use in Indian and other recipes where the clarity of ghee can be appreciated. The absence of milk proteins helps to keep ghee from scorching or burning when it is used in cooking.

Figure 8.1
Ghee often is prepared in Indian homes, but it also can be purchased in cans in Egypt and other Mediterranean and Middle Eastern countries. Courtesy of Plycon Press.

enhance keeping quality; unsalted butter (also called sweet butter) is available in most markets, too. Carotene may be added for color.

Margarine

Margarines (occasionally called oleomargarine) represent some remarkable achievements in food technology. The goal of the extensive research in margarines originally was to develop a product from vegetable oils with the characteristics of butter. To do this, oils from plants (corn, soybean, cottonseed, safflower, sunflower, or canola) are hydrogenated to change them into spreadable solid fats. Hydrogenation of the unsaturated fatty acids causes some ***trans* fatty acids** to form. Recognition of these fatty acids as possibly raising the risk of coronary heart disease resulted in the federal requirement that *trans* fatty acid content be listed on the Nutrition Facts label (Figure 8.2).

Stick margarines are marketed as a spread that can be substituted for butter in any of the preparations for which butter is designated. Their labels will indicate the ingredients used in making the specific margarines. As is true with all labels, the ingredients must be listed in descending order of weight in the product, beginning with the most abundant item. A comparison of margarine labels allows consumers to make choices between margarines made of only one specific type of oil or a mixture of oils. It also indicates whether an oil or a hydrogenated fat is the most abundant ingredient, a matter of interest to people seeking a high intake of polyunsaturated fats in relation to saturated fats. When an oil is listed as the first ingredient, the margarine will be higher in polyunsaturated fatty acids than if a partially hydrogenated or hydrogenated fat is the first item. All margarines, however, are higher in polyunsaturated fatty acids than butter is.

Soft margarines are marketed in tubs because they contain such a high proportion of polyunsaturated fatty acids that they will not remain in the form of a molded stick at room temperature. Oil sources for making soft margarines are the same as those used in manufacturing stick margarines. The lower melting point of tub margarines makes them easy to spread on bread, but even stick margarines are much easier to spread than butter when they are first removed from the refrigerator.

Diet margarines offer yet another choice to consumers. These are products formulated with a percentage of water far exceeding the usual 16 percent in other margarines. By replacing much of the fat with water, the caloric contribution of diet margarines is reduced appreciably. The high water content limits the use of diet margarines to serving as a spread. They have no cooking applications.

Whipped Spreads

Both butter and margarine are also marketed in whipped form. Whipping adds air and increases the volume of these spreads, which tends to limit the amount normally spread on bread or a roll. On a volume basis, whipped butter or margarine contains approximately half as many calories as the regular form.

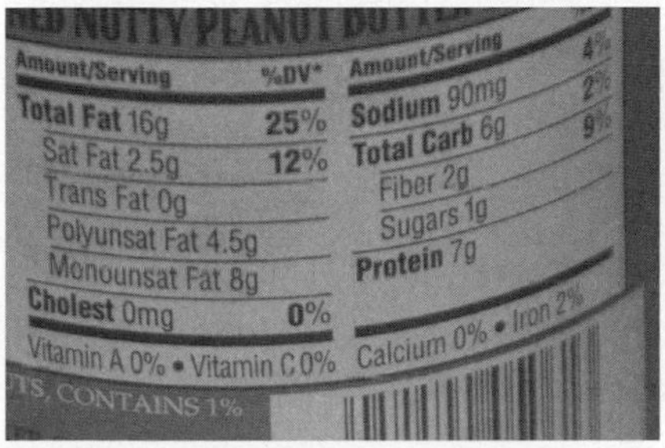

http://www.margarine.org/historyofmargarine.html
—Background on the development of margarine.

trans *fatty acid* Form of fatty acid sometimes created when hydrogen is added to a double bond in an unsaturated fatty acid.

www.margarine.org
—National Association of Margarine Manufacturers; information on margarines for professionals.

http://www.fda.gov/Food/ResourcesForYou/Consumers/ucm079609.htm
—Information on *trans* fats.

http://www.fda.gov/Food/LabelingNutrition/ConsumerInformation/ucm109832.htm
—Information on labeling of *trans* fat.

Figure 8.2
The Nutrition Facts label must list not only total fat but also saturated and *trans* fat content. Courtesy of U.S. Food & Drug Administration (FDA).

phytosterol or stanol ester Plant compounds occurring naturally in some plant oils that can help reduce LDL and total cholesterol levels.

omega-3 fatty acids Polyunsaturated fatty acids essential in the diet: α-linolenic acid (ALA), eicosapentaenoic acid (EPA), and docosahexaenoic acid (DHA).

http://benecolusa.com/index.jhtml

—Information on Benecol spreads.

http://www.smartbalance.com/

—Information on Smart Balance.

http://www.promisehealthyheart.com/Home.aspx

—Information on Promise spreads.

http://www.fao.org/ag/agn/agns/jecfa/cta/69/Phytosterols_CTA_69.pdf

—Article on phytosterols and stanols.

http://www.iseo.org/

—Site of the Institute of Shortening and Edible Oils.

http://www.crisco.com/Cooking_Central/

—Information on Crisco products and their use.

http://www.businessweek.com/news/2010-11-07/edible-oil-prices-to-rise-on-supply-curbs-mistry-says.html

—Overview of edible oils supply and prices.

NUTRITION INPUT
CHOLESTEROL AND SPECIAL SPREADS

In response to long-standing concerns about the relationship between serum cholesterol levels and heart disease, the food industry has developed some butter-like soft spreads as possible substitutes for butter. The key component in such spreads is either a **phytosterol or stanol ester** having a structure similar to, but somewhat different from cholesterol. Corn and soybean oils are among the plant sources of the sterols and stanols; these are then combined with fatty acids to form esters for incorporation into the spread. When consumed in recommended amounts (one to two tablespoons) as part of the day's fat intake, these spreads help lower LDL (low-density lipoproteins) and total cholesterol levels. This is due to limited absorption of dietary cholesterol. In addition to the plant sterols or stanols, these spreads contain **omega-3 fatty acids**, which also are associated with promoting heart health. People with risk factors for heart disease are the intended audience for these products, which include Benecol®, Promise®, and Smart Balance®. Not surprisingly, these alternatives are considerably more expensive than butter or margarine.

Shortenings

In a sense, shortenings are the first cousins of margarines, for they are products manufactured from the same types of oils used in making margarines. The oils are modified in a solid fat by adding hydrogen, a process called hydrogenation. A key difference is that shortenings do not contain water. Artificial butter flavoring and/or yellow food coloring often will be added to shortenings to enhance their appeal in baked products. Shortenings do not become rancid as readily as lard, which makes it possible to store them at a cool room temperature.

Shortenings, available in cans or in sticks, have been designed primarily for use in baked products. The inclusion of monoglycerides and diglycerides aids in emulsifying the ingredients in cake batters to promote a fine texture and retards staling.

Salad Oils

Salad oils commonly are the oils expressed from one or more of the following: corn, safflower, cottonseed, soybean, peanut, canola, sunflower seed, or olive (Figure 8.3). These oils from plant sources are generally high in polyunsaturated fatty acids, although olive and palm oils are rather low. The distinctive flavor of olive oil is prized by some as an ingredient in vinegar and oil dressings and in a number of recipes for pasta and vegetable dishes of Italian, Greek, or Middle Eastern origins (Figure 8.4). Other salad oils also are utilized as ingredients in salad dressing.

Oils are of great importance as the frying medium for shallow-fat or deep-fat frying because of their high smoke point. Most salad oils can be used several times for deep-fat frying before their smoke point drops below frying temperature (about 375°F [190°C]). The absence of water in oils contributes to their stability at high temperatures. Unlike butter and margarine, salad oils consist entirely of fatty compounds and do not contain either water or milk solids, both of which promote breakdown during frying.

Cooking Sprays

Cooking sprays have gained a niche in food preparation as a convenient product that can be applied quickly to help prevent food from sticking to pans during heating. Part of the appeal of cooking sprays is that they add almost no calories because so little is used. In addition, flavored cooking sprays may add appeal to vegetables while adding only an insignificant amount of fat.

Figure 8.3
Olive oil, such as that produced by the Agricultural Cooperative of Kritsa on the island of Crete, is a prominent ingredient in many Mediterranean dishes.
Courtesy of Plycon Press.

Several types of oils are used in the various cooking sprays found in today's markets, but all of them contain an emulsifier (lecithin) and a propellant. Corn, canola, and olive oils are the primary ingredient in several cooking sprays. A few contain water or an alcohol, in addition to the basic three ingredients. Although all cooking sprays contain one or more oils, they are used so sparingly that their nutrition labels indicate that zero calories are provided in a serving.

Figure 8.4
These olive groves near Kritsa produced the olives that were pressed for the olive oil shown in Figure 8.3. Courtesy of Plycon Press.

TECHNOLOGY OF FATS

Origin of Fats

Fats vary in their natural characteristics, depending upon their origin. For example, in milk fat, fatty acids range in chain length from 4 to 26 carbon atoms, with nine different saturated and seven unsaturated fatty acids being prominent. In contrast, many other fats will have only three saturated and two unsaturated fatty acids in abundance in their structures. Cattle fat is higher in saturated fatty acids than is the fat from chickens and other poultry, pigs, or lambs. Even the location of the fat within the animal influences the composition of the fat; fats near the surface are softer and higher in polyunsaturated fatty acids than are those in the leaf fat surrounding the internal organs.

Some changes in the fatty acid composition of non-ruminants can be accomplished by modifying the diet. The fat of pigs can be changed somewhat in this way. However, changing the diet of cattle does not alter the composition of their fat, because bacteria in their rumen modify dietary fats prior to passage into the intestinal region, where they are absorbed.

The fats of commercial interest from animals are milk fat, lard, and tallow. Milk fat is the forerunner of butter and is made available by churning milk until the emulsion in milk

SCIENCE NOTE
CHEMISTRY OF FATS

glycerol Alcohol containing three carbon atoms and three hydroxyl groups; common to the fats used in food preparation.

All fats of concern in food preparation contain one component in common—**glycerol**. Although it is a small alcohol containing only three carbon atoms, glycerol is unique in that it has three hydroxyl (—OH) groups (in contrast to the single functional group usually found in alcohols). Each of these hydroxyl groups can combine with a fatty acid to form an ester linkage by eliminating a molecule of water.

Glycerol   Fatty acid   Monoglyceride showing ester linkage (dashed lines)

fatty acid Organic acid containing between 4 and 26 carbon atoms; combines with glycerol to form a fat.

Fatty acids are responsible for the varying characteristics of different fats. The fewer the carbon atoms present in a fatty acid, the lower is the melting point compared with a fatty acid with a longer chain. Fats containing fatty acids with 16 or more carbon atoms will be firmer at room temperature than will those with short chains because of the difference in melting point of the fatty acids.

Another variation in fatty acids that helps to determine whether a fat will be a fluid or a solid is the amount of saturation with hydrogen. Each carbon atom within the fatty acid chain is capable of holding two hydrogen atoms. When this situation exists, the fatty acid is saturated; that is, it cannot hold any more hydrogen.

Sometimes adjacent carbon atoms will each have only one hydrogen atom, thus creating a double bond or an unsaturated fatty acid. Many plant oils contain molecules of fat that have fatty acids containing two or three double bonds. These fatty acids are designated as being polyunsaturated. An increase in the amount of unsaturation lowers the melting point temperature. Thus, vegetable oils, with their comparatively high amount of polyunsaturation, will remain fluid at room temperature, in contrast to the firm saturated fats in butter and other firm solid fats.

The carbon chain in a fatty acid ordinarily proceeds in a linear fashion, but at double bonds there is the possibility of altering the direction of the next portion of the chain. The configuration at a double bond that causes the chain to continue in its linear fashion is a *trans* form; the *cis* form is the arrangement causing a change in the direction of the molecule at the double bond. The *cis* form causes the melting point of the fatty acid to be significantly lower than is the comparable fatty acid in the *trans* form.

Fats not only differ in chain length and degree of saturation of the fatty acids they contain, but they also differ in the number of fatty acids in a molecule. When a fat contains a single fatty acid, it is called a monoglyceride. This fatty acid can be esterified at the terminal carbon or at the central carbon position. Diglycerides will have two fatty acids esterified to glycerol either at the two terminal carbon atoms or at two adjacent carbon atoms. The ultimate configuration of most fats used in food preparation is that of a triglyceride, in which all three carbon positions have been esterified with fatty acids. These various possibilities are depicted in Table 8.1.

trans Configuration at the double bond of an unsaturated fatty acid resulting in a continuation of the linear chain.

cis Configuration at the double bond of an unsaturated fatty acid resulting in a change in the direction of the fatty acid.

TABLE 8.1
GENERAL STRUCTURES OF FATS IN FOODS[a]

Type of Fat	Possible Structures	
Monoglyceride		or
Diglyceride		or
Triglyceride		

[a]R, R′, R″, and R‴ represent the remainder of the carbon–hydrogen chain; R = (–CH$_2$)$_x$CH$_3$, in which x represents between 2 and 22 CH$_2$ groups.

lard Fat rendered from the fatty tissue of pigs.

tallow Fat rendered from the fatty tissue of cattle.

breaks and reverses to form the water-in-oil emulsion of butter. The fat that will be marketed ultimately as **lard** or as **tallow** must be extracted from the fatty tissues of pigs and cattle, respectively.

Rendering

The first step in producing lard or tallow is extraction of fat from tissues, a process known as rendering. This is accomplished by chopping fatty tissues into fine pieces and then subjecting them to between 40 and 60 pounds of steam pressure to transform the solid fats into liquid for removal. Cooking fatty tissues in an open kettle is another way of rendering lard. The dry rendered lard resulting from this processing has a cooked flavor, which some people prefer.

Oils are extracted from some plant seeds (e.g., corn, sunflower) by pressing to express the oils or by treating with a solvent to extract the fat-soluble materials. Following extraction, the oils are heated briefly in steam to coagulate any protein that might be present and make the protein insoluble.

Refining

The fats and oils resulting from rendering or extraction are contaminated with such undesirable materials as free fatty acids and other substances. To improve the quality of fats and oils, it is necessary to refine the raw material by adding alkali to the fat to form an emulsion, which then is heated, broken, and separated. Additional washings and centrifugation continue until the free fatty acid content is decreased to between 0.01 and 0.05 percent, a degree of purity essential to the production of a fat with a reasonable shelf life. Once the fats and oils have been purified to this extent, they are bleached to lighten the color and deodorized to improve odor and flavor.

Hydrogenating

hydrogenation Process of adding hydrogen to polyunsaturated fatty acids to change oils into solid fats.

Hydrogenation, the addition of hydrogen to unsaturated fatty acids, is a key process in making margarines and shortenings. Through the action of a nickel catalyst in an environment held between 212°F and 392°C (100°C and 200°C) and at 15 atmospheres of pressure, hydrogen is added (two atoms of hydrogen at each double bond) to transform oils into solids. The melting points of fatty acids rise as unsaturation decreases.

Hydrogenation can be controlled to achieve the degree of saturation desired. To maintain as high a content of polyunsaturated fatty acids as feasible, margarines may be manufactured by mixing unhydrogenated oil with some fat that has undergone a fairly thorough process of hydrogenation. This permits the manufacture of a product that can be spread, yet one with the desired high content of polyunsaturated fatty acids.

Hydrogenation results in formation of some *trans* as well as some *cis* fatty acids. Concerns about the potential negative impact of elevated levels of *trans* fatty acids on heart health have resulted in an FDA regulation requiring that the amount of *trans* fat be listed on nutrition labels. This recent attention on the matter triggered increased efforts by margarine and shortening manufacturers to reduce formation of this configuration during hydrogenation. The results to reformulate products can be seen on the labels of fats in markets today; many contain little or no *trans* fatty acids. These health-promoting changes have been accomplished by making changes in the oils, as well as using such techniques as inter- and intraesterification to alter the arrangements of fatty acids in the molecules.

Blending and Tempering

Fats can be tailored to provide the physical characteristics desired for a particular application. Oils can be blended with solid fats to produce a fat with excellent spreading and creaming characteristics over a wide temperature range. To obtain the fine crystalline structure desired, solid fats are warmed and mixed thoroughly with the oils being added. Then this mixture is supercooled rapidly with agitation to achieve a matrix of very tiny fat crystals in which the oil droplets are trapped. This supercooling and rapid crystallization is accomplished by placing the fluid fat into a closed system containing nitrogen to cool the fat to 65°F (18°C) in 30 seconds. Then the fat is worked for up to four minutes to help achieve the desired fine crystals. A holding period at a controlled cool temperature for a couple of days to temper the fat completes the

SCIENCE NOTE
FAT CRYSTALS

Solid fats are composed of many, many crystals of fat with some oil trapped between them. The ease with which these crystals form is influenced by the fatty acids in the fat molecules.

The crystal forms in solid fats (Figure 8.5) may be any of four different types: alpha (α), beta prime (β′), intermediate, or beta (β). The β′ form is a transitory crystal that melts very quickly and recrystallizes in the fairly stable β form. The β′ crystals are actually very small and give the appearance of an extremely smooth surface, as seen when a can of shortening is opened. If shortenings and other solid fats are held at cool storage temperatures, the desirable β′ crystals will be retained for months. However, if they are warmed a bit, the crystals will begin to melt, and when they recrystallize, they will be in the larger intermediate crystal form. The intermediate crystals give a somewhat coarse appearance to the surface of a fat.

If butter or margarine is melted and then allowed to cool undisturbed, the surface is rather granular because very large β crystals are formed. Fats with β crystals are not recommended for use in shortened cakes in which the fat is creamed with sugar, because these large crystals create a coarse-textured cake.

Actually, any melted fat will cool in the form of β crystals unless quick cooling and thorough agitation are used to crystallize the fat. The procedure used in the solidification or crystallization of fats in making margarines and shortenings is designed to precipitate β′ crystals rather than intermediate or β crystals. These desirable β′ crystals are stable during storage and marketing as long as temperatures are fairly cool.

It is particularly important in warm weather to avoid letting margarine get warm, for the β′ crystals will melt, and the transition to the intermediate and even to the

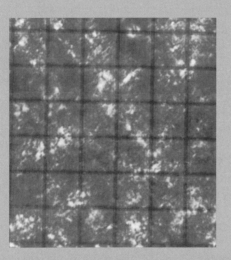

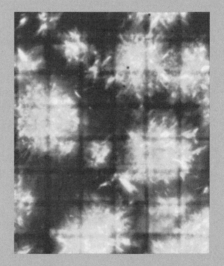

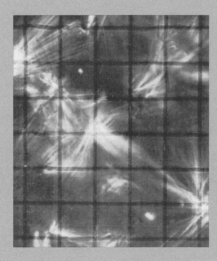

Figure 8.5
Photomicrographs of beta prime fat crystals (top left), intermediate crystals (top right), and beta crystals (left) in polarized light (200x). Grid lines represent 18 microns (top left). Courtesy of Plycon Press.

(Continued)

(Continued)

very stable β crystals may take place with prolonged warm storage. Shortenings and lard need cool storage (60°F [15.5°C] for shortening and 40°F [4.5°C] for lard) to keep β′ crystals.

Lard crystals are particularly unstable, which tends to cause a grainy appearance. The fatty acids on the molecules of lard can be stripped off during manufacturing and rearranged to modify the form of the fat crystals. Lard that has undergone this special treatment is called **rearranged lard**. Adding flakes of a fat in the β′ form to the cooling lard helps seed the crystallizing lard into the desired β′ form.

---

rearranged lard Lard that has been processed to remove the fatty acids from the glycerol and then to reunite the molecule in a somewhat different configuration to achieve a product that tends to form β′ crystals.

winterizing Process of chilling oil to 45°F (7.2°C) and then filtering it to remove any fat crystals.

manufacturing process. This tempering period aids in achieving stable, fine crystals that are of considerable benefit in any solid fat.

Winterizing

Salad oils are designed so that they can be kept chilled without having crystals of fat forming in them. To accomplish this, the oils are chilled to 45°F (7.2°C) and then filtered to remove any crystals that have formed. This chilling and filtering process is called **winterizing**. Following this process, it is possible to store salad oils and salad dressings containing these oils in the refrigerator and to pour them from their bottles without warming them to melt crystals.

STORING FATS

Cold temperatures are helpful in extending the shelf life of any fat or oil because enzyme action leading to the development of hydrolytic rancidity is retarded. However, room temperature storage eliminates the need for waiting for cold fats to warm enough to be easy to use; it also saves space in the refrigerator. If fats are to be used within a short time, refrigerator storage may not be necessary. This is particularly true for salad oils. Salad oils can be stored in a cool, dark cabinet for several weeks without becoming rancid. Generally, this is the preferred way to store these products because of convenience, but refrigerator storage extends shelf life. Shortenings also can be stored in a cool, dark place. They should be covered tightly to help keep out air and retard oxidative rancidity.

Storage of olive oil presents a real dilemma. It becomes rancid more quickly than other oils at room temperature, but develops fat crystals in the refrigerator and cannot be poured until it is warmed. With proper planning, olive oil can be stored in the refrigerator and removed well in advance of use. Room temperature storage is practical if the oil is bought in a small enough quantity that it will be used fairly soon.

Butter, margarines, and lard should be stored in the refrigerator to extend their shelf life. They need to be covered tightly to minimize oxidation and to avoid absorbing volatile flavors from other foods in the refrigerator. Fats take up volatile flavors from onions, cheeses, or other aromatic foods if they are not kept securely packaged.

SELECTING FATS

Selection of the best fat for a particular task in cookery is an important part of preparing a top-quality product, yet simply buying the most expensive fat is not a guarantee of the best choice. The role that fat is to play in making the product will determine the type to choose.

Spreads

The choice of a spread is largely an individual matter. Butter is more difficult to spread immediately after being removed from the refrigerator than are the various margarines. If many sandwiches are to be made quickly, margarine may be a time-saver. Preference for a specific brand of margarine or of butter often is based on flavor and level of polyunsaturated fatty acids rather than on plasticity or ease of spreading.

Tub margarines are particularly easy to spread because of their softness, the result of a high ratio of polyunsaturated fats in their formulation. This softness makes attractive service of these margarines at the table very difficult, a disadvantage that causes some people to avoid them.

If margarine is to be used as an ingredient in a batter or dough product or for frying, choice of a diet margarine will prove unsatisfactory. The low fat content and high water level will create tough baked products, and considerable splattering will be a problem in frying. The smoke point of diet margarines is very low, which is another reason for not frying with them.

Butter or regular margarines generally can be used interchangeably because of their similar composition and characteristics. Some people maintain that they can distinguish between butter and any margarine and are willing to pay the higher cost of butter. Others do not detect any important difference and opt for margarines, either on the basis of economy or the desire for fewer saturated fats and a higher level of polyunsaturated fatty acids. Clearly, this is a matter of individual preference.

Frying

Some people like to use butter or margarine for shallow-fat frying because of the flavor and color contributed by these fats. However, both butter and margarine can be used only a very short period of time before they begin to smoke and break down (Table 8.2). This is due to their fat composition and the presence of water as well as to the presence of milk solids. Burning of these fats (actually, the milk solids in them) also can be a problem affecting both appearance and flavor. Clarified butter burns less readily than butter.

Lard and shortenings are other fats sometimes used for frying (Figure 8.6). Unfortunately, these have comparatively low smoke points, which usually make both lard and shortening poor choices. The addition of mono- and diglycerides to shortenings during manufacturing reduces shortenings' suitability for frying, for those types of glycerides break down and start smoking soon after frying is begun.

TABLE 8.2
SMOKE POINT OF SOME FATS AND OILS[a]

Fat/Oil	Smoke Point	
	°C	°F
Safflower oil	267	513
Sunflower oil	213	415
Soybean oil	248	478
Canola oil	243	470
Corn oil	242	468
Peanut oil	234	453
Mid-oleic sunflower oil	232	450
Olive oil	191	375
Lard	183–205	361–401
Shortening	180–188	356–370
Butter	≈177	≈350

[a]Smoke points drop during prolonged heating.

Figure 8.6
Lard is the fat used for frying potato chips and many other foods in Peru and other Hispanic countries. Courtesy of Plycon Press.

Salad oils are good choices for frying. Peanut oil has a slightly distinctive flavor enjoyed by some, but avoided by others. Olive oil, despite its relatively low smoke point, is the popular choice for frying in countries bordering the Mediterranean Sea (Figure 8.7). The other salad oils have high smoke points and are essentially tasteless, characteristics that make them particularly well suited to use in deep-fat frying. Their content of antioxidants is an aid in extending shelf life.

Salad Dressings

Salad oils are often selected for making salad dressings; their viscosity and clarity make them key components of dressings. Although the flavor of many dressings is derived from the seasonings and vinegar used in them, olive oil sometimes is chosen for its distinctive contribution to flavor. A disadvantage of using olive oil is that it will start to crystallize when stored in the refrigerator, making it necessary to warm the oil enough to be poured. Other salad oils usually have had their components with a high melting point removed during processing to prevent crystals from forming and immobilizing the oil during refrigerator storage.

Figure 8.7
Olive oil is this chef's choice for frying loukamades, a dessert treat for his customers on the island of Crete. Courtesy of Plycon Press.

Baked Products

Breads Fat is a minor ingredient in most breads and sometimes is not even included, as is the case in French bread. In yeast breads, butter or margarine often is chosen because of the flavor and color contributions despite the fact that only a small amount is used. It is possible to use shortening or an oil (Figure 8.8), although the color and flavor contributed by the butter or margarine will be lacking. Firm fats promote high volume and a fine crumb in yeast breads.

Quick breads are so varied that it is necessary to comment on the type of fat best suited for several different products. For instance, muffin preparation requires the fat to be in liquid form. That liquid may be a salad oil or melted shortening. Butter and margarine usually are not used unless the recipe is adjusted because they would provide less fat and more liquid.

Biscuits are prepared by cutting the fat into the dry ingredients. To do this, the fat must be capable of being split apart easily and remaining separated. Shortenings have this capability and hence are preferred for this purpose. Butter and margarine are difficult to cut into small pieces when cold and will tend to cream together during mixing when warm.

Some quick loaf breads, such as banana nut bread, are made by creaming the fat with the sugar to establish a fine grain in the bread. Shortenings are excellent choices in these breads because they are very plastic and readily creamed without becoming too soft. Butter has the disadvantage of sometimes becoming too soft during creaming, so that the emulsion in the batter ultimately breaks, resulting in a slightly coarse texture.

Cakes Shortened cakes require thorough creaming of the fat and sugar as the initial step in mixing the ingredients. Although butter and margarine can be creamed, they may become too soft. They also do not have the emulsifying agents (mono- and diglycerides) that are added to shortenings to enhance their performance in making fine-textured cakes. There is a trade-off between the flavor and color contributions of butter and margarine and the fine texture resulting from the use of shortening. Shortenings that are flavored and colored to mimic butter are available to contribute all three desirable qualities to baked products. Sometimes lard is used in cakes, but its compact nature and lack of emulsifying agents cause these cakes to be somewhat compact, with a slightly greasy crumb.

Chiffon cakes are unique among the foam cakes because they use oil in the recipe. Foam cakes, which rely on light egg white foams for their airy quality, cannot be made with solid fats. Salad oil, however, can be blended with the other ingredients to give added tenderness to chiffon cakes without making them heavy.

Pastry The ratio of fat to liquid in pastries is particularly crucial. With too much water or too little fat, a pastry can quickly become very tough. Excellent results can be obtained using either lard or hydrogenated shortening, for both of these are entirely fat and do not contain water.

Figure 8.8
A commercial baker pours in a generous amount of olive oil to help tenderize and flavor his popular Greek artisanal bread. Courtesy of Plycon Press.

If butter or margarine is substituted into a pastry, the recipe needs to be adjusted by increasing the fat and reducing the water. These changes are needed because the amount of fat in butter is about 16 percent less than in shortening or lard, and some water actually is being added by the butter, both changes being clearly counter to producing a high-quality pastry. Puff pastries are specialty items prepared by placing butter between thin layers of dough to aid in keeping the layers separated and also add color and flavor. The water in butter helps to generate steam between the layers during baking, which promotes puffing of the numerous layers to make a high pastry. Shortening and lard are not used in puff pastry because they lack flavor and the water needed for steam development.

Cookies   The melting characteristics of butter, margarines, and shortenings are different, and these differences are quite evident in making cookies. Most cookie recipes create moderately rich doughs. During mixing, the doughs may seem very similar in their handling characteristics, regardless of which of these three types of fats is used. However, drop cookies will spread quite differently during baking, depending upon the type of fat used. Cookies made with shortening will hold their shape and flow less readily than will those containing butter or margarine. With careful development, a cookie recipe can be formulated for a particular type of fat. Butter and margarine can be used interchangeably, but they cannot be substituted for shortening unless the recipe is adjusted.

The type of fat used plays a significant role in determining the flavor of cookies because they usually are made with a high ratio of fat. Butter is often chosen because it adds a rich, full flavor. Margarine in cookies may also add a satisfactory flavor that is quite similar to that of butter. Lard is used less often because it adds a distinctive flavor.

FUNCTIONS IN FOOD PREPARATION

Palatability

Color, flavor, and aroma are aspects of palatability that can be influenced by the type of fat selected. The golden color of butter, margarines, and yellow-colored shortenings is considered to improve palatability of the products in which they are used. Regardless of the color of the fat used, baked products containing them will have a pleasing golden-brown color.

The flavors and aromas of butter, olive oil, lard, and most margarines are important in determining palatability of foods. Usually butter and margarines add important flavor. Lard has a flavor that is enjoyed by some people, while others may not like it. Olive oil, like lard, has its devotees and its detractors.

Textural Influences

Two textural qualities, tenderness and flakiness, are influenced by fats. Tenderness is one aspect of texture that is of great importance in baked products. Cakes and pastries usually are assessed for their tenderness, and the amount and type of fat selected can have a significant effect on this characteristic. Fats promote tenderness by impeding the contact of water with the protein (gluten) in flour, which toughens the product. The fat also adds a lubricating quality, another factor in preventing toughness. The consequence of these actions of fats during the mixing of batters and doughs is increasing tenderness with increases in the proportion of fat.

Solid fats can be cut into pieces, as is done in making pastry and biscuits. These pieces melt during baking and become incorporated in the cell walls, leaving holes where the pieces had been in the initial mixture. This contributes significantly to the textural characteristic called flakiness (thin layers forming numerous small pockets that shatter when cut). It should be noted that when fat is in small pieces to create a flaky texture, there actually is less fat coating the gluten strands to promote tenderness. This reduced tenderness can be noted when the pastry is cut with a fork. In products in which flakiness is desired, the use of a hard fat is important.

Cooking Medium

Fats and oils can be heated to 375°F (190°C) and higher (temperatures much hotter than boiling water), thus adding considerable opportunity for variety in food preparation. When foods are fried, they develop a crisp character on the outside and remain pleasingly moist in the interior. The flavors of fried foods are a combination of the richness afforded by the absorbed fat, possible unique flavors of the specific fat used, and the cooked food itself.

PERFORMANCE OF FATS IN FOOD PREPARATION

Shortening Value

The ability of a fat to aid in tenderizing baked products is called its **shortening value**. This terminology is derived from the ability of fats to shorten gluten (protein) strands, the structural protein network in wheat-containing batters and doughs. In other words, fats contribute to structural weakness, helping to keep baked products tender. This is accomplished by spreading the fat into thinner and thinner layers along the gluten strands that develop during mixing. This slippery coating of fat helps to inhibit hydration of the gluten. The type of fat used will influence the tenderness of a product. The plasticity of a fat and its ability to cover surface area are two important qualities determining its shortening value.

shortening value Ability of a fat to interfere with gluten development and tenderize a baked product.

Plasticity An ideal fat for tenderizing will be soft enough to be spread easily, but not so fluid that it runs out of the mixture. Hard fats are limited in their effectiveness as shortening agents because they resist efforts to spread them into thin layers during mixing, thus limiting the protective action of the fat. Fats that are soft enough to be spread into rather thin films during mixing are said to possess **plasticity**. Shortenings are good examples of fats that are plastic over a rather wide temperature range, making them excellent choices in many baked products. In contrast, butter has a narrow temperature range over which it exhibits plasticity. When first removed from the refrigerator, it is too hard to spread, yet in a warm room, butter becomes quite fluid. This limited plasticity makes butter less effective as a shortening agent than shortening.

plasticity Ability of a fat to be spread easily into quite thin films.

Surface Area The composition of a fat will determine how effectively it blocks water from reaching gluten. Fats with added mono- and diglycerides are useful shortenings because the hydroxyl (−OH) group(s) will be attracted to the interface between water and fat. Similarly, polyunsaturated fatty acids in salad oils are able to cover a large surface area along the gluten strands because the double bonds also are drawn to both water and fat. When molecules have structural features attracted to the interface between water and oil, fats are very good shortening agents. Figure 8.9 illustrates the particularly effective configuration of a fatty acid with three double bonds, a situation common in salad oils. Note that fatty acids with either one or two double bonds are equally effective in covering surface area because it is physically impossible for the second double bond to be drawn back to the interface. However, any unsaturated fatty acid is more effective at covering the surface at the interface than is a saturated fatty acid.

Figure 8.9
Orientation of fatty acids at oil/water interface. Note surface area covered when three double bonds are present. Courtesy of Plycon Press.

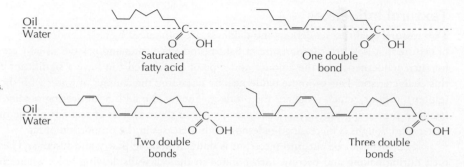

Frying

Fat is the cooking medium utilized in both shallow-fat and deep-fat drying. Many different fruits, vegetables, meats, eggs, poultry, fish, and even some doughs and batter-dipped products may be fried. In fact, frying is a quick and popular way of preparing many foods, in large part because of the crisp texture that develops on the surface of well-prepared fried foods.

Shallow-Fat Frying   Good heat control is the key to successful shallow-fat frying. The food should be frying briskly, but with little spattering and no smoking of the fat. If the heat is too high, the fat will start to smoke, which is irritating to the eyes and also causes a greasy buildup on kitchen walls over a period of time. Moreover, the food will become tough and dry or may even be burned on the exterior if the fat is too hot. Too low a heat creates greasy food due to the absorption of extra fat during the extended frying period.

Deep-Fat Frying   A thermometer is an important adjunct to successful deep-fat frying, for temperature control must be maintained if the food is to be cooked through without burning or becoming greasy. Most deep-fat frying is done at 375°F (190°C), and the fat should be heated to this temperature before any food is added. If it is not hot enough, excess grease will be absorbed by the food. The addition of food to hot fat will cause the temperature of the fat to drop below the desired frying temperature of 375°F (190°C), but a fast rate of heating will quickly restore the desired temperature unless large quantities of food are added at one time. Four pounds of oil drop almost 18°F (10°C) when even as little as two ounces of potatoes are being French-fried. A thermostatically controlled fryer will quickly regain the desired temperature because the drop immediately triggers the unit to heat. Despite this action, it still is important to avoid overloading a fryer so that food will be fried at the correct temperature rather than becoming greasy due to too low a temperature.

The appearance of deep-fat fried foods can be a deceptive indication of doneness, particularly if the frying oil is too hot. Even at 375°F (190°C), foods brown very readily and look wonderful, while still being almost raw in the center. This is a greater problem when thick pieces (such as chicken) are being fried than when something thin (like onion rings) is being prepared. Fortunately, the browning process proceeds far more slowly after the initial browning, which makes it possible to fry foods until they are done in the center without burning them if the temperature is controlled properly. When the correct amount of time has elapsed for deep-fat frying, a final check can be made by cutting a very small slit in the product to the center and checking for doneness. If the food is done, it should be drained on a paper towel to remove excess fat clinging to the surface. For optimum quality, fried food should be served just as soon as possible. If holding is necessary, it should be placed between layers of paper towels and held at 140°F (60°C) in the oven until served.

Oil for deep-fat frying can be used more than once. However, even when care is taken to store the oil properly, the smoke point will drop gradually, causing the foods fried in it to be less appealing than they would be if fresh oil were used. The useful life of a frying oil can be maximized by heating it as briefly as possible. Preheating should be done just long enough prior to frying to reach the proper temperature before frying begins. Cooling should start as soon as the food has been fried.

Keeping the water in foods to be fried to an absolute minimum will also help to extend the useful life of the oil. For example, when water comes in contact with hot oil, there is considerable splattering, which introduces oxygen into the oil and also adds water. Both water and oxygen accelerate the breakdown of oil, thus causing the smoke point to drop. Using paper towels to blot potatoes for French fries and other foods that may contain water before frying will reduce this problem.

Foreign particles in oil for deep-fat frying also hasten chemical breakdown and lowering of the smoke point. After frying, the cooled oil can be strained to help filter out small particles of food that may have fallen into the oil during frying. Frying oil can be used more than once, but it should be changed when it begins to darken and appears somewhat viscous.

SCIENCE NOTE
CHEMICAL CHANGES IN FATS

Heat Reactions

The high temperatures used in frying cause fats to undergo hydrolysis and polymerization of the fatty acids. The first stage in the breakdown of fats in frying is hydrolysis, in which a molecule of water is utilized to split a free fatty acid from the fat molecule, ultimately releasing glycerol. The glycerol molecule then loses two molecules of water, forming a very irritating aldehyde called acrolein. This reaction is shown here:

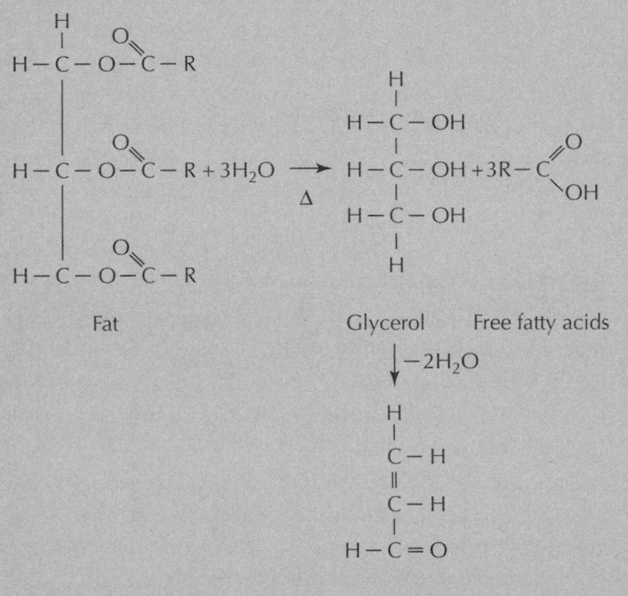

Fat   Glycerol   Free fatty acids

Acrolein

The free fatty acids released during extended use of oils gradually polymerize into long chains. The long carbon chains resulting from this chemical change present much more resistance to movement than does a single fatty acid. Polymerization increases viscosity in oils that have been used for a period of time for deep-fat frying, a change that gradually becomes evident.

The release of free fatty acids and formation of acrolein are accompanied by smoking of the fat. The temperature at which this can be seen is the smoke point (see Table 8.2, p. 163). The smoke point is not a constant value, but instead drops gradually as the fat begins to break down. Oils will have a smoke point well above the temperature needed for frying when they are first used, but they will begin to smoke during frying after a period of time. Hydrogenated shortenings are not suitable for deep-fat frying because their monoglycerides will quickly lose the single fatty acid, and the free glycerol will promptly form acrolein, causing smoking to occur at the temperature used in frying.

Rancidity

Fats slowly undergo deteriorative chemical changes that create undesirable odors and flavors due to oxidation or hydrolysis. The first detectable change, reversion, is noted in polyunsaturated fats when they develop a slightly fishy flavor and aroma. This precedes actual rancidity.

Oxidative Rancidity

Unsaturated fatty acids in fats become rancid when they take up oxygen at the double bonds following removal of a hydrogen atom from the carbon atom adjacent to the point of unsaturation. Heat and light promote the initial oxidation process, but the reaction will continue even in the dark once rancidity is started. The result is the formation of peroxides due to the uptake of oxygen. Consequently, oxidative rancidity is measured by determining the peroxide value of a fat; the higher the peroxide value, the lower is the quality of the fat.

Oxidative rancidity is retarded by antioxidants, such as the tocopherols, that may be present naturally in oils or added during processing. Antioxidants are effective because they take up the oxygen more readily than the fatty acids do. Metals (particularly copper, iron, and nickel) catalyze oxidative rancidity by lowering the energy needed for peroxide formation. Traces of these minerals need to be kept from contact with fats. Hematin (an iron-containing

(Continued)

(Continued)

compound in meat) can catalyze oxidative reactions in the fats of meat even during frozen storage. Lipoxidases are enzymes in vegetables capable of catalyzing oxidative rancidity. However, freezing or heat will inactivate lipoxidases.

Hydrolytic Rancidity

Hydrolytic rancidity occurs when free fatty acids are split from fat molecules as a result of the action of lipases (enzymes catalyzing the breakdown of fats) during

storage. It is determined by measuring the level of free fatty acids in the fat.

Cold temperatures retard development of hydrolytic rancidity, but even frozen storage does not halt this gradual deterioration of quality. Flavor changes are particularly objectionable when hydrolytic rancidity results in free fatty acids with 12 or fewer carbon atoms. Fortunately, heat is effective in inactivating lipases.

SUMMARY

Wise selection and use of fats and oils is important from the standpoint of nutrition and weight control as well as food quality. There are numerous fats and oils from which to choose. Lard and butter are familiar animal fats, while margarines, shortenings, salad oils, and cooking sprays are produced commercially from several plant sources, including corn, soybeans, safflower, cottonseed, sunflower, palm, and olives.

In many areas of food preparation, fats are used to enhance palatability by modifying texture, color, and flavor and by promoting tenderness. Oils and fats are used for frying foods, too. Butter and margarine are used for spreads and sometimes in cakes and cookies. Frying is most satisfactory when salad oils are used, but butter or margarine can be used if frying is to be brief. Salad oils are well suited to making salad dressings, with olive oil being a favorite choice for some. For most baked products, shortenings are particularly suitable, although some people may prefer lard for making pastry. Specific baked products may be made using oil; chiffon cakes require oil as the lipid, and muffins can be made with oil rather than melted fat, if desired.

Refrigerator storage extends the shelf life of fats and oils, although shortening and salad oils usually can be stored at room temperature for weeks without becoming rancid. Butter, margarine, and lard should be stored in the refrigerator to retard the development of rancidity unless they are to be used promptly.

Fats are composed of glycerol and fatty acids (usually three fatty acids) in each molecule. The melting point of fats is determined by the number of carbon atoms and the amount of unsaturation in the fatty acids. To prepare fats and oils for the commercial market, the fats are rendered or extracted from their animal or plant sources, after which they are refined and sometimes hydrogenated to convert some oils into solid fats.

Blending and tempering are done to achieve the desired mix of fats and oils to achieve a fat that will be quite stable in the beta prime (β') crystal form. Oils are winterized to remove crystals of fat that form at refrigerator temperatures.

When fats are used to tenderize baked products, their shortening value is of importance, for this determines how much protection from water a particular fat will afford gluten during mixing. Fats with short chain fatty acids and polyunsaturated fatty acids will spread readily to give good coverage. Monoglycerides and fatty acids with at least one double bond will help to block water from gluten by collecting at the interface between the fat and water.

Frying—either shallow-fat or deep-fat frying—causes some breakdown of fats. Careful temperature control aids in producing a high-quality fried product with a minimum of fat clinging to it. Extended heating of fat during frying causes fatty acids to split from glycerol; the free glycerol then breaks down to acrolein. The fatty acids polymerize as heating continues, causing increased viscosity of the oil. The smoke point drops as these changes take place.

Rancidity develops as a result of oxidation or of hydrolysis during extended storage of fats. Oxidative rancidity can be catalyzed by lipoxidases and is evidenced by an increase in the peroxide number due to the loss of hydrogen at double bonds and the uptake of oxygen. Metals and oxygen in the presence of stored fats promote oxidative rancidity, while antioxidants retard this change by reacting readily with oxygen that may be present. Hydrolytic rancidity, the splitting off of fatty acids, results in an increasing level of free fatty acids as rancidity develops. The presence of water promotes this reaction, but lipases can catalyze hydrolytic rancidity even in dehydrated foods. Heat inactivates lipases.

STUDY QUESTIONS

1. Make an inventory of the various types of fats and oils available in a supermarket. How do the ingredients compare among (a) brands and (b) types of products? Compare the price per pound of each item.

2. Using the same recipe for each product, prepare pastry using each of the following fats: shortening, butter, stick margarine, lard, and salad oil. Compare the ease of preparation and the palatability characteristics of each pastry.

3. What factors influence the fluidity of a fat?

4. Why is it important that fat crystals be in the β′ form when fats are used for making cakes? Does their type of fat crystal have significance if fats are to be used for frying?

5. What changes occur in a fat during prolonged heating?

6. In what ways do fats become rancid? How can use and storage practices help to delay the onset of rancidity?

7. What fats are the most effective tenderizing agents? Why?

8. What fat or oil would you recommend for deep-fat frying shrimp? Explain why you made your selection.

SELECTED REFERENCES

Albers, M. J., et al. 2008. 2006 marketplace survey of *trans* fatty acid content of margarines and butters, cookies and snack cakes, and savory snacks. *J. Am. Dietet. Assoc. 108*(2): 367.

Berry, D. 2005. Designer lipids. *Food Product Design 14*(12): 118.

Berry, D. 2009. Digging into our fatty-acid dilemma. *Food Product Design 19*(6): 70.

Blumenthal, M. M. 1991. New look at chemistry and physics of deep-fat frying. *Food Technol. 45*(2): 67.

Borra, S., et al. 2007. Update of *trans*-fat reduction in American diet. *J. Am. Dietet. Assoc. 107*(12): 2048.

Carr, R. A. 1991. Development of deep-fat frying fats. *Food Technol. 45*(2): 95.

Clark, J. P. 2005. Fats and oils processors adapt to changing needs. *Food Technol. 59*(5): 74.

Decker, K. J. 2005. ABCs of omega-3s. *Food Product Design 14*(11): 81.

Decker, K. J. 2011. Healthier fried foods. *Food Product Design 21*(1): 42.

Duxbury, D. 2005. Analyzing fats and oils. *Food Technol. 59*(4): 66.

Duxbury, D. 2005. Omega-3s offer solutions to trans fat substitution problems. *Food Technol. 59*(4): 34.

Esquivel, T. 2008. Understanding acrylamide. *Food Product Design 18*(11): 16.

Fortin, N. D. 2005. Fats in the fast lane. *Food Product Design 14*(12): 148.

Foster, R. J. 2008. Cholesterol control. *Food Product Design 18*(9): 56.

Foster, R. J. 2009. Checking the oil for snacks. *Food Product Design 19*(11): 54.

Galloway, R. 2011. Soybean oil innovations. *Food Product Design 21*(1): 20.

Hazen, C. 2004. Understanding fats and oils today. *Food Product Design 14*(11): 38.

Hazen, C. 2009. Better trans-fat baked goods. *Food Product Design 19*(1): 26.

Hazen, C. 2010. Baking sans *trans. Food Product Design 20*(8): 32.

Hicks, K. B., and R. A. Moreau. 2001. Phytosterols and phytostanols: Functional food cholesterol busters. *Food Technol. 55*(1): 63–67.

Hoerr, C. W. 1960. Morphology of fats, oils, and shortenings. *J. Am. Oil Chem. Soc. 37*: 539.

Hollingsworth, P. 2001. Margarine: Over-the-top functional food. *Food Technol. 55*(1): 59–62.

Jacklin, S. 2004. Food manufacturers in the frontline against obesity. *Food Product Design. Functional Foods Annual* Sept: 15.

Juttelstad, A. 2004. Marketing of *trans*-fat-free foods. *Food Technol. 58*(1): 20.

Kalua, C. M., et al. 2008. Changes in virgin olive oil quality during low-temperature fruit storage. *J. Agr. Food Chem. 56*(7): 2415–2422.

Kuntz, L. A. 2001. Fatty acid basics. *Food Product Design 11*(8): 93–108.

Kuntz, L. A. 2005. *Trans*-lating formulas. *Food Product Design 15*(7): 14.

Leake, L. L. 2007. *Trans* fat to go. *Food Technol. 61*(2): 66.

List, G. R. 2004. Decreasing *trans* and saturated fatty acid content in food oils. *Food Technol. 58*(1): 23.

Luff, S. 2004. Ascendancy of omega-3s. *Food Product Design. Functional Foods Annual* Sept.: 67.

Mermelstein, N. H. 2009. Analyzing for *trans* fats. *Food Technol. 63*(3): 71.

Miraglio, A. M. 2002. The low-down on *trans* fatty acids. *Food Product Design 12*(1): 31–34.

Narasimmon, R. G. 2009. Say low-fat cheese. *Food Product Design 19*(1): 24.

Ohr, L. M. 2005. Functional fatty acids. *Food Technol. 59*(4): 63.

Ohr, L. M. 2006. Functional fats. *Food Technol. 60*(3): 81.

Ohr, L. M. 2008. Not all fats are bad. *Food Technol. 62*(6): 101.

Ohr, L. M. 2009. Following functional oils. *Food Technol. 6*(2): 65.

Ohr, L. M. 2009. Matters of the heart. *Food Technol. 63*(5): 123.

Pszczola, D. E. 2004. Fats: In *trans*-ition. *Food Technol. 58*(4): 52.

Pszczola, D. E. 2006. Future strategies for fat replacement. *Food Technol. 60*(6): 61.

Remig, V., et al. 2010. *Trans* fats in America: Review of their use, consumption health implications, and regulation. *J. Amer. Dietet. Assoc. 110*(4): 585.

Sloan, A. E. 2005. Time to change the oil? *Food Technol. 59*(5): 17.

Spano, M. 2010. Heart health and fats. *Food Product Design 20*(3): 22.

Spano, M. 2010. Reconsidering ALA omega-3s. *Food Product Design 20*(6): 22.

Tiffany, T. 2007. Oil options for deep-fat frying. *Food Technol. 61*(7): 46.

Westman, E. C. 2009. Rethinking saturated fat. *Food Technol. 6*(2): 26.

Workers in a candy factory in Sri Lanka busily pack their morsels for shipment to distant markets.

9
Carbohydrates: Sugar

Chapter Contents

INTRODUCING THE CARBOHYDRATES

Carbohydrates are recognized in nutrition as an important source of energy, a function viewed negatively by some weight-conscious people. It is true that some foods are rather concentrated sources of carbohydrate, but pure carbohydrates still provide less than half as many calories per gram as are derived from a comparable amount of pure fat.

In food preparation, the various carbohydrates serve some key roles meriting special discussion. The simplest of the carbohydrates are the sugars. Many foods, particularly fruits, naturally contain sugars, which are responsible for pleasingly sweet flavors. However, sugars in various forms often are added when making candies, desserts, and even sauces for meats and vegetables.

Other carbohydrates that are larger molecules than sugars also are found in a wide array of foods. Starch is perhaps the most familiar complex carbohydrate, but the fiber in fruits and vegetables also contains carbohydrates in such forms as cellulose, hemicelluloses, pectic substances, and gums. These different forms are valued in food preparation for their contributions to the texture and structure of foods.

At first glance, it would seem that sugar and its sweet flavor would have almost nothing in common with the complex structural carbohydrates that contribute a range of textures. Why are these simple and complex substances clumped collectively into the category of organic compounds called carbohydrates? The answer lies in the fact that they are all made up of the same elements—carbon, hydrogen, and oxygen—and in approximately the same proportions. The term *carbohydrate* is a combination of *carbon* and *hydrate* (H and OH, or water). This relationship of hydrate to carbon holds regardless of the size and complexity of a particular carbohydrate.

Key Concepts

1. Mono- and disaccharides, which are simple carbohydrates capable of undergoing hydrolysis and caramelization, are available in a variety of products to sweeten food products.

2. Several alternative sweeteners have entered the market to provide sweetness in various products with reduced calories from carbohydrates.

3. Crystalline candies are made by creating a supersaturated solution and then controlling cooling and crystallization to produce a smooth texture.

4. The sugar solution in amorphous candies reaches such a high temperature and concentration of sugar that an organized crystalline structure cannot form.

carbohydrates Organic compounds containing carbon, hydrogen, and oxygen, with the hydrogen/oxygen ratio being the same as water (H_2O); includes sugars, starches, pectic substances, cellulose, gums, and other complex substances.

SUGARS IN THE MARKETPLACE

The sugars marketed today are quite different in quality, quantity, and price from the first sugar known in the Near East. Although sugar was once a rare item available only to royalty, today it is a household item in most kitchens around the world. The history of sugar began sometime between 300 and 600 A.D. when various techniques were developed in the Near East to refine and crystallize sugar. News of this remarkable food was carried to Europe by the returning Crusaders and eventually reached the New World when Columbus introduced sugar to Santo Domingo in 1493.

Of course, changes in sugar production have taken place over the centuries, but perhaps the single most important discovery was the realization by a 19th-century German chemist that the sugar beet is an outstanding source of sugar. By the beginning of 20th century, the sugar beet was approaching sugarcane as a source of sugar for commercial production. Levels of consumption of cane versus beet sugar vary in different sections of the country.

Cane sugar is produced by washing the cane stalks, squeezing out the juice from the cane stalks (Figure 9.1), heating the juice in the presence of lime to aid in removing impurities, and then evaporating the mixture to a highly viscous syrup and to raw sugar crystals (Figure 9.2). These raw sugar crystals are the starting material for the refining process. The coarse, yellow raw sugar is transformed from its sticky state into white, fine crystals by the use of charcoal and careful control of the crystallization process.

Beet sugar, the product of sugar beets, is extracted from these beets and processed to the refined sugar product in much the same manner as the process used for making cane sugar. The end product of both of these manufacturing processes is the same sugar, sucrose, and is marketed simply as granulated sugar or in related sugar products. Since there is no difference between cane and beet sugars, either type can be chosen. The market for both types is regulated by the federal government, which establishes the levels of sugar imports authorized each year.

An interesting by-product of sugar manufacturing is monosodium glutamate, often referred to simply as **MSG**. This is a sodium derivative of sugar, yet is not itself sweet tasting. Its merit is as a flavor enhancer to help heighten the existing flavors in foods. It is a familiar ingredient in various Asian cuisines.

MSG Monosodium glutamate (MSG), a by-product of sugar processing, is a flavor enhancer often used in Asian cuisines.

Granulated Sugar

Between 50 and 85 percent of factory sugar production is devoted to granulated sugar because of its important roles in many food products. The source of granulated sugar, whether cane or beet, will be found on the package label, although both products are the same.

Figure 9.1
Juice is squeezed from sugarcane as the first step in manufacturing cane sugar.
Plycon Press.

Figure 9.2
Balls of unrefined cane sugar are ready to go to the market in India, where they are called jaggery. Plycon Press.

White or refined granulated sugar may be purchased in different granule sizes, ranging from superfine to regular granulated sugar. The name dessert sugar, a synonym for superfine, indicates that this type of sugar is preferred for making hard and soft meringues and other desserts where the ease of solubility of these very tiny crystals is important. Regular granulated sugar is perfectly suitable for most uses and has the advantage of being less expensive than dessert sugar.

Cube sugar is simply granulated sugar that has been moistened with a colorless syrup, molded into cubes, and then dried in that shape. These cubes are used for sweetening individual cups of tea and coffee.

Powdered (Confectioner's) Sugar

One problem with any sugar is its tendency to cake when stored in a moist environment. To counteract the tendency to lump when sugar that is pulverized to a fine powder is stored, cornstarch is added in the manufacturing of powdered sugar. A mixture that contains 3 percent cornstarch is sufficient to absorb the moisture that would otherwise cause caking in this sugar with very fine particles. Powdered sugar customarily is used for making icings and for sweetening certain fruits, such as strawberries.

Raw Sugar

Raw sugar, a semirefined sugar that is a light tan color, has gained a place on the market shelf because of consumers' demand for natural products. However, there is no nutritional merit in using raw sugar in place of granulated sugar. (Raw sugar in the market is not actually the unrefined product, for the unrefined product is not safe to eat and cannot be sold.) Sugar that is marketed in this country as raw behaves much like brown sugar in food preparation and is sometimes used to sweeten fruits or to make cookies and other baked products. The tan color will show when this sugar is used in light-colored baked products. The cost of raw sugar is surprisingly high in view of the fact that the processing is slightly easier than that for white granulated sugar and there are no significant nutritional benefits.

Brown Sugar

Because of its pleasing and distinctive flavor, brown sugar frequently is used in baked products. The color and flavor of brown sugar are correlated with the state of refinement: a dark, strong-flavored brown sugar has undergone less filtration and purification than has a light, mild-flavored

Figure 9.3
This tap in a sugar maple tree drips sugary sap as the prelude to maple syrup and sugar. Courtesy of Debra McRae.

product. Either can be used very satisfactorily. The comparatively high moisture content of brown sugar tends to promote the development of hard lumps during storage. Packaging in plastic bags with tight closures that can be resealed helps to minimize this problem. A pourable, pellet-like brown sugar is also available, although this is more costly than regular brown sugar.

Maple Sugar and Maple Syrup

The tapping of sugar maple trees (Figure 9.3) and boiling of the collected sap to make maple syrup and maple sugar date back to colonial days in America. It still is possible to buy maple syrup and sugar, but limitations in the production process have hampered output and caused prices to be relatively high for these products.

Maple syrup and sugar have a sweet taste and a pleasing, distinctive flavor, which contributes to their popularity. The demand for maple flavoring has stimulated considerable effort to develop a synthetic counterpart, and the result is a reasonably comparable flavoring at a significantly reduced price. Synthetically flavored maple syrup is a familiar and widely used topping for pancakes and waffles and may even be used occasionally in baked products for sweetening.

Molasses

Molasses is a sugarcane derivative that may be marketed as unsulfured, sulfured, or blackstrap. Sulfured molasses ranges in color from rather light to a medium dark brown, depending on whether it is prepared by centrifuging the first (the lighter color) or second boiling of the sugarcane juice. Sulfured molasses is a by-product remaining after cane sugar has been crystallized and removed from the cane juice. Sulfur fumes are in contact with the liquid when sugar is the principal product being prepared, and molasses is merely a by-product.

Unsulfured molasses is a full-flavored, reddish-brown liquid that has not been exposed to sulfur fumes. Aging enhances the flavor of unsulfured molasses. Blackstrap molasses, often used as animal food, is the material remaining after the sugar has been extracted from the boiled cane juice.

Corn Syrup

All of the sweeteners discussed so far are produced from parts of plants that are high in their sugar content. Corn syrup is unique in that it is produced from starch, a complex carbohydrate, by a series of chemical changes called hydrolysis. This hydrolytic breakdown is accomplished by treating starch from corn with hydrochloric or sulfuric acids in the presence of heat and pressure to produce a mixture of breakdown products. Although cornstarch itself does not have a sweet taste, the small units splitting from the starch (glucose, maltose, and some dextrins) are sweet. Corn syrup, which is a very viscous liquid, gains much of its sweetness from its high glucose content. Light corn syrup is light in color (not in calories) and has a slight flavor of vanilla; dark corn syrup has a more intense flavor from a little addition of a molasses derivative. These two can be used to suit the recipe or the preference of the chef, but color and flavor differences will be evident.

The abundance and comparatively low cost of cornstarch are valued qualities that have helped to make corn syrup a popular sweetener. However, there still is a need to find ways of using or marketing the surplus cornstarch available, and this has prompted efforts to derive new products from it. One creative approach has involved the development of a corn syrup called **high-fructose corn syrup**. Chemically, this is an interesting product; the enzyme isomerase is used to convert some of the glucose in the corn syrup into another sugar, fructose. Theoretically, this high-fructose corn syrup (actually only about 30 percent fructose) has an advantage over the original corn syrup because fructose is about twice as sweet as glucose. This means that less fructose-containing corn syrup can be used to sweeten a product than would be needed if ordinary corn syrup were used. This difference is an advantage in beverages or other fluid applications but not in baked products. Nevertheless, there are many applications of high-fructose corn syrup by food manufacturers. High-fructose corn syrup is not available directly to consumers at the marketplace level.

http://www.international sugars.com/ISI_-_Home.html
—Information on sugars available for commercial use.

http://www.mayoclinic. com/health/high-fructose-corn-syrup/AN01588
—Mayo Clinic discusses high-fructose corn syrup.

http://www.karosyrup.com/ products.html
—Information on various corn syrups.

high-fructose corn syrup (HFCS)   Corn syrup in which isomerase has converted some of the sugar to fructose.

isomerase   Enzyme used to convert glucose to fructose to make high-fructose corn syrup.

CORN SYRUP CONTROVERSY

The crisis over America's weight problems is front and center as a major health issue. Clearly this is an important issue, but weight control is a confounding personal problem for growing numbers of people. As publicity has focused increasingly on weight loss, considerable information is circulating via all possible modes of communication and from numerous people, ranging from leading medical and nutrition authorities to opportunists with strong voices and opinions, but little accurate knowledge.

Sweet foods are frequently the target when weight-loss diets are being devised, which makes sense because of the comparatively high calorie count in relation to essential nutrients. One response to letting people have their cake and eat it too has been the development of several zero- or low-calorie sweeteners. Unfortunately, many dieters seem to think that means the food itself can be eaten in any quantity without adding calories, which ignores the fats that often are included in sweet treats.

The gathering storm regarding sweets in the diet has settled on HFCS, charging that it is the cause of childhood obesity and many related problems. No doubt HFCS has contributed, but so has every other food that was consumed beyond the amount needed for a healthy weight. There is nothing unique about HFCS. Like other digestible carbohydrates, it contributes four kilocalories per gram. People need to reduce intake of foods providing few nutrients in relation to calories. Protesting against HFCS will not solve the problem, but eating less will.

INGREDIENT HIGHLIGHT
HONEY

Honey is the only sweetener derived from animal sources. Bees, using nectar from different flowering plants, produce this distinctive sweetening liquid (Figure 9.4). Frequently, the sources of nectar for the bees are clover and alfalfa, but there are many types of honey, such as orange blossom, available with varying flavor qualities. Honey is an excellent sweetener because it contains an abundance of fructose and adds a distinctive flavor to products containing it.

The disadvantages of honey are the comparatively high price and the fast browning when batters and doughs containing honey are baked. This difference in the rate of browning is due to the large amount of fructose, which causes more rapid browning than sugar does.

Honey can be substituted in some recipes for as much as half the sugar, but adjustments will be needed. For each cup of honey used, liquid needs to be reduced by one-fourth cup and one-half teaspoon soda added to compensate for the acidity of the honey. If the measuring cup is sprayed with nonstick cooking spray before adding honey, the viscous honey will drain quickly from the cup. The baking temperature should be reduced by 25F° (15C°).

Liquid honey should be stored at room temperature to retard crystallization; refrigerator storage causes crystals to start to form. Crystallized honey can be liquefied by placing the container in hot water or by microwaving very briefly just until the crystals disappear.

Figure 9.4
This beekeeper dons protective gear when he harvests honey from his beehives.

http://www.fda.
gov/Food/default.htm
—Information can be traced
by searching for specific
sugar substitutes.

Other Sweeteners

Saccharin, which is not a carbohydrate, is a non-nutritive sweetener that has been used as a sweetener (Sweet'N Low®) by diabetics for years, but it also is chosen by some weight-conscious people in order to reduce their caloric intake. Saccharin is marketed in many commercial food products and in the granular and fluid forms for sweetening foods at home. Saccharin can be used in products, such as beverages, where sugar serves only a sweetening function, although some people find the aftertaste objectionable. Saccharin is not a suitable substitute for sugar in traditional candy recipes or batter and dough products where sugar performs other roles in addition to sweetening.

Other non-nutritive sweeteners are being developed and several are marketed today. Extensive tests on the safety of any proposed new additive, including sweeteners, must be completed and approved by the U.S. Food and Drug Administration before it can be used in any food. Cyclamates are available in some countries but not in the United States because some evidence of carcinogenicity was found in experimental animals fed unrealistically high doses of the sweetener. Aspartame (Equal, NutraSweet®) is a low-calorie sweetener approved for use in many different food products (Figure 9.5). This substance is a dipeptide composed of two amino acids, aspartic acid and phenylalanine, the latter being a concern for people with phenylketonuria. Because of its chemical composition, aspartame behaves like a protein and loses its sweetness when heated. A gram of aspartame will provide four kilocalories of energy, but the sweetness contribution is sometimes as great as 200 times that of sucrose. Since only small amounts of aspartame are needed, its use as a sweetener can reduce the calorie content of beverages and some other food items in which sucrose traditionally would be used.

$$HO-\overset{\overset{\displaystyle O}{\|}}{C}-CH_2-\underset{\underset{\displaystyle NH_2}{|}}{CH}-\overset{\overset{\displaystyle O}{\|}}{C}-NHCH-\overset{\overset{\displaystyle O}{\|}}{C}\overset{\displaystyle O}{\underset{\displaystyle OCH_3}{}}$$

Aspartame

Figure 9.5
NutraSweet® packages carry not only nutrition and ingredient information but also a statement that it contains phenylalanine and another that says it is safe for diabetics.

Neotame, also a sweetener, is another dipeptide. It has far greater sweetening ability than aspartame and has the added advantage that it does not yield phenylalanine as a breakdown product.

Sucralose (Splenda®) is a very sweet product (sucrose with three chlorines). This is being marketed for consumers to use in place of sugar in various applications, including baked products. Tagatose (Gaio®) is a sweetener derived from dairy products, which qualified it to be approved as GRAS (generally recognized as safe).

Acesulfame-K (Sweet One®, Sunette®), derived from acetoacetic acid, is being used widely because of its intense sweetness and suitability in a number of commercial food products. In 2008, the FDA approved the use of stevia, a very sweet compound from a plant native to Paraguay. Rebaudioside A (often referred to as Reb A) is the main compound in this no-calorie sweetener. It is being marketed currently as Truvia™. Isomalt (derived from sucrose) is used widely in food technology, but it is only about half as sweet as sucrose. Researchers are developing combinations of these various sweeteners in an effort to obtain optimum sweetening and performance characteristics in various sweetened food items.

http://www.caloriecontrol. org/sweeteners-and-lite/ sugar-substitutes
—Summary information about several sweeteners.

SWEETENING POWER

The sweetening power of pure sugars and of products containing sugars is of importance in formulating recipes, for the sweet taste of any food must please the diner's palate. People vary in their taste sensitivity, with some being able to detect sweetness at a far lower concentration than others can. One way of considering sugars as ingredients is to determine how sweet one sugar is in comparison with another. The sweetest sugars can be detected as being sweet at much lower concentrations than those that are only slightly sweet. Such tests ordinarily are conducted using dilute sugar solutions tested at room temperature.

REACTIONS OF SUGARS

Hydrolysis

Sucrose can undergo the severe chemical breakdown involved in caramelization, or it can be subjected to a milder change—that of hydrolysis. Hydrolysis of sucrose results in the formation of **invert sugar** (equal amounts of two simple sugars, glucose and fructose). This change, specifically called inversion, affects the sugar-containing products in which hydrolysis occurs because the usual end result is a mixture of sucrose and invert sugar, which together will crystallize less easily than will sucrose alone.

invert sugar A mixture of equal amounts of glucose and fructose resulting from the hydrolysis of sucrose.

http://www.nyu.edu/pages/ mathmol/library/sugars/
—Models of sugar structures.

INDUSTRY INSIGHT
FRUCTOOLIGOSACCHARIDES

Fructooligosaccharides (**FOS**) are sugars in which sucrose is joined with two or three fructose units, resulting in a somewhat more complex carbohydrate molecule that is not easily digested, but that does increase sweetness. These fructooligosaccharides are found naturally to a limited extent in bananas, tomatoes, onions, honey, and some other foods. Experiments in which Spiegel and co-workers (1994) added FOS to yogurt demonstrated that FOS was effective in improving the flavor and texture. The motivation for such research is the hope of obtaining highly palatable foods that appeal to consumers while also providing fewer calories. The fact that humans cannot digest FOS makes it possible to obtain a satisfactory yogurt without adding calories along with sweetness. FOS affords but one example of non-nutritive sweeteners and the search for low-calorie foods.

FOS Fructooligosaccharide, non-nutritive, sweet carbohydrate comprised of one molecule of sucrose and two or three fructose units.

SCIENCE NOTE
MONO- AND DISACCHARIDES

The sugars found naturally in foods are classified on the basis of the number of carbon atoms in their basic units and on the complexity of the total molecule. Some five-carbon sugars, called pentoses, are found in foods, but they have limited application in home food preparation. Ribose and arabinose are pentoses. Of more importance in food preparation are the hexoses, which are named because of their content of six carbon atoms. Glucose, fructose, and galactose are the three hexoses of particular interest. Their structures are shown below.

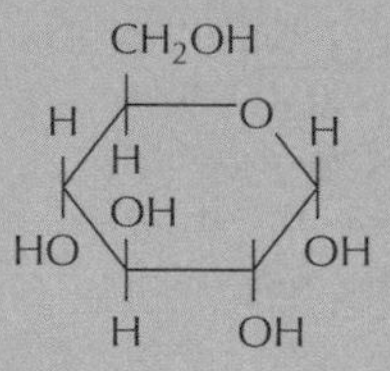

Glucose 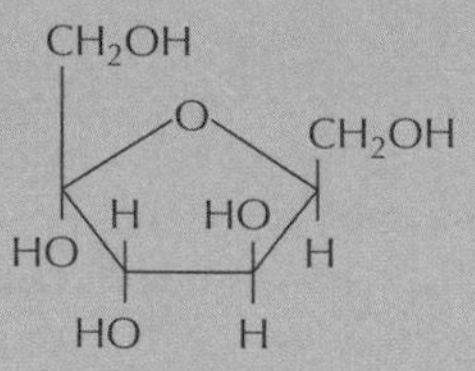   Fructose 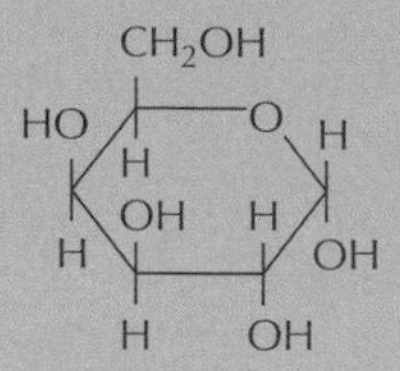   Galactose

These three monosaccharides are used in the formation of three common disaccharides. Each molecule of a disaccharide is composed of two monosaccharides that have been united with the expulsion of a molecule of water. All three of the disaccharides of greatest importance in food contain one unit of glucose. In fact, maltose contains two units of glucose. Lactose contains galactose in addition to glucose, and fructose is the second monosaccharide in sucrose. Their structures are presented below.

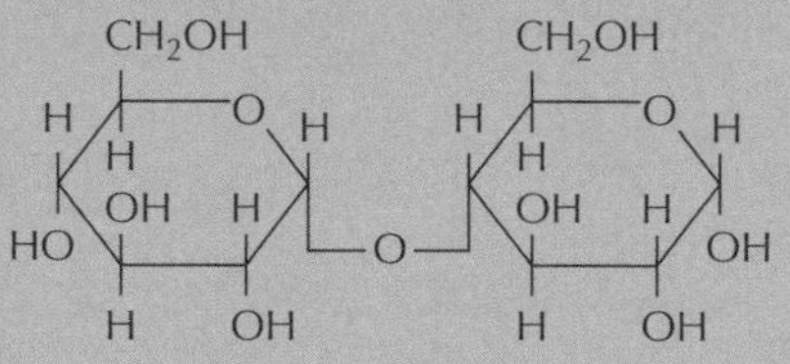

Maltose 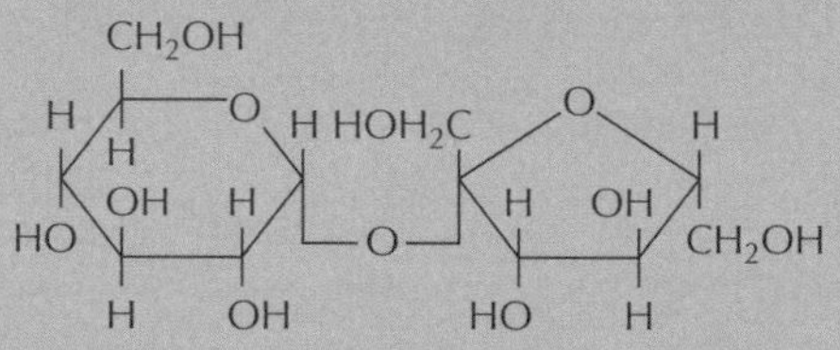   Sucrose

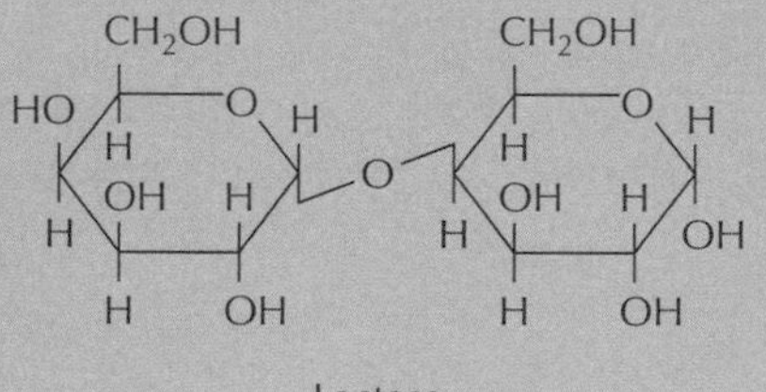

Lactose

Sucrose is the most common of the disaccharides and is used widely in food preparation. Lactose is the sugar in milk and sometimes is referred to as milk sugar.

---

inversion Specific term for the hydrolysis of sucrose to glucose and fructose.

Inversion is promoted when sugar is cooked in a solution to which an acid has been added. In making crystalline candies, cream of tartar frequently is added as the acid ingredient to ensure that a moderate amount of invert sugar will be formed to help in achieving a smooth texture. A moderate to slow rate of cooking will result in an appreciable amount of inversion, while a fast rate of boiling a crystalline candy will permit less time for inversion to occur.

Some inversion is desirable when making crystalline candies because the presence of more than one sugar helps to inhibit crystal formation during the cooling period, thus aiding in creating a smooth-textured candy. However, excessive inversion presents a problem; too

> ### SCIENCE NOTE
> ## CARAMELIZATION REACTIONS
>
> When heated without water, sucrose crystals melt, and then chemical breakdown begins. First, the linkage between the fructose and glucose units of sucrose breaks. Continued heating then creates many different chemical compounds as a result of the breaking of the ring structure of both monosaccharides. Prominent among the compounds created by caramelization are organic acids. Evidence of the formation of these acids is seen when baking soda is added to caramelizing sugar; the alkaline ingredient combines with the acids to form carbon dioxide, causing the caramelized liquid to bubble and become porous. An application of this reaction to produce CO_2 is the making of peanut brittle, for this type of candy is heated to the point where caramelization is occurring, and then baking soda is added before the very viscous mixture has an opportunity to cool enough to become solid. The reaction of the soda with the organic acids in the candy causes the brittle to become opaque and porous as a result of the large amount of carbon dioxide generated.

much inversion of sucrose to glucose and fructose can interfere with crystal formation so much that the resulting candy will be too soft. The addition of a small amount of cream of tartar, combined with a moderate rate of heating, will provide the combination needed to produce an appropriately firm, smooth-textured crystalline candy.

Another means of causing hydrolysis is with the use of the enzyme **invertase**. Invertase is used commercially to catalyze the inversion of sucrose. As is true with any enzyme, invertase must not be heated if it is to retain its catalytic ability. Consequently, commercially produced chocolate creams are made by creating a fairly firm center filling that is mixed with invertase prior to dipping the chocolate. After a period of several days of storage, invertase will have inverted enough sucrose so that the filling softens to the desired consistency.

invertase Enzyme mixed with fondant-type fillings to invert some of the sucrose and soften the consistency of commercial chocolates.

Caramelization

Sucrose can be heated by itself until it becomes so hot that it melts and fairly rapidly goes from a colorless liquid to a golden brown and then to a deep brown, followed by black if heating is continued. At the same time that the color is changing, the aroma becomes caramel-like and eventually will smell like burning sugar unless cooled promptly. The temperature of caramelizing sugar is very high, and the chemical breakdown of the sugar proceeds so rapidly that boiling water usually is poured into the molten sugar at the desired stage to cool the mixture and halt caramelization. Even when the added water is boiling, there is a large temperature differential between the molten sugar and the boiling water, which results in some spattering briefly. This added water not only halts caramelization but also dilutes the sugar to make a caramelized sugar syrup for use in recipes. Otherwise, the undiluted sugar will solidify into a hard, brittle mass that cannot be incorporated with other ingredients.

www.exploratorium.edu/ cooking/candy/sugar

—Science of making candy.

TYPES OF CANDIES

Candy is called *khandi* in Arabic and sweets in England, but it has universal appeal regardless of the name. From the perspective of nutrition, candy certainly is not essential, but its popularity in various forms around the world indicates that candy likely is here to stay as a pleasure of life. The various candies are classified as crystalline or amorphous, depending upon their internal organization. **Crystalline candies** are the candies that can be bitten easily and can be cut with a knife. When viewed under a microscope, there are many areas in crystalline candies where organized crystal structure can be seen, along with some liquid. Fondant, fudge, panocha, divinity, and creams are examples of *crystalline candies.*

Amorphous candies, as the name implies, lack an organized structure. These candies generally have a higher concentration of sugar than the crystalline candies. Their cooked syrups

crystalline candies
Candies with an organized crystalline structure; easily bitten or cut with a knife.

amorphous candies
Candies with a very high concentration of sugar, making them too viscous to form an organized crystalline structure; texture ranges from chewy to very hard and brittle.

are so viscous that sugar crystals cannot form any type of organization. The amorphous candies, with their lack of organized crystal structure, are not chewed easily or cut with a knife. They range in texture from extremely chewy caramels to very hard or even brittle products, such as toffee.

Although crystalline and amorphous candies are both examples of sugar cookery, their preparation problems are unique. They both require careful cooking to the correct final temperature, but the problems associated with making crystalline candies are quite different from those involved in making high-quality amorphous candies.

Crystalline Candies

The concentration of sugar in crystalline candies is appreciably lower than in the amorphous candies, which means that they are not boiled as long or to as high a temperature (Table 9.1). As a result, the likelihood of scorching and of obtaining an inaccurate temperature reading is reduced significantly. As with amorphous candies, however, a pan with even heating characteristics must be used. Since the temperature of boiling candies reflects the sugar concentration, very accurate temperature control is vital to obtaining the correct firmness of crystalline candies. A small error on the low side will cause the candy to be too soft, and a degree or two above the correct temperature will create a crumbly, hard product.

Two other factors, in addition to the final temperature reached, influence the firmness of a crystalline candy. One is the rate of heating. If a candy is heated unusually slowly, the amount of inversion that occurs will be excessive. The large proportion of the resulting glucose and fructose will interfere more than normally in the crystallization process, and the candy will be a little softer than the final temperature would suggest. This problem can be avoided by being sure to use a pan large enough to allow the boiling candy to boil vigorously without splashing over the top.

hygroscopic Attracting (or absorbing) water.

The second factor that might cause a crystalline candy to be too soft relates to making candy on a rainy day. This is not an old wives' tale; there is scientific evidence to support the result. Sugar is very **hygroscopic**—that is, it attracts or absorbs water readily; this is particularly true when it is in a hot solution. Thus, while crystalline candies are cooling in an extremely humid environment, moisture will be removed from the air and held in the cooling candy. The result is that the candy will have higher moisture content after standing than it did when it was first removed from the heat.

In crystalline candies, the moisture level is so critical to the firmness of the candy that this small amount of absorbed moisture will make the candy just a bit too soft. To compensate for this, on a rainy day crystalline candies should be cooked about one degree Fahrenheit higher than the recipe states. This adjustment is unnecessary for amorphous candies because their moisture level is slightly less critical.

TABLE 9.1
INGREDIENTS AND FINAL TEMPERATURES FOR SOME TYPICAL CANDIES

Candy	Basic Ingredients	Final Temperature °F (°C)
Crystalline		
Fondant	Granulated sugar, corn syrup or cream of tartar, water	238 (114)
Fudge	Granulated sugar, cocoa or chocolate, milk, corn syrup, butter	234 (112)
Panocha	Brown sugar, granulated sugar, milk, corn syrup, butter	234 (112)
Amorphous		
Caramels	Granulated sugar, corn syrup, butter, cream	245 (118)
Taffy	Granulated sugar, corn syrup, water	260 (127)
Toffee	Granulated sugar, butter, water, corn syrup	300 (149)

In addition to the firmness, crystalline candies are evaluated on their smoothness. Ideally, a crystalline candy will feel perfectly smooth when rubbed with the tongue against the roof of the mouth. There should be no suggestion of grittiness or rough crystals even though these candies are defined as having an organized crystalline structure. For success, the crystals must be very small, rather than in large aggregates, for it is these large clumps of crystals that feel rough on the tongue.

There are three factors of particular importance in achieving a very smooth, velvety texture: (1) interfering agents, (2) adequate beating, and (3) rapid crystallization.

Interfering agents are ingredients or components that make it difficult for sugar crystals to form and clump together in large aggregates. Butter and the fat in chocolate are examples of interfering agents in fudge because they help to keep sugar crystals from bonding tightly to each other. The use of corn syrup is another; its viscous quality and the presence of a mixture of sugars (maltose and glucose) are useful in blocking crystals from aggregating. Increased viscosity makes it more difficult for sugar crystals to align closely enough to hydrogen bond to each other, and the different shapes of maltose and glucose molecules also help to prevent bonding between crystals. Cream of tartar and other acidic ingredients interfere indirectly by promoting the inversion of sucrose to give a mixture of sugars.

Beating is an important part of preparing high-quality crystalline candies. By beating these candies continuously from the time crystallization is starting, the sugar crystals are kept in motion and are not able to bond together into coarse aggregates. To achieve the desired very smooth crystalline candy texture, it is necessary to continue beating from the time crystallization begins until the candy softens slightly just before becoming firm. However, even diligent and vigorous beating cannot prevent a slight amount of graininess if crystallization begins too early in the cooling process.

Beating does not cause the candy to get hard; it simply influences how readily the crystals grow together. It also modifies the color by trapping air throughout the solidifying, crystallizing candy. The combination of the air and the numerous sugar crystals produces an opaque, white or lighter-colored candy than would result if beating were omitted.

The last factor influencing the smoothness of crystalline candies is the point when crystallization begins. If crystals are formed very rapidly, the candy will become locked into a fine crystalline structure that will change very little over time. The fine crystals remain separated; they do not rearrange into large aggregates if the total crystallization process can occur within an extremely brief period of time. This circumstance occurs when all of the sugar in a crystalline candy is dissolved during the boiling period and the candy is allowed to cool to about 110°F (43°C) without any disturbance. If beating is initiated at this point, there will be extremely rapid formation of many sugar crystals and little opportunity for crystals to clump and create a grainy texture.

When beating crystalline candies, it may be difficult at first to spot the exact point when beating should be stopped and the candy should be spread in preparation for cutting into pieces. The clue to the stopping point is the very slight softening of the candy due to the **heat of crystallization** (heat energy released when the very viscous sugar solution changes into crystals). With experience, this softening can be detected, but it is difficult to see in small batches of candy because the heat is dissipated so rapidly. If the candy is not spread in time, the crumbly mass can be kneaded gently into a cohesive, attractive candy and shaped to the desired thickness (Figure 9.6).

Sometimes crystalline candies do not meet expectations. Perhaps they are too hard or too soft, or maybe they have a gritty texture. Unlike a number of food products, such candies can be salvaged. Water needs to be added to the candy in a pan, and then the dissolved candy should be reheated until the correct final temperature is reached. The cooling and beating are done the same as they would be done for any crystalline candy.

When a high-quality crystalline candy has been prepared, it will improve even more by undergoing a 24-hour ripening period in a tightly covered container. During this period, there will be a slight softening and an increase in smoothness. However, longer storage will allow small crystals to dissolve in the **mother liquor** and recrystallize on larger

interfering agents Butter, corn syrup, or other ingredient inhibiting crystal formation.

heat of crystallization Heat energy released when a viscous sugar solution crystallizes and forms a solid mass.

mother liquor Saturated sugar solution between the crystals in crystalline candies.

Figure 9.6
Crystalline candies soften slightly (due to the heat of crystallization) just before they solidify; this is the critical time to spread them quickly and thus avoid kneading.

saturated solution
Homogeneous mixture that has as much solute in solution as possible at that temperature.

supersaturated solution
Solution in which more solute is dissolved than theoretically can be dissolved; created by boiling a true solution to a high temperature and then cooling it very carefully.

co-crystallization   Addition of gum or other ingredient to a highly concentrated sugar solution just before beating very fast, a process that traps the second substance in a mass of microcrystals.

crystal aggregates. The mother liquor is the saturated sugar solution found between the sugar crystals throughout the candy. This liquid helps to soften a crumbly, overbeaten candy into a workable mass during kneading. Since the smallest sugar crystals in a candy are the ones most susceptible to being dissolved in the saturated mother liquor, crystalline candies gradually become grainy during prolonged storage.

Amorphous Candies

During the cooking of amorphous candies, water is evaporated until the correct concentration of sugar has been achieved. This is determined by the temperature of the boiling candy, which ranges from about 260° to 300°F (127°–149°C), depending upon the type of amorphous candy being prepared. As water is being evaporated, the sugar concentration is effectively increasing, with the result that the boiling point of the solution keeps rising. The effects of sugar on vapor pressure and the temperature of boiling are discussed in Chapter 4.

These candies become extremely viscous in the later stage of cooking, making it difficult to keep the candy in total contact with the thermometer. If air is trapped around the bulb, the reading will be inaccurately low, and overcooking to the point of scorching may occur. Scorching may also be a problem if amorphous candies are boiled in pans that heat unevenly; a heavy aluminum pan with a perfectly flat bottom provides uniform heat distribution to avoid possible burning of any portion of the candy. Careful stirring during the

---

SCIENCE NOTE
SATURATED AND SUPERSATURATED SOLUTIONS

In sugar cookery, sugar is a solute that is dissolved in a solvent (water or milk usually) to make a true solution. This is a true solution because it is homogeneous; that is, the content of samples taken from different portions of the mixture will all be the same. The ability of water to dissolve sugar varies with the temperature of the solution. This is quite apparent when making candy. At first, the solution is gritty no matter how much it is stirred because much of the sugar cannot be dissolved until the temperature rises. Gradually, the sugar all goes into solution, and the temperature of the boiling mixture starts to rise. This is now a **saturated solution**, which means that no more sugar can be dissolved in that amount of water at that temperature. However, the percentage of sugar in solution continues to rise in the boiling candy as the temperature rises and water evaporates. Throughout this boiling and evaporation period, the candy is a saturated solution, although the percentage of sugar in solution continues to increase until the final temperature is reached and the candy is removed from the heat.

Once the candy has been removed from the heat, the solution will begin to cool. This may seem to be perfectly natural, but in candy cookery, the cooling needs to be considered in relation to the sugar in the solution. Remember that less sugar should be in solution at a cooler temperature than could be dissolved in a saturated solution at the higher temperature reached during cooking. In other words, more sugar has been placed in solution by going to the higher final temperature than theoretically can be in solution as the candy cools. And yet, it is possible to keep this extra sugar in solution for quite a long time during the cooling period. By this careful cooling, a **supersaturated solution** is created, which means that more sugar is in solution than theoretically can be in solution at that temperature. The cooler the candy gets, the less stable the supersaturated solution becomes because

less and less sugar can be dissolved as the temperature drops. Ideally, a highly supersaturated state will be created.

If some nucleus is introduced into a supersaturated solution, the excess sugar in solution begins to crystallize and precipitate. The presence of a crystal of sugar, a piece of lint, or any other object can serve as the starting point for crystals of sugar to form. If this occurs when the candy has cooled only a little, there will be rapid crystallization of the small amount of dissolved sugar that should not have been in solution. Gradually, as the candy continues to cool, the extra sugar will continue to crystallize, adhering to the existing crystalline nucleus and creating a gritty texture even if beating is done continuously from the time the crystals start to form until the candy becomes solid.

In the ideal circumstance, a crystalline candy will cool to 110°F (43°C) before any crystals form, a condition creating an extremely unstable situation. If beating is started at this point, the large excess of dissolved sugar will start to crystallize almost simultaneously, and the candy will become a solid mass within a matter of a very few minutes. Crystal aggregates simply cannot grow large under this circumstance if beating is vigorous until the candy solidifies. This is the reason that careful cooling to create a highly supersaturated solution is so important to success in making smooth crystalline candies.

During the manufacturing of granulated sugar, it is possible to trigger instantaneous formation of crystals from a pure, highly concentrated sugar solution with extremely rapid beating; this procedure is called spontaneous crystallization. The result is extremely minuscule crystals. A second component (a gum or oil, for example) can be stirred with the sugar solution just prior to crystallization. The tiny sugar crystals entrap this second ingredient uniformly and promote a very smooth texture. This process is referred to as **co-crystallization**.

entire boiling period is an additional aid in making high-quality amorphous candies.

Amorphous candies are evaluated on the basis of their texture and flavor, characteristics that vary with the specific type of candy. Caramels should be wonderfully chewy, while taffy (Figure 9.7) can be pulled while cooling, but ordinarily is a bit too hard to bite once it cools; toffees and brittles break easily when hit with a knife handle. A particular amorphous candy is judged on whether or not it fits the expected chewiness or hardness for the specific candy being made. The flavor should not have any trace of scorching or burning and should be pleasingly rich and characteristic of the ingredients and flavorings used.

Commercially, candies are divided into three categories, according to their ingredients:

1. Candies made entirely of sugar with or without flavor and color (hard candies, creams, stick candies).
2. Candies containing at least 95 percent sugar and a maximum of 5 percent non-sugar ingredients (pectin jellies, marshmallows, nougats).
3. Candies with a minimum of 75 percent sugar, and between 5 and 25 percent non-sugar ingredients (fudge, caramels, starch jellies, chocolates).

Figure 9.7
Saltwater taffy is being pulled by machines that not only achieves the desired texture for the candy but also attracts customers to eat it.

The problems encountered in commercial confectionery are a composite of the problems encountered in making homemade candies, plus storage and shipping hazards. Some of these problems can be alleviated by the use of appropriate additives. For instance, glycerol and large quantities of corn syrup are helpful in maintaining moisture in candy and in retarding the development of a gritty texture in creams and mints. Various emulsifiers, including monoglycerides, are helpful in retarding staling and toughening of candies having a starch-gelled base.

Inversion to promote a mixture of sugars and a smooth crystalline candy is aided by adding cream of tartar in commercial candies. Invertase is a vital additive in softening cream centers after chocolates have been dipped.

CULTURAL ACCENT
TURKISH DELIGHT

Turkish delight, a national favorite of that country, is a unique gelatinous candy that many feel definitely deserves its name. Apparently this candy (also known as lokum) was developed for one of the Ottoman sultans because the sultan wanted a confection to delight wives in the harem. The chef tried many combinations of ingredients until he finally combined cornstarch with a gum (probably gum arabic), sugar, rose water, and various nuts. The result was an overwhelming success, and it continues to be a favorite in Turkey.

This candy has a gummy mouthfeel and is only moderately sweet, although it usually is coated lightly with confectioner's sugar. Rose water, a familiar aromatic ingredient in Middle Eastern cookery, provides a delicate, flowery flavor in the candy. Pistachios are ubiquitous in Turkey, so it is not surprising that Turkish delight made with pistachios is the favorite type of lokum.

For candies that are gels (orange slices, for example), gums are essential to form the gel. Most gums used in candy production are carbohydrates derived from seaweed, plant seeds, or tree exudates. The seaweed extracts, such as agar and Irish moss, have been used commercially for a long time, but often now are replaced in commercial candy-making by starch and pectin. Carrageenan (Irish moss) is used to prevent the "oiling off" that occurs in high-fat candies such as caramels, toffees, and nougats in hot weather. Two tree exudates, gum arabic and gum tragacanth, have the dual functions of preventing crystal growth and emulsifying fat to avoid fat separation in candies.

SUMMARY

Carbohydrates are important sources of energy in the diet, whether in the form of various sugars or starch; other complex carbohydrates are valued as roughage. In food preparation, the simple carbohydrates, the sugars, are used as sweeteners to add to the pleasure of eating. The word *carbohydrate* is etymologically derived from the fact that, chemically, all compounds in this class are hydrates of carbon.

Among the many sweeteners available to consumers today, the various types of cane and beet sugars are used in by far the greatest quantity, with granulated sugar being the most common form selected. Dessert sugar and powdered or confectioner's sugar are other refined sweeteners, the latter having cornstarch added to it to keep the fine powder from lumping. Raw sugar, a partially refined sugar, is nutritionally comparable to refined sugar and is more expensive. Light and dark brown sugars contain impurities that alter their color and flavor. Maple syrup and sugar have unique flavors attributable to the impurities in the maple sap from which they are made. Molasses is another distinctive sweetener and is the by-product, either sulfured or unsulfured, resulting from the processing of cane sugar.

Corn syrup is made from cornstarch by hydrolysis. A variation produced from corn syrup is high-fructose corn syrup, the result of the action of isomerase (an enzyme) on the sugars in corn syrup. Honey also is a fluid sweetener, this one being naturally high in fructose. The distinctive flavor of honey varies with the source of the nectar the bees collect, but all types result in very rapid browning in baked products.

Saccharin is a non-nutritive sweetener used by many to avoid calories from sugar and by diabetics as a means of limiting sugar intake. The bitter aftertaste is objectionable to some people. Aspartame, a dipeptide, is a low-calorie sweetener. Its intense sweetness means only small amounts of aspartame are needed to sweeten a beverage or other food item.

Sucralose (Splenda®) is a sweetener derived from dairy products, which qualified it to be approved as GRAS (generally recognized as safe). Acesulfame-K (Sweet One®, Sunette®), Tagatose (Gaio®), and FOS are other sweeteners.

Sugars are classified as monosaccharides and disaccharides, with the disaccharides being made up of two units of the monosaccharides. Glucose, fructose, and galactose (all hexoses) are the common monosaccharides; these are combined in various ways to form sucrose (table sugar), maltose, and lactose (milk sugar).

Sucrose, the sugar commonly used in cookery for sweetening, tenderizing, browning of baked products, and other purposes, undergoes a severe chemical breakdown when it is heated to very high temperatures. This process, called caramelization, results in the formation of many different compounds, including organic acids. Hydrolysis is a less severe reaction and results in the formation of an equal mixture of two sugars (glucose and fructose); the mixture is called invert sugar.

The two types of candies are crystalline and amorphous, the difference being that crystalline candies have organized crystals of sugar throughout, while amorphous candies are completely disorganized and range from chewy to very hard. The type of candy, whether crystalline or amorphous, is determined in large measure by the final cooking temperature; crystalline candies are cooked to lower temperatures than amorphous candies. The lower temperature of crystalline candies means that the concentration of sugar is somewhat lower, a difference that enables the sugar crystals to form an organized network in the cooling, fairly viscous crystalline candies.

Amorphous candies should be the correct texture for the type of candy (ranging from chewy caramels to brittle toffees) and should not have any trace of scorching, the most common problem in their preparation. In contrast, crystalline candies are evaluated on the basis of being firm yet soft enough to bite easily and having a velvety smooth texture. This texture is the result of achieving a highly supersaturated solution and then beating adequately until the structure sets. Commercial candies are categorized according to the percentage of sugar they contain. Many of these have various additives to enhance the quality of the candy when it reaches consumers.

STUDY QUESTIONS

1. What is the result of a very slow rate of heating on a crystalline candy? Explain the reaction that occurs.
2. What influence does the amount of beating have on a crystalline candy?
3. Does the time of initiation of beating influence the quality of a crystalline candy? Explain.
4. Explain the purpose and action when each of the following ingredients is added to a basic fondant recipe: cream of tartar, corn syrup, chocolate, butter. Explain the action of each.
5. Why does the temperature of boiling candy rise gradually?

SELECTED REFERENCES

Awad, A., and A. C. Chen. 1993. New generation of sucrose products made by co-crystallization. *Food Technol.* 47(1): 146.

Berry, D. 2008. Low-cal sweet tooth satisfaction. *Food Product Design* 18(9): 24.

Berry, D. 2010. Coloring confections. *Food Product Design* 20(7): 38.

Chinachoti, P. 1993. Water mobility and its relation to functionality of sucrose-containing food systems. *Food Technol.* 47(1): 134.

Clark, J. P. 2004. Crystallization is key in confectionery processes. *Food Technol.* 58(12): 94.

Clark, P. J. 2007. Lessons from chocolate processing. *Food Technol.* 61(12): 89.

Clemens, R., and P. Pressmann. 2007. HFCS—A sticky matter. *Food Technol.* 61(12): 19.

Dea, P. 2004. Chewy confections. *Food Product Design* 14(6): 63.

Dea, P. 2004. Sweet success: Nutty confections. *Food Product Design* 13(11): 62.

Dea, P. 2005. Secrets of chocolate and confectionery coatings. *Food Product Design* 15(9): 80.

Decker, K. H. 2009. A little chocolate luxury. *Food Product Design* 19(5): 26.

Decker, K. J. 2010. Grown-up confections. *Food Product Design* 20(9): 32.

Deis, R. C. 2009. Seamlessly sugar-free sweets. *Food Product Design* 19(6): 50.

Deis, R. C. 2005. How sweet it is—Using polyols and high-potency sweeteners. *Food Product Design* 15(7): 57.

Hartel, R. W. 1993. Controlling sugar crystallization in food products. *Food Technol.* 47(11): 99.

Hollingsworth, P. 2002. Artificial sweeteners face sweet 'n sour consumer market. *Food Technol.* 56(7): 24–27.

Kuntz, L. A. 2010. Stevia's sweet story. *Food Product Design* 20(6): 16.

McQuate, R. S., and R. C. Kraska. 2009. Where are stevia-derived sweeteners headed? *Food Product Design* 19(4): 18.

Nabors, L. O. 2002. Sweet choices: Sugar replacements for foods and beverages. *Food Technol.* 56(7): 28–34.

Nabors, L. O. 2007. Regulatory status of alternative sweeteners. *Food Technol.* 61(2): 24.

Natchay, K. 2010. Thinking outside the box of chocolates. *Food Technol.* 64(12): 22.

Palmer, S. 2004. Sweetening power of polyols. *Food Product Design* 14(2): 30.

Prakash, I., et al. 2002. Neotame: Next-generation sweetener. *Food Technol.* 56(7): 36–40.

Pszczola, D. E. 2004. Confection: Sweet acronym. *Food Technol.* 58(10): 50.

Spiegel, J. E., et al. 1994. Safety and benefits of fructooligosaccharides as food ingredients. *Food Technol.* 48(1): 85.

Taylor, T. P., et al. 2008. Physical properties and consumer liking of cookies prepared by replacing sucrose with tagatose. *J. Food Sci.* 73(3): S145–S151.

Tragash, K., and Y. Tomiyama. 2005. Aspartame revisited. *Food Product Design* 15(7): 73.

Turner, J. 2003. Honey of an option. *Food Product Design* 13(4): 14.

Wallace, T. C., et al. 2009. Unlocking the benefits of cocoa flavanols. *Food Technol.* 63(10): 34.

Barley and oats are two cereal crops that produce grains with a high starch content. Courtesy of Agricultural Research Service.

10

Carbohydrates: Starches and Cereals

Key Concepts

1. Starch is a plant polysaccharide that can undergo chemical and physical changes during food preparation to alter physical characteristics of foods.
2. Gelatinization of starch in the presence of water and heat causes starch mixtures to thicken (e.g., cream sauces, soups).
3. Gelatinized starch mixtures can form gels (e.g., starch-thickened puddings) by a process called gelation.
4. Cereals are high in starch, which needs to be gelatinized by heating with water.

STARCH, A KEY POLYSACCHARIDE

Starch, the form in which plants store energy, is a carbohydrate that is classified as a polysaccharide. Although it is made up of long chains of glucose units linked to very large molecules, it surprisingly lacks the sweet taste of glucose. The importance of starch in food preparation is due to its unique ability to swell and thicken food mixtures when heated with water. Despite their very different properties, glucose and starch contribute the same energy (4 kilocalories per gram).

Sources

Cereals are rich sources of starch. Those used as commercial sources include corn, wheat, waxy corn, and rice; cornstarch is a particularly common starch, but flour (which contains wheat starch) often is used in the home when making gravy and sauces (Figure 10.1). **Tapioca**, potato, and arrowroot are familiar starches obtained from the roots or tubers of plants (Figure 10.2). Less familiar to consumers is sago, a tree starch from the pith of the sago palm.

    Whether from cereal, root (Figure 10.3), or tree, each type of starch behaves uniquely when used to prepare various food products. This is not surprising, because each looks quite different when viewed under a microscope. For example, potato starch is very large and fairly round, and rice starch is quite angular and tiny.

starch Complex carbohydrate (polysaccharide) made of glucose units; valued as a thickening agent.

tapioca Starch from the root of cassava (also called manioc).

http://www. nationalstarch.com/ Pages/home.aspx

—National Starch and Chemical Company website.

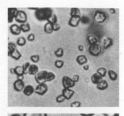
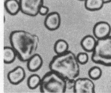
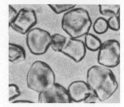
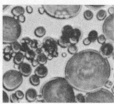

Figure 10.1
Cereal starches (top to bottom) are rice, corn, waxy corn, and wheat (500x). Courtesy of Plycon Press.

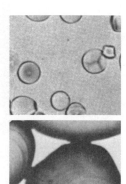

Figure 10.2
Root starches include tapioca (top) and potato (500x). Courtesy of Plycon Press.

Starch in Food Preparation

Starch functions as a thickening agent in many sauces, soups, gravies, puddings, pie fillings, and other foods. The **rheology** (study of flow properties) of such foods as sauces and soups is important to palatability. The appropriate characteristics for a particular product can be acquired by selecting the starch that will take up water during heating to create the desired flow and mouthfeel. If the correct amount of that starch is used, the food will thicken to the appropriate viscosity during cooking.

In some starch-containing foods, the first step is thickening, which is achieved by heating to gelatinize the starch. Subsequently, cooling can transform the thickened paste (sol) into an apparent solid (gel). Starch-thickened puddings and cream pies are foods that take advantage of these physical transitions that can occur when starch is an ingredient. Another example of starch taking up water and then forming a gel when cool can be seen in baked products; starch in wheat flour is responsible for binding some of the liquid to help transform cake batter into a baked cake with a firm, yet tender structure.

Heat alters the behavior of starch. The presence of water is critical in determining what type of change occurs when starch is heated. If starch is heated to a high temperature without water, a chemical change (dextrinization) occurs and alters its physical properties. However, only a physical change (gelatinization) takes place when starch is heated with water; chemical change does not occur. The significance of these changes when preparing foods containing starch is discussed in more detail in the following sections.

Dextrinization

Sometimes starch (usually flour) is heated alone in a heavy skillet to develop browned flour for preparing a brown sauce or gravy. This same browning occurs on the surface of a piece of bread when it is toasted. When starch is subjected to dry heat, it will undergo **dextrinization**, a chemical change. The large molecules of starch are broken into shorter chains of glucose units called **dextrins**. Dextrins are more soluble than starch, and they have less thickening ability. This chemical change is illustrated when gravy is made using browned flour; more browned flour is required to thicken that gravy than is needed if regular flour is used.

Gelatinization

At various temperatures, starch dispersed in water will exhibit different characteristics. In cold water, a limited amount of swelling will occur, but for the most part, starch in cold water can be maintained in suspension only by stirring. The root starches are somewhat more soluble in cold water and will swell a bit more than the cereal starches without applying heat.

Figure 10.3
Cassava roots, the source of tapioca starch, are arranged directly beyond the sweet potatoes the vendor is bagging at an outdoor market in Kenya. Courtesy of Plycon Press.

For starch to serve as an effective thickening agent, both adequate heat and water must be present. If either the heat or the water is missing, thickening will not occur. This thickening action of starch is the result of a process called gelatinization. Gelatinization occurs as water is gradually absorbed into starch granules in the presence of adequate heat. Although this sounds quite simple, unattractive lumps form readily unless the starch is dispersed thoroughly and gelatinization is done with careful control of heating and stirring.

The first step is the complete dispersion of the starch granules in water. Three different procedures can be used to thoroughly distribute the starch:

1. Mixing the starch with cold water to make a smooth slurry (thin paste).
2. Mixing the starch with oil or melted fat to make a smooth paste.
3. Combining the starch with a fairly large quantity of another dry ingredient before adding liquid.

Notice that in each of these techniques, the requirements of both water and heat are not satisfied. Consequently, the gelatinization process does not begin during this period, and mixing can be accomplished without lumps forming.

Once the ingredients have been combined smoothly, the mixture is heated to gelatinize the starch and thicken the product. Stirring is essential when gelatinizing starch. Without adequate stirring, the temperature will vary from one part of the mixture to another, and the hottest areas will have gelatinized starch granules, which are thicker than the other areas and will form lumps in the product.

During gelatinization, some of the water in the product will be absorbed into the individual starch granules and held there tightly, actually becoming bound water (Figure 10.4). Bound water no longer is able to flow; the water that is bound in the granules causes the granules themselves to swell significantly. It is the combination of less free water actually available in the system and the physically swollen starch granules that is responsible for the very obvious thickening that occurs during gelatinization of starches.

As the starch mixture thickens during gelatinization, there is an increase in the translucency of the system, a clear change from the milky, opaque quality of ungelatinized starch suspensions. This change in translucency is caused by the solution of some of the portions of crystalline structure within the granules and the loss of some of the amylose from the granule

rheology Study of flow properties of matter.

dextrinization Chemical breakdown of starch to shorter chains of glucose when starch is subjected to intense dry heat.

dextrin Polysaccharide made of glucose units; smaller and more soluble than starch and with reduced thickening ability.

amylose Linear starch fraction (1,4-α-glucosidic linkages) that is somewhat soluble in water and capable of forming gels.

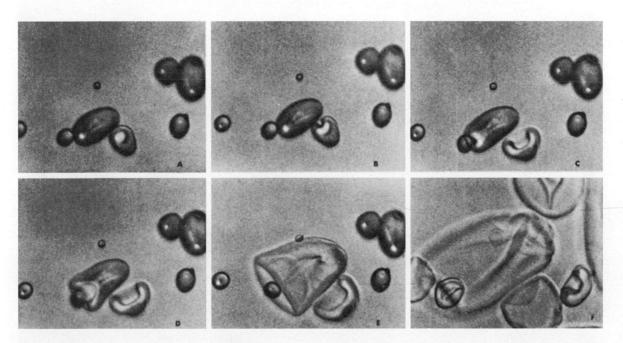

Figure 10.4
Potato starch gelatinization between initial swelling (a) and complete swelling (f). Note the change in size and translucency. Courtesy of Plycon Press.

amylose: can form gel linear

amylopectin cant form gel linear – then branches

SCIENCE NOTE
A CHEMICAL AND PHYSICAL PORTRAIT

Starch is a very short word representing the complex polysaccharide in plants that can cause thickening when heated in water. However, this is not a very specific term. Chemists have differentiated between two components of starch—**amylose** and **amylopectin.** These two carbohydrates are both made up of glucose as the single building unit, but amylose is basically a linear molecule in which the glucose units are linked by an alpha (α)-glucosidic linkage between the first carbon of one glucose and the fourth of the next unit. This linearity is important, for it permits

amylose molecules to escape from the starch granule by dissolving to an extent in the water. It also makes it possible for amylose molecules to cross-link to each other in fairly low-energy systems to form gels. The structure for amylose is shown, in part, below. Actually, there are probably more than 600 glucose units in a single molecule of amylose.

The other starch fraction, amylopectin, has many portions in which the glucose units are linked by the same 1,4-α-glucosidic linkage seen in amylose. However, after 20 to 25 units arranged linearly, a 1,6-α-glucosidic linkage occurs. It is this linkage to the carbon outside the ring structure that causes a branching in the amylopectin molecules, giving them a bulky structure. As a consequence, amylopectin molecules are rather insoluble and do not link together readily to form gels. The smallest of the amylopectin molecules probably contains at least 1000 glucose units, and complex ones are as large as 1500 glucose units. The structure has many branch points, a portion of the molecule being shown below.

Amylose

Amylopectin

Starch granules are the organized units in which starch—actually, amylose and amylopectin—molecules are deposited in the leucoplasts in plants. The shape of the granules varies with the type of plant (refer back to Figures 10.1 and 10.2), but the basic features are the same in all starch granules. The most common ratio of amylose to amylopectin is about one molecule of amylose to four amylopectin molecules, but this varies.

The molecules are arranged in concentric spheres, much like the organization of a child's toy in which a ball is contained within a ball within a ball, and so forth, until finally

the central, very tiny ball is reached. However, the layers of the granule are composed of regions where amylose molecules are aligned quite neatly, creating some crystalline areas, while the amylopectin molecules are random in their associations. All of the molecules are held to each other in the concentric layers by hydrogen bonds. There is no skin or other protective coating surrounding the assembled granule. It is this granule that can be gelatinized.

With this picture in mind, gelatinization can be visualized and appreciated. The heat being applied during gelatinization increases the energy in the system. The energy causes some of the hydrogen bonds to break within the granule, thus allowing some water to move into the voids created. This water keeps moving in toward the center of the granule as continuing heating breaks more and more of the hydrogen bonds responsible for the original, rather tight granular structure. The solution of some of the freed amylose molecules causes them to begin to leave the granule, but the water continues to enter the granule and to be bound there.

As more and more water enters, the granule gets larger and larger, but the density of the starch molecules within the granule is reduced due to the dilution by the water. This causes the desired thickening, but it also makes the swollen granules somewhat susceptible to damage when the gelatinizing mixture is being stirred because of the potential distances between amylose and amylopectin molecules within the granules. This disruption of the somewhat crystalline areas of amylose within the starch granule and the reduced density within the granule both contribute to the increased translucency noted in gelatinized starches.

When gelatinization has been completed, the system is a sol in which the starch granules and amylose are the discontinuous phase and the liquid is the continuous phase. The viscosity of this starch sol (often called a hot starch paste) is influenced by several factors, one of the most important being temperature.

When a starch paste is hot, the system contains a considerable amount of energy, and the amylose molecules outside the granules move about within the total system. However, the system loses energy as the sol begins to cool. The result is slower and slower movement of the solids in the sol. Gradually, hydrogen bonds will begin to form between the various amylose molecules outside the granules, making a random network in which the swollen starch granules become enmeshed. The ultimate result is that a continuous network of the solid develops, and the liquid becomes the discontinuous or dispersed phase. In other words, the system becomes just the opposite of the sol that was formed originally. The new colloidal system is a gel.

into the surrounding water. In fact, one way of telling when gelatinization is completed is the translucent quality. However, there is a considerable variation in this characteristic, depending on the type of starch being gelatinized. The root starches (e.g., potato) are more translucent than cereal starches such as corn (Figure 10.5). Flour, which is often gelatinized in cookery, remains opaque even when gelatinization is completed; the protein in the flour continues to block the transmission of light through the starch paste, even when the starch itself is altered enough to let light pass through.

Factors Influencing Properties

The type of starch undergoing gelatinization influences the properties of a starch system. One of the differences is the amount of water that can be absorbed into the starch granule before it ruptures. Ruptured starch granules are undesirable because they can create a somewhat gummy mouthfeel. Cereal starches have a limited ability to absorb water compared with root starches. Corn and wheat starch granules will rupture when the equivalent of about 40 percent of their weight in water has been absorbed; that is, rupturing is likely to occur if 100 grams of either of these starches absorbs 40 grams of water. Remarkably, potato starch can absorb considerably more water (as much as 100 grams of water per 100 grams of starch) before the granules disintegrate.

The temperature range over which gelatinization occurs also varies with the type of starch. Root starches begin to swell at about 150°–160°F (65.6°–71.1°C), and gelatinization is completed at temperatures well below boiling, forming quite clear pastes. In fact, root starches will tend to disintegrate when they are heated to temperatures just below boiling. However, cereal starches are quite resistant to water penetration in the early phases of gelatinization, and these types of starch must be heated to temperatures ranging from 200 to 212°F (93.3°–100°C) for gelatinization to be completed. Even when gelatinization has been finished, cereal starches will be less translucent than root starches. These characteristics are summarized in Table 10.1.

Several factors determine the viscosity of starch sols and gels:

1. Concentration of starch
2. Type of starch
3. Extent of gelatinization
4. Addition of acid or sugar
5. Thoroughness of the dispersion of the starch

amylopectin The rather insoluble fraction of starch; contains both 1,4- and 1,6-α-glucosidic linkages, resulting in a bulky, branching molecule that does not form a gel.

starch granule Units of starch (usually consisting of about 20 percent amylose and 80 percent amylopectin) deposited in concentric layers within the leucoplasts in plant cells.

www.iowacorn.org
—Iowa Corn Growers website.

Figure 10.5
Cornstarch is a cereal starch that often is used to thicken a cherry pie filling or other product where translucency is important to the finished product. Courtesy of Plycon Press.

The concentration of starch is very important in determining the viscosity of starch-containing products. The higher the ratio of starch to liquid, the thicker the product will be. Thinner starch pastes result when either the starch content is decreased or the liquid is increased. Conversely, to make a thicker soup or sauce, the starch must be increased or the liquid decreased (Figure 10.6).

The type of starch used in thickening products also influences the viscosity of the gelatinized mixture. Substitution of root starches for cereal starches results in more tender gels than those produced with rice starch. Therefore, tapioca and arrowroot starches will need to be used in increased quantities if they are to be substituted for cereal starches.

There is not only a distinct difference between the thickening ability of the more-effective cereal starches and the less-effective root starches, but there also are differences within the groups. Rice starch has less thickening ability than cornstarch or arrowroot starch. Wheat flour has only about half as much thickening ability as cornstarch, a reflection of the difference in the thickening ability of wheat versus cornstarch and also the replacement of starch by some protein in the flour, which means that flour actually has less starch per measure than cornstarch has. If

TABLE 10.1
COMMONLY USED STARCHES AND THEIR CHARACTERISTICS

Starch	Type	Relative Thickening Ability	Characteristics of the Paste
Cornstarch	Cereal	Great	Optimum thickening by heating to 200°–212°F (93.3°–100°C); moderately translucent
Flour[a]	Cereal	Half as great as cornstarch	Optimum thickening by heating to 200°–212°F (93.3°–100°C); more opaque than cornstarch
Rice starch	Cereal	Moderate	Optimum thickening by heating to 200°–212°F (93.3°–100°C); moderately translucent
Potato starch	Tuber	Less than cornstarch	Optimum thickening by heating to 190°F (87.8°C); thins when boiled; tendency to become gummy; quite translucent
Tapioca	Root	Less than cornstarch	Optimum thickening by heating to 160°F (71.1°C); thins when boiled; tendency to become gummy; quite translucent
Arrowroot	Root	Less than tapioca	Optimum thickening by heating to 175°F (79.4°C), thins when boiled; tendency to become gummy; quite translucent

[a]Contains wheat starch and protein.

flour is to be substituted for cornstarch in a recipe, the measure of flour should be increased to twice the amount of cornstarch indicated. Conversely, half as much cornstarch can replace the amount of flour indicated as the thickening agent in a recipe. For people watching calories, this may be a useful substitution (Figure 10.7).

The final temperature to which a starch paste is heated has an important influence on viscosity. To obtain maximum thickening from any specific starch, the starch sol must be heated to a high enough temperature to ensure complete gelatinization. For the cereal starches, this means approaching boiling. However, the root starches require less severe heat treatment. In fact, tapioca and arrowroot starches reach maximum viscosity at a comparatively low temperature (see Table 10.1) and will actually begin to thin as the mixture approaches boiling.

Many cookbooks suggest cooking a starch mixture in a double boiler over boiling water, but this arrangement requires a considerable amount of time to bring the starch mixture to a high enough temperature for maximum gelatinization of cereal starches. At high elevations, it is physically impossible to heat the starch mixture to a high enough temperature using a double boiler. Cereal starches can be heated fairly quickly to achieve maximum gelatinization over moderate direct heat; a double boiler is helpful in avoiding overheating root starch products.

If starch mixtures also have eggs as a thickening agent, the starch should be gelatinized first just by heating to the boiling point. Then the protein should be added carefully and the entire mixture heated over boiling water just enough to coagulate the protein.

Figure 10.6
Cream of potato soup recipes may be thickened to the desired consistency by using cornstarch or flour, but less is needed than in other cream soups because the potatoes slough off some starch, which also increases viscosity. Courtesy of Plycon Press.

Figure 10.7
Cream of mushroom soup can be thickened with flour because milk in the soup causes the soup to be opaque regardless of the type of starch chosen.
Courtesy of Plycon Press.

syneresis Separation of liquid from a gel.

Sugar has a significant effect on several aspects of gelatinized starch products, including a tenderizing effect on the starch gel. The very hygroscopic nature of sugar enables it to compete with starch for the water in the recipe; in other words, less water will be available to aid in gelatinizing the starch as the sugar level is increased. Because of this competition for water, sugar in starch mixtures causes the following changes:

1. The temperatures at which the initial swelling and maximum swelling occur are higher for the sugar–starch mixture than for a starch product without sugar.
2. The maximum viscosity of the starch paste is reduced when sugar is present because the sugar competes for the water and reduces the uptake of water into the starch granules.
3. Less disintegration of starch grains occurs when sugar is present because there is less swelling of the granules.
4. The resulting gel is less rigid because less amylose is released into the liquid to form the gel network when sugar is present.
5. **Syneresis**, the loss of liquid from the gel, is increased as the level of sugar in the starch product increases.
6. Increased sugar increases translucency.

If the concentration of sugar exceeds 20 percent by weight in the product, the foregoing effects are quite pronounced.

Lumping in a gelatinizing starch mixture can be the cause of reduced viscosity in the product because there will be dry starch granules trapped inside the lumps. Since these dry granules cannot obtain water for gelatinization, they will remain in their original, ungelatinized state. In effect, lumpy starch products contain less gelatinized starch to thicken the paste than they were expected to contain. Aside from the detrimental characteristic of being a little too thin, lumpy products are unattractive in appearance and do not have a good mouthfeel. These are all important reasons for following one or more of the procedures described earlier for dispersing the starch with the other ingredients.

acid hydrolysis Cleavage of a molecule by utilizing a molecule of water in the presence of an acid, which serves as a catalyst.

The addition of acid prior to heating a starch mixture causes a thinning of the product during gelatinization due to **acid hydrolysis** of some of the starch. This is why, when preparing such acid-containing gelatinized starch products as Harvard beets or lemon meringue pie filling, the starch should be gelatinized before adding the acid. The lemon juice or vinegar can be stirred in following gelatinization without having a significant amount of acid hydrolysis to occur.

Reduced thickening ability also occurs when flour is dextrinized or browned; the darker the flour has been browned, the less is the thickening ability of the browned flour. A practical solution to the reduced thickening ability is to add some non-dextrinized flour to augment the thickening ability of the browned product and achieve the desired viscosity in a brown sauce.

Starch Gels

gelation Formation of a gel, a colloidal dispersion in which the solid forms a continuous phase and liquid forms the discontinuous or dispersed phase.

Gelation   Most gelatinized starch pastes lose their ability to flow when they become cool. This formation of a gel is called **gelation**, a term unfortunately similar to *gelatinization,* yet meaning something very different. To avoid possible confusion, this change in colloidal state is often referred to simply as *gel formation*. In the preparation of cream pie fillings and in puddings and some other desserts, starch is the ingredient used to achieve the desired firmness. These products are expected to hold their shape and not flow, yet they are supposed to be sufficiently tender to sag just a bit or to bulge out very slightly when cut, without actually moving at the base of the

SCIENCE NOTE
CHEMICAL DEGRADATION

The linkages between the glucose units comprising starch molecules are covalent bonds, but they still are susceptible to cleavage by acid or intense dry heat. When starch is being gelatinized, the presence of acid results in some acid hydrolysis of the molecules, particularly of the amylose molecules released from the swelling granules. The reaction involves the uptake of a molecule of water to form hydroxyl groups on the carbon atoms involved in this reaction. The result is two fragments, each of which is shorter than the original molecule. These fragments are more soluble and have less thickening ability than the original, longer chain molecule. In prolonged heating, this reaction can be repeated many times to produce quite short fragments. The reaction of hydrolysis is:

Dextrinization is another means of degrading starch molecules. In this process, dry starch is heated to temperatures well above the boiling temperature possible when water is the cooking medium. This intense energy from the heat enables some of the linkages between glucose units in starch molecules to split, with the uptake of a molecule of water. This water is available from the very limited moisture content naturally present in flour and other starch-containing foods. In effect, the chemical change occurring during dextrinization results in the same type of products that are liberated in acid hydrolysis, and the actual reaction involves the formation of a hydroxyl group on each carbon involved in the linkage between glucose units, just as is shown in the

$$\text{starch chain} \xrightarrow[\text{acid}]{+ \text{HOH}} \text{fragments}$$

above reaction. The difference between the two reactions is the amount of energy required: Without acid as a catalyst, a great deal of energy is required, which is provided by heat in the dextrinization process.

cut (Figure 10.8). Too much starch causes such a stiff texture that the pie or other product will remain absolutely rigid when cut, rather than bulge. It also will have an excessively firm mouthfeel. Conversely, too little starch, too much sugar, lumping, or acid hydrolysis can cause a product to be too thin to serve easily.

Not all gelatinized starch systems will undergo gelation. For this transition to a gel to occur, there must be a sufficient concentration of gelatinized starch, with a reasonable amount of free amylose molecules. Without the free amylose, the necessary interlocking structure will not form. Also, if there has been too much hydrolysis of the amylose molecules, the molecular strands will be too short to form an entrapping network, and the gelatinized system will remain a sol.

Syneresis Gels appear to be solids, with little propensity for change, but in fact the amylose network is held in place by hydrogen bonds between molecules. These bonds are constantly breaking and reforming, resulting in molecular movement within the gel. The liquid (the dispersed phase) in the gel is trapped within the interstices of the amylose network. However, the constant rearranging of the amylose provides opportunity for liquid to escape from the gel. This draining of liquid from a gel is called syneresis. By cutting through a starch gel, many trapped pockets of liquid will be revealed, and syneresis will slowly begin to be noticeable.

Retrogradation When starch gels are established, they will undergo a gradual change called **retrogradation**. This change occurs as hydrogen bonds between amylose molecules break and the molecules rearrange themselves; subsequently, new bonds form and enmesh molecules and granules. The tendency is to group closer and closer together in a somewhat organized, crystalline relationship. This crystalline aggregation that develops during retrogradation is perceived as a gritty texture. The somewhat tougher, slightly crisper texture that gradually develops as bread ages is an example of retrogradation.

Retrograded starch is resistant to digestion in the small intestine and acts as dietary fiber when foods containing it are eaten cold. The starch in cold cooked potatoes and legumes is a source of resistant starch classified as RS3,

retrogradation Formation of crystalline aggregates in a gelatinized starch product during storage.

Figure 10.8
The base of this dessert is blancmange (vanilla pudding), which has been thickened with cornstarch. Note that the pudding shows a slight softening without flowing, the mark of the desired consistency.
Courtesy of Plycon Press.

which makes them a source of dietary fiber if eaten cold. However, their starch content becomes digestible if they are eaten while warm or hot.

Retrogradation is a reversible process. Simply by heating the starch gel, the hydrogen bonds will begin to break, allowing the amylose to move freely once again. However, the crystalline areas will form again upon cooling. The formation of crystalline areas in bread is noted in stale bread, which becomes seemingly fresh and soft again when heated. Another example is gravy or a white sauce that has been stored in the refrigerator. The retrograded starch sauce will lose its crystalline character when reheated.

Starch Products

waxy starches Starches from plants bred to produce a starch that is virtually all amylopectin and is free of amylose; valued for use in products where a gel is not desirable.

Special Starches Selective breeding is being done to produce new varieties of starch-yielding plants with the desired physical characteristics. A particularly important product has been the development of strains of plants that produce starches containing almost no amylose. These starches, which are almost 100 percent amylopectin, are called **waxy starches**. Amioca, also called waxy cornstarch, is the result of genetic research aimed at providing useful variations in starch. Waxy starches are valued because they will thicken but will not form a gel, due to the absence of amylose. This type of starch sol is ideal for commercial fruit pie fillings, as well as in some salad dressings and instant puddings.

In low concentrations, waxy starches produce pastes comparable in viscosity to pastes made with potato starch; however in high concentrations and with longer cooking, the paste from amioca will be slightly thicker than tapioca and distinctly less viscous than a comparable potato starch paste. A nice feature of waxy starches is that they do not form a scum or skin on top because there is no amylose present to retrograde on the surface.

edible starch films Films made from special starches containing about 80 percent amylose.

Edible starch films are gaining in interest, partially as a novelty and partly because of their utility. Geneticists in 1957 developed a corn that deposited starch with about 20 percent amylopectin and 80 percent amylose, a ratio just about the reverse of regular cornstarch. The interesting feature of this special starch is that the increased concentration of amylose makes it possible to produce thin, edible films of this starch when it has been gelatinized. Edible starch films can be used in such applications as wrappers for candies; these chewable and digestible wrappers can be consumed along with the candy. Japanese candies wrapped in rice paper are familiar examples of this application of high-amylose starch products. Casings for meat products and soluble packets for foods to be boiled are other possible applications.

Pregelatinized Starches The first of the treated starch products was Minute® rice, a product of five years of research, which was first marketed in 1946. This product is cooked to gelatinize the starch until the process is about 60 percent complete and then is dried. Minute® tapioca is another pregelatinized starch product. Instant puddings and instant mashed potatoes are other examples of the types of special precooked starch products on the market. These products require rehydration before being served, but they do not need the boiling or other heating ordinarily required to gelatinize the starch.

Frozen Products   Consumers who want desserts but who are pressed for time to make them have created a market for frozen cream pies. These are ready to serve after they have been removed from the freezer and allowed to thaw. Because these desserts are not reheated or stirred before serving, stability of the gel structure after freezing and thawing is a major factor in assessing palatability. Retrogradation of the starch gel may impart a detectable grittiness; syneresis may lead to a soggy crust.

A crunchy candy can be made by gelatinizing a 5 percent starch paste, cooking, and then freezing it to produce a fragile starch sponge that can be dipped in chocolate.

Some frozen puddings and pie fillings are made using waxy rice flour as a replacement for egg and cornstarch thickeners. Use of waxy rice flour in frozen commercial puddings causes the thawed product to have a desirable consistency, with little syneresis compared with similar products made with other starches. Puddings made with waxy rice flour (sometimes called glutinous rice flour) can be stored at 0°F (−18°C) for up to nine months and still have satisfactory characteristics when thawed. The chief objection to waxy rice flour is the raw starch flavor that persists.

Modified Starches   Another approach to producing frozen starch-thickened products is to use a starch with phosphate cross-linkages. Phosphate or acetyl can be esterified on the carbon atoms external to the rings of glucose comprising the starch molecules. This arrangement helps to minimize the tendency to retrograde and to exhibit syneresis. These cross-linked starches with their esters are sometimes called **stabilized** or **modified starches**.

One complaint about starch-thickened products is the pasty or stringy quality that occurs sometimes due to fragile starch granules. Various phosphorus-containing compounds (metaphosphate, for example) can be used to cross-link starch molecules within the uncooked starch granules. This change in the chemical nature of the granules results in resistance to rupturing during the gelatinization process, which reduces the pasty quality of the gelatinized product. These **cross-linked starches** have undergone less processing than the stabilized starches, for they do not undergo sufficient treatment to form the ester linkages typical of the stabilized starches.

Thin-boiling starches are useful in some commercial applications, such as making gumdrops, where their thin, fluid nature allows the gelatinized starch to be poured easily. However, these starches form desirably stiff gels when cooled after gelatinization. These unique starches are made by allowing limited acid hydrolysis to occur when the raw starch is heated gently in a dilute acid.

Resistant starches are unique starches that resist digestion by **carbohydrases** in the small intestine, thus providing some fiber and little energy when they are eaten. Such starches are of particular interest to food manufacturers today as they work to develop products that are reduced in calories. Some resistant starch is contained naturally in legumes, seeds, and grains that have been milled only partially. Producers of some ready-to-eat cereals are including resistant starches as ingredients because they can be marketed for their health-promoting qualities.

stabilized (modified) starches   Starches resistant to retrogradation and syneresis because of formation of phosphate or acetyl esters of starch; often called modified starches.

cross-linked starches   Starches treated with various phosphate compounds prior to gelatinization to reduce rupturing of the starch granule.

resistant starch   Starch that passes out of the small intestine without being digested.

carbohydrase   General term for enzyme that catalyzes the digestion of carbohydrate.

http://www.resistantstarch. com/ResistantStarch/

—Information on resistant starch and Hi-maize.

INGREDIENT HIGHLIGHT
HI-MAIZE® RESISTANT STARCH

Corn has been bred to produce plants that carry desired variations, some of which increase crop yields and some that modify specific characteristics. Hi-maize, a high-amylose cornstarch, is a resistant starch that has become available through this type of research. It is of interest from a nutrition perspective; it is a starch classified as RS2 and is a source of dietary fiber.

Although it is a starch, its high amylose content reduces its ability to thicken a sauce during heating. However, it can be incorporated to replace as much as a fourth of the flour in bread and other baked products. This substitution reduces calories a little because the reduced digestibility means that people actually derive between two and three calories per gram of the starch versus four calories that flour would have provided. In addition, the added fiber helps promote motility.

Figure 10.9
Cheese sauce (a medium white sauce and a tasty cheese) can add color and flavor appeal to broccoli and other vegetables. Courtesy of Plycon Press.

STARCH COOKERY

White Sauces

Starch-thickened sauces are used widely in cooking, and the ability to prepare a smooth sauce of the appropriate viscosity for the desired end use is key to making such diverse products as soufflés and cream soups (Figure 10.9). Basic white sauces and their variations can be prepared successfully if certain basic knowledge has been acquired. One of the key pieces of information is the appropriate viscosity of white sauce for different applications. The four viscosities of white sauces and their suggested uses are

1. Thin sauce: cream soups.
2. Medium sauce: creamed vegetables, cheese sauce, and gravy.
3. Thick sauce: soufflés.
4. Very thick sauce: binding agent for croquettes.

These sauces vary in the proportion of flour and fat they contain in relation to the milk. The fat used may be butter, margarine, shortening, or salad oil, depending upon the flavor and color characteristics desired in the finished product. The proportions for making the different white sauces are presented in Table 10.2.

White sauces utilize two of the techniques mentioned previously to disperse starch uniformly prior to gelatinization. First, the starch is stirred thoroughly with melted fat or with oil to help separate the starch granules. Then this fat–starch slurry is blended with cold liquid to disperse the starch still more before any heat is available to start gelatinization. When making large quantities of white sauce, about a fourth of the milk is used cold to disperse the starch, while the remainder is scalded before being added. This helps to shorten the cooking time without causing the lumping that would result if the scalded milk were added all at once directly to the fat–starch mixture. An absolutely smooth product must be achieved before any heat is applied to the starch mixture. Any lumps present prior to heating will remain throughout the preparation, for the starch on the outside of the lumps will gelatinize and trap dry starch within each of the lumps, resulting in a poor texture and a product that is slightly thinner than desirable.

When the sauce is completely smooth, heating is initiated at a moderate rate. Constant stirring around the sides and all across the bottom of the pan throughout the heating period is essential if a smooth sauce is to be produced. Otherwise, the starch will start to gelatinize rather quickly along the edges and across the bottom of the pan where the mixture heats most quickly; then when these areas are stirred, some of the thickened portions will be scraped free and become large lumps in the sauce.

Evaluation of white sauces is based on their consistency, texture, flavor, and surface appearance. Consistency varies with the type of sauce being prepared. A thin sauce should be thickened very slightly, but should have a definitely fluid nature. In contrast to the thin sauce,

Table 10.2 *Proportions for White Sauces*				
Type	**Flour**	**Fat**	**Milk**	**Salt**
Thin	1 tbsp	1 tbsp	1 c	1/4 tsp
Medium	2 tbsp	2 tbsp	1 c	1/4 tsp
Thick	3 tbsp	3 tbsp	1 c	1/4 tsp
Very thick	4 tbsp	4 tbsp	1 c	1/4 tsp

JUDGING POINTS
WHITE SAUCES

- Appropriate viscosity for the type of sauce (thin: somewhat thickened; medium: flows slowly after spoon leaves a path; thick: spreadable; very thick: paste-like)
- Smooth, free of lumps
- No fat film
- No raw starch flavor

---

the medium sauce should flow rather slowly so that a creamed dish will not flow all around the plate quickly. Since a thick sauce needs to be folded into beaten egg whites, it must be spreadable but should flow extremely slowly. A very thick, paste-like sauce serves as glue to bind ingredients together for deep-fat frying.

Regardless of the viscosity of the sauce, the product should be perfectly smooth. Lumps may result from inadequate mixing of the starch with other ingredients prior to gelatinization. They may also result from too little stirring in all areas of the pan during gelatinization. If a sauce starts to get lumpy during cooking, the heat should be reduced to allow time for the stirring to keep up with the gelatinization process.

Flavor of a white sauce ordinarily is quite uncomplicated. There should be no trace of a raw starch flavor. Adequate gelatinization should eliminate this problem. Also there should be no suggestion of scorching. Use of a heavy pan when heating a white sauce can be invaluable in helping to eliminate scorching, because the combination of sugar and protein in milk can scorch very easily if any hot areas develop in a pan. The type of fat selected for use in making the sauce may make a positive contribution to the flavor, and the salt (possibly plus some other seasonings) will help to create a flavorful sauce.

An undesirable fat film sometimes appears on a white sauce; the cause on a thin or medium white sauce usually is failure to gelatinize the starch completely or using too little starch in relation to the amount of fat used. If a film is evident, the first corrective measure is to bring the sauce to a boil to ensure that gelatinization has been completed. Often this treatment will solve the problem. If not, a smooth slurry of some starch and cold liquid needs to be made and added to the sauce with stirring, followed by adequate heating to gelatinize the newly added starch and bind the fat.

In thick or very thick white sauces, a fat film usually is the result of excessive evaporation of liquid. This is particularly likely to happen if a small amount of sauce is being prepared and the heating is being done very cautiously. In contrast, the very rapid thickening that occurs when thick and very thick sauces are being prepared rapidly can result in lumping unless the heat is reduced drastically. This circumstance often results in loss of so much liquid through evaporation that the sauce breaks, releasing a very noticeable layer of fat in the sauce. Although this looks terrible, the problem is remedied easily by slowly stirring in a small amount of liquid to help reform the emulsion and bind the fat in. Before thick sauces can be utilized in soufflé preparation, the separated fat must be recombined with the sauce.

Gravies

Gravies are medium white sauces in which the drippings from the meat serve as the fat for the sauce. The technique for preparing the gravy depends upon the cookery method used for the meat. The drippings from fried or roasted meat are mostly fat and can be used to combine directly with the flour to help separate the starch granules before adding liquid and gelatinizing the sauce. In these cases, the drippings must be measured, using two tablespoons of drippings for each cup of gravy desired (the proportions for a medium white sauce); the remainder of the drippings should be removed from the pan. Failure to do this will result in a gravy with a fat layer because there will be too much fat to be bound by the flour or starch in the gravy. The starch is stirred directly into the measured drippings of fat, a method called the **roux method**.

roux method   Preparation of gravy by stirring starch into the measured drippings from fried or roasted meats.

Braised and stewed meats are cooked in liquid, which means that the liquid in the pan from braised or stewed meats can cause gelatinization of the starch to begin as soon as it comes in contact with the dry starch. A lumpy gravy almost inevitably results unless a smooth slurry of starch and cold water or milk is made and then added slowly, with stirring, to the hot liquid. This method sometimes is called the kettle method of making gravy.

Regardless of the technique used for making the gravy, the desired result is a pleasingly flavored and colored sauce with a perfectly smooth texture and the consistency of a medium white sauce. There should be no fat film. The most likely cause of a fat film is failure to measure the fat accurately for the amount of gravy being prepared. Lumpiness may be the result of failure to disperse the starch uniformly before gelatinization or of inadequate stirring during thickening. The problem of inadequate stirring is exaggerated when gravy is made in a skillet or other pan with a very large surface.

Cream Soups

Cream soups are thin white sauces with puréed vegetables or other food added for color, flavor, and general interest. Various seasonings appropriate to the type of cream soup being prepared are added to heighten the appeal of the soup. Although by strict definition cream soups should contain only puréed foods, many people precook the foods to be added and chop (rather than purée) them so that the soup acquires textural interest. The one exception to using the proportions for a thin sauce in making cream soups is cream of potato. The starch in the potatoes will add to the viscosity of the soup, making it necessary to reduce the amount of starch used in making the thin white sauce itself.

Preference regarding the amount of puréed vegetable to use in cream soups varies with individual taste and also with the vegetable, but usually ranges between 2 and 4 tablespoons per cup of soup. Spinach, for instance, is used in the smaller measure to produce the desired color and flavor, for the large measure would be overpowering. On the other hand, celery is so bland and has such a subtle color that the large amount produces a more appealing soup.

Most cream soups require careful attention to correct measurements, proper dispersion of the starch, and uniform gelatinization with stirring to prepare an excellent product. However, cream of tomato soup adds another dimension because of the acidity of the tomatoes. The milk proteins in the cream soup will curdle if they are placed in too acidic a medium, and tomatoes have the potential for causing curdling. The acidic tomatoes must be added slowly and with stirring to the white sauce so that the milk will never become acidic enough to precipitate the proteins. By also being sure to use milk that is fresh (but pasteurized), and by keeping the heating period as short as possible, the tendency to curdle is minimized. In other words, add the tomato purée to the soup just in time to heat to the desired temperature and serve immediately.

The color of homemade cream of tomato soup is very important for palatability. If only tomato juice is used, the product will have a sickly orange-red color and will lack appeal. However, if the pulp is pressed vigorously through the mesh used for puréeing, it will contribute a pleasing red color, and wholesome flavor as well.

Cream soups should be perfectly smooth, free of any trace of a fat film, well seasoned, and an appropriate color and flavor for the type of soup being prepared. All cream soups should be the viscosity of a thin white sauce.

JUDGING POINTS
CREAM SOUP

- Somewhat thickened, but still flowing
- Smooth, free of starch lumps
- No oil film on surface
- Appropriate color for the type of soup
- Pleasing flavor, no scorching

Cornstarch Puddings

Whether called *blancmange* or simply cornstarch pudding, these puddings are nourishing, simple ways of providing a considerable amount of milk (Figure 10.10). The preparation follows that for many other starch-thickened products. Since cornstarch puddings have very little fat (actually, just enough butter to provide a flavor highlight), the starch is dispersed by mixing it thoroughly with the sugar in the recipe and then blending in about a fourth of the milk (cold) to form a slurry. Through these two steps, the cornstarch should be dispersed uniformly, thus eliminating much of the potential for lumping.

Then the scalded milk can be added with stirring to assure uniform heat distribution. By scalding three-fourths of the milk, the actual heating period for gelatinizing the starch is kept reasonably short, which reduces the labor involved and also helps to minimize the sticky texture that can develop when starch granules begin to rupture due to excessive stirring. Stirring must be done throughout the gelatinization process to avoid lumps—as is true in making any starch-thickened product. A moderate rate of heating is recommended, for that allows control of the gelatinization in a smooth, uniform fashion without injuring the starch from prolonged stirring. Gelatinization is done when a spoon pulled through the pudding leaves a distinct path, but not a broad freeway.

A well-prepared cornstarch pudding will be perfectly smooth, with a light, rather delicate mouthfeel and an appealing flavor with no hint of raw starch. When the pudding has been chilled, the edge should soften slightly when cut with a spoon, but should not actually flow. The flavor should not indicate any evidence of scorching.

Figure 10.10
A sprinkling of ground nutmeg and a generous garnish of cherry sauce (thickened with cornstarch for clarity) add color and flavor appeal to this simple blancmange.
Courtesy of Plycon Press.

CEREALS

Cereals in the Diet

Cereals, which are named after the Roman goddess of grain Ceres, have been the mainstay of people's diets for countless centuries, since the very earliest efforts at cultivating crops. Depending upon the land and climatic conditions, the staple cereal crop may be corn, wheat, rice, oats, rye, or millet; rice and wheat are of particular importance. Interestingly, about equal amounts of calories are provided for feeding the world by both wheat and rice, but the farming of rice is done so intensively that only half as much land is used to raise the world's rice as is used to raise the wheat. When all grain crops are considered, more than 70 percent of the total cultivated land on earth is used for growing cereals.

The relative abundance of cereals and their nutrient contribution have caused them to occupy a prominent spot in menus. Rice consumption in the United States has increased, partly as a consequence of increased immigration by people from regions where rice has been the traditional cereal and partly due to a developing image of rice as a special or gourmet cereal. Wheat, long

Figure 10.11
Short-grain rice is harvested from a small rice paddy in the mountains on Japan's Honshu Island. Courtesy of Plycon Press.

the traditional cereal grain in the United States, is being purchased increasingly in baked products and ready-to-eat cereals rather than in flour or cereals requiring cooking.

Corn, unlike many of our foods that originated in other parts of the world, is considered to be a rather special American crop: Its ancestor, maize, was flourishing here when the ships of Columbus arrived. In fact, corn spread to Europe from the American continent when explorers took seeds back to the European continent. Presently, a large percentage of the corn consumed by people and also by livestock in the United States is grown in the Midwest, an area of the country often referred to as the Corn Belt. There are three basic types of corn: sweet corn for human consumption, field corn for feeding animals, and popcorn, a popular snack item.

Rice is the staple grain in the Far East, ranging from Japan and China through India, and has been the number one grain for centuries there. Although rice is spoken of as a single cereal, there really are three different types available—short, medium, and long grain. The short-grain rice (sometimes called sticky rice) is particularly popular in Japan (Figure 10.11), while the long-grain rice is preferred in the United States. Production in the United States is limited, with Missouri, Arkansas, Mississippi, Louisiana, Texas, and California accounting for most of the rice grown here.

Wheat, the staple grain in the U.S. diet, includes several different types: hard red spring, hard red winter, soft red winter, white, and durum. The hard red spring and hard red winter wheats are grown intensively in Kansas, Montana, Nebraska, Minnesota, and Texas to provide the wheat for flour used in making most baked products. Soft red winter wheat is grown in states primarily south and east of Illinois, while the white wheat is the product of the Pacific Northwest. These types of soft wheat are used to make cake and pastry flours.

durum wheat A very hard, high-protein wheat grown primarily in North Dakota and particularly well suited to making pastas.

Durum wheat is a unique, amber-colored wheat of a different species and is valued for making macaroni, spaghetti, and the various other alimentary pastes or pastas. This variety is the hardest of all of the wheat varieties. Since it was first imported from the Crimea in the middle of the 19th century, this crop has been bred for high protein content and resistance to disease. Remarkably, 13 counties in North Dakota (in the northeastern part of the state) produce about 85 percent of the durum wheat grown in the United States, with the remainder being primarily from Minnesota and Montana.

Oats are grown along the northern tiers of states, from the Dakotas and Nebraska to Pennsylvania and New York, plus Texas. Barley, a somewhat less-familiar cereal grain, is grown in the northern tier of states from Washington to Minnesota and in California. Oats and barley are used primarily for breakfast cereals and have limited use in baked products. Rye is another cereal valued for its flavor and also for its structural capability in baked products, sometimes being used in combination with wheat flour to make bread. Triticale, a comparatively new type of cereal, is a cross between wheat and rye that has been developed by geneticists. The supply of triticale is somewhat limited, but it is an interesting grain for use in baked products.

Grain Structure

All cereal grains are comprised of three distinct parts: bran, endosperm, and germ (also called the embryo). The bran portion actually consists of several outer layers covering the endosperm and germ (Figure 10.12). These bran layers are high in cellulose and hence valued as good sources of fiber, as well as providing useful amounts of several of the B vitamins (Table 10.3).

The endosperm is the region of the kernel where starch is deposited in a protein matrix. This area, comprising the large majority of the kernel, is a source of starch and protein, plus rather limited amounts of the B vitamins. It is the fraction utilized primarily in the milling of wheat flours.

By far the smallest portion of the grain is the germ or embryo, for it constitutes only about 2.5 percent of the kernel. However, this is the portion that can produce viable sprouts. A unique feature of the germ is that it contains fat. It also is a rich source of thiamin. The presence of fat in the germ limits the storage life of whole grains because the fat will become rancid over a period of time, particularly if the storage temperature is hot.

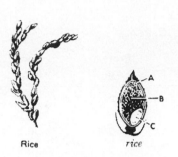
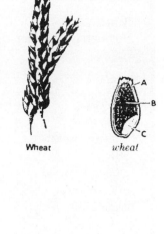
Rice · rice · Wheat · wheat

Nutritional Contribution

Cereals undergo varying degrees of processing, resulting in some variations in nutrient content from one cereal product to another. However, some generalizations can be drawn. The protein content of cereals is modest, but very important amounts of protein are provided when cereals occupy a prominent part of the diet. For example, a person eating four cups of rice daily would obtain 16 grams of protein, which is almost 30 percent of the daily need for an adult man. This protein is classified as being incomplete, because it does not provide adequate amounts of all the essential amino acids. However, the protein from cereals is utilized quite well when combined with animal protein, which is the case when cereals are eaten with milk added. Cereals also complement the protein from legumes and nuts, enabling these plant protein sources to be utilized with increased efficiency. The complementary nature of cereal and legume proteins is particularly important for people on vegetarian diets.

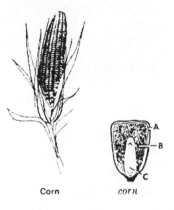
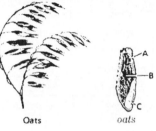
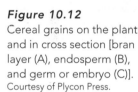
Corn · corn · Oats · oats

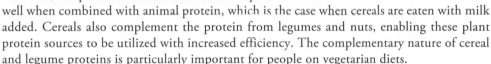

Figure 10.12
Cereal grains on the plant and in cross section [bran layer (A), endosperm (B), and germ or embryo (C)].
Courtesy of Plycon Press.

All cereals are excellent sources of starch, which makes them useful as inexpensive sources of energy. Thiamin, riboflavin, and niacin occur naturally in cereal grains in abundance; the bran and germ are appreciably higher in their vitamin content than the endosperm is, while the protein is most abundant in the endosperm (see Table 10.3 on p. 205). Whole grain cereals also are good sources of fiber.

Table 10.4 contains information about the actual nutrient content of a variety of cereals and cereal products. In addition to the nutrients mentioned, cereals contain small amounts of other vitamins and trace minerals. However, these may be lost during processing, particularly if refined cereal products are being manufactured, for then the bran and embryo are removed.

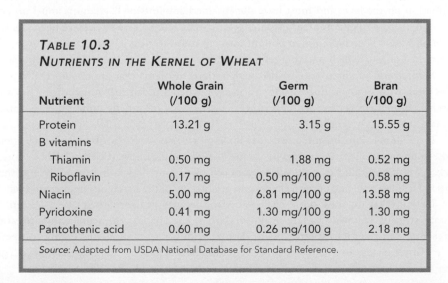

TABLE 10.3
NUTRIENTS IN THE KERNEL OF WHEAT

Nutrient	Whole Grain (/100 g)	Germ (/100 g)	Bran (/100 g)
Protein	13.21 g	3.15 g	15.55 g
B vitamins			
Thiamin	0.50 mg	1.88 mg	0.52 mg
Riboflavin	0.17 mg	0.50 mg/100 g	0.58 mg
Niacin	5.00 mg	6.81 mg/100 g	13.58 mg
Pyridoxine	0.41 mg	1.30 mg/100 g	1.30 mg
Pantothenic acid	0.60 mg	0.26 mg/100 g	2.18 mg

Source: Adapted from USDA National Database for Standard Reference.

TABLE 10.4
NUTRIENT CONTENT OF SELECTED CEREALS[a]

Food	Energy (kcal)	Protein (g)	Iron (mg)	Thiamin (mg)	Riboflavin (mg)	Niacin (mg)
Bran flakes	128	4	10.5	0.50	0.57	6.7
Bread, slice						
Cracked wheat	65	2	0.7	0.48	0.06	0.9
Rye	83	3	0.9	0.14	0.11	1.2
White, enriched	66	2	0.9	0.11	0.08	1.1
Whole wheat	69		0.7	0.11	0.06	1.3
Bulgur	154	6	1.8	0.18	0.05	1.8
Corn flakes	101	2	5.4	0.38	0.04	0.5
Corn grits, enriched	182	4	1.4	0.22	0.15	1.0
Farina	105	3	0.7	0.12	0.07	1.9
Macaroni, enriched	221	8	1.8	0.38	0.19	2.4
Noodles, enriched	221	7	2.4	0.46	0.21	3.3
Oatmeal	166	6	2.1	0.17	0.04	0.5
Rice, white enriched	194	5	2.9	0.34	0.03	3.6

Source: United States Department of Agriculture.
[a]All items are reported as cooked or ready to eat. Portions are 1 cup (1 slice for breads).

Commercial Processing

Of the many different techniques used in processing cereals, refining, or fractionation, is most common. Fractionation may be done by hulling (as is done with popcorn), milling (used in making flour), and polishing (rice); the purpose is to remove the bran, germ, or endosperm to facilitate cooking and/or enhance storage life. When wheat is refined in making white flour, the bran and germ are removed, resulting in the white color, a product with enhanced shelf life (due to removal of lipids in the germ) and loss of fiber and some of the vitamins. Refined cereal products clearly have advantages as well as disadvantages.

To compensate for the loss of vitamins resulting from refining cereal products, enrichment is often done to replace thiamin, riboflavin, niacin, folate, and iron at required levels, with the addition of calcium and vitamin D being optional. **Enriched cereals** must indicate this information on the label and must have the specified amounts of B vitamins and iron added (Table 10.5). Although a number of states require that refined cereals be enriched, this is not true in all states. Therefore, it is important for consumers to read labels to be sure to purchase the enriched product when selecting refined cereals.

Some cereal products are fortified with various nutrients that are not normally present in the food, with some products having so many nutrients added that much of the day's total nutrient requirement is provided by a bowl. These cereals are usually quite expensive and are not mandatory for good nutrition.

In addition to enrichment, cereals may undergo a variety of changes as a result of technology. Whole-grain cereals often are broken by various means into smaller particles to facilitate cooking. Cracked wheat and rolled oats are whole-grain cereals that are broken mechanically into smaller pieces to facilitate softening of the cellulose and gelatinizing of the starch during preparation.

New breakfast cereals, both ready-to-eat and hot, enter the marketplace in a seemingly constant stream. The wide variety of types, flavors, and shapes represents a vast investment in creativity and resources in attempts to capture significant shares of this highly competitive market. Breakfast cereals usually are processed into one of six categories: extruded, flaked, gran-

enriched cereals Refined cereals to which thiamin, riboflavin, niacin, folate, and iron have been added at specified levels.

TABLE 10.5
FEDERAL STANDARDS FOR ENRICHED RICE AND MACARONI PRODUCTS

Nutrient	Macaroni Products (nutrient/pound)	Rice (nutrient/pound)
Required		
Thiamin	4.0–5.0 mg	2.5–4.0 mg
Riboflavin	1.7–2.2 mg	1.2–1.4 mg
Niacin	27.0–34.0 mg	16.0–32.0 mg
Folate	0.9–1.2 mg	0.7–1.4 mg
Optional		
Calcium	500–625 mg	
Vitamin D	250–1000 USP units[a]	

[a]One USP unit equals one international unit (IU).

ulated, puffed, rolled, or shredded. Additional variety is achieved by combining products from more than one cereal grain and by adding varying levels of fiber.

Among the hot cereals, quick-cooking or instant products compete with untreated ones. Disodium phosphate is added to produce **quick-cooking cereals** and rice. This addition does speed softening by reducing the heat energy needed for water to penetrate starch granules. On the negative side, the resulting product is more gummy and sticky than the untreated cereal. **Instant hot cereals** have undergone gelatinization prior to being dehydrated and packaged; hence, these need only to be rehydrated with boiling water before being served.

Corn and Barley

Although corn is popular as sweet corn in various forms, fresh, frozen, and canned sweet corn represent only a portion of the food items that may be made from corn. **Hominy** and grits are two processed corn items popular among many people, particularly in the South. Hominy is made by removing the bran and germ of the corn kernel (utilizing a lye treatment) to yield a unique form of corn endosperm. **Grits,** another lye-treated corn product closely related to hominy, is coarsely chopped hominy. Hominy and grits can be made from either white or yellow corn, the white being traditional in the South and the yellow being common in the northern states.

Another familiar cereal product from corn that is often an ingredient in cooking is cornmeal. Cornmeal is finely ground corn from which the germ has been removed to enhance shelf life. Cornmeal and hominy grits, regardless of whether they are produced from white or yellow corn, usually are marketed as enriched products because of the loss of nutrients during their manufacturing.

Cornstarch, a familiar product derived from corn, is a popular thickening agent in food preparation. The endosperm, separated from the remainder of the corn kernel by wet milling, serves as the source of cornstarch and corn syrup. Production of cornstarch requires separation of the starch from protein and other extraneous compounds in the endosperm. Corn syrup then may be produced from the cornstarch by acid hydrolysis and/or enzymes appropriate to the desired end product.

Barley is used to only a very limited extent in the United States. The customary form in which it is marketed for use as a food ingredient is as pearl barley, which is the portion remaining after the bran has been removed. It also is used in malted products and in making whiskey.

Rice

Rice is enjoying more popularity in this country than ever before. The combination of increased interest in creative cookery and the marketing of rice in various forms as a gourmet item has contributed to a growing market for this cereal. Several types of rice are found in most markets.

quick-cooking cereals
Cereals treated with disodium phosphate to hasten softening during cooking.

instant hot cereals
Cereals that have been precooked to gelatinize the starch and then hydrated to produce a product requiring only rehydration to serve.

hominy Endosperm product made by soaking corn in lye.

grits Coarsely chopped hominy.

www.irri.org

—International Rice
Research Institute website.

Brown rice is whole-grain rice containing the bran and germ, as well as the endosperm; despite the fact that it takes about twice as long to cook as polished rice, brown rice is quite popular, particularly among people who are seeking the fiber and vitamin and mineral content provided by this whole-grain cereal. Instant brown rice is available for those who wish to avoid the 40-minute cooking period required to prepare brown rice. A distinctive nutty flavor, slightly crisp texture, and light brown color are characteristic of brown rice that has been prepared carefully.

At one time, and in some circles, polished rice was a status symbol. The snowy white of boiled, polished rice was considered to be far more desirable than the slightly brown color of brown rice. The fact that polished rice can be ready to serve in 20 minutes (half the time needed for brown rice) doubtless added to its appeal. However, the removal of the bran and germ during polishing or milling also meant the removal of many of the nutrients present in useful quantities in the whole-grain brown rice. The enrichment of polished rice often is done to replace the thiamin, riboflavin, niacin, folate, and iron lost during milling, making enriched polished rice only slightly less nourishing than brown rice. If polished rice is the form selected, it is important to be sure that it has been enriched, a fact that will be stated on the label.

Parboiled rice is another choice in the market. This rice is slightly more yellow than polished rice, but otherwise is very similar in appearance. To produce parboiled rice, the rice grains are steamed under pressure and then are dried prior to being polished. This steaming period drives the water-soluble B vitamins from the bran into the endosperm of the grains, where these vitamins remain following milling. It is the yellowish color of riboflavin that contributes the yellow cast to parboiled rice. After this process, about 92 percent of the thiamin, 70 percent of the riboflavin, and almost 78 percent of the niacin present in the bran will be retained in the polished grains of parboiled rice. This processing adds significantly to the cost of this form, but it still is well below the price of the instant or dehydrated, pregelatinized rice.

CULTURAL ACCENT
MOCHI

A special tradition for people in Japan and for many Japanese Americans is making mochi. Mochi is made by boiling sweet glutinous rice in water to gelatinize the starch granules until they begin to rupture. This warm mass then is pounded over and over with a massive mallet until the rice evolves into an extremely sticky, glue-like mass (Figure 10.13). Pounding is often done in a ceremonial fashion, with at least two energetic people alternating turns in lifting their mallets above their heads and driving them down hard on the rice. Small portions may be removed from the mass to be served as a very chewy treat, which may have bean paste or other flavoring added to it if desired.

Figure 10.13
Mochi is made traditionally in Japan by pounding boiled sweet glutinous rice with a massive mallet until it forms a cohesive, sticky paste. Courtesy of Plycon Press.

Special rice varieties now are being imported to provide still more options when serving rice. Two very sticky rices preferred by many Asians are mochigome and calmochi. Basmati is a type of rice with an unusually long grain and a hint of fragrance. Paella is a Spanish dish in which arborio, a medium-grain rice, shows off to advantage.

Another "rice" product on the market—wild rice—is not truly a rice. Instead, it is the seeds of a wild grass grown in cold marshlands in northern Minnesota and southern Canada. Indigenous people who live in the area are the only people allowed to harvest the crop. They do this by pushing canoes through the marshes and shaking the mature seeds from the grasses into the canoes—not exactly a modern harvesting technique. The limitations on harvesting wild rice have caused the price to remain very high. However, the distinctive flavor, crisp texture, and excellent nutritive value of wild rice make this a pleasing and healthful, yet costly, item when used in menus.

Although wild rice can only be grown in the harsh climate of northern Minnesota and the neighboring region in Canada, a very similar plant has been developed in northern California and is competing in the marketplace with wild rice. California wild rice is not identical to true wild rice, but consumers are buying it because of its availability and competitive pricing.

SCIENCE NOTE
CHARACTERISTICS OF RICE GRAINS

The previous discussion has focused on the merits of different methods of processing rice to influence color, textural characteristics, and cooking time. However, the type of rice selected for the processing is also of great importance in influencing the characteristics of the cooked rice. The length of the rice grain (short, medium, and long) is the means commonly used for differentiating types of rice (Figure 10.14). Their cooking characteristics vary because of the general differences in the ratios of amylose to amylopectin.

Long-grain rice, characterized by being long and slender, becomes fluffy when cooked; medium-grain rice is an intermediate between the long- and the short-grain varieties; and short-grain rice is easily distinguished by its fat and stubby shape and sticky quality after cooking.

Long-grain rice is the type preferred by many people because it cooks into well-defined grains and has a fluffy character. Properly prepared, long-grain rice has a pleasing, non-sticky character when being chewed. This type absorbs

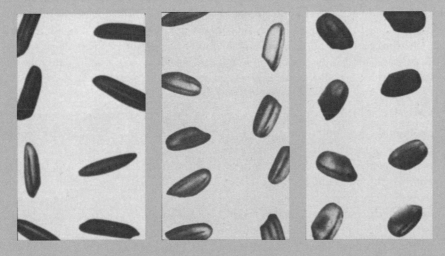

Figure 10.14
Long-grain rice (left) becomes fluffy; medium grain (center) is somewhat fluffy, but a bit sticky; short grain (right) is sticky when cooked. Courtesy of Plycon Press.

a considerable amount of water during boiling, when compared with the amount absorbed by the medium- or the short-grain varieties. These characteristics of long-grain rice appear to be the result of the comparatively high proportion of amylose in the starch granules in this type of rice grain.

Short-grain rice has a rather cohesive, sticky quality when properly prepared. These characteristics are valued when using rice to make sushi or a ring or when it will be eaten using chopsticks. The stickiness is thought to be due to the tendency of short-grain rice to split on the ends during cooking, thus releasing some starch into the cooking water and also disrupting the general structure of the individual grains. Both medium- and the short-grain rice have a reduced content of amylose in comparison with the long-grain variety. The gelatinization process takes place at a somewhat lower temperature in the short-grain than in long-grain rice.

couscous Wheat cereal product made by adding a small amount of water to a mixture of semolina and a little flour and then rubbing it together into small granules that are subsequently steamed or simmered in water.

bulgur Parboiled, cracked wheat; has a chewy and nut-like flavor.

pastas Various dough pastes containing durum wheat and water and extruded or rolled and cut in a variety of flat and rounded or twisted shapes.

semolina Granular, milled durum wheat, with a maximum of 3 percent flour.

kasha Buckwheat groats (hulled and fragmented particles).

Figure 10.15
Semolina (milled durum wheat) is extruded as spaghetti by a technician who will dry and cook it to help evaluate the quality as part of breeding experiments.
Courtesy of Agricultural Research Service.

Wheat

Wheat is an extremely versatile cereal grain, adaptable to many uses. Its importance as the source of the principal flour used in baked products accounts for much of the wheat consumed in this country (Chapters 15–17). However, there are other wheat products of merit in the diet. Wheat is utilized in both hot and cold cereals. Farina, a traditional hot cereal, is made of small pieces of the endosperm of wheat and contains no bran and a maximum of 3 percent flour. Rolled wheat can be purchased as wheat flakes for use as a ready-to-eat cereal or as an ingredient in baked products and casseroles.

Couscous is a cereal product made by mixing semolina (coarsely ground hard wheat flour) and a little all-purpose flour with a small amount of water and then rubbing it between the hands to form countless small granules. Often it is steamed or simmered with water; sometimes seasonings and other ingredients such as golden raisins or nuts are added. In North Africa, couscous has been prominent in meals for centuries, and it is becoming popular as an occasional alternative to potatoes or rice in the United States.

Bulgur is an ancient form of wheat that has been popular for centuries in Middle Eastern cuisines and that recently has been gaining in popularity in the United States as a substitute for rice or potatoes. The cooked product has a distinctly chewy texture and a nut-like flavor. To produce bulgur from wheat, the wheat grains are parboiled and dried before part of the bran layer is removed. Although bulgur with whole kernels is available, the more common form is cracked bulgur.

Pastas of numerous shapes and formulations are also wheat products, but these are ordinarily made from durum wheat (Figure 10.15). The doughs used in making the three forms of pastas (spaghetti, macaroni, and noodles) contain a large proportion of **semolina**, which is a granular product produced by milling durum wheat and restricted to a maximum of 3 percent flour. Macaroni and spaghetti and their variations are extruded from doughs containing semolina, granulars (milled durum with more flour than is allowed in semolina), and water. Noodles differ in that they also contain more than 5 percent egg solids or yolks in their doughs.

Pasta variations include green noodles, which feature spinach as an ingredient. Green noodles are particularly appealing when served topped with grated cheese or sesame seeds. A popular trend is the use of fresh pastas rather than the familiar dehydrated products. Fresh pastas require refrigeration and must be boiled and used promptly before any fermentation occurs in the dough. Fresh pastas are available in some markets. Pasta makers are a popular piece of equipment in U.S. kitchens, where people have gained an appreciation for the high quality of the fresh pastas.

Buckwheat, a relative of wheat, is the source of **kasha**, which is similar to bulgur. The hull of the grain is removed before the kernel is fragmented to produce kasha.

Other Grains

Spelt, millet, and quinoa are grains that were important in widely scattered regions of the world and are gaining renewed interest today. Spelt apparently originated in the region called Mesopotamia (present-day Iraq). Its grains are ground into flour and is a familiar grain there and also in other markets today. Millet is a grain crop that is grown in many places where farming conditions are rather arid. Its grains have a rather tough husk, which contributes texture and fiber when consumed as a cooked cereal. Quinoa is a grain from Peru and countries in the northern part of South America, where it is particularly valued when ground into flour. Recently, Indian rice grass (a seed-bearing grass in Montana) has been developed as a crop to produce a flour marketed under the name Montina. Montina and flours from other grains that are not genetically linked to wheat are of particular interest in preparing baked products and other foods for patients with gluten allergies or intolerance (e.g., celiac disease).

Storage

There are two basic problems in the storage of cereals and pastas in the home: possible hatching of larvae and potential uptake of moisture and off-flavors. Desirable storage conditions are a cool, dry cupboard, for these conditions delay deteriorative changes. Under these conditions, the maximum storage time for unopened or tightly closed

INGREDIENT HIGHLIGHT
QUINOA

Although quinoa originated in Peru (Figure 10.16), some Canadian and Colorado farmers are raising this unique grain today, too. It is marketed as both a grain and as a flour. Because this flour lacks gluten, it needs to be combined with some wheat flour when making leavened baked products. However, pasta can be made with quinoa flour, a product of particular interest to people with celiac disease.

Quinoa grain naturally has a bitter taste because of saponins, compounds on the surface of the seeds that contribute to foaming during cooking. Washing removes saponins, effectively reducing foaming and improving the flavor of the cooked grain. For a somewhat nutty flavor, the dry grains can be roasted in a skillet at low heat while stirring for about 5 minutes before cooking. Boiling for 15 minutes in twice as much water as quinoa gelatinizes the starch, develops translucence, and splits the germ off enough to form a white tail on each grain.

Figure 10.16
Quinoa, a native grain grown in the Andes, is a mainstay of the diet and a key ingredient in this traditional Peruvian soup. Courtesy of Plycon Press.

packages of cereals ranges between two months and a year (Table 10.6). Whole-grain products are limited in their shelf life by the onset of rancidity of the fat in the germ.

Occasionally, refrigerated or frozen storage of cereals may be desirable, for these temperatures prevent the hatching of larvae during extended storage and also greatly retard onset of rancidity. Of course, such cold storage is more costly than is use of a cool kitchen cabinet. Counterbalancing that cost may be the prevention of spoilage losses and the opportunity to take advantage of low

www.quinoa.com/
—Northern Quinoa Corporation website.

http://www.fmi.org/ consumer/foodkeeper/
—Information on safe storage of cereals and other foods.

TABLE 10.6
APPROXIMATE STORAGE TIME FOR CEREALS AND PASTAS

Product	Maximum Storage Recommended (months)
Breakfast cereals	2–3
Bulgur	6
Cornmeal and grits	4–6
Pasta	
Macaroni and spaghetti products	12
Egg noodles	6
Rice	
White, parboiled, packaged, and precooked	12
Brown and wild	6

sale prices. If dry cereals have lost their crispness because of absorbing moisture from the air, they may be heated in a 350°F (175°C) oven until they have lost their excess moisture.

Preparation of Cereals

The objectives for cooking the various types of cereals are: (1) to soften the cellulose and (2) to gelatinize the starch. Specific directions for preparation usually are provided on the packages, and these often are the best guide for preparing the cereal. Variations may include using milk as the cooking medium rather than water, a change that modifies the flavor and increases the nutritive value of the prepared cereal. Well-prepared hot cereals will be free of lumps; will be light on the tongue rather than pasty; will have a pleasing flavor with no suggestion of a raw starch flavor; and will pile softly when hot.

Hot Breakfast Cereals   One of the basic problems in preparing hot cereals is avoiding lumps when the cereal and water are combined and then heated to gelatinize the starch. The technique used for adding cereals to the boiling, salted water varies with the size of the cereal particles. Fine cereals, such as cornmeal, will lump badly if they are added directly to boiling water. To avoid this problem, cornmeal and similar products should be mixed with some cold water before being stirred into boiling water. Other cereals may be stirred in as dry particles. Cereals are added when the water has already reached a boil to help reduce the cooking time, which reduces the amount of stirring required. Because boiling granular cereals need to be stirred while being cooked in order to achieve uniform gelatinization of the starch and a smooth product, there will be some tendency toward a sticky product if the cooking time, and consequently the stirring time, is long.

The actual length of time required to reach the desired end point in a cooked cereal is determined by: (1) size of the cereal particles (large particles take longer), (2) the amount of cellulose present, (3) previous treatment of the cereal, and (4) the elevation of the cooking site. Since cellulose softens comparatively slowly, the more cellulose in a cereal, the longer is the cooking time. Previous treatment might include gelatinization and dehydration, a circumstance requiring merely the addition of boiling water prior to service. Disodium phosphate, which speeds the gelatinization process, may have been incorporated as an additive.

Cereals usually are added to a measured amount of boiling, salted water and are boiled over direct heat (with stirring, if a granular product) until the desired end point is reached. The amount of water to use varies with the type of cereal being prepared and is dependent on the character of the particles, as can be seen in Table 10.7. When available, package directions should be followed. To reduce problems of foaming and possible boiling over, a small amount of margarine, butter, or oil may be added to the boiling water. If milk is being used as the liquid medium, use of a double boiler is recommended, because its moderate heat will prevent scorching the milk and avoid the likelihood of boiling over, both being common problems when using direct heat with milk. If a cooked cereal needs to be held at all after it has been prepared, the pan should be covered to prevent or at least minimize formation of a skin on the surface.

Rice Cookery   Unless otherwise specified on the package, polished rice should be boiled in 2 to 2 1/4 cups salted water per cup of rice; a little olive or other oil can be added to help keep

TABLE 10.7
PROPORTIONS FOR PREPARING CEREALS[a]

Type of Cereal	Quantity of		
	Cereal	Salt	Water
Rolled, flaked	1 c	1/2 tsp	2–3 c
Coarse or cracked	1 c	1 tsp	3–4 c
Fine granules	1 c	1 1/4 tsp	4–5 c

[a]Package directions are a better guide to preparing specific cereals. This table is only a general guide.

long-grain rice from clumping together. Ideally, all the water will have been absorbed just when the rice is done. This eliminates the problem of losing water-soluble B vitamins into the cooking medium, but it does mean that enough water must be provided to allow the starch to be gelatinized. Otherwise, the rice will not soften adequately. If it is not done when the cooking water is gone, more water will need to be added to complete the gelatinization process.

The average time for boiling polished rice is about 20 minutes, while brown rice requires about 40 minutes, and some wild rice takes as long as 60 minutes. Minute rice and quick-cooking brown rice require significantly less time than their conventional counterparts. The tests for doneness vary with the type of rice: polished rice should be soft when rubbed between the fingers; brown rice should be tender, yet somewhat crisp; and wild rice will start to curl open on the ends of the grains.

Other variations for preparing rice include baking. This is done by pouring either boiling water or scalded milk over the rice in a baking dish, covering tightly, and baking for about 35 minutes at 350°F (176.7°C) until the rice tests done. Another variation, sometimes referred to as the pilaf method, is to sauté the raw rice grains lightly and then to add water or other cooking liquid and boil or simmer until done. Bouillon often is used as the liquid in this method.

Bulgur and Other Cereals The methods used for preparing rice are equally applicable to the preparation of bulgur. Like rice, bulgur takes about 20 minutes of boiling in a covered pan to reach the desired degree of doneness. Both cereals swell appreciably due to the gelatinization of the starch in them, actually about tripling the original uncooked volume. Couscous should be prepared according to package directions because instant couscous does not require as much time for hydration.

Kasha (buckwheat groats) will boil to the desired degree of doneness in about 15 minutes following a brief period of sautéing in butter or oil. Only twice as much water as kasha is usually an adequate ratio for preparing this cereal product. Preparation of pearl barley also is similar, although more time is required to complete the softening of pearl barley than is required for rice.

Hominy grits require five times as much water as dry grits when they are being prepared. This is more than double the amount of water required for preparing rice and bulgur. Therefore, it is not surprising that grits expand to about four times their original volume after cooking (in contrast to rice expanding about three times). Grits become softened and ready to eat after about 15 minutes of boiling.

Pasta Directions for preparing pastas usually are provided on the packages, but the following are some general suggestions that can be used if specific guidelines are not provided. About 6 cups of water should be brought to a boil before half a pound of pasta is added. For this amount, 1 teaspoon of salt and 1 teaspoon of oil generally are added, the latter being helpful in reducing foaming and preventing pieces from sticking readily to each other. Long pieces of pasta need to be added by pushing them slowly into the boiling water as the first portion softens and bends. All of the pasta must be immersed in the boiling water so that cooking will be uniform. The time required to reach the desired *al dente* ("to the tooth") stage varies with the type of pasta and usually is close to the length of time indicated on the package. The pasta can be checked for doneness by pressing a piece with a fork against the side of the pan or by sampling a piece. The piece should feel firm and chewy, yet have just the tiniest suggestion of a firm core. An important part of pasta preparation is thorough draining before serving. A colander or strainer works well for this task. Unless this is done carefully, a plate of pasta may turn into a small lake with an island of pasta.

www.thenibble.com/ reviews/main/pastas/ glossary.asp
—Overview of pasta types.

SUMMARY

Although much of the starch used in cooking is obtained from cereals, some root and tree starches are also used in thickening a number of food products. Starch is composed of two fractions—amylose and amylopectin; these fractions are deposited in an organized fashion in granules. When heated to extremely high temperatures by dry heat, dextrinization occurs, and the ability to thicken is reduced somewhat. When starch is heated in the presence of water, gelatinization, or the uptake of water into the starch granules, and the resultant swelling cause a noticeable thickening. Some of the slightly soluble, linear amylose will leave the granules and move freely in the water, while some of the water will enter the granule and become bound inside. A dispersion of gelatinized starch that flows is called a sol; if the flow properties are lost upon cooling, the dispersion is termed a gel.

The concentration, type of starch, final temperature during cooking, amount of sugar, presence of lumps, addition of acid prior to gelatinization (causing acid hydrolysis), and extent of dextrinization (if dextrinized starch is used) all influence the viscosity of starch sols and the firmness of their resulting gels. Gels undergo changes during storage. Syneresis is the loss of some of the liquid from a gel and occurs particularly where there is a cut surface. The amylose molecules that are outside the granules gradually rearrange themselves into some more organized crystalline areas while the gel is being stored, a process called retrogradation. This results in a tendency toward some crystalline areas, causing a gritty character.

Starches bred to contain almost entirely amylopectin are called waxy starches and are useful when gels are not desired, yet the product needs some thickening. High-amylose starches are bred to provide edible thin films. Regular starches (about 20 percent amylose and 80 percent amylopectin) may be precooked and then dehydrated to make "instant" starch products. Waxy rice starch or other starches with phosphate cross-linkages are stabilized sufficiently to undergo frozen storage with little retrogradation occurring. Resistant starches (such as Hi-maize and cold potato or legume starches) provide some fiber in the diet because they are not digested in the small intestine. Thin-boiling starches for use in making candies containing starch gels undergo some acid hydrolysis, but not enough to interfere with the ability to form a strong gel.

Examples of products using starch as the thickener include white sauces (thin, medium, thick, and very thick), gravies, cream soups, and cornstarch puddings. Thorough dispersion of the starch using a fluid fat, cold liquid, or dry ingredients must be done before the starch comes in contact with hot liquid if lumps are to be avoided. Stirring is necessary throughout the gelatinization period to make a smooth product. Layers of fat on top are not desirable and may be the result of (1) incomplete gelatinization, (2) too little starch or too much fat, or (3) excessive moisture loss when making thick and very thick products.

Cereals occupying important places in the diet as sources of starch, energy, and the B vitamins include corn, wheat, rice, oats, and millet. Wheat is particularly important in the United States because its flour is used in most baked products, and durum wheat is the main ingredient in pastas. All cereal grains are comprised of the bran (rich in nutrients), the germ (a source of B vitamins and fat), and endosperm (high in starch and some protein). In cereals the bran and embryo are often removed to give the refined product a longer shelf life (without the fat) and a reduced cooking time (removal of the fibrous bran). Enrichment frequently is done to replace some of the nutrients removed from refined cereals. Parboiling is done in processing some rice as a means of shifting nutrients into the endosperm before polishing the grains.

Storage of grains is limited by the possibility of insect infestation and by development of rancidity in whole-grain products. A cool, dry storage area and possibly even refrigerator or freezer storage extend shelf life.

The preparation of cereals is directed toward softening the cellulose and gelatinizing the starch. Lumping may be a problem in some hot breakfast cereals, but rice and other individual grain products do not present this problem, and hence do not require stirring during cooking. When done, cereals should have no trace of a raw starch flavor, and grains should be tender. Rice and other cereals and their products expand significantly (usually three or even four times, in the case of hominy grits) as a result of the gelatinization of their starch. Pasta is usually added to boiling water containing salt and a little oil and boiled until tenderized to the al dente stage.

STUDY QUESTIONS

1. What is the relationship between glucose and starch? Between amylose and amylopectin?
2. Describe a starch granule and the changes it undergoes during gelatinization.
3. What is the difference between a starch sol and gel? What are some uses of both of these forms in foods?
4. What factors influence the viscosity of starch sols and gels?
5. What are the ways in which starch can be dispersed uniformly without introducing lumps into starch-thickened products?
6. Explain each of the following and indicate why each is important in working with starch: dextrinization, hydrolysis, retrogradation.
7. Describe the differences between instant and quick-cooking starch products.
8. What kinds of rice are available? How does the type of rice influence its preparation?
9. Identify five foods that could be served as the starch in a dinner menu and explain how each is prepared.

SELECTED REFERENCES

Benedict, T. 2009. Cheese and sauce—Perfect match. *Food Product Design. 19*(6): 60.

Berry, D. 2003. New times for cereals. *Food Product Design 13*(1): 35–60.

Berry, D. 2009. Breakfast cereals go organic. *Food Product Design 19*(2): 70.

Chauhan, G. S., et al. 1992. Nutrients and antinutrients in quinoa seed. *Cereal Chem. 69*(1): 85.

Clark, J. P. 2006. Ethanol growth inspires advances in cereal milling. *Food Technol. 60*(9): 73.

Davis, R. C. 1998. The new starches. *Food Product Design 7*(11): 40.

Darling, K. 2009. Starch on the side. *Food Product Design 19*(11): 46.

Foster, R. J. 2008. Morning brings the grain event. *Food Product Design 18*(12): 42.

Grenus, K. 2004. Natural state of breakfast cereals. *Food Product Design 14*(5): 88.

Hazen, C. 2002. Breakfast cereal—Original functional food. *Food Product Design: Functional Foods Annual*. Sept.: 47.

Hazen, C. 2008. Grain-based ingredients. *Food Product Design 18*(8): 70.

Henrich, S. 2010. Battling obesity with resistant starch. *Food Technol. 64*(3): 22.

Jane, J. L., and J. F. Chen. 1992. Effect of amylose molecular size and amylopectin branch chain length on paste properties of starch. *Cereal Chem. 69*(1): 60.

Marquart, L., and E. A. Cohen. 2005. Increasing whole grain consumption. *Food Technol. 59*(12): 24.

Miraglio, A. M. 2003. Fiber in the morning. *Food Product Design 13*(4): 131.

Ohr, L. M. 2006. Go with the grain. *Food Technol. 60*(9): 63.

Ohr, L. M. 2009. Good-for-you grains. *Food Technol. 63*(1): 57.

Pszczola, D. E. 2001. Rice: Not just for throwing. *Food Technol. 55*(2): 53–59.

Pszczola, D. E. 2003. New ingredient developments are going with the grain. *Food Technol. 57*(2): 46–61.

Pszczola, D. E. 2006. Which starch is on first? *Food Technol. 60*(4): 51.

Pszczola, D. E. 2008. Reawakening of breakfast foods. *Food Technol. 62*(1): 46.

Pszczola, D. E. 2010. Pondering the pasta possibilities. *Food Technol. 64*(11): 43.

Worrell, B. 2010. Peruvian culinary wonders. *Food Product Design 20*(9): 71.

Artisanal feta cheese is being made by this Greek cheese maker who patiently stirs with a wand from an olive tree as the milk and rennin begin to form a curd. Courtesy of Plycon Press.

11

Proteins: Milk and Cheese

Chapter Contents

Key Concepts

1. Milk, a protein-rich food, is usually pasteurized and homogenized prior to being marketed as fluid, canned, or dried products with varying fat content.

2. The solubility of milk proteins is influenced by heat and acidity, both of which need to be considered when preparing foods containing milk to avoid scorching, curdling, and/or boiling over.

3. Foams of varying stability can be made using cream or dried milk with adequate fat or protein, respectively.

4. Milk and/or cream mixtures can be frozen to make ice creams with desired textural and flavor qualities.

5. Natural and processed cheeses are made by clotting milk and draining the whey from the curd; sometimes suitable molds or bacteria or other flavoring agents are added to natural cheeses prior to aging, whereas process cheeses are not aged.

INTRODUCTION

The composition of milk, the fluid secreted by lactating mammals, varies with the source, but its merits from the nutritional as well as from the culinary perspective are appreciated widely. Actually, milk is a complex fluid containing protein, fat, and carbohydrate (in the unique form of lactose). Its high nutrient value has made milk an important food for people, and it has also made milk a nourishing medium for microorganisms that may invade it.

This chapter examines the nutritional merits of milk and its various products, the control of microorganisms during milk storage, processing techniques to produce the desired products, and the cookery principles involved in preparing foods using the various milk products, with their protein content. In fact, much of the discussion on milk and cheese cookery is based on the behavior of protein under various circumstances in foods.

Figure 11.1
Milk from goats provides an option for people who are allergic to the protein in cow's milk or those who enjoy its flavor. Courtesy of Plycon Press.

www.fao.org/DOCREP/003/X6528E/X6528E00.htm

—Background on camel's milk.

www.indiadairy.com/info_buffalo_milk.html

—Production of water buffalo milk.

In the United States, milk is assumed to be cow's milk unless the product is specified to be from a different source. Goat's milk is another type of milk found in some stores (Figure 11.1). This may be the milk of choice for children who are allergic to cow's milk. The difference in the proteins may mean that goat's milk does not cause an allergic response. Other customers may choose goat's milk because they like the distinctive flavor. In some countries around the world, milk may more commonly be from goats, ewes, or such exotic sources as water buffalo.

CULTURAL ACCENT
EXOTIC SOURCES

In some other countries, dairy cattle are not raised in large numbers to provide milk. Instead, milk may be available from mammals that are typically found in the region. In India and Southeast Asia, milk from water buffalo is a familiar food. Camels are a source of milk in desert regions around the world, notably in the Sahara, the Arabian Peninsula, and northern India (Figure 11.2). Vicuñas and llamas, which are relatives of the camel, produce milk for their young and for the people living in the high Andes in South America. In Tibet, the yak is the source of milk, its shaggy coat having served effectively to insulate it from the harsh winters over the centuries. In fact, sufficient milk is obtained from yaks to prompt China to establish a factory producing dried yak milk. Lapps in the Arctic region of the Scandinavian Peninsula drink milk obtained from their reindeer herds.

The composition of milk from these diverse sources varies, although all types are very nourishing. The proteins in each are unique to the species, and as mentioned previously, this may be important for children who are allergic to cow's milk. The fat content is far higher in reindeer, yak, camel, and water buffalo milk than in cow's or even goat's milk.

Figure 11.2
Camel's milk is available in North Africa, the Middle East, and northern India. Courtesy of Plycon Press.

NUTRITIONAL VALUE OF MILK

Whole milk is about 87 percent water, with the remainder being about 4.9 percent carbohydrate, 3.5 percent fat, 3.5 percent protein, and a residue of ash. The carbohydrate in milk is lactose, which accounts for the sweet taste of milk. Lactose, like other sugars that can be metabolized, serves as a source of energy (4 calories per gram). Milk is the major source of lactose in the food supply; this sugar is responsible for the abdominal discomfort some people experience from milk because they have a deficiency of **lactase**, the enzyme needed to digest lactose.

Milk fat, like many animal fats, is relatively low in polyunsaturated fatty acids. The most abundant fatty acids in milk fat are oleic, palmitic, and stearic acids; butyric and other fairly short-chain fatty acids contribute to the flavor of milk, as well as to its energy value.

Milk is a useful source of complete protein. In fact, milk contains a variety of proteins, some of which are water soluble, others of which may precipitate under conditions employed in cooking or in manufacturing cheese. **Casein** is the chief protein fraction in milk (Figure 11.3). Whey proteins, the water-soluble proteins that are part of the **whey** formed in the production of cheese, include lactalbumin and lactoglobulin. The body utilizes various milk proteins very well.

The nutritive merits of milk are so high that milk almost seems to possess a halo. Certainly, the useful amounts of protein and carbohydrate are significant to good nutrition, but these nutrients alone do not explain the significance of milk in the diet. The levels of most vitamins and many minerals are quite high in milk (Table 11.1).

Riboflavin, one of the B vitamins, is present in significant amounts in milk and contributes a delicate greenish yellow color to the whey produced in cheese making. Since this vitamin is very sensitive to light and it is present in abundance in milk, careful packaging and storage to prevent exposing milk to sunlight are important to the level of riboflavin when the milk is consumed. Cardboard or brown-tinted glass containers are important

Figure 11.3
Casein is the main protein in the curd formed when making cheese; other proteins can be precipitated subsequently from the fluid whey remaining in the kettle by adding acid. Courtesy of Plycon Press.

lactase Enzyme needed for digesting lactose.

casein Main protein in milk; precipitated in manufacturing cheese from milk.

whey Liquid removed from clotted milk in cheese production.

TABLE 11.1
NUTRIENT CONTRIBUTIONS OF 1 CUP (8 FL OZ) NON-FAT MILK

Nutrient	% DV[a]
Fat	0
Cholesterol (less than 5 mg)	0
Sodium (120 mg)	5
Total carbohydrate (12 g)	
Fiber (0 g)	0
Sugar (12 g)	4
Protein (9 g)	20
Vitamin A	10
Vitamin C	4
Vitamin D	25
Calcium	30
Iron	0

[a]Percent Daily Values, based on a 2000-calorie diet.

devices for conserving riboflavin during marketing. Milk also contributes useful amounts of thiamin and vitamin A (if the milk is whole milk or has been fortified with vitamin A in the case of non-fat milk). Milk ordinarily is fortified with vitamin D at the level of 400 IU (international units; 10 micrograms) per quart so that a quart of milk daily provides all of the vitamin D a child requires.

Among the minerals contained in milk, calcium and phosphorus are present in particularly significant amounts. In fact, milk serves as such an important source of these two key minerals that it is extremely difficult to get enough of either of them (particularly enough calcium) without using milk generously in the diet. The favorable ratio of calcium to phosphorus and the addition of vitamin D make the utilization of calcium and phosphorus particularly effective.

KEEPING MILK SAFE

Milk and foods containing milk require careful handling to avoid the possibility of food-borne illnesses. Some microorganisms that can thrive in milk are capable of causing tuberculosis, undulant fever, scarlet fever, septic sore throat, typhoid fever, gastroenteritis, and diphtheria. These microorganisms may be in milk if a cow is infected. Milk handlers who are sick may also be a source of microorganisms. Thus, the point of contamination may be the dairy, or it may be the home.

On the Farm

To reduce the possibility of milk-borne infections in dairies, efforts are made to ensure that the herd and the handlers are all in good health. All dairy cattle are tested for bovine tuberculosis, and many are tested for *Brucella abortus,* the bacterium causing undulant fever in humans. Adequate housing for the cows and high sanitation standards are essential in maintaining dairy herds in excellent health. Dairies also have a significant responsibility for being sure that all equipment used in handling the milk is absolutely clean. Rapid cooling of milk is essential to help to keep the growth of microorganisms to a minimum before milk can be pasteurized (Figure 11.4).

Pasteurization

An extremely important treatment in assuring the safety of milk is **pasteurization**. This process is a heat treatment developed by Louis Pasteur as a method for inactivating disease-producing microorganisms. There is no way to prevent the presence of some microorganisms in the raw milk obtained from the cow. Even when very high levels of sanitation are maintained in a dairy, there will be live microorganisms in the milk, and some of these microorganisms may be harmful. It is for this reason that pasteurization is so vital.

Various heat treatments can be used for pasteurizing milk. The hold method is done by heating milk to 145°F (62.8°C), holding it at that temperature for 30 minutes, and then cooling it rapidly to at least 45°F (7.2°C) or cooler. The method used most commonly today is the high-temperature short-time (sometimes called HTST) method, in which milk is heated to 161°F (71.7°C) and is held there for at least 15 seconds before being cooled to 50°F (10°C) or below. Other temperature treatments also are authorized and include 191°F (88.3°C) for 1 second, 204°F (95.6°C) for 0.05 second, or 212°F (100°C) for 0.01 second.

A fairly new development is ultra-high-temperature (**UHT**) pasteurization. This process involves rapid heating to 280°F (137.8°C) for at least 2 seconds, an extreme treatment that makes it possible for the milk to be stored in a sterile container at room temperature until it is opened. This aseptically packaged product can

pasteurization Heat treatment to kill disease-producing microorganisms in milk.

http://www.ext.colostate. edu/safefood/newsltr/v10n2 s04.html

—Discussion of pasteurized and raw milk.

UHT Ultra-high-temperature pasteurization of milk (280°F [137.8°C] for 2 seconds) to sterilize the milk in its package so that it can be stored at room temperature until the package is opened.

Figure 11.4
Sanitation in milking barns is of paramount importance to minimize possible contamination of milk with harmful microorganisms. Courtesy of Agricultural Research Service.

CONSUMER ALERT
RAW MILK CONTROVERSY

Pasteurization of milk has protected consumers from a wide range of food-borne illnesses such as listeriosis, tuberculosis, and undulant fever for well over a century. The heat of pasteurization is sufficient to kill *E. coli*, *Campylobacter*, *Salmonella*, and other harmful microorganisms so that the nutritional benefits of milk can be gained without the risk of a food-borne illness.

Despite this long record of benefits from pasteurization, some people feel that they can only get the best nutrition from raw milk, which they claim is safe and more nourishing because it is natural. Remarkable claims about its virtues are delivered, usually with more emotion than scientific evidence. Arguments over the right to buy raw milk break into the news sporadically, and proponents continue their quest to convert others to their cause. Some people have even bought their own or are sharing a cow with others so they can get raw milk without having to find it in markets. Milk that enters interstate commerce is marketed under federal regulations and must be pasteurized. However, states have the power to write their own legislation for milk sold within their borders, and these laws vary from state to state. Consumers need to be aware of the importance of pasteurization so they can make a safe choice when buying milk.

be stored up to six months on the shelf if it is not opened. Once opened, the contents must be refrigerated to avoid spoilage. Creams of various fat percentages are sometimes prepared for marketing by use of UHT. The high temperature involved in processing milk and cream by UHT results in a slight "cooked" flavor, but the convenience of storage at room temperature makes this treatment a useful one for some applications.

http://www.foodsafety.gov/ keep/types/milk/index.html

—Information on safety of milk.

Storage of Milk and Cream

Milk and milk products are quite perishable, which makes it important that all fresh products be kept in refrigerated storage to extend shelf life. This is true not only for these milks but also for canned milks after they are opened and for reconstituted dry milk. The practice of removing milk from the refrigerator just long enough to pour the amount needed is a useful one in retarding spoilage of milk. Suggestions regarding home storage of various milk products are presented in Table 11.2.

http://www.fda.gov/ Food/ResourcesForYou/ Consumers/ucm079516.htm

—FDA statement regarding raw and pasteurized milk.

TABLE 11.2
HOME STORAGE OF DAIRY PRODUCTS[a]

Product	Storage Conditions	Duration of Safe Storage
Fresh whole milk	Covered, refrigerator	3–5 days
Fresh skim milk	Covered, refrigerator	3–5 days
Reconstituted non-fat dry milk	Covered, refrigerator	3–5 days
Evaporated milk		
Unopened can	Room temperature	6 months
Opened can	Covered, refrigerator	3–5 days
Sweetened condensed milk		
Unopened can	Room temperature	Several months
Opened can	Covered, refrigerator	3–5 days
Dry milks		
Whole	Refrigerator	Few weeks
Non-fat	Room temperature	Few months
Cream, table and whipping	Covered, refrigerator	3–5 days
Whipped cream (aerosol can)	Refrigerator	Few weeks

Source: Adapted from Milk in family meals. *Home and Garden Bulletin No. 127,* U.S. Dept. Agriculture, Washington, DC, Rev. 1972, p. 5.

[a]Open dating is a guide to freshness at store.

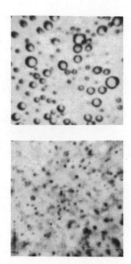

Figure 11.5
By forcing milk through tiny apertures under pressure, the large fat globules of milk (top) are split into very tiny spheres, which remain suspended in homogenized milk (bottom). The smallest gradations on the scale are two microns. Dark-field illumination was used to make these photomicrographs.
Courtesy of Plycon Press.

http://www.foodsci. uoguelph.ca/dairyedu/ homogenization.html
—Description of homogenization process.

www.nationaldairycouncil. org
—Website of National Dairy Council.

www.wisdairy.com
—Wisconsin Dairy Council website.

www.dairycouncilofca.org
—Website of Dairy Council of California.

reduced-fat milk   Milk with its fat content reduced 25 percent (to a level of about 2 percent fat).

low-fat or light milk   Milk with fat reduced to 1 percent.

MODIFYING MILK

Homogenization

The cream in milk, because of its low specific gravity, naturally floats to the top, where a layer can be observed and even poured off or separated from the rest of the milk. Although this milk, often referred to as "cream-top" milk, used to be the only type available, consumers found that their milk tended to vary in richness because of inadequate shaking of the bottle. Researchers responding to this complaint developed a technique in which heated milk is forced through tiny apertures at a pressure between 500 and 2500 pounds per square inch. This force causes the fat globules to be broken up into droplets so small that they remain suspended and distributed uniformly throughout the milk (Figure 11.5). This process also denatures some of the milk proteins (notably casein) as they are being forced through the tiny openings, a change that makes homogenized milk somewhat more digestible than its non-homogenized counterpart.

Fortification

The addition of vitamin D to milk is a measure that has been invaluable in helping to reduce the incidence of rickets among young children in this country. Milk was chosen as the vehicle for fortification because vitamin D promotes absorption of the large amount of calcium that is present. There are three different ways in which the specified 400 IU of vitamin D per quart may be added: feeding irradiated yeast to the cows, irradiating milk by letting a thin stream of milk run under an ultraviolet light prior to pasteurizing, or adding a vitamin D concentrate prior to pasteurization. The impracticality of the first two methods virtually mandates that the third method—that of adding a vitamin D concentrate—be the technique used.

MILK PRODUCTS

Fluid Milks

Whole Milk   Whole milk marketed today generally has been homogenized and pasteurized, and these processes are indicated on the label. By legal definition, whole milk must contain a minimum of 3.25 percent fat and at least 8.25 percent non-fat milk solids. Usually, the milk also is fortified with 400 IU of vitamin D per quart. This is the type generally assumed when the term *milk* is used. Its level of richness provides a flavor pleasing to many and also contributes some fat to products prepared using whole milk (Figure 11.6).

Reduced-Fat Milk   The national interest in reducing fat in the diet and in losing weight has resulted in an increasing market for **reduced-fat milk**, the milk produced when 25 percent of the cream is removed from whole milk. The amount of fat in reduced-fat milk is about 2.0 percent. Pasteurization and homogenization ordinarily are key parts of the preparation of reduced-fat milk for market. The non–fat milk solids content must be at least 8.25 percent. Since vitamin A is lost when the fat is being removed, it is mandatory to add 2000 IU of vitamin A; the addition of vitamin D is optional. The retention of the low level of fat makes the flavor acceptable to many people who are interested in reducing their calorie intake without giving up much flavor pleasure.

Low-Fat or Light Milk   **Low-fat or light milk** is processed the same as for reduced-fat milk, but with even more fat removed to bring the fat content to 1 percent.

Non-Fat or Fat-Free Milk   Specifications require that milk marketed as **non-fat or fat-free milk** has a maximum fat content of 0.1 percent or less and a minimum of 8.25 percent non-fat milk solids. Usually this type of milk is homogenized, despite its minimal fat content; it also is pasteurized and fortified with 2000 IU of vitamin A and 400 IU of vitamin D per quart.

Figure 11.6
Pasteurized milk choices available in refrigerated cases in the market include fat-free, 1 percent, 2 percent, and whole milk, as well as organic and lactose-free. Courtesy of Plycon Press.

The virtual elimination of the fat results in a reduction of calories by almost half when skim milk is compared with whole milk.

This removal of fat is attractive to dieters and to people who are trying to lower their intake of fat, particularly animal fats. The reduced fat level results in a loss of the richness of flavor preferred by many people. However, nutritionally, non-fat milk is an excellent choice. In fact, the concentration of nutrients is very slightly higher (with the exception of fat) in non-fat milk than in whole milk, and the protein content (identified as "protein fortified") is at least 10 percent non-fat milk solids.

Flavored Milks Chocolate milk, available as the whole milk product or at lesser fat levels, is flavored with a chocolate syrup or a cocoa powder, with the chocolate solids ranging from 1.0 to 1.5 percent. The sucrose or other sugar, added at a level of between 5 and 7 percent, adds to the calorie content. The fat level (whole, reduced-fat, low-fat, or non-fat) is indicated on the label, and so are such processing steps as pasteurizing, homogenizing, and fortifying with vitamins A and D.

Cultured Milks **Acidophilus milk** has had the bacterium *Lactobacillus acidophilus* added to it. This results in the production of lactic acid from lactose as the bacterial colony metabolizes the carbohydrate. Nutritionally, acidophilus milk is comparable to the non-fat milk from which it is made, although the price will be significantly higher than the ordinary non-fat milk. However, this cost may be very acceptable to people who ordinarily have trouble digesting milk because of lactose intolerance. The flavor of acidophilus milk also is appealing to a moderate-sized audience, who appreciate it as a beverage or an ingredient in various recipes.

Cultured buttermilk is made by adding lactic acid–producing bacteria to pasteurized non-fat milk, whole milk, concentrated fluid milk, or reconstituted non-fat dry milk. Usually, non-fat milk is used to make cultured buttermilk, which despite its name, is actually low in fat. Sometimes flecks of butter are added to increase the palatability, with the result that cultured buttermilk may have as much as 1 percent fat.

Yogurt is not a fluid milk product, but because it is marketed in its fresh state and is a cultured product, it is discussed here. The consistency of yogurt is custard-like rather than fluid. This texture is the result of the fermentation of milk, either whole or skim, by an inoculum of *Streptococcus thermophilus* and *Bacterium bulgaricus*. The acid produced by these lactose-digesting bacteria results in precipitation of the protein in the milk to form the familiar soft curd of yogurt. Fruits and other flavorings often are added to provide a variety of flavors to yogurt

fat-free or non-fat milk Milk that has been skimmed to a fat level of 0.1 percent or less.

acidophilus milk Milk containing *Lactobacillus acidophilus*, which metabolizes the lactose in milk.

cultured buttermilk Cultured skim milk that sometimes contains flecks of butter.

yogurt Milk-based food produced when milk is clotted by lactic acid–producing bacteria.

Figure 11.7
Lactase is introduced into milk to digest lactose before milk reaches consumers who do not naturally have enough of the enzyme. Courtesy of Agricultural Research Service.

http://silksoymilk.com/
—Information and recipes using a soy drink.

evaporated milk Canned milk made by evaporating about half of the water prior to canning; available in various levels of fat.

http://www.verybestbaking. com/Carnation/ Products.aspx
—Information on evaporated milks.

sweetened condensed milk Canned milk product made by evaporating about half the water and adding about 44 percentage sugar.

http://www.tastethedream. com/recipes/index.php
—Information and recipes using a rice drink.

in the marketplace. These products have gained popularity as dressings for fruit salads, as dessert items, and as snack foods. Those made from skim milk can be useful in weight-reduction diets.

Frozen yogurt, a sweetened, flavored yogurt that has been frozen, is a popular dessert item. The high sugar content often found in frozen yogurts adds significantly to the calorie content of this dessert, which is viewed as being competitive with ice cream.

Lactose-Reduced Milk Some people have an inadequate amount of lactase, the enzyme needed to digest lactose, and the result is stomach cramps due to gas formation. For these people, lactose-free milk is produced by addition of lactase, which digests the disaccharide in the milk before it reaches the consumer (Figure 11.7).

Milk Alternatives An allergy to casein or other proteins in milk may prevent some people from including milk in their diet. In response to this problem "milks" containing soy or rice proteins have been developed (Table 11.3). These are designed to be consumed as a beverage, but they also can be used in recipes adapted to their unique composition.

Canned Milks

Evaporated Milks Although evaporated whole milk was, for years, the only type of **evaporated milk** on the market, the widespread acceptance of low-fat and non-fat fluid milks made it feasible to consider producing evaporated milks with these reduced fat levels (Figure 11.8). These have found a satisfactory place in the market. Regulations regarding composition of evaporated skim milk stipulate a fat content of not more than 0.5 percent and a milk solids content of at least 20 percent. Vitamins A and D must be added. Evaporated milks sometimes are used undiluted and sometimes reconstituted with an equal amount of water. The undiluted milk can be whipped and used as a topping.

Sweetened Condensed Milk. Since both evaporated milk and **sweetened condensed milk** are marketed in cans, some consumers are confused about the two types. They have a significant feature in common—a bit more than half of the water has been evaporated from the milk. However, sweetened condensed milk, as the name suggests, contains a high percentage of sucrose and/or glucose (actually, 44 percent) to help retard bacterial growth. Thus, canned sweetened condensed milk can be stored very satisfactorily at room temperature for as much as a year or more if the can is not opened.

The high sugar content adds to the viscosity of sweetened condensed milk as well as to browning when it is heated slowly for a period of two hours or more. Also the high concentration

---

TABLE 11.3
NUTRIENTS IN 1 CUP MILK AND ALTERNATIVE BEVERAGES

Type of Milk	Calories	Protein	Fat	Carbohydrate	Calcium	Vitamin D
		(g)	(g)	(g)	(mg)	(IU)
Non-fat	83	8.26	0.2	12.47	299	115
Silk, soy	100	7.00	4.00	7.99	299	119
Rice drink, unsweetened	113	0.67	2.33	22.01	283	101

Source: United States Department of Agriculture.

of milk protein, combined with the tendency to precipitate and thicken fairly readily with the addition of acid or the application of heat, makes sweetened condensed milk a useful ingredient in some desserts.

Dry Milks

Non-fat dry milk solids are the most common of the powdered milk products. This type of milk usually is prepared by evaporating part of the water from pasteurized non-fat milk with the use of a vacuum. This concentrated product next is sprayed into a drying chamber to remove the remainder of the water. The solids are collected, and then the dried milk is moistened with steam so that it clumps into aggregates that disperse readily when reconstituted in water. Vitamins A and D may be added to enhance the nutritive value.

Often non-fat dry milk can be stored at room temperature, and it is much less bulky and heavy than the original skim milk from which it was produced. Although there is a slight "processed" flavor when reconstituted, thorough chilling of the reconstituted milk and/or mixing some fluid milk with the reconstituted milk may make non-fat dry milk acceptable as a beverage. This milk, when only partially reconstituted (equal amounts of solids and water) can be whipped to provide a low-calorie, low-cost whipped cream alternative.

Whole milk and low-fat milk also can be dehydrated to produce their dried milk counterparts. Unfortunately, the fat in these products limits their shelf life owing to potential rancidity. Therefore, these forms of dried milk are not always available in the retail market. However, they are used in commercial chocolate and candy manufacturing as well as in infant feeding formulas in some instances.

Creams

Creams with different levels of fat are available for various applications (Table 11.4). These creams have designations that may confuse shoppers. Half-and-half, the cream with the lowest fat content, usually is used on cereals or in coffee and other beverages. Some people prefer light cream, also called coffee cream or table cream, because they like a richer addition to their cereals and coffee.

Light whipping cream is sometimes simply labeled as **whipping cream**, which indicates its ability to be beaten into a foam. Heavy whipping cream, with its slightly higher fat content, whips into the stiffest of the cream foams. Unless the fat content is at least 30 percent, the cream will not whip into a foam that is useful. There are also whipped toppings marketed commercially, often with stabilizers added to them, and their fat content may vary significantly from one product to another.

Sour cream is a popular cream for use in making dips and salad dressings, as well as in some baked products. The fat content is at least 18 percent, which makes it well below the

Figure 11.8
Evaporated milk (right) is quite different from sweetened condensed milks (left and center) because no sugar is added to it. Courtesy of Plycon Press.

http://www.eaglebrand. com/
—Information on nutrient content in sweetened condensed milks.

http://extension.usu.edu/ foodstorage/htm/ dried-milk/
—Information on use and storage of dried milk.

whipping cream Cream with a fat content high enough to be whipped (at least 30 percent).

sour cream Viscous, acidic cream containing at least 18 percent fat; acidified by action of lactic acid bacteria on lactose.

TABLE 11.4
FAT CONTENT OF CREAMS[a]

Type of Cream	Percent Fat
Half-and-half	10.5–18.0
Light cream (coffee or table)	18.0–30.0
Light whipping cream (whipping)	30.0–36.0
Heavy cream (heavy whipping)	36.0
Sour cream (cultured sour)	18.0

[a]Terms in parentheses are alternative names under which the cream may be marketed.

fat content for butter, and therefore a comparatively low-calorie topping for baked potatoes. Pasteurization is done for 30 minutes at temperatures between 165° and 180°F (73.9° and 82.2°C), a procedure not only adequate for killing harmful bacteria but also helpful in producing the desired firm body characteristic of sour cream. A controlled culture of lactic acid bacteria is added to develop the desired acidic tang and to promote firmness. Since sour cream curdles rather readily with heat, it should be added to heated sauces or meats just long enough to be heated to the desired temperature.

Butter

Butter is unique among milk products, for it is primarily fat (at least 80 percent) and is not useful as a source of calcium and the other nutrients for which milk is recommended. Nevertheless, butter is popular as a fat in food preparation because of its color and flavor. Either sweet or sour cream may be churned to make butter, with the buttermilk being drained from the fat to concentrate the butter to its required fat content of at least 80 percent. Other steps in the production of most butter include washing, salting, working (squeezing some water out), and cutting into blocks.

Some recipes call for sweet or unsalted butter. If a recipe requiring unsalted butter also specifies the addition of salt, there is little reason to purchase the sweet butter. The added salt can be reduced or eliminated and regular butter or margarine utilized instead.

Whipped butter is a variation of solid butter. This sometimes is used as a table spread by people who wish to reduce the amount of fat and calories in their diets. Substitution of whipped butter for regular butter in recipes should be done on the basis of weight rather than volume.

Frozen Milk Products

Frozen milk products of various compositions are available in today's markets. Ice cream is a sweetened, often flavored, frozen milk product with a minimum fat content of 10 percent, unless the flavoring is a bulky substance, in which case the minimum fat level is 8 percent. Ice milk is lower in calories than ice cream because its fat content is between 2 and 7 percent. Sherbets contain so little milk solids (limited to between 2 and 5 percent) that they are really not considered milk products. They also have only 1–2 percent milk fat, giving them a granular texture. Even ice milk has at least 11 percent milk solids, and ice creams range as low as 16 percent for bulky flavored ice creams and 20 percent or more in other ice creams.

Some markets sell an imitation ice cream. This product must be labeled "imitation." Some imitations are called **mellorine**, indicating that the original milk fat has been replaced by another fat. Others are of the type known as **parevine**, which indicates that no dairy ingredients are contained in this frozen dessert. Tofutti®, a frozen tofu-based (soybean curd) food, is another non-dairy "ice cream."

In addition to the milk fat, ice creams and related products contain varying amounts of sugar, milk solids, stabilizers, flavorings, and coloring to achieve the desired characteristics.

http://cfr.vlex.com/vid/135-130-mellorine-19705055

—Federal regulation defining mellorine.

www.pacode.com/secure/data/007/chapter39/s39.32.html

—Regulations on parevine.

mellorine   Frozen dessert usually made with a vegetable fat.

parevine   Frozen dessert usually made without any dairy or meat products.

These ingredients are mixed and pasteurized before being frozen either in a batch process or continuous freezer. Agitation in the batch freezer permits incorporation of air, whereas the continuous freezer introduces fixed amounts of air as the ice cream moves through the freezer section. Either method increases the volume through the addition of air; this addition and the expansion due to freezing water into ice result in the phenomenon known as **overrun**. Some overrun is desirable in promoting a pleasingly light consistency and smooth texture, but too much creates unpleasantly airy, fluffy ice cream. Stabilizers contribute to the texture of the frozen product by facilitating development of small ice crystals. They also aid in retarding the melting of ice creams when they are served.

Imitation Milk and Whiteners

Certain foods in the marketplace must be labeled as imitations. Imitation milks can be manufactured to resemble milk and be substituted for milk. However, their formulations may be quite different from milk. For example, vegetable fat may replace milk fat in some products; dextrose or corn syrup may replace lactose in others; sodium caseinate, which is derived from milk, often serves as the protein source. No standards have been established for these imitation milks; hence, label reading is necessary before deciding to use an imitation milk.

Filled milk was defined in the Filled Milk Act (PL-513) of 1923 as follows:

…any milk, cream, or skimmed milk whether or not condensed, evaporated, concentrated, powdered, dried, or desiccated, to which has been added or which has been blended or compounded with any fat or oil other than milkfat, so that the resulting product is an imitation or semblance of milk, cream, or skimmed milk whether or not condensed, evaporated, concentrated, powdered, dried, or desiccated.

Under this definition, coconut oil, a vegetable oil with more than 90 percent saturated fatty acids, may be used as the replacement for milk fat; this substitution clearly provides no advantage over the saturated fatty acid content of about 60 percent in milk fat.

Interest in imitation milks today is so low that there is little concern over regulating the production of these types of products. However, coffee whiteners or lighteners are popular among consumers because of their excellent storage life (six months when stored at 100°F [38°C] or two years when stored at 70°F [21°C]). Such longevity is a distinct advantage to people who rarely use cream. Although whiteners may vary somewhat in their ingredients, they usually are a combination of a vegetable fat (often coconut oil), a protein (sodium caseinate), corn syrup or other sweetener, emulsifiers, stabilizers, coloring, and flavoring. These products generally can be added directly into a hot beverage or reconstituted with hot water and chilled for service as the fluid cream imitation. The caloric content of coffee whiteners and light cream is about comparable.

INSPECTION AND GRADING

The Agricultural Marketing Service of the U.S. Department of Agriculture (USDA) is the agency responsible for maintaining surveillance of milk and other dairy products entering interstate commerce (Figure 11.9). Individual states are responsible for control within their boundaries, although their regulations for intrastate inspection must conform, as a minimum, to federal guidelines. Monitoring responsibilities include inspection of dairy plants and surrounding areas to ensure clean, orderly, and well-maintained physical facilities for production. Incoming raw materials are checked regularly for safety, and all products are subjected to rigorous quality control standards before leaving the plant. The top grade of milk, the grade reaching consumers, is Grade A.

Butter is graded according to U.S. grade standards as U.S. Grade AA (highest quality), U.S. Grade A, or U.S. Grade B. U.S. Grade B usually is made from sour cream, causing it to have a slightly acidic, but generally acceptable, flavor.

overrun Increase in volume of ice cream as a result of expansion as water turns to ice and as air is incorporated during freezing.

Figure 11.9
Grade shields (top to bottom) for butter, instant non-fat dry milk, and cottage and process cheeses.
Courtesy of Plycon Press.

amino acid Subunit of protein; contains an amino (–NH₂) and an organic acid group (–COOH).

peptide bond Bond formed between the carboxyl of one amino acid and the amino group of a second amino acid with a loss of a molecule of water.

SCIENCE NOTE
PROTEINS AND DENATURATION

Proteins are organic compounds containing two unique structural features—an amino group ($-NH_2$) and an organic acid radical.

$$-C{\overset{O}{\underset{OH}{}}}$$

These features are found in each of the basic units of a protein and are called **amino acids**. They all have the following basic structure, with R representing a range of different structures, from simply a hydrogen atom in glycine to quite a complex double-ring structure in tryptophan. The R group for each amino acid differs, giving the unique quality to each specific amino acid (Table 11.5).

$$R-C\overset{|}{\underset{HNH}{}}-C{\overset{O}{\underset{OH}{}}}$$

Amino Acid

TABLE 11.5
THE R GROUPS OF SOME AMINO ACIDS

Amino Acid	Formula of R Group
Alanine	$-CH_3$
Arginine	$-(CH_2)_3-NH-C-(NH_2)_2$
Glycine	$-H$
Histidine	$-CH_2-CH-CH$ $HN \quad N$ C
Isoleucine	$-CH-CH_2-CH_3$ CH_3
Leucine	$-(CH_2)_4-NH_2$
Lysine	$-CH_2-CH_2-CH_2-CH_2-NH_2$
Methionine	$-CH_2-CH_2-S-CH_3$
Tryptophan	$-CH_2-C$ ... N H
Tyrosine	$-CH_2-\bigcirc-OH$
Valine	$-CH-(CH_3)_2$
Phenylalanine	$-CH_2-\bigcirc$

Proteins are made up of many amino acids joined together by a linkage called a peptide linkage or **peptide bond**. The peptide linkage is a covalent, very strong bond between the acid (carboxyl) group of one amino acid and the amino group of another amino acid, a linkage that is formed with the loss of a molecule of water. An example of the peptide bond and the union of two amino acids to form a dipeptide is given below. This is repeated again and again to form protein molecules, all of which are extremely large.

Amino acid   Amino acid   Dipeptide

Primary Structure

The linkage of one amino acid to another and then to another creates a backbone chain consisting of a repeating pattern of a carbon atom (with the R group attached) joined to a second carbon atom (with an oxygen attached to make a carbonyl or –C==O) and then attached to a nitrogen atom (with a hydrogen atom). Thus, the repeating pattern of the basic chain of a protein is –C–C–N–C–C–N–C–C–N– throughout the extremely large molecule. Note that throughout the long molecule, all of the linkages in the backbone chain are covalent, which gives this basic backbone structure a linear structure with considerable strength. This basic backbone chain is called the primary structure of protein, and it is formed entirely by covalent bonding. The general appearance of the primary structure is shown below, with one of the peptide bonds indicated by a dashed line.

Primary structure

During food preparation, this primary structure is resistant to change. However, some enzymes, called **proteolytic enzymes** because they attack protein, can cause a cleavage along this backbone. When this happens, enzymatic hydrolysis will result in an uptake of water at the peptide linkage, and two shorter peptides, or chains of amino acids, will result.

This backbone or primary structure is the same in all proteins. The difference in individual proteins is due to the R groups of the various amino acids comprising the specific protein molecule. The amino acid sequence of individual proteins varies with the specific protein and with the species synthesizing the protein.

Secondary Structure

Proteins in nature are found in a more complex arrangement than that seen in the primary structure. Instead, the primary structure of protein molecules is coiled into a less strained, lower energy state in nature; this arrangement is the secondary structure, often referred to as the helical structure, and is superimposed on the primary structure. The secondary structure, unlike the primary structure, is held in position only by secondary bonding forces in most instances.

The arrangement for this secondary (helical) structure is in a right-handed alpha helix, which is quite a stable, non-stressed form. The bonding forces operating within the secondary structure are hydrogen bonding, van der Waals forces, and disulfide bridges (covalent bonding). Hydrogen bonds and van der Waals forces are the predominant bonds. They are secondary bonding forces and are more susceptible to alteration than the covalent bonding comprising the primary structure. The spherical configuration is strengthened by hydrogen bonding between the oxygen of the carbonyl in one amino acid and the hydrogen linked to a nitrogen in an amino acid at a comparable position on the adjacent coil of the helix.

The coiled secondary structure resembles a spring in which the primary structure corresponds to the wire of the springs, representing the continuous covalently bonded chain. This appears in the diagram.

The linkage between portions of the protein molecule is illustrated by the hydrogen bonding in the diagram, which shows a small portion of the protein structure in its secondary configuration. This secondary structure is quite a low energy state and is further stabilized by the hydrogen bonding occurring between every fourth amino acid residue (Figure 11.10).

A few proteins are categorized as fibrous proteins, which assume a somewhat different structure, usually referred to as the pleated sheet structure. In these fibrous proteins, the rather tightly coiled alpha helix is extended distinctly into a zigzag extension known as the beta configuration. This pleated sheet structure is found in wool and hair, both of which meet the requirement of being rather stretchy because of the pleated arrangement. This configuration is of limited importance in food products.

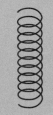

Secondary structure

A unique fibrous protein of importance in food preparation is the connective tissue known as collagen. Proline and hydroxyproline are repeated with frequency in collagen, but these amino acids provide a distinctly rigid character wherever they occur along the amino acid chain. This is explored in the context of the connective tissue in meat in Chapter 13.

Tertiary Structure

Yet another level of organization in protein molecules is referred to as the tertiary structure. A distortion of the helical structure appears to exist in some protein molecules in nature, causing them to be convoluted into a spatial arrangement resembling a globe or globular shape; some parts of the coiled helix become a bit compressed, while other areas may be quite stretched out. This tertiary arrangement can be visualized by twisting a spring into a globular (spherical) shape. Note that some areas of the helical spring become compressed, and others are stretched. The tertiary arrangement of proteins in nature is held in place by secondary bonding forces, but the greater distortion of low-energy bond angles in this tertiary structure causes it to be susceptible to change more readily than is true for the non-stressed secondary structure. A possible visualization of the tertiary structure of protein is shown in the diagram, with the line itself representing the primary structure, the recognizable helical coils showing the secondary structure, and the overall configuration being the tertiary structure (Figure 11.11).

(Continued)

(Continued)

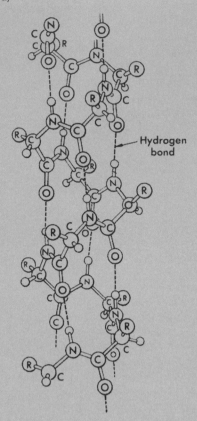

Figure 11.10
Schematic drawing of portion of an
alpha helix of a protein molecule.
Courtesy of Commonwealth of Scientific and
Industrial Research Organization.

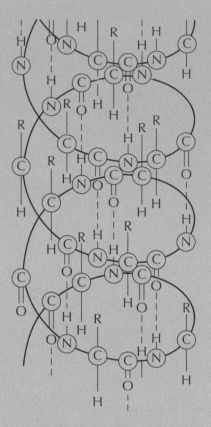

Figure 11.11
Sketch of the tertiary structure of a
globular protein. Courtesy of Plycon Press.

Quaternary Structure

Some very large protein molecules, with molecular weights exceeding 50,000, may have more than one peptide chain associated together. This association is referred to as the quaternary structure. An example of this is seen in meat (Chapter 13).

Denaturation

Proteins in foods as they are harvested are referred to as native proteins. Their structures conform to the previous levels of organization and arrangements just described. However, these native proteins are capable of undergoing some physical changes during certain treatments used commonly in preparing foods. A key change is that of **denaturation,** a physical change altering the behavior of proteins from native to denatured protein.

Denaturation is the unfolding of the tertiary structure of the protein as heating or beating supplies enough energy to break the secondary bonding forces responsible for holding the native protein in its convoluted, usually globular, shape. The physical shape of the protein molecule begins to resemble the helical secondary structure, exemplified by a coiled spring. When this happens to many protein molecules, it is possible

for some of these "coiled springs" to align themselves sufficiently to begin to form hydrogen bonds between molecules. This binding together of molecules reduces the flow properties of the system because these large aggregates or clumps of protein present considerable resistance to movement. In other words, the protein becomes less soluble and tends to precipitate or to resist movement, that is, it is denatured.

In addition to the larger aggregates that are formed, proteins are also altered in their behavior because of the different R groups exposed by the changes in the physical contours of the individual molecules. The various R groups will have the ability to be attracted to or to be repelled by other protein molecules as the result of the types of substances comprising the individual R groups. Thus, electrical charges on protein molecules are subject to change during the denaturation process as the physical shape and conformation of the molecule changes.

Another term associated with physical changes in protein is **coagulation.** Often coagulation is used interchangeably with denaturation. However, there actually is a fine distinction between these two terms. Technically coagulation, which is the clumping together of the partially denatured molecules, refers only to the second step of the process of denaturation.

U.S. Extra Grade is the designation on instant non-fat dry milk of optimal quality, having a sweet and pleasing flavor, a natural color, and the ability to dissolve immediately in water. Instant non-fat dry milk bearing the shield stating "USDA Quality Approved" has been processed under sanitary conditions and is of good quality.

Cheeses sometimes are graded. Cheddar cheese may be graded AA, the top grade, with A being just slightly lower in quality. A shield stating "USDA Quality Approved" is placed on cottage cheese and pasteurized process cheese that meet U.S. Department of Agriculture standards for quality and production.

Problems in Milk Cookery

Milk is a valued ingredient in many different food products, but certain precautions must be observed when heating milk. The changes of particular concern are those associated with scum formation, curdling, and scorching. These outcomes are attributable to the proteins in milk, and they are undesirable because they detract from the quality of the finished product. Since proteins in milk are at the root of these difficulties, the avoidance of problems will be more understandable if the nature of proteins is explained.

Scum Formation

When milk is heated, a scum or a skin tends to form over its surface, particularly when the pan is not covered. The skin effectively traps steam, creating pressure and causing milk to boil over unless the heat is reduced greatly. This scum appears to be the result of evaporation from the surface of the milk, which concentrates the protein (particularly casein) at the surface.

The skin traps milk solids, including proteins and calcium salts, all of which can be removed by spooning the skin off frequently. Unfortunately, this spooning off is not a cure for scum formation, for a new scum begins to form as soon as the existing skin is removed. Covering a pan in which a hot cream soup is being held for a time or placing a cover of foil or plastic wrap directly on the surface of a cooling milk-based pudding keeps scum formation on these products to a minimum.

Cocoa and hot chocolate are notorious for forming a scum. To reduce the problem for these drinks, they should be beaten until a foam is formed on the surface. Another approach is to add a marshmallow or a topping of whipped cream, both of which form a barrier that prevents air from coming in contact with the surface of the beverage.

Scorching

Use of a heavy pan or double boiler for heating milk helps eliminate scorching, which is caused by overheating the serum proteins that precipitate during cooking. These proteins are altered by heat and rapidly undergo denaturation. The denaturation of the serum proteins also carries some calcium phosphate to the bottom of the pan, trapped in the protein precipitate. The sugar in milk interacts with the protein precipitate to cause browning, called a **Maillard reaction**. Along with the precipitation of the serum proteins, a cooked milk flavor also develops. This is the result of the formation of sulfur-containing compounds, notably hydrogen sulfide.

Scorching can be alleviated by keeping the heating time to a minimum and by stirring frequently to keep the precipitated serum proteins from sticking to the bottom of the pan and

proteolytic enzyme Enzyme capable of catalyzing a break in a protein at a peptide linkage.

denaturation Unfolding of tertiary structure and clumping of protein molecules due to heating or beating.

coagulation Clumping of partially denatured protein molecules to make a relatively insoluble protein mass.

Maillard Reaction Browning reaction in food caused by reaction between protein and a sugar.

JUDGING POINTS
MILK-CONTAINING PRODUCTS

- No or minimal scum
- No brown flecks or scorched flavor from scorching
- Uniform appearance with no evidence of curdling

overheating. A double boiler is particularly effective in preventing scorching because the water beneath the pan of milk provides a slow rate of heating, allowing excellent heat distribution throughout the milk.

Curdling

A significant problem in working with milk is the formation of unsightly curdled products. These curds are precipitated protein aggregates and may be caused by various factors. Some foods containing milk are more likely to curdle than others because they contain acidic ingredients or may be rather high in salt; either of these characteristics can cause curdling, although for different reasons.

When fruits are combined with milk, the milk tends to curdle. As acidic fruits are added, the milk protein becomes less soluble. These precipitated proteins, notably casein, form the curds that are so distracting to the eye. One way of helping to reduce the likelihood of curdling when milk and fruits or tomatoes will be heated together is to be sure that the milk is fresh, because milk gradually may become more acidic as it ages. This acidity enhances the action of the acidic ingredients being added, and curdling is likely to occur. When working with milk, heating times should be as short as possible, for heating tends to destabilize the protein, making curdling more likely.

The effect of salt on curdling can be seen when scalloped potatoes are baked with generous amounts of salty ham cubes. The saltier the ham, the greater the prospect the milk-based sauce will curdle. This curdling is attributed to the fact that the ions of sodium and chloride from the salt interact with the electrical charges on the surface of the milk proteins. When the normally repulsive (similar charges causing molecules to be prevented from approaching each other) charges on the protein molecules are canceled by the ions from the salt, the protein molecules can form aggregates as hydrogen bonds link them. These molecular aggregates of milk protein are seen as curdled sauce in the scalloped potatoes.

Clotting of Milk

rennin Protein-digesting enzyme from a calf's stomach.

In most milk products, the goal is to avoid curdling the milk protein so that the result will be the desired smooth, fluid texture. However, sometimes the ability of casein to form a precipitate is utilized to produce clotted (clabbered) milk products. In fact, cheeses are clotted milk products that are subjected to a variety of techniques following the actual clotting process. Cheeses are such an important part of the diet that these are treated in a separate section of this chapter.

There are two types of clotted milk products that sometimes are produced in the home—**rennin** (or rennet) puddings and yogurt. These two products are of interest because different clotting mechanisms are used for each of them.

SCIENCE NOTE
pH AND PROTEIN DENATURATION

pH

The effect of acids and bases on such food components as pigments and carbohydrates has been pointed out in preceding chapters. Proteins undergo particularly dramatic changes as a result of acids. The acidity or alkalinity of a food or other substance is expressed in terms of its *pH*, which is defined as the negative logarithm of the hydrogen ion potential. This pH scale ranges from 0 to 14, with pH 7 representing neutral (neither acidic nor alkaline). The range between 0 and 7 is acidic, and the smaller the number, the more acidic is the substance. Between pH 7 and 14, the food is alkaline, becoming increasingly alkaline as the number gets larger.

Isoelectric Point

Proteins are **amphoteric** compounds (capable of behaving either as acids or bases, depending upon the medium in which they are found). This dual nature is the result of the presence of both the carboxylic acid and the amino groups in the molecules of proteins. At varying pH values, the carboxylic acid groups may ionize (COO^-), resulting in an overall negative charge on the protein molecules, while under other conditions, the amino groups may ionize to form NH^+, thus giving an overall positive charge. Because of this ability to ionize at the carboxyl or amino group, and also because of their various R groups, proteins will carry different electrical charges, depending upon the pH of the medium.

At a specific pH (which differs for each protein), the electrical charge on a protein will be neutralized (neither plus nor minus) on the surface of the molecule. When this electrical charge is at its minimum or neutral point, the protein is said to be at its **isoelectric point.** At this point, the protein molecules are very unstable or insoluble; they precipitate or form curds because the molecules get close enough to each other to form hydrogen bonds that hold them in clumps. Sometimes this is the action being sought (as in the making of cheese); other times the curdling is a culinary catastrophe.

The isoelectric point of casein in milk is pH 4.6. The pH of milk will vary with its freshness, but usually will be 6.5 or higher. If milk is added to a fruit with a pH of maybe 3.5, the combination of the two foods will clearly result in a pH approaching the isoelectric point of casein. In fact, if a small amount of milk is blended with the fruit or with tomatoes, that milk will pass through the range of the isoelectric point of casein, and curds will form.

If the converse is done, that is, if some fruit is stirred into a quantity of milk, the acid will gradually reduce the pH of the mixture as more and more fruit is added, but none of the milk protein will be in the pH of the isoelectric point of casein unless enough fruit is added to reduce the whole system to a pH approaching 5 or lower.

When working with protein, be it milk proteins or other foods with a significant quantity of protein, it is important to consider the isoelectric point of the specific protein system if the pH of the system is going to be modified by any ingredients. Techniques of preparation or ratios of ingredients can be modified to achieve the desired results if the likelihood of precipitation of protein at the isoelectric point is kept in mind.

Rennin puddings are made by the addition of rennin, a protein-digesting enzyme available synthetically or from the lining of calves' stomachs. The action of this enzyme results in the formation of a soft gel in which the precipitated protein serves as the continuous solid network. The water of the milk is trapped within this protein network, making a delicate, tender gel that, with suitable flavorings, is an easily digested, nourishing dessert. Although this clotting procedure is not complex, temperature control at about 100°F (38°C) is essential. If the rennin is subjected to too high a temperature, the enzyme will denature because it is a protein and will no longer be effective in catalyzing clot formation. Too cool a temperature delays the gel formation, the extent of delay being dependent on how cool the mixture is.

Yogurt relies on the growth of a bacterial culture of special lactic acid bacteria inoculated into the milk. Temperature well above room temperature (about 115°F [46°C]) is maintained to promote the digestion of lactose to lactic acid by the bacteria. As lactic acid accumulates, the pH of the milk decreases until the fluid begins to approach the isoelectric point of casein, at which point the casein begins to precipitate and forms the soft gel structure characteristic of yogurt.

As is true in making rennin puddings, temperature control is vital, although the reason is different. In the case of yogurt, too high a temperature would kill the microorganisms, and no more lactic acid would be produced. Electric yogurt makers provide the controlled temperature needed for producing the desired quality.

A few people make cottage cheese in the home. This process can be accomplished by use of rennin or by acid coagulation. Regardless of the clotting mechanism used, the gel structure formed will trap the large quantity of water normally found in milk. In order to produce a cottage cheese at home, it is necessary to cut through the gel structure in a number of places to allow the liquid (called whey) to drain from the curd. A modest amount of heating of the curd or squeezing the cut curd in cheesecloth helps to concentrate the protein curd.

amphoteric Able to act as an acid (carrying a + charge) or a base (a – charge). Their carboxyl and amino groups permit proteins to do this.

isoelectric point pH at which the electrical charge of a protein is essentially neutral.

DAIRY FOAMS

Protein-containing foods often are capable of forming foams (Chapter 12), and some of these are quite useful in food preparation. The dairy products used for foams include whipping cream, evaporated milk, and non-fat dry milk solids. The ease of forming and the stability of the resulting foams are qualities of particular interest when deciding which product to use.

Whipped Cream

Whipped cream is the dairy foam with the highest fat content; in fact, at least 30 percent fat is required for cream to foam satisfactorily. The stability of whipped cream is excellent if the cream is kept chilled, for the foam is stabilized by the aggregation of very small fat particles in the films of liquid that form the confining walls of the air bubbles. If the foam is slightly warm, the fat begins to soften, and the foam loses the strength originally contributed by the clumps of solid fat in the chilled foam. The protein in whipping cream is of some assistance in forming whipped cream foams, but this is quite insufficient to form the desired foam without the high fat content.

In addition to being sure that the cream to be whipped is well chilled, it is important in preparing whipped cream to stop beating before the emulsion reverses itself. Cream is an oil-in-water emulsion, but the beating involved in making whipped cream is sufficient to begin to make the emulsion somewhat less stable. If beating is not stopped at the right point, the emulsion will break, and clumps of butter (a water-in-oil emulsion) quickly result. Unfortunately, this change cannot be reversed.

Often sugar is added to whipped cream to provide a touch of sweetness. It also helps keep fat from clumping within the films surrounding the air bubbles, thus requiring additional beating if it is added before the desired end point. Overbeating is less likely to occur if sugar has been added to the foam during whipping than afterwards, but it may be added satisfactorily at either time.

Frozen or refrigerated whipped cream and toppings can be purchased ready to use. Stabilizing agents are added during the manufacturing of these products to achieve the necessary stability. Some of these are formulated with reduced-fat and low- or no-calorie stabilizers and sweeteners to appeal to dieters.

Evaporated Milk Foams

Evaporated milk can be used to make a less expensive, lower calorie foam than is available when whipping cream is the starting material. However, stability in evaporated milk foams can be a real challenge. Undiluted evaporated milk makes the most stable foam when the milk has been chilled in an ice cube tray to the point where some ice crystals are forming in it. Chilling the bowl and beater blades to be used in whipping the evaporated milk also is an aid in keeping the developing foam as cold as possible.

An evaporated milk foam is stabilized primarily by the viscous nature of the concentrated milk protein dispersion. The fat content is only about 7.5 percent, well below the 30–35 percent found in whipping cream; the protein content is about three times that in whipping cream. The composition of an evaporated milk foam clearly is quite different from that of whipped cream.

Non-Fat Dried Milk Foams

Non-fat dried milk foam, when diluted with an equal quantity of cold water (preferably a ratio of 1.5 parts solids to 1.0 part chilled water), can be beaten into a fine foam that can be held in the refrigerator for a few hours. This type of foam has the distinct advantage of being much lower in calories than other dairy foams because of the lack of fat. The disadvantage is the lack of a rich flavor.

The stability of this type of foam, while somewhat limited, is adequate for use as a topping. The addition of lemon juice helps to bring the mixture closer to the isoelectric point of casein, thus helping to denature the protein to add some stability to the resulting foam. Non-fat dried milk solid foams are stabilized by the denaturation of part of the protein during beating. The protein concentration varies with the amount of water added to the solids, but often will be 20 percent or even higher, which far exceeds the less than 3 percent found in whipping cream. This large amount of protein facilitates stabilization of the foam by protein denaturation. Of course, the fat content is essentially nil, making the stabilizing effect of the protein vital to non-fat dried milk solid foams.

ICE CREAMS AND OTHER FROZEN DESSERTS

Many people enjoy ice cream and related frozen desserts for their pleasing flavors, refreshing coolness, and smoothness in the mouth. An important aspect of these desserts is the presence of very small ice crystals, along with a somewhat light feeling on the tongue. Much of the technology associated with ice creams and other frozen desserts is focused on the factors influencing crystal size. Important among these factors is the role of the various ingredients included in the mixture to be frozen.

Ingredients and Their Influence

Sugar   The obvious role of sugar in ice cream is to sweeten the product. However, it also plays a role in determining the textural characteristics of the frozen ice cream, because sugar causes the freezing temperature of the mixture to drop. In fact, a cup of sugar in a quart of the ice cream mixture will decrease the freezing point approximately 2°F (0.7°C). This means that the ice cream must be chilled below the normal freezing temperature of water if ice crystals are to form.

The greater the content of sugar in an ice cream, the lower is the freezing point. This reduced freezing temperature helps to keep the size of crystals in the ice cream very small because a reasonable amount of stirring can be done during the freezing process to help break up any ice crystal aggregates as they slowly form. There is a counterbalancing negative role of sugar in ice cream. Very sweet ice creams will melt more quickly when served than will those with very little sugar in them, a direct result of the effect of sugar on freezing (and, conversely, melting) points.

Dairy Ingredients   Cream of various fat content often will be used as the liquid in making ice cream, not too surprising a fact in view of the name of the products. The cream is valued for its fullness of flavor, a contribution of the fat in the cream. The fat also helps to interfere with aggregation of ice crystals in the freezing mixture, a desirable influence in obtaining velvety smooth ice cream. Homogenized creams are even more effective in promoting a smooth texture than are non-homogenized creams because of the greater number of very small fat globules formed during homogenization.

Some milk solids may be added to help promote the desired texture. These solids help to develop a smooth texture because they increase the viscosity of the mixture to be frozen. They also contribute a bit to lightness in the mouth because of the tendency toward foaming introduced by the added protein content. The action of evaporated milk, when the milk is used without adding water to dilute it to normal strength, is similar to that of the non-fat dried milk solids. However, both these products introduce added lactose, which adds not only to the sweetness but may tend to introduce a sandy texture when frozen. This textural problem is a good indication of the fact that lactose is comparatively poorly dissolved and tends to precipitate in coarse crystalline aggregates when it is increased beyond the normal concentration in cream.

Juices   The liquid in sherbets and ices is primarily fruit juices. These juices contribute delightful flavors, but their acidity may necessitate using an increased amount of sugar, which adds to the calories and tends to create melting problems during service. In the event that both fruit juices and milk are to be used, curdling of the cream mixture is likely to be a problem, although prompt freezing can keep curdling to a minimum. Interestingly, because these tart mixtures need more sugar for adequate sweetening, the added sugar increases the viscosity of the mixture, thus helping to promote the formation of small crystals rather than large aggregates.

Freezing the Mixture

With Agitation   Commercial ice creams are pasteurized, homogenized, and often allowed to be refrigerated for a short period of time to allow blending of flavors and hydration of any added stabilizers before freezing. However, home-prepared ice cream mixtures frequently are not heated prior to being frozen. If mixtures are heated first, they should be allowed to cool to refrigerator temperature before placing them in the container for freezing. The freezing process may be done either with or without agitation, although agitation usually is considered desirable whenever possible because of the smoother, lighter texture achieved when stirring is done during freezing (Figure 11.12).

Designs for ice cream freezers vary somewhat, but most are composed of a bucket with a small drain in which a container holding the ice cream and a rotating dasher are suspended, with a motor or a mechanical crank being attached to the dasher. A variation of this device is a small

Figure 11.12
Ice cream achieves optimal texture by being agitated during freezing. Courtesy of Plycon Press.

container with a motorized agitator that can be operated within the freezer unit of a refrigerator, thus eliminating the need for a large bucket and ice. Although this device is small and convenient, the rate of freezing is considerably slower than in the conventional bucket assembly.

The conventional ice cream freezer is designed to permit rapid cooling of the ice cream mixture while agitating the freezing dessert. Rapid freezing is accomplished by packing the bucket surrounding the ice cream container with a mixture of ice and rock salt, the usual ratio being 1 part rock salt (a coarse ice cream salt) to 8 parts ice. The freezing process involves the removal of heat from the ice cream mixture until the product becomes so cool that ice crystals start to form. Removal of heat is facilitated by the use of a metal container to hold the ice cream because the metal helps to conduct the heat out of the ice cream and transfers the energy into melting the ice. As the ice melts, a salt brine is formed, with the salt dissolving into the brine. The presence of the sodium and chloride ions from the dissolved salt lowers the freezing (or the melting) point progressively as the amount of salt used is increased.

The recommended ratio freezes the mixture slowly enough to permit some air to be incorporated into the increasingly viscous mixture and also breaks up large aggregates of ice crystals that might be starting to gather. Sherbets, which have a lower freezing point than ice creams, require a ratio of 1 part salt to only 6 parts ice so that the melting ice-salt brine will be sufficiently cold to freeze even these foods. The coldest temperature that can be reached by this technique is –6°F (–21°C), the result of using a ratio of 29 percent salt and 71 percent ice (by weight). This approach to freezing ice cream is unsatisfactory, however, because the ice cream will cool so rapidly that not enough air will be incorporated to give the desired smooth texture before the mass freezes.

The rate of cranking the freezing mixture needs to be varied, depending upon the stage in the freezing process. To start, slow cranking is appropriate to help keep the entire mixture a relatively uniform temperature, rather than having freezing starting to take place around the edges of the container while the center is still comparatively warm. As the mixture begins to freeze, the rate of cranking should be increased to help maintain small crystals of ice and avoid the coarse aggregates that cause the finished ice cream to feel rough.

As more and more ice crystals form, the mixture becomes increasingly viscous, making it necessary to crank more slowly until further agitation is too difficult. The ice cream then is allowed to chill, covered, without further agitation while still standing in the brine solution for about half an hour. During this standing period, the ice cream becomes the desired firm consistency. The dasher needs to be removed as soon as agitation is stopped and before it freezes into the ice cream.

The key to preparing frozen desserts is stirring at the appropriate rate throughout the freezing process. Very rapid cranking before ice crystals begin to form may cause the butterfat to clump together in the ice cream and contributes to curdling. Insufficient agitation during active formation of ice crystals contributes to the rough texture characteristic of ice cream containing large aggregates of ice crystals. These aggregates will occur unless the dasher or other device regularly passes through the freezing ice cream to break up developing clusters before they solidify.

Without Agitation   Desserts also may be frozen without agitation, a process often referred to as *still-freezing*. This method of freezing ice cream can be done in any freezer with no other special equipment. Sometimes these mixtures are removed briefly from the freezer as the ice crystals start to form and are stirred a bit. This method helps to lighten and smooth the texture, but it still results in a product that has a rather heavy consistency and a suggestion of grittiness.

To help overcome these drawbacks, recipes for still-frozen ice creams frequently contain interfering substances to help minimize the tendency of ice crystals to congregate. A recipe using whipping cream or another rich source of fat increases the viscosity of the mixture and reduces the likelihood of coarse crystals of ice forming. If the cream used is whipped or some other type of foam (perhaps beaten egg whites, whipped gelatin, or whipped undiluted evaporated milk), the frozen product will have a reasonably light texture, albeit not as pleasing as ice cream made with agitation.

Evaluating Ice Creams

Ideally, frozen desserts of all types should have a rather light, yet not frothy, smooth feel on the tongue. The texture should be free of curdling and grittiness. Both flavor and color should be pleasing, yet distinctive. These frozen desserts should be able to be served and consumed without softening very much.

CHEESES

Origins and Applications

Cheese making is a skill that existed as long ago as 9000 B.C. and possibly even earlier. As far as is known, cheese production began in Arabia and flourished in Europe (Figure 11.13) during the Middle Ages, especially in the monasteries. Cheese was typically made in the home in the United States until the middle of the 19th century, when a cheese factory was built in New York State. Most of the cheese consumed in the United States today is commercial cheese.

Figure 11.13
Artisanal cheese making is still done in some villages around the Mediterranean and other parts of the world.
Courtesy of Plycon Press.

Cheese and milk have many nutritional attributes in common, although the actual amounts of the various nutrients in cheese depend on the type. Most cheeses are high in fat and calories and are good sources of complete protein; cottage cheese and other cheeses made from skim milk are low in fat. The nutrients generally are fairly concentrated in cheeses. This is because cheeses are made from milk from which most of the natural water content has been removed. Thus, calcium, phosphorus, and vitamin A are abundant in many cheeses.

Types of Cheeses

The two principal divisions in categorizing cheeses are natural and process. Natural cheeses may be classified on the basis of the following criteria: means of clotting (lactic acid or rennin), amount of ripening (cured or uncured), firmness, and source of the milk (cow, goat, or sheep). Process cheese products are differentiated into categories on the basis of moisture and fat content.

Natural Cheeses   Production of **natural cheeses** begins with the clotting of milk proteins to form a curd, which then is cut and worked to force much of the liquid from the gel. The liquid separated from the curd is whey, a distinctly fluid product with a yellowish-green tint caused by riboflavin and a rather sweet taste due to its lactose content. The curd is pressed into a compact mass and then is subjected to any of several treatments to achieve the desired end product. Some cheeses will have coloring added, while others may be inoculated with bacteria and/or molds to modify the flavor and texture. At this point, some natural cheeses are marketed as unripened cheeses, but many are stored to allow various changes to take place, resulting in ripened cheeses with characteristics unique to the particular type being ripened (Figure 11.14).

natural cheese
Concentrated milk curd; ripening is optional.

Ripening of cheeses may be very brief, or it may take months to achieve the desired changes typical of a particular variety. Ripened natural cheeses lose some of their naturally tough and rubbery characteristics, enabling them to blend readily with other ingredients in recipes.

Textures of ripened natural cheeses vary, depending upon the treatment. Some become very soft, whereas others may become quite hard and even a bit crumbly. Some become distinctly porous: Swiss cheese is a particularly good example of this quality. Another important area of change is in flavor, which usually becomes increasingly distinctive and full as the aging process continues. The actual extent of these various changes during ripening depends on storage time and temperature, with warm storage temperatures accelerating flavor development.

Table 11.6 provides an overview of many of the popular cheeses available to consumers, information about the type of milk used, and the ripening process (or lack of ripening). The firmness of the cheese is a common way of differentiating between the various natural cheeses. Ripening is another distinction often made in cheese classifications.

Figure 11.14
Feta cheese is a ripened cheese commonly made from the milk of sheep, although goat's milk also may be used. Courtesy of Plycon Press.

These characteristics were used to provide the classifications in Table 11.6: soft, unripened; firm, unripened; soft, ripened; semisoft, ripened; firm, ripened; very hard, ripened; and blue-vein mold, ripened.

Soft Natural Cheeses Cottage cheese is made commercially or at home from skim milk clotted by rennin and/or lactic acid. *Streptococcus lactis*, lactic acid producing bacteria, will convert lactose to lactic acid when milk is allowed to stand at a moderately warm temperature for a period of time, causing the milk to begin to approach the isoelectric point of casein. Under these conditions, the casein precipitates, leaving much of the calcium in the milk whey in the form of calcium lactate, a soluble calcium salt. This explains why cottage cheese made by precipitating casein with acid is lower in calcium than the milk was from which it was made.

Rennin frequently is used to clot milk when making cheese (Figure 11.15). When rennin is the mechanism for clotting the milk to make cheese, the calcium will be retained in the curd rather than being lost in the whey, because the calcium forms an insoluble salt with casein (calcium caseinate). Although cottage cheese ordinarily does not contain fat in the curd because of the lack of fat in the skim milk being clotted, some cottage cheese has cream added back to the cheese. When this is done, the fat content is 4 percent, and the cheese is identified as creamed cottage cheese.

Cream cheese is another soft natural cheese, but it is made from whole milk with some cream added, which explains its name. Lactic acid is the agent responsible for curd formation. Neufchâtel is quite similar to cream cheese, the difference being that this type of cheese contains somewhat less cream than is used in making cream cheese.

Camembert is a soft, ripened cheese cured with *Penicillium camemberti*. Characteristically, the center is rather fluid when fully ripened. Brie is closely related to Camembert, but is firmer.

Figure 11.15
This device is used to cut the curd that forms after rennin is added to milk to make cheese. Courtesy of Plycon Press.

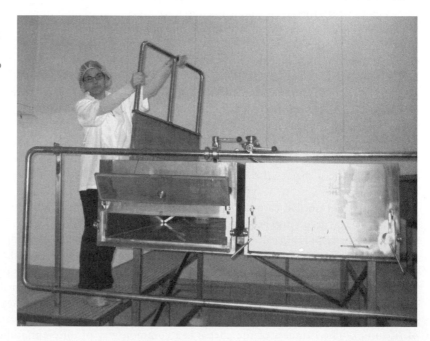

TABLE 11.6
CHARACTERISTICS OF SOME POPULAR VARIETIES OF NATURAL CHEESES

Kind or Name (Place of Origin)	Kind of Milk Used in Manufacture	Ripening or Curing Time	Flavor	Body and Texture	Uses
Soft, Unripened Varieties					
Cottage, plain or creamed (Unknown)	Cow's milk skimmed; plain curd, or plain curd with cream added	Unripened	Mild, acid	Soft, curd particles of varying size	Salads, with fruits, vegetables, sandwiches, dips, cheesecake
Cream, plain (United States)	Cream from cow's milk	Unripened	Mild, acid	Soft and smooth	Salads, dips, sandwiches, snacks, cheesecake, desserts
Neufchâtel (France)	Cow's milk	Unripened	Mild, acid	Soft and smooth, similar to cream cheese but lower in milk fat	Salads, dips, sandwiches, snacks, cheesecake, desserts
Ricotta (Italy)	Cow's milk, whole or partly skimmed, or whey from cow's milk with whole or skim milk added; in Italy, whey from sheep's milk	Unripened	Sweet, nut-like	Soft, moist or dry	Appetizers, salads, snacks, lasagna, ravioli, noodles, and other cooked dishes, grating, desserts
Firm, Unripened Varieties					
Mysost, also called Primost (Norway)	Whey from cow's milk	Unripened	Sweetish, caramel	Firm, buttery consistency	Snacks, desserts, served with dark bread
Mozzarella (Italy)	Whole or partly skimmed cow's milk	Unripened	Delicate, mild	Slightly firm, plastic	Snacks, pizza, lasagna, casseroles
Soft, Ripened Varieties					
Brie (France)	Cow's milk	4–8 weeks	Mild to pungent	Soft, smooth when ripened	Appetizers, sandwiches, snacks good with crackers and fruit, dessert cheese
Camembert (France)	Cow's milk	4–8 weeks	Mild to pungent	Soft, smooth, very soft when fully ripened	Appetizers, sandwiches, snacks; good with crackers, and fruits such as pears and apples, dessert cheese
Limburger (Belgium)	Cow's milk	4–8 weeks	Highly pungent, very strong	Soft, smooth when ripened; usually contains small irregular openings	Appetizers, snacks; good with crackers, rye or other dark breads, dessert cheese
Semisoft, Ripened Varieties					
Muenster (Germany)	Cow's milk	1–8 weeks	Mild to mellow	Semisoft, numerous small mechanical openings, contains more moisture than brick	Appetizers, sandwiches, snacks, dessert cheese

(Continued)

TABLE 11.6 (Continued)

Kind or Name (Place of Origin)	Kind of Milk Used in Manufacture	Ripening or Curing Time	Flavor	Body and Texture	Uses
Firm, Ripened Varieties					
Cheddar (England)	Cow's milk	1–12 months or more	Mild to very sharp	Firm, smooth, some mechanical openings	Appetizers, sandwiches, sauces, on vegetables, in hot dishes, toasted sandwiches, grating, cheeseburgers, dessert cheese
Edam (Netherlands)	Cow's milk, partly skimmed	2–3 months	Mellow, nutlike	Semisoft to firm, smooth, small irregularly shaped or round holes, lower milk fat than Gouda	Appetizers, snacks, salads, sandwiches, seafood sauces, dessert cheese
Swiss also called Emmentaler (Switzerland) *Very Hard, Ripened Varieties*	Cow's milk	3–9 months	Sweet, nut-like	Firm, smooth with large round eyes	Sandwiches, snacks, sauces, fondue, cheeseburgers
Parmesan also called Reggiano (Italy)	Partly skimmed cow's milk	14 months to 2 years	Sharp, piquant	Very hard, granular, lower moisture and milk fat than Romano	Grated for seasoning in soups, vegetables, spaghetti, ravioli, breads, popcorn; used extensively in pizza and lasagna
Romano also called Sardo Romano or Pecorino Romano (Italy)	Cow's milk; in Italy, sheep's milk (Italian law)	5–12 months	Sharp, piquant	Very hard, granular	Seasoning in soups, casserole dishes, ravioli, sauces, breads; suitable for grating when cured for about 1 year
Blue-Vein Mold, Ripened Varieties					
Blue, spelled bleu on imported cheese (France)	Cow's milk	2–6 months	Tangy, peppery	Semisoft, pasty, sometimes crumbly	Appetizers, salads, dips, salad dressing, sandwich spreads; good with crackers, dessert cheese
Gorgonzola (Italy)	Cow's milk; in Italy, cow's milk or goat's milk or mixtures of the two	3–12 months	Tangy, peppery	Semisoft, pasty, sometimes crumbly, lower moisture than blue	Appetizers, snacks, salads, dips, salad dressing, sandwich spreads, good with crackers, dessert cheese
Roquefort(France)	Sheep's milk	2–5 months or more	Sharp, slightly peppery	Semisoft, pasty, sometimes crumbly	Appetizer, snacks, salads, dips, sandwich spreads, good with crackers dessert cheese
Stilton[a] (England)	Cow's milk	2–6 months	Piquant, milder than Gorgonzola or Roquefort	Semisoft, flaky; slightly more crumbly than blue	Appetizers, snacks, salads, dessert cheese

Source: Adapted from Fenton, F. E., How to buy cheese, *Home and Garden Bulletin, No. 193,* U.S. Dept. Agriculture, Washington, DC, 1971. P. 8–17.

[a]Imported only.

INGREDIENT HIGHLIGHT
MASCARPONE

Mascarpone is a soft cheese that originated south of Milan, Italy. It is made by heating cream to 185°F (85°C), acidifying it with tartaric acid, and allowing it to clot for 24 hours in cold storage. The clot is squeezed to remove the whey before it is packaged for sale. Mascarpone needs to be consumed within a week; its high moisture content means that it will spoil faster than firmer cheese. Tiramisu, a popular rich Italian dessert, features mascarpone as a main ingredient. Honey can be blended with mascarpone to make a delectable accompaniment to fresh berries or other fruits. It also can be served as a savory spread for crackers when flavored with herbs.

Two popular dessert cheeses classified as soft cheeses—Limburger and Liederkranz—are noted for their highly developed aromas and flavors, which are the result of the ripening process.

Semisoft Natural Cheeses   There are three similar cheeses laced with a characteristic blue-green color and a distinctive flavor. These rennin-clotted cheeses, which are distinctly firmer than the soft cheeses, include Gorgonzola, Roquefort, and blue (or bleu). *Penicillium roqueforti,* or a similar mold, injected into the cheese will grow impressively during the ripening period of between 2 and 12 months to develop the desired textural and flavor changes. Gorgonzola and blue are produced using cow's milk, while Roquefort is made from sheep's milk. The other distinctive requirement for a cheese to be called Roquefort is that it be ripened in the caves near Roquefort, France, where the atmospheric conditions are quite uniform and uniquely suited to accomplish the desired ripening.

Muenster is a cheese reflecting the locale where it has been produced. Muenster from the United States is mild in comparison with the well-developed flavor of Muensters from Europe.

Brick gets its name from the ability of this cheese to be formed into brick-like shapes. The flavor is mild and comparatively sweet.

Hard Natural Cheeses   Cheddar cheese, named for the town in England where it was first made, is produced by using lactic acid bacteria to acidify the milk to the pH where rennin will be effective in bringing about curd formation. Annatto (an extract from the seedpods of a Central American tree) usually is added to produce the characteristic yellow-orange color often associated with cheddar cheese. The repeated cutting of the curd and draining of the whey, a process called cheddaring, is done to achieve the desired moisture content before salting and ripening are done.

Commonly, cheddar cheese will be found in the market in various stages of ripening, ranging from mild to very sharp. The cost of extended storage for ripening cheddar long enough to produce the distinctive and permeating flavor of very sharp cheddar is reflected in its comparatively higher cost compared with mild, the least costly.

Edam and Gouda are hard dessert cheeses that gain distinction by sporting colorful wax coatings. Holland is the home of these two types of hard cheeses. Another popular cheese sometimes used for dessert (as well as for many other occasions) is Swiss cheese, or Emmentaler. *Streptococcus thermophilus* and *Lactobacillus bulgaricus* are the microorganisms used to precipitate the curd. However, it is the gas production stemming from the inclusion of *Propionibacterium shermanii* that causes the impressive holes in ripened Swiss cheese.

Parmesan cheese, developed in Italy, is virtually synonymous with Italian cookery. To help this very hard cheese ripen satisfactorily over a period of between 16 months and several years, the exterior is rubbed with an oily mixture that gradually causes a dark green to black exterior to develop.

Process Cheeses

Process cheese is made from a mixture of natural cheeses and an emulsifier blended together with controlled heating. The various flavors of process cheeses are the result of the natural cheeses selected for making a particular process cheese. The emulsifier added may be sodium

process cheese   Blend of natural cheeses heated to at least 145°F (63°C) with the addition of an emulsifying agent and water; never ripened.

citrate, disodium phosphate, or other additive that will be effective in binding the high fat content of the natural cheese ingredients with the water that is added to the process cheese to produce the desired consistency. By heating this mixture to at least 145°F (63°C) and no hotter than 165°F (74°C) and stirring to achieve a homogeneous mixture, a cheese with excellent keeping qualities and usually a bland flavor is produced. The heat enhances shelf life because bacterial and enzymatic action are halted, thus preventing ripening. This process produces a pasteurized product, the accurate name being pasteurized process cheese.

For some purposes, cheese products with varying textural characteristics may be useful. Pasteurized process cheese products have a slightly higher moisture content than do the natural cheeses used to make them, which makes process cheeses a bit softer. However, variations of the process cheese contain even more moisture and less fat than process cheese. **Process cheese food** contains about 4 percent more water than does the comparable process cheese, while process cheese spreads have at least 4 percent more water than does the process cheese food. This additional water in the **process cheese spreads** results in excellent spreading characteristics.

Although process cheese products do not undergo flavor changes due to ripening, some variation in flavor is possible through the addition of such ingredients as pimiento, crushed pineapple, or bacon bits. Added seasonings are used in various process cheese spreads to heighten the flavor of these basically bland products.

Cold pack cheese is not a process cheese despite its similar formulation, for no heat is applied in manufacturing it, hence its name. (Cold pack is also known as club cheese.) The lack of heat in cold pack cheese processing results in flavors similar to the natural cheeses used in the product, but with enhanced spreading qualities due to the addition of the emulsifier.

Packaging and technological advances have resulted in the availability of a wide choice of process cheeses, process cheese foods, and process cheese spreads, a number of which can be stored in their packaging without refrigeration until they are opened.

Cheese Cookery

Process cheeses and related products are simple ingredients to use in cooking because they melt and blend readily with other ingredients. The emulsifier in them helps to prevent oil from separating and forming a greasy product. The somewhat lower fat content of process cheeses enhances their performance in heated foods. The disadvantage of these types of cheeses is the lack of distinctive flavors.

Natural cheeses afford a pleasing and distinctive range of flavors for use in different foods. Ripened natural cheeses will melt and combine well with other foods because the casein in the cheese is modified by the action of molds or bacteria to make this protein easier to disperse. A natural cheese that has not been ripened very much will be difficult to disperse and will lack the well-developed flavor of the fully ripened cheese.

The exciting flavors of ripened natural cheeses explain why many people select these cheeses over process cheeses in cooking. As just noted, unripened natural cheeses blend less readily than do ripened counterparts, but even the ripened counterparts tend to separate more readily than the process cheeses. Natural cheeses also may become tough and rubbery when held at serving temperatures for a period of time or when heated to too high a temperature.

process cheese food Process cheese product with about 4 percent more water than in process cheese.

process cheese spreads Process cheese product with about 4 percent more water than in process cheese food, or about 8 percent more than in process cheese.

JUDGING POINTS
CHEESE-CONTAINING PRODUCTS

- Pleasing flavor of cheese
- No oil separation or oiliness
- No stringiness or rubbery texture

Success in cooking with natural cheeses is achieved when attention is paid to certain factors, beginning with careful selection of well-ripened natural cheeses because of their ease in blending with other ingredients. Moreover, during the actual heating process, it is important to:

1. Avoid high temperatures.
2. Keep the heating period as short as possible.

These precautions are consistent with the fact that natural cheeses are high in protein and fat. The low temperatures and short heating periods are designed to keep the denaturation changes of protein to a desirable level. If subjected to too much heat, protein molecules will clump together very tightly, squeezing out considerable fat and making a rough, stringy protein curd. The longer the heating period and/or the higher the temperature, the more severe these changes will be. A cheese pizza that is baked at too high a temperature is a familiar example of these deteriorative changes. The toughening of the cheese proteins is evident when a piece of the pizza is accompanied by seemingly endless strands of cheese and an oily residue.

Often cheese-containing products are thickened by starch. The best results are obtained when the starch mixture is gelatinized prior to the addition of the cheese. Basically, the cheese only needs to be added long enough to melt completely before the fondue, cheese soup, rarebit, or other dish is served (Figure 11.16). Clearly, such items should not be boiled once the cheese is incorporated; grainy and stringy sauces will be the result when cheese is overheated.

When making casseroles and other baked products containing cheese, oven temperatures should be as low as feasible for the overall quality, and the baking time should be kept short. When possible, the cheese should be protected from oven heat by a layer of buttered bread crumbs, a sauce, or other insulation. The sides and bottom of a casserole, such as in macaroni and cheese, can be protected by placing the casserole dish in a pan of hot water, thus insulating the cheese in the casserole from some of the oven heat. In some instances, cheese is used to garnish the top of casseroles. This can be added just long enough before the end of the baking period to allow the cheese to melt.

Figure 11.16
Cheese rarebit, basically cheese sauce over toast, is a classic dish in England, which is noted for its outstanding cheddar cheese.
Courtesy of Plycon Press.

SUMMARY

Milk is a key food nutritionally, being a particularly valuable source of calcium, phosphorus, vitamin D, riboflavin, and protein, along with other nutrients. Pasteurization and refrigeration are invaluable in helping to maintain the safety of milk. Homogenization and fortification are valued for their contributions to convenience, palatability, and nutrient content. These processes are used in treating fresh milks of varying fat content, as well as processing in canned and dry milks. Butter, creams, ice creams, and imitation products, as well as the various milk products, are handled and stored under rigorous state and federal controls.

Protein structure (from the amino acid units comprising a single molecule through the primary to even the quaternary structure) is very complex and is subject to change when various forms of energy are applied, notably when heat or mechanical agitation is used during food preparation. Denaturation involves physical changes, particularly in the tertiary structure of proteins, and a clumping together of molecules.

Milk proteins are of concern in food preparation because of their participation in such changes as scum formation, scorching, curdling, and clotting. Control of the acidity of protein-containing mixtures can help to keep the protein away from the isoelectric point, thus reducing the likelihood of detrimental changes in the protein.

Whipping cream with a fat content of 30 percent or more will whip readily to a foam with reasonable stability. Evaporated milk foams can be made if the undiluted milk is chilled until crystals start to form on the edges. Stability of evaporated milk foams is very limited unless gelatin or other stabilizer is used. Dried milk foams can be made when the solids are diluted with water in a 3:2 ratio.

Natural cheeses are valued for their distinctive flavors and wide range of textures. However, in food preparation, the toughening of the protein and the tendency for the fat to separate are potential problems that can be minimized by keeping temperatures low and heating times short.

Process cheese, process cheese food, and process cheese spread are mixtures of natural cheeses blended with an emulsifier and water and then pasteurized to produce rather bland cheeses that are easy to use without becoming unduly tough or exhibiting fat separation. Cold pack cheese is virtually the same as process cheese except that heating is not involved.

STUDY QUESTIONS

1. What useful changes occur in milk as a result of the homogenization process?
2. Compare the ease of formation and stability of foams made from whipping cream, coffee cream, evaporated milk, and non-fat dried milk solids. What contributes stability to the different foams?
3. Why is the calcium content of cottage cheese clotted with acid lower than that clotted with rennin?
4. Describe the result of using a process cheese versus a well-ripened natural cheese in a grilled cheese sandwich. What advantages and disadvantages can you cite for the two types of cheeses used in this preparation?
5. Compare ice cream made without agitation and the same recipe made with agitation. Explain the differences.
6. Why is the cranking of an ice cream freezer done slowly at first? What may happen if the cranking is much faster than recommended?
7. Why is salt added to the ice used in an ice cream freezer?
8. Diagram the (a) primary, (b) secondary, and (c) tertiary structures of a protein.
9. Why is the isoelectric point of a protein important?
10. Why does heat cause denaturation of protein?

SELECTED REFERENCES

Baggs, C. 2002. Saying more than just cheese. *Food Product Design* 11(12): 72–79.

Beardmore, G. 2006. Cheese, the right stuff(ing). *Food Technol.* 60(5): 21.

Beckley, J., and H. Ashman. 2008. Developing compelling dairy foods. *Food Technol.* 62(12): 26.

Brody, J. 2010. Say Mozzarella. *Food Product Design* 20(4): 22.

Bullens, C., et al. 1994. Reduced-fat cheese products using carrageenan and microcrystalline cellulose. *Food Technol.* 48(1): 79.

Burrington, K. J. 2002. New dairy ingredients "moove" to enhance products. *Food Product Design* 12(1): 63–74.

Burrington, K. J. 2002. More than just milk. *Food Product Design* 12(7): 37–64.

Burrington, K. J. 2004. 21st century ice creams. *Food Product Design* 14(2): 88.

Burrington, K. J. 2006. Fine-tuning cheese performance. *Food Product Design* 15(10): 45.

Criado, M. T., et al. 1994. Importance of bacterial adhesion in the dairy industry. *Food Technol.* 18(2): 123.

Crick, F. H. C., and J. C. Kendrew. 1957. X-ray analysis and protein structure. *Adv. Prot. Chem. 12:* 133.

Decker, K. J. 2009. Yogurt in a high state of ferment. *Food Product Design* 19(3): 76.

Feder, D. 2009. Smile and say *formaggio*. *Food Product Design* *19*(10): 30.

Foster, R. J. 2009. Reduced-fat dairy indulgences. *Food Product Design 19*(1): 18.

Handojo, A., Y. Zhai, G. Frankel and M. A. Pascall. 2009. Measurement of adhesion strengths between various milk products on glass surfaces using contact angle. *J. Food Eng. 92*(3): 305–311.

Hazen, C. 2004. Cultured dairy products. *Food Product Design 13*(12): 73.

Hazen, C. 2009. Stabilizing ice cream. *Food Product Design 19*(2): 32.

Hazen, C. 2010. Crafting better dairy stability. *Food Product Design 20*(11): 28.

Hazen, C. 2011. Dairy-based beverages. *Food Product Design 21*(1): 32.

Hollingsworth, P. 2003. Culture revolution. *Food Technol. 57*(3): 20.

Hollingsworth, P. 2003. Frozen desserts: Formulating, manufacturing, and marketing. *Food Technol. 57*(5): 26–45.

Klahorst, S. 2002. Nutrients from dairy sources. *Food Product Design: Functional Foods Annual*. Sept.: 89.

Knehr, E. 2004. Whey protein gives beverages a boost. *Food Product Design. Functional Foods Annual*. Sept.: 29.

Koski, S. 2008. Power of whey. *Food Product Design 18*(8): 22.

Kuntz, L. A. 2010. Concentrating on whey protein isolate. *Food Product Design 20*(3): 18.

Light, A., et al. 1992. Hedonic responses to dairy products: Effects of fat levels, label information, and risk perception. *Food Technol. 46*(7): 54.

Marshall, R. T., and D. Goff. 2003. Formulating and manufacturing ice cream and other frozen desserts. *Food Technol. 57*(5): 32–45.

Miraglio, A. M. 2004. Wheying the positives. *Food Product Design 13*(11): 33.

Miraglio, A. M. 2006. Better-tasting, better-for-you ice cream. *Food Product Design 16*(2): 82.

Morr, C. V. 1992. Improving texture and functionality of whey protein concentrate. *Food Technol. 46*(1): 110.

Narasimmon, R. G. 2009. Say low-fat cheese. *Food Product Design 19*(1): 24.

Ohr, L. M. 2007. Technological advances spur dairy innovation. *Food Technol. 61*(7): 77.

Olson, N. F., and M. E. Johnson. 1990. Light cheese products: Characteristics and economics. *Food Technol. 44*(10): 93.

Pszczola, D. E. 2009. Uses for dairy deepen. *Food Technol. 63*(1): 46.

Pszczola, D. E. 2010. Permissible indulgence in dairy. *Food Technol. 64*(2): 49.

Rittman, A. 2005. From cheese to sauce. *Food Product Design 14*(12): 75.

Rockwell, B. P. 2010. Healthier kid's beverages. *Food Product Design 20*(10): 88.

Salminen, S., et al. 1991. Fermented whey drink and yogurt-type product manufactured using Lactobacillus strain. *Food Technol. 45*(6): 112.

Sloan, A. E. 2002. Got milk? Get cultured. *Food Technol. 56*(2): 16.

Spano, M. 2010. The many faces of soy. *Food Product Design 20*(10): 26.

Spano, M. 2010. Whey to better health. *Food Product Design 20*(11): 14.

Tharp, B. W., and T. V. Gottemoller. 1990. Light frozen dairy desserts: Effect of compositional changes on processing and sensory characteristics. *Food Technol. 44*(10): 86.

Turner, J. 2004. Fine-tuning the art of cheese making. *Food Product Design 14*(11): 126.

Van Hekken, D. L., and N. Y. Farkye. 2003. Hispanic cheeses: The quest for queso. *Food Technol. 57*(1): 32–38.

Young, J. 2008. Ethnic cheeses perceptions. *Food Product Design 18*(9): 48.

Immunologist Peter Holt (foreground) and veterinarian Lara Vaughn collect and label eggs that will be tested for *Salmonella enteritidis*. Courtesy of Agricultural Research Service.

12

Proteins: Eggs

Chapter Contents

Key Concepts

1. Eggs are a nutritious, high-protein food that needs to be refrigerated at all times to maintain safety and quality.

2. In food preparation, eggs contribute color and flavor, promote emulsion formation, act as an agent to thicken or to clarify, and contribute structure and texture.

3. To prepare high-quality egg products, avoid overheating by using moderate temperatures and heating just long enough to achieve the desired end point.

4. Egg foams need to be beaten to the correct end point to achieve the volume and texture required in soufflés, fluffy omelets, and foam cakes.

5. Consumers and food manufacturers can choose among fresh eggs, designer eggs, egg substitutes, dried, and frozen eggs.

INTRODUCTION

If only one word could be used to describe eggs in food preparation, that word would be *versatile,* for eggs are used not only as a dish by themselves but also in many other complex food systems. They may be prepared alone: perhaps fried, poached, baked, scrambled, or cooked in the shell. Some of the more complex recipes featuring eggs include soufflés, omelets, and angel food and sponge cakes.

In food preparation, eggs are valued for their ability to:

1. Emulsify
2. Thicken
3. Clarify and bind
4. Foam

Food systems containing both fat and a liquid can be emulsified with the aid of eggs, particularly egg yolks. This emulsifying property is used in stabilizing salad dressings, cream puffs, cake batters, and many other foods. The thickening ability of eggs is of importance in preparing such items as custards and some sauces. This ability is used to clarify some clear soups or beverages. Also, the batter used in deep-fat frying vegetables illustrates the use of egg as a binding agent. Egg white foams add to the volume and texture of such food products as sponge and angel food cakes, as well as being baked as meringues. Yolk foams also are used occasionally.

NUTRITIONAL VALUE

Eggs are one of the most cost-effective means of obtaining complete protein. They each provide about 6 grams of animal protein, and the price per serving is quite low in comparison with beef and other animal protein foods. The fat content of eggs (6 grams) is entirely in the yolk. The combination of the protein and fat adds up to approximately 80 calories per egg. Most vegetarian diets permit generous use of eggs as a means of ensuring adequate protein intake and also providing other nutrients.

The yolk is a source of other nutrients as well as fat. For instance, the iron in the yolk (0.9 milligrams) is valuable in helping to meet the required intake of this key mineral. Another positive nutritional benefit of the egg yolk is the presence of useful amounts of vitamin A, even though the actual level varies somewhat with the diet of the hen. A negative contribution of the yolk is cholesterol, a substance to be avoided or minimized by people who are deemed by physicians to be at risk of a heart attack. The yolk of an egg provides 186 milligrams of cholesterol. Eggs marketed as being high in polyunsaturated fats and egg substitutes developed in response to the concern over cholesterol are rather costly alternatives to fresh eggs.

Whether white or brown, the color of an eggshell is determined by the kind of chicken that laid it. For example, White Leghorns always lay eggs with white shells, and Rhode Island Reds lay brown-shelled ones. The color is a matter of esthetics because it has no impact on the nutritional value of the egg.

STRUCTURE

The various structural features of eggs are all of importance because of their contributions toward the practical aspects of marketing and storage, as well as the functional roles played in food preparation. The shell, made up largely of calcium carbonate, serves as a protection for the contents of the eggs, despite the fact that it is perforated with innumerable tiny holes. These holes hold the potential for bacterial contamination and infiltration into the interior and also provide the avenue for the loss of some water and carbon dioxide

INGREDIENT HIGHLIGHT
YOLK COLOR

Yolk color is influenced by the diet of the hen and is an indicator of the level of xanthophylls. Deeper, brighter orange yolks are desirable nutritionally because they contain more lutein and zeaxanthin, phytochemicals contributing to eye health. In the human eye, lutein and zeaxanthin are found in the macula lutea, where they may prevent ultraviolet light from entering the eye.

Marigold petals and paprika are particularly rich sources of xanthophylls, and these are sometimes used in commercial feed to improve the nutritive value of egg yolks. The marigold enhances the yellow, and paprika brings out the red to contribute the desired richly colored yolk (with enhanced levels of lutein and zeaxanthin). Corn, which is commonly fed to hens, naturally contains xanthophylls, too, but the levels drop as the corn sits in storage. The addition of marigold petals and paprika in small amounts brings the corn or wheat feed to desirable levels of xanthophylls.

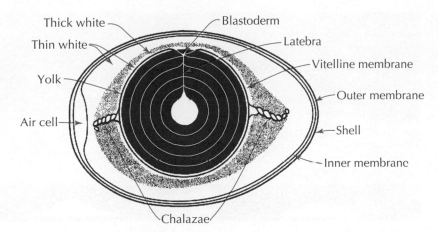

Figure 12.1
Cross-sectional diagram of an egg.
Courtesy of Plycon Press.

Labels on figure: Thick white, Thin white, Yolk, Air cell, Blastoderm, Latebra, Vitelline membrane, Outer membrane, Shell, Inner membrane, Chalazae

from the egg. A mucin layer, called the bloom, coats the exterior of the shell until the egg is washed or buffed.

Inside the shell, yet another protective device is found. In fact, there are two protective membranes (the inner and the outer); both membranes aid in blocking passage of materials through the shell. An air cell is situated between the two membranes at the end of the egg. Immediately inside the inner membrane (Figure 12.1) there is a layer of thin white. Sandwiched between this first layer and another layer of thin white is the thick white. Trapped by the three-layered white is the yolk, which is contained within the **vitelline membrane.** The **chalazae,** two fibrous tissues, extend on either side of the yolk, helping to keep the yolk centered within the egg and restricting its movement. The germ spot or **blastoderm** is seen as an indistinct spot on the yolk. The latebra is the white column extending under the blastoderm to the center of the yolk. Although difficult to see, the yolk actually is composed of layered sections of white and yellow yolk.

The composition of the white is quite different from that of the yolk. The white is very high in water (87 percent) and contains essentially no fat. In contrast, the yolk is about 35 percent fat and only about 50 percent water. These differences help to explain the distinctive behavior of the yolk and the white in food preparation.

vitelline membrane
Membrane surrounding the yolk.

chalazae Fibrous structures at the sides of the yolk, aiding in centering the yolk within the white.

blastoderm Germ spot in the egg yolk.

SELECTION

Deteriorative Changes

Although all eggs have the same structural features, the quality will vary as a result of storage conditions and deteriorative changes. One obvious change in eggs as they lose quality is the increasing size of the air cell. This is the consequence of the loss of some moisture and carbon dioxide from the egg through the pores in the shell. The rate at which this happens is dependent upon the storage conditions and the retention of the protective covering on the shell. The loss of carbon dioxide stems from the white, a loss that causes the egg white to become increasingly alkaline as deterioration proceeds.

Accompanying this loss of carbon dioxide and increase in alkalinity is a thinning of the thick white. As the thick white decreases, the yolk is able to move through the white more readily than through the original thick white, and the yolk tends to float toward the upper surface within the white. This movement within the white is possible despite the impedance provided by the chalazae. In addition, the vitelline membrane weakens.

When eggs are broken from the shell, these changes can be noted (Figure 12.2). The white spreads over a large surface area and fails to pile up around the yolk. The yolk is flattened on the surface, rather than being held in a rounded shape, a consequence of the weakening of the vitelline membrane. There also is considerable likelihood of the yolk breaking. These changes are the basis for the grading of eggs.

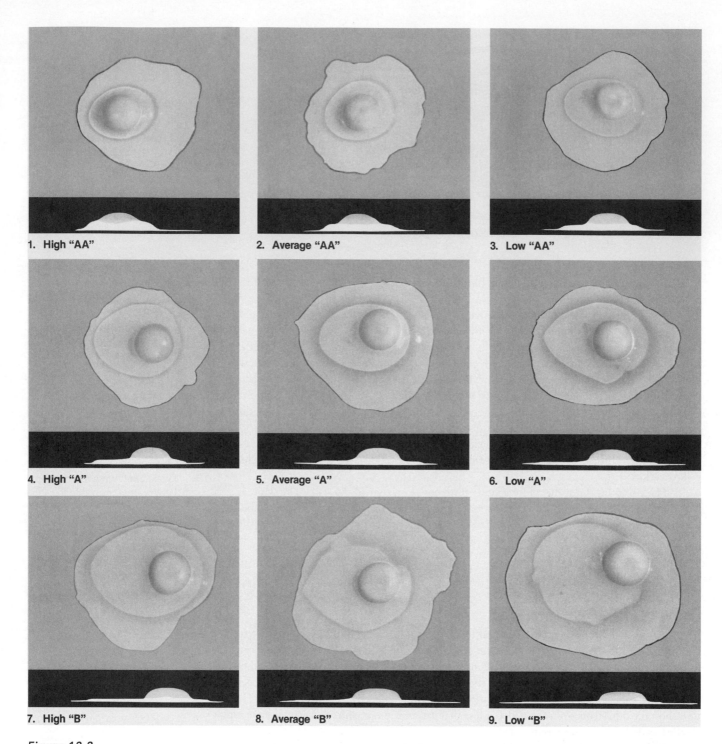

1. High "AA"   2. Average "AA"   3. Low "AA"

4. High "A"   5. Average "A"   6. Low "A"

7. High "B"   8. Average "B"   9. Low "B"

Figure 12.2
Grading standards for eggs are based on the comparative deteriorative changes that have occurred. Grades range from top-quality Grade AA to Grades A and B. Note the greater surface area covered by the white and the reduced height of the yolk with decreasing grades. Courtesy of U.S. Department of Agriculture.

Safety Oversight

Eggs have the potential for being contaminated with microorganisms even before they are laid until they are eaten. This span means that various government agencies and several people play a role in bringing safe eggs to the table.

When eggs are forming in the hen, there is a remote potential that a transovarian infection may transmit *Salmonella enteritidis* into the egg, where the bacteria remain viable until killed by heat during cooking. Prevention of this infection requires good sanitary measures where the eggs are being laid.

There are also opportunities for microorganisms to contaminate eggs by entering through the pores of the shell. If eggs do become contaminated internally, microorganisms multiply. The rate of multiplication is dependent on storage temperatures, so careful control of sanitation and storage temperatures throughout the marketing process must be maintained to assure the safety of eggs in the marketplace.

Several government agencies at state and federal levels are involved in monitoring eggs and their safety. Among those at the federal level are the U.S. Department of Agriculture, Animal and Plant Health Inspection Service (APHIS), Food Safety and Inspection Service (FSIS), Food and Drug Administration (FDA), Agricultural Research Service (ARS), and National Agricultural Statistics Service (NASS). Many state agencies also are involved in state safety programs.

Grading

Federal grading of eggs is done under the direction of the U.S. Department of Agriculture. Since this grading often is done in concert with state programs, the joint program is referred to as the Federal–State Grading Program. The grades for eggs reaching retail markets are U.S. Grade AA (the top grade), U.S. Grade A, and U.S. Grade B (Figure 12.3).

To be graded as AA, shell eggs must have a clean, unbroken shell, an air cell less than 1/8 inch deep, and a yolk that is well centered and free of defects. When the air cell is a maximum of a quarter of an inch deep, the yolk is centered fairly well and is relatively free of defects, and the shell is clean and sound, the egg is of U.S. Grade A quality. Grade B, the lowest quality grade for consumers, is assigned if the yolk is somewhat mobile with a flattened appearance, the air cell is a maximum of 3/4 inch deep, and the shell is only slightly stained.

The grades are established in advance of the marketing process, often being determined prior to an extended storage period. Hence, the grade indicated on eggs tells the condition at grading and may not necessarily reflect the actual grade at the time of purchase. This is a problem for consumers, but no suitable alternative has been found.

In the Shell. **Candling** is the process used for grading eggs in the shell before eggs enter the consumer market. This process is a simple one in which eggs are rotated as they pass in front of a light (Figure 12.4). The size of the air cell, the position and mobility of the yolk, and the possible presence of such foreign substances as rots, molds, and blood spots can be seen as silhouettes. The viscous nature of the white in a high-quality egg will prevent the yolk from moving readily, and the yolk will appear as an indistinct, dark silhouette in the center of the egg, while a Grade B egg will have a yolk that reveals a rather distinct silhouette moving near the edge of the egg (Figure 12.5 a, b, c).

A blood spot on the yolk is not graded down, for it can be removed easily, but blood in the white is not acceptable since this condition causes rapid spoilage. Eggs with a porous shell are graded down because of the increased ease of moisture and carbon dioxide loss. The color of the shell is ignored in determining egg grades, for this characteristic has absolutely no influence on the quality of the egg or its nutritive value. The shell color is simply a characteristic determined by heredity.

Out of the Shell. For the commercial food industry, eggs often are sold in bulk after being shelled. These shelled eggs are graded by various methods. One system uses the **yolk index,** a figure derived by measuring and dividing the height by the diameter of the yolk. Another measurement is the height of the thick albumen (thick white), expressed in arbitrary units called

Figure 12.3
Shell egg grade marks. U.S. AA is the top grade. Note that the size is indicated on the label in the top shield. Size is not related to grade.
Courtesy of Plycon Press.

http://www.foodsafety.gov/keep/types/eggs/index.html
—Government information on egg safety and other consumer information about eggs.

candling Procedure used to grade eggs in the shell.

http://www.ams.usda.gov/AMSv1.0/getfile?dDocName=STELDEV3004502
—Egg grading manual.

http://www.fsis.usda.gov/fact_sheets/Focus_On_Shell_Eggs/index.asp
—Extensive information on eggs in the shell.

yolk index Measure of egg quality out of the shell; height of yolk divided by diameter.

Figure 12.4
An ARS-developed procedure makes tiny cracks (microcracks) in this candled egg visible. Courtesy of Agricultural Research Service.

Figure 12.5
Eggs graded by candling are backlighted to reveal the quality of the egg while still in the unbroken shell: (a) yolk outline slightly defined (Grade AA), (b) yolk outline fairly well defined (Grade A), and (c) yolk outline plainly visible (Grade B). Courtesy of U.S. Department of Agriculture.

(a)

(b)

(c)

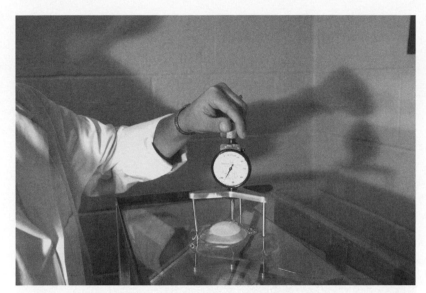

Figure 12.6
A micrometer is used to grade quality when eggs are graded out of the shell. The height of the thick albumen, measured in Haugh units, is progressively less from Grade AA to Grade B.
Courtesy of U.S. Department of Agriculture.

Haugh units. In this system, Grade AA whites have a minimum value of 72 Haugh units; Grade A, 60–71; and Grade B, 31–59 (Figure 12.6). The color of the yolk is ignored in establishing egg grades out of the shell, for the color is merely an indication of the hen's diet, not the quality.

Weight Classes

Egg cartons in the retail market identify not only the grade quality but the weight class (on the basis of a dozen eggs). The largest (jumbo) eggs weigh 30 ounces per dozen, and the smallest (peewee) weigh only 15 ounces per dozen. The weight classes (per dozen) are as follows:

Jumbo	30 oz
Extra large	27 oz
Large	24 oz
Medium	21 oz
Small	18 oz
Peewee	15 oz

These weight designations provide an indication of the general size of the eggs within the container, but the actual size of individual eggs may vary considerably within a single carton. For example, a small egg may compensate for a large one so that the weight of the dozen will average out appropriately.

Recipes usually are based on the use of large eggs, although most recipes have sufficient tolerance to permit the use of extra-large eggs. In fact, recipes relying on egg white foams often are superior when made using extra-large eggs.

Grade and weight classes are two independent features of egg marketing. Grade clearly designates quality at the time the candling was done. Weight denotes only size and carries no implication of the quality of the egg. Most markets offer choices both in sizes and grades. The most common choices are between extra large and large in sizes and between AA and A in grading.

In general, if the difference in price between sizes is less than 9 cents per dozen, the larger size is less costly than the smaller size per ounce. Conversely, a price difference of more than 9 cents makes the smaller size the more economical buy. For many egg dishes, including frying and poaching, U.S. Grade AA is the wise choice, but U.S. Grade A or even B can be used satisfactorily in puddings and many baked products. Angel food cakes and other foam products are best when prepared with high-quality eggs.

Designer Eggs

Consumers now have additional options when they are shopping for fresh eggs. Some eggs are being marketed as cage free or free range (Figure 12.7). The benefits of such treatment may be nice for the hens, but eggs laid by caged hens have a more sanitary environment than do the

http://www.egglandsbest.com/home.aspx

—Eggland's Best website; information on special eggs.

Figure 12.7
In this market, free-range eggs are more than two times as expensive as those laid by caged hens. Courtesy of Plycon Press.

http://edis.ifas.ufl.edu/ PS048

—Consumer information on designer eggs.

www.aeb.org

—American Egg Board website; variety of information on eggs.

eggs laid in a free setting. Organic eggs are another option. This designation can only be used if the hen feed meets federal regulations for being labeled "organic."

Omega-3 eggs are being produced and marketed as a dietary source of omega-3 fatty acids that may help to reduce the risk of heart disease (Figure 12.8). The amounts of these fatty acids in eggs increase when hens are fed a special diet that often includes flaxseed and fish oil. A darker yellow yolk is also created by this diet.

Egg ranchers also are producing eggs with reduced levels of cholesterol and/or saturated fat. For these eggs to be marketed as lower in cholesterol or saturated fat, they must have a reduction of at least 25 percent compared with regular eggs. Prices for eggs requiring special diets for the hens are usually higher than other eggs.

Figure 12.8
Omega-3 and organic eggs are options available to consumers willing to pay more for them. Courtesy of Plycon Press.

> **INDUSTRY INSIGHT**
> ## EGG SUBSTITUTES
>
> As a response to the public concern over the cholesterol content of egg yolks, egg substitutes are now on the market. Formulas in different brands vary, but basically the egg white is retained and the yolk is replaced with vegetable oil products and carotenoids (as coloring agents) and a nutritional additive. Other substances also are added to make the final product simulate fresh whole egg. These substitutes are available in both frozen and fluid (refrigerated) forms. The nutritional analyses vary with the product, with the calorie value ranging from higher to lower than fresh whole egg.
>
> All egg substitutes are alike in that they do not contain cholesterol, and they are significantly more expensive than eggs. These substitutes can be used in various recipes where whole fresh egg is an ingredient as suggested by the manufacturers, but the results frequently are not identical to those made with eggs. Nevertheless, most products are quite acceptable to those who have been instructed to curtail cholesterol intake because of diagnosed health problems. Use of egg substitutes in scrambled eggs and French omelets has been more satisfactory than in some more elaborate egg preparations. Consumers do need to be aware of the fact that cartons of egg substitutes usually contain less than the equivalent of a dozen eggs.

ALTERNATIVES TO FRESH EGGS

Frozen Eggs

In institutional feeding operations, frozen eggs represent a valuable time-saver because of the great deal of time required to break eggs in quantity and the even greater amount of time required to separate the yolks and whites after they are broken. Add to that labor cost the fact that yolks may be dropped into the whites when eggs are being separated, and it is obvious that frozen eggs are a viable alternative to fresh eggs in quantity cookery.

One of the important problems in freezing eggs is the control of microorganisms. To reduce contamination, the shells are washed just before the eggs are broken from the shell. Freezing then is done just as quickly as possible, with attention being directed throughout the processing to eliminating any contamination. Pasteurization of the white, yolk, or whole egg is an aid in reducing microorganism counts. The heat treatment of pasteurization has only a very slight effect on the baked products made with pasteurized frozen egg products.

Frozen whole egg and egg white are more satisfactory than the frozen yolks because the yolks begin to thicken during frozen storage and then do not blend well with other ingredients after being thawed. The addition of salt or sugar to yolks or whole eggs prior to freezing reduces this tendency, however. It is important to consider the end use intended for frozen yolks or whole eggs, because those containing sugar can be used very satisfactorily in dessert items, but are not acceptable in scrambled eggs and similar items.

Whites can be frozen commercially or in the home without adding other ingredients. They can be thawed and used just as fresh whites would be.

Dried Eggs

Packaged mixes provide a familiar example of the use of dried eggs, with angel food cake mix being a popular one. Institutional feeding operations also are customers for dried eggs. Dried eggs are produced by forcing liquid egg through an atomizer as a fine spray, which then is dried quickly, cooled, and packaged. Bacterial control is vital to the production of a high-quality dried egg. The yolk, the white, or the whole egg may be converted into a dried product, but objectionable changes in color, flavor, odor, and solubility occur when either dried yolks or whole eggs are held at storage temperatures above 40°F (4°C). Commercial bakeries using dried egg products are able to incorporate them with other ingredients quite satisfactorily if mixing is done at high temperatures (as high as 154°–176°F [68°–80°C]).

STORAGE

One of the remarkable features of eggs is their capability of undergoing storage for even longer than six months if the conditions are controlled carefully. By utilizing such storage, the supply of eggs to markets can be kept quite constant throughout the year, thus helping to keep eggs comparatively low in cost. Eggs naturally have an excellent protection in the form of the shell, but certain techniques are utilized to enhance the maintenance of quality during storage. Appropriate storage conditions include a controlled atmosphere of carbon dioxide and very cool temperatures (between 29°F and 31°F [–2°C and –1°C]). These conditions reduce carbon dioxide loss and inhibit enzymatic and microbiological action. The humidity must be sufficiently low to inhibit mold formation on the shells.

Since the pores in the shells represent the potential for deteriorative mechanisms to function, eggs needing cleaning before storage will be washed, which removes the bloom as well as the dirty material. The pores are resealed by coating the shells, usually by dipping them in mineral oil held at 110°F (43°C), a temperature high enough to keep the oil from being drawn through the pores into the egg during dipping.

A crucial aspect of maintaining quality during storage is controlling temperature, for eggs lose quality rapidly when they are not chilled. At no time during the marketing process should eggs reach even 60°F (16°C), and preferably the temperature should be maintained just above freezing. Unless eggs are shipped and marketed under refrigeration, their quality will be something less than their grade classification indicates.

Consumers are not able to observe much of the storage and marketing process, but they do have an opportunity to observe how eggs are handled in the display area of the market. Clearly, eggs displayed in market aisles with no refrigeration will be of lower quality than will those kept properly chilled. Even display cases that are overflowing with egg cartons do not afford adequate refrigeration for optimal maintenance of quality. Adequacy of refrigeration of eggs in the back of the store and in all previous phases of the marketing process can only be assessed by the actual quality of the eggs when they are used.

Egg selection needs to be based on the known quality of eggs purchased from a store as well as on the grade indicated on the carton because of the many opportunities for inadequate refrigeration and loss of quality. In other words, shopping for egg quality is based on selecting a store with high standards for maintaining good control of temperature for eggs.

Consumers need to assume responsibility for safe egg storage after buying them. Guidelines are presented in Table 3.3, page 46.

EGG COOKERY

Functional Roles

Coloring and Flavoring Agent When egg yolks are included in products, they add a pleasing richness of color in addition to enhancing flavors. For instance, in a lemon meringue pie filling, it is the egg yolk and not the lemon that contributes the expected yellow color. Cream fillings and cream puddings gain their creamy color from the egg yolks they contain.

Emulsifying Agent The ability of egg yolk to act as an emulsifying agent is due, at least in part, to lecithin, a phospholipid in the yolk. Lecithin is attracted to the interface between the aqueous and lipid phase of an emulsion. In essence, lecithin helps to form a protective, monomolecular layer around the droplets in an emulsion. This layer prevents the droplets from coalescing and breaking the emulsion because the lecithin blocks direct contact of the oil droplets with each other in most food emulsions. Hollandaise sauce and cream puffs are two classic examples of foods that rely heavily on their egg yolk content for successful emulsions.

Thickening Agent The ability to serve as a thickening or binding agent depends upon the change in solubility occurring when proteins are denatured by heat. Proteins in the yolk are different from those in the white, which results in slightly different behaviors of these two portions of egg when heated. However, both the white and the yolk are capable of thickening when heated.

The heating of egg-thickened mixtures requires much more careful attention to temperature control than is necessary for gelatinizing starch in preparing starch-thickened mixtures. Egg mixtures should be heated just to the point where they achieve maximum thickening without any sign of curdling, and then they should be served immediately or cooled to prevent curdling due to the residual heat in the mixture. Such precautions are not necessary when thickening with most starches. Novices may overheat products when learning to use egg as a thickening agent, because they expect the same dramatic thickening with egg as occurs with starch. In fact, the thickening occurring with egg is fairly subtle.

Clarifying Agent   The thickening ability of egg proteins also is used in some recipes to bind particles during coagulation. For example, soup stock can be clarified by stirring in beaten egg white (one egg per quart of stock) and then blending it completely with the stock. While the stock is simmering for about 10 minutes, the proteins coagulate and capture particles. After a cup of cold water is added, the fat is removed from the surface, and the scum is removed by pouring the stock through a fine strainer. The result is a clear stock. A similar technique sometimes is used by campers when they add eggshells to boiled coffee to settle the grounds.

Structural and Textural Agent   When egg proteins are denatured, they become rather rigid and are capable of providing structural strength and texture to food products, particularly if the concentration of egg is high. Perhaps the best example of the importance of eggs as a structural agent is in the preparation of popovers. The high concentration of egg explains the rigid, yet somewhat elastic, quality of the cell walls in popovers, a texture quite different from the usual character of breads. Similarly, the walls of sponge cakes and angel food cakes gain much of their character from the egg foams they contain.

Divinity is a candy that illustrates a unique contribution of egg white protein to texture. In this case, the egg white foam and the hot, concentrated sugar syrup are beaten together. The egg white proteins are denatured by the combination of beating and the heat from the syrup. These denatured proteins aid in separating sugar crystals in the divinity, thus blocking the aggregation of crystals that would result in a gritty candy.

Foams, particularly egg white foams, are both structural and textural aids in several different types of products. Fluffy omelets, soufflés, and foam cakes (sponge, angel food, and chiffon) are familiar examples of the use of foams to attain a large volume and a light, somewhat porous texture. Skillful preparation and careful incorporation of these foams with other ingredients are necessary if a high-quality product is to result.

Foams can be prepared using egg whites, egg yolks, or even a mixture of the two, but the largest volume by far is obtained using only egg whites. Foams need to be beaten to the correct point and then incorporated very gently with any other ingredients to avoid as much loss of air as possible. Finally, the product containing the foam usually is baked to help stabilize the foam by denaturing the protein to strengthen the cell walls. Immediate baking in a preheated oven reduces the time available for cells to collapse and for volume to be lost from the foam.

ovalbumin   Heat-sensitive, abundant protein in egg white.

ovomucin   Structural protein abundant in thick egg white.

SCIENCE NOTE
FACTORS INFLUENCING DENATURATION

There are several proteins in egg whites of interest in studying denaturation. **Ovalbumin,** the most abundant of these proteins, can be denatured by mechanical agitation and by heat. **Ovomucin** and lysozyme are two other proteins that have been studied in relation to heat denaturation. Ovomucin is responsible for much of the structure in thick egg white and is about four times as abundant in the thick as in the thin white. Initiation of the actual coagulation of egg white is thought to be the result of formation of a complex between ovomucin and lysozyme molecules in the white, a change that causes an increasing opacity as denaturation progresses.

Egg yolks contain a mixture of proteins. The water-soluble protein fraction in egg yolk is called livetin. Two other proteins contribute to the emulsifying ability of the yolk, as well as adding to the thickening power of yolks. These proteins, lipovitellin and lipovitellinin, are lipoproteins; the combination of protein and lipid in their structures accounts for their emulsifying power.

(Continued)

(Continued)

Type of Protein

Proteins in egg white are more responsive to heat denaturation than are those in the yolk. Denaturation begins at about 125°F (52°C) under extremely controlled laboratory conditions. Under ordinary conditions of heating, whites will start to coagulate perceptibly at about 140°F (60°C) and will cease to flow at about 149°F (65°C). The yolk starts to coagulate at just about the temperature where the whites cease flowing (149°F [65°C]). The flow character of the yolks is lost at about 158°F (70°C).

Since there is a difference in coagulation temperatures between the yolks and the whites, it is not surprising that the use of whites, yolks, or whole egg will cause a small difference in the temperature to which egg-thickened products will need to be heated to achieve optimum thickening. A product containing only egg whites will thicken more readily than will one thickened only with yolks, while whole egg mixtures will thicken over an extended temperature range.

Rate of Heating

A slow rate of heating permits coagulation to be completed at the lower end of the temperature range for the type of protein being heated because there is adequate time for the necessary unwinding of the tertiary structure and aggregating of several of these relaxed molecules before the temperature rises very much. When heat input is great and the temperature is rising rapidly, there is very little time for the relaxation and subsequent aggregation of protein molecules to occur before the temperature is at the upper end of the range for denaturation.

Time is an important factor to consider when denaturing egg proteins, for it is interwoven intimately with temperature and possible curdling of products. The very gradual temperature rise resulting from a slow rate of heating provides adequate time to assess the progress of the denaturation process and to remove the product from the heat before curdling can occur. Intense heat input causes denaturation to occur at a comparatively high temperature, but there is almost no time between reaching the desired degree of denaturation and the onset of curdling, which is, unfortunately, an irreversible and unattractive condition.

Added Ingredients

The addition of acids, such as lemon juice and cream of tartar, lowers the coagulation temperature because they help to reduce the alkalinity of the egg, bringing the proteins toward their isoelectric points. Since the electrical charges on the surface of the protein molecules are reduced as the isoelectric point is approached, the electrical repulsion of the molecules will be reduced on the surface, and the clumping together of molecules will be facilitated by the addition of acid ingredients. Although it is possible theoretically to add so much acid to a food system that the pH drops below the isoelectric point of the protein, this does not occur in normal food products. Thus, it is realistic to say that the addition of acid reduces the temperature for coagulating egg proteins.

Sugar has the opposite effect of acid on the coagulation temperature of egg-thickened products. When sugar is added, the coagulation temperature rises, too. This effect is due, at least in part, to the dilution of the protein concentration by the added sugar. The dilution of protein, whether by sugar or other ingredient in a reasonable quantity, will cause a detectable rise in the coagulation temperature of the protein system. This is even true when milk is added, despite the fact that adding milk is adding some protein. The overall effect of adding milk is to dilute the protein, because milk contains mostly water. The reverse arises if the concentration of egg protein is increased by increasing the amount of egg used or decreasing the level of sugar, milk, or other significant ingredient. The increased concentration of protein causes the denaturation temperature range to drop and resemble rather closely the range for concentrated egg white, whole egg, or yolk.

The effects of the rate of heating, the type of protein, and the concentration of the protein, as well as the pH of the medium, are important to recognize, for they clearly influence the preparation of successful products. Salts, because of their ability to ionize, are recognized as being involved in denaturation of egg proteins. However, this is not of practical significance, since virtually any food being prepared will have sufficient salts to permit denaturation. This can be demonstrated by baking a custard prepared with distilled water rather than milk. This water custard will fail to gel properly until a salt is added to provide the electrical ions needed to interact with the electrical charges on the surface of the protein molecules. Once the ions are available, the complete coagulation process can be observed. Milk and other ingredients commonly used in egg-thickened products provide adequate ions for normal denaturation to occur; hence, salts need not be added.

Safety Measures

Only about 0.005 percent of the eggs in the market are infected with *S. enteritidis*, yet even this small risk of infection makes it wise to assure that any fresh eggs have been heated to at least 160°F (71°C) (or 140°F [60°C] for 3 1/2 minutes) to kill any *S. enteritidis* that might be present (Figure 12.9). Various egg-containing products require different techniques to assure adequate heating. The process to use on egg yolks when making mayonnaise is described in Chapter 7. Stirred custard, eggnog, or egg-containing ice cream mixtures need to be heated to 160°F (71°C). Scrambled eggs are heated sufficiently when no liquid is visible. Poached and fried eggs should be cooked until the whites are coagulated and the yolks are starting to thicken.

Meringues that are to be baked will be heated sufficiently when baked for at least 15 minutes at 325°F (163°C). If meringues are being used in unbaked recipes, such as cold soufflés, the egg whites and sugar need to be heated over hot water while being beaten until the whites form soft peaks. This meringue will get hot enough to kill the harmful bacteria that might be present.

In the Shell

Eggs may be soft cooked or hard cooked by placing them gently in boiling water and then maintaining a simmering temperature (185°F [85°C]) until the desired stage of doneness is reached (Figure 12.10). For soft-cooked eggs, between 3 and 5 minutes will be sufficient to thicken the white and perceptibly thicken the yolk without hardening it; about 18 minutes will complete the coagulation of the yolk of a hard-cooked egg if the egg is at room temperature before being simmered, but somewhat more time will be needed if the egg is colder at the start of heating.

The use of a simmering temperature during egg cookery is recommended to avoid toughening the protein of the white before the heat has had sufficient time to penetrate and coagulate the yolk. To reduce the likelihood of cracking the eggs when they are being added to the boiling water, each egg should be dunked a couple of times with the aid of a slotted spoon to allow an opportunity for the expanding gas in the air cell to escape through the pores at a moderate rather than an explosive

Figure 12.9
Eastern Regional Research Center chemical engineers Sudarsan Mukhopadhyay (left) and Peggy Tomasula examine a ceramic membrane module for use in microfiltration of liquid egg whites to eliminate potential pathogens such as *Salmonella enteritidis*. Courtesy of Agricultural Research Service.

Figure 12.10
When preparing hard- or soft-cooked eggs, water should be maintained at a simmering temperature to avoid toughening the proteins. Courtesy of Plycon Press.

Figure 12.11
A well-prepared hard-cooked egg has a tender white and completely coagulated yolk with no trace of ferrous sulfide surrounding it. Courtesy of Plycon Press.

rate. When simmering is completed, hard-cooked eggs should be immersed immediately in cold water and then peeled in order to cool them rapidly.

A well-prepared soft-cooked egg will possess a white that is tender yet completely coagulated, while the yolk will flow somewhat lazily when cut. The flavor should be pleasingly fresh. Hard-cooked eggs of high quality should have a firm and tender white surrounding a well-centered, completely coagulated, non-waxy yolk with no discoloration surrounding the yolk (Figure 12.11).

Success in preparing soft-cooked eggs depends upon using an egg of acceptable quality and accurate timing. Hard-cooked eggs present similar requirements, but the quality of the egg is of greater importance than is true for soft-cooked eggs. The hard cooking of eggs immortalizes the quality so that a portrait of that quality can be seen when the egg is peeled and sliced in half. If the yolk is close to one side and the air cell is large, the egg is of low quality.

Additional evidence of low quality is the formation of a dark ring of ferrous sulfide on the surface of the yolk. This combination of iron and sulfur from the yolk and the white, respectively, is unattractive evidence of a low-quality egg, poor control of simmering and cooling conditions, or both. The comparatively high alkalinity of a low-quality egg promotes formation of ferrous sulfide, but this compound will form even in an egg of high quality if the cooking period is extremely long or if the egg is not cooled rapidly following the simmering period.

Hard-cooked eggs sometimes are resistant to peeling. The problem of having some of the white peel off with the shell leaves a distressing topographic outline, yet this is the sign that the egg is of high quality. Ease of peeling is associated with eggs having whites with a pH of at least 8.9, which means that carbon dioxide has been lost from the egg and that quality is deteriorating. The only eggs having a pH lower than 8.9 are those less than two days old or those that have been dipped to seal their pores and prevent loss of carbon dioxide.

JUDGING POINTS
SOFT-COOKED EGGS

- Yolk slightly thickened throughout, but without any firm areas
- White all coagulated, but not tough
- Pleasing, fresh flavor

JUDGING POINTS
HARD-COOKED EGGS

- Yolk firm, but tender, with no traces of undenatured yolk
- No trace of a dark ring around the yolk
- Well-centered yolk
- White firm, but tender

Out of the Shell

Fried Eggs Eggs prepared in very simple ways are included frequently in meals, particularly at breakfast. Fried eggs, a favorite way of preparing eggs out of the shell, are prepared by heating eggs of high-quality in fat in a frying pan using either of the following methods. One technique is to fry eggs slowly in an excess amount of fat, with the hot fat being spooned over the upper surface to baste the egg and coagulate the protein fairly uniformly, including the thin layer of white coating the yolk surface. In the other method, just enough fat is used to keep the eggs from sticking, and a small amount of water is added to form steam within the tightly covered frying pan. The steam aids in coagulating the upper surface.

Either method should result in an egg that has a tender white and a slightly thickened, unbroken yolk covered by a film of coagulated white. There should be no evidence of crisp browning on the white, for this is an indication of extreme overheating of the proteins in the white and results in unnecessary toughness. Careful control of the heat is needed for either method of frying to avoid making the egg tough.

Poached Eggs With the emphasis on weight control and keeping the fat content of the diet low, poaching is an appropriate way of preparing eggs. Only eggs of high quality will be satisfactory when poached, because low-quality eggs will spread badly when slipped into the simmering water. A high-quality egg, with its abundance of thick white, will have little tendency to spread away from the yolk.

Poaching is done by heating water almost to boiling before slipping the egg in very gently, directing it toward the side of the pan to help retain the desired shape (Figure 12.12). Water is retained at simmering to coagulate the egg without unduly toughening the protein. The turbulence associated with boiling would also tend to fragment the structure of the egg, resulting in

Figure 12.12
A pleasing poached egg is prepared by sliding a high-quality egg very gently into simmering water and removing it carefully with a slotted spoon when the white is completely coagulated and the yolk is thickened slightly. Courtesy of Plycon Press.

JUDGING POINTS
FRIED EGGS

- Completely coagulated white occupying a relatively small area and without evidence of frying around the edges
- Unbroken, nicely rounded yolk with a veil of coagulated white on the surface
- Yolk that flows slowly when cut, but is not hardened in any region

---

JUDGING POINTS
POACHED EGGS

- Most of white coagulated in a firm, but tender mass surrounding the yolk
- Yolk unbroken and slightly coagulated, but not firm any place
- Fresh flavor
- Well drained

a less attractive egg than can be achieved in simmering water. Simmering should be continued only until the white has coagulated into a solid mass, and the yolk is very slightly denatured to a honey-like consistency. Just as soon as this point is reached, the egg should be removed gently with a slotted spoon to allow any extra water to drain.

A poached egg should have a firm, tender white piling well around a slightly thickened, unbroken yolk. No part of the yolk should be coagulated to the point where it begins to solidify. The white should be in a single mass and not display streamers of denatured thin white. If desired, an egg poacher can be used to avoid the spread of eggs during poaching.

Baked Eggs   Baking is another way of preparing eggs with little or no fat. Baked eggs are prepared by breaking eggs into individual ramekins or custard cups and baking in a 325°F (163°C) oven. Although butter, salt, and pepper sometimes are added to the surface of the egg before baking, this is not necessary for those who are watching fat and salt intake. High-quality eggs are desirable for baking because they will have a fresher flavor than will those of lower quality.

The white of a well-prepared baked egg will be tender and completely coagulated, and the yolk will be viscous but not set when it is cut. There should be no trace of browning around the edge.

Scrambled Eggs   Scrambling is a good way of preparing eggs below U.S. Grade AA, for the eggs are beaten gently to blend the whites and yolks completely before they are heated. A weak yolk and a limited amount of thick white are not particular problems when scrambling eggs, and the usual addition of milk to tenderize the product by diluting the egg protein has the added benefit of enhancing flavor, which might otherwise be dull. Of course, high-quality eggs can be used to make scrambled eggs, too.

When the ingredients have been blended completely, but without creating a foam, the mixture is poured into a greased or nonstick skillet and heated slowly. Continuous, slow stirring is done during the entire cooking period to scrape moderately large pieces of coagulated egg from the skillet bottom and allow the undenatured fluid egg to reach the heat of the pan. This procedure is continued until no more egg mixture actually flows, but the large pieces of scrambled egg are still quite shiny on their surfaces. For best results, the eggs are served immediately; holding scrambled eggs increases toughness of the product and may lead to syneresis (liquid separating from the coagulated masses).

Evaluation of scrambled eggs is done on the basis of appearance and eating qualities. The pieces should be solid (not porous), moderately large, and a uniform, yellow color throughout. There should be no trace of browning, for that is evidence of too intense a heat. The surfaces should be just slightly shiny, but there should not be any tendency to flow. In the mouth, the eggs should be tender, and the flavor should be pleasing.

JUDGING POINTS
BAKED EGGS

- Tender, but completely coagulated white
- Rounded yolk, with coagulated white veiling the surface
- Slightly thickened but not solidified yolk
- Fresh flavor

JUDGING POINTS
SCRAMBLED EGGS

- Homogeneous yellow with no flecks of white or brown
- Tender
- Moderately large, irregular pieces that are slightly moist on the surfaces
- Pleasing, fresh flavor

French Omelet A French omelet could be described as a golden brown half-moon of a cooked egg mixture (Figure 12.13). Actually, the mixture cooked for scrambled eggs is the same as that used in making a French omelet; only the cooking method is different. However, the results are startlingly different.

The eggs are blended thoroughly with a tablespoon of milk (the same as is used for scrambled eggs) for each egg and a bit of salt for flavor; care is taken in making both products to avoid beating air into the mixture so that the finished products will not be porous. Unlike the preparation of scrambled eggs in a rather cool skillet, butter is heated in the skillet until it is sizzling before the egg mixture is added when a French omelet is being prepared. This rather intense heat is desired so that the egg in contact with the pan will begin to coagulate almost immediately and will start to develop the desired golden brown color and smooth surface on the outside of the finished omelet.

As the egg is cooking, the omelet is lifted in places with a narrow spatula to allow uncooked egg to flow to the bottom of the skillet. When no more uncooked egg can be tipped to flow to the bottom, lifting of the omelet ceases except for a quick examination to be sure the desired golden brown color has been achieved. If not, the heat is turned up briefly to finish browning. Then the filling is scattered on half the omelet, and the omelet is folded over or rolled so that the browned bottom surface is on the outside.

A French omelet should have a pleasing, golden brown exterior surface, and the interior should be a uniform, yellow color with no evidence of streaks of white or of porosity. The center should be glossy, but not runny. The flavor should be pleasing, and the omelet should be tender, except for the slightly toughened crust.

Custards

Stirred Custard In contrast to the egg products already discussed that are made with only egg and perhaps a very small amount of diluents, stirred custard is a mixture of a comparatively large amount of milk, flavored with sugar and extract and thickened with a rather small amount of

Figure 12.13
A French omelet, unlike scrambled eggs, should be browned pleasingly before being folded and served. Browning is promoted by having the butter sizzling when the egg mixture is added. Courtesy of Agricultural Research Service.

JUDGING POINTS
FRENCH OMELET

- Uniformly yellow color throughout the interior with no flecks of white
- Golden brown exterior
- Interior coagulated, but slightly moist
- Tender, except for exterior
- Pleasing flavor
- Neatly folded in half or rolled

Figure 12.14
To avoid curdling from residual heat, stirred custard must be cooled very rapidly as soon as it is heated enough to coagulate the mixture enough to coat a spoon when it is dipped in. Courtesy of Agricultural Research Service.

egg. When prepared carefully, stirred custard will be a very smooth, delicately flavored sauce with a viscosity about that of heavy cream (Figure 12.14). The content of milk and egg makes stirred custard a very nourishing sauce to serve over fresh fruit, gingerbread, or other baked desserts.

Preparation of stirred custard requires some patience and diligence to achieve the desired viscosity without curdling. First, the ingredients are beaten gently together and then strained to remove the chalazae. Then, very gentle heating is done in a double boiler over simmering water or over very low direct heat. Stirring is done slowly and constantly to assure uniform heating and denaturation of the egg protein. Slowly, the mixture will approach the temperature range at which denaturation will occur.

Heating is continued until a metal spoon is coated evenly when dipped in the custard. Just as soon as this test is noted, the custard is poured into a shallow dish resting on a bed of ice for very rapid cooling. This is necessary to avoid having the residual heat curdle the mixture by overheating the denaturing protein. Once the egg proteins have been overheated and the custard has curdled, there is no way of reversing the process, although judicious use of an eggbeater will make the texture somewhat smoother. The recommended slow rate of heating not only helps to obtain uniform denaturation but also provides a somewhat extended period of time to determine when the desired end point has been reached and to initiate cooling before curdling can happen. Regardless of the rate of heating, residual heat can cause curdling of the custard after it has been removed from the heat unless cooling is done very rapidly.

Baked Custard   Either baked or stirred custard can be prepared from the same milk–egg mixture, the difference being only in the method used to heat the two products. Stirred custard retains its flow properties because the constant stirring prevents the formation of a gel structure. However, baked custard is heated quiescently in the oven at 350°F (177°C) until a thin knife can be inserted halfway between the center and the edge of the custard and come out clean (Figure 12.15). The center still will shake a bit when the custard is moved at this point, but the residual heat in the hot custard will be sufficient to set it by denaturing the egg protein even in the center of the dish. This test is not performed at the center of the custard because the residual heat will overheat the protein severely if the custard is baked until a knife comes out clean in the center. Overbaking causes a

---

JUDGING POINTS
STIRRED CUSTARD

- Uniform light yellow throughout
- Smooth texture, with no evidence of curdling
- Consistency of heavy cream
- Pleasingly sweet flavor

porous texture in a baked custard and syneresis. On the other hand, underbaked custard will fail to set (form a gel) in the center, and the product will be rather soft and runny.

The ideal baked custard will be tender enough to shake just a tiny bit in the center, but will hold a sharp edge when sliced. The interior texture is perfectly smooth, with no holes, and there will be no evidence of syneresis. The upper surface may have a touch of golden brown but will not have even a trace of burning. No traces of white will interrupt the golden yellow of the interior. Crème brûlée, with its topping of caramelized sugar, is but one of the variations that can be made utilizing a custard base.

Custard pies and quiches also are popular. These pies should be tested with a knife halfway between the center and the edge to determine whether they have been baked sufficiently. Overbaking of pumpkin, pecan, or plain custard pies is the most common reason for a soggy crust in them. Another means of helping to avoid a soggy crust is to bake the crust partially, but not enough to brown it, before adding the filling. For the adventurous, the crust can be baked in one pie pan and the filling in another. After cooling, the filling is slipped cautiously into the crust.

Cream Puddings and Pies

Nourishing and pleasing desserts can be made by combining egg yolk with cornstarch-thickened puddings to enrich the color and flavor. Cream puddings, such as the cornstarch pudding described in Chapter 10, are prepared by gelatinizing the starch completely over direct heat.

Figure 12.15
Baked custard (insulated by simmering water during baking to avoid overheating the outer portions) is done when a knife inserted halfway between the edge and center comes out clean.
Courtesy of Plycon Press.

CULTURAL ACCENT
QUICHE

Quiche Lorraine and other kinds of quiche are among the flavorful dishes that come to mind when thinking about egg cookery and cultural adaptations. French cuisine features quiches, which are custard tarts made with various ingredients that add variety and flavor. The first step is preparation of the crust that lines the quiche pan. This special pan is a round baking pan with rather straight, low sides. The bottom often is removable to help facilitate service of the

baked quiche. The custard mixture traditionally is made with eggs and cream, plus the desired additional ingredients. For dieters, milk may be substituted for the cream. Because the filling is thickened with eggs, it is important to bake the quiche just until the custard is set. Overbaking causes the egg proteins to draw together and gradually force liquid from the coagulated egg. This liquid soaks into the crust, causing the crust to lose its crispness and become soggy.

Then the pudding is removed from the heat, and a spoonful is stirred vigorously into the beaten yolks to be sure that the hot pudding is dispersed immediately throughout the yolks, gradually causing them to approach coagulation temperature. This process is repeated three more times to dilute the egg yolks and help to raise the coagulation temperature of their proteins before they are stirred into the hot pudding. The warm, diluted egg-protein mixture is stirred into the cream pudding, and heating is continued gently for about 5 minutes to ensure that the yolk proteins are coagulated. This heating is imperative, for upon standing, uncoagulated yolks will cause the pudding to become quite thin. Coagulation of the yolks is evidenced by a subtle increase in the viscosity of the hot pudding and a slight loss of glossiness.

Overheating of the yolk-containing pudding by boiling or by heating too long should be avoided so that the pudding will not develop a curdled texture. Use of a double boiler or a very low heat setting will aid in avoiding this problem. It should be noted that the starch gelatinization process, with its extended period of intense heating, is completed before the egg is added to help prevent overheating the egg proteins.

Whether preparing a cream pudding or a cream pie, the procedure just outlined is used. Puddings are usually poured into appropriate serving dishes and chilled before being served. Cream pie fillings are poured into baked pie shells and then are usually topped with a meringue and baked. Both cream puddings and cream pies need to be held in refrigerated storage as soon as they have had an opportunity to cool a bit, because their content (egg and milk) can support strong growth of microorganisms that might be present. Refrigeration is important to food safety.

A well-prepared cream pudding or pie filling will be perfectly smooth, showing no lumps from the starch or from overheated egg protein. When chilled and cut, the product should soften very slightly but should not flow. In other words, it is just a bit softer than a baked custard. Cream puddings should have a rather light feel on the tongue, with no trace of stickiness or pastiness. Overstirring, often the result of too slow a rate of cooking during gelatinization, leads to a pasty quality. The flavor should be pleasing and appropriate for the specific type of product being prepared; scorching should not have occurred.

Meringues

Stages of Beating   Egg white foams form the basis of hard and soft meringues, as well as being utilized in many cakes and other baked products. The characteristics of the foams vary with the extent of beating, and these stages need to be recognized if optimum quality is

---

JUDGING POINTS
CREAM PUDDINGS

- Smooth consistency with no pastiness or lumps
- Softens slightly, but does not flow when cut
- Pleasing flavor with no overtone of raw starch or scorching

to be obtained in products utilizing them. Egg whites are beaten to the **foamy stage** before other ingredients are added. The foamy stage is characterized by a porous texture, with large, uneven air cells, and a transparent appearance. At the foamy stage, cream of tartar or lemon juice may be added to aid in stabilizing the foam. Sugar also is added very gradually at the foamy stage.

Continuation of beating beyond the foamy stage gradually increases the viscosity and also the opacity of the foam. The texture becomes increasingly fine and more uniform with beating beyond the foamy stage. Sugar continues to be added gradually during this period, if sugar is a part of the recipe. For most recipes, beating should be continued until the beater can be pulled slowly out of the foam, and the resulting peaks will just bend over. This is often referred to as the **soft peak stage** (Figure 12.16). At this point, the foam will have some elasticity if it is used immediately yet will be sufficiently stable to maintain a good volume while being blended with other ingredients and baking in the oven.

The soft peak stage is the stage used most frequently in cookery. This stage is reached rather rapidly if whites are beaten without adding sugar or acid but is delayed significantly when either of these ingredients is used. An electric mixer is convenient for forming these latter foams.

With a bit more beating, the egg white foam will continue to get even stiffer than it is at the soft peak

Figure 12.16
When the peaks just bend over when a spatula is pulled up slowly from the beaten whites, the foam is at the soft peak stage, the point at which most egg white foams are used or folded in with other ingredients.
Courtesy of Plycon Press.

stage. The peaks will stand up straight when the beater is withdrawn at this point, yet the surface has a sheen, and the foam remains intact. This **stiff peak stage** is used in making hard meringues and chiffon cakes.

If beating is continued beyond the stiff peak stage, a very few revolutions of the beater will result in the whites being overbeaten and so stiff that they become brittle and the foam breaks apart. This **dry stage** is unsuitable for any application in food preparation. The rigidity of the cell walls is due to considerable denaturation of the protein by mechanical action.

Care should be taken to be sure that beating is stopped at the correct point. However, if this dry stage is reached, a partial reversal can be accomplished by beating in some sugar, which helps in softening the foam and facilitating folding in of ingredients. Unfortunately, this will result in too much sugar in the product. Avoidance of overbeating is the best solution.

Soft Meringues Egg whites beaten with an acid and sugar beginning at the foamy stage can be whipped to the soft peak stage and then spread on a pie filling or other suitable dessert in preparation for baking. The usual amount of sugar added in making soft meringues is 2 to 2 1/2 tablespoons per egg white, the latter producing a sweeter, higher calorie product that cuts better than the one with less sugar. Addition of sugar needs to be started gradually at the foamy stage; the texture and volume will not be as pleasing if the foam is beaten beyond this point before the sugar addition is initiated.

Adequate beating to achieve the soft peak stage where the peaks just bend over is essential to obtaining the desired fine texture and volume. Underbeaten soft meringues have poor volume and will tend to shrink because they start to collapse during baking. Overbeaten whites are difficult to spread attractively, and the surface looks quite dry after baking.

foamy stage Transparent, coarse, somewhat fluid foam; stage appropriate for adding acid and gradually adding the sugar, but not suitable for use in food mixtures.

soft peak stage Egg white foam beaten until the peaks just bend over; point where other ingredients usually are folded in because of its flexibility and stability.

stiff peak stage Point at which egg white peaks stand up straight, but the foam does not break when ingredients are folded in; used in making hard meringues and chiffon cakes.

dry stage Point at which beaten egg white foam becomes brittle and loses the sheen seen normally on egg white foams.

SCIENCE NOTE
EGG FOAMS

Foams are colloidal dispersions in which bubbles of air are surrounded by thin layers of liquid, which sometimes contain protein. Egg foams are but one example of foams found in foods. Other types of foams are formed with gelatin and with some dairy products. All these foams gain their stability from the protein. These foams can be formed because the protein-containing liquid has a relatively low **surface tension,** which allows the liquid to increase its surface area around the gas bubbles without squeezing out the air too quickly. Another important characteristic besides low surface tension is low vapor pressure of the liquid; low vapor pressure assures that the liquid will not evaporate quickly.

Egg proteins have excellent foaming qualities because of their low surface tension and low vapor pressure. With a limited amount of effort, the liquid can be stretched out into thin films encompassing air to form the desired high-volume foams. This is particularly true of egg white proteins. Ovomucin in thick egg white is sheared by the beater blades into comparatively short fibers, which can be spread by additional beating into monomolecular films to help stabilize the forming foam. Ovalbumin and the other proteins in the whites also are spread into thin films to aid in forming the egg white foam. The comparatively low surface tension of these proteins explains why egg whites can be spread into thin films with the aid of an eggbeater. The fact that the foams have some degree of stability is attributed to some denaturation of the protein during beating, but more important is the fact that the vapor pressure of egg protein liquids utilized in the foams is quite low, showing only a limited tendency to evaporate.

Stability and ease of formation are two characteristics of interest when preparing egg foams. The ease of formation is decreased when sugar or acid ingredients are added to the foam during its preparation. Presumably, the delay in forming a foam when sugar is added is due largely to the dilution of the protein by the sugar. This addition appears to inhibit the denaturation of the protein by agitation, although eventually a fine-textured, stable foam results. The fine texture is achieved because of the increased amount of agitation required. The continuing beating constantly stretches and modifies the size of the individual cell walls into finer and finer cells with thinner walls.

The delay in foam formation noted when cream of tartar or other acid ingredient is added appears to be due to the fact that the pH of the egg white is shifting away from the isoelectric point of **lysozyme,** one of the proteins involved in foam formation. This delay in foaming is beneficial to the formation of a fine-textured foam, for the extended period of agitation permits continuing stretching into thinner cell walls and smaller cells.

The temperature of egg whites influences the ease of foam formation; whites at room temperature can be beaten easily into a foam of fine texture, while chilled egg whites are more viscous and difficult to beat, requiring more beating to form a foam of lesser volume and coarser texture.

Other factors influencing ease of foam formation of whites are the presence of fat and the use of dried egg whites. The presence of even a trace of fat greatly retards foam formation of egg whites. This is the reason that absolutely none of the yolk, with its content of fat, should contaminate whites that have been separated to make a foam.

Stability of egg foams is determined by several factors: quality of the egg (amount of thick white), concentration of the protein, pH of the system, the presence of sugar, and the extent of beating. Eggs of comparatively low-quality foam readily because of their abundance of thin white, but this foam is less stable than is one created with more effort using high-quality eggs with abundant thick white. The addition of water or other liquid to egg whites or egg yolks increases initial foam volume but has a markedly negative effect on the stability of such foams, due to the reduced concentration of protein.

The proteins, which are denatured by the mechanical action of beating, are essential to the strength and stability of cell walls in foams. The addition of an acid provides a stabilizing influence on egg foams, and so does the use of sugar. In addition, sugar imparts a somewhat elastic, resilient quality to foams, enabling them to be folded into other ingredients with a minimum loss of air. Egg white foams are beaten to different stages for specific applications, but foams are less stable when underbeaten than they are when beaten to the point where the peaks will just bend over.

surface tension   Tendency of a liquid to present the least possible surface area (to form a sphere rather than spread into a film); low surface tension is essential to foam formation and stability.

lysozyme   Protein involved in egg white foams; isoelectric point is pH 10.7.

Soft meringues should be spread on their appropriate substrate and baked immediately in a preheated oven (350°F [177°C]) until the surface is a pleasing, golden brown (about 15 minutes or slightly longer). Baking should result in coagulation of the protein throughout the soft meringue (Figure 12.17). This is somewhat difficult to do without overbaking the upper surface because of the insulating effect of the air in the foam.

When possible, the meringue should be placed on the filling in the pie shell while the filling is still in the temperature range of 140°–170°F (60°–77°C) and baked immediately. The heat of the filling will help to begin to denature the protein in the meringue from beneath, while the oven heat exerts its effect from above. The motivation for this haste in baking the meringue on a hot filling is to produce a pie with less *leakage* or **weeping,** terms used to describe

Figure 12.17
Soft meringues are prepared by beating egg whites and sugar to the soft peak
stage, spreading over a cream pie or other dessert, and baking until a light
golden brown.

the collection of liquid between the meringue and the filling. Leakage apparently is caused by inadequate denaturation of the protein in the meringue.

Spreading a meringue to a comparatively uniform thickness over the entire surface of a pie facilitates adequate heating of the entire meringue. This means that high peaks should be avoided, for they will be overbaked and may even burn before the rest of the meringue has been baked enough. A pleasing appearance is created by making a shallow, swirling pattern with a rubber spatula without pulling up any sharp points.

A spatula also can be used effectively to seal the meringue tightly to the crust all around the edge. This helps to keep the meringue from shrinking and pulling away from the crust. It also reduces the possibility of overbaking and burning peaks and forming golden brown droplets of syrupy liquid on the surface of baked meringues, a problem termed **beading.**

Beading occurs when protein is overcoagulated during the baking of meringues, which seems to force out some of the sweetened liquid in the form of little beads resembling beads of perspiration. Beading is particularly obvious if meringues are placed on hot fillings and then the meringues are overbaked. To avoid weeping, the recommendation still must be to use a hot filling, but also to bake meringues only to a golden brown. Even with these precautions, leakage and weeping can occur if a meringue pie has to stand more than a very few hours before being served.

In summary, a soft meringue will be of excellent volume and fine texture, with no leaking between the filling and meringue and no beading on the surface. The color will be a pleasing golden brown. It can be cut easily without the meringue clinging to the knife. An underbaked meringue will have considerable leakage; an overbaked one will exhibit beading and will stick to the knife when cut.

A unique use of the soft meringue is the preparation of a baked Alaska. For this dessert, the oven is preheated to 450°F (232°C). To make a baked Alaska, the meringue must be prepared before starting the rest of the preparation. Then a hard block of ice cream is arranged on a bottom layer of cake, and a thick coating of soft meringue is spread attractively on all sides and the top. This is baked immediately at 450°F (232°C). The intense heat quickly browns the meringue before the heat penetrates and softens the ice cream. The temperature contrast between the hot meringue and the very cold ice cream makes this a seemingly magical, yet simple, dessert to prepare. Since this meringue is eaten right after baking, there is no concern about the formation of beads despite the fact that the very intense heat of the oven actually causes some overbaking.

weeping Leakage of fluid between the filling and meringue due to inadequate denaturation of the proteins in the meringue; also called syneresis.

beading Droplets of moisture that form on a meringue due to overbaking.

Hard Meringues   Hard meringues need to be made with the aid of an electric mixer; the high sugar content (almost twice as much as is recommended for soft meringues) delays foam formation significantly. The easiest technique is to add half of the sugar in the same manner used for making soft meringues and then to continue beating vigorously while adding the final half. Beating should be continued until the peaks stand up absolutely straight. Even then, the large amount of sugar makes it possible to shape the very stiff mixture into the desired shells or drop cookies on a nonstick baking sheet or brown paper. Baking is designed to dry out the whites and denature the protein (Figure 12.18). There is no need to be hasty about the duration of the baking period, for the foam is extremely stable as a result of the large amount of sugar. The baking is done at the low setting of about 200°F (93°C) or slightly higher to avoid browning while the meringues are being dried to the point of becoming crisp, but not brittle.

A desirable hard meringue is an appropriate size, easy to cut, not sticky, and is white, with no more than a trace of browning. Sticky meringues are due to underbaking or underbeating. Hard, tough meringues are the result of overbaking. Browning is the result of using too high an oven temperature for baking.

Figure 12.18
Hard meringues contain twice as much sugar as soft meringues, which requires very extensive beating to reach the soft peak stage before they are baked at 200°F (93°C) until dry and crisp, but not brown. Courtesy of Plycon Press.

Fluffy Omelets

Fluffy omelets are an example of a product utilizing both yolk foams and white foams. After separation, the yolks need to be beaten until they are very thick and will pile, a process requiring extended, energetic beating. Then the whites are beaten (with added liquid) to the soft peak stage. Immediately, the yolks are poured gently over the whites and folded in until absolutely no streaks of yellow show and no yolk is at the bottom of the bowl. While this folding is being done, butter is heated until bubbling in a heavy skillet, and the oven is preheated to 325°F (163°C).

Just as soon as folding is completed, the omelet is transferred gently into the skillet and heated half a minute to brown the bottom surface and begin the denaturation process. Then the skillet is transferred to the hot oven and baked until the upper surface is dry and the protein is coagulated, as evidenced by inserting a knife in the center and finding it clean when it is withdrawn. For service, the omelet is folded in half and served with or without a sauce (Figure 12.19).

There is a strong tendency for a layer of the yolk mixture to collect in the bottom of a fluffy omelet because of the comparative instability of the egg white foam, which has been diluted with additional liquid. However, by beating to the correct end point, folding until all of the yolk foam is completely blended with the whites, and then immediately heating at a fairly rapid rate, little drainage can occur before the foam and its contents are denatured and held in position.

A person who works quickly is more likely to be successful than is one who works slowly. However, even very slow workers can make excellent fluffy omelets if they use

Figure 12.19
A fluffy omelet (rear) has a high volume from the egg white foam compared with a French omelet (foreground), which is made without the foam. Courtesy of Plycon Press.

acid to help stabilize the egg white foam and if they beat the yolk foam long enough to get the yolks very thick. Tomato juice, lemon juice, or cream of tartar can be used effectively to reduce drainage and help stabilize the egg white foam. Also to be avoided are underbeating or overbeating the egg whites, inadequate folding, and allowing the foams or omelet to stand at all before completing the mixing and baking.

Maximum volume is achieved by beating the yolks and whites to just the right stages, efficiently and gently folding the two foams together just until they are blended, baking immediately, and avoiding too little or too much baking. Underbeaten foams of yolks or whites lack stability and do not have the maximum amount of air incorporated in them, thus contributing to poor volume. Overbeaten whites lack the elasticity needed for stretching a little in the oven. In addition, they are difficult to fold into the yolks because they break into pieces. This problem requires additional folding to eliminate the white chunks and causes loss of volume even before baking. An underbaked omelet will tend to collapse when removed from the oven, while an overbaked one will start to lose volume in the oven because the protein will become overcoagulated and will tend to shrink.

A well-prepared fluffy omelet will be light, tender, and of good volume, with a pleasingly golden brown exterior. There will be absolutely no suggestion of a layer, nor any streaks of unblended white or yolk. Only slight shrinkage will be evident when the omelet is removed from the oven.

Soufflés

Soufflés and fluffy omelets have many features in common, for they both are products in which a viscous yolk mixture is combined with an egg white foam and baked. However, there are several differences. To begin, the yolk mixture in a soufflé actually is a thick white sauce in which yolks are incorporated. The starch in this thick sauce must be gelatinized (Chapter 10) by bringing the sauce to a boil, after which the yolks are combined in the same fashion described in the discussion of cream puddings earlier in this chapter; that is, by stirring a spoonful of the gelatinized starch sauce into the beaten yolks, followed by three more additions prior to stirring the yolk mixture into the sauce.

This sauce is set aside, covered, while the whites are beaten to the soft peak stage. The foam is formed most effectively by adding cream of tartar or some other acid at the foamy stage and beating with an electric mixer until the soft peak stage is reached. Gently but quickly, the warm yolk mixture is poured down the side of the bowl containing the egg white foam, and the two are folded together efficiently and gently just until there are no streaks and no yolk mixture remains on the bottom.

Then the soufflé is transferred to a deep soufflé dish, a circle is traced around the surface an inch away from the edge of the dish (This defines an inner circle that will rise higher than the outer circle), and the dish is placed in the oven that has been preheated to 350°F (177°C). About an hour usually is needed for the soufflé to be set enough so that a thin knife inserted in the center will come out clean. Soufflés need to be served just as soon as they are removed from the oven because they will settle a bit even when they are done and will look less dramatic than when they first emerge. Holding in the oven after baking is completed is not satisfactory, because the overheating will cause the protein to begin to shrink together and much volume will be lost.

One of the problems sometimes encountered in preparing a soufflé is the breaking of the emulsion in the thick sauce. This is likely to happen when a cheese or chocolate soufflé is being prepared because of the added fat from either of these ingredients. The usual cause is too much evaporation of liquid during gelatinization. Although the sauce looks dreadful when the emulsion is broken, the addition of only a very small amount of milk or water and some stirring will return the sauce to its original smooth state, and preparation of the soufflé can be continued. This remedy must be applied before the sauce is combined with the egg yolks or with the white foam so that the soufflé can be folded together easily.

Soufflés should be very high and light, pleasingly browned, and well blended, with no suggestion of a layer on the bottom (Figure 12.20). A good soufflé is tender and flavorful. The impression of a particularly light soufflé can be created by baking it in a dish that is a bit too small and putting an aluminum foil collar around the rim to contain the soufflé as it rises. When baking is completed, the collar is removed, leaving a soufflé rising well above the dish. This has dramatic psychological benefit, but is a little difficult to do successfully.

Volume and the possible presence of a layer are the two concerns to be addressed when preparing a soufflé. Proper beating of the egg white foam to the soft peak stage and appropriate folding of the yolk mixture into the whites are two aids in achieving maximum volume. Immediate baking at the desired temperature to just the correct end point also helps. Note that the position for testing a soufflé is the center rather than the point midway between the center and the edge used in testing custards. The center of a soufflé must be set before the product is removed from the oven. Otherwise, the cool room temperature will cause the expanded hot gas in the soufflé to contract; the undenatured egg foam will not have the strength to hold itself up, and the soufflé will fall.

Figure 12.20
Soufflés should be high, pleasingly browned, and without a layer in the bottom.
Courtesy of Plycon Press.

A layer in a soufflé can be the result of a sauce that is too thin, so that the sauce drains toward the bottom of the soufflé before the structure is set. Inadequate folding of the sauce into the whites may cause a similar problem. As would be expected, allowing the completed soufflé to stand before it is baked in a preheated oven or failing to preheat the oven can cause even a properly prepared soufflé to undergo some drainage so that the sauce begins to form a layer.

Some soufflés contain vegetables and are served as the main course for a luncheon or as a side dish in a dinner, while sweet ones are used as desserts. Sauces sometimes are served on soufflés. Spoon bread is a cornmeal soufflé (originating in the South) that is enjoyed with butter as a substitute for mashed potatoes at a meal.

Foam Cakes

Foam cakes are special types of cakes using a large proportion of egg white foam to provide high volume and a comparatively open structure. The foams for these are prepared according to the principles discussed in this chapter. However, there are additional ingredients and principles involved in making cakes. This discussion is presented in Chapter 17. The problems of foam formation and possible settling of layers during baking are of concern in making foam cakes, just as they are in preparation of soufflés and other egg dishes utilizing foams.

JUDGING POINTS
SOUFFLÉS

- High volume, minimum shrinkage
- No layer
- Deep golden crust
- Uniform interior with no flecks of egg white

SUMMARY

Eggs are used alone or in food combinations to perform several different functions in cookery. They are valued for their ability to emulsify ingredients, thicken products, form foams, and bind ingredients. They are able to perform these various roles because they contain a useful amount of proteins in both the yolk and the white. They are also sources of other nutrients; the yolk is a source of vitamin A, cholesterol, some fat, and some other vitamins and minerals.

The egg is packaged in a slightly porous, protective shell, which encompasses the white (thick and thin whites), as well as the yolk, with its vitelline membrane and chalazae extending on either side. Key changes when eggs are not stored under good, cold storage conditions are a weakening of the vitelline membrane, an increase in alkalinity, increased space in the air cell, an increase in thin white, and a decrease in thick white. These changes can be assessed by candling eggs in the shell to classify them as U.S. Grade AA through U.S. Grade B. Weights range from jumbo to peewee, with extra large and large being the most common sizes in the retail market.

Dried and frozen eggs are utilized commercially. Frozen yolks and whole eggs need some added salt or sugar to prevent the development of an extremely gummy texture. Egg substitutes are available in frozen and liquid form to provide a product simulating eggs, but without the cholesterol of egg yolks. These are more costly than regular eggs, but may be important for people on restricted diets since they can be substituted satisfactorily in some products for fresh eggs.

Eggs are important ingredients in omelets (French and fluffy), custards (stirred and baked), cream puddings and pies, meringues (hard and soft), soufflés, and foam cakes. They also are prepared individually in the shell (soft- or hard cooked) and out of the shell as fried, poached, baked, and scrambled. In several of these products, egg foams are important for volume and texture. The coagulation temperature of eggs is influenced by the type and concentration of protein, rate of heating, and added ingredients. Eggs need to be heated to 160°F (71°C) to avoid the small risk of *Salmonella enteritidis*.

Eggs, particularly the whites, are used often to form foams to enhance volume and modify texture of food products. The low surface tension and vapor pressure of egg whites are important characteristics in forming stable foams. Sugar and acid stabilize foams but delay foam formation. Dilution of protein and inadequate beating reduce foam stability. The presence of fat interferes with forming egg white foams.

The desirable characteristics and techniques for achieving these qualities for several different egg preparations are included in this chapter. Products and appropriate tests for doneness are presented for eggs cooked in the shell (hard- and soft cooked), out of the shell (fried, poached, baked, and scrambled), omelets (French and fluffy), stirred and baked custards, cream puddings and pie fillings, hard and soft meringues, soufflés, and foam cakes (sponge, angel food, and chiffon). Foams are stabilized by adding acid at the foamy stage and continuing beating until the soft peak stage is reached. For hard meringues and chiffon cakes, beating is continued to the stiff peak stage. Overbeating foams reduces final volume and quality.

STUDY QUESTIONS

1. How are eggs graded in and out of the shell? What changes take place in eggs as they gradually deteriorate?
2. What factors determine the coagulation temperature of an egg mixture?
3. Compare the causes of a layer in the bottom of a fluffy omelet with the causes in a soufflé.
4. What, if anything, can be done to remedy the separation of fat from the thick white sauce used in making a soufflé?
5. Compare the tests for doneness of baked custard and a soufflé. Why are the tests different?
6. Describe the results of overbaking a baked custard; a stirred custard.
7. What are four functions eggs can perform in food preparation? Cite an example of each in a food prepared in the home.
8. Compare the size of package and the cost of equivalent amounts between fresh eggs and egg substitutes.

SELECTED REFERENCES

Berry, D. 2008. Lifetime of egg nutrition. *Food Product Design* *18*(9 supplement): 3.

Blumenthal, D. 1990. *Salmonella enteritidis:* From the chicken to the egg. *FDA Consumer 24*(3): 6.

Cannon, R. 2008. Organic vs. natural. *Food Product Design 18*(8): 26.

Esquivel, T. 2010. Egg safety. *Food Product Design 20*(10): 14.

Grisanti, G. 2004. Whipping up dessert. *Food Product Design 23*(10): 78.

Hazen, C. 2004. Proteins: Nutrition and function. *Food Product Design 14*(5): 34.

Hester, E. E., and C. J. Personius. 1949. Factors affecting beading and leakage of soft meringues. *Food Technol.* *3*: 346.

Luff, S. 2002. Phytochemical revolution. *Food Product Design: Functional Foods Annual.* Sept.: 77.

Miraglio, A. M. 2005. Return of the egg. *Food Product Design* *15*(1): 93.

Sauter, E. A., and J. E. Montoure. 1972. Relation of lysozyme content of egg white to volume and stability of foam. *J. Food Sci. 37*: 918.

Schmidt, R. H. 1981. *Gelation and coagulation.* ACS Symposium Series 147. p. 131.

Shane, S. M. 2007. Health, market stimulate interest in yolk color. *Egg Industry* Aug.: 1.

Stadelman, W., et al. 1982. Thermally processed hard cooked eggs. *Poultry Sci. 61*(2): 388.

Wang, A. C., et al. 1974. Effects of sucrose on quality characteristics of baked custard. *Poultry Sci. 53*: 807.

Zuromski, W. 2010. Cracking open new egg ideas. *Food Product Design 20*(11): 44.

Lamb barbecued on a spit over an open fire is ready to be the feature of a spring picnic. Courtesy of Plycon Press.

13

Proteins: Meats, Poultry, and Fish

Chapter Contents

Key Concepts

1. Meats (composed of muscle, connective tissue, and fat) are inspected and graded before being cut into primal and retail cuts; for safety, refrigeration and careful sanitation (HACCP) are important during marketing and continuing until prepared and consumed.

2. Tender cuts of meat can be prepared successfully using dry heat methods (roasting, pan frying, deep-fat frying, pan broiling, and broiling), but less tender cuts need moist heat (braising and stewing or cooking in liquid).

3. Chickens and other poultry can be prepared by the same methods as red meat; they require very careful refrigeration and high sanitation standards.

4. Fish have a short shelf life because they are particularly susceptible to spoilage; cooking time should be short to avoid toughening and drying.

5. Soy protein foods are healthful and can add variety to menus.

6. Vegetarians need to plan menus carefully to meet nutritional needs.

MEATS

Meat is defined in food preparation as the edible flesh of animals. According to this definition, the meats commonly utilized in the United States include beef, veal, pork, and lamb. These red meats are cornerstones of the diets of many Americans and are prominent not only for the portion of the food dollar spent for them but also because of the quantity consumed. Other types of protein foods (poultry, fish, eggs, and cheese) are eaten in much smaller quantities than are the red meats, although there is an increasing consumption of these. Of the red meats, beef clearly is the favorite; in fact, approximately one-and-a-half times as much beef is eaten as the total of the other red meats consumed annually by Americans.

The expense of protein-rich foods and particularly of meat makes the entrée selection a logical place to start when planning a menu. All aspects of meats, from selection, through storage, preparation, and service, deserve careful attention because meat serves as the focal point of a meal, as well as the largest item in the food budget. A thorough understanding of all aspects of meat in the menu

TABLE 13.1
OVERVIEW OF MEAT CLASSIFICATIONS[a]

Name	Age	Description
Cattle		
Veal	Less than 18 weeks, 450 pounds	Very light in color, delicate flavor
Calf (baby beef)	Less than about 9 months, 750 pounds	Medium color, moderate flavor, high proportion of connective tissue
Beef	Over 1 year	Bright red, full flavor
Pork	5–12 months	Grayish-pink, some marbling, full flavor
Sheep		
Lamb	To 1 year	Cherry-red, delicate flavor, tender
Mutton	Over 1 year	Deep cherry-red, strong flavor, less tender than lamb

[a]The classification of animals is based on the sex, age, and sexual condition of cattle, swine, and sheep. These classes include the following:

Beef—steer: male castrated at a young age; heifer: female that has never borne a calf; cow: female that has borne a calf; bull: mature, uncastrated male; stag: mature, castrated male

Swine—barrow: young castrated male; gilt: young female; sow: female that has borne young; boar: mature, uncastrated male; stag: mature, castrated male

Sheep—lamb: less than a year old, with a wether being a young castrated male; yearling: a year-old sheep; mutton: older sheep, with a ram being male and a ewe being female

will enable the consumer to obtain maximum pleasure and effectiveness from tender, flavorful, and juicy meats.

This chapter is divided into three main sections—meats, poultry, and fish, which are the three major categories of muscle-type foods. The underlying principles for handling and preparing these various types of protein foods are essentially the same, although there are specifics that require emphasis. Nutritional aspects of vegetarian diets also are discussed.

Definition of Meats

Various terms are used to designate particular animals and particular types of meat. These designations are helpful in indicating what characteristics might be expected because the color, flavor, and tenderness vary with the age of the animal. As animals mature and age, the color of the muscles becomes darker. The flavor becomes more intense with the age of any of the animals and is particularly noticeable in sheep. Similarly, beef also has a richer, fuller flavor than does veal. The designations for meats from animals at different ages are presented in Table 13.1.

Muscle

Structure   Meats are composed of muscle, connective tissue, fat, and bone. The bone is peripheral to the portions that are consumed and hence is of interest because of the type and amount associated with a particular meat cut. Whereas bone is cut from the muscle either at the market or at the table, the muscle, connective tissue, and some of the fat may be eaten. The changes occurring in these components of meat are of special interest.

Muscle is approximately 75 percent water and 20 percent protein, with the remaining 5 percent representing a combination of fat, carbohydrate, and minerals. The percentage of water in meat varies with the type of muscle, the kind of meat, the season of the year, and the pH of the meat. The ability of meat to hold water, termed its **water-holding capacity**, is important to the juiciness of the meat.

water-holding capacity
Ability of muscles to hold water; an important contribution to juiciness of meats.

The structure of muscle is much more complex than it appears to the naked eye, for it consists of several levels of organization (Figure 13.1). The basic structure begins with a protein sol called the sarcoplasm being bound by a very fine membrane, the sarcolemma, to make a muscle fiber. Within the structure of these fibers are units called myofibrils.

To break this structure down still farther in exploring the structure of muscle, the myofibrils are comprised of thick and thin myofilaments. These myofilaments give a striated or striped appearance to muscle tissue when viewed under magnification. Apparently the number of these muscle fibers ceases to increase following birth of the animal, but the existing fibers grow, resulting in the observable growth of young animals.

The fibers are held into bundles of fibers, or fasciculi, by connective tissue. These fasciculi are large enough to be seen by the naked eye and are perceived as strands within muscles. The connective tissue surrounding each of the fasciculi in a muscle is called the endomysium. The total muscle is comprised of many of these fasciculi plus some fatty deposits, all arranged in an orderly fashion and held in position by a surrounding sheath of connective tissue, the perimysium. Clearly, a great deal of organization is involved in the complex arrangement, from the thick and thin myofilaments of the myofibrils to the fibers, fasciculi, and the total muscle.

Muscle Proteins   **Myosin**, the most abundant of the muscle proteins, increases the toughness of the muscle fibers when heated. Tropomyosin, another muscle protein with properties similar to myosin, and actin, a globular protein, are important in muscle fibers. Muscle contraction is theorized to be due to a complexing of actin and myosin to form **actomyosin**.

The colors in meats are the result of the presence of some other proteins. **Myoglobin** is the central pigment in meat coloration. This iron-containing pigment, a protein similar in structure to hemoglobin, is capable of combining with several different substances, including oxygen. With oxygen, oxymyoglobin is formed, which gives meat a particularly bright red color. In combination with water, a brownish-red color develops as metmyoglobin is formed. Also, the central iron atom in myoglobin can change valence, resulting in color changes.

Cured meats have nitrates added to form **nitric oxide myochrome**, a compound contributing the permanent pinkish color of cured meats. Sometimes, the porphyrin ring of heme is oxidized, causing an iridescent, greenish color on the surface of ham or other cured meats. Exposure to oxygen and ultraviolet light hastens the development of this condition.

Problems with discoloration of meat can be retarded by wrapping meat cuts in relatively airtight packages and storing them away from light. Ordinarily, discoloration should be minimal for as long as three days when displayed in a refrigerated meat case in a store. Freezing causes some fading, although the change in color is minimized by carefully wrapping to exclude most of the air.

Connective Tissue

The two types of connective tissue proteins in meat cuts are collagen and elastin. **Collagen** is of particular significance in meat cookery, for this is the structural protein for the connective tissue sheaths throughout the muscles. Sometimes it is called simply white connective tissue. Collagen molecules are elongated, fibrous molecules and are arranged randomly sometimes in parallel.

Elastin is found in rather concentrated deposits, where this type of connective tissue appears as a yellow, almost rubbery mass. This type of connective tissue protein usually is discarded as gristle because it essentially remains unchanged and tough throughout any type of cookery technique.

Fat

Fat in meats is found between muscles and within muscles, and in both locations fat contributes to the overall flavor and juiciness of meats. These fatty deposits in animals consist of many aggregates of fat cells that are formed early in life and then enlarged. Fat first is laid down subcutaneously as a protective layer around the organs in the abdominal cavity, and then it begins to accumulate around and between muscles, with the intramuscular fatty deposits being laid down last.

The deposition of fat within muscles is known as **marbling**. In beef, marbling is considered desirable if a person is seeking a particularly juicy, flavorful, and tender cut. However, in pork,

Figure 13.1
Cross-sectional view of raw beef semitendinosus (small muscle of bottom round), as seen in a scanning electron micrograph. Courtesy of Plycon Press.

myosin   Most abundant muscle protein.

actomyosin   Complex muscle protein composed of actin and myosin formed during muscle contraction.

myoglobin   Iron-containing pigment in meat; compound similar to hemoglobin and capable of reacting with various substances to effect color changes in muscle.

nitric oxide myochrome   Compound contributing pink color to cured meats.

collagen   White connective tissue in meats; fibrous structural protein encasing muscle proteins.

elastin   Extremely strong connective tissue; a yellow-colored protein in meat that is not tenderized by cooking.

marbling   Fatty deposits in muscle of meats.

SCIENCE NOTE
COLLAGEN AND GELATIN

Collagen is the connective tissue that forms the sheaths encasing muscle proteins in muscles. The fibrous nature of collagen derives from the fact that two somewhat unusual amino (actually imino) acids—proline and hydroxyproline—are repeated frequently in the amino acid chain constituting the primary organization of the molecules. These two acids (see the following structural formulas) interfere with the helical coiling as collagen attempts to assume the normal helical (secondary) structure of most proteins. The difficulty in achieving a helix is due to the fact that the nitrogen needed for the peptide linkage between amino acids is actually part of a ring structure of the two acids, which limits the ability of the backbone chain of the protein to bend.

Hydroxyproline   Proline

These elongated chains are somewhat more complex than is suggested by simply examining the unique linearity caused by the hydroxyproline and proline. In collagen, usually three of these chains are twisted together loosely in an arrangement comparable to that of a three-ply cord. The chains are held together by hydrogen bonding between the individual strands to make a collagen molecule. The association of the strands in this way makes collagen quite a tough fiber and contributes significantly to the apparent toughness of meat in which collagen is abundant. The analogy of the three-ply cord can be used to demonstrate the increased strength resulting from the three-ply arrangement rather than testing single strands.

These three-ply molecules of collagen are instrumental in holding the muscles of meat together in an organized fashion. Their fibrous nature, however, is susceptible to some change when heat is supplied to begin to allow the hydrogen bonds holding the three strands together to break. When heat, particularly moist heat, is applied, these bonds start to break. Over an extended period of time, enough of these hydrogen bonds will break to cause the loosely twisted chains to start to pull away from each other. No chemical breakdown is occurring within a single chain; rather, the change is a dissociation between chains. Gradually, single strands will begin to drift individually, resulting in a distinct, tenderizing effect in the meat. These individual strands that separate from collagen are gelatin. Since they represent strands with only a third the cross section of collagen, these gelatin molecules present much less resistance to cutting than does the native collagen. For this reason, meats braised for an extended period of time become literally "fork tender" and can be cut without using a knife.

---

abundant marbling is rated undesirable because of the greasy quality imparted by excessive fat (pork naturally has a comparatively large amount of marbling). Selective breeding is being used in pork production to attempt to minimize fat content and reduce the richness of pork, an effort that has met with considerable success.

Nutritional Contributions

All red meats are significant sources of complete protein, with the actual contribution ranging between 9 and 19 percent, depending upon the particular species (beef is higher than pork) and cut. This protein is utilized efficiently within the body unless extreme heat is used in preparing the meat.

The fat in meats is a source of calories and of saturated fatty acids, with beef being criticized particularly for its content of saturated fatty acids. In fact, it is because of the abundance of fat, particularly saturated fatty acids, that Americans have been encouraged to shift meat consumption patterns to reduce the amount of red meats and increase poultry and fish. However, with judicious removal of fatty deposits around muscles and servings of appropriate size, red meats can be utilized as a nourishing food at least three or four times a week by most people.

Red meats are excellent sources of iron and copper, as well as some other minerals, and for this reason, beef and other red meats are important components of the diet. In fact, people who avoid red meats often have difficulty in meeting the Recommended Dietary Allowance for iron. The organ meats, particularly liver, are especially rich sources of the various minerals, although all of the red meats are useful sources.

Thiamin, riboflavin, and niacin are B vitamins that are particularly abundant in red meats. Of the meats, pork is the highest in thiamin content, although all the red meats are good sources. Vitamin B_{12} also is provided by red meats. Since the liver is the storage area for vitamin A, it is not surprising that liver from any type of meat animal is a useful source of this vitamin.

Figure 13.2
Livestock can graze as much as they like in fields with abundant grass, but feed must be purchased when they are in feedlots rather than pasture. Courtesy of Plycon Press.

When meat is prepared by dry heat cookery methods, the retention of vitamins is quite good. However, moist heat cookery methods cause some of the B vitamins (thiamin, riboflavin, and niacin) to migrate into the cooking liquid. If the liquid is consumed with the meat, this does not present a problem, but if the liquid is discarded, some of the B vitamins will be lost.

PREPARING MEAT FOR MARKET

Production Practices   One of the major concerns among meat producers is the cost of getting livestock to the meat packers (Figure 13.2). The longer an animal is fed prior to marketing, the more costly is its production. Feed costs, feedlot space, and labor are all involved in fattening an animal for slaughter.

Animals can be brought to maturity and to market more rapidly if sex hormones are administered (either orally or as implants) than if no hormones are provided. Extensive research has been conducted over many years to determine (1) effectiveness in promoting growth of animals and poultry intended for the dining table and (2) safety of meat from animals raised with hormone supplementation. Based on this body of research, the FDA currently approves use of the following natural and synthetic hormones: estradiol, progesterone, testosterone, trenbolone acetate, zeranol, and melengestrol acetate (MGA). Administration of any of these hormones

---

INDUSTRY INSIGHT
HIGH TECH AND CATTLE

Some feed yards and dairy operations are using electronic ear tags and careful monitoring of all aspects of production to achieve higher profits per head of cattle. The weight of each animal, the amount and type of feed consumed, inoculations, and even ultrasonic images to determine the marbling can be measured and monitored throughout the entire feeding period to obtain a clear picture of weight gain, quality, and expense at any time. Information gathered in this way can also be analyzed to aid breeders as they seek to produce cattle that have optimal characteristics for the marketplace. The expense for such a sophisticated approach to cattle production is increased, but the higher profits more than offset the cost for large operations.

Presently, electronic monitoring is being used more in dairy cattle operations than in beef production. Electronically tagged cattle trigger a sensor when they are placed in a milking station. The amount of milk and the amount of fat in the milk given by the cow are entered into a computer. Even the health of the animal can be monitored by noting the white blood cell count in the milk. A sensor in the hindquarter of a dairy cow can be used to note the brief (6–12 hours) period of maximum fertility, which promotes maximum breeding productivity to keep milk production coming.

must be done under conditions stated by the FDA; pellet implants in the ear are effective and can be easily removed.

Cattle feed has been undergoing tight scrutiny as the incidence of bovine spongiform encephalopathy (**BSE**) and the possibility of transmission to humans via contaminated beef have been in the news. This fatal brain disease of cattle can apparently be transferred to humans, where it manifests itself as Creutzfeldt–Jakobs disease. Initial concerns were raised in the United Kingdom in 1986, but an infected cow in Washington State in 2004 brought the problem to this country via Canada. Steps taken to control the problem include banning the use of brain tissue in cattle feed and developing and enforcing regulations regarding the health status of cattle to be used in feed and meat supplies.

Consumers with concerns about eating only what they view as natural foods have created a niche market for poultry or meat that is identified as free range. Farmers raising what they tout as free range or organic meat, poultry, or eggs suggest that their products are not only more humane for the animals while they are living on the farm but also that the resulting food is better for the health of consumers. The merits of promoting the psyche of the animals need to be evaluated by consumers in relation to the pain that can be experienced in the pocketbook when free-range products are purchased. The nutritional benefits are not proven.

Rigor   Progressive chemical changes occur following the slaughtering of an animal, with these changes leading to the onset and ultimately the passing of **rigor mortis**. The live animal will have some glycogen (carbohydrate) stored, but this source of energy varies considerably in quantity and is particularly dependent upon the circumstances at the time of slaughter. A comparatively high level of glycogen at slaughter is desired so that the carcass will develop a low pH during rigor. To help to achieve this, a calm, quick dispatch is very helpful. Any exercise, nervous exhaustion, insulin release, or fasting prior to slaughter will reduce the amount of glycogen in reserve.

The level of **glycogen** in the animal is important because this carbohydrate is the source of energy for chemical reactions and also for the formation of lactic acid in the carcass during rigor. With an adequate supply of glycogen at the time of slaughter, the acidity of the carcass will drop to a pH of about 5.3. When meat reaches this acidic pH, the color of the meat, its tenderness, and juiciness will be optimal. However, if there is little glycogen in reserve at slaughter, the pH of the carcass will not drop sufficiently low. The resulting meat will be an undesirable, dark color and sticky and gummy in character. Beef in which the pH has remained too high is designated as **dark-cutting beef** and is considered lower in quality.

Rigor mortis, the stiffening of the muscles in the carcass, appears to be due to the formation of actomyosin from actin and myosin as the glycogen breaks down and ATP (adenosine triphosphate, a high-energy compound) and lactic acid form. First the trend is toward reduced pH due to lactic acid formation, but then ammonia ultimately is liberated when ATP breaks down. Ammonia production causes the pH of the carcass to rise a bit, and the stiffening of the muscles passes. Rigor mortis usually reaches its peak in cattle in about 24 hours, with softening of the muscles occurring gradually after that.

Cold Storage   High standards of sanitation and maintenance of a low relative humidity and constant low temperature are essential during the initial chilling of carcasses and storage of meats until they reach the consumer. Meats, like other protein-rich foods, are very susceptible to spoilage by microorganisms unless storage conditions are controlled carefully. Since spoilage takes place on the surfaces, storage problems can be kept to a minimum if the carcasses are cut to yield the largest possible pieces that can be handled.

BSE   Abbreviation for bovine spongiform encephalopathy, a fatal brain disease that can occur in cattle.
http://www.cdc.gov/ncidod/dvrd/bse/
—CDC website; information on BSE.

rigor mortis   Series of chemical changes occurring in the carcass following slaughtering.

glycogen   Polysaccharide in muscle, which breaks down to produce energy and lactic acid in the carcass following slaughter.

dark-cutting beef   Darkly colored beef with a sticky, gummy character, the result of too little glycogen at slaughter, usually due to exhaustion or inadequate feeding at dispatch.

CULTURAL ACCENT
KOBE BEEF

Kobe beef, which was first produced in Kobe, Japan, is the most expensive beef in the world to produce and also to buy. Production costs are linked to the way in which some beef cattle are groomed for the market. Sake (rice liquor) is rubbed on the animal as muscles are massaged to promote tenderness. These pampered animals also are fed beer, which is mixed into their feed during hot summer months to promote appetite. The goal is to bring a contented steer to market that is well marbled, tender, and juicy—characteristics prized by beef aficionados. This beef, which is the most costly on the market, has carved a special niche for itself in some upscale markets in this country, as well as in Japan.

At packing houses, carcasses ordinarily are split in half to allow thorough cleaning of the interior region. The introduction of ozone or carbon dioxide into the chilling and holding rooms at packing plants, as well as the maintenance of temperatures just above freezing, help to extend the length of time that carcasses can be held in packing houses before being shipped and sold to as long as 10 days.

All meats are held in cold storage until rigor passes before they are marketed or frozen. The holding of meat until the muscles relax again is important in achieving optimal water-holding capacity. If meat is frozen before a carcass passes through rigor, the water-holding capacity will be minimal, with the result that there will be considerable drip loss when the meat is thawed. In contrast, meat frozen after rigor has passed will have a high water-holding capacity so that much of the water will be bound when the meat is frozen. This bound water will continue to be held in the meat following thawing, thus allowing only limited drip loss.

Aging　A small amount of top-grade prime beef is held in cold storage for a ripening period of 15 to 40 days before being marketed. During this holding period, mold grows on the outer surface of the side of beef, but the layer of fat on the surface is so thick in prime beef that the mold and some of the fat can be trimmed easily from the **aged beef** as the carcass enters the marketing chain. Lower quality beef and also veal do not have enough fat to permit ripening or aging. Pork cannot be aged even though it has a thick coating of fat, because the fat will start to become rancid during the storage period.

Beef aged or ripened for a period between 10 and 29 days will become increasingly tender due to the action of proteolytic enzymes on the various proteins in the muscles. There also is increased hydration of the protein during ripening. Connective tissue remains unchanged during the aging process, but color and flavor changes of significance occur. The fresh red color gives way to a gray-brown at lower cooking temperatures than are required for color change in unripened beef. Even before cooking, ripened beef is noticeably darker than unripened beef. The flavor becomes increasingly distinctive and intense as aging progresses and is usually judged to be best when beef is ripened for 20–40 days. All these changes occur more slowly at temperatures just above freezing than they do at warmer temperatures, but the microbiological problems at warmer temperatures make very cold (not frozen) storage important.

Curing　Both beef and pork may be preserved by **curing**, the former product being called corned beef and the latter ham. The permanent reddish color is the result of treatment by a combination of salt, sodium nitrate, and heat. During the brining period, the original nitrate is reduced to nitrite, which then reacts with myoglobin in the meat to produce the familiar red color and to prevent botulism.

The possible carcinogenicity of nitrates and nitrites has generated a good bit of dialogue regarding the allowance of these chemicals in curing meat products. Although there is apparently an extremely small risk of nitrates contributing to the development of cancer, the risk (if indeed there really is one) is so very small that these chemicals are still permitted in curing. The risk of botulism in sausages and other meats cured without these chemicals is considerably greater than any possible cancer hazard if nitrates were to be banned in the manufacturing of cured meat products. The controversy over the use of nitrates in curing meats resulted in a flurry of research activities which culminated in a reduction in the level of nitrates used, but not an elimination of these important preservatives.

The extent of penetration of curing agents varies with the pH of the meat being cured, with meat at about pH 5.2 achieving far higher penetration than that at the less acidic pH 6.6. The meats that are not very acidic are more susceptible to spoilage than are those approaching pH 5.2. However, heating of the meats at the higher pH levels is a help in reducing spoilage because heating enhances the penetration of the curing agents. Sage, black pepper, and salt hasten rancidity of fats in cured meats, whereas other spices retard this problem.

Smoking　**Smoking** of ham and sometimes other meats is done to enhance flavors and to promote shelf life. The smoking, preferably done using sawdust from hardwoods, dries the surface and also adds distinctive flavors, depending upon the type of wood being used as fuel for the smoking process. Not only does the surface become dry, but the proteins in the meat are denatured slowly by the heat from the smoking fuel.

Freezing　Meats may be frozen by sharp freezing or by quick freezing. Sharp freezing is done by holding meat in a storage room with rapidly moving air and a temperature of –10°F (–23°C).

aged beef　Prime beef that has been held in very cold storage for 15–40 days to intensify flavor and tenderize the muscles.

curing　Treating of meats with salt, sodium nitrate, and heat to achieve color and flavor changes and to promote shelf life and reduce spoilage.

smoking　Means of helping to promote shelf life of meat by hanging it in a smokehouse to dry out the surface and add flavor to the meat.

This method is slow in comparison with quick freezing. As a result, the ice crystals in meats that have been sharp frozen tend to be quite large (Chapter 19).

Quick freezing is a term for any technique that results in extremely fast freezing. The methods are (1) immersion, (2) contact, and (3) convection. Immersion freezing employs use of a brine solution to achieve temperatures below the point of freezing water. A blast of cold air is the technique used in convection freezing. Any of the quick-freezing methods will result in a frozen meat with small ice crystals and with extremely low bacterial, yeast, or mold growth because of the rapid cooling to temperatures unfavorable for microbiological activity.

Drip loss will be comparatively less for thin pieces of frozen meat than for thicker cuts because thick pieces will freeze slowly in the center. This means that moisture will tend to be drawn out and frozen between the fibers, while the thin pieces will freeze so rapidly that the moisture is trapped within the fibers. Beef should be held at least 48 hours after slaughter before being frozen; the other meats need to be held at least 24 hours to allow changes necessary to keep drip loss of frozen meats to a minimum.

In frozen storage, meats can be held for several weeks without serious loss of quality, whereas the fresh meat would need to be consumed within a matter of very few days. Another advantage of freezing meats is that the meats become more tender. The meats should be held in frozen storage at –10°F to 0°F (–23°C to –18°C) to achieve a satisfactorily long, safe storage period.

The packaging used for the frozen meat is another important factor in determining how long the frozen meat can be held. A packaging material resistant to damage and yet capable of being fitted tightly around the meat is needed. The packaging should keep air from reaching the meat. If the package has any tears or other openings, the very dry environment of the freezer will result in formation of a dried, tough area because of desiccation on the surface of the cut, a circumstance termed **freezer burn**. Once freezer burn has occurred, the area will never return to its former hydrated state, regardless of the treatment applied.

Freeze-drying   Drying has long been a means of preserving meats, but the addition of a second process, freezing, makes a unique and effective way of preserving meat. **Freeze-drying**, as the name suggests, involves freezing the meat and then sublimating the ice from the meat to produce a very lightweight product that does not require refrigeration for storage. This preservation method has proven to be particularly useful in the formation of dehydrated soups with meat.

Inspection

Meat's potential for carrying harmful microorganisms prompted legislation for inspection as far back as 1890, when the Meat Inspection Act was passed (Figure 13.3). Since that time, other laws governing inspection have been passed by the federal government and cover the sanitation standards required for meat and poultry entering interstate commerce. In fact, the Wholesome Meat Act of 1967 and the Wholesome Poultry Products Act of 1968 mandated that meats and poultry involved in intrastate commerce be inspected under state programs at least as rigorous as the standards required for interstate marketing. This legislation effectively ensured that any meat reaching consumers would have been slaughtered under sanitary conditions and would be from animals free of disease at the time of slaughter.

In 1996, the Food Safety and Inspection Service (FSIS) in the U.S. Department of Agriculture began to implement the Pathogen Reduction and Hazard Analysis and Critical Control Points (HACCP) Final Rule. This heightened inspection of meat and poultry was triggered by some serious episodes of ground meat contaminated with *E. coli* O157:H7. The regulations required at each plant include:

1. HACCP-based process controls
2. Microbial testing for *E. coli*, which is an indicator of fecal contamination
3. Pathogen reduction performance standards to assure that Salmonella contamination is below the national baseline
4. Sanitation standard operating procedures

Authorized inspectors are responsible for inspection of meat and poultry (Figure 13.4). States can elect to have their own inspectors for meat being marketed within the state, or they can utilize federal inspectors. Only federal inspectors are authorized to inspect meat for interstate commerce. The

freezer burn Desiccation of part of the surface of frozen meat, a result of improper packaging that allows air to be in contact with the meat surface.

freeze-drying Process of drying frozen foods.

Figure 13.3
Inspection stamp, required for all meat carcasses crossing state lines, bears the number of the inspector and the message "U.S. Inspected and Passed." It is imprinted on each primal cut. Courtesy of United States Department of Agriculture.

inspection includes assessment of the entire slaughtering and packing operation, from checking the healthiness of the animal through all packing plant patterns of sanitation and refrigeration.

The fact that a meat carcass bears the inspection stamp on each primal cut means only that the meat was safe for consumption at the time of inspection. This stamp carries no guarantee that subsequent handling has met the same standards of cleanliness. Also, the inspection stamp is not a statement of the palatability or eating quality of the meat. It simply indicates that the meat has been inspected and passed, and identifies the packer by number. Consumers may often buy retail cuts that show no sign of the inspection stamp, for only one small stamp is imprinted with a safe (usually red or yellow) vegetable dye on each primal cut.

The one potential hazard in meat that is not revealed by inspection is *Trichinella spiralis* (Chapter 3). This is a parasitic worm sometimes found in pork if hogs have been fed on uncooked garbage. Despite the requirement by all states that any garbage fed to hogs must be cooked, inadequate heat treatment is still a possibility. If viable trichinae are present in pork, the parasite can infect humans too, resulting in the condition called **trichinosis**. Trichinae usually can be killed by holding frozen meats in storage at temperatures no higher than 5°F (–15°C) for 20 days, by heating fresh pork to 170°F (76.7°C) or hams to 160°F (71.1°C), or by heat processing for a period of time at 137°F (58.3°C) internal temperature.

Grading

Unlike inspection, which is mandatory, grading is done at the discretion of meat packers who may elect any of three options: (1) federal grading, (2) packer grading, or (3) no grading. If federal grading is the choice, federal graders are hired by the packers to classify the meat according to government specifications into the appropriate grade (Chart 1). Occasionally, packers may wish to use their own grading system, a practice seen most commonly in the marketing of hams under the packers' grade names. The chief value of grading for the consumer is as a guide to meat quality. However, the range of quality in some grade categories still makes it useful to be able to make educated choices within the grade.

Beef The grades for beef have been established by the U.S. Department of Agriculture, the federal unit also responsible for administration and enforcement of federal meat grading standards. The descriptions of the characteristics required in each grade have been altered occasionally, with the result that U.S. Choice, the grade commonly available to consumers in the markets, encompasses a wide range of quality. Although the grade designation is helpful in this case, consumer knowledge of quality is essential to making the best choices within the grade.

The top grade of beef is U.S. Prime (Table 13.2); restaurants are the primary market for this grade. If beef achieves this grade, the shield-shaped grade marker (Figure 13.5) will show this in a continuously repeating pattern imprinted by a roller, which repeats the grade stamp

Figure 13.4
Sides of beef inspected and graded by federal inspectors carry the round inspection stamp at points that will mark each of the primal cuts. The shield-shaped federal grade stamp is imprinted in a continuous strip by running an inked roller down the carcass. Courtesy of Agricultural Research Service.

trichinosis Illness caused by viable *Trichinella spiralis*, a parasite sometimes found in pork and transmitted to humans if infected pork is heated inadequately.

Relationship Between Marbling, Maturity, and Carcass Quality Grade*

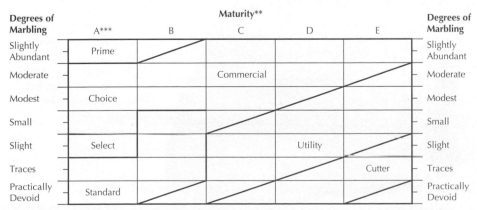

* Assumes that firmness of lean is comparably developed with the degree of marbling and that the carcass is not a "dark Cutter."
** Maturity increases from left to right (A through E).
*** The A maturity portion of the Figure is the only portion applicable to bullock carcasses.

TABLE 13.2
U.S. DEPARTMENT OF AGRICULTURE GRADES FOR BEEF, VEAL, AND LAMB

Beef	Veal	Lamb	Pork
Prime	Prime	Prime	Not graded because of uniformity
Choice	Choice	Choice	
Select	Select	Select	
Standard	Standard	Commercial	
Commercial	Commercial	Utility	
Utility	Utility	Cull	
Cutter	Cull		
Canner			

Figure 13.5
Grading by federal personnel is optional, but meat indicating USDA Prime or other federal grade must be graded by federal personnel and meet the criteria established for the imprinted grade. Courtesy of United States Department of Agriculture.

http://www.askthemeatman.com/hog_cuts_interactive_chart.htm

—Interactive chart on pork cuts.

http://www.beef.org

—Extensive information on various aspects of beef.

http://www.americanlamb.com/

—Information on lamb.

http://www.askthemeatman.com/beef.htm

—Information about beef cuts.

along the entire length of the carcass. A similar stamping is done for the USDA Choice and other grades. Because of the continuous strip of grading symbols, many retail cuts will have at least a portion of the shield showing on the outer side of the cuts (Figure 13.6).

Pork   Pork considered to be acceptable for the consumer market is rated from the high U.S. No. 1 to U.S. No. 4, grades that are based more on yield than on quality distinctions, because there are only minimal differences between carcasses for palatability. The designation is of use in the wholesale market because it indicates the relative yield of the four major lean cuts, but the grade designation is not evident in the retail meat case. Soft and watery pork is rated only as USDA Utility, considered to be an unacceptable rating for the consumer market.

Lamb   The quality of lamb varies far more than pork does, despite the fact that both species generally are marketed at a much younger age than beef. Lamb has six quality grades (USDA Prime through USDA Cull), as shown in Table 13.2. Mutton begins with USDA Choice as the top grade and is followed by Good, Utility, and Cull. The yield designations range from 1 to 5, with the rating being determined by the amount of fat covering the outside of the carcass and the fat deposited inside.

Selection and Care

Decisions regarding choice of meat cuts begin with the planning of the menu. The amount of time available for preparation and the amount of money for meat in the food budget are two important concerns when selecting meats. A general way of looking at meats in relation to these two factors is to classify meats into tender and less tender cuts.

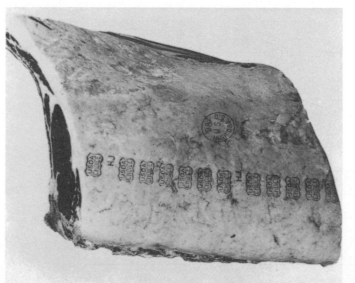

Figure 13.6
This beef rib (primal cut) is graded as U.S. Choice because of its relatively heavy covering of fat, as well as marbling within the muscle. Note the single round inspection stamp on the primal cut and the repeating shield-shaped imprint for the grade. Courtesy of United States Department of Agriculture.

Tender cuts often require little preparation time, but usually are comparatively costly; less tender cuts are best when prepared using a long cooking period, but they usually cost less than the tender cuts. Persons working outside the home may decide against buying less tender cuts unless they can use a crock pot or they can cook the meat on the weekend or other times when at home.

The classification of a particular cut is dependent upon the location on the carcass, the type of meat, and the grade. Generally, portions of the animal that receive little exercise will be more tender than the cuts from areas that are used extensively by the animal. In fact, the tenderloin muscle receives almost no exercise, regardless of the type of animal, and is tender regardless of the grade of the carcass. In beef, the cuts from the shoulder, rump, and belly are classified as less tender, while the rib, short loin, and sirloin primal cuts are the sources of tender cuts. However, the rump of USDA Prime beef is classified as tender, while USDA Choice and lower grades yield rump classified as less tender.

The designation of tender or less tender for a particular part of the animal differs with the type of animal. Whereas the rump of beef usually is classified as less tender, the rump of pork is tender. In fact, pork usually is classified as tender, regardless of the cut. Veal, although it is from a very young animal, is only moderately tender because there is a reasonably high proportion of connective tissue in relation to the muscle proteins. There also is very little fat deposited in veal. Lamb, from the leg primal cut (with the exception of the shank) through the rib, is classified as tender. However, the shank of the leg, the neck, shoulder, and the breast of lamb are all considered to be less tender cuts, reflecting the heavy exercise in these areas.

Identification of Cuts Recognition of the various cuts is a tremendous help in making selections at the meat counter. The first point is to determine the type of meat, which can be done by looking at the size of the cuts, the color of the muscles, and the character of the fat. Beef cuts are the largest of the meats in the meat case, with veal being somewhat smaller, followed by pork, and finally lamb.

The muscle color adds more information because beef is red, while veal is an extremely light to moderate pink, pork is a grayish-pink, and lamb is a dark red. Even the fat serves as a means of distinguishing between the meats. Beef has a hard fat which usually is white but may begin to assume a yellowish overtone in very mature beef. Veal has very little fat, and what fat there is will have a pink overtone. Pork fat is the softest of the fats, and it has a somewhat pink color. Lamb fat is the hardest and is quite white.

Recognition of cuts needs to be developed at two levels—the primal cuts and the retail cuts (Table 13.3). The **primal cuts** are the first cuts made on each half of the carcass. Primal cuts are designated for the various meat animals in Figures 13.7 through 13.10. Note that more primal cuts are made in beef than in the smaller animals. This is done so that the butcher can handle a primal cut; beef cuts comparable to those in pork would be so heavy that they would be very difficult for the butcher to manage.

Within each of the primal cuts, a number of **retail cuts** will be made to provide the cuts of meat available at the market (Figure 13.11). The bones can serve as aids in identifying

http://www.uen.org/
Lessonplan/preview.
cgi?LPid=5365
—Extensive information about beef by Utah Education Network.

http://www.ams.usda.gov/
LSG/stand/imps.htm
—Institutional Meat Purchases Specifications (IMPS).

http://www.ams.usda.gov/
AMSv1.0/getfile?dDocNam
e=STELDEV3002633
—Agricultural Marketing Service website; meat buying.

primal cuts First cuts (wholesale cuts) to provide large sections, yet small enough to be handled by the butcher.

retail cuts Meat cuts available to consumers.

TABLE 13.3
PRIMAL CUTS OF BEEF, VEAL, PORK, AND LAMB

Beef	Veal	Pork	Lamb
Chuck	Shoulder	Jowl	Shoulder
Rib	Rib	Boston shoulder	Rib (hotel rack)
Short loin	Loin	Loin	Loin
Sirloin	Sirloin	Leg	Sirloin
Round	Round	Spare ribs	Leg
Tip	Breast	Picnic shoulder	Breast
Flank	Shank	Foot	Shank
Short plate			
Brisket			
Foreshank			

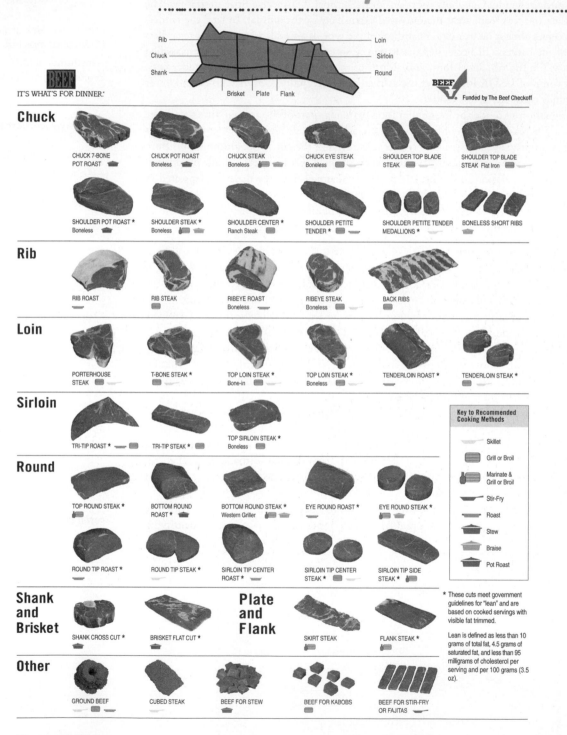

Figure 13.7
Primal and retail beef cuts. Courtesy of the Beef Checkoff.

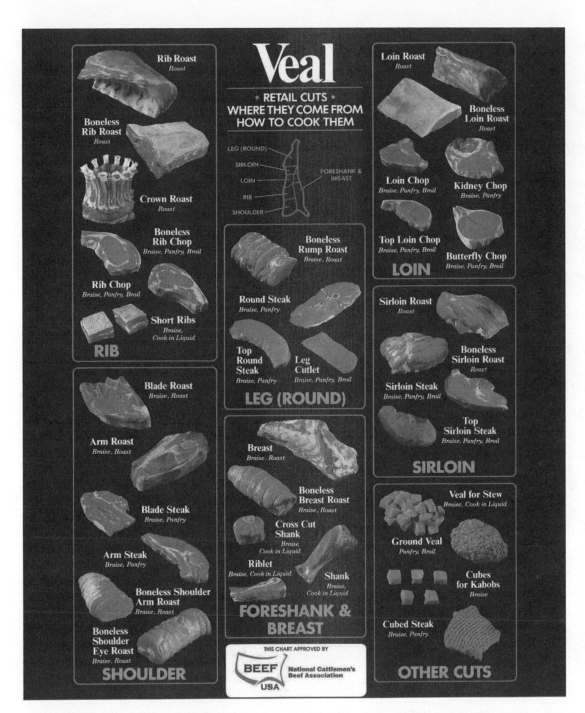

Figure 13.8
Primal and retail veal cuts. Courtesy of National Cattlemen's Beef Association.

a specific meat cut, for the bones from various parts of the carcass have unique and readily recognizable shapes. For example, the presence of a round bone clearly indicates that the cut is from either a front or back leg, and the "T-bone" is a backbone. These and other examples are presented in Table 13.4.

When the location of the cut is known and the type of meat has been identified, the classification of the cut as tender or less tender can be made readily. This classification is very important, for selection of a cooking technique appropriate to the tenderness of the cut is essential to success in meat cookery. Tender and less tender cuts can be very pleasing to eat when they are prepared correctly, while even the most tender of cuts can be disappointing when cooked improperly.

Pork Basics

pork
Be inspired

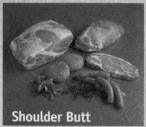

Shoulder Butt

Upper row (l-r):
Bone-in Blade Roast,
Boneless Blade Roast

Lower row (l-r):
Ground Pork,
Sausage, Blade Steak

Picnic Shoulder

Upper row (l-r):
Smoked Picnic,
Arm Picnic Roast

Lower row:
Smoked Hocks

Side

Top:
Spareribs

Bottom:
Slab Bacon, Sliced
Bacon

Leg

Upper row (l-r):
Bone-in Fresh Ham,
Smoked Ham

Lower row (l-r):
Leg Cutlets, Fresh
Boneless Ham Roast

Loin

**Tenderloin &
Canadian-Style Bacon**

Left: Tenderloin
Right: Canadian-Style Bacon

Ribs

Left: Country-Style Ribs
Right: Back Ribs

Roasts

Upper row (l-r):
Center Rib Roast (Rack of Pork),
Bone-in Sirloin Roast
Middle:
Boneless Center Loin Roast
Lower row (l-r):
Boneless Rib End Roast,
Boneless Sirloin Roast

Chops

Upper row (l-r):
Sirloin Chop, Rib Chop,
Loin Chop

Lower row (l-r):
Boneless Rib End Chop,
Boneless Center Loin Chop,
Butterfly Chop

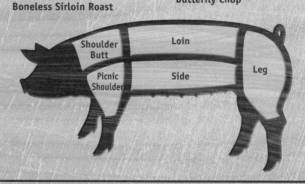

THE MANY SHAPES OF PORK ROASTS

Cut Loose!

When shopping for pork,
consider cutting traditional
roasts into a variety of
different shapes

CHOPS: Dinner, backyard barbecue or gourmet entree

CUBES: Great for kabobs, stew & chili

STRIPS: Super stir fry, fajitas & salads

CUTLETS: Delicious breakfast chops & quick sandwiches

www.PorkBeInspired.com   #03342 04/2011

Figure 13.9
Primal and retail pork cuts. Courtesy of the Pork Checkoff.

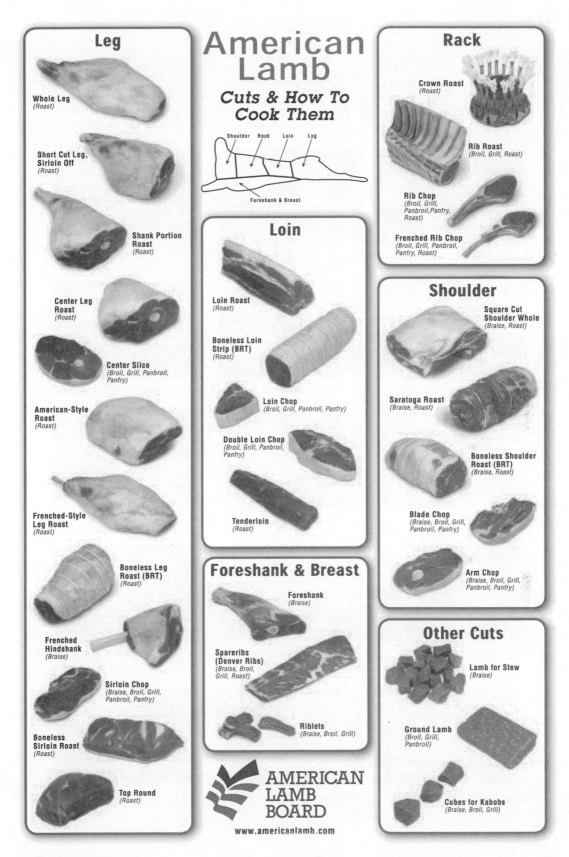

Figure 13.10
Primal and retail lamb cuts. Courtesy of the American Lamb Board.

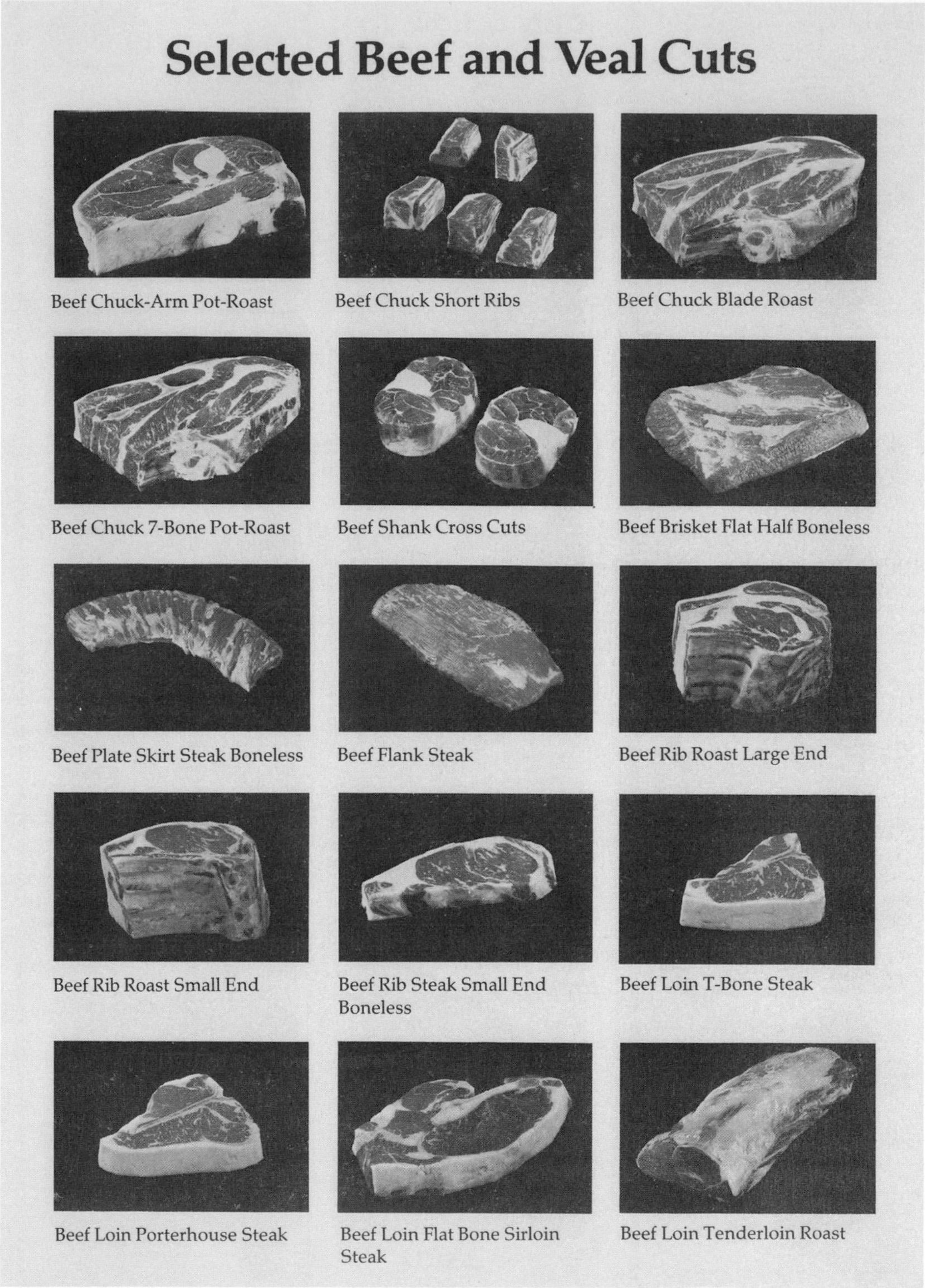

Selected Beef and Veal Cuts

Beef Chuck-Arm Pot-Roast

Beef Chuck Short Ribs

Beef Chuck Blade Roast

Beef Chuck 7-Bone Pot-Roast

Beef Shank Cross Cuts

Beef Brisket Flat Half Boneless

Beef Plate Skirt Steak Boneless

Beef Flank Steak

Beef Rib Roast Large End

Beef Rib Roast Small End

Beef Rib Steak Small End Boneless

Beef Loin T-Bone Steak

Beef Loin Porterhouse Steak

Beef Loin Flat Bone Sirloin Steak

Beef Loin Tenderloin Roast

Figure 13.11
Selected retail cuts of beef, veal, pork, and lamb. Courtesy of National Cattlemen's Beef Association.

Pork and Lamb Cuts

Beef Round Steak

Beef Round Rump Roast

Veal Loin Chops

Pork Loin Rib Chops

Pork Loin Chops

Pork Spareribs

Pork Leg (Fresh Ham) Shank Portion

Pork Leg (Fresh Ham) Rump Portion

Smoked Pork Shoulder Picnic Whole

Lamb Shoulder Blade Chops

Lamb Shoulder Arm Chops

Lamb Breast

Lamb Loin Chops

Lamb Leg Sirloin Chops

Lamb Leg Frenched Style Roast

Figure 13.11
(Continued)

TABLE 13.4
IDENTIFICATION OF RETAIL CUTS BY BONE SHAPE

Name	Bone Shape			Cuts
Arm bone				Shoulder, arm cuts
Blade bone	(Near neck)	(Center)	(Near rib) 	Shoulder blade cuts
Back bone and rib bone				Rib cuts
Back bone (T-bone)				Short loin cuts
Hip bone	(Pinbone)	(Flat bone)[a]	(Wedge bone)[b] 	Hip (sirloin) cuts
Leg or round bone				Leg or round cuts
Breast and rib bones				Breast or brisket cuts

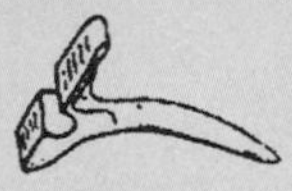

[a]Formerly part of "double bone," but today the backbone usually is removed, leaving only the "flat bone" (also called "pinbone") in the steak.
[b]Wedge bone, which is near the round, may be wedge shaped on one side of sirloin steak wile on the other side the same bone may be round.

Making the Selection   In most markets, decisions may be made between two or more packages of the same cut of meat. One obvious guide in making the selection is whether or not a specific package contains the approximate amount of meat needed to serve those to be fed. The following figures are a general guideline for the amount of meat to purchase per person, although individuals vary rather widely in just how much they eat at a meal:

Boneless cuts	1/4 lb
Small bones	1/3 lb
Average bone	1/2 lb
Large bone	3/4–1 lb

Buyers should look for packages with the smallest amount of bone in relation to meat when selecting among packages of the same cuts. Also the size of the fatty deposits surrounding the edible portion of the cut should be noted. Since both bone and fatty deposits generally are discarded, they can represent significant waste and expense in comparison with possibly a similar cut that has been trimmed closely.

Texture of the meat cuts is also important. The finer the texture appears to be for a specific cut, generally the more tender is the cut. A bright color characteristic of the particular type of meat is yet another clue to selecting optimum quality and freshness. However, money can be saved by purchasing a package that has been reduced because it was cut the day before. This is recommended only when the meat will be cooked and served the same day it is purchased, for such meat will spoil more quickly than will freshly cut meats.

Storage   Meat is a highly perishable food and must be kept refrigerated. The time between leaving the refrigerated meat counter in the store until meat packages (unopened) are refrigerated or frozen in the home should be kept to a minimum to reduce the potential for spoilage by microorganisms. Even canned hams should be refrigerated unopened in their containers unless the package indicates refrigeration is not necessary. This precaution is needed because some

TABLE 13.5
STORAGE GUIDE FOR FRESH, PROCESSED, AND COOKED MEATS

Product	Storage Period to Maintain Quality	
	Refrigerator 40°F or below (4.4°C) (days)	Freezer 0°F (–17.8°C) (months)
Fresh Meats (beef, veal, lamb, pork)		
Roasts	3–5	4–12
Steaks	3–5	6–12
Chops	3–5	4–6
Ground	1–2	3–4
Variety meats	1–2	3–4
Sausage (pork)	1–2	1–2
Processed Meats		
Bacon	7	1
Hot dogs	7	1–2
Ham (whole)	7	6
Ham (half)	3–5	6
Ham (slices)	3–5	1–2
Luncheon meats	3–5	1–2
Sausage (raw)	2	1–2
Sausage (dry and semidry)	14–21	Not recommended
Cooked Meats		
Cooked meats and meat dishes	3–4	2–3
Gravy and meat broth	1–2	2–3

http://www.fsis.usda.gov/ fact_sheets/Ham/index.asp

—Fact sheet about ham.

http://www.foodsafety.gov/ keep/charts/storagetimes. html

—Site for federal information on safe storage.

canned hams have not undergone sufficient heat treatment during canning to permit safe storage at room temperature.

Many refrigerators have a special meat compartment that should be maintained at 35° to 40°F (1.7°C to 4.4°C), preferably at 35°F (1.7°C). If this compartment is not available, the meat should be stored in the coldest part of the refrigerator for short-term storage (Table 13.5). For somewhat longer periods, meats can be stored in the freezer section of the refrigerator. However, the freezer of a refrigerator does not sustain a temperature uniformly low enough for extended frozen storage. A separate freezer must be maintained at a maximum temperature of 0°F (–17.8°C) if the meat is to be stored for the extended times suggested in Table 13.5.

http://www.fsis.usda. gov/fact_sheets/Meat_ Preparation_Fact_Sheets/ index.asp

—Fact sheets on meat preparation.

Selecting an Appropriate Cookery Method

Sometimes preparation of meat begins with applying a dry rub mixture of herbs and/or spices over the surface or marinating it in a flavorful combination of wine, juice, or other ingredients. Thin or small pieces of meat are able to absorb more of the flavors because the rub or the marinade penetrates only a short distance. Both techniques enhance flavor. Marinades also may make the meat more tender, as a result of the action of the acid on the proteins in the meat. Marinating may be done for a rather short time or for several days, as is done when making sauerbraten. Regardless of the length of time involved, meats should always be marinated in the refrigerator to assure safety. Used marinade is a fine medium for the growth of harmful microorganisms. If the marinade is to be used in basting or for any other purpose, it must be boiled to kill any microorganisms that may be present.

A major decision in meat cookery is deciding whether to use a dry heat or a moist heat method. For tender cuts of meat, dry heat is preferred, whereas less tender cuts need the long,

http://www.ams.usda.gov/ LSG/stand/imps.htm

—Institutional Meat Purchases Specifications (IMPS).

Figure 13.12
Tenderloin, the most tender muscle, is best prepared by using a dry heat cookery method and cooking just to the desired final temperature [145°F (63°C) for medium rare]. Courtesy of National Cattlemen's Beef Association.

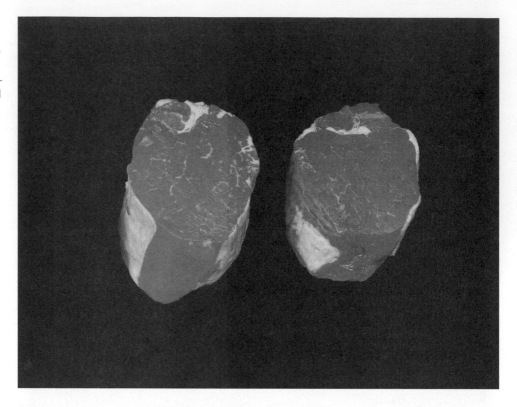

slow cooking provided by moist heat methods. This distinction is based on the major protein components found in the tender versus the less tender cuts.

In tender cuts, the muscle proteins are the dominant consideration (Figure 13.12). Since muscle proteins are fairly soluble and tender prior to cooking, the heat will only serve to toughen the overall character of the meat by denaturing the muscle proteins. As a result, tender cuts of meat will become progressively less tender the longer they are cooked because the muscle proteins draw closer and closer together as they denature. Roasting, broiling, pan broiling, pan frying, and deep-fat frying are the methods for dry heat cookery of meat.

On the other hand, less tender cuts are dominated by a comparatively high content of collagen (Figure 13.13). A cookery technique that proceeds slowly and takes an extended period

Figure 13.13
Beef bottom round steak is a less tender cut and is best when prepared by a braising or stewing (moist heat methods). Courtesy of National Cattlemen's Beef Association.

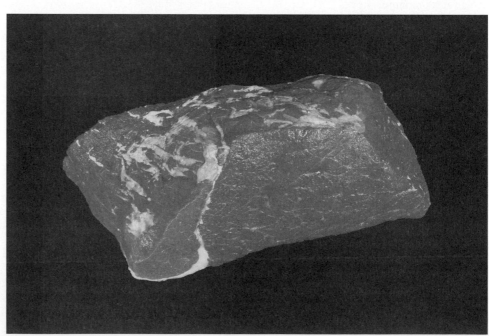

of time provides just the right circumstance for the collagen molecules to relax and release the individual gelatin strands. The extremely tender results of moist heat cookery on less tender cuts emphasize the merits of selecting this type of preparation. The two basic types of moist heat cookery are braising and cooking in liquid (also called stewing).

Regardless of the type of cookery method selected, tests for doneness are important guides to achieving a high-quality product. Tender cuts of meat are tested most accurately using a meat thermometer to indicate the temperature on the interior. The final temperature for beef, veal, and lamb is dependent on personal preference. For medium rare, the internal temperature should be 145°F (62.8°C); for medium, 160°F (71.1°C); and for well done, the center of the meat should reach 170°F (76.7°C). Ground meats should be heated to at least 160°F (71.1°C). The potential risk of viable trichinae mandates that pork should be cooked to an interior temperature of 160°F (71.1°C) to allow a margin of safety. Hams that have not been heat treated during processing should be heated to at least 160°F (71.1°C) and preferably to 170°F (76.7°C). Fully cooked hams should be reheated to an interior temperature of at least 140°F (60°C).

Less tender cuts of meat are done when a fork can be inserted into them and removed easily. In all instances, this will mean that the meat has been cooked to well done. However, a thermometer is not necessary to determine this; the fork test is a convenient and sufficiently accurate means of determining doneness in home cookery.

The rate at which various meats will reach the desired end point varies somewhat from one piece to another. Variations are due to the amount of bone, the amount of fat, and the dimensions of the cut. Of course, minor variations in temperature control during the cooking period will add to the possible variations in time needed for meat to be ready to serve. Despite these many influences, some guide is needed to help decide when the meat should be started for a meal. Timetables have been worked out for various meats, various cuts, and different cookery methods. These timetables are intended merely as guides. The foregoing tests for doneness should be applied (by using a thermometer or fork, depending on the cookery method being used) to ensure that the desired end result is achieved.

DRY HEAT METHODS

Roasting   Roasting is an appropriate technique for large cuts of tender meat, such as a rib roast. Preparation by roasting is a very simple process, beginning with assembling the roast on a rack in a shallow pan and then inserting the thermometer (unless it is not ovenproof) so that the sensing portion is in the center of the roast, but touching neither bone nor fat (Figure 13.14). Rib roasts with the bone in can stand on their own bone structure rather than needing a rack to hold them out of the drippings; hence the name "standing rib roast."

The assembled meat, with its thermometer and roasting pan, is placed without any cover in the center of the oven and positioned so that the meat thermometer can be read quickly and easily while the meat is roasting. Since this is a dry heat method, no covering, not even aluminum foil, should be used. Ovenproof thermometers are used rather than plastic-covered thermometers since plastic will melt at temperatures used for roasting. Plastic thermometers are inserted when it is close to time for the meat to be at the desired final temperature and then removed if more time is needed in the oven.

The temperature used for roasting is influenced by the size of the roast. Small roasts ordinarily are roasted at 325°F (163°C), while large roasts are placed in ovens set at 300°F (150°C), the lower temperature being used to provide more uniform heat penetration through the large mass of muscle. When these comparatively low oven temperatures are used, meats show less drip loss, less shrinkage, increased juiciness,

http://www.beefits whatsfordinner.com/
—Suggestions on meat cookery.

http://www.beefits whatsfordinner.com/ meatcase.aspx
—Interactive site about cooking various beef cuts.

http://www.beefits whatsfordinner.com/ cookinglessons.aspx
—Chart of recommended methods for cooking various beef cuts.

Figure 13.14
Standing rib roast, a tender cut, resting on its bones with the fat side up in a shallow, uncovered pan is ready for roasting in a 325°F (163°C) oven. Courtesy of Plycon Press.

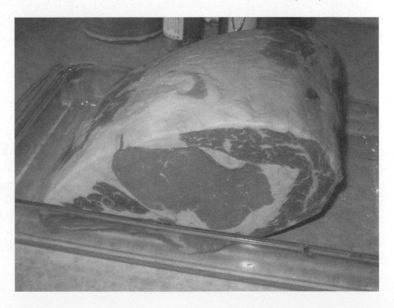

TABLE 13.6
TIMETABLE FOR ROASTING

Cut	Weight (lb)	Oven Temperature (°F)	Interior Temperature When Removed from Oven (°F)	Approximate Cooking Time (min/lb)
Beef				
Standing rib	6–8	300–325	145 (rare)	23–25
			160 (medium)	27–30
			170 (well done)	32–35
	4–6	300–325	145 (rare)	26–32
			160 (medium)	34–38
			170 (well done)	40–42
Rolled rib	5–7	300–325	145 (rare)	28–34
			160 (medium)	38
			170 (well done)	48
Veal				
Leg	5–8	300–325	170 (well done)	25–35
Loin	4–6	300–325	170 (well done)	30–35
Rib (rack)	3–5	300–325	170 (well done)	35–40
Pork (fresh)				
Loin	5–8	325–350	160 (medium)	20–30
			170 (well done)	30–35
Leg (ham), bone in (half)	5–8	325–350	160 (medium)	30–35
			170 (well done)	35–40
				25–30
Pork (cured)				
Ham (cook before eating)	10–14	300–325	160	18–20
Ham (fully cooked)	10–14	325	140	15
Lamb				
Leg	5–8	300–325	145 (medium rare)	15–20
			160 (medium)	
			175–180 (well done)	20–25
				25–30
Shoulder, rolled	3–5	300–325	145 (medium rare)	25–30
			160 (medium)	30–35
			175–180 (well done)	35–40

and more uniformity in heat penetration than if meats are roasted in ovens between 425°F and 450°F (218°C and 232°C). The low temperatures also cause less spattering and burning, which eases the cleaning of the oven and roasting pan. Basting can be done during roasting, but this step is not at all necessary.

Roasting times can be calculated based on the figures indicated in the timetable shown in Table 13.6. In addition to the actual roasting time, a standing time of between 10 and 20 minutes should be allowed at room temperature to allow the meat to become slightly firm for ease in carving.

Some people start to roast meat by searing the roast or browning it quickly on the surface in a 500°F (260°C) oven and then continuing roasting at 300°F (150°C). There is no particular benefit in using this technique; the disadvantages are greater fuel consumption and high drip and evaporative losses. This method is not recommended for these reasons.

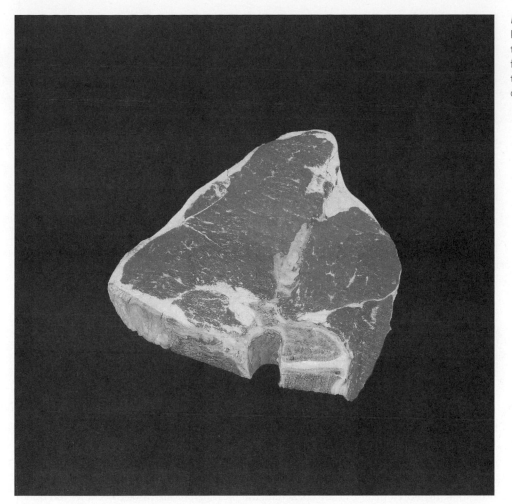

Figure 13.15
Porterhouse steak is a
tender cut ideally suited
for broiling because it is a
tender cut. Courtesy of National
Cattlemen's Beef Association.

Broiling **Broiling** is the only preparation utilizing direct heat to cook meat. Broiling may be done on a charcoal broiling unit or hibachi in which the heat comes from beneath, or it may take place in an oven or special broiler compartment. In either of these types of compartments, the heat comes from the top onto the upper surface of the meat. In a sense, charcoal broiling may be considered as "upside down" broiling.

Both approaches to broiling require tender cuts of meat an inch or more in thickness, with the thickness being uniform throughout the cut to be broiled. Thinner cuts will become unpleasantly dry during broiling. Porterhouse, T-bone, club, and rib steaks of beef, cured ham slices, lamb chops, and bacon all broil well (Figure 13.15).

Oven broiling requires a special broiler pan that allows the fat to collect on the bottom below a rack that serves the dual function of keeping the meat out of the drippings and protecting the collecting fat from the intense heat of the broiler unit. This type of broiler pan minimizes smoking of fat during broiling and, what is more important, sharply reduces the possibility of a fire in the broiler.

Since broiling is done by means of a rather intense, continuous heat, it is important that the entire surface of the meat be at a uniform distance from the heat source. In other words, meats being broiled need to remain flat during the broiling period rather than curling up. When meat curls during broiling, pockets of fat collect on the surface and present a fire hazard; furthermore, the meat nearest the heat source is likely to burn, while the remainder will not yet be done. This entire problem can be avoided by scoring the edges of the steak at intervals of about an inch, being sure to cut entirely through the connective tissue surrounding the muscle without making a cut into the meat itself (Figure 13.16). These breaks in the connective tissue

broiling Cooking by direct heat, usually at a distance of about three inches; fat is allowed to drain away from the meat.

Figure 13.16
Steaks remain flat during broiling if they are scored around the edges by cutting through the collagen. Courtesy of Plycon Press.

prevent the meat from curling due to the shrinkage of the connective tissue at the perimeter of muscle during broiling, and the meat remains flat.

Usually the top surface of meat to be broiled is positioned about three inches from the heat source. However, if the meat is to be broiled until well done, the meat should be lowered a little to allow more time for heat to penetrate the meat before the surface becomes too done. The meat is broiled on the first side until about half done, at which time the top surface is salted, if desired, and the cut is turned over. Then the second side is broiled until the desired degree of doneness is reached. The meat is not turned a second time during broiling. To maintain constant direct heat, most broilers must be operated with the door ajar.

When the cut being broiled is thick enough, a thermometer should be inserted from the side and parallel to the two cut surfaces so that the temperature in the center of the cut can be measured. However, this often is not feasible. The timetable for broiling (Table 13.7) serves as a guide in such instances, but the actual degree of doneness can be determined by making a small incision in the finished piece of meat.

To add flavor interest to meats to be broiled, the meat can be marinated for at least an hour before broiling. Acid fruit juices in a marinade can also help to promote tenderness. Another treatment prior to broiling is adding meat tenderizer according to the package directions to less tender, less expensive cuts of meats. Papain, a proteolytic enzyme from papaya, often is the enzyme used. Unfortunately, this enzymatic digestion frequently results in a powdery surface texture.

pan broiling   Cooking meat in a skillet, being careful to keep removing fat as it drains from the meat.

Pan Broiling   Both broiling and **pan broiling** are cookery methods producing a comparatively low fat content in the finished product, for in both these methods, the fat is removed from the meat as it drains out. Cuts that can be broiled can also be pan broiled. In addition, tender cuts of meat too thin for broiling can be pan broiled satisfactorily (Figure 13.17).

Success in pan broiling requires a heavy, ungreased skillet so that heating can be done relatively slowly without burning the meat. During pan broiling, fat is removed from the pan as it drains from the meat. It is this removal of the collecting fat that differentiates pan broiling from pan frying. Unlike broiling, pan broiling is done by turning the meat several times with tongs to help achieve the desired degree of doneness without overheating the exterior surface and drying out the meat.

		Approximate Total Cooking Time (min)	
TABLE 13.7 **TIMETABLE FOR BROILING**			
Cut	Thickness (in.)	Rare	Medium
Beef			
Rib steak	1	15	20
	1 1/2	25	30
	2	35	45
Club steak	1	15	20
	1 1/2	25	30
	2	35	45
Sirloin steak	1	20	25
	1 1/2	30	35
	2	40	45
Porterhouse steak	1	20	25
	1 1/2	30	35
	2	40	45
Ground beef patties	1	15	25
Lamb			
Shoulder chops	1		12
	1 1/2		18
	2		22
Rib chops	1		12
	1 1/2		18
	2		22
Loin chops	1		12
	1 1/2		18
	2		22
Ground patties	1		18

Pan Frying Tender cuts of meat half an inch to an inch in thickness are suitable for **pan frying**. The requisite for successful pan frying is a heavy skillet with uniform heat conduction. This allows the meat to be fried uniformly and without burning before it is done to the desired end point. Preparation of meat for pan frying requires scoring the fat and connective tissue in the same fashion as is done for broiling and pan broiling. Then the meat is placed in the skillet containing just enough fat to keep the meat from sticking. Careful temperature control during frying is important to the quality of the finished product. If the heat is too intense, the fat draining from the meat will begin to smoke, irritating the eyes and giving a burned flavor to the meat.

The principal difference between pan broiling and pan frying is the treatment of the fat released from the meat. In pan frying the fat is allowed to collect in the pan throughout the frying period. This results in the development of a suggestion of crispness on the surface of the fried meat and also a higher fat and calorie content in the meat when it is served. For persons concerned with reducing fat intake, pan frying is not as suitable for preparing tender cuts of meats as are broiling, pan broiling, or roasting.

Deep-Fat Frying **Deep-fat frying** is the dry heat method employing enough fat to immerse the frying food completely in hot fat. Often this is done using a deep-fat fryer

Pan Frying Cooking meat in a frying pan and allowing the fat to accumulate in the pan.

deep-fat frying Dry heat method in which meat is immersed in very hot fat.

Figure 13.17
T-bone steak is a tender cut well suited to pan broiling, broiling, or pan frying.
Courtesy of National Cattlemen's Beef Association.

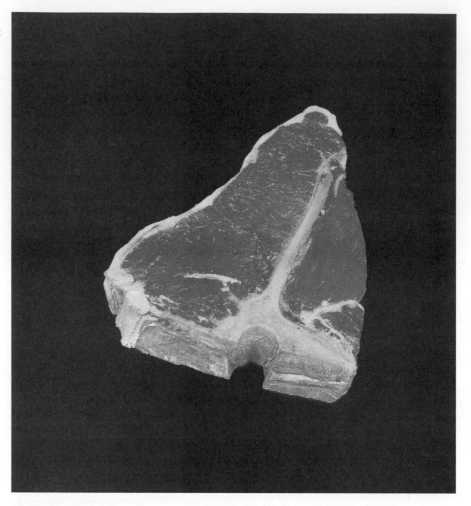

(Figure 13.18), but a deep pan on a thermostatically controlled heating element also may be used satisfactorily. Careful control of the temperature in deep-fat frying is very important, for if the fat is too hot, the food will be burned on the outside before the center is done. Fat that is too cool results in a prolonged cooking time, and the absorption of extra fat will give a greasy feel to the food.

The temperature can be maintained reasonably well once the correct frying temperature (usually 350°–375°F [175°–190°C]) has been reached if only a small amount of food is added at a time. If a large quantity is added, the cold food will cause the temperature to drop considerably, and several minutes will be required to reheat the fat to the correct frying temperature.

Deep-fat frying is used fairly commonly for frying chicken and fish. Only rarely are the red meats prepared in this fashion. However, bite-sized pieces of beef tenderloin or other tender steak sometimes are prepared in this general fashion as a beef fondue.

Care should be taken to blot food to eliminate extra water if chunks of beef or other items are to be deep-fat fried. This will reduce the foaming and splattering that can occur if hot fat and cool water come in contact. Deep-fat fried foods should be drained well and blotted on a paper towel before serving. This technique also reduces the amount of fat consumed when deep-fat fried foods are served.

Questions have arisen about the safety of **acrylamide**, a compound that forms when meats and other foods are subjected to very high temperatures. Research is being conducted to determine more about the carcinogenicity of acrylamide, but answers about safe levels and possible harm are not yet available. Among the foods noted to be potential sources of

acrylamide Potential carcinogen that forms when meats, vegetables, and baked products reach extremely high temperatures.

acrylamide are fried and broiled meats, for the surfaces of these meats reach temperatures well in excess of the temperature of boiling water. (Baked products and fried vegetables are other sources.)

Moist Heat Methods

Braising   **Braising** is used very frequently in preparing less-tender cuts of meat (Figure 13.19). This moist heat method sometimes is begun by browning the cut of meat thoroughly on all sides before adding a small amount of liquid and covering the pan for an extended period of simmering. The initial fast browning gives the meat a pleasing color and develops a full flavor, both of which add to the palatability of the liquid as well as to the meat itself. Sometimes this initial browning is omitted, which results in a satisfactory product but one lacking the heightened color and flavor obtained by browning.

During the simmering period, the liquid level needs to be checked occasionally and more liquid added to compensate for evaporation that has taken place. If the simmering is being done on the range top, the heat needs to be set very low, and the pan should be equipped with a lid that fits snugly. Even with these precautions, evaporation will occur during the two or three hours of simmering needed to achieve the desired degree of tenderness. Braising is continued until a fork can be inserted and removed easily, which means that braised meats always are at the well done stage.

One of the nice features of braising is that a variety of flavors can be introduced to add interest to the entrée for the meal. For instance, tomatoes, such seasonings as thyme and basil, onions, and numerous other flavorful ingredients may be added to intermingle with the flavors of the meat during the long period of simmering. Also, the acidity of tomatoes or other ingredients helps to promote the tenderizing of the meat. However, an extended simmering period still is necessary for the meat to reach the desired degree of tenderness.

Many different types of meat cuts are well suited to braising. Any cuts classified as less tender can be prepared very satisfactorily in this way. Veal, regardless of the cut, benefits from braising because the comparatively high proportion of collagen in the meat will be converted to gelatin, making veal that is extremely tender. The other benefit to veal that is braised is the added flavor, for veal itself has an extremely delicate, if not bland, flavor. Thick pork chops also should be braised to ensure that the interior reaches the necessary 160°F (71.1°C) in the center before the chops are too dark and dry on the exterior.

Stewing (Cooking in Liquid)   The other method categorized as moist heat cookery is stewing or cooking in liquid (Figure 13.20). Braising and stewing are very similar methods, the primary difference being that stewed meats have enough liquid added to cover them, while braised meats have only enough liquid added to cover the bottom of the pan and keep the meat from sticking. Browning of meats to be stewed is optional, although often meats being made into stews are browned on all sides of the cubes prior to adding the water or other liquid.

Figure 13.18
Deep-fat frying a turkey can be dangerous because it displaces a large amount of very hot fat when it is lowered into the fryer, but the results are juicy and flavorful when the temperature and quantity of the oil are controlled. Courtesy of Plycon Press.

braising   Moist heat method in which meat is cooked very slowly in a covered pan in a small amount of water until fork tender.

Figure 13.19
A 7-bone pot roast is a less tender cut until it is transformed to a fork-tender meat by braising (a moist heat method). *Courtesy of National Cattlemen's Beef Association.*

Figure 13.20
Stewing is a moist method that not only tenderizes less tender cuts of meat but also provides opportunity for blending flavors from added spices and other ingredients. *Courtesy of Plycon Press.*

In most instances, the liquid used in stewing is water, often with a bouquet garni or selected seasoning being added. Once the liquid is added, the temperature needs to be controlled to maintain a simmering temperature. Boiling will promote production of a slightly tougher product than will be the result of simmering. Somewhat less energy will be required to maintain the simmering temperature than is needed for boiling, which is an added advantage of temperature control.

Stewed meats are tested in the same way that they are for braising (by inserting a fork and removing it to be sure that this can be done easily). Although the time will vary somewhat with the size of the piece(s) of meat being stewed, the usual stewing period is about three hours.

Often vegetables are added to meats being stewed. The size and types of vegetables will influence the time required to achieve the desired degree of tenderness, but the length of time for the vegetables will always be far less than that for the meats. Therefore, the vegetables are added to the stewing meats fairly near the end of the stewing period to avoid overcooking the vegetables. Stews may be thickened, if desired, by blending the thickening agent (usually flour) with some cold water until perfectly smooth before stirring this slurry into the stew containing the tender meat and vegetables. The entire stew then is heated, with thorough stirring, until the starch is gelatinized (Chapter 10).

In addition to cubed stew meats, several of the variety meats are well suited to cooking in liquid. Tongue, kidney, heart, tripe, sweetbreads, and brains are all appropriate for this cookery technique. The times range from as long as three to four hours for beef heart and tongue to as little as 15–20 minutes for sweetbreads and brains. Smoked country hams and picnics, as well as corned beef, are suitable for cooking in liquid, the time required for the hams being approximately 20–30 minutes per pound. Smoked picnics and corned beef require about 45 minutes per pound.

POULTRY

Interest in reducing serum cholesterol levels, and possibly the incidence of heart attacks, and also the desire to reduce fat intake have spurred considerable gains in poultry consumption. From the standpoint of nutrition, poultry of all types can be recommended highly. Food budgets also benefit from the use of poultry, particularly chicken and turkey.

Classification

The types of poultry available most commonly in the United States include chickens, turkeys, ducks, and geese. Chickens are popular throughout the year, but turkeys are beginning to augment chickens in the markets at times far removed from the traditional holiday feasts. Each type of poultry has specific classes, as follows:

Chickens

1. Cornish game hen or Rock Cornish game hen. Young chicken (either Cornish chicken or a cross between a Cornish and another breed) usually 5–7 weeks old and weighing a maximum of two pounds.
2. Broiler or fryer. Usually 9–12 weeks old.
3. Roaster. From 3–5 months old.
4. Capon. Castrated male usually under 8 months old.
5. Stag. Male under 10 months old.
6. Hen or stewing chicken. Mature female less than 10 months old.
7. Cock. Mature male having coarse skin and toughened, darkened meat.

Turkeys

1. Fryer-roaster turkey. Usually under 16 weeks old.
2. Young hen turkey. Female, usually 5–7 months old.
3. Young tom turkey. Male, usually 5–7 months old.
4. Yearling hen turkey. Female under 15 months old.
5. Yearling tom turkey. Male under 15 months old.
6. Mature or old turkey. More than 15 months old.

Ducks

1. Broiler or fryer duckling. Usually under 8 weeks old.
2. Roaster duckling. Usually under 16 weeks old.
3. Mature or old duck. Usually over 6 months old.

Geese

1. Young goose. Tender flesh, windpipe easily dented.
2. Mature or old goose. Toughened flesh, hardened windpipe.

INGREDIENT HIGHLIGHT
OSTRICH

If you are interested in trying a new dish, you might like to try ostrich meat, a red meat that originated in Africa (Figure 13.21). This super-sized fowl is flightless despite its big wings; its legs are powerful and enable it to run as fast as 45 miles per hour. The nutritional merits of ostrich meat have been part of the reason that some ostriches are now being raised commercially in the United States. Protein content is high and the cholesterol content is low. The fat content varies with the specific cut, but generally ranges between 1.9 and less than 4.0 percent, compared with around 15 percent for beef. For dieters, ostrich meat may be an interesting meat to try because of its lower calories. On the other side of the coin is the comparatively high cost and the rather dry mouthfeel of ostrich.

Figure 13.21
Ostriches are wild in Kenya, but some are raised on farms in the United States for sale as poultry meat.
Courtesy of Plycon Press.

http://www.ostriches.org/
recipes.html

—Information about preparing ostrich cuts.

Shopping for Poultry

Poultry must be inspected by the appropriate federal or state inspectors before interstate and intrastate marketing can commence. These inspectors check according to the guidelines for wholesomeness of poultry outlined in the Wholesome Poultry Products Act of 1968. Grading often follows inspection, with the federal grade standards serving as the usual basis for evaluating quality. Under federal guidelines, poultry may be graded as U.S. Grade A, U.S. Grade B, and U.S. Grade C. However, the U.S. Grade A is the grade commonly seen in the markets. This grade is based on a good overall appearance denoting good conformation and meatiness, a well-developed layer of fat in the skin, and skin virtually free of defects. The lower two grades sometimes may be sold on the retail market, but their grade usually is not displayed. Common use of the lower grades is in processed poultry products.

Shoppers must decide whether to buy whole fowl or part(s). In the case of chickens, those that have been cut up cost more than do those that are purchased whole. However, some time is saved by not having to cut the pieces. For people who have a strong preference for certain parts, the purchase of only those parts may be satisfactory, though more costly than buying the entire fowl.

TABLE 13.8
SUGGESTED QUANTITIES OF POULTRY NEEDED PER SERVING

Type	Purchasing Guide
Turkey	Just less than 1/2 lb
Duckling	More than 1/2 lb
Goose	More than 1/2 lb
Chicken	
Barbecuing or broiling	1/4 chicken (2 1/2–lb chicken)
Frying	1/2 lb

The breast is the most expensive part, followed in decreasing order by the thighs, drumsticks, and wings. Often consumers will have the options of buying poultry skinless, boneless, and tenders.

The ratio of muscle to bone varies a good deal with the type of poultry being selected, which makes the amount of poultry to purchase sometimes puzzling. Usually, a whole Cornish hen is served as a single portion, which may be really more than some people desire unless the hen is quite small. For people with light appetites, half a Cornish hen is quite adequate. Similarly, other types of poultry may require a fairly heavy portion to provide enough meat if the fowl has a high ratio of bone to meat. Examples of the amount to allow per serving of various poultry choices are given in Table 13.8.

Storage

Particular care is necessary when storing poultry because microorganisms grow readily, particularly on the surfaces of the body cavity. Refrigeration just as soon as possible after purchase is extremely important to keep potential hazards to an absolute minimum. Table 13.9 outlines satisfactory storage periods in the refrigerator and the freezer.

Much of the poultry purchased is in the frozen form. Ideally, this poultry will be thawed completely just when preparation is ready to begin. For a small bird, thawing can be done within a reasonable length of time in the refrigerator, although room temperature is significantly faster, as can be seen in Table 13.10. A convenient thawing technique is intermittent heating and standing time provided by use of a microwave oven. Other methods involve immersing the poultry (in a watertight bag) in cold water, making frequent changes of water to help promote thawing. When it is possible to separate pieces and to remove the giblets and neck from the interior body cavity of whole fowl, thawing will be accelerated. A concern with room temperature thawing of very large birds is that the exterior portions will be at a temperature conducive to growth of microorganisms before the interior is thawed. However, the heat during roasting or frying will be sufficient to kill these microorganisms.

TABLE 13.9
REFRIGERATOR AND FREEZER STORAGE PERIODS FOR POULTRY

	Storage Period to Maintain Quality	
Type of Poultry	Refrigerator 35°–45°F (1.7°–7.2°C) (days)	Freezer 0°F (–17.8°C) (months)
Fresh Poultry		
Chicken	1–2	12
Turkey	1–2	12
Cooked Poultry		
Pieces covered with broth	1–2	2–6

http://www.foodsafety.gov/keep/charts/storagetimes.html

—Site for federal information on safe storage.

TABLE 13.10
ESTIMATED THAWING TIME FOR CHICKEN AND TURKEY

Frozen Poultry to Be Thawed	Refrigerator[a]	Cold Water[b]
	Time Required	
Chickens		
Less than 4 pounds	12–16 hours	1–1 1/2 hours
4 pounds or more	1–1 1/2 days	2 hours
Turkeys		
4–12 pounds	1–3 days	4–6 hours
12–20 pounds	3–5 days	6–8 hours
20–24 pounds	5–6 days	10–12 hours

[a]Leave in original wrapping with poultry resting on a tray.
[b]Cover poultry, wrapped in watertight bag, with cold water. Change water frequently.

Cookery

The various cookery methods described for meats also are utilized in preparing poultry. Whole fowl, particularly turkey and other large birds, frequently are roasted. In preparation for roasting, the giblets and neck are removed from the interior cavity, and the carcass is scrubbed carefully on the outside and the interior. Any remaining pinfeathers or other feathers should be removed. Just before roasting is to begin, the body and neck cavities are stuffed, if desired, and roasting is started to avoid an opportunity for potentially hazardous development of microorganisms. Clearly, a turkey should never be stuffed and then refrigerated overnight before roasting. The stuffing should not be packed firmly in the cavities because it needs some room to expand from the juices. The skin flap is pulled over the neck cavity and skewered to hold the dressing inside.

The trussed turkey can be roasted particularly easily if it is held inverted in a V-shaped rack placed in a shallow pan to catch the drippings. The turkey and pan are placed on the oven rack, located usually at the bottom position so that the turkey will be fairly well centered for good heat circulation. A meat thermometer placed in the dressing should reach 165°F (73.9°C).

When roasting unstuffed turkeys, the thermometer needs to be positioned with the sensing device in the center of the thigh, at which position the temperature indicating doneness is 165°F (73.9°C). Timing of meals featuring roast turkey can be facilitated by calculating the approximate time required for roasting, according to weight. Guidelines are presented in Table 13.11.

Because roasting is a dry heat method, no cover is placed over the turkey, despite the fact that turkey roasting pans traditionally have a cover (Figure 13.22). Use of aluminum foil surrounding a turkey results in a moist heat approach to preparing the fowl, a situation in which the skin assumes a grayish pallor rather than the golden brown traditionally visualized with roast turkey. Even when the oven temperature is increased to 425°F (220°C) to compensate for the insulating effect of the foil, this poor color remains a problem, and the energy required for roasting is increased significantly. The advantage is that oven splattering is minimal, although splattering will occur if the foil is opened for the final phase of roasting as a means of achieving some browning. Fowl can also be prepared in a special clay pot that has a relatively tight lid. Again, this device steams rather than roasts.

One reason given by people electing to these moist heat cookery methods is that they feel that turkey is too dry when roasted. Indeed, turkey meat will be quite dry when roasted—if, and only if, the turkey is roasted too long. When roasted to the correct final temperature, turkey is a very juicy meat. When overheated, the meat will be dry—even when moist heat is used.

Other dry heat meat cookery methods also may be used very successfully to prepare poultry unless the fowl is too mature and tough. Suitable methods include deep-fat frying, broiling, and frying. Oven frying is a variation of frying deserving mention as a means of saving time

TABLE 13.11
TIMETABLE FOR ROASTING POULTRY

	Ready-to-Roast Weight (lb)	Estimated Roasting Time at 325°F (163°C) (hr)
Chickens		
Whole broilers and fryers	3–4	1 1/4–1 1/2
Whole roasters	5–7	2–2 1/4
Capons	4–8	2–3
Ducks	4–6	2–3
Geese	6–8	3 1/2–4 1/2
Turkeys, whole[a, b]	6–8	3–3 1/2
	8–12	2 3/4–3
	12–16	3 1/4–4 1/2
	16–20	4 1/2–4 1/2
	20–24	4 1/2–5
Halves, quarters, pieces	3–8	2–3
Boneless roasts	3–10	3–4

[a]Add approximately 15 minutes per pound if turkey is stuffed.
[b]If roasting from the frozen state, at least 50 percent more time will be needed.

when preparing chicken. Pieces of chicken are prepared by washing them carefully, rolling in flour or crumbs, and then coating very lightly with oil or melted fat before placing them in a shallow baking dish. Baking is at 400°F (205°C) until done, with the pieces being turned once to promote uniform browning.

Very mature poultry needs to be prepared by moist heat methods. Although braising can be done, stewing is more common. Poultry for stewing may be left whole if a container sufficiently large is available; an option is to cut individual pieces before stewing. Use of a pressure saucepan or cooker saves considerable time. Stewed poultry will be done when tender enough for a fork to be inserted easily. This usually requires about two hours.

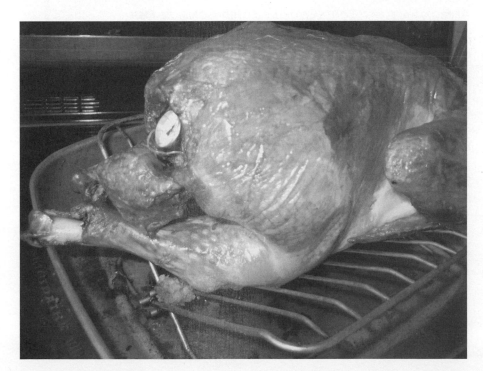

Figure 13.22
Turkey is juicy and tender when roasted uncovered with the breast down in a V-shaped rack placed inside a large shallow pan to catch the drippings. Courtesy of Plycon Press.

FISH

fish Cold-blooded aquatic animals, usually used to designate those with fins, a backbone, skull, and gills.

Fish have been swimming upstream for years in an attempt to gain a reasonable place in the nation's menus. Today the publicity encouraging the increased use of fish to replace meats, with the latter's high saturated fat and cholesterol content, has enhanced consumption of fish significantly. Nutritionally, fish generally are much lower in fat than the red meats and consequently are also lower in calories. The fat they do contain is high in polyunsaturates. From the perspective of cookery, fish have the advantage of usually being quick and easy to prepare.

Kinds of Fish

shellfish Subcategory of fish; equipped with shell or horny outer covering.

mollusk Shellfish protected by an outer shell, for example, scallops, clams, and oysters.

crustacean Shellfish covered by a horny protective layer; for example, shrimp, lobsters, and crabs.

More than 240 types of fish and **shellfish** are available to consumers in different parts of the United States. In differentiating fish from shellfish, the former are defined as a cold-blooded aquatic animal equipped with fins, a backbone, skull, and gills for removing air from water, whereas the latter are equipped with a shell or horny outer covering. Fish are categorized according to their oil content (Table 13.12); shellfish are divided into **mollusks** with shells (oysters, scallops, mussels, and clams) and **crustaceans** (Figure 13.23) with horny outer coverings (shrimp, lobsters, and crabs).

Fish may live in freshwater or saltwater, or they may spend part of their lives in freshwater and part in saltwater (anadromous). Because of their differences in habitat, fish frequently are labeled as freshwater or saltwater fish. Both of these water sources have the potential for being polluted, which can influence the safety of the fish obtained from them. Such pollution may

---

TABLE 13.12
APPROXIMATE FAT CONTENT OF SELECTED COMMON FISH

Oily Species (6–20% Oil or More)	Intermediate (2–6%)	Non-Oily Species (Less Than 2% Oil)
Chub, lake	Anchovies	Clams
Herring, sea	Bass	Cod
Mackerel	Carp	Flounder
Salmon, king	Crab	Haddock
Salmon, silver (medium red)	Oysters	Halibut
Salmon, sockeye (red)	Salmon, chum	Lobster
Sardines	Salmon, pink	Mullet
	Shrimp	Ocean, perch
		Octopus
Smelt		Oyster
Swordfish		Pike, lake
Tuna, canned		Rockfish
White fish, lake		Scallops
		Squid
		Sole
		Whiting

Figure 13.23
Crabs, lobsters, and shrimp (left to right) are classified as crustaceans, but diners will call them absolutely delicious. Courtesy of Plycon Press.

be from natural causes, such as the red tide (Chapter 3), which can cause paralytic shellfish poisoning at certain times of year. Also, industrial waste or improper sewage treatment may be prominent among the sources of contamination of both fresh and saltwater.

Increasing consumption of fish for health reasons and concern for developing all possible food sources to meet the needs of the burgeoning world population have stimulated considerable activity in developing food supplies from the sea and also from freshwater. Fish farming is resulting in controlled production of selected fish, such as trout and salmon. However, this type of farming is in its infancy compared with the sophisticated approaches that have been developed for farming crops on land.

Inspection and Grading

The National Marine Fisheries Service, part of the National Oceanic and Atmospheric Administration (NOAA) within the U.S. Department of Commerce, is the governmental unit responsible for the inspection and grading of fish. Inspection encompasses surveillance of the condition of the fish prior to processing and the conditions throughout the plant handling the fish. Since fish are very susceptible to spoilage, sanitation and temperature control are absolutely vital to maintaining acceptable microbiological limits. Inspection standards are directed toward these types of controls.

Grading identifies whether the quality of a fish meets Grade A, B, or substandards. The top quality is Grade A. Grade B is of very satisfactory quality, but more variation in size and more blemishes are acceptable than in the higher grade. Fish monitored and graded by federal standards will have a shield printed on their packaging stating U.S. Grade A or a shield announcing that the fish were packed under continuous inspection of the U.S. Department of Commerce.

http://www.seafood.nmfs.noaa.gov/ServicesBrochure.pdf
—Brochure on grading and inspection.

Selection and Care

Fish can be very costly or quite inexpensive, depending on the type selected. Live lobsters airfreighted to market are at the top end of the scale, while local catches usually are comparatively inexpensive (Figure 13.24). The difficulty of maintaining high quality in fresh fish has resulted in a broad frozen fish market as a means of maintaining excellent and safe fish during the marketing process. Because of the significant reduction in waste effected by freezing, frozen fish can be marketed at very competitive prices.

Criteria for selecting fresh fish include a shiny and unfaded skin, red gills, and clear eyes (Figure 13.25). The odor should be mild. If the fish has cut surfaces, these should look fresh

Figure 13.24
A huge tuna, a prize from the sea, is being readied for sale to sushi bars. Courtesy of Plycon Press.

dressed fish Fish from which the gills, fins, head, tail, and entrails have been removed.

fillets Lengthwise pieces of fish cut free of the backbone and associated bones.

steak Cross-sectional slice of a uniform thickness.

Figure 13.25
Fish are resting on a bed of crushed ice to help retain their shiny skin, red gills, and clear eyes. Courtesy of Plycon Press.

and not dry. Frozen fish should be encased in airtight packaging and frozen solidly. Fish visible in the package should have a plump appearance rather than a spongy, somewhat desiccated look.

Fish may be prepared for market in several ways. **Dressed fish** are fish that have had the heads and tails, the scales, and the entrails removed, but the bones are still present. Fish are made into **fillets** by stripping the flesh lengthwise from the backbone. **Steaks** are simply cross-sectional slices from a large dressed fish, such as salmon. The recommended portion size for a serving of fish is as follows:

Dressed	1/2 lb
Fillet	1/3 lb
Steaks	1/3 lb
Sticks	1/4 lb
Canned	1/6 lb

For optimal quality, fresh fish should be refrigerated immediately after purchase and prepared the same day, or no later than the next day. If fresh fish is not to be used in three days, it should be frozen as soon as it is brought into the kitchen from the market. Frozen storage should be limited to an absolute maximum of six months, but the quality will be best if the fish is used within a period of about three months. During storage, whether on shipboard when the fish is first caught or in the home, contamination begins in the slime of the skin, causing loss of firmness and color in the flesh beneath. Trimethylamine, a compound contributing heavily to the smelly odor of fish, is formed during storage unless great care is taken to regulate sanitation and temperature.

Fish Cookery

Fish have a limited amount of connective tissue, and even this connective tissue is more tender than that found in land animals (Figure 13.26). As a result, fish cookery basically becomes a problem of heating to a desirable serving

Figure 13.26
Fish fillets can be prepared quickly by pan frying because they are thin and have little connective tissue.
Courtesy of Plycon Press.

temperature without causing the fish to become dry and tough. The protein will coagulate when the fish is hot enough to serve, and the flesh will tend to flake apart when probed with a fork. Beyond this point, continued heating will reduce the quality of the fish because the protein will continue to draw together more tightly, causing the flesh to be tougher and forcing liquid out, which reduces the juiciness. Optimum juiciness and tenderness are achieved by brief cooking.

Fish cookery is unusual in that either moist heat or dry heat methods can be used successfully. Baking requires the longest time of the various methods, possibly up to an hour depending upon the size of the fish. Broiling and oven frying or baking (at 450°F [232°C] or less) require approximately 15 minutes, assuming that the fish is close to an inch thick. Pan frying is slightly faster because of the efficiency of heating with the very hot fat. In fact, deep-fat frying usually requires three to five minutes to achieve the desired end point. Although sauce or seasonings can be placed on fish being baked, the other dry heat methods do not add flavors.

One of the reasons for using moist heat cookery is the possibility of adding a subtle flavoring to the fish. Poaching and steaming are favorite moist heat methods. Poaching is done by placing a single layer of fish in a large frying pan containing simmering milk, water, or white wine. The fish should be simmered until the flesh flakes readily when tested with a fork, which usually requires about 5–10 minutes. Steaming is done by placing the fish on a rack above boiling water and then covering the pan tightly to trap the steam around the fish. The test for doneness also is flaking with a fork, and the steaming time is essentially the same as that required for poaching. Poaching is preferred by some people over steaming because of its potential for adding flavor, whereas steaming simply heats the fish and coagulates the protein without adding flavors.

JUDGING POINTS
FISH COOKERY

- Attractive appearance
- Fish flesh is flaky and tender to chew
- Moist in the mouth
- Pleasing, fresh flavor

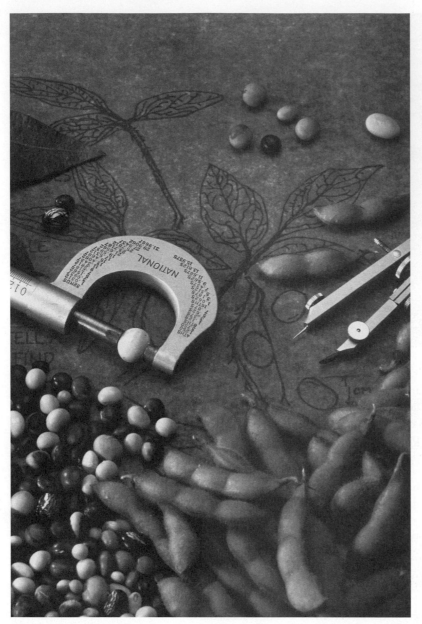

Figure 13.27
Soybeans are valued for their high-quality plant protein and their ability to be made into a wide array of edible protein products, including textured meat extenders. Courtesy of Agricultural Research Service.

textured soy protein (TSP)   Concentrated soy protein product from defatted soy flour; plant protein meat substitute.

SOY PROTEIN PRODUCTS

Textured Soy Protein

Interest in developing **textured soy protein (TSP)** has been spurred by a combination of factors, including the vegetarian movement, the comparatively high cost of meat, and anticipated food shortages in feeding the world's soaring population. The amino acid profile of soy protein is the most complete of the vegetable proteins, which makes this bean a particularly appropriate choice from the standpoint of nutrition (Figure 13.27). Farmers find this a good cash crop because of its ease of growth and its ability to put nitrogen back into the soil, leaving it more fertile than before the soybeans were planted.

Several different types of products have been developed from soybeans by food technologists (Table 13.13). Textured soy protein, also referred to by such synonyms as TSP (textured soy protein) and TVP (textured vegetable protein), can be used with considerable success as a meat extender to save meaningfully in the meat budget. It can be substituted at levels of up to 30 percent and still be acceptable to consumers. In fact, substitution at this level is authorized in the school lunch program. Use of TSP in meat loaf results in increased thiamin content, reduced drip losses, and retention of fat. Although the soy protein does not contain as much fat as ground beef, the ability of TSP to absorb fat during the baking period results in comparable fat levels in substituted and unsubstituted baked meat loaves. It is this ability to absorb fat that contributes to the pleasing juiciness of ground beef products containing TSP.

Among the various commercial items developed with TSP, imitation bacon is one of the most successful. TSP "bacon" bits are popular additions to salads because of their crisp texture and bacon-like flavor. Some fabricated meats have been made from TSP, and they have found a market among people avoiding meats.

Tofu

In a sense, tofu is the soybean equivalent of cheese. It is manufactured by coagulating the proteins in soymilk and then cutting and draining the coagulum to produce the familiar curd. The firmness of the tofu curd varies from soft or silken tofu to medium soft, firm, and even extra firm. Silken tofu is suitable for blending with other ingredients to make sauces, dips, and icings. If tofu is to be incorporated into cheesecakes, puddings, and pies, medium soft is the consistency that works best. When chunks or pieces of tofu are needed, the appropriate type to use is firm or extra firm.

Tofu is marketed in sealed tubs containing water to cover the block of tofu. Refrigerated storage and daily changes of cold water are needed to store tofu as long as a week. If necessary, tofu can be frozen, although the texture will be somewhat mealy after thawing.

TABLE 13.13
SELECTED MEAT AND SOY PRODUCTS AND SOME NUTRITIVE VALUES

Food	Calories	Protein (g)	Fat (g)	Carbohydrate (g)	Calcium (mg)	Iron (mg)	Thiamine (mg)	Riboflavin (mg)	Niacin (mg)	Vitamin B_{12} (mcg)
"Animal Protein Sources										
Chuck roast, 1/8 fat trim[a, b]	318	27.33	22.35	0.00	13	3.20	0.070	0.250	2.460	2.310
Beef, ground, 15% fat, broiled	232	24.62	14.02	0.00	20	2.68	0.043	0.178	5.778	2.810
Chicken breast meat, roasted	231	43.43	5	0.00	21	1.46	0.098	0.160	19.197	0.480
Egg, chicken, large, uncooked	72	6.28	4.75	0.36	28	0.88	0.020	0.229	0/037	0.450
Milk, non-fat fluid	83	8.26	0.2	12.15	299	0.07	0.110	0.446	0.230	1.230
Soy Products										
Vanilla yogurt	150	5.00	2.99	25.01	199	1.45	NA	NA	NA	NA
Soy flour, defatted	346	49.36	1.28	40.29	253	9.70	0.733	0.266	2.743	0.000
Soy protein concentrate[a]	328	63.63	0.46	25.41	363	10.78	0.316	0.142	0.716	0.000
Soy protein isolate[a]	338	80.69	3.39	7.36	178	14.50	0.176	0.1	1.438	0.000
Soymilk, unsweetened	335	6.95	3.91	4.23	301	1.12	0.374	0.503	0.401	2.700
Tofu, raw, firm, $CaSO_4$	290	31.56	17.44	8.54	1366	5.32	0.316	0,204	7.620	0.000

Source: USDA Nutrient Database; values are for 1 cup portion.
[a]Portion is 100 grams.
[b]Select grade beef.

CULTURAL INSIGHT
VEGETARIAN ADAPTATIONS

This chapter addresses animal protein in the diet, but many people today are vegetarians, at least to some degree. Those who consume eggs and dairy (ovo-lacto vegetarians) in addition to a plant diet can obtain the nutrients needed for good health by increasing their intake of the various foods they prefer to eat; they basically need to replace the nutrients lacking because of the absence of meat.

One of the challenges nutritionally for vegetarians who completely eliminate food from animal sources is to obtain the necessary quantity and balance of essential amino acids from plant foods. Even soy protein, the most complete of the plant proteins, does not contain as useful an amino acid profile as is found in eggs, milk, or meat. Fortunately, an appropriate combination is available when two or more complementary protein sources are eaten: cereal, legume, and nuts. The traditional combination of rice and beans in a Mexican meal provides the complete protein blend to meet the body's need. Other combinations that provide adequate essential amino acids are cereal and nuts, nuts and legume, or all three types together.

Iron from plant sources is absorbed with greater difficulty than from animal sources (refer to Table 13.13). If eggs are eaten, they help to meet the need for that mineral; milk is too low to provide much, but it is an important source of calcium. Vitamin B_{12} is found only in animal foods so strict vegetarians need to be sure to take a supplement for this vitamin as well as for iron. They also may need to be sure they are eating enough calories to maintain a desirable weight. This aspect of vegetarianism may attract some overweight people to at least reduce the amount of meat they are eating; meat definitely carries a fairly high calorie count unless portion sizes are controlled. A portion the size of a deck of cards is recommended.

SUMMARY

Red meats (beef, veal, pork, and lamb), poultry, and fish are very important sources of protein in the diet. Meat cuts comprise muscle, connective tissue, fat, and bone. In muscle, the sarcoplasm is bound by the sarcolemma to make a muscle fiber in which myofibrils and their thick and thin myofilaments are found. The fibers are in bundles (fasciculi), each of which is encased in connective tissue (endomysium), and fasciculi are clustered and surrounded by the perimysium.

Myosin, actin, actomyosin (in contracted muscle), and tropomyosin are important muscle proteins. Myoglobin and related pigments provide the color in meats. Connective tissue may be elastin or collagen; collagen can be converted to gelatin by a slow, long cooking period to tenderize meats. Fats add to the flavor and juiciness of meats. In addition to their fat and protein, meats are excellent sources or iron and copper, as well as providing thiamin, riboflavin, and niacin.

Meat passes through rigor following slaughter, with the conditions at slaughter influencing the drop in pH occurring during rigor. The ease of spoilage of meats requires that careful sanitation and refrigeration be provided for all meats, but prime beef being aged for two to sometimes more than five weeks in order to heighten the flavor needs particularly well-controlled conditions. Curing, smoking, freezing, and even freeze-drying are techniques used for extending the shelf life of meats. Inspection by government inspectors is used to monitor meat packing to assure safety of meat supplies. *Trichinella spiralis*, a parasite for which pigs sometimes are hosts, is not detected by inspection, making it necessary to heat pork to an internal temperature of 160°F (71.1°C) to assure its safety.

Grading of carcasses of beef, pork, and lamb can be done as an optional aid to consumers, whereas the inspection is legally mandatory. Beef is the type of meat most likely to be graded. This grading is based on quality considerations of palatability, texture, and marbling, and on yield.

Identification of cuts is important to consumers so that they will be knowledgeable about how the cut should be prepared. Carcasses are divided first into primal cuts and subsequently into retail cuts. Consumers can deduce much about the identity of a cut by examining the color of the meat, the size and shape of the bone, and the type of fat. Meat can be stored up to about five days (depending on the cut) in the refrigerator, but cuts should be frozen if they will be held longer than the recommended storage time.

The first decision in meat cookery is whether to use one of the moist heat or one of the dry heat methods, the former being recommended specifically for less tender cuts of meat, most veal cuts, and thick pork chops. Dry heat cookery is the appropriate category for most other cuts. Dry heat cookery methods include roasting, broiling, pan broiling, pan frying, and deep-fat frying. Braising and stewing, the two moist heat methods, require an extended cooking period to form gelatin from collagen and achieve the desired tender entrée.

Poultry (chickens, turkeys, ducks, and geese) are generally tender, although old fowl may be quite tough. Inspection divides poultry into U.S. Grades A, B, or C. Excellent refrigeration and thorough cleaning and rinsing of carcasses of poultry are other important measures to assure safety when poultry reaches consumers.

Roasting is an appropriate method for preparing turkeys and other fowl, with the exception of less tender, old poultry, such as stewing hens. Stewing or cooking in liquid is necessary to tenderize these fowl. Roasting should be done without any type of covering until the thermometer indicates 165°F (73.9°C) in the dressing or 185°F (85°C) in the thigh.

Fish (freshwater, saltwater, or anadromous) may be categorized as fish (fins and gills) or shellfish, which are subdivided further into mollusks and crustaceans. Inspection and grading are the responsibility of the U.S. Department of Commerce's Bureau of Commercial Fisheries. Three grades of fish, A, B, and substandard, have been established.

Fish are usually dressed and marketed as the fresh or frozen product, sometimes being cut into steaks or into fillets. Careful cleaning and controlled temperature storage are vital to the quality and safety of fish as they reach the marketplace and the consumer. The minimal amount of connective tissue dictates that fish be heated just enough to reach the desired serving temperature; longer heating toughens fish. Either moist heat or dry heat methods can be used.

Textured vegetable proteins (TVP) can be spun using soy protein. Several acceptable products have been developed, one of these being imitation bacon bits and another being the TVP used as a meat extender with ground beef, at levels up to 30 percent. Soy protein is the most complete of plant proteins, but vegetarians need to eat at least two types (cereal, legume, nuts) together for optimum protein intake. Other nutrients requiring attention unless eggs and milk are in the diet are iron, calcium, and vitamin B_{12}.

STUDY QUESTION

1. What federal departments are responsible for inspecting the following when they enter interstate commerce: (a) beef, (b) pork, (c) lamb, (d) veal, (e) poultry, (f) fish, and (g) shellfish?

2. Identify the types of connective tissue. What means can be employed for tenderizing meats containing a high percentage of connective tissue? What is the significance of connective tissue in fish cookery?

3. Describe the process of aging meat, including the suitability of various meats for aging.

4. Why is inspection of meat mandatory, and what types of characteristics are inspected?

5. Describe the grading process and what is meant by the grades for various types of meats.

6. Outline the process of preparing meats by each of the following cookery methods and identify several cuts that can be cooked appropriately by each: (a) broiling, (b) braising, (c) frying, (d) roasting, (e) pan broiling, (f) stewing, and (g) deep-fat frying.

7. Compare the results of cooking fish a very long time with the braising of a pot roast for the same length of time. Why are the results so different?

SELECTED REFERENCES

Berry, D. 2010. Label-friendly meat shelf-life solutions. *Food Product Design 20*(9): 44.

Borresen, T. 2009. Seafood for improved health and well-being. *Food Technol. 63*(1): 88.

Brody, A. L. 2002. Case-ready fresh red meat: Is it here or not? *Food Technol. 56*(1): 77–78.

Clark, J. P. 2008. Navigating seafood processing. *Food Technol. 62*(10): 91.

Clemens, R., and P. Pressman. 2005. Avian flu, Chicken Little, Owl Wise. *Food Technol. 59*(11): 20.

Cole, B., and B. Kuecker. 2002. Packaging up case-ready profits. *Food Product Design 11*(11): 113–115.

Decker, K. J. 2003. Where there's smoke, there's flavor. *Food Product Design 13*(4): 85.

Decker, K. J. 2004. Meat analogues enter the Digital Age. *Food Product Design 14*(1): 106.

Decker, K. J. 2008. Omnivore's opportunity: Formulating for the flexitarian. *Food Product Design 18*(11): 20.

Decker, K. J. 2009. Lean, mean protein machine. *Food Product Design 19*(1): 44.

Decker, K. J. 2009. Yogurt in a high state of ferment. *Food Product Design 19*(3): 76.

DeLoia, J. 2005. "Shrimply" irresistible. *Food Product Design 15*(1): 70.

Duxbury, D. 2004. Acrylamide in food: Cancer risk or mystery? *Food Technol. 58*(12): 91.

Egbert, R., and C. Borders. 2006. Achieving success with meat analogs. *Food Technol. 60*(1): 28.

Esquivel, T. 2008. Understanding acrylamide. *Food Product Design 18*(11): 16.

Foster, R. J. 2004. "Meating" consumer expectations. *Food Product Design 14*(9): 38.

Foster, R. J. 2008. Nothin' but nut. *Food Product Design 18*(11): 44.

Giese, J. 2004. Testing for BSE. *Food Technol. 58*(3): 58.

Grün, I. U., et al. 2006. Reducing oxidation of meat. *Food Technol. 60*(1): 36.

Hazen, C. 2004. Mainstreaming soy protein. *Food Product Design: Functional Foods Annual*. Sept.: 87.

Hazen, C. 2005. Antioxidants "meat" needs. *Food Product Design 15*(1): 61.

Hazen, C. 2006. Adding soy ingredients for health. *Food Product Design 16*(2): 63.

Hazen, C. 2010. Richer meat flavors. *Food Product Design 20*(3): 48.

Hegenbart, S. 2002. Soy: The beneficial bean. *Food Product Design 11*(10): 82–97.

Hogan, B. 2004. Beef—Beyond the burger. *Food Product Design 14*(1): 14.

Huang, G. 2009. Almonds: Versatile, stable safe. *Food Product 19*(4): 22.

Huston, W., and C. M. Bryant. 2005. Understanding BSE and related diseases. *Food Technol. 59*(7): 46.

Klapthor, J. N. 2004. Wall-to-wall mad cow coverage. *Food Technol. 58*(2): 91.

Kolettis, H. 2004. It's a mad, mad world. *Food Product Design 13*(11): 21.

Lynch, B. 2002. From sea to shining sea. *Food Product Design Food Service Annual* Nov.: 56–62.

Mandigo, R. W. 2002. Ingredient opportunities in case-ready meats. *Food Product Design 11*(11): 96–110.

Mermelstein, N. H. 1993. Controlling E. coli O157:H7 in meat. *Food Technol. 47*(4): 990.

Mermelstein, N. H. 2009. Analyzing for mercury in food. *Food Technol. 63*(9): 76.

Mermelstein, N. H. 2010. Analyzing for histamine in seafood. *Food Technol. 64*(2): 66.

Pszcola, D. E. 2009. Bean benefits. *Food Technol. 63*(3): 49.

Ravishankar, S., et al. 2009. Edible apple film wraps containing plant antimicrobials inactivate foodborne pathogens on meat and poultry products. *J. Food Sci. 74*(10): M440.

Resurreccion, A. V. A., et al. 2009. Peanuts: Bioactive food in a shell. *Food Technol. 63*(12): 30.

Santerre, C. R. 2004. Farmed salmon: Caught in a numbers game. *Food Technol. 58*(2): 108.

Shapiro, L. S. 2001. *Introduction to Animal Science*. Prentice Hall. Upper Saddle River, NJ.

Sierengowski, R. 2004. Ethnic sausages. *Food Product Design 13*(11): 76.

Silver, D. 2003. Oceans of opinions. *Food Product Design 13*(4): 120–129.

Sloan, A. E. 2006. Prime time for meats and poultry. *Food Technol. 60*(3): 19.

Spano, M. 2010. The many faces of soy. *Food Product Design 20*(10): 26.

Spano, M. 2011. Plant-based proteins. *Food Product Design 21*(2): 20.

Westman, E. C. 2009. Rethinking saturated fat. *Food Technol. 6*(2): 26.

Zino, D. 2005. Taking a closer look at beef. *Food Product Design 15*(9): 62.

Chemical leavening results from combining sour cream (an acid) with baking soda (an alkali) and releasing carbon dioxide; a similar reaction occurs when baking powder is dampened. Courtesy of Plycon Press.

14

Leavening Agents

Chapter Contents

Key Concepts

1. Leavening in baked products may be due to air, steam, and/or carbon dioxide.

2. Air can be incorporated by beating a batter and/or by carefully blending in a foam.

3. Steam that is generated from liquids in a batter or dough during baking contributes a significant leavening (e.g., in popovers).

4. Carbon dioxide, whether created from acid ingredients reacting with baking soda or from baking powder, generates a reliable amount of leavening in baked products.

OVERVIEW

Most baked products undergo some rather remarkable changes during baking, one of the most dramatic often being a large increase in volume. Sometimes the increase triples the volume of the original mixture, and frequently there is at least a doubling of the size during baking. Although this growth may seem to be an act of magic, tricks are not the secret. The key lies in the formation and expansion of gases with heat. This chapter explores the development and expansion of these gases in baked products.

Air, carbon dioxide, and steam are the gaseous components causing impressive increases in volume. The sources of these three gases are rather varied in foods, yet they all are important because gases expand when they are heated. When the oven heat begins to reach the gases in the interior of a food, pressure starts to build within each cell as the gas pushes with increasing force. The pressure causes elastic, undenatured, protein-containing cells to stretch ever thinner and occupy a larger and larger volume.

When this protein in the cell walls denatures from the oven heat, the cell walls lose their elasticity and become fixed in their extended position. Clearly, leavening of a baked product is a very dynamic occurrence, one with tremendous potential for expansion, but also one carrying the possibility of potential problems in quality control. The problems are to generate the desired amount of pressure within the cells of the product and to set the cell walls permanently at the maximum volume.

AIR

Any baked product will receive at least some leavening action from air. Even pastry, a seemingly compact dough, undergoes some increase in volume during baking because of air trapped in the stiff mixture. At the opposite end of the spectrum of leavened baked items is a soufflé. The lightness of the egg white foam in the soufflé mixture prior to baking provides ample evidence that air is

http://food.oregonstate.
edu/learn/leavening.html

—Basic information on leavening agents.

http://www.foodsubs.com/
Leaven.html

—Background information on leavening agents.

http://www.orbitals.com/
self/leaven/index.html

—Overview of leavening agents.

Figure 14.1
Air is essential to leavening in pound cake (left), in which the creaming of butter and sugar creates a foam that traps air in the batter. The volume of a cake with the same ingredients, but without creaming and trapping air (center), is only about half as great as the control on the left. Air was removed from the batter before this same formula was baked (right), resulting in a still smaller volume. Courtesy of Plycon Press.

present in abundance in a soufflé, and this air expands in the heat of the oven to contribute to the leavening.

The importance of air as a leavening agent in cake can be demonstrated by a special experiment. If air is evacuated from a cake batter and the cake is baked, the cake fails to rise. Without air to provide the necessary pressure within each cell, rising fails to occur during baking, even when steam is generated. The air-lightened cells are needed as spaces in which steam and carbon dioxide can collect and expand.

Although air frequently is not the most effective of the gases in increasing volume, it must be present, even if only in small quantities. The actual contribution of air to the total volume of leavening is influenced by several factors: (1) the amount of manipulation, (2) the viscosity of the batter, (3) the nature of the ingredients, and (4) the length of time elapsing before baking (Figure 14.1).

Amount of Manipulation

Frequently, increased mixing increases the amount of air incorporated into a product, but this is not always true. Perhaps the best example of the use of manipulation to incorporate air is the beating of egg whites into foams. Increasing the amount of beating increases the volume of the foam up to an optimum point, after which the egg white proteins begin to lose some of their extensibility.

The rigidity of overbeaten egg white foam makes the incorporation of other ingredients difficult, and increased folding is required to distribute the white foam uniformly. With each stroke during folding, air is lost from the foam. In other words, overbeating of egg whites results in reduced leavening because of the loss of air from the foam during folding.

Quick, skillful folding of ingredients into a foam can make a significant difference in the volume of a foam-containing product because of the variation in the amount of air lost from a foam with careless, slow, or excessive folding. Experience is an important factor in getting maximum leavening from air, particularly from air in a baked product based largely on the presence of an egg white foam.

Viscosity of the Batter

One of the most viscous mixtures containing air is a creamed combination of shortening and sugar, such as that prepared in making conventional cakes. Directions optimistically say to cream the fat and sugar until they are light and fluffy. Although it is true that vigorous action results in digging little air pockets in the fat, using the sharp crystals of sugar to cut into the fat is ineffective in making a foam that even remotely resembles the light foam available with egg whites. The viscous nature of the fat, however, traps most of the air within this very heavy foam, providing the vital and numerous small cells needed to trap leavening gases in the basic structure where they expand during baking. Air trapped in a foam contributes a proportionately small, but highly significant, leavening action.

The temperature and proportions of the ingredients play important roles in determining how much air is incorporated in a mixture. To illustrate, a chilled fat is so hard that only a little air can be trapped within it to make a fat/air foam. At the opposite extreme is a melted fat or oil, which is so fluid that any air caught within it by mixing is not held because the liquid fat quickly forces the air out as it flows to minimize its surface area. Plastic fats (those that can be creamed easily without becoming excessively soft) are optimal for trapping air to provide leavening, and this characteristic is obtained at approximately room temperature for most solid fats.

Similarly, the ingredients and temperature of the batter itself influence the amount of air held within the batter. A cool batter will be more viscous than a warm one; consequently, air will be held more readily within the cool batter. If a batter has sufficient flour to make a stiff dough or so little flour that the batter flows readily, air will be held less well than in one that can be beaten with some difficulty or stirred fairly vigorously to add air during mixing.

Nature of the Ingredients

Foams are an effective way of introducing air into baked products, and egg foams are the lightest of the foams. Egg foams may be of three types: yolk, whole egg, and white. With considerable effort, yolks can be beaten into foams that are reasonably stable for blending with other ingredients. If enough patience is exercised in beating the yolks, sponge cakes and fluffy omelets can gain a moderate amount of their leavening from the air incorporated in the yolk foam. Whole-egg foams ordinarily represent a very modest incorporation of air because of the limited foaming ability of the proteins, yet they do introduce some air into the products in which they are used. The most significant source of air for leavening is egg-white foams. The whites can be extended rather easily into fine-textured, thin-walled foams trapping large amounts of air, and properly beaten whites are elastic enough to be able to be folded into other ingredients with only a modest loss of air. The addition of sugar during beating adds to the stability, but also introduces a sweet taste, which may not be suitable for some applications.

The type of fat selected is another factor influencing the amount of air that might be held within a batter or dough. Oils are detrimental to the inclusion of air because they increase fluidity of the mixture. Fats that are spread with moderate ease at room temperature are good choices when air leavening is of considerable importance, as is true in shortened cakes.

Bench Time

Air is an elusive commodity in batters and doughs. Just because air has been trapped in a foam or in the mixture itself at one point, there is no guarantee that it will still be there when the product is being baked. Time is the enemy of air leavening. Mixing times need to be kept relatively short after the air has been introduced, and standing time prior to baking following completion of mixing should be avoided. The period of time the mixture is either being mixed or is standing prior to baking is referred to as bench time. Air will provide its maximum leavening in baked products if bench time is kept short by mixing efficiently and avoiding any delays between mixing and baking.

STEAM

The heat of the oven causes water or other liquid to be converted to steam in any baking product, and this steam provides a remarkable increase in volume—actually an expansion of 1,600 times from the original volume of the water. Even a comparatively dry cookie dough contains enough water to gain some leavening from steam. In fact, steam, like air, is a source of leavening in all baked products.

The most dramatic examples of steam as a leavening agent are provided by popovers, puff pastry, and cream puffs. These products rely on an extremely hot oven at the beginning of baking (Figure 14.2) to generate steam rapidly before the structure becomes set by the denatured proteins. The large amount of steam almost seems to explode these items. Popovers, puff pastry, and cream puffs get so much leavening from steam and a little air that no additional leavening

Figure 14.2
The combination of a very fluid batter and an extremely hot oven generates so much steam in a baking popover that the volume almost triples during baking.
Courtesy of Plycon Press.

needs to be provided. In most other products, steam and air are augmented by other leavening agents to achieve the desired volume in baked products.

CARBON DIOXIDE

Carbon dioxide is a gas that can be generated within batters and doughs by either biological or chemical means. Yeasts are microbiological sources of carbon dioxide, and these one-celled plants produce carbon dioxide for leavening when they are allowed to grow within a dough. Bacteria in batters and doughs can contribute indirectly to leavening by producing lactic and acetic acids that can react with alkaline ingredients in a chemical reaction to yield carbon dioxide or that can promote the growth of certain yeast. The yeast, in turn, produces the carbon dioxide.

Chemical reactions to produce carbon dioxide occur in a batter or dough when an acid ingredient and an alkaline substance both are present. These may be separate ingredients in a recipe, as was often the case in the past. Formulated baking powders are the most common source of carbon dioxide today.

BIOLOGICAL AGENTS

Yeast   **Saccharomyces cerevisiae**, the strain of yeast used in yeast-leavened batters and doughs, produces the carbon dioxide needed for achieving the desired volume (Figure 14.3). This one-celled plant uses various sugars as sources of energy for growth and survival. In the course of metabolizing the sugars, carbon dioxide and ethyl alcohol are released into the batter or dough. Of course, this reaction is dependent upon the survival of the yeast until an adequate amount of carbon dioxide has been produced.

Figure 14.3
Saccharomyces cerevisiae (shown under 1200 × magnification) is the yeast used in yeast-leavened baked products to generate carbon dioxide during the fermentation period. Courtesy of Plycon Press.

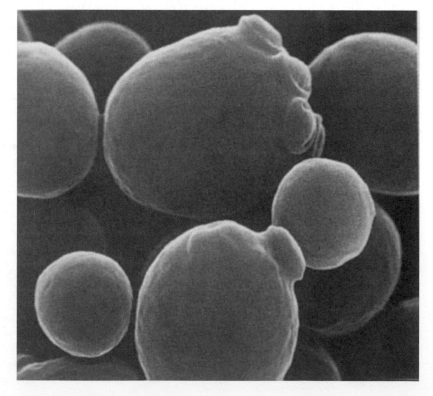

Saccharomyces cerevisiae
Strain of yeast used to produce carbon dioxide in yeast-leavened products.

http://www.breadworld. com/products.aspx
—Information on baking with yeast.

http://www.redstaryeast. com/
—Information on yeast.

Yeast can be purchased in compressed form as cornstarch-containing cakes, which are preferred by some people because of their rapid action. These cakes, with their high moisture content of about 72 percent, require refrigerated storage and have a maximum viable shelf life of only about five weeks. Even with careful storage, the yeast cakes tend to dry out around the edges within their foil-wrapped packages, limiting their viability after the expiration date stamped on the package.

Active dry yeast is a popular form of yeast because of its long shelf life. The expected shelf life of active dry yeast is six months if stored at 90°F (32°C), but when stored at 40°F (4°C), active dry yeast will be active even after a period of two years. This type, like compressed yeast, can even be frozen without harm. The expiration date stamped on an envelope of active dry yeast is based on storage at room temperature.

Through careful genetic research, a new strain of active dry yeast was produced that cut in half the time required for adequate carbon dioxide production. **Quick-rise active dry yeast** can save about an hour in the total time required for making bread.

Production of active dry yeast begins with a propagation period on dilute molasses at 86°F (30°C), after which the yeast is recovered and made into press cake. This press cake is extruded to facilitate dehydration to a moisture content of only about 8 percent before the product finally is ground to produce the granular active dry yeast contained in the individual packets in the market.

The biggest drawback to using active dry yeast is the need to rehydrate the yeast, although this can be done very quickly in water at 100°–115°F (38°–46°C). The granules also can be combined directly with flour for incorporation into batters and doughs. When using this method, the liquid being added to the mixture should be at a temperature of 120°–130°F (49°–54°C) so that the batter or dough will be warmed sufficiently for adequate hydration to occur. Quick-rise active dry yeast should be hydrated at the same temperatures used for the traditional active dry yeast.

The production of carbon dioxide and alcohol from sugar in yeast-containing doughs is termed fermentation. For fermentation to take place, the yeast mixture must contain a fermentable sugar. Sucrose (granulated sugar) often is added to batters and doughs to provide food for the yeast. An enzyme in the yeast, **sucrase,** catalyzes the breakdown of sucrose to its two component sugars, glucose and fructose. These two sugars, in turn, are metabolized into the desired gas (CO_2) and alcohol.

In addition to the sugar that may be added to batters and doughs, there is some sugar naturally available from the flour. About 1–2 percent of flour is glucose, which can be used immediately by the yeast to start fermentation. The starch in flour is a rich potential source of glucose for fermentation. The first step in this breakdown is catalyzed by β-**amylase,** which progressively attacks the long starch chains until maltose is produced, and then maltose is split into two molecules of glucose. Other enzymes aiding β-amylase in this extensive breakdown are R-enzyme, Z-enzyme, and limit dextrinase.

quick-rise active dry yeast Strain of yeast capable of reducing rising time of yeast-leavened products by half.

sucrase Enzyme in yeast that catalyzes breakdown of sucrose to glucose and fructose to initiate production of carbon dioxide in batters and doughs containing yeast.

beta (β) amylase Enzyme prominent in the catalytic release of maltose and glucose from starch to provide food for yeast.

http://www.baking911.com/ bread/starters_baking.htm —Background information on starters.

INGREDIENT HIGHLIGHT
HOME-GROWN STARTERS

Starters combine the romance of yesteryear with the pleasure of doing something relaxing and mundane. So, what is a starter? It is a viable mixture of yeast, flour, and water which springs to life to generate carbon dioxide when added to a batter or dough. When these simple ingredients are combined and held at room temperatures, the yeast will feed on the sugar available from the flour. Slowly, carbon dioxide will be produced by the yeast, and bubbles will start to form, creating a lively source of carbon dioxide.

Part of the bubbling starter is added as an ingredient to the batter or dough being made; the remainder is fed by stirring in flour and water in amounts equal to the quantity removed. The refreshed starter is stored in a jar covered with plastic wrap until 12 hours before it will be used again. Then it is held at room temperature for about half a day so that the yeast will resume active generation of carbon dioxide.

This procedure can be followed for years if the starter is fed once a week or every time some is removed for baking. If no starter is needed, it still is necessary to remove part of the starter and replenish the water and flour. Otherwise, the levels of some of the other compounds produced by the yeast may interfere with normal yeast metabolism.

The production of carbon dioxide by yeast requires time, but the precise length of time needed is variable, depending largely on the temperature of the medium. Yeast can grow at 50°F but multiplies far more rapidly when in a medium at 85°–95°F (29°–35°C), the range considered optimal for the **proofing** of batters and doughs with yeast. Fermentation, the period when alcohol, acids, and carbon dioxide are being generated to double the volume of a yeast-leavened batter or dough, ordinarily requires about one hour for the first rising when the surrounding temperature is between 85°–95°F (29°–35°C), but about eight hours will be required if the mixture is fermented in the refrigerator. Proofing, the rising period following shaping and placing in a baking pan, takes about half the time to double in volume that is needed for the first fermentation period.

Too warm a temperature during fermentation and proofing is detrimental to the quality of the finished product, for the flavor and texture may be less pleasing as a result of too much alcohol and carbon dioxide production. If the temperature rises to 110°F (43°C), the yeast will be killed by the heat in about an hour, and dead yeast no longer can produce carbon dioxide. At 140°F (60°C), yeast will be killed in about five minutes. However, carbon dioxide production undergoes considerable stimulus when the yeast temperature is first elevated to warm oven temperatures. In fact, the increase in volume in the preliminary phase of baking is recognized as **oven spring**, a phenomenon that is expected prior to the killing of the yeast.

Sugar is added as an ingredient to many batter and dough products to promote the desired fermentation reaction and produce carbon dioxide. As a regulatory measure to partially counteract the effect of sugar, salt also is added in the recipe. Salt has an inhibitory regulatory function in moderating the growth of yeast, and hence the production of carbon dioxide.

Although yeast must be maintained within a comparatively narrow temperature range for optimal production of carbon dioxide, frozen storage of yeast-containing doughs is not detrimental to the yeast activity upon thawing and warming to normal fermentation temperatures. This capability of yeast to remain viable during frozen storage in batters and doughs has led to the development of unbaked frozen bread doughs that, upon thawing and baking, are accepted widely as a satisfactory replacement for home-baked breads.

Bacteria and Yeast   *Saccharomyces cerevisiae* produce carbon dioxide readily at the comparatively neutral reaction of most batters and doughs. Two other yeasts are involved in the popular sourdough breads. These yeasts, **Saccharomyces exiguus** and *Saccharomyces inusitatus*, are active in a distinctly acidic medium. In fact, *S. exiguus* can grow very well at the very acidic pH of 4.6.

The acidity needed for the sharp flavor and the growth activity of *S. exiguus* and *S. inusitatus* is the result of bacterial action in the mixture. The type of bacteria capable of producing acid in the batter or dough is *Lactobacillus sanfrancisco*, the strain bearing the name of the city of its origin. Happily, *L. sanfrancisco* ferments maltose to produce the acid responsible for the decline in the pH of the proofing mixture to the comparatively low pH range where *S. exiguus* and *S. inusitatus* become active in producing the desired carbon dioxide.

This combination of bacteria and yeast needed to produce sourdough bread (often referred to as San Francisco sourdough) requires an extensive incubation period for the necessary acid formation (about eight hours) and reproduction of yeast to maintain the starter and another very slightly shorter proofing period for the dough prior to baking. Careful maintenance of the starter is essential to quality control, with care being required to avoid contamination of the culture with undesirable bacteria or yeast.

Chemical Agents

Separate Ingredients   Recipes may obtain part of their leavening from the reaction of acid and alkaline ingredients when both are present. The alkaline ingredient in recipes is **baking soda**, also called sodium bicarbonate or bicarbonate of soda. Baking soda alone is not able to produce carbon dioxide for leavening. However, when this white powder is dissolved and placed in contact with an acid, a chemical reaction occurs, and carbon dioxide is produced. It is this gas that is responsible for the actual leavening.

Several familiar ingredients can be used to provide the acidic reaction needed to combine with soda to produce carbon dioxide. Sour milk and sour cream, as their names indicate, are

---

proofing   Fermentation of yeast-leavened batter or dough in the baking pan to produce enough carbon dioxide to double the volume; usually at 85°–95°F (29°–35°C).

oven spring   Sharp increase in volume in early phase of baking due to accelerated carbon dioxide production in a hot oven.

Saccharomyces exiguus   Yeast primarily responsible for the production of carbon dioxide in acidic, sourdough breads.

baking soda   Bicarbonate of soda, an alkaline ingredient ($NaHCO_3$).

acidic ingredients. If sour milk is not available, the addition of vinegar or lemon juice (1 to 1 1/2 tablespoons per cup) to milk is sufficient to produce the desired acidity. This acidic milk, when combined with about 1/2 teaspoon soda per cup of milk, will be neutralized, and carbon dioxide will be released in appropriate quantities to leaven quick breads and cakes containing about 2 cups of flour. Cream of tartar is another acid often available in the home. Honey, molasses, and fruit juices are also acidic ingredients that can produce carbon dioxide when combined with soda.

A couple of limitations are noted when carbon dioxide is to be produced as a result of combining acid and alkaline ingredients. Reasonable speed in completing the mixing and initiating the baking is necessary if an adequate volume is to be achieved using this approach to leavening, for the chemical reaction begins as soon as the dissolved soda and acid are combined.

http://whatscookingamerica.net/History/BakingPowderHistory

—Traces the history of the development of different types of baking powders.

http://www.clabbergirl.com/consumer/products/rumford/

—Information on monocalcium phosphate baking powder.

SCIENCE NOTE
BAKING POWDERS

When an acid reacts with baking soda, a salt residue remains after the carbon dioxide has been released. The taste of some of these salt residues sometimes can be noted as an aftertaste. Since the residue flavors may be objectionable to some people, baking powders are judged on the basis of strength of aftertaste as well as such other characteristics as ease of reaction and cost.

Tartrate Salts

Tartrate baking powders are deemed to be very desirable, for they can be used at adequate levels with little or no aftertaste. Two of the forms of tartrate salts that are used in making tartrate baking powders are tartaric acid and cream of tartar (properly termed acid potassium tartrate). The reaction of tartaric acid with baking soda is as follows:

$$2\,NaHCO_3 + H_2C_4H_4O_6 \rightarrow Na_2C_4H_4O_6 + 2\,H_2O + 2\,CO_2 \uparrow$$

Cream of tartar in baking powder produces carbon dioxide according to the following reaction:

$$NaHCO_3 + KHC_4H_4O_6 \rightarrow NaKC_4H_4O_6 + H_2O + CO_2 \uparrow$$

The disadvantages of tartrate baking powders are their completeness of reaction at room temperature and their comparatively high cost. Although people who are experienced and efficient in preparing baked products are able to obtain excellent baked goods using tartrate baking powders, the volume obtained by slower workers may be disappointing. As a result, the tartrate baking powders generally have disappeared from the marketplace. However, 1/2 teaspoon cream of tartar may be blended thoroughly with 1/4 teaspoon soda and used in place of 1 teaspoon of commercial baking powder if a tartrate powder is desired.

Phosphate Salts

Sodium acid pyrophosphate (SAPP) and monocalcium phosphate (MCP) are two phosphate salts that can be used to combine with baking soda in making a baking powder. Although it is true that the phosphate salts react a little slower than the tartrate, the phosphates are capable of reacting almost completely at room temperature.

The reaction of monocalcium phosphate with baking soda is as follows:

$$8\,NaHCO_3 + 3\,CaH_4(PO_4)_2 \rightarrow Ca_3(PO_4)_2 + 4\,Na_2HPO_4 + 8\,H_2O + 8\,CO_2 \uparrow$$

The ready reaction of both the tartrates and the phosphates at room temperature helps to develop a fairly fine texture in baked products as long as the mixing and baking proceed rapidly enough to denature the protein and set the structure before the carbon dioxide all escapes from the baking product. A poor volume can result if delays occur or if mixing is unduly long.

Sulfate Salt

Sodium aluminum sulfate is a salt that, when combined with water, forms sulfuric acid and then reacts with soda to form carbon dioxide primarily at oven temperatures; when the reaction does occur, it leaves a residue with a penetrating, bitter taste. When used as the sole acid in a baking powder, sodium aluminum sulfate (often referred to simply as SAS) generates carbon dioxide so late in the baking period that the crust may set before very much volume has developed. The reaction of this somewhat reluctant sulfate salt occurs in two steps:

$$Na_2Al_2(SO_4)_4 + 6\,H_2 \rightarrow 2\,Al(OH)_3 + Na_2SO_4 + 3\,H_2SO_4$$

$$3\,H_2SO_4 + 6\,NaHCO_3 \rightarrow 3\,Na_2SO_4 + 6\,H_2O + 2\,CO_2 \uparrow$$

Sulfate–Phosphate Salts

To obtain the desired release of some carbon dioxide during mixing to help promote a fine and uniform texture, and also to have sufficient gas available in the baking period, a combination of two acid salts was selected for incorporation with baking soda. The two chosen were a sulfate salt for gas generation in the oven and a phosphate salt for the necessary production of gas during the mixing of a batter or dough. To indicate these two different contributions, the resulting powder was dubbed a double-acting or sulfate–phosphate baking powder. The approximate ratio of the two types of acid salts is 1 part SAS (sulfate) to 4 parts phosphate. The reactions from the two salts are those already presented for the respective salts.

TABLE 14.1 COMMERCIAL BAKING POWDERS		
Brand	**Type**	**Acid Ingredients**
Calumet	Double-acting	Sodium aluminum sulfate and calcium phosphate
Clabber Girl	Double-acting	Sodium aluminum sulfate, calcium acid phosphate
Rumford	Phosphate	Monocalcium phosphate
Magic[a]	Phosphate	Calcium acid phosphate

[a]Available only in Canada.

A delay in finishing the mixing and starting to bake will permit much of the carbon dioxide to escape from the batter or dough, which results in a poor volume in the finished product.

The other problem is that the varying acidity of the acid ingredients makes it difficult to know just exactly how much soda is needed to neutralize the batter. If too much soda is used, the alkaline reaction will contribute a soapy flavor and a yellowish color. If too little soda is used, too little carbon dioxide will be produced. In short, the volume of products leavened with soda and an acid ingredient will vary from time to time and will be influenced significantly by the experience of the chef.

Baking Powder   Baking powder was developed more than a century ago. This invention was lauded because it provided reliable and consistent leavening in baked products. Dr. Price's baking powder was made by combining 60 parts of cream of tartar, 30 parts of baking soda, and 10 parts of potato starch. In this mixture, the cream of tartar provided the acid salt, the baking soda contributed the alkaline salt, and the potato starch served as an absorbent to take up any moisture that might be present and prevent interaction of the two active components. Following this formulation, other acid salts were used to produce baking powders with varying characteristics.

Today's baking powders for the home market are surprisingly similar to the baking powder of Dr. Price's day. Basically, they still are composed of baking soda, starch, and acid salts (Table 14.1). The chief difference is that some of the baking powders on the grocery store shelves contain two different acid salts; these explain why they are dubbed **double-acting baking powders**. These powders contain a phosphate salt capable of reacting at room temperature when dissolved and a sulfate salt requiring oven temperatures for reaction.

By law, these powders must provide 12 percent carbon dioxide; by practice, they usually provide 14 percent. Cornstarch is added to protect the viability of the baking powder by absorbing moisture entering the can and preventing reaction of the acid and base during storage. The other function of cornstarch is to serve as a filler so that a measure of the powder will generate the required 12 percent or slightly more carbon dioxide.

double-acting baking powder   Baking powder containing two acid salts: an acid salt that reacts at room temperature (phosphate salt) and one requiring heat for reaction (sulfate salt); common type of baking powder in the retail market.

INDUSTRY INSIGHT
ACID SALTS FOR BAKERS

Food processors have choices in leavening that are not available to the consumer. Various acid salts are used to combine with soda in the commercial mixes presently being marketed.

Commercial food manufacturers select the specific acid salts needed to optimize the quality of the particular product being prepared. T are added as separate ingredients, but in amounts calculated to react completely and thus to avoid changes in the acidity or alkalinity of the batter or dough. By keeping the acid salts separated from the soda until mixing is being done, the production of carbon dioxide is not a problem during shelf storage. Among the acid salts used commercially, there are several phosphate salts commonly used in the baking industry: sodium acid pyrophosphate (SAPP), monocalcium phosphate (MCP), dicalcium phosphate (DCP), and sodium aluminum phosphate (SAP). Sodium aluminum sulfate and aluminum sulfate salts often are used in addition to the fast-acting phosphate salts to add increased leavening during baking.

SUMMARY

Leavening of baked products is achieved by the inclusion of air and steam, often augmented by carbon dioxide. The contribution of air in leavening baked products is influenced by several factors: the amount of manipulation, the viscosity of the batter, the nature of the ingredients, and the length of time elapsing before baking. Steam is particularly important in leavening popovers, puff pastry, and cream puffs, but it is of some significance in leavening any baked product.

Carbon dioxide is a very effective gas in promoting leavening. It is the result of the reaction of an alkaline ingredient (baking soda) with an acid ingredient or an acid salt in a baking powder mixture. Acid ingredients in foods include sour milk, sour cream, cream of tartar, molasses, honey, and fruit juices. Baking powders in the retail market are double-acting baking powders containing a sulfate and a phosphate salt as acid ingredients. Baking soda is the alkaline ingredient.

Carbon dioxide is available in a more leisurely fashion when *Saccharomyces cerevisiae* (baker's yeast) is included in the batter or dough and allowed to ferment until enough carbon dioxide is produced to double the volume. Sugar is used as food for the yeast to metabolize and produce the desired carbon dioxide. Salt serves as a means of controlling the rate of yeast growth in yeast-leavened products. Temperature control is vital to maintaining viable yeast for the desired gas production at a reasonable fermentation rate. Sourdough bread provides another example of the use of microorganisms as sources of carbon dioxide: *L. sanfrancisco* produces acid from maltose; *S. exiguus* and *S. inusitatus* thrive in the acidic environment and generate carbon dioxide for leavening.

STUDY QUESTIONS

1. Identify and explain the factors that influence the leavening contribution of air in various batters and doughs.
2. Will yeast be able to produce carbon dioxide in a dough that does not contain sugar as an ingredient? Explain your answer. Describe the leavening developing in a yeast-leavened dough with added sugar and in one made without added sugar.
3. What are the three basic constituents of baking powder? Explain the function of each.
4. What are the pros and cons for using a double-acting baking powder?

SELECTED REFERENCES

Cooper, E. J., and G. Reed. 1968. Yeast fermentation—Effect of temperature, pH, ethanol, sugars, salt, and osmotic pressure. *Baker's Digest 42*(6): 22.

Dunn, J. A., and J. R. White. 1939. Leavening action of air included in cake batter. *Cereal Chem. 16*: 93.

Golal, A. M., et al. 1978. Lactic acid and volatile (C_2—C_5) organic acids of San Francisco sourdough French bread. *Cereal Chem. 55*: 461.

Hood, M. P., and B. Lowe. 1948. Air, water vapor, and carbon dioxide as leavening gases in cakes made with different types of fat. *Cereal Chem. 25*: 244.

Oszlanyi, A. G. 1980. Instant yeast. *Baker's Digest 54*(4): 16.

Pomper, S. 1969. Biochemistry of yeast fermentation. *Baker's Digest 42*(2): 32.

Ponte, J. G., Jr., et al. 1970. Studies on the behavior of active dry yeast in breadmaking. *Cereal Chem. 37*: 263.

Ray, B. 2001. *Fundamental Food Microbiology*. 2nd ed. CRC Press. Boca Raton, FL.

Reiman, H. M. 1977. Chemical leavening systems. *Baker's Digest 51*(4): 33.

Saunders, R. M., et al. 1972. Sugars of flour and their involvement in the San Francisco sour dough French bread process. *Cereal Chem. 49*: 86.

Sugihara, T. F., et al. 1970. Nature of the San Francisco sour dough French bread process. II: Microbiological aspects. *Baker's Digest 44*(2): 51.

Tenbergen, K., and H. B. Eghardt. 2004. Baking ammonia: The other white leavening. *Food Product Design 14*(6): 110.

White, J. W., Jr., 1978. Honey. *Adv. Food Res. 24*: 304.

Wheat flour is the basic ingredient in almost all types of baked products including yeast and quick breads, cookies, cakes, and pastries. Courtesy of Plycon Press.

15

Basics of Batters and Doughs

Chapter Contents

Key Concepts

1. Wheat flour contains glutenin and gliadin, proteins that can be manipulated in the presence of water to form gluten, a somewhat elastic and cohesive complex capable of providing much of the structure of baked products.

2. Other ingredients (e.g., eggs, sugar, salt, leavening agents, liquids, fats, or oils) may be added to contribute their unique functions in various baked products.

3. Ratios of ingredients and the techniques used in mixing batters and doughs, as well as baking conditions, all play roles in determining the characteristics of the end product.

4. Altitude influences the ratio of ingredients required to make successful baked products, particularly cakes.

BASICS OF FLOUR MIXTURES

Breads have been baked as a mainstay of the diet for many civilizations over the centuries. Ancient Egyptians apparently had the ability to make leavened bread more than 5,000 years ago. Today breads take many different shapes and include diverse ingredients, depending upon the particular staple grain available and the cultural preferences of consumers.

Interest in bread has undergone a resurgence as people have become increasingly aware of the nutritional merits of complex carbohydrates and fiber. The enthusiasm for natural foods without preservatives has prompted the bakery industry to market breads containing a variety of whole-grain cereals. Consequently, the standards that people formerly used for selecting breads in the market have undergone some significant changes from the "balloon" loaves of earlier years. This same movement is reflected in the increase in baking bread at home, particularly breads made with mixtures of different flours.

Bread and other baked products, such as cakes, cookies, and pastries, are made using flour as the primary ingredient, which is mixed with a liquid and usually various other ingredients to create a batter or a dough. When these are baked, their structures set so that they can be cut and often may be held in the hand.

Batters and doughs have varying physical properties because of the different flour-to-liquid ratios in them. Batters fluid enough to be poured (approximately equal parts of liquid and flour) are classified as **pour batters**. Popovers, pancakes, and shortened cakes are baked from pour batters (Figure 15.1). A **soft batter** (made with twice as much flour as liquid) can be dropped from a spoon. Dumplings, some cookies, muffins, and various other quick breads are products made with soft batters (Figure 15.2).

pour batter Flour mixture with approximately equal amounts of flour and liquid (1:1 ratio); popovers and shortened cakes are examples.

soft batter Flour mixture with twice as much flour as liquid (2:1 ratio); muffins and drop cookies are examples.

Figure 15.1
Popovers are made using a pour batter (ratio of 1 part flour to 1 part liquid). Courtesy of Plycon Press.

Figure 15.2
Muffins are made using a soft batter (ratio of 2 parts flour to 1 part liquid). Courtesy of Plycon Press.

soft dough   Flour mixture with approximately three times as much flour as liquid (3:1 ratio); biscuit and bread doughs are examples.

stiff dough   Flour mixture with about eight times as much flour as liquid (8:1 ratio); pastry and pasta doughs are examples.

Doughs contain much less liquid in relation to flour, creating a mixture that can be handled if hands are lightly floured. **Soft doughs** (approximately three times as much flour as liquid) are somewhat resilient when they are kneaded (Figure 15.3). Yeast breads and baking powder biscuits are examples of baked products made from soft doughs. If about six to eight times as much flour as liquid is used, a **stiff dough** will result. Pastry dough is an example of a stiff dough (Figure 15.4) using six times as much flour as liquid, and pasta dough is even stiffer and drier (eight times as much).

All baked products possess a structural network, a combination of protein and starch, responsible for holding the baked item together. Many studies of batters and doughs are directed toward the development and solidification of this network. Wheat, with its unique proteins, is the basis of high-quality batter and dough products. No other cereal or other type of food possesses the specific characteristics that can be developed when wheat flour is used in mixing and baking batters and doughs. The nature of wheat flour and its contributions to batters and doughs, as well as the roles of other ingredients of batters and doughs, are discussed in this chapter.

Figure 15.3
Biscuits are made using a soft dough (ratio of 3 parts flour to 1 part liquid). Courtesy of Plycon Press.

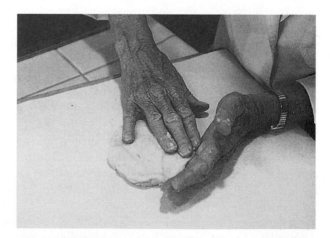

Figure 15.4
Pastry is made using a stiff dough (ratio of 6 parts flour to 1 part liquid). Courtesy of Plycon Press.

WHEAT FLOUR

Flour is the name applied to any finely ground cereal grain, although many people use the term to mean specifically the product resulting from grinding wheat (Figure 15.5). The protein in wheat makes it possible to produce breads capable of withstanding the force involved in spreading butter or margarine on them. Protein also is responsible for the fact that cakes and pastries made with wheat flour can be cut and served without disintegrating.

Gluten, the key protein complex in wheat flour, is responsible for the elastic and cohesive nature of batters and doughs made with this type of flour. The starch in that same flour is of value in strengthening structure and absorbing the extra liquid during baking. However, the starch from any type of flour can perform these functions. It is the protein in wheat that is so distinctive.

Figure 15.5
The kernels of wheat are milled to make the flour that provides much of the structure of most baked products. Courtesy of Agricultural Research Service.

Milling

To obtain the flour used in making baked products, the wheat grains undergo a grinding and refining procedure, a process called **milling** (Figure 15.6). Milling begins with the grinding of whole wheat kernels after a very brief preliminary steam treatment (tempering), which facilitates separation of the outer layers and the germ from the endosperm (Chapter 10). Grinding shatters the endosperm and splits off the bran coating, although the bran tends to remain intact. At the same time, its fat content allows the germ to be pressed into flakes, and these separate readily from the endosperm.

Separation of the various fractions of the kernel is done by using air currents. The differing weights of the various fractions cause them to be tossed with varying ease by the currents. The different fractions can be directed and collected in streams ranging from whole wheat flour to very refined for use in making particular flour products.

milling Grinding and separating of the desired fractions of the cereal kernel to produce flour.

Bleaching and Maturing

Freshly milled wheat flour tends to produce products with reduced volume and rather sticky doughs, characteristics that do not exist if a mature flour is used. Unfortunately, maturing or aging is costly because of the cost of the storage space and also because of prospective loss due to insects or rodents during prolonged storage. To overcome the performance objections and to shorten the storage times, the milling industry adds bleaching and maturing agents to the freshly milled flour. Additives approved for use include chlorine dioxide gas, acetone peroxides, and oxides of nitrogen. Soft wheat flours may be matured and bleached with chlorine gas and nitrosyl chloride. These bleaching agents lighten the pigments (xanthophyll and anthoxanthins) in the flour. The improved baking performance is attributed to a change in the chemical structure of the protein (see Science Note—Flour Proteins and Lipids on page 335).

Enrichment

Since the milling of flour splits the vitamin- and mineral-rich bran and germ from the endosperm and removes these fractions in refined flours, much of the nutritive value of flour is lost. The advantage of milling is that the keeping quality of the refined flour is improved due to the removal of the germ and its fat (with its potential for becoming rancid). To compensate for the removal of important nutrients, a federal enrichment program requires the addition of 2.9 milligrams of thiamin, 1.8 milligrams of riboflavin, 24.0 milligrams of niacin, 0.7 milligrams of folic acid, and 20 milligrams of iron per pound of flour. Calcium is an optional additive, but if added, it is to be added at the rate of 960 milligrams per pound of flour.

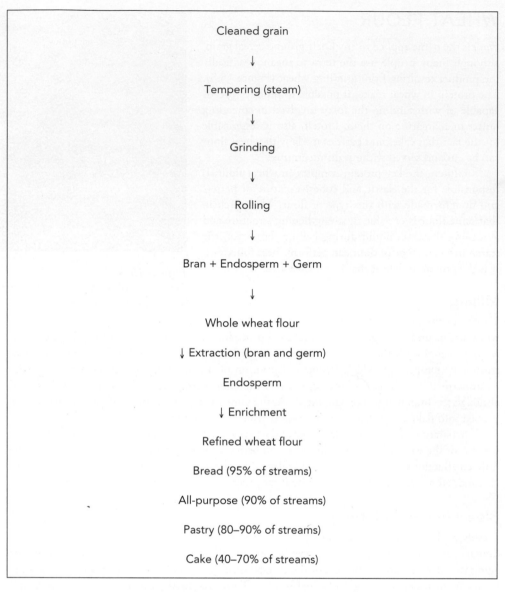

Cleaned grain

↓

Tempering (steam)

↓

Grinding

↓

Rolling

↓

Bran + Endosperm + Germ

↓

Whole wheat flour

↓ Extraction (bran and germ)

Endosperm

↓ Enrichment

Refined wheat flour

Bread (95% of streams)

All-purpose (90% of streams)

Pastry (80–90% of streams)

Cake (40–70% of streams)

Figure 15.6
Overview of the steps in milling wheat. Courtesy of Plycon Press.

http://food.oregonstate. edu/learn/flourmixgen.html

—Background information on flours.

http://www.bettycrocker. com/products/gold-medal-flour

—Extensive suggestions and information about baking.

http://www.kingarthurflour. com/

—Information on flours and baking.

http://www.cookeryonline. com/Bread/index.html

—Basic information on various flours.

http://www.joyofbaking. com/RecipeIndex.html

—Wide range of baking ideas and recipes.

http://www.pillsburybaking. com/

—Extensive suggestions and information about baking.

Flour that has been enriched must bear a label indicating this, but there is no federal legislation requiring enrichment of refined flour. However, most states now have legislation mandating that all refined flour and bakery products made with refined flour must be enriched. Although the enriched flours are not enriched with all of the nutrients lost in milling and refining wheat, they are very wholesome and nourishing, and they do provide important sources of four B vitamins and iron.

Enriched refined flour produces lighter baked products with finer textures and volume than can be made using the whole-grain flour or blends of whole-grain flour with other cereal flours. However, the nutritive value of the whole-grain products is slightly higher, and their ranges of flavor, color, and texture are greater than in products made of enriched refined flour. The choice can be based on personal preference, for either flour represents an intelligent approach to good nutrition.

Types of Flour

Bread Flour   Bakers utilize bread flour when making breads because of the strong structure provided by the gluten it contains. The comparatively high protein in this hard wheat flour is ideal for developing the cohesive crumb quality needed in breads. Bread flour ordinarily is not available for home use.

All-Purpose Flour   **All-purpose flour** is made from hard wheat or a blend of hard and soft wheat. These types of wheat, commonly grown in the central part of the nation, usually result in a flour with a protein content of about 10.5 percent. The protein content is sufficient to make satisfactory breads, yet it is not so strong that cakes will be unpleasantly tough. Consequently, all-purpose flour can be used with reasonable success to make any type of baked product for families, which explains its other name—family flour.

All-purpose flour is available bleached and unbleached, to suit individual consumer preferences. The unbleached version is preferred by people who are concerned about additives in food and are willing to accept baked goods of somewhat reduced quality in preference to consuming additives. This clearly is a matter of individual choice, for there is no evidence of harm from the use of additives approved for bleaching flour.

Cake Flour   The desired tenderness and fine texture in cakes are promoted by the use of **cake flour**. This type of flour, made from soft wheat, has a protein content of only about 7.5 percent. Not only is it significantly lower in protein than all-purpose flour, but the protein structure resulting from use of cake flour is more tender and finer than the comparable all-purpose product (Figure 15.7).

Pastry Flour   **Pastry flour** is quite similar to cake flour in that it contains about 7.5 percent protein and also is made from soft wheat. However, it is not ground to as fine a particle size as is cake flour. This is the type of flour preferred by commercial bakers for making cookies and pastries, but it is not commonly available to home bakers.

Whole Wheat Flour   As the name implies, the entire wheat grain is used in making **whole wheat flour.** The presence of the bran adds a slightly crunchy texture and a light brown color. Unfortunately, the presence of the germ limits the shelf life of whole wheat flour, because of the fat present in this portion of the grain. Products made with whole wheat flour are a bit more compact, lower in volume, and more chewy than those made with refined all-purpose flour.

Self-Rising Flour   **Self-rising flour** is, in a sense, a partial mix for baking. It contains not only flour but also an acid salt (usually monocalcium phosphate), baking soda, and salt (sodium chloride), the amounts of these providing the equivalent of half a tablespoon of baking powder and half a teaspoon of salt per cup of self-rising flour.

Recipes stipulating self-rising flour have already been adjusted to compensate for these additions, but the salt and baking powder need to be omitted if using self-rising flour in recipes based on use of all-purpose flour. Similarly, self-rising flour is not well suited for use in yeast-leavened products. The wheat used in producing self-rising flour is a blend of hard and soft wheat to give a total protein content of about 9.3 percent, somewhat lower than the usual level in all-purpose flour. Self-rising flour is particularly popular in the South, where it is often preferred for making biscuits.

Gluten Flour   The protein level in gluten flour is raised to about 41 percent by the addition of vital wheat gluten, a dry form. This gives a distinctly chewy texture to breads (usually marketed as gluten bread) made with this type of flour. From the perspective of nutrition, there is no need to use gluten flour, for the average American diet contains far more protein than is needed. However, it does add variety to the types of breads in the diet and clearly is an appropriate choice for those who like it.

Other Flours   Rye flour is used in conjunction with wheat flour in making rye bread. Although rye flour has some capability in contributing to structure, the protein in rye is less cohesive and elastic than is that comprising the gluten in wheat.

Triticale is a comparatively new grain developed by crossbreeding wheat and rye. It carries some of the characteristics of both parent grains, but it cannot be used in place of wheat in achieving optimum quality in baked products. However, continuing research efforts exploring the utilization of triticale flour in baking may eventually make such products

all-purpose flour   Flour from hard or hard and soft wheat blended; protein content of about 10.5 percent and suitable for making most baked products.

cake flour   Fine-textured flour from soft wheat; contains about 7.5 percent protein.

pastry flour   Moderately fine textured soft wheat flour; about 7.5 percent protein.

whole wheat flour   Flour containing the bran and germ, as well as the endosperm.

self-rising flour   Flour containing the necessary amounts of baking powder and salt for preparing batters and doughs, making it necessary to eliminate these two ingredients from recipes if substituting self-rising flour.

triticale   Grain produced by crossing rye and wheat; its flour has a protein mixture with some potential for making good baked products.

Figure 15.7
Gluten ball from cake flour (left) and from all-purpose flour (right). The smaller content of protein in cake flour is evident when compared with the all-purpose flour product. The balls are essentially all protein, the starch having been removed by washing them under cold running water until no starch remains before baking.
Courtesy of Plycon Press.

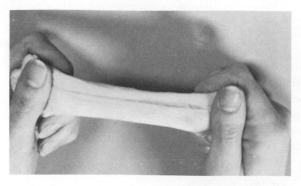

Figure 15.8
Gluten, an elastic protein complex formed when wheat flour and liquid are manipulated together, is able to stretch during baking until the temperature becomes so hot that the protein denatures. Denatured gluten is responsible for much of the structure of baked products. Courtesy of Plycon Press.

http://www.bobsredmill. com/flours-meals/

—Information on flours from various grains.

gluten Protein complex formed in batters and doughs when wheat flour is mixed with water or other aqueous liquids.

quite acceptable without the addition of wheat flours. The somewhat higher level of lysine in triticale, in comparison with wheat proteins, makes triticale of interest nutritionally because lysine is a limiting amino acid in wheat. Partial substitution of wheat flour with triticale flour in breads and other baked products can be done with good results.

Use of Flour in Baked Products

Gluten   When water and wheat flour are mixed together, a cohesive quality begins to develop in the dough or batter, leading to increased resistance to mixing and an elasticity. These characteristics are the result of an association between insoluble proteins in the flour to form a complex known collectively as **gluten** (Figure 15.8). Gluten can be stretched into fairly thin strands to form cell walls in batters and doughs during the early phase of baking and then to become rigid in the extended conformation as heat denatures the protein. In essence, this describes the significance of wheat gluten in providing the structure in baked products.

Development of the optimum gluten network is central to making batter and dough products of excellent quality. Too little gluten development is evidenced by a crumbly baked product that is difficult to serve. Too much gluten development results in a tough, chewy product with slightly reduced volume. The amount of mixing actually needed to develop gluten optimally depends upon the presence of other ingredients.

When the ratio of flour to liquid is high (1:1), as it is in popover batter, gluten is developed with difficulty. However, in muffins, which have a flour to liquid ratio of about 2:1, the batter is so sticky that the gluten strands tend to adhere to each other during mixing, causing them to develop readily. A similar situation is found in the somewhat more viscous 3:1 ratio of flour to liquid in biscuits, although the increased viscosity makes it possible to do somewhat more mixing in biscuits than in muffins before a tough product results.

The presence of added fat interferes with gluten development, making it necessary to increase the amount of mixing as the amount of fat in a recipe increases. The coating provided by the fat, coupled with the difficulty that water has in penetrating the fat coating to interact with

CELIAC DISEASE AND GLUTEN-FREE

One of the food product areas emerging recently is gluten-free foods, which are targeted to meet the special dietary needs of people who have **celiac disease,** an autoimmune disease in which gluten in the diet damages villi lining the small intestine and interferes with absorption of nutrients. A diet free of gluten helps to prevent further damage to the intestinal wall. This may sound simple, but significant changes in the diet need to be made if this is to be achieved because gluten, the protein complex in wheat, is vital to making baked products with the desired texture.

Most breads, crackers, cookies, cakes, and pastries need to be eliminated because of their gluten content, and flours from rice, potato, quinoa, and a few other sources substituted. Additional possible alternatives to work with include corn, soy, tapioca, beans, sorghum, millet, buckwheat, teff, nuts, amaranth, and arrowroot. The problem is that the resulting products tend to have quite different textural properties compared with their counterparts containing wheat flour.

To make appropriate choices for a gluten-free diet, it is important to be aware that gluten is used in many food mixtures and products that are surprising. The only way to be sure is to read ingredient labels and watch for any of the following sources: durum wheat, semolina, graham, spelt, triticale, barley, rye, malt and malt vinegar (containing barley), breading, soup bases, imitation seafood and bacon, lunch meats, stuffing, beer, and even Communion wafers and vitamin and herbal supplements.

Some assistance in identifying safe food choices is becoming available as labeling requirements to protect against food allergens are implemented. However, the definition of gluten-free for labeling purposes is still not legally defined. Nevertheless, some products now are clearly identified as gluten-free, a situation that is of some help to shoppers needing these items. The food industry is working to meet the demand for safe foods for this significant part of the market, and many innovative products can be expected to appear in grocery stores in the coming years.

the gluten, is the apparent explanation for the increased need for mixing. Sugar also delays gluten development, seemingly because it competes for some of the moisture needed by the gluten.

The amount of liquid absorbed by gluten in batters and doughs varies according to the specific flour and its gluten-forming properties. Flours made with soft wheat absorb less water than do hard wheat flours. This difference in absorptive ability is very noticeable in preparing pastries, where the ratio of water to flour is particularly critical to the tenderness of the finished product. Typically, flours purchased in the South absorb less water than do flours purchased in the Midwest.

SCIENCE NOTE
FLOUR PROTEINS AND LIPIDS

Soluble Proteins—Albumins and Globulins

The various proteins found in flour often are classified according to solubility. Two types of proteins—the albumins and globulins—are classified as soluble proteins. The comparatively small amount of these proteins (only about 15 percent) and the seemingly minimal significance of either of these globular proteins in relation to structure have caused the globulins and albumins in flour to gain little research attention.

Gluten

Gliadin The remaining 85 percent of the flour protein is said to be insoluble, although about half is soluble in alcohol. This protein, which is soluble in 70 percent alcohol, is called **gliadin.** When isolated from the other proteins, gliadin (molecular weight of 50,000) is a viscous liquid. The gliadin molecules, which are polypeptide chains in an apparently fairly spherical, compact shape, contribute to the sticky, flowing character of the gluten complex, partly because of their high glutamic acid content and consequent ability to form secondary bonds between molecules. People with celiac disease are sensitive to gliadin.

Glutenin Glutenin (molecular weight of 2–3 million) is considered to be the protein fraction responsible for the elastic quality of the gluten complex. Actually, glutenin is not a single protein, but consists of two and probably more fractions that have a somewhat fibrous character. Proline, which is abundant, limits the physical, spatial configurations the molecules may assume. Cystine, another amino acid occurring in glutenin, contributes disulfide bonds. In fact, the sulfhydryl groups and disulfide bonds, both of which are subject to change from oxidation and reduction, are involved in the elasticity of the gluten complex, a characteristic of considerable importance in achieving the desired volume.

The Complex For gliadin and glutenin to form an elastic and cohesive complex, manipulation is needed to bring these two fractions together in a complicated and intimate association. It is probable that the glutenin molecules associate to form a loose network of these elongated molecules, with the more compact gliadin molecules being trapped in this network in a somewhat random fashion. The fluid nature of the gliadin probably permits some slippage of the glutenin fibers over each other during mixing.

Lipids

Surprisingly, the elaborate combination of gliadin and glutenin to make gluten is not sufficient by itself to produce the familiar elastic and tenacious qualities seen in batters and doughs. The lipids naturally present in flour also are important, even though their quantity (less than 2 percent) may seem rather insignificant. The fats are present primarily as phospholipids and glycolipids. The glycolipids are primarily galactose combined with fat, giving molecules that can use hydrogen bonds and van der Waals forces effectively to bind with the proteins in the flour. It is hypothesized that the glycolipids in flour act almost like a sandwich filling between layers of the gluten complex.

Although the importance of lipids and of the two principal fractions of gluten (gliadin and glutenin) has been studied extensively, there still is much to be learned about the complex formation of the structure in baked products. Research is ongoing in this field of proteins and lipids and their interactions.

---

http://www.nlm.nih.gov/ medlineplus/celiacdisease. html
—Information on celiac disease and diet.

http://www.abcr.com/doc/ Gluten%20Allergen%20 Analysis.pdf
—Summary of status of gluten-free labeling.

http://www.fda.gov/Food/ LabelingNutrition/Food AllergensLabeling/Guidance ComplianceRegulatory Information/ucm111487.htm
—FDA site for status of regulations about gluten-free labeling.

gliadin Sticky fraction of gluten.

glutenin Very large, elastic component of gluten.

Starch   During mixing, starch in flour plays a relatively minor role. It is not until the starch begins to undergo gelatinization in response to the heat in the oven that much water is absorbed into the granules. During baking, starch aggressively absorbs water in an attempt to gelatinize the granules. In very fluid batters, considerable swelling and gelatinization occur because there is sufficient liquid there for this physical change to progress smoothly.

Gelatinized starch contributes meaningfully to the strength of the cell walls in which the granules are embedded. In fact, moderately acceptable cakes can be made using pure starch as the primary structural ingredient when gluten-free baked goods are needed for special diets. This is in contrast to the high-quality cakes that can be prepared when flour, with both its protein and starch, is the principal structural agent.

CULTURAL ACCENT
RICE PAPER

Wheat flour is the flour of choice for most types of bread products, but rice provides the structure for the delicate wrappers used in making Vietnamese spring rolls. Rice flour lacks the structural qualities provided by the gluten complex in wheat flour, but the protein and starch in it can provide sufficient structure to allow cooks to form rice paper wrappers. These look like very thin, semitransparent pancakes after they have been dried on long bamboo racks under the hot Vietnamese sun (Figure 15.9). Surprisingly, these rice papers are strong enough to be used as wrappers for spring rolls containing a variety of tempting fillings.

Figure 15.9
Rice paper drying on racks in the sun in Vietnam before being used to make spring rolls. Courtesy of Plycon Press.

FUNCTIONS OF OTHER INGREDIENTS

Eggs

Eggs, depending on the quantity used and the treatment prior to inclusion in the batter, may fulfill a variety of important functions in addition to adding to the nutritive value of the product. During the mixing of a batter or dough, eggs act as a liquid to help moisten dry ingredients and to assist in developing the gluten. The coagulation of egg proteins during baking adds to the stability of the structure of baked products, with the actual importance of this added strength being dependent on the amount of egg used. In popovers and angel food cakes, for example, the amount of protein provided by the eggs is an important adjunct to the structure provided by the flour. Additionally, eggs contribute flavor, and, when the yolks are used, color also is enhanced.

Beaten eggs add to the leavening of baked products because of the air they hold trapped within the foam. Egg white foams are particularly important in aiding with leavening. However, the egg yolk foam used in sponge cakes is a good example of the fact that yolks can also be significant sources of air.

The emulsifying ability of egg yolks is an important factor in producing smooth cake batters. Another example of the use of egg yolks as emulsifying agents is in the preparation of cream puffs, for they contain a very large proportion of fat, which would separate from the flour and liquid were it not for the binding ability of the egg yolks, with their content of lecithin, a noted emulsifying agent.

Sugar

The obvious function of sugar in baked products is to provide a sweet taste. If light or dark brown sugar is used in place of refined sugar, additional flavors are added. Honey is yet another source of sweetness and accompanying flavor variations. Sugar substitutes afford an alternative means of sweetening baked products. However, these variations in the form of sweetening, when substituted in batters and doughs for refined sugar, quickly reveal that sugar does far more than merely sweeten baked products.

One of the important contributions of sugar is to aid in the browning of the crust of baking products. Although the sucrose (refined sugar) itself does not participate in the Maillard reaction, glucose and fructose liberated by hydrolysis from the original sucrose can react with protein to cause surface browning. In fact, when honey or fructose is substituted for refined sugar in batters and doughs, the Maillard reaction is much more intense because of the abundance of reducing sugar available from either of these sources.

Tenderness and volume of baked products are important characteristics influenced by the amount of sugar in relation to other ingredients in batters and doughs. The strongly hygroscopic (water-attracting) nature of sugar introduces a strong competition with flour for the liquid, which means that sugar will decrease the amount of liquid actually available to the developing gluten complex. This change means that additional mixing is needed to develop the gluten satisfactorily in products containing sugar.

The amount of mixing needed increases directly with the increase in the quantity of sugar. This can be illustrated by comparing the preparation of muffins and shortened cakes. Muffins have a very small amount of sugar added, and a minimal amount of mixing is required to develop the gluten appropriately. On the other hand, shortened cakes have a comparatively large amount of sugar (and other interfering ingredients, too), necessitating a considerable amount of manipulation to develop the desired gluten network. Actually, sugar is a helpful ingredient during mixing because it allows sufficient time for adequate blending of the ingredients before the gluten is developed too much.

Sugar also has a tenderizing effect, due to two actions. As just noted, gluten development is delayed by sugar, and this delay helps to keep gluten from becoming so developed that it is tough and chewy. The second action to help tenderize products by adding sugar is involved in the baking period. An increase in the amount of sugar in a recipe results in a somewhat higher coagulation temperature of the protein present.

If a baking flour mixture has to be heated to an elevated temperature before the gluten denatures and sets the structure, the elastic nature of the gluten will be maintained for a longer time than if no sugar is present. During this extended period when the gluten remains elastic, the pressure of the hot gases within the cells keeps stretching the cell walls thinner and thinner. Thin cell walls are more tender than thick ones. In short, the sugar causes a higher coagulation temperature and longer period of time for stretching the gluten into thin cell walls before denaturation occurs; this is the second reason for regarding sugar as a tenderizing ingredient.

The increased temperature of denaturation of the gluten when sugar is increased also explains the way in which sugar influences volume. Up to a certain critical point, increasing sugar will increase volume because of the extended period of stretching cell walls. However, if cell walls get stretched too thin before the gluten denatures, the cells will explode when the gluten strands break from the pressure generated by the hot gases. This situation is analogous to blowing up a balloon until it is stretched so thin that the material simply cannot stretch enough to accommodate the pressure of the enclosed air and it pops. When the cells in baking products reach the point of exploding, the product falls and remains extremely compact no matter how much longer it is baked.

Sugar substitutes do not have effects comparable to sugar on the tenderness and volume of baked products because they have little influence on the development and coagulation temperature of the gluten. Even the use of sugars other than sucrose will give somewhat different results in tenderness and volume.

Salt

Salt is used to enhance flavors in baked products. Its other function is to regulate the growth of yeast in yeast doughs, where it serves to counterbalance the stimulating effect of sugar and to help tighten the gluten, both of which aid in avoiding a coarse texture.

Leavening Agents

Leavening agents, as discussed in Chapter 14, are necessary to increase the volume and promote development of the desired texture in baked products. They need to be included in amounts adequate to achieve the desired volume without imparting an undesirable flavor or aftertaste, usually 1–2 teaspoons of baking powder per cup of flour for most baked products.

Liquids

Milk is the liquid used most commonly in batters and doughs, though water, sour milk, sour cream, or fruit juices sometimes are used. Liquid aids in the development of the gluten. Without liquid to help hydrate the mixture, gluten does not develop. Liquid also is needed to gelatinize starch during the baking period; gelatinized starch adds rigidity and strength to cell walls. Fruit juices and the other liquids with distinctive flavors add to the flavor of the baked product, but they may affect the denaturation of protein and the gelatinization of starch.

Leavening action is provided by liquids when they are converted to steam during baking. They also serve as a solvent to activate the reaction of baking powder to produce carbon dioxide. Unless baking powder is dissolved, the reaction between the soda and acid salt will not occur. Similarly, baking soda must be dissolved if it is being used in conjunction with an acid ingredient. For example, the liquid in sour milk dissolves the soda, and the acid in the milk then reacts with the soda to generate carbon dioxide for leavening.

Fats and Oils

An important function of fats and oils is to tenderize baked products by impeding gluten development. The coating of fat that develops on gluten strands tends to block water from the flour proteins needing the liquid for gluten development. This coating of fat also has a lubricating effect.

The texture of various baked products reflects the type of fat used, particularly in recipes where the fat content is comparatively high. For instance, pastry made with oil tends to have a granular texture in contrast to the flaky, layered texture of a pastry made with a firm fat, such as shortening. Fats also promote a soft crumb in breads and cakes.

Fats contribute to the flavor of baked goods, especially when a flavorful one (butter or margarine) is used. Even when the fat itself has little apparent flavor, there is a richness of flavor that is promoted by the presence of the fat. Yellow margarine, butter, and other colored fats may add to the creamy color of breads, cakes, and other items. This color often is perceived as indicating a particularly rich and flavorful product.

The specific contributions made by a fat are dependent in part upon the type being used (Chapter 8). Selection of the appropriate fat for making a specific batter or dough can result in a product with optimum characteristics. Since the physical properties and composition vary from one type of fat to another, it is necessary to modify recipes when substitutions of fat are made.

MIXING TECHNIQUES

Individual technique in preparing batters and doughs can have a very significant effect on the final volume, texture, and tenderness of baked products. Certain key words are used in recipe instructions to indicate the operations to be used during preparation. Each of the following terms has a specific meaning in relation to preparing batters and doughs. These need to be understood and then practiced until quality products are prepared each time.

Creaming is the creation of a heavy, air-in-fat foam by agitating solid fat and sugar together until the mixture is somewhat light and fluffy. This may be done with the aid of an electric mixer or by mixing fairly vigorously with a wooden spoon or paddle. Creaming should be discontinued if the mixture begins to lose volume and becomes soft.

Beating is rapid agitation of a mixture of foods with the aid of an electric mixer or a wooden spoon. This action is more vigorous than creaming and is applied on a wide range of ingredients. Usually the purposes are to beat in air and to develop gluten.

Stirring is gentle mixing of ingredients to blend them thoroughly. This technique is used when trapping of air is not necessary and when excessive gluten development needs to be avoided.

Folding is a gentle motion designed to bring ingredients up from the bottom of the mixing bowl and spread them across the upper portion of a foam or batter with minimum disruption. This process is repeated, with every fifth stroke coming up through the middle to facilitate uniform blending, until the entire mixture is homogeneous. A rubber spatula is particularly well suited for folding, because it scrapes the ingredients up from the bottom efficiently. Other utensils suitable for folding include a narrow metal spatula or a wire whip or whisk. The important action in folding is to blend ingredients thoroughly with a minimum development of gluten or loss of air from the foam.

Cutting in is the technique used to cut solid fats into small particles in the preparation of pastries and biscuits. A pastry blender (see Figure 4.8) is designed specifically for doing this task efficiently, but two table knives can be used in a crosscutting motion to accomplish the desired result. A light, tossing motion with the pastry blender is important in avoiding packing the fat into a solid mass while the cutting in is being done.

Kneading is the mixing together of ingredients with the hands or a dough hook on a mixer. Techniques for kneading vary, depending upon the amount of gluten needing to be developed. In yeast breads, considerable gluten needs to be developed, so the kneading technique involves a folding over the dough and then a vigorous push with the heel of both hands simultaneously. The dough is rotated a quarter of a turn, and the process is repeated in a

creaming Mixing fat and sugar together vigorously to create an air-in-fat foam.

beating Very vigorous agitation with a wooden spoon or on a mixer at high speed to trap air and/or to develop gluten.

stirring Gentle blending of ingredients when trapping of air and development of gluten are not needed.

folding Very gentle manipulation with a wire whisk, narrow metal spatula or rubber spatula to bring ingredients up from the bottom and spread them over the upper surface to aid in blending them uniformly.

cutting in Process of cutting solid fat into small pieces using a pastry blender or two table knives.

kneading Folding over a ball of dough and pressing it with either the fingertips or the heels of both hands, depending on the amount of gluten needing to be developed and the ratio of ingredients.

INGREDIENT HIGHLIGHT
COOKING SPRAYS

Cooking sprays have been available for more than half a century, and they have found a niche in many kitchens because of their convenience, versatility, and long shelf life. Because they can be sprayed directly onto baking pans and sheets, bakers can avoid the messy task of greasing them to prevent sticking. This treatment makes it practical to use baking equipment that does not have a nonstick coating, thus avoiding any possible effects from eating food baked on coated surfaces.

Although any cooking spray can be used successfully for coating baking pans, special baking sprays containing a small amount of flour have been formulated specifically for this task. If people with celiac disease will be eating the products,

a regular cooking spray should be used instead of the baking spray. Also, butter-flavored cooking spray will have a small amount of lactose, which makes this a type of cooking spray to be avoided by those who have severe lactose intolerance.

People who bake and prepare other foods at home may wish to keep a container of at least the general-purpose cooking spray handy in a cupboard for quick use whenever preparations require it. The can has a shelf life of two years, which means that it will be safe to use for a long time, a fact that is important in view of the small amount used for each application. For optimal results, the can needs to be shaken vigorously to disperse the components uniformly before spraying.

rhythmic pattern until the gluten is developed to the point where blisters can be seen under the surface of the dough, but the dough itself has a smooth surface.

Since gluten develops very readily in preparing biscuit dough, the folded dough is pushed gently with just the fingertips of both hands, after which it is rotated a quarter of a turn, and the process is repeated. Only a brief period with this gentle kneading stroke is used for making biscuits to avoid causing them to become tough. Kneading not only mixes ingredients; it also develops the necessary gluten network and contributes to the desired flaky quality of biscuits. In contrast, so much kneading is done when making yeast bread doughs that the layers of the folded dough tend to merge together into a continuous gluten network, and layering or flakiness is not present.

BAKING

Preparation of pans for baking varies with the product and with the container selected. Breads being baked in pans with sides can be removed easily if the sides and bottom of the pans are sprayed with nonstick cooking spray or greased lightly (unless the pan has a coating). If the bottom of the cake pan is lined with a layer of wax paper, sprayed with nonstick cooking spray, or greased, layer cakes can be removed easily. The sides are not greased, which helps the cake cling to the sides and pull upward during baking.

Foam cakes (angel food, sponge, and chiffon) can be removed easily when baked in ungreased tube pans of two-part construction. Nonstick coatings on tube pans are not recommended when foam cakes are being prepared, because the cakes are likely to fall out when the pan is inverted to maintain the cake at maximum volume during cooling. Usually, cookies are baked on nonstick cookie sheets or jelly roll pans or simply on ungreased sheets. A spatula is used to remove cookies from the baking sheet when they come out of the oven because they tend to break if they cool before being loosened. Ungreased cookie sheets save the problem of burning and polymerizing fat in all of the areas where the bare pan is exposed between the cookies.

The rack position should be checked and shifted if necessary before the oven is turned on. When baking in a preheated oven, baking pans should be placed in the center rack position, with sufficient space between pans and between the pans and the oven edges to permit good air circulation and achieve relatively uniform browning. Pans should not be placed directly underneath one another—the top pan will not bake adequately on the bottom, and the bottom pan will be too done on the bottom and very pale on the top.

Preheating allows baking to begin immediately at the desired temperature, but this practice wastes energy. Yeast breads should be baked in a preheated oven when volume has doubled, or else they should be started in a cold oven before they have doubled in volume. Too much oven spring occurs, and a coarse texture results if a cold start is used on rolls that already have doubled.

If starting cakes, quick breads, or other baked products in a cold oven, the oven rack should be positioned just above the center. This added distance from the heating element at the bottom will eliminate excessive browning (or possibly burning) while the oven is being heated to the appropriate temperature. When baking from a cold start, more time is necessary than is indicated in the recipe to reach the desired end point because of the low temperature during the early phase. Foam cakes have the potential to lose gas from the foams and for the heavier ingredients to begin to drain toward the bottom to form a layer if baking is delayed; starting in a cold oven adds to this problem.

The structure of baked goods is most delicate immediately prior to denaturation of gluten, for this is when the expanding gases are still stretching the cells. Until denaturation occurs, gluten is extensible and requires that gases in the product maintain pressure. However, denaturation halts stretching and sets the structure. At that point, baked products can be removed from the oven, because the cell walls are strong enough to maintain the structure and no longer need to be supported by hot gases.

Tests for doneness need to be made for baked products to be sure that the structure has been set throughout. However, testing should not be done until the product should be done; this avoids letting cold air into the oven at the most critical stage of baking. Tests in the center give information about the exact state of affairs at the coolest point. Shortened cakes and loaves of quick breads are tested by inserting a toothpick in the center and checking to be sure that no batter is clinging to it when it is withdrawn. Foam cakes are done when they spring back after being touched lightly on the surface. Yeast breads, pastries, cookies, and many quick breads are checked on the basis of elapsed time and appropriate browning.

TREATMENT FOLLOWING BAKING

The strength of the structure immediately after baking determines the way in which a specific product will be cooled. Drop cookies, for example, usually are strong enough to be lifted off the baking sheet gently with a spatula when they come from the oven, whereas they will tend to break if allowed to cool on the sheet before they are loosened. Cakes, with the exception of foam cakes, are placed upright on a rack to permit air to circulate under the pan and hasten the cooling. Layers can be cut loose from the edges of the pan, covered with an inverted plate, and then turned over abruptly to unmold them onto the plate while the pan feels warm, but not hot, to the hand.

Foam cakes have weak structures when they first come from the oven, and the weight of the cake pushing down on itself in the pan will cause loss of volume while the cake is cooling. This problem is avoided by inverting the tube pan as soon as the cake is taken from the oven and letting the cake hang suspended until the pan is cool (Figure 15.10). This stretches out the cells during the cooling period, resulting in maximum volume. Once foam cakes have cooled, they can be removed from the tube pans by cutting them loose around the outer edge and the tube, removing the tube with the cake, and then cutting the cake loose from the bottom of the pan before inverting the tube and cake onto a suitable plate.

Quick breads and yeast breads are quite strong even when first removed from the oven. Therefore, there is no reason to delay taking them from their pans (Figure 15.11). Unless they are being served at once, breads should be transferred from pans onto cooling racks immediately. Otherwise, the crusts will become soggy from condensing steam.

ADJUSTMENTS FOR ALTITUDE

The decreased atmospheric pressure at elevations of 3,000 feet or more causes detectable changes in the quality of baked products unless some modifications in the formula are made. The recommended changes are based on the fact that expansion occurs more readily at high altitudes than at sea level, where atmospheric pressure is greater. This creates greater resistance to expansion at low elevations than in the mountains. To avoid having cell walls rupture, recipes are modified in the mountains to strengthen cell walls and decrease pressure within the cells (Chapter 17, Science Note—High-Altitude Baking).

Figure 15.10
Foam cakes are inverted to cool as soon as they are removed from the oven so that the cells will be stretched by gravity to help retain maximum volume until cool enough to be removed from the pan. Courtesy of Plycon Press.

Figure 15.11
Breads have a strong structure even when first taken from the oven. To avoid soggy crusts, breads should be removed immediately from baking pans and cooled on a rack. Courtesy of Plycon Press.

INDUSTRY INSIGHT
ANTISTALING ENZYME

Staling of baked products is a problem in commercially prepared breads, cakes, cookies, and pies, for this quality limits their shelf life. Amylose, the linear starch fraction, begins to undergo retrogradation as the product cools. Eventually, amylopectin (the branched fraction of starch) also begins to retrograde, resulting in a somewhat rapid, partially crystalline texture.

Boyle and Hebeda (1990) reported that a rather heat-resistant enzyme, Multifresh®, is able to prevent rapid staling. The enzyme, an α-amylase produced by *Aspergillus niger*, hydrolyzes some of the branches of the amylopectin starch molecules. These less-branched amylopectin residues are not able to bond easily with other amylopectin molecules, and staling is delayed. Multifresh is approved by the Food and Drug Administration for use in bakery products.

SUMMARY

Wheat flour is the basic ingredient in most baked products because of its unique combination of insoluble proteins. When water is added and the mixture is manipulated, these proteins can be worked into a cohesive, elastic complex called gluten. To obtain wheat flour suitable for the consumer market, the wheat grain is milled, bleached, matured, and enriched (if the bran and germ have been removed to make a refined flour).

Bread flour is a high-protein flour available primarily to commercial bakers. All-purpose flour, made from hard wheat or a blend of hard and soft wheat to give a protein content of about 10.5 percent, is well suited to the preparation of breads, cookies, pastries, and even some cakes. Cake flour has a protein content of only about 7.5 percent; the rather tender protein from this soft wheat flour is well suited to making cakes. Pastry flour is similar, but a bit coarser than cake flour. Other flours on the market include whole wheat flour, self-rising flour (contains an acid salt, soda, and salt), gluten flour, and flours from other cereals (rye and triticale, for example).

Wheat flour is able to provide the basic structure of baked products because of the protein strands that are developed during the mixing of batters and doughs. Gluten (the protein complex) is a combination of gliadin, a sticky and viscous protein, and glutenin. Glutenin contributes the necessary elasticity to the unbaked protein complex.

Lipids in flour are also involved in the formation of the structure during mixing and baking. Sugar and fat delay the development of gluten; the ratio of liquid to flour also influences how readily gluten develops during mixing. Gluten needs to be developed sufficiently to hold the baked product together, but not so much that it becomes tough. When properly developed, gluten will be able to stretch into appropriately thin cell walls during baking, yielding a good volume and a tender product.

Starch is also an important structural component of flour. During the baking period, starch absorbs water as gelatinization occurs. The gelatinized starch granules are embedded in the gluten matrix to help add rigidity to the structure after baking.

Eggs add another element to the structure of many baked products. They also contribute air for leavening when they are beaten into a foam. Other contributions are flavor, color, and emulsifying ability.

The pleasing golden-brown crust on baked products is due in large measure to the Maillard reaction, a combination of sugar with protein. Of course, sugar contributes a sweet taste, too. Sugar promotes volume and tenderness by modifying the rate of gluten development during mixing and by raising the coagulation temperature of gluten during baking. Sugar substitutes do not have these effects.

Salt is primarily a flavoring substance, although it does serve to retard carbon dioxide production by yeast. Leavening agents are valued primarily because of their influence on volume. Between 1 and 2 teaspoons of baking powder per cup of flour usually are sufficient to leaven products appropriately without leaving an objectionable aftertaste.

Liquids are needed to develop gluten and to gelatinize starch. They aid leavening by dissolving baking powder and baking soda, as well as providing steam during baking. Most liquids also contribute some flavor.

Tenderness and fullness of flavor are two characteristics promoted by the use of fats or oils. By interfering somewhat with gluten development, they aid in producing a tender product. The form of fat used and the way in which it is incorporated often influence the texture. Flavor and color may also be a reflection of the type of fat used.

For production of high-quality baked products, it is important to know and to practice the basic mixing techniques (creaming, beating, stirring, folding, cutting in, and kneading) and to follow appropriate baking guidelines. Optimal results are obtained when the correct pans are prepared appropriately and when the panned product is arranged in the correct position in the oven and baked until the correct end point is reached.

STUDY QUESTIONS

1. What are the differences between all-purpose flour, cake flour, and whole wheat flour? What are the effects of using each of these types of flour in making batter and dough products?

2. What factors influence the rate of gluten development in batters and doughs?

3. What adjustments are needed if self-rising flour is to be substituted for all-purpose flour in a recipe?

4. Why is the starch content of flour important in baked products?

5. In baked products, what are the functions of (a) eggs, (b) sugar, (c) butter, (d) shortening, and (e) liquids?

SELECTED REFERENCES

American Home Economics Association. 1993. *Handbook of Food Preparation.* 9th ed. AHEA. Washington, DC.

Berry, D. 2004. Breads on the rise. *Food Product Design 14*(7): 106.

Bullock, L. M., et al. 1992. Replacement of simple sugars in cookie dough. *Food Technol. 46*(1): 82.

Bushuk, W., and E. N. Larter. 1980. Triticale: Production, chemistry, and technology. *Adv. Cereal Sci. & Tech. 3*: 115.

Carroll, L. E. 1990. Functional properties and applications of stabilized rice bran in bakery products. *Food Technol. 44*(4): 74.

Carroll, L. E. 1990. Stabilizer systems reduce texture problems in multi-component foods and bakery products. *Food Technol. 44*(4): 94.

Clemens, R., and J. Dubost. 2008. Catering to gluten-sensitive consumers. *Food Technol. 62*(12): 21.

Danno, G., and M. Natake. 1980. Susceptibility of wheat glutenin to enzymatic hydrolysis. *Ag. Biol. Chem. 44*(9): 2155.

Decker, K. J. 2002. The gourmet cookie experience. *Food Product Design 11*(10): 34–52.

Decker, K. J. 2005. Looking at the whole-grain picture. *Food Product Design 15*(9): 49.

Freeman, R. P., and D. R. Shelton. 1991. Microstructure of wheat starch: From kernel to bread. *Food Technol. 45*(3): 162.

Haber, T., et al. 1976. Hard red winter wheat, rye, and triticale. *Baker's Digest 50*(6): 24.

Hazen, C. 2008. Grain-based ingredients. *Food Product Design 18*(8): 70.

Hazen, C. 2009. Better trans-fat baked goods. *Food Product Design 19*(1): 26.

Hazen, C. 2010. Baking sans *trans. Food Product Design 20*(8): 32.

He, H., and R. C. Hoseney. 1992. Effect of the quantity of wheat flour protein on bread loaf volume. *Cereal Chem. 69*(1): 17.

Hodge, S. 2009. Old world breads. *Food Product Design 19*(5): 44.

Hoseney, R. C. 1992. Factors controlling gas retention in nonheated doughs. *Cereal Chem. 69*(1): 1.

Hoseney, R. C., et al. 1971. Functional (breadmaking) and biochemical properties of wheat flour components. VIIII: Starch. *Cereal Chem. 48*: 191.

Hosome, K., et al. 1992. Studies on frozen dough baking. I: Effects of egg yolk and sugar ester. *Cereal Chem. 69*(1): 89.

Huebner, F. R. 1977. Wheat flour proteins and their functionality in baking. *Baker's Digest 51*(5): 25.

Hulse, J. H., and D. Spurgeon. 1974. Triticale. *Sci. Am. 231*(2): 72.

Kahn, K., and W. Bushuk. 1978. Glutenin: Structure and functionality in breadmaking. *Baker's Digest 52*(2): 14.

Kobs, L. 2001. "C" is for cookie. *Food Product Design 11*(9): 31–40.

Kulp, K., et al. 1991. Functionality of carbohydrate ingredients in bakery products. *Food Technol. 45*(3): 136.

Leung, H. K., et al. 1983. Water binding of wheat flour doughs and breads as studied by the deuteron method. *J. Food Sci. 48*(1): 95.

Magnuson, K. 1977. Vital wheat gluten update '77. *Baker's Digest 51*(10): 108.

McWilliams, M. 2012. *Foods: Experimental Perspectives.* 7th ed. Prentice Hall. Upper Saddle River, NJ.

Ohr, L. M. 2009. Good-for-you grains. *Food Technol. 63*(1): 57.

Pomeranz, Y. 1980. What? How much? Where? What function? in bread making. *Cereal Foods World 25*(10): 656.

Pszczola, D. E. 2005. Ingredients for bread meet changing 'kneads'. *Food Technol. 59*(1): 55.

Pszczola, D. E. 2009. Rediscovering ingredients of antiquity. *Food Technol. 63*(10): 43.

Pszczola, D. E. 2011. Breads and beyond. *Food Technol. 65*(1): 50.

Ranhotra, G. S., et al. 1992. Total and soluble fiber content of air-classified white flour from hard and soft wheats. *Cereal Chem. 69*(1): 75.

Rice, E. W. 1972. *Baking and Cooking at High Altitudes.* Laramie, WY.

Ryadchikov, V. G., et al. 1981. Study of glutenins and gliadins of wheat flour. *Appl. Biochem. Microbiol. 17*(1): 18.

Sikka, K. C., et al. 1978. Comparative nutritive value and amino acid content of triticale, wheat, and rye. *J. Ag. Food Chem. 26*(4): 788.

Spano, M. 2009. Celiac disease feeds gluten-free need. *Food Product Design 19*(10): 28.

Tenbergen, K. 2008. Flat breads: Old world meets new. *Food Product Design 18*(11): 38.

Tenbergen, K., and H. B. Eghardt. 2004. Baking ammonia: The other white leavening. *Food Product Design 14*(6): 110.

Tu, C. C., and C. C. Tsen. 1978. Effects of mixing and surfactants on microscopic structure of wheat glutenin. *Cereal Chem. 55*: 87.

Zandonadi, R. P., et al. 2009. Psyllium as a substitute for gluten in bread. *J. Amer. Dietet. Assoc. 109*(10): 1781.

Zeringer, H. J., Jr., et al. 1981. Triticale lipids: Composition and bread making characteristics of triticale flours. *Cereal Chem. 58*(1): 351.

Breads seemingly offer infinite variety when different grains, seeds, flavorings, and leavening agents are incorporated. Courtesy of Plycon Press.

16
Breads

Chapter Contents

THE WORLD OF BREAD

Around the globe, most cultures have at least one bread-like product that fills a major, vital role in the cuisine. These **breads** range from the chapatis of India and the pita (also called pocket bread) of Middle Eastern cuisines to the familiar sliced loaves of bread and English muffins that are staples of the U.S. diet. Although the breads of the world assume many different shapes and flavors, they generally can be characterized as being prepared from a cereal flour (usually wheat) and possessing a structure sufficiently strong to permit butter or another soft product to be spread over the surface without disintegrating into crumbs.

Generally, breads are classified according to the type of leavening action used (Figure 16.1). If yeast is used to produce carbon dioxide, the bread is classified as a yeast bread, whereas breads leavened primarily with steam or with carbon dioxide produced from the chemical reaction of soda and an acid salt are termed quick breads. Actually, the designation of quick breads is a key to the sharp distinction between the two categories. Yeast-leavened breads take much longer to make than do quick breads because of the time required for fermentation and proofing (producing carbon dioxide) of the dough before baking. Conversely, quick breads can be produced quickly, for they do not have to wait for living organisms (the yeast) to generate carbon dioxide.

QUICK BREADS

Ingredients for Variety

Considerable variety is found among the **quick breads**. They vary in their ingredients and their ratios of liquid to flour, as well as in their mode of cooking. The quick breads popular in the United States usually have wheat flour as the

Key Concepts

1. Breads are classified as quick breads or yeast breads, based on whether or not they are leavened by yeast.

2. Popovers, pancakes, and waffles are quick breads made from pour batters, with popovers being a 1:1 ratio of flour to liquid, pancakes with slightly less liquid, and waffles still less.

3. Muffins are made from a drop batter, a 2:1 flour-to-liquid ratio that is so sticky that gluten can quickly develop too much during mixing.

4. Biscuits sometimes have enough liquid to make a drop batter, but more commonly are a 3:1 ratio of flour to liquid, which makes a soft dough that can be kneaded lightly, rolled, and cut into the desired shape for baking.

5. Yeast breads are stiff doughs that require vigorous kneading after mixing by the straight dough method or the sponge method, or by using a bread-making machine.

bread A flour (usually wheat) mixture that is baked, but sometimes is steamed or fried.

http://www.baking911.com/bread/101_intro.htm
—Several different aspects of breads.

http://www.cooks.com/rec/ch/breads.html
—Wide variety of bread recipes.

Figure 16.1
Breads are classified into quick and yeast breads on the basis of the type of leavening used. Courtesy of Agricultural Research Service.

quick bread Bread leavened with steam or carbon dioxide produced by a chemical reaction; bread that does not require time for biological agents to produce carbon dioxide.

http://recipes. howstuffworks.com/ bread.htm
—Basic information and experiments on bread making.

http://www.breadworld. com/
—Broad range of information on making yeast breads.

principal ingredient, but there may be other grains combined with all-purpose flour to add flavor and textural contrasts. Corn bread is a familiar example of the use of another cereal being combined with all-purpose, refined wheat flour to obtain a different flavor, texture, and even a distinctive color. Buckwheat is a popular grain added to some pancake batters to make buckwheat pancakes. These are but a couple of examples of the use of different grains for variety.

Although flour and an occasional use of other cereal grains would seem to dominate the quick bread scene, other ingredients add to the assortment classified as quick breads. For instance, the use of butter, shortening, or oil can make quite a difference in the textural characteristics and the flavor of the baked breads. The use or absence of eggs, as well as the use of only the yolks or whites, provides other modifications in quick breads. Sugar adds sweetness and color to some quick breads, although most usually are rather low in this sweetener.

The type and the amount of liquid used in making quick breads can also vary. Ordinarily, milk is used, but occasionally orange juice, water, or other liquid may be chosen. The liquid used influences flavor, texture, and browning.

Comparison of Quick Breads

The range of products classified as quick breads is indeed impressive. Popovers and cream puffs are quick breads that rise so dramatically during baking that they appear literally to have exploded. Muffins are baked from a rather soft batter dropped into individual containers or cups in a special muffin pan. Biscuits are rolled and cut from a dough that is stiff enough to be baked in individual shapes on a cookie sheet. Cake doughnuts are cut from a dough rolled into a thickness of about half an inch and then fried in deep fat. Loaves of fruit and nut breads basically are a viscous drop batter and are fairly similar to muffins in their consistency. In contrast, waffle and pancake batters flow. The most important distinction between waffles and pancakes is their method of baking.

Quick breads are comparatively complex mixtures in which the accuracy of measuring ingredients begins to be evident in the finished product. For instance, the thickness and the spread of a pancake are determined primarily by the ratio of liquid to flour in the batter. Even small variations in the measure of either of these key ingredients will cause noticeable changes in quality of the baked pancake. The same is true of other types of quick breads.

The diversity of batters and doughs comprising the array of quick breads is interesting to review. A comparison between common types is given in Table 16.1. Typical ratios of ingredients are only a part of the study of ingredients. The physical state of the fat, whether liquid or solid; the use of egg, baking powder, and sugar; and the method of mixing are all of importance in determining the properties of the final product.

TABLE 16.1
TYPICAL FORMULAS FOR QUICK BREADS

Type	Flour (cups)	Milk (T)	State	Fat Amount (T)	Egg	Sugar (T)	Baking Powder (tsp)
Muffins	1	7	Liquid	2	1/2	1 1/3	1 1/2
Biscuits	1	5 1/2–6	Solid	2	—	—	1 1/2
Popovers	1	16	Liquid	1/2	1	—	—
Cream puffs	1	16[a]	Liquid	8	4	—	—
Waffles	1	11 1/2	Liquid	4 1/2	1+	—	1 3/4
Pancakes	1	13	Liquid	1 2/3	1	1	2 1/2
Doughnuts	1	3 1/2	Liquid	1	1	3 1/2	1 1/2

[a]Liquid is water.

Muffins

Muffins can be a tender, flavorful quick bread, but they may turn out to be crumbly or even very tough. Technique in preparing muffins will have a particularly important effect on the quality of the baked product, largely because the sticky ratio of flour to liquid (2:1) causes considerable gluten development with each stroke used in mixing. A small miscalculation in mixing can make a significant difference in the baked muffin.

muffins Quick bread with a cauliflower-like, rounded surface resulting from careful mixing and baking of a batter with a 2:1 ratio of flour to liquid.

SCIENCE NOTE
FLOUR-TO-LIQUID RATIOS

The ratio of flour to liquid is perhaps the most critical component of quick bread formulas. A quick, but useful, preliminary evaluation of quick bread recipes can be done by comparing the amount of flour with the amount of liquid when both ingredients are expressed in the same units of measure. This comparison is simplified arithmetically to gauge whether the mixture will be a batter (pourable or capable of being dropped onto a flat surface for baking) or a dough that needs to be rolled.

The thinnest batter ordinarily made will have a ratio of 1:1 (1 part flour to 1 part liquid). When equal amounts of liquid and flour are used, the mixture will be fluid or very pourable, as is the case in the preparation of popovers. In fact, the 1:1 ratio is so fluid that gluten fails to form well because of the limited interaction between individual gluten strands during mixing.

A very different product with this 1:1 ratio is cream puffs. Anyone who has made cream puffs will recognize that the dough must be viscous enough to stand up almost in a ball when dropped from the spoon onto the baking sheet. Although the 1:1 ratio of flour to liquid makes this sound impossible, the egg yolks used in the puff dough are such effective emulsifying agents that, augmented by starch in the flour, they are able to bind all of the fat and liquid in an emulsion within the dough.

Muffins are a batter product capable of being spooned into cups or a baking pan and flowing a bit to conform to the shape of the container. This viscosity is achieved by using a flour:liquid ratio of approximately 2:1, that is, 2 parts flour to 1 part liquid. This ratio is a very sticky combination, in which the gluten strands receive enough liquid to cause them to begin to develop and to tend to cling to each other and stretch during mixing. This 2:1 ratio results in very rapid gluten development; overmixing quickly becomes a problem.

Biscuits are a good example of a 3:1 ratio of flour to liquid. This large amount of flour in relation to liquid means that the flour proteins hydrate more slowly and develop into gluten with greater difficulty than is found in working with the 2:1 ratio of muffins. Somewhat more manipulation of the mixture is necessary to develop gluten appropriately in biscuits than is needed for muffins. Nevertheless, overmixing in biscuits can be a problem, albeit less so than in muffins. This 3:1 ratio results in a dough that can be handled with reasonable ease, being neither so sticky that it would be impossible to knead with the hands nor so stiff that it would be hard to keep in a cohesive, yet tender, mass. Cake doughnuts, another quick bread, may have a ratio of 4:1, that is, 1 cup of flour to only 1/4 cup of liquid.

muffin method Method in which dry ingredients are sifted together in one bowl and the liquid ingredients (including melted fat) are combined in a second bowl; the liquid ingredients are poured all at once into the dry mixture and stirred just enough to moisten all dry ingredients.

In addition to the sticky ratio of flour to liquid, muffins contain only a moderate amount of fat and little sugar to help retard the effect of mixing. If either of these ingredients were increased, muffins would be far less likely to be overmixed than they are in the typical recipe, but then they would lose their bread-like quality and begin to assume the characteristics of a cake. Consequently, their preparation focuses primarily on achieving just the right amount of gluten development—neither too much nor too little.

Muffins are mixed using the **muffin method**. This method begins with the thorough blending of dry ingredients by sifting them together into a bowl. A second bowl is used to blend all of the liquid ingredients together completely. The fat is melted and treated as a liquid ingredient. Then liquid ingredients are poured all at once into a well in the dry ingredients and stirred just enough to moisten the dry ingredients. This results in a lumpy batter, but one with no areas with dry flour. It is the lumpy batter that produces the cauliflower-like surface of muffins, which is the desirable product. If mixing is continued until the lumps are removed, the baked muffin will be tough and full of tunnels.

Surprisingly, gluten develops so readily in muffins that it is necessary to avoid extra manipulation of the batter even while spooning the batter into the greased muffin cups. Care must be taken to get a large spoonful of batter, enough to fill a muffin cup half full, so that a single spoonful will make one muffin. This gives the desired surface appearance, whereas the addition of a bit more to the batter in a muffin cup frequently produces a misshapen, lopsided muffin.

Evaluation of muffins involves careful examination of the top surface and also a close look at the cross section of the interior, for these areas reveal quickly the quality of preparation (Figure 16.2). The upper surface of muffins should be rounded and have a cauliflower-like appearance and a golden-brown color. The cross section inside should reveal a moderately coarse texture, which is comparatively uniform throughout and does not reveal any pockets or tunnels. Cell walls should be of moderate thickness and should not show any trace of a waxy appearance. The structure should be sufficiently strong to make it possible to spread butter or margarine on its surface with only a little crumbling, yet the muffin should be able to be bitten and chewed with ease.

Undermixed muffins will have a poor volume and flat surface, perhaps with even some flecks of dry flour showing. Some sharp points also seem to erupt from the surface, rather than being rounded. The poor volume is due to failure to moisten all the baking powder so that not

Figure 16.2
Undermixed muffin (left) exhibits poor volume and a crumbly texture; proper mixing (center) develops a slightly rounded, cauliflower-like top and a fairly uniform, rather coarse texture; excessive mixing (right) causes a peaked top and a smooth exterior surface with tunnels inside (usually directed upward toward the peak). These characteristics demonstrate the development of gluten throughout the mixing of muffin batter. Courtesy of Plycon Press.

all of the gas needed for leavening is released. Undermixing also causes them to be very crumbly, because the gluten has not been developed sufficiently to give the amount of structure required. Cell walls also usually are quite thick, and the cells range from very small to some that are quite large within the same muffin.

Overmixing develops the gluten more than is desirable. This can be spotted readily by looking at the contour and texture of the upper crust. When a muffin is fairly pointed and the texture of the crust has the smooth appearance of a yeast bread, the batter has been overmixed. In fact, the top of an overmixed muffin often resembles the shape of a lopsided miniature mountain, the peak being the point where the last of the batter was pushed from the spoon into the muffin pan. The interior will reveal tunnels leading toward this peak. These tunnels are passageways in which the expanding carbon dioxide pushed its way toward the surface, with the overdeveloped gluten directing its movement upward. This visual message of overmixing is accompanied by a detectable toughness. These various symptoms of overmixing develop so rapidly that it often is possible to examine a batch of muffins and tell by their surface appearance the sequence in which they were spooned into the pan; the small amount of manipulation in spooning the batter can be sufficient to cause overmixing in the last ones.

Commercial muffin mixes can be mixed more than muffins made using the basic ingredients. This difference in the rate of gluten development is the result of the higher content of sugar and fat used in mixes, a formula designed to help novices be successful. Busy cooks sometimes opt for using a muffin mix because of the time it saves.

Fruit and Nut Breads

Date nut, banana, and certain other fruit- or nut-containing breads are quick breads (Figure 16.3). Often these are made by the muffin method, although a few of them contain so much fat and sugar that they resemble cakes more closely than muffins and consequently are prepared by the same method used for making shortened cakes (Chapter 17). These breads are baked in loaf pans until a toothpick inserted in the center of the loaf comes out clean. This test ensures that the batter in the center has had an opportunity to become hot enough for the gluten to denature and the starch to gelatinize. The visual test of a golden-brown exterior used in muffins cannot be used for these breads because of the potential for inadequate heating of the interior in the center of the loaf. Elapsed baking time is a good guide to knowing when to test with the toothpick, for the volume of the loaf will be affected if the oven is opened and the bread is tested when the structure is stretched to its maximum but has not yet been denatured.

Ideally, the loaf will be gently rounded on the top and with a slightly cauliflower-like surface, and the interior will be tender and a little coarse, but not crumbly. The volume should be good, and without tunnels. The amount of mixing and its effect on fruit and nut breads made by the muffin method is similar to that on muffins. Overbaking dries out the loaf and may cause an overly brown crust. Underbaking causes the loaf to fall as a consequence of allowing the expanded gases to cool and contract before the structure sets.

Figure 16.3
Fruit and nut breads often contain more sugar and fat than muffins and, therefore, require somewhat more mixing to develop the gluten enough for easy slicing. Excessive mixing will cause tunnels. Courtesy of Plycon Press.

As soon as baked loaves are removed from the oven, they should be eased from the pan onto a wire rack to cool. This avoids the problem of condensed moisture on the bottom and side crusts. The structure of these breads is strong enough to allow this type of handling without losing volume. However, slicing is done more readily the day after baking than when the loaves are fresh because the structure will become increasingly rigid and will hold the sliced edge with ease.

Biscuits

biscuits Quick bread made by cutting in solid fat and using a flour-to-liquid ratio of 3:1, which results in a dough that can be kneaded, rolled, and cut into straight-sided, round disks for baking.

The ingredients in **biscuits** are combined in a totally different way to achieve this unique type of quick bread. An important feature of biscuits is that the fat is used in a solid form, being cut into pieces. These pieces are partially responsible for the flaky texture desired in biscuits, a texture completely unlike that of muffins. To make these flour-covered fat particles, a pastry blender usually is used with a light flipping motion that coats each piece of fat with a layer of flour while slicing the fat into progressively smaller particles. The coating of flour helps to keep the fat particles separated while the dough is being mixed. During baking, these pieces of fat melt, leaving little pockets where the carbon dioxide and steam can expand and create a flaky texture.

After the fat has been cut into the dry ingredients, all of the liquid is added at once. This mixture is stirred briefly with a fork to moisten all of the ingredients, using an occasional cutting motion to penetrate the thick dough and help to moisten the dry ingredients that may not be contacting the liquid. Gluten develops a little less readily in biscuit dough than in muffin batter because the flour-to-liquid ratio in biscuits is about 3:1, which is not as sticky as the 2:1 ratio in muffins. This slight inhibition of gluten development in biscuit dough makes it possible to stir the ingredients about 20 strokes and then to knead the dough. Biscuits are kneaded gently by folding the dough in half and pressing lightly in a rhythmic motion with the fingertips, a technique that is repeated 10–20 times to promote the development of flaky layers as the gluten develops. As kneading progresses, the dough tightens noticeably and becomes smooth. Kneading must be stopped before the dough starts to spring back or take on a rubbery character.

After kneading, the dough is rolled to a thickness about half that of the desired height of the baked biscuit, for biscuits will just about double in height during baking. They expand upward, but not sideways. Thin biscuits (only about half an inch high when baked) will be crusty and dry. Usually, biscuit dough is rolled about half an inch thick, which results in a high biscuit with a pleasing crispness on the surface and bread-like, flaky interior.

The rolled dough is cut with a sharp cutter pressed evenly downward through the dough to help produce biscuits that stand up straight during baking. For crisp-sided biscuits, the unbaked biscuits are positioned at least an inch apart on the baking sheet. However, placing biscuits so that their sides touch helps to hold them in position and prevents their leaning over during baking. Either arrangement is satisfactory. Since the oven heat does not reach the sides of biscuits arranged so that they touch, these biscuits will be soft on the sides, rather than crisp. By brushing milk lightly on the surface of the biscuits before baking, the top surface will develop a shiny, golden-brown crust free of the tiny brown "freckles" of undissolved baking powder that show on the crust of biscuits not brushed with milk.

Evaluation of biscuits involves the appearance of the exterior and also the palatability characteristics of the interior (Figure 16.4). A high-quality baking-powder biscuit will have straight sides, a flat top, and a pleasingly browned crust. Some horizontal cracks will show in the sides, which are clear indications of the flaky texture within. The top surface should be crisp, and the interior crumb should be tender.

If biscuits have a somewhat rough surface and poor volume, the dough was not kneaded sufficiently. On the other hand, too much kneading develops the gluten too much, resulting in a smooth surface, tough crumb, and small volume. Tough biscuits may be the result of too much stirring or kneading, or they may be

Figure 16.4
Baking-powder biscuits should have straight sides and cracks along the side indicating a flaky interior.
Courtesy of Plycon Press.

due to using too little liquid. Optimal results are obtained when the dough is just slightly sticky, but still able to be kneaded. At this moisture level, the edge of the biscuit right at the bottom crust will curl up ever so slightly.

Drop biscuits are a variation of rolled biscuits. Although the ingredients are the same, drop biscuit recipes include too much liquid for the resulting mixture to be kneaded. The biscuits are dropped from a spoon onto the baking sheet, rather than being rolled and cut with a biscuit cutter. The result is a rather casual appearance—a rough surface and poorly defined shape. However, they are quick to make and often are enjoyed for their crisp crust. A close relative is the dumpling, which simply is dropped on bubbling gravy or other liquid and steamed until cooked throughout. Dumplings, due to steaming, do not have a crisp exterior.

Cake Doughnuts

Cake doughnuts are a quick bread that usually is fried rather than baked. The dough is made with a small amount of liquid fat and with only a little over half as much liquid as is used in biscuits. Doughnut dough is toughened with excessive handling. The key to making tender cake doughnuts is to avoid working in any extra flour, using just enough to be able to roll the dough with ease. The dough should be chilled before being rolled or extruded, as the increased viscosity and reduced stickiness result in less toughening of the dough during this phase.

Careful control of the fat at 375°F (190°C) during frying of doughnuts is important to the quality of the finished product. When the fat is too hot, the doughnuts will brown very rapidly on the surface, but the interior will not be hot enough to denature the protein and gelatinize the starch until the exterior is practically burned. This leads to undercooked doughnuts with gummy interiors. An even greater problem involves the rapid breakdown of the overheated fat to acrolein (an eye irritant) and free fatty acids, which together impair flavor of the doughnuts and aggravate the cook. Conversely, frying at too low a temperature extends the length of time required to achieve the desired internal temperature and exterior browning. Moreover, the dough absorbs fat from the frying medium, which results in a greasy doughnut. The best doughnuts are made by carefully maintaining the fat at 375°F (190°C).

Waffles and Pancakes

Unlike many of the other quick breads, waffles and pancakes are eaten with a fork and are often topped with syrup or sauce. The proportions of flour to liquid vary slightly among different recipes, but generally pancake batters are slightly more fluid mixtures than waffle batters. Waffles contain not quite 3/4 cup milk to 1 cup of flour, while pancakes are made with a little over 3/4 cup of milk to 1 cup of flour. Although neither of these batters is quite a 1:1 ratio, they both are very fluid mixtures that can be beaten vigorously to make a smooth batter without developing the gluten extensively. Waffle batter, although leavened with baking powder, sometimes is made by folding an egg white foam into the batter to help introduce additional air and promote lightness.

Temperature control on waffle irons and pancake griddles is a tremendous aid to making products of high quality. If there is no temperature control, the iron or griddle should be preheated until drops of cold water seem to dance, rather than sizzle (not quite hot enough), when they touch the surface. Pancakes are poured to make a circle of the desired size on the griddle and then are allowed to bake on the first side until bubbles rise through the batter and burst at the surface and the bottom is a pleasing brown. At this time they are flipped to brown the second side. They should be served with the surface that was browned first on top. Waffles are poured onto a preheated iron, which is closed for baking until steam stops issuing from the iron. Attempts to open the iron sooner usually tear the waffle because the batter will stick.

Pancakes should be a picture-perfect golden brown on the surface and should be round. The size is strictly a matter of personal preference. They should be light and tender. Overmixing of the batter or too much flour in relation to the milk can cause pancakes to be tough.

Waffles should be crisp and golden brown on the exterior and tender to chew. The waffle should fill the grid pattern of the iron completely. In case appetites are less than the amount of batter for waffles, the remaining batter can be baked, and the cooled waffles can be frozen for subsequent reheating in a toaster. Commercially produced frozen waffles have gained a reasonable market segment because of their convenience. Moreover, people who do not have a waffle iron can enjoy them.

Variations of both waffles and pancakes are popular items. Pecans and blueberries are typical ingredients that can be added to batters to enhance nutritive value as well as create intriguing variations of these products. Additional variety is gained by using fruits and sauces for toppings. Crêpes are pancakes with extra liquid added to the batter, creating a very fluid mixture that produces pancakes that are almost paper thin. Crêpes sometimes are made using a special pan that is heated and then dipped into a shallow bowl of batter; a small frying pan is recommended as a suitable substitute. Crêpes can be rolled with fillings of chicken, fish, or other protein foods in sauces to serve as an entrée, or they may have sweet fillings or be cooked in sweet sauces to create an exotic dessert. Waffles also have their sophisticated gadgetry. A Belgian waffle iron permits the preparation of waffles with a very crisp texture and deep squares that effectively trap any of a wide variety of syrups and toppings.

Popovers

popovers Dramatic quick bread leavened primarily by steam, the result of a very fluid batter (1:1 ratio of flour to liquid) and baking in a very hot oven.

Popovers, one of the most dramatic quick breads to make, are steam leavened. They can be characterized as "wonder bread," for popovers often triple in volume during baking. The explanation is that steam is generated very rapidly in this fluid batter as it is heated in a very hot oven, and this steam forcefully expands the gluten from the flour and the protein from the egg, particularly the protein from the white. Then the proteins denature in this greatly extended position and the starch gelatinizes, resulting in the familiar shell-like structure of popovers.

Preparation of popovers is simple and quick, merely involving beating milk, flour, eggs, and salt together until the batter is smooth. This very fluid batter, with its ratio of equal amounts of milk and flour, permits fairly extensive beating without overdeveloping the gluten. Actually, the gluten and starch of the flour are augmented considerably in popovers by the protein of the egg white; adequate egg white is essential to obtain the desired degree of popping during baking. The extensibility of egg white proteins during the early part of baking and the strength contributed to the structure by the denatured egg white protein in the finished product are vital to the success of popovers. In short, popovers with an inadequate amount of egg white protein fail to "pop." Popovers are definitely one product for which extra-large eggs are an asset.

Ideally, popovers are poured directly into lightly oiled, preheated custard cups or popover pans and are baked immediately in an oven preheated to at least 425°F (220°C) (Figure 16.5). Under these conditions, a large volume of steam will be generated quickly, causing the essential rapid expansion of the batter. This high temperature causes rather rapid browning, gelatinization of the starch, and setting of the structure, but the interior may not be dried out sufficiently unless the baking time is extended to about 45 minutes total. If browning starts to become excessive, the oven temperature can be lowered to 350°F (175°C) after the first 15 minutes of baking.

The ideal popover will have a crisp texture and a pleasingly browned exterior. The volume will be very big, with a large central cavity surrounded by reasonably thin walls defining the total popover. There should be no sogginess in the cavity, although the walls will be slightly moist. The most vexing problem in making popovers is failure to pop. This difficulty is due most likely to having too little egg white in the batter. However, an oven that is too cool can also be at fault.

Cream Puffs

Technically, **cream puffs** are quick breads that are served as a base for an entrée or a dessert rather than as an accompanying bread product. Cream puffs are of special interest because of their similarities and dissimilarities with popovers. Both are steam-leavened quick breads and hence must be baked in a very hot oven to generate sufficient steam to create the desired volume and large cavity. The cavity is the unique feature of both of these quick breads. In the case of cream puffs, this cavity is essential so that it can serve as the site for holding various fillings.

The intriguing aspect of cream puffs is that the unbaked mixture is a dough, not a fluid batter, despite the fact that equal amounts of liquid and flour are used. Since popovers contain the same flour-to-liquid ratio, it would be natural to expect that cream puffs would also form a batter. However, cream puffs contain not only starch gelatinized in a boiling water–butter mixture but also a large amount of eggs—enough to emulsify the butter in the cream puff mixture (Table 16.1), forming an oil-in-water emulsion that very significantly modifies the flow properties of the system to create a dough.

Sometimes too much water may be evaporated during preparation of cream puff dough, causing the oil-in-water emulsion to break. If the dough begins to look curdled and fat oozes from the mixture, a small amount of water must be stirred in to reestablish the emulsion and provide the water needed for leavening by steam during the baking period. Just enough water is added to produce a smooth dough in which the fat is emulsified; too much water causes so much thinning that the baking cream puff cannot contain the steam, and the puff then fails to live up to its name.

Cream puffs should be large and pleasingly golden brown, with a large interior cavity and somewhat crisp walls. The puff is accomplished by baking an emulsified dough containing sufficient egg protein in an oven hot enough to generate the steam needed to stretch the gluten network and create the large cavity. If too little butter, egg, or water is present, the desired large volume and cavity will not be achieved. Other causes of failure to puff are too cool an oven or too much water.

Figure 16.5
Popovers are a dramatic quick bread leavened primarily by steam, the result of a very fluid batter (1:1 ratio of liquid to flour) and baking in a very hot oven. Courtesy of Plycon Press.

cream puffs Quick bread used as a container for dessert fillings or main course mixtures; crisp shell with a large cavity made possible by the combination of butter, water, egg, and flour dough baked in a very hot oven.

Naan is one of several unique breads that are typical in India's cuisine. This bread serves as an appropriate bridge between quick and yeast breads because recipes vary with regard to their source of leavening. Some recipes use yogurt to add biological leavening and others use yeast. These biological agents require time for carbon dioxide to be generated and start to leaven the dough. Therefore, they are not really quick breads.

The dough is basically flour, egg, milk or yogurt, a little salt and sugar, and a source of microbiological leavening. Various seeds and other flavorings may be added to create variations of naan. Some recipes recognize the variations in ambient temperature in different parts of India by suggesting a much longer rising time for doughs being prepared in cooler places than for those in a hot environment. After rising time, naan dough is rolled into balls about the size of a peach and then shaped into discs for baking in a tandoori oven, the traditional cylindrical charcoal-burning oven of India (Figure 16.6). In the United States, the dough can be placed on preheated oven tiles and baked in a convection oven, a suitable substitute.

Figure 16.6
Naan, a favorite bread in India, traditionally is baked in a tandoori oven.
Courtesy of Plycon Press.

http://www.tandoors.
com/?gclid=CPDm_
KjpnqcCFQcnbAodMSU3Lq
—Information on tandoori
ovens.

http://www.indiaforvisitors.
com/food/bread/naan.htm
—Website about India,
including its food;
descriptions and recipes for
making breads typical of
India.

YEAST BREADS

Yeast breads take time to make because of the time required for the yeast to produce adequate amounts of carbon dioxide for leavening the dough as it bakes. The generation of carbon dioxide requires careful control of fermentation conditions to maintain viable yeast within an optimal temperature range (Chapter 14). The level of sugar and of salt must be consistent with the conditions needed by the yeast for normal metabolic reactions to take place. Regardless of whether yeast breads are intended to become loaves, bread sticks, or various types of rolls, the doughs generally are prepared by the straight dough method, although the sponge method sometimes is used.

Managing Yeast Bread Preparation

Time management in making yeast breads sometimes is critical. Although not a great deal of time is required to mix and knead a bread dough, the two periods required for fermentation and proofing and the subsequent baking period dictate the need for a comparatively long time span for completing the project, usually about three hours. However, the fermentation and proofing times can be shortened by increasing the amount of yeast added to the dough. Another technique used by some is to prepare the dough in the evening, covering it and allowing it to proof in the refrigerator during the night. By morning the dough will have doubled, and the remainder of the preparation can proceed. It also is possible to shape rolls on the baking sheet and let them rise in the refrigerator. The baking time will need to be extended somewhat to offset the cold temperature of the dough at the start of baking.

Straight Dough Method

The initial step in preparing the dough by the **straight dough method** is to soften the yeast. Compressed yeast cakes are placed in lukewarm water (about 104°F [40°C]), while active dry

straight dough
method Method of
making yeast bread dough
by combining scalded milk,
sugar, salt, butter, egg with
softened yeast (added after
mixture is sufficiently cool),
and flour; kneading and
proofing precede baking.

yeast should be rehydrated in water at a temperature of 100°–115°F [39°–46°C]). While the yeast is softening, the milk is scalded by holding it at almost 200°F (93°C) for a minute and then is poured into a bowl containing the fat, sugar, and salt. The heat of the milk should be sufficient to melt the butter, which helps to cool the milk to around 100°F (39°C) or slightly cooler so that the softened yeast can be added safely. If eggs are being used, they are added just before the yeast so that their cool temperature will provide additional security against killing the yeast by exposing them to too high a temperature during mixing.

Use of shortening as the fat in the dough promotes production of a bread with excellent volume and a fine crumb. This effect is the result of the adsorption of β′ crystals at the gas–liquid interface of bubbles as they expand in the dough during fermentation. During baking, the fat becomes so fluid that it spreads and becomes part of the surface of the bubbles. This facilitates stretching of the bubbles to promote the desired increase in volume. Some of the fat forms crystals again after the bread is baked.

The addition of approximately a third of the flour creates a batter that can be beaten vigorously to help initiate development of a strong gluten network. Additional flour is stirred in to create a soft dough, one that can be kneaded vigorously without becoming too sticky (Figure 16.7). The kneading process for yeast breads is a far more vigorous technique than is that used in kneading biscuits. Although the dough is folded in half and then pushed with the hands, this type of kneading involves using the heels of both hands rather than a gentle push with the fingertips. However, kneading in yeast breads should not be done so vigorously that gluten strands tear. The dough is rotated a quarter of a turn each time the kneading motion is done. Then it is folded over, pressed with the heels of the hands, and rotated in a repetitive sequence, creating a rhythm that facilitates development of the necessary amount of gluten. Kneading can be done with a mixer or food processor, if desired. When blisters begin to show just under the surface of the dough when it is folded over gently, an adequate amount of gluten has been developed (Figure 16.8). The ball of dough then is oiled on its surface and is placed in a bowl, where it is covered and then held for fermentation, preferably at a temperature of about 80°F (27°C).

Fermentation is allowed to proceed until the dough has doubled in volume, a process that helps to promote extensibility of gluten, as well as produce acids and alcohol. When the ball is doubled, the fist is used to push the dough down in preparation for the proofing period. Unlike the fermentation period, which is completed in a covered bowl in about an hour's time, the proofing period is done after the dough has been shaped into the desired form and placed in the baking pan (Figure 16.9). Rising is allowed to continue without a cover until the dough has again doubled in volume, a process requiring about half as much time as was needed for the initial fermentation.

Baking is done in a preheated oven, usually at about 400°F (204°C), until the bread is a pleasing golden brown and the appropriate amount of time has elapsed. Breads high in sugar or containing raisins or other sweet ingredients need to be baked at about 350°F (175°C) to avoid scorching or burning. The baking period is marked by the phenomenon called **oven spring**, which is an obvious increase in volume due to volatilization of alcohol and to rapid carbon dioxide production by yeast in the warm environment until the yeast is killed by the heat.

The straight dough method is the method commonly used in the home for making yeast breads because mixing is

Figure 16.7
In the early stage of kneading yeast bread dough, the mixture is quite rough and may need additional flour to help keep the dough from sticking to the hands. Courtesy of Plycon Press.

oven spring Increase in volume of yeast breads in the early part of baking, the result of rapid yeast growth and gas expansion.

Figure 16.8
Vigorous kneading, accomplished using the heels of both hands in a rhythmical motion while rotating the dough, is necessary for the development of an adequate amount of gluten. The appearance of the dough will progress from a rough surface (left) to undermixed dough with gluten strands beginning to show (center), and finally to a satin-like surface when sufficient gluten has been developed (right). Courtesy of Plycon Press.

relatively quick. The resulting product is excellent, but a good bit of physical effort is needed to develop the gluten sufficiently by this method. Some people enjoy the task of kneading the dough by hand; others use food processors.

Sponge Method

The other traditional method of mixing yeast doughs is the **sponge method**. Much of this method is comparable to the straight dough method. The principal difference is that part of the flour and all of the salt are withheld until after an initial fermentation period. During this fermentation of the fairly fluid batter, the carbon dioxide being formed causes the mixture to begin to develop a spongy appearance, which explains why this is called the sponge method of mixing. Following the first rising period, the salt and remaining flour are added, and the remaining preparation steps are the same as in the straight dough method (kneading, rising, shaping, rising, and baking). This method used to be necessary some years ago because the yeast that was available at that time required a long rehydration and activation period, a problem no longer encountered. Consequently, only a few recipes now are made using the sponge method. The time required for development of the sponge is a real disadvantage.

Rapid-Mix Method

Some time can be saved when preparing yeast breads at home by using the rapid-mix method—by mixing the active dry yeast directly with two cups of flour before pouring in warm milk or very hot tap water and the fat. This mixture is beaten vigorously with an electric mixer to develop the gluten before the remaining flour is stirred in. The subsequent handling of the dough is the same as in the straight dough method. Some time is saved in the early steps of mixing. The very warm liquid in the rapid-mix method does not harm the yeast because the mixture cools to a safe temperature for the yeast before it becomes hydrated.

Bread Machines

Bread machines currently are being used in some homes to provide the pleasure of homemade bread with very little time and effort on the part of the baker. The ingredients are measured into the machine by the cook, but the remainder of the mixing, kneading, proofing, and baking are functions performed by the bread machine. Time and temperature are programmed into the machine. The resulting bread is round, rather than the traditional loaf shape, and the texture is somewhat porous. However, the aroma, flavor, and texture are sufficiently pleasing to have captured a large market for bread machines.

Factors in Yeast Bread Quality

The amount of flour incorporated into the yeast doughs has a significant influence on the quality of the finished product, but there is no simple way of communicating to the novice just how much flour is needed in a specific recipe. The vague indication of how much flour to use in a yeast dough can be disconcerting, for exact measurements when preparing new recipes help to generate a feeling of confidence. Some yeast bread recipes do indicate a measure of sifted flour to use, but this may not prove to be the optimal amount. The problem stems from the fact that the absorptive qualities of flour vary among lots, and they vary particularly among different parts of the country. The goal is to add enough flour to allow the dough to be kneaded without sticking to the hands. The dough should have an alive, springy feel and should sag a little when resting on the breadboard after kneading. If dough appears rigid and feels resistant to kneading, it contains too much flour and will be tough and somewhat dry when baked.

Control of fermentation is absolutely essential to production of high-quality yeast breads. Temperatures must be kept below 115°F (46°C) any time hydrated yeast is present. Temperatures above this will kill yeast quickly, resulting in poor volume. The most likely points where the system may be too hot are when the yeast is added to the scalded milk mixtures and

Figure 16.9
Dough decorations may be added to the shaped dough before the final proofing.
Courtesy of Plycon Press.

sponge method Method of preparing a yeast dough, in which the salt and part of the flour are withheld until the batter has generated enough carbon dioxide to give a sponge-like quality to the mixture; addition of the rest of the flour and the salt precedes the completion of the kneading and subsequent steps.

Figure 16.10
A professional baker is ready to load three proofed loaves into his fiery hot brick oven. No wonder locals flock to his shop to buy fresh bread.
Courtesy of Plycon Press.

when fermentation may be taking place in an oven that is too warm, which may be the case if a gas oven has a high pilot light.

In addition to temperature regulation, fermentation can be controlled partially by the amount of sugar contained in the formulation. Sugar needs to be available throughout the fermentation period to serve as food for the yeast. When this situation exists, carbon dioxide will continue to be generated until the structure has stretched and set during baking. To counterbalance the effect of sugar, some salt is necessary to act as an inhibitor on the metabolism of yeast, thus regulating carbon dioxide production and helping to prevent formation of too much of this gas.

Bread loaves and rolls are best baked in a preheated oven when the shaped dough has just doubled in volume (Figure 16.10). The oven spring occurring when baking is initiated will add the finishing touch to the desired volume. The texture will become too porous and the product may even fall if the proofing time is extended to permit too much carbon dioxide production to occur before baking kills the yeast.

Elapsed time is one of the key tests for doneness of breads and rolls. A golden-brown crust color is a misleading guide to doneness, for a pleasing crust color usually develops prior to the time the bread actually is denatured inside. An underbaked loaf of bread or roll will have a doughy center.

When done, most breads should be removed immediately from the baking pan and transferred to a cooling rack or to a breadbasket for prompt service to diners. The structure of yeast breads is tenacious and more than strong enough to hold its original volume and shape when handled while hot, which is fortunate, for crusts become soggy from condensed moisture if products are allowed to cool in their baking pans. However, sweet rolls baked in a syrup coating the bottom of the pan should be cooled in the baking pan until the syrup has started to cool and become viscous. At that point, the pan should be inverted and the syrup allowed to drip onto the rolls until most of the topping has been transferred.

Quality of yeast breads is assessed by examining the exterior and interior carefully (Figure 16.11). The product should be shaped pleasingly and be appropriate in size for the occasion. The crust should be a tempting golden brown and have a sheen. Melted butter or margarine brushed over the crust immediately after baking creates this sheen. The crust should not be soggy; breads made without milk or fat should have a crisp crust. The interior of the bread should be uniform, with cells of moderate size and cell walls of medium thickness, characteristics clearly coarser than the texture in cakes. An extremely coarse texture, however, is a clear sign of excessive fermentation. Bread and rolls should be easy to chew, but should not be so tender that butter or other spreads cannot be spread without creating a large quantity of crumbs. Attention should be directed toward shaping rolls into a uniform size, a means of enhancing the beauty of home-baked rolls.

Figure 16.11
For special occasions or holidays, breads sometimes are decorated with sculpted dough or a design pressed on the surface. Courtesy of Plycon Press.

Figure 16.12
Sourdough breads are
leavened by use of a starter
containing microorganisms
to produce carbon dioxide.
Consequently, sourdough
breads require fermentation
and proofing. Courtesy of
Plycon Press.

Sourdough

Sourdough breads conjure up vivid images of bearded prospectors joining in the Gold Rush, but this popular type of bread is also very familiar today. Many colorful stories have been spun about the miners who slept with their sourdough starter placed right next to their guns so that nothing could happen to the starter. Actually, the care and feeding of sourdough starters is a subject vital to bakers today, too, just as in the past, for maintenance of the proper strain requires proper feeding of the desired microorganisms and avoidance of new, undesirable strains (Figure 16.12).

A sourdough starter is made with flour, sugar, yeast, and water and is stored at room temperature. A portion of this starter is saved for making the next product, and flour and water are added to feed the starter before storing this sponge in the refrigerator. Uses for sourdough starter are rather varied and include bread, pancakes, waffles, biscuits, muffins, and cakes. The flavor of the sourdough starter adds a distinctive quality to products in which it is used.

http://www.breadtopia.
com/sourdough-starter-
management/
—Management of
sourdough starters.

SUMMARY

Breads are baked products containing a large proportion of flour (usually wheat) and a liquid with leavening agents, eggs, and flavoring agents rounding out the list of ingredients. On the basis of the type of leavening they contain, baked bread products are divided into quick breads and yeast breads. Quick breads are leavened by air, steam, and/or carbon dioxide, which is provided by a chemical reaction between an acid and an alkaline ingredient. Although carbon dioxide, air, and steam also serve as the leavening agents in yeast breads, the carbon dioxide is generated slowly by the metabolic reactions of yeast (*Saccharomyces cerevisiae*, a one-celled plant) during proofing at a controlled temperature.

Quick breads contain a variety of ingredients, but one of the most significant aspects of ingredients in influencing the characteristics of quick breads is the flour-to-liquid ratio, which has considerable impact on gluten development. Muffins, with a ratio of two parts flour to one part liquid (2:1), can be easily mixed too much because of the very sticky nature of the dough

and its gluten. On the other hand, the very fluid nature of a 1:1 ratio, which is found in popovers and cream puffs, permits considerable mixing without overdeveloping the gluten. The 3:1 ratio used in biscuits can be handled somewhat more than muffins without becoming tough.

With the proper amount of mixing, the surface of muffins will have a cauliflower-like look, be somewhat rounded, and have a golden-brown color. The interior will be slightly coarse but will not have tunnels. Overmixed muffins rise toward a peak, with interior tunnels leading up it; they also will be tough. Undermixed muffins will have some areas of dry ingredients that have not been moistened with any liquid. The baking powder in these dry areas will not be able to react because it is not dissolved, which results in smaller volume. The crust will appear somewhat rough or jagged, and the muffins will be quite crumbly when they have not been mixed enough.

Other quick breads include fruit and nut breads, biscuits (kneaded and drop), cake doughnuts, waffles, pancakes, popovers, and cream puffs. Some of these are batters of an appropriate viscosity for dropping or baking in a loaf pan or muffin pan; others are doughs that can be rolled out and cut. Although baking is the usual method of cooking quick breads, cake doughnuts are fried in deep fat.

Yeast breads usually contain enough flour to enable the dough to be kneaded, either by hand or machine. After a fermentation period after mixing that doubles the volume, the dough is shaped in the baking container and then proofed to double the volume again as the yeast generates carbon dioxide. During baking, an initial oven spring increases the volume due to the stimulating effect of the heat on the yeast. However, the

yeast is killed quickly, thus limiting the additional leavening action. Baking is done until the appropriate time has elapsed and the crust is a pleasing golden brown. As soon as the bread is removed from the oven, loaves are taken from their baking pans and are placed on racks to cool, just as is done with quick breads, to avoid developing soggy crusts.

Sourdough breads are popular because of their tart flavor. This tartness is due to the development of acid by bacteria introduced into the dough via the sourdough starter. This acidic medium promotes the development of yeast, which serves as the source of the carbon dioxide for leavening.

STUDY QUESTIONS

1. Compare the method of preparing muffins with that used in making biscuits.
2. Why does gluten develop so easily in muffins? Describe the changes in the appearance of the batter and the baked muffins with different amounts of mixing.
3. What differences can be identified between popover batters and cream puff pastes? Why are the physical properties of

the two so different when their flour-to-liquid ratios are comparable?
4. Contrast the straight dough, rapid-mix, and sponge methods of making yeast breads.
5. What precautions are necessary when making yeast breads of good volume?

SELECTED REFERENCES

American Home Economics Association. 1993. *Handbook of Food Preparation.* 9th ed. AHEA. Washington, DC.

Berry, D. 2004. Breads on the rise. *Food Product Design 14*(7): 106.

Brooker, B. E. 1996. Role of fat in the stabilization of gas cells in bread dough. *J. Cereal Sci. 24*: 187.

Carroll, L. E. 1990. Stabilizer systems reduce texture problems in multicomponent foods and bakery products. *Food Technol. 44*(4): 94.

Clemens, R., and J. Dubost. 2008. Catering to gluten-sensitive consumers. *Food Technol. 62*(12): 21.

Decker, K. J. 2005. Looking at the whole-grain picture. *Food Product Design 15*(9): 49.

Foster, R. J. 2008. Morning brings the grain event. *Food Product Design 18*(12): 42.

Freeman, T. P., and D. R. Shelton. 1991. Microstructure of wheat starch: From kernel to bread. *Food Technol. 45*(3): 162.

Friend, C. P., et al. 1993. Effects of hydrocolloids on processing and qualities in wheat tortillas. *Cereal Chem. 70*(3): 252.

Gao, L., et al. 1992. Structure of glutenin based on farinograph and electrophoresis results. *Cereal Chem. 69*(4): 452.

Golal, A. M., et al. 1978. Lactic and volatile C_2–C_5 organic acids of San Francisco sourdough French bread. *Cereal Chem. 55*: 461.

Hazen, C. 2006. New fiber options for baked goods. *Food Product Design 15*(10): 80.

Hazen, C. 2008. Grain-based ingredients. *Food Product Design 18*(8): 70.

Hazen, C. 2009. Better trans-fat baked goods. *Food Product Design 19*(1): 26.

He, H., and R. C. Hoseney. 1992. Effect of the quantity of wheat flour protein on bread loaf volume. *Cereal Chem. 69*(2): 17.

Hodge, S. 2009. Old world breads. *Food Product Design 19*(5): 44.

Hoseney, R. C. 1992. Factors controlling gas retention in non-heated doughs. *Cereal Chem. 69*(1): 17.

Hoseome, K., et al. 1992. Studies on frozen dough baking. I: Effects of egg yolk and sugar ester. *Cereal Chem. 69*(1): 89.

Inoue, Y., and W. Bushuk. 1992. Studies on frozen dough. II: Flour quality requirements for bread production from frozen dough. *Cereal Chem. 69*(4): 423.

Kaldy, M. S., et al. 1993. Influence of gluten components and flour lipids on soft wheat quality. *Cereal Chem.* *70*(1): 77.

Ohr, L. M. 2009. Good-for-you grains. *Food Technol. 63*(1): 57.

Pszczola, D. E. 2005. Ingredients for bread meet changing 'kneads'. *Food Technol. 59*(1): 55.

Pszczola, D. E. 2011. Breads and beyond. *Food Technol. 65*(1): 50.

Ranhotra, G. S., et al. 1992. Total and soluble fiber content of air-classified white flour from hard and soft wheats. *Cereal Chem. 69*(1): 75.

Ryu, G. H., et al. 1993. Effects of some baking ingredients on physical and structural properties of wheat flour exudates. *Cereal Chem. 70*(3): 291.

Siffring, K., and B. L. Bruinsma. 1993. Effects of proof temperature on the quality of pan bread. *Cereal Chem. 70*(3): 351.

Slaughter, D. C., et al. 1992. Quality and classification of hard red wheat. *Cereal Chem. 69*(4): 428.

Spano, M. 2009. Celiac disease feeds gluten-free need. *Food Product Design 19*(10): 28.

Tenbergen, K. 2008. Flat breads: Old world meets new. *Food Product Design 18*(11): 38.

Chocolate cake topped with sculpted chocolate and icing is a delectable treat.

17

Cakes, Cookies, and Pastries

Chapter Contents

Key Concepts

1. Foam cakes (angel food, sponge, and chiffon) have fairly large cells and a light texture because of the egg foams that add considerable air and some steam for leavening during baking.

2. Shortened cakes are higher in fat and sugar than foam cakes, and they are leavened by carbon dioxide (usually derived from baking powder).

3. Cookies are classified as bar, drop, or rolled, depending on the handling characteristics of the mixture, which characteristically is high in sugar and fat and low in liquid.

4. Pastry requires skill to produce a tender, flaky crust because the large amount of flour in relation to water (6:1 ratio) and the distribution of the fat in particles result in a dough in which gluten can easily develop too much.

"SHORT AND SWEET"

Although breads are increasing in popularity, the study of quick breads and yeast breads actually represents but a fraction of the total possibilities in flour-based mixtures. Many cake recipes are very similar to those for quick bread, except that they contain appreciably more sugar and fat. Because of this sweet richness, cakes are served as the finale to a meal or as a snack. Cakes are classified either as shortened cakes (a term signifying their fat content) or foam cakes (named to indicate the egg foams that contribute so significantly to their structure).

Cookies comprise yet another category of baked product. The physical characteristics vary rather widely; some doughs are dropped, while others can be rolled and cut, and still others are baked as a sheet or layer and cut into bars. They range in texture from crisp and chewy to tender and fairly light.

Pastries are used most commonly as the crusts for pies. However, puff pastries form the basis for patty shells and French pastries. Other pastries are made utilizing very thin sheets of dough; for example, baklava is a popular Middle Eastern dessert made of numerous layers of filo dough. These different pastries usually are dessert items. The popularity of quiche has brought attention to pastry for the main course. In addition, meat pies, chicken à la king in patty shells, and spanokopita (spinach in layers of phyllo dough) expand the use of pastries in the main course (Figure 17.1).

These baked products certainly cover a broad range of characteristics and applications. Nevertheless, they all have in common dependence on gluten for much of their structural integrity. The variety is a result of varying

Figure 17.1
Spanokopita, a favorite Greek main dish, is made with a spinach and egg filling encased in phyllo.

proportions and kinds of ingredients combined and baked in different ways. Imagination and careful culinary techniques are important ingredients in preparing any baked product. In addition, a fundamental knowledge of the various types of cakes, cookies, and pastries helps to ensure success.

CAKES

The two basic categories of cakes—foam and shortened—are distinctly different in their preparation and baked characteristics. The ratios of ingredients and procedures for mixing and baking are related to quick breads, yet each type of cake has certain unique features that need to be identified and respected.

Foam Cakes

Foam cakes gain their name from the fact that much of their basic structure is due to the use of an egg foam into which other ingredients are blended. The foams used may be egg white, egg yolk, or both; foams of whites are the most common basis of foam cake recipes. Regardless of the type of foam used, the structure of foam cakes is quite weak and benefits from use of a tube cake pan to help the batter pull itself upward to achieve maximum volume during baking. Additional assistance is provided by cooling the baked cake in an inverted position to help stretch out the foam cell walls until they gain strength by cooling. These foam cakes are categorized as angel food, sponge, and chiffon. Although all are foam cakes, certain unique features distinguish each type.

Angel Food Cake **Angel food cakes** are the simplest of the foam cakes to make, for they really are just an egg white foam stabilized with some sugar and combined with cake flour to strengthen the structure. Persons on weight reduction diets or on low cholesterol diets particularly appreciate angel food cakes because of their lack of fat and cholesterol. Formulas for them contain neither shortening nor baking powder.

Not surprisingly, the key to a successful angel food cake is the creation and handling of an optimal egg white foam (Chapter 12). This challenge is met in part by the use of cream of tartar and part of the sugar, beginning at the foamy stage of beating the whites. The whites are beaten until the peaks just bend over, a point at which the foam maintains reasonable elasticity and stability. Use of high-quality eggs with a large amount of thick white is a further aid in achieving optimal quality.

http://food.oregonstate. edu/learn/pastry.html

—Background information on cakes of different types and other baked products.

http://www.joyofbaking. com/cakes.html

—Recipes and information on cakes.

http://www.joyofbaking.com/ FoamCakes.html

—Information on foam cakes.

angel food cake Foam cake consisting primarily of egg white foam, sugar, and cake flour, with no fat or baking powder.

The rest of the sugar is combined with the cake flour before the dry ingredients are added, a fourth at a time, and folded into the egg white foam. By mixing the cake flour with the sugar, the tendency of the cake flour to ball up in the mixture is reduced, and the sugar–flour combination blends readily with the foam, allowing the folding operation to be done efficiently. Even though it tends to ball up because of its fine texture, cake flour is the flour of choice in making angel food cake. The tender gluten and somewhat reduced amount of protein in it are pluses in making angel food cakes, for the flour is needed only as a supplemental aid to the egg white protein for the necessary structural strength of the baked cake.

The flour–sugar mixture is folded in as efficiently as possible, with the process beginning just as soon as the egg white foam has been formed (Figure 17.2). The goal is to keep as much of the air trapped in the foam as possible, for it is this air (in combination with moisture from the egg whites) that is responsible for the leavening of the cake.

After the batter has been transferred very gently into an ungreased tube pan, a knife is used to cut through the batter once to eliminate any large pockets of air trapped in the batter, because they would be unattractive in the baked cake. The pan is not greased, thus helping the cake cling and pull itself up the sides of the pan. Baking should be initiated immediately, preferably in a preheated oven to avoid loss of air from the batter while the oven is heating.

The test for doneness is to touch the cake lightly with a finger when the appropriate length of time has elapsed. If done, the cake will spring back, but one that is not quite done will retain the indentation from the finger and may even fall. Such testing needs to be done quickly to avoid cooling the cake if it is not done; cool air will contract the air within the cake, which reduces the pressure within the cells and causes the cake to shrink or even fall.

When the cake is done, the pan should be removed from the oven and inverted immediately to allow the fragile structure to hang and stretch to maximum volume while cooling. Ideally, the tube pan has legs to keep the surface of the cake from contacting the counter while cooling. If this is not available, the pan should rest on a rack to allow air to circulate underneath, thus avoiding condensation. An underbaked angel food cake will fall from the pan when inverted, whereas an overbaked cake will be slightly dry and tough due to loss of moisture and overcoagulation of the egg white and gluten proteins in the cell walls.

Angel food cake of high quality is very tender, seeming to virtually "melt in the mouth." It will have an excellent volume, and the air cells will be rather uniform, of moderate size, and with thin walls. The crumb should be slightly moist, and there should not be any dry flour. The crust should be a pleasing brown.

Angel food cake mixes are popular because they eliminate the problem of what to do with the egg yolks left when making angel food cake "from scratch." They are also something of a time-saver. The dried egg whites used in angel food cake mixes require extensive beating, preferably with an electric mixer, to achieve the correct end point. The peaks need to just barely stand up straight when the beater is extracted from a foam of dried egg whites, which is an extension of beating beyond that required for fresh egg whites. Volume is affected adversely if dried egg whites are not beaten sufficiently.

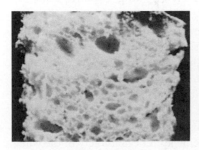 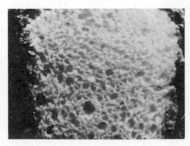 

Figure 17.2
Inadequate manipulation of flour and sugar in angel food cake batter results in uneven and coarse texture with low volume (left) in comparison with angel cake made with the correct amount of folding (center). Too much folding (right) develops the gluten so much that the texture becomes rather compact and tough.

sponge cake Foam cake comprised of an egg yolk foam and an egg white foam, plus a small amount of cake flour, water, lemon, and sugar, and usually baked in a tube pan.

Sponge cakes are similar to angel food cakes, with some features that differ. Perhaps the most apparent distinction is that sponge cakes have an egg yolk foam as well as an egg white foam. In fact, the egg yolk foam is unique because of the extensive amount of beating that is done to obtain a foam that is almost thick enough to pile, despite the addition of a small amount of water. Stability of the egg yolk foam is enhanced by the addition of a small amount of lemon.

The yolk foam is combined with the cake flour by gentle folding and then allowed to stand briefly while the egg white foam is being prepared, for the yolk foam retains its volume and elasticity better than the foam of the whites. The whites are whipped into a comparatively stable foam, due in part to the stabilizing effect of added cream of tartar and sugar. The two foams are folded together gently but quickly, just until a completely homogeneous batter develops, and no streaks of the yolk or white foam can be found. Extra folding should be avoided because it will cause excessive gluten development and also will release air from the foams unnecessarily.

Sponge cakes usually are baked in an ungreased tube pan so that the batter will cling to the pan and will help to increase the volume during baking. The tube permits air to circulate in the center area as well as around the outside edge of the cake; it also has the advantage of reducing the total distance that heat has to travel to reach the center of the cake and coagulate the proteins (Figure 17.3). If a sponge cake is to be a jelly roll, the batter is spread over the entire surface of a jelly roll pan in an even layer. The baking time is fairly short due to the thinness of the cake layer.

Sponge cakes are tested in the same manner as angel food cakes (by touching them gently and having them spring back, leaving no indentation in the surface). Unless being baked as a jelly roll, sponge cakes should be inverted to cool before being removed from the pan. A jelly roll needs to be removed and rolled in a towel while still warm so that the layer can be rolled without cracking.

A high-quality sponge cake has fairly fine, uniform cells and thin cell walls. When examined in cross section from top to bottom, the color should be a uniform yellow, with no streaks of yellow or pieces of egg white and no tendency toward formation of a layer toward the bottom. The exterior should be a pleasing, golden brown, and the volume should be very high.

Figure 17.3
Sponge cake, like other foam cakes, is baked in an ungreased tube pan; a knife is used to release the cake before removing it from the pan.

Technique is important in preparing a sponge cake, for inadequate beating of the egg yolks can cause thick cell walls, poor volume, and a tendency for a layer to form in the bottom of the cake. Underbeating of whites causes similar problems: The whites will not contain enough air in them, and they will tend to be a little fluid and drain from the yolk foam before the structure is set. Inadequate folding of the yolk and white foams can also cause a layer to begin to form, because the yolk foam is fairly heavy and will start to move toward the bottom. Overbeating of whites avoids this problem, but it will reduce volume due to some loss of extensibility of the white foam and also the increased amount of folding needed to blend the stiff white foam with the yolks. Toughness is due to too much development of gluten, which occurs fairly easily if extra folding is needed to blend the yolk and white foams.

JUDGING POINTS
SPONGE CAKE

- Golden-brown crust
- Large volume
- Uniform color (no layer and no pieces of white)
- Uniform medium-sized cells
- Tender, yet very slightly chewy

Chiffon Cakes   In some ways, **chiffon cakes** represent a transition between foam and shortened cakes, although they are classified as foam cakes. The formula for chiffon cakes includes oil and baking powder, neither of which is found in the true sponge or angel food cakes. Baking powder commonly is used as a source of leavening in both types; shortened cakes are made with fat, albeit usually not oil. The presence of these two ingredients promotes distinct differences between chiffon cakes and either angel food or sponge cakes. Chiffon cakes typically have the greatest volume, are finer in texture, and are more tender than angel food or sponge cakes.

Preparation of chiffon cakes begins by combining all of the ingredients except the egg white, part of the sugar, and the cream of tartar and then beating until the batter is smooth. Since this batter is quite fluid, extensive beating can be done without developing the gluten excessively. The whites then are beaten in a separate bowl until they reach the foamy stage, at which time the cream of tartar is added all at once, and the remaining sugar is added gradually. Beating of whites for chiffon cakes needs to be continued until the foam is stiff enough that the whites just barely stand up straight when the beater is pulled upward gently. This slightly exceeds the stage of beating for other egg white foam uses, but is necessary because of the distinctly fluid nature of the yolk–flour mixture that needs to be folded into the beaten whites.

Folding of the whites and the yolk–flour mixture must be done with careful attention to be sure that all of the fluid mixture gets blended uniformly throughout the whites. Unless this is done, there will be a tendency for the yolk–flour mixture to drain toward the bottom before the structure sets. Chiffon cakes are much more likely than sponge cakes to have evidence of a layer starting to form toward the bottom because of the fluidity of the yolk–flour mixture. This layer not only is unattractive to the eye, but it has a rather rubbery texture due to the egg yolk. The problem of separation is reduced considerably by being sure to use part of the sugar in the recipe (2 tablespoons per white) to help stabilize the egg white foam rather than placing all the sugar in the yolk–flour mixture. This sugar-stabilized egg white meringue has the elasticity necessary to permit thorough blending and folding of the yolk–flour mixture with the whites.

A chiffon cake of excellent quality is attractive, for its volume usually is greater than either angel food or sponge cakes. When well prepared, a chiffon cake will be tender, slightly moist, and uniform in texture from top to bottom, with no evidence of separation of a layer. The cells will be moderate in size and uniform, and the cell walls will be just a little thicker than those seen in shortened cakes. A chiffon cake is detectably more tender than a sponge cake, due in large measure to the oil in the chiffon cake and the extensive stretching of the cell walls, making them thinner and, therefore, more tender than those in sponge cake.

chiffon cake   Foam cake containing oil and baking powder, as well as the ingredients used in other foam cakes, which are combined and folded into an egg white foam beaten until the peaks just stand up straight.

JUDGING POINTS
CHIFFON CAKE

- Very large volume
- Golden-brown crust
- No evidence of a layer or pieces of white
- Uniform, moderately small cells
- Tender

TABLE 17.1
A COMPARISON OF FOUR BASIC TYPES OF CAKES

Type of Cake	Flour	Liquid	Eggs Number, Part	Eggs Method of Adding	Fat Type	Fat Amount	Leavening Agent
Angel food	1c	—	12 whites	Foam, folded in	—	—	Air (egg white foam stabilized with sugar and acid), steam
Sponge	1c	5 T water	4 yolks and whites	Foams, folded in	—	—	Air (egg white and yolk foams stabilized with acid and sugar), steam
Chiffon	1 1/3 c	6 T water	2 yolks and 4 whites	Yolks added with liquid, white foam folded in	Oil	2/3 c	Baking powder (1 1/4 tsp), air (egg white foam stabilized with sugar), steam
Shortened	1 c	1/4 c milk	1 whole	Creamed with the fat and sugar foam	Plastic fat	2/3 c	Baking powder (3/4 tsp), air, steam

Comparison of Foam Cakes   Foam cakes all contain an egg white foam to help promote volume and a pleasing, uniform texture. They also all are made with cake flour. Beyond these similarities, there are crucial differences in the various foam cakes. For example, in the use of eggs, angel food cake contains no yolk, whereas sponge cake uses a well-developed, fairly viscous yolk foam, and chiffon cake merely has the yolks beaten in with the other ingredients to make a satin-smooth batter to be folded ultimately with the whites. As can be seen in Table 17.1, chiffon cakes are the only type of foam cake using a fat (actually oil) and baking powder.

Stable egg foams, particularly stable egg white foams, are fundamental to successful foam cakes, even to chiffon cakes that contain baking powder for leavening. The use of sugar and cream of tartar is almost like an insurance policy, helping to assure good volume and a desirable texture in foam cakes. In Chapter 12, the action of sugar in promoting elasticity and a fine texture due to delaying foam formation was discussed; also of importance is the shift toward the isoelectric point of a key egg white protein that results when cream of tartar is added.

INDUSTRY INSIGHT
BAKERY BLENDS

America's concerns about overweight and its impact on health have generated extensive research to develop tempting foods with reduced calories. Fat substitutes have the potential for use in rich dessert formulations as a means of creating commercial bakery items for those who are watching their fat intake. However, these substitutes do not perform exactly like fats in cakes and other high-fat baked products. Formulas need to be adjusted extensively to achieve cakes and other bakery items that have satisfactory tenderness, moisture, texture, and volume.

Bakery blends have been developed in the food industry to provide an appropriate combination of special components that work in concert with the selected fat substitute to achieve the desired characteristics in the batter or dough and in the baked product. Examples of these components include whey protein concentrate, mono- and diglycerides, and sodium lactylate. In addition to the bakery blend, gums and/or starches and fiber may be added to help adjust the formula. The fact that these various blends and individual ingredient additions are needed emphasizes the important roles performed by fat in rich bakery items.

Shortened Cakes

Usually, the word *cake* conjures up visual images of a cake baked as a sheet or a layer in a round or rectangular pan approximately 2 inches deep. Such cakes have a finer texture, more tender crumb, and a richer flavor than characteristically will be found in foam cakes. These cakes are often called **shortened cakes**, a term denoting their comparatively high fat content. Variations are great within the category identified as shortened cakes. The liquid used may vary, the portion of egg (yolk and/or white) used and its treatment may differ, flavoring agents may cover a wide range, and even the leavening agents may be somewhat diverse.

The simplest of the shortened cakes often is referred to simply as a plain cake. This term designates one made with whole egg and just the basic ingredients (fat, sugar, cake flour, liquid, baking powder, and flavoring). White cakes are very similar, with the exception that only the egg white is used, usually in the form of a foam. Chocolate or **devil's food cakes** are a very popular form of shortened cake. The color range in chocolate cakes is quite remarkable, depending upon the pH of the cake batter. If extra soda is added to bring the batter well into the alkaline range, the chocolate cake will become a rich, deep-red mahogany color due to reaction of a pigment in the chocolate. Such a cake usually is called a devil's food cake. Chocolate cakes with a definitely brown color tone are neutral or even slightly acidic. Variations in color are the result of using an acidic ingredient (sour milk or cream, for example) and soda to react and form carbon dioxide.

Shortened cakes can be mixed in a variety of ways to achieve varying results. The methods are based on the conventional method, but also include variations to meet special requirements. In addition to the conventional method, the modified conventional, conventional sponge, muffin, and single-stage methods are suited to certain shortened cake formulas.

Conventional Method   The **conventional method** of making shortened cakes begins with a thorough creaming to create a very heavy fat–sugar foam, one in which the crystals of sugar actually dig tiny air pockets to create the cells entrapping air. This foam provides the framework of the structure, helping to create a uniform, fine texture as the air starts to expand during baking. Creaming should be terminated if the fat starts to melt at all from the physical action, for a very soft fat is unable to trap air effectively.

During the latter part of creaming, vanilla or any other flavoring agent should be added to the creamed mixture. This step is recommended because fats retain the flavor and aroma of extracts effectively and carry that flavor throughout the batter uniformly.

When creaming has been completed, the beaten eggs are blended in to establish an emulsion, with the yolks serving as the primary emulsifying agent. Formation of an emulsion in the cake batter is important to helping to produce a shortened cake with a fine texture. The combined manipulation involved in the creaming process and the blending in of the eggs should be stopped before the butter or other fat in the mixture becomes extremely soft. This precaution needs to be observed to avoid producing a curdled-looking batter, the result of breaking the emulsion. The texture of a cake batter containing a broken emulsion will be somewhat coarser than that of a cake produced with an emulsified batter.

The dry ingredients (flour, salt, and baking powder, plus cinnamon or other spices being used in certain recipes) should be sifted together prior to beginning the actual mixing of the cake so that the preparation of the batter can proceed without delay. Approximately a third of the dry ingredients is stirred carefully into the creamed mixture containing the eggs. This addition thickens the batter, which helps to avoid curdling or breaking of the emulsion when the first half of the liquid is added and stirred in. The second third of the dry ingredients is added and stirred until no dry flour is evident. At this point, the rest of the liquid is added, with stirring; finally, the last third of the dry ingredients is added and stirred (Figure 17.4). The best results are obtained when a cake recipe has been standardized, with a given number of strokes to be stirred after each of the dry ingredient and the liquid additions if mixing by hand, or a specified number of minutes at a designated speed on the electric mixer.

The conventional method frequently is chosen for making shortened cakes because this will produce a cake with a tender crumb, a fine texture, and excellent keeping qualities. The disadvantages of the comparatively long mixing time and the energy demands deter some individuals from using this method.

---

shortened cakes Cake containing a solid fat (commonly creamed with sugar), sugar, (usually) leavening agent, flour, eggs, and liquid.

http://www.joyofbaking. com/ButterCakes.html —Information on shortened cakes.

devil's food cake Shortened cake made with some excess of soda to achieve the desired deep mahogany color.

conventional method Method of preparing shortened cakes, in which fat and sugar are creamed, the beaten eggs added, and the sifted dry ingredients added (in thirds) alternately with the liquid (in halves).

Figure 17.4
Chocolate cake batter (made using the conventional method) is being mixed by Greece's leading pastry chef.

modified conventional method   Method of mixing a cake using the conventional method, but separating the eggs and adding the whites as a foam folded in at the end of mixing.

Modified Conventional Method   The **modified conventional method** of making shortened cakes differs from the conventional only in the way that the eggs are incorporated. In this instance, the eggs are separated, and the yolks are beaten together and added to the creamed mixture (rather than the whole eggs). When the other ingredients have been combined, the egg whites are beaten until the peaks just bend over and then are folded gently into the batter. By using the egg whites as a foam, additional air is incorporated into the batter to help promote a light cake.

Conventional Sponge Method   Yet another variation of the conventional method is the conventional sponge method, a technique particularly good for cakes low in fat. For this method, the eggs are separated. Part of the sugar (2 tablespoons per egg white) is reserved for making a meringue with the egg whites at the end of the mixing period, while the rest of the sugar is used for creaming with the fat as the first step in the mixing process. The yolks are added in the same fashion as in the modified conventional method, and the remainder of the mixing generally is comparable to the modified conventional method. The only difference is that the egg white foam is prepared by gradually adding the reserved sugar, beginning at the foamy stage. The added stability of the egg white foam as a result of the sugar is valuable in preparing a light cake with good volume and a fine texture.

Muffin Method   The muffin method of making cakes is the same as that used in making muffins (Chapter 16). To utilize this method, the fat must either be melted or an oil must be used so that the fat can be blended with the liquid ingredients, including the beaten whole eggs. All the dry ingredients are sifted together to blend them thoroughly before the liquid ingredients are added all at once and stirred in. This method is very fast compared with the rather deliberate techniques required in the conventional method and its variations. However, the lack of creaming of the solid fat and sugar causes cakes made by the muffin method to be rather coarse in texture. This method also results in rapid staling, as contrasted to the conventional method. For instances when the quality of the finished product is somewhat less important than the time required to prepare it, the muffin method may be acceptable.

single-stage method   Method combining all of the ingredients except the egg and possibly part of the liquid, mixing, and then adding the egg and any remaining liquid with beating.

Single-Stage Method   The **single-stage method** of making shortened cakes is basically the method used in making cake mixes; that is, the dry ingredients (sifted together) are combined all at once with the soft shortening and most or all of the milk. Usually a mixer is used for a designated length of time to combine these ingredients. Then the egg and any remaining liquid are added and are mixed into the batter for a specified period. This method is very fast, but it produces a fairly coarse texture, and the cake stales rapidly.

TABLE 17.2
COMPARISON OF METHODS FOR MAKING SHORTENED CAKES

| Method | Method of Adding | | |
	Eggs	Fat	Liquid and Flour
Conventional	Whole, beaten, blended into creamed mixture	Creamed with sugar	Alternately (1/3 flour, 1/2 liquid, 1/3 flour, 1/2 liquid, 1/3 flour)
Modified conventional	Yolk, beaten and blended with creamed mixture; whites, beaten with no sugar, folded in at end	Same as conventional method	Same as conventional method
Conventional sponge	Same as modified conventional except half of sugar used to make white foam	Same as conventional	Same as conventional method
Muffin	Whole, beaten and added with liquid ingredients	Oil or melted shortening added with liquid ingredients	All of liquid and dry ingredients combined at one time
Single stage	Whole, near end of mixing when last liquid added	With all dry ingredients and most of liquid	Dry ingredients and most of liquid added at same time as shortening; remainder of liquid added with egg after initial mixing period

These five variations of preparing the batter for a shortened cake are compared in Table 17.2.

Baking Prior to preparing the batter, the pans for shortened cakes can be lined on the bottom with wax paper if the cake is to be removed after baking. The sides do not need to be greased, for the cake can be released easily from the edges with a spatula or a knife. If a shortened cake is to be stored in the pan, the bottom of the pan is greased lightly, but wax paper is not used.

As soon as mixing has been completed, the batter should be poured gently into the prepared cake pan(s), and the pan should be placed in the center of a preheated oven. The oven temperature for shortened cakes usually is about 365°F (185°C), for this temperature is sufficiently hot to generate carbon dioxide rather rapidly from baking powder and to promote leavening from steam and air, yet it is not so hot that the structure sets before the cake has expanded to a desirable volume. Shortened cakes are baked until a toothpick inserted in the center comes out clean, a quick and easy means of being sure that the protein has denatured (Figure 17.5). They are overbaked if the cake is pulling away from the pan.

The cakes are cooled in the pan until the pan feels warm, but not hot, on the bottom. At this point layer cakes are removed by inverting the cake and pan onto a plate, then carefully removing the pan and peeling the warm wax paper away. Shortened cakes are not inverted to cool; their fat content weakens the cell walls to the point where the cake would fall out of the pan.

The changes occurring in a cake during baking are indeed remarkable. What starts as a fluid batter of small dimensions emerges from the oven as a light and tender, yet rigid, structure that can be cut and served easily. The cells have grown in size, and their walls have stretched and become considerably thinner than they were in the original batter. The liquid responsible for the flowing character of the batter has been used to gelatinize the starch in the flour. The combination of the binding of water in gelatinizing the starch and in developing the gluten and the evaporation occurring during baking explains the shifts in water occurring during the transition of the batter from the liquid state into a rigid structure.

The growth in volume during the baking process results from the expansion of air and carbon dioxide and the development of steam from water in the batter. Gases expand tremendously when heated, and these expanding gases push against the cell walls, which are able to stretch because of

Figure 17.5
When a toothpick inserted in the center comes out clean, the structure of a shortened cake is set, and the cake should be removed from the oven.

Figure 17.6
These shortened cakes have excellent volume and a level surface, indicators of their excellent quality.

their content of gluten. The elasticity of gluten permits the cell walls to keep stretching and stretching as the gases and steam within the cells push against the walls. Ideally, these cell walls will be quite thin, yet still strong enough to support the weight of the cake when the protein in the walls has denatured and cooled.

The transition from elastic protein to the rigid, denatured gluten occurs as a result of adequate heating during baking. This transformation occurs rather slowly, but it will take place first at the edges and the top and bottom of the cake where the oven heat first contacts the batter. If the oven temperature is too hot, the crust will set before the protein on the interior is denatured. Since the interior will still have elastic gluten and gases pushing against it, considerable pressure to expand builds up inside the cake until there is so much pressure that the crust breaks open. Then the interior batter will push upward through the break, resulting in a cracked, humped cake.

The converse occurs if the oven heat is somewhat below 365°F (185°C), for the fat in the batter will melt, and the cells in the cake will start to move around and bump into each other, sometimes coalescing into larger cells. Ultimately, the baked cake will have a coarse cell structure and thick cell walls because of this migratory mode. Some of these changes will occur if cakes are started in a cold oven. This is why preheating the oven is recommended for baking shortened cakes.

Evaluation   Shortened cakes should be very tender and have a fine, velvety texture, a pleasing flavor, and good volume (Figure 17.6). The texture should be uniform, with no evidence of tunneling. The crust should be golden brown and gently rounded, being neither humped nor sunken.

Deviations   Variations from the ideal shortened cake may result from several factors. A proper balance of ingredients and a good technique that traps air in the batter are required to achieve excellent volume. Volume and tenderness are factors that are closely related; an increase in the volume of a given amount of batter means thinner cell walls, as the same amount of solid material is stretched to cover a larger total surface area. An appropriate amount of baking powder promotes the desired volume. Too much baking powder can contribute so much carbon dioxide that the cake will collapse from the pressure generated (Table 17.3). There also likely will be an objectionable residue flavor when an appreciable excess of baking powder is used. On the other hand, too little baking powder results in a very heavy cake.

TABLE 17.3
POSSIBLE CAUSES OF LOSS OF QUALITY IN CAKES

Problem	Possible Cause
Too dark a crust	Too hot an oven; use of fructose or honey; position too near the top or bottom of the oven
Fallen center	Too much sugar; too much fat; too much baking powder; inadequate baking; too cool an oven; oven door opened during baking
Peaked or humped	Too much flour; too little sugar, fat, or milk; overstirring (too much gluten developed); too deep a pan
Poor volume	Not enough leavening; too cool an oven; too much fat or liquid
Large cells and tunnels	Too much baking powder; excessive mixing
Dry, tough crumb	Too much flour; too much egg; too little fat; too little sugar; too little liquid
Sticky, sugary crust	Too much sugar
Overflowing pan	Too small a pan; too much sugar; too much baking powder

---

JUDGING POINTS
SHORTENED CAKES

- Golden-brown, gently rounded crust
- Good volume
- Fine, uniform cells, no tunnels
- Tender
- Slightly moist crumb
- Pleasing flavor

Sugar has a tenderizing effect by promoting an increased volume. One effect of increasing the sugar is the need for an increased amount of mixing to develop the gluten. Of course, sugar influences the sweet taste of a cake; sugar also promotes browning of the crust. Small increases in the amount of sugar in many cake recipes will be acceptable, but large increases are likely to cause the cake to fall because of excessively high temperatures needed for the gluten to denature and set the structure.

Too much fat can cause a cake to fall and to have a greasy crumb. Increased fat also enhances browning. The tenderizing effect of fat in interfering with gluten development can be offset, in part, by increasing the mixing.

Most shortened cakes are made with cake flour to take advantage of the tender, less abundant gluten in this type of flour. If all-purpose flour is used, the cake will be less tender.

Eggs are valuable in shortened cakes because of their emulsifying ability, as well as their capacity to form foams. However, too much egg is a toughening factor in shortened cakes and can cause the crumb to have a somewhat waxy character.

All these ingredients clearly contribute to the characteristics of a specific cake. In addition to the factors noted, the extent of mixing is a vital influence on cake quality. There must be sufficient gluten developed to hold the cake together, but extra stirring will promote the development of very strong gluten strands. The manifestation of too much mixing will be the formation of tunnels and a tough cake.

SCIENCE NOTE
HIGH-ALTITUDE BAKING

The greatly reduced atmospheric pressure experienced at altitudes exceeding 3,000 feet influences the preparation of many different foods. For example, water boils at temperatures significantly below the 212°F (100°C) characteristic of sea level, which means that boiled foods require more cooking time as altitude increases. Similarly, baked products, particularly cakes, are affected significantly by altitude. Water will also evaporate more readily at high altitudes than at sea level.

Of particular importance at high elevations is the reduced pressure of the atmosphere bearing down on the surface. This means that the expanding gases and stretching cell walls in a shortened cake or other baked product will have reduced opposition to their stretching. This can cause cakes to fall before the structure is set.

To avoid having cakes fall when being baked at high altitudes, they should be baked at a temperature of 400°F (204°C) to help set the structure rapidly. Depending on the altitude, the baking powder should be decreased by between an eighth and a fourth (for every teaspoon, use 7/8 teaspoon at 2,000–5,000 feet or 3/4 teaspoon at 5,000–7,000 feet). A decrease of 1 tablespoon of sugar per cup of sugar up to 5,000 feet and of as much as 3 tablespoons between 5,000–7,000 feet also helps to strengthen the structure and prevent the cake from falling. To compensate for the increased loss of moisture, liquid can be increased by about 1 tablespoon at 3,000 feet and up to 4 tablespoons per cup of liquid at 7,000 feet. Fat may need to be reduced by between 1 and 2 tablespoons per cup to help strengthen the structure. When using foams, the egg whites should be beaten slightly less than normal to avoid trapping too much air if the cake is being prepared at a high elevation.

Cakes are very sensitive in their balance between ingredients and the pressures that they can withstand within their cells during baking. Therefore, these suggestions are merely guidelines. Experimentation is necessary to determine just what the ratio of the various ingredients will need to be to achieve the optimal product at different elevations. The general approach is to reduce the pressure within the cells and to strengthen the cell walls by modifying the amounts of the appropriate ingredients, specifically by reducing baking powder and sugar (and probably fat) and by increasing liquid to compensate for excessive moisture loss.

Figure 17.7
Drop cookies are baked from a dough that is stiff enough to be dropped from a spoon onto a baking sheet with little spreading.

http://www.joyofbaking. com/cookies.html
—Information on cookies.

COOKIES

Cookies generally are somewhat less delicate and sensitive than shortened or foam cakes. Nevertheless, there are guidelines to preparing and evaluating this type of baked product. Cookies can be categorized into three groups: drop, bar, and rolled cookies. Ordinarily, cookies are mixed by the conventional method, the same as is used for making shortened cakes. The proportions of the ingredients are quite different from those in shortened cakes, with the limited amount of liquid being the most obvious difference. Cookies frequently contain special textural and flavoring ingredients, such as raisins, chocolate chips, and nuts.

Drop cookies, compared with shortened cakes, are richer, and the dough is stiffer, which is necessary to keep them from flowing on the baking sheet. The added stiffness is achieved by reducing the liquid. Ordinarily, drop cookies are dropped from a spoon onto the baking sheet, but they also can be forced through a cookie press to create special shapes. Baking usually requires between 10 and 15 minutes at 375°F (190°C) to achieve the desired golden-brown color (Figure 17.7). The appearance is the criterion for determining that drop cookies are done.

Bar cookies ordinarily are slightly softer in their consistency than drop cookies are before baking. This permits the dough to be spread into a fairly uniform thickness in a rectangular baking pan. After baking, bar cookies are cut into the desired size and are removed from the pan. Sometimes they are frosted before they are cut and served. Their structure is strong enough that they can be cut while still warm.

Rolled cookies require a dough sufficiently stiff to be able to be rolled, cut, and transferred to a baking sheet. These doughs often are refrigerated to chill them thoroughly so that they can be rolled out with a minimum of flour. Extra flour adds to the toughness of the baked cookies and should be avoided as much as possible in rolled cookies. Stiff cookie doughs can also be made into logs, refrigerated, and sliced and baked even several days after mixing the dough if the logs are wrapped tightly to prevent loss of moisture.

The texture of cookies varies considerably, depending upon the specific type being prepared. Some cookies are quite crisp, while others may be chewy, or even soft. During baking, cookies should spread only a little, and they definitely should not be burned or underbaked. Cookies with too much fat in relation to the flour in the mixture will tend to spread too much, brown too quickly, and be greasy. On the other hand, cookies with too much flour will be tough and dry.

To preserve quality after baking, drop and rolled cookies should be removed from the baking sheet while they are still warm but not so hot that they tend to fall apart when lifted with a spatula. Warm cookies can be placed in a single layer on paper towels to finish cooling. When completely cooled, they can be transferred to an airtight container for storage. Brief storage can be very satisfactory at room temperature, but excellent quality can be maintained for an extended storage period when baked cookies are frozen in tightly sealed containers.

INGREDIENT HIGHLIGHT
WHAT'S IN A NAME?

Springerle and other old European cookie recipes sometimes call for hartshorn, a name that reflects the fact that this ingredient was actually ground hart's (stag) horn that contained ammonium carbonate. This substance (marketed as baker's ammonia) serves as a leavening agent because ammonia is generated from it when the cookie dough is heated in the oven, a fact that is evident from the smell during baking. Although it is not safe to eat raw dough containing baker's ammonia, the resulting baked cookies are both safe and delicious. Springerle are the anise-flavored "picture" cookies that are made by rolling the dough with a special rolling pin carved deeply with designs or pictures that are seen on the surface of the baked cookies.

PASTRY

Pastry is the simplest of the baked products in terms of ingredients, but may be the most difficult to prepare well. The simplicity explains the confounding difficulties that may arise during the preparation of a pie crust, for only the necessary materials are there—water and flour to provide for the gluten development necessary for the structure and some fat to promote flaky texture.

Gluten develops very easily in pastry, both because of the limited amount of water and because of the limited distribution of the fat. Water has to be provided at a level that allows the tenacious gluten to develop and hold the product together without making the dough too sticky and fluid to handle and roll out. This ratio is approximately 6 parts flour to 1 part water. This 6:1 ratio promotes gluten development readily, even with only a little handling.

Ordinarily, a flour product with an abundance of fat will be extremely tender because the fat coats gluten very effectively and blocks some of the water from interacting with the flour proteins easily. This happens to an extent in pastry, but the fat is not used to its maximum advantage. Instead, it is cut into pieces, leaving much of it encapsulated and unable to interact with the flour. In essence, the net effect of the fat in pastry dough is comparable to using a much smaller amount of fat, but completely coating the flour with the fat. The inefficient use of fat in typical pastry dough is responsible for much of the problem of tough pastries when people are learning to make pie crusts. Fortunately, tender and flaky pastries can be made with practice and understanding of the process.

Ingredients

In the home, pastry ordinarily is prepared using all-purpose flour that has been sifted once before being measured carefully. Pastry flour is used commercially because of its lower protein content and consequent tenderizing effect; however, it is not generally available to consumers in retail markets. All-purpose flour can be used quite satisfactorily as long as it is measured carefully and the dough is handled delicately and skillfully. The ratio of flour to liquid is extremely critical in preparing pastry doughs; hence, the need for careful measuring of sifted flour.

Salt in pastry dough is there simply for flavor. In fact, its omission is consistent with the recommendation today that salt intake should be reduced where feasible. Since pastry ordinarily is the foundation of a dessert or main dish with a flavorful filling, deletion of salt in the pastry is likely to go unnoticed.

Fat contributes flavor and tenderness. It also promotes flakiness and browning. Interestingly, although fat is included primarily for its tenderizing effect, its inclusion by being cut into small pieces is productive in promoting flakiness but counterproductive to tenderness. However, so much fat is used in pastry that it is possible to make an extremely tender crust despite the limited surface area of the fat.

The ratio of flour to fat can be varied considerably, depending upon the skill of the person making the dough. Practically anyone can make a tender pie crust using a ratio of 2 parts flour to 1 part fat (2:1). This ratio provides a considerable amount of surface area of fat, even when the fat is left in small pieces, and protects the flour rather effectively from the water. Of course, the calorie content of such a rich pastry is very high. Consequently, the somewhat leaner ratio of 3 parts of flour to 1 part fat (3:1) is the one used most commonly. This reduced amount of fat requires more skill on the part of the baker than is needed with the 2:1 ratio, but a tender crust can be prepared with a little practice. For those who are intent on reducing fat as much as possible and still making pastry, a ratio of 4 parts flour to 1 part fat (4:1) is the answer. However, this lean mixture is something of a challenge to handle without overdeveloping the gluten.

Water is added as sparsely as possible, yet it must be included to develop the gluten sufficiently to bind the crust together. With the proper amount of water, pastry dough will feel slightly dry, but the dough will stick together when pressed firmly. If too little water is used, the dough will crumble at the edges when being rolled. Even a small excess needs to be avoided because water promotes toughness.

Preparation

Technique is fundamental to the quality of pastry, and this technique begins with extremely careful measuring of the ingredients. The ratio of flour to water is particularly crucial to the ease of handling and the tenderness of the final product. Both of these ingredients require

http://www.joyofbaking. com/tarts.html
—Information on pies and tarts.

Figure 17.8
Pastry can be rolled easily into a thin, round sheet of the desired size when it is shaped into a flat disk and rolled evenly on a floured pastry cloth using a sock-covered rolling pin.

Figure 17.9
The edge of this crust is resting on the lip of the pie plate and holes are being made with a fork before baking so that the crust will hold its shape and not form blisters during baking.

especially careful measurements to ensure correct quantities. The actual preparation begins with a careful mixing of the salt and the flour, followed by cutting in of the fat. The cutting-in process is done most efficiently using a pastry blender, wielded with a light, tossing motion to help maintain the fat in the small, discrete pieces desired to promote flakiness. A relaxed flick of the wrist helps to avoid pressing the dough mixture into a compact mass. If a pastry blender is not available, a couple of table knives can be used in a cross-cutting motion. Cutting in should be done until the fat is in pieces about the size of rice grains.

The addition of the water is a critical process in making a tender, high-quality pastry, because this is when gluten development begins. The goal is to get uniform distribution of the water with an absolute minimum of manipulation of the dough mass. This goal can be reached by adding the water, only a drop at a time, while lightly tossing the flour-coated fat particles with a table fork. This action requires considerable coordination, for one hand is doing a flipping motion with the fork while the other is controlling the drop-by-drop addition of water all around the mixing bowl.

Care must be taken to add water throughout the dough, not just in a small area. The most effective distribution is done at the time the water is being dropped into the dough. By being careful to deliver the drops into dry area at all times, the problem of soggy dough in one area and a crumbly section in another part can be avoided. Ideally, the entire dough mass will be moistened slightly but not really adhering when all the water has been added. At this point, the back of a table fork is used to mash the dough together just enough to make it stick together in a ball. Minimum action should be used, for gluten develops very easily at this point.

In preparation for rolling, enough dough for one crust should be removed to a 10-inch piece of wax paper and worked in it very gently and quickly with the hands to form a ball. Then this ball is crafted quickly, on a lightly floured pastry cloth, into a flattened disk with a smooth circumference and no indication of cracks. In other words, this shaping prepares the dough to be rolled easily into the desired round shape needed for lining the pie plate.

Gentle pressure is needed in rolling out the crust so that the gluten strands in the dough will be eased into position and not be torn or stretched unduly. The pressure is eased toward the edge of the dough to help achieve a uniform thickness throughout the dough (Figure 17.8). The desired circular shape is maintained by continually changing the angle of the strokes of the rolling pin. Rolling is completed when the dough shows only a slight imprint when touched lightly with the finger and is large enough to fit into the pan with an extra half-inch margin for the edging.

Care must be exercised to avoid stretching or tearing when transferring the pastry from the cloth into the pie plate. An easy way to accomplish the transfer is to fold the pastry delicately in half and then into quarters. This permits easy handling and allows the dough to be unfolded and gently eased into the pie plate. The pastry needs to be fitted into the pan by letting the weight of the crust pull the crust down to the junction between the side and bottom of the pan, being careful to avoid stretching the dough to make it go into this portion of the pan.

A technique for helping the crust of a one-crust pie retain its desired shape is to trim the crust about half an inch beyond the edge of the pie plate, fold the edge under so that it stands on the lip of the plate, and then flute or do other trim finishing so that the edge continues to rest firmly on the lip. This keeps the edge from collapsing into the pie plate during baking. A pie shell that is to be baked before filling needs to be perforated with number of holes in the crust before baking (Figure 17.9). This can be done quickly using a table fork. These holes allow steam to escape during baking and help to prevent the development of pressure in pockets that would form large blisters or cause humps in the baked crust.

Baking of unfilled pie shells is done in an oven at 425°F (218°C) until the crust is a light golden brown. The baked crust should be a uniform golden brown, conform to the pie plate shape, and be tender and flaky. The quality of rolling and handling of the dough into the pie plate is evident in the finished crust, for a crust that has been rolled unevenly will brown unevenly, with the thin areas being much darker than the thicker areas. A stretched crust will pull away from the sides of the pan and may be almost bowl-shaped rather than have an angular junction between the sides and bottoms.

Flakiness is judged by looking at a cross section and is seen most easily by examining the edge trim area. The desired appearance is one of fine layers of dough so that the crust almost shatters or flakes when cut. Tenderness also is evaluated most easily at the trim area because the extra layer adds to the difficulty of cutting with a fork. This makes differences in tenderness apparent between pastry samples.

Factors Influencing Tenderness

The efficiency with which fat is protecting gluten from water in the dough is a key factor in influencing tenderness of a baked pastry. A soft, warm fat coats the gluten strands effectively. In fact, in one method of making pastry, the fat is whipped into boiling water before combining with the dry ingredients. This melts the fat and gives a very thorough protective coating. Oils, because of their fluid nature, are particularly effective in coating gluten strands to develop a tender crust. Even soft, but not fluid, fats are able to provide a reasonably good covering. Clearly, to make the most tender crust possible, fat needs to be sufficiently warm to be able to be spread easily. Chilled fats lack the ability to be spread enough to be very effective in promoting tenderness.

Tenderness also is promoted by keeping all manipulation to a minimum after the water has been added. The drop-by-drop addition of water (rather than the pouring it all in at one time) is very helpful in maintaining tenderness in a pastry because this technique reduces the amount of mixing required to distribute the water uniformly. Only enough mixing should be done to get the dough to stick together and to roll it out. Beyond this minimal mixing, the gluten will become too developed, and the crust will be unpleasantly tough.

The amount of water used is vital to the tenderness of the pastry when baked. Extra water means extra toughness as a result of increased gluten development. Increased flour or decreased fat also will have a toughening effect. Substitution of margarine or butter for shortening in pastry also results in a tougher product, for both of these table fats have water comprising about 15 percent of their total, which means that the fat level is reduced. Therefore, the actual content of such a pastry includes an excess of water and a deficiency of fat. Although table fats can be used satisfactorily to make pastry with a pleasing golden color and a distinctive flavor, it is necessary to modify the usual formulation to increase the fat measure, decrease the water, and eliminate the salt.

Flakiness in Pastry

Flakiness is the layered texture in a pastry when thin layers of cells are interspersed with flat holes between the layers. To achieve this, the flour, with its gluten strands, must provide a network incorporating small pieces of fat and some air pockets. During baking, the fat particles melt and flow a bit, often being adsorbed by the gluten strands. Moisture in the dough is converted into steam during baking, and this steam can collect in the little spaces left by the melting fat. Quickly, the steam expands, creating an even larger space between the gluten strands, and a flaky pastry is the result (Figure 17.10). Flakiness is promoted by using a firm fat rather than a very soft one or an oil, for these latter fats tend to be spread into thin layers throughout the dough, resulting in a mealy or grainy texture.

Flakiness and tenderness are two desirable characteristics in pastry, but they are not necessarily going to be developed simultaneously. For instance, oil will provide the most tender pastry, but such a pastry usually is mealy, not flaky.

Figure 17.10
Flakiness in these three layers of pastry is evidenced by the numerous cavities formed when the cells trap steam and air during baking and stretch the walls until the gluten denatures and the structure sets.

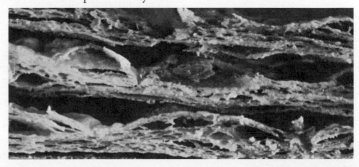

On the other hand, a hard fat can be cut in just until fairly large particles of fat are achieved. This circumstance will give a distinctly flaky quality, but the ineffective distribution of fat will promote a tough pastry. Fortunately, a reasonable compromise is achieved by using a firm, yet slightly soft, fat and cutting it in until it is the size of rice grains. This situation provides the potential for steam to collect in little pockets to create the flaky character and also distributes the fat fairly extensively so that the gluten will be inhibited reasonably in its development.

The choice of flour also influences flakiness versus tenderness. Pastry or cake flour reduces flakiness because of the weak gluten, but promotes tenderness; the gluten in hard wheat flours is sufficiently strong to promote the desired flaky quality but reduces tenderness.

Evaluation of Pies

One-Crust Pies   Custard, chiffon, and meringue or cream pies are familiar one-crust pies. The crust for chiffon and meringue pies always is baked before filling, and often the custard pies also are made with baked or partially baked shells to help reduce the soaking of the crusts of custard-type pies. These pies are evaluated in relation to the quality of their crusts and their fillings. The desired qualities of cream fillings and meringues are presented in Chapter 12.

Chiffon pies require (1) the thickening of egg yolk protein, (2) forming a stable egg white foam, and (3) folding a partially congealed protein mixture with the egg white foam to form a light gelatin-containing foam filling capable of being sliced and served. Chiffon fillings should be rigid when they are cut, yet not rubbery. They should hold a straight line along the cut edge but should not be difficult to cut. The fillings should be light, airy, flavorful, tender, and uniform in appearance and texture, with no rubbery bits of gelatin present. Due to the airy nature and the large volume of the foam, it is important to make the flavoring strong enough to present the desired result.

Custard pies are basically simply custard with a pastry base. Evaluation of the filling is the same as was outlined in Chapter 12 for baked custards. Perhaps the greatest difficulty in preparing a custard pie is avoiding a soggy bottom crust. If the filling is baked in the crust, a fairly long time passes before the liquid filling coagulates, which permits a fair amount of liquid to be absorbed by the crust as it is baking.

One solution is to bake the crust without the filling until the crust just begins to get a bit crisp, but is not browned before adding the filling. Thus, the crust can be baked adequately without overbaking the filling. Also, the hot crust begins to warm the filling from the bottom, which facilitates the baking of the filling. Overbaking the filling is to be avoided, for the resulting syneresis causes the crust to become quite soggy after baking. The filling is done when a knife inserted halfway between the center and the edge comes out clean. This test should be applied to any custard-type pie, including pumpkin and pecan (Figure 17.11).

One-crust pies should be made the same day they are to be served. The crust of even a well-prepared custard pie will gradually become a bit soggy if the pie must be held until the following day. Chiffon fillings and meringues are very difficult to cut and are rather tough the second day (Chapter 12). The fillings used in one-crust pies do not freeze well (Chapter 10); they should be made fresh when they are planned on a menu.

Two-Crust Pies   Two-crust pies are evaluated on the basis of both the crust and the filling. The top and bottom crusts should have no suggestion of sogginess. The crust should be about an eighth of an inch thick and should be flaky and tender. The appearance should be attractive,

Figure 17.11
To avoid syneresis, custard-type pies (e.g., pumpkin) should be baked only until a knife inserted halfway between the edge and center comes out clean. The residual heat will set the center portion as the pie stands after leaving the oven.

including a golden-brown color and a neatly crafted edge. By baking the pie as soon as the filling has been added and the top crust has been completed, the amount of time available for the juiciness of the filling to soak the bottom crust is kept to a minimum. Another way of helping to keep the crusts crisp is to be sure to cut an adequate steam vent in the upper crust. This permits the steam from the filling to escape in the oven during baking, which prevents a soggy upper crust. It also helps to keep the crust from being pushed way above the filling.

The filling of a two-crust pie should have a pleasing flavor and be somewhat thickened, yet not have a pasty character. The upper crust should be very close to, or resting on, the surface of the filling. This is facilitated in fresh fruit pies by packing the fruit quite firmly before baking to help eliminate wasted space between pieces (Figure 17.12). The pie should be beautiful

Figure 17.12
Two-crust pie ready for the oven. Note the edging resting on the lip of the pie plate and the cuts in the upper crust to vent steam.

to look at and boast a beautiful, golden-brown color. The crusts should be crisp and tender, preferably with a flaky texture. Although these pies usually can be held overnight without the significant loss of quality seen in one-crust pies, two-crust pies do lose desirable characteristics when held more than a few hours. If at all possible, two-crust pies should be served the same day they are made. If necessary, they can be prepared and frozen without baking until the day they are to be served. Two-crust pies generally freeze quite satisfactorily in their unbaked state. Then the baking period restores the desirable qualities of these pies.

Puff Pastry

Although the pastry used for pies is far more common than puff pastry, puff pastry is used with sufficient frequency to warrant at least passing mention here (Figure 17.13). Puff pastries are very flaky, rich pastries comprising many layers of thin pastry rolled with butter spread generously between layers. These pastries provide a graphic illustration of the fact that tenderness and flakiness are not necessarily parallel characteristics, for puff pastries always are extremely flaky and voluminous, but they often are rather tough to cut.

A well-prepared puff pastry is very flaky and high in volume because of the puffed up layers of dough. It will be only moderately tender. There will be numerous layers of dough that have a rich flavor as a result of the butter used to form layers between the dough layers. The high volume in puff pastry is promoted by baking in a hot oven, which generates generous amounts of steam quickly and almost seems to levitate the layers. These pastries form the foundation of such famous French pastries as Napoleons and patty shells, the latter being used as a base for various creamed entrées as well as for desserts.

Figure 17.13
Thiples (pronounced "thee-ples," are deep-fat fried spiral Greek pastries served with a drizzle of honey.

MIXES

Food companies have invested vast amounts of time, energy, and resources in developing mixes and convenience foods. There are frozen cakes, cookies, and pies, some being ready to eat, while others still need to be baked. The bakery section provides other items that are ready to eat, and the packaged mixes afford yet another alternative for people who do not wish to make their own items. Some mixes offer only a limited saving of time, while other products such as frozen patty shells are tremendous time-savers. An angel food cake mix saves having to separate a dozen eggs and resolves the dilemma of what to do with the remaining 12 yolks. Refrigerated biscuit and cookie doughs afford quick solutions to preparing something hot and fresh when an unexpected food need emerges.

With the large numbers of two-income families and the increasing pressures on time, the presence of mixes and convenience foods clearly is here to stay. These items not only save time but also may provide quality superior to the product that can be prepared by inexperienced people. Price comparisons between mixes and comparable products prepared in the home need to be made on an individual basis; products and consumer requirements vary widely.

Many people find food preparation is a satisfying outlet for their creativity. Mixes may tend to stifle creativity, but certainly it is possible to invent new applications of the mixes if creativity is a high priority. Even so, some cooks clearly will prefer to start with the basic ingredients, either because of possible savings or because of creative satisfactions.

Mixes contain additives that enable them to survive the rigorous demands imposed by the extended marketing period. These additives are listed in the ingredient label on each package, often with the explanation of the reason for their inclusion. Extensive testing has been done on the safety of the various additives; the general agreement is that our food supply is very safe and that the additives used in mixes are safe in the amounts used. Nevertheless, people who wish to avoid additives where possible can prepare baked products from the basic ingredients. Actually, the decision regarding the use of mixes versus preparation in the home is a very individual matter. Either approach can provide wholesome and nourishing food for consumers.

SUMMARY

Cakes, cookies, and pastries are desserts using flour as the basic structural ingredient, with sugar, fat, and other ingredients being added to produce a wide range of products. Foam cakes include angel food cake (which contains only the egg whites and no baking powder or fat), sponge cake (made with both yolk and white foams, but with no baking powder or fat), and chiffon cakes (made with baking powder, oil, yolks, and an egg white foam). These cakes are baked in tube pans and are inverted to stretch out their weak structures while they cool. Technique is important in each of the foam cakes to achieve a high volume and a tender product with a pleasing texture.

Shortened cakes are more tender and finer in texture than foam cakes because they contain a solid fat that is creamed with sugar to provide a very fine cellular framework. The basic method for making shortened cakes is the conventional method: The fat and sugar are creamed together, the eggs are added, and finally the dry ingredients and liquid are added in alternating order. Variations include the modified conventional method, the conventional sponge method, and the single-stage method. The ratios of ingredients and the baking conditions can cause variations in the finished products. For high-altitude baking, cake recipes need to have the baking powder and sugar reduced and the liquid increased slightly.

Cookies are categorized as drop, bar, or rolled. Their formulas are far more flexible than the ones used for making cakes. However, proper proportions of ingredients, careful mixing, and appropriate baking techniques still are important in obtaining products of high quality.

Technique is particularly important in making pastry, for its simple formula of flour, fat, liquid, and salt has the potential for making tender or tough products. A ratio of 3 parts flour to 1 part fat usually makes a satisfactory pastry, and a ratio of 4 parts flour to 1 part water produces a tender product when manipulation is done properly. Flakiness is promoted by cutting a solid fat into pieces the size of rice grains. Tenderness is promoted by keeping the water content to a minimum and by limiting handling of the dough as much as possible. These doughs need to be rolled to a thickness of about an eighth of an inch and then fitted carefully into pie plates. Either one- or two-crust pies can be made. The fillings should be prepared carefully to meet the criteria for the specific type of pie being prepared. In general, pies should be eaten the same day that they are baked.

Puff pastry is made with a very rich dough, and more fat is lavished between layers. By baking at a high temperature, the pastry is puffed up by the steam within the dough. Although very flaky, puff pastry generally is not as tender as pie pastry.

Mixes are available for quick preparation of baked products. Their use needs to be considered on an individual basis. For some people, mixes are an important part of the diet, while others prefer to make products from the basic ingredients because of the possibly improved quality, the creative experience, the possible saving in money, and the reduced amount of food additives.

STUDY QUESTIONS

1. What differences are found among the ingredients used in angel food, sponge, and chiffon cakes? How does each of the differences influence the characteristics of the baked cakes?
2. Prepare similar cakes from mixes and from recipes using the basic ingredients. Compare the time of preparation, cost, and palatability. When is a mix the best choice? When is a homemade cake preferred?
3. What ingredients are used ordinarily in making a shortened cake? What are the functions of each of these ingredients?
4. Why are modifications needed in a recipe for a cake being prepared at an elevation of 5,000 feet? What changes probably need to be made?
5. Describe the conventional method for making cakes. What is the reason behind each procedure?
6. Prepare three samples of pastry: one with butter as the fat, one with hydrogenated shortening, and one with salad oil. Evaluate each baked sample and explain how the fat influenced the quality of each pastry.
7. Compare the preparation of a puff pastry using the frozen ready-to-bake product and one made from the basic ingredients. Considering both cost and the value of time, which product better suits your needs?

SELECTED REFERENCES

Albers, M. J., et al. 2008. 2006 marketplace survey of *trans* fatty acid content of margarines and butters, cookies and snack cakes, and savory snacks. *J. Am. Dietet. Assoc. 108*(2): 367.

American Home Economics Association. 1994. *Handbook of Food Preparation*. 9th ed. AHEA. Washington, DC.

Anonymous. 1988. *Baking for People with Food Allerg*ies. House and Garden Bulletin No, 246. U.S. Dept. Agriculture. Washington, DC.

Bullock, L. M., et al. 1992. Replacement of simple sugars in cookie dough. *Food Technol. 46*(1): 82.

Charon, J. 2009. Chocolate dessert obsession. *Food Product Design 19*(1): 36.

Decker, K. J. 2005. High-profile flatbreads. *Food Product Design 15*(1): 97.

Elgidaily, D. A., et al. 1969. Baking temperature and quality of angel cakes. *J. Am. Diet. Assoc. 54*: 401.

Giese, J. 1993. Alternative sweeteners and bulking agents. *Food Technol.* 47(1): 113.

Hartel, R. W. 1993. Controlling sugar crystallization in food products. *Food Technol.* 47(11): 99.

Hazen, C. 2006. New fiber options for baked goods. *Food Product Design* 15(10): 80.

Hazen, C. 2009. Better trans-fat baked goods. *Food Product Design* 19(1): 26.

Hazen, C. 2010. Baking sans *trans. Food Product Design* 20(8): 32.

Hosome, K., et al. 1992. Studies on frozen dough baking. I: Effects of egg yolk and sugar ester. *Cereal Chem.* 69(1): 89.

Howard, N. B. 1972. Role of some essential ingredients in formation of layer cake structure. *Baker's Digest* 46(5): 28.

Howard, N. B., et al. 1968. Function of starch granule in the formation of layer cake structure. *Cereal Chem.* 45: 329.

Kaldy, M. S., et al. 1993. Influence of gluten components and flour lipids on soft wheat quality. *Cereal Chem.* 70(1): 77.

Koeller, K. and R. LaFrance. 2005. *Let's Eat Out: Your Passport to Living Gluten and Allergy Free.* R & R Publishing. Chicago, IL.

Kulp, K., et al. 1991. Functionality of carbohydrate ingredients in bakery products. *Food Technol.* 45(3): 136.

Pszczola, D. E. 1994. Blends reduce fat in bakery products. *Food Technol.* 48(6): 168.

Ranhotra, G. S., et al. 1992. Total and soluble fiber content of air-classified white flour from hard and soft wheats. *Cereal Chem.* 69(1): 75.

Ryu, G. H., et al. 1993. Effects of some baking ingredients on physical and structural properties of wheat flour exudates. *Cereal Chem.* 70(3): 291.

Tenbergen, K., and H. B. Eghardt. 2004. Baking ammonia: The other white leavening. *Food Product Design* 14(6): 110.

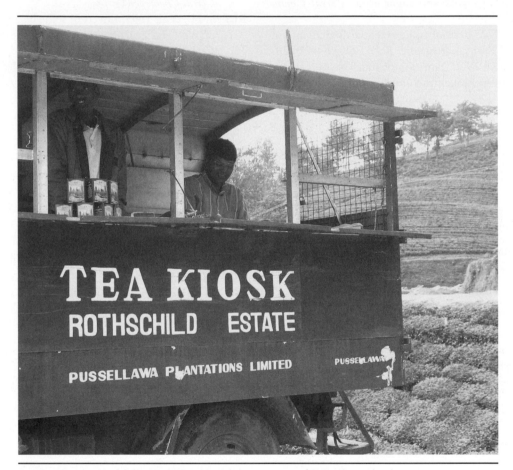

Tea is an important, labor-intensive crop in the mountains of Sri Lanka and India. Courtesy of Plycon Press.

18

Beverages

Chapter Contents

THE SYMBOL OF HOSPITALITY

Beverages, more than any other food item, are the symbol of hospitality among people. Whether they meet in an office or informally in a home, a beverage of some type frequently is served to welcome the visitor and set a friendly mood. Often coffee or tea will be prepared, depending upon the time of day and the cultural heritage of the host (Figure 18.1).

In recent years, a vast array of beverages began arriving in markets across the country, until now the choices are almost overwhelming. Bottled beverages are popular because of their convenience. However, coffee, tea, and hot chocolate (or cocoa) require preparation. This chapter focuses primarily on these beverages and their preparation, for the ability to prepare these hallmarks of hospitality is a very important part of the study of foods in the context of the social aspect of food.

COFFEE

In the United States, coffee is a symbol of hospitality, despite the fact that large numbers of people also consume other beverages, such as tea, particularly in the evenings. The tempting aroma and stimulating flavor of coffee are catalysts to help get conversations and ideas flowing, especially in the early morning hours. In business offices and industrial settings across the nation, the coffee break has become a respected tradition. In the home, coffee is synonymous with friendship and relaxation; students, however, often use the stimulating properties of coffee to help them stay awake while cramming for exams.

Key Concepts

1. Coffee and its variations are popular because of the pleasing range of flavors, which are due to differences in the source and roasting of the beans, and the lift provided by the caffeine.

2. Tea, a beverage brewed from tea leaves that may have been fermented (black tea), partially fermented (oolong), or dried with no fermentation (green), is popular with or without added flavors; variations include decaffeinated tea and herb teas without caffeine.

3. Hot chocolate and cocoa are popular beverages that usually are made with milk, which enhances their nutritional value while causing some scum formation.

4. Fruit beverage combinations need to be made with fruits that will maintain a desirable color.

5. Alcoholic beverages, such as wine, can be useful as cooking ingredients, as well as beverages; the alcohol boils off when food mixtures are heated, but the flavor remains.

Figure 18.1
In Abu Dhabi (one of the United Arab Emirates) and the Middle East, mint tea is often served from a pot of this design to honor guests.
Courtesy of Plycon Press.

Figure 18.2
Coffee originated in Ethiopia, but is enjoyed throughout the world today.
Courtesy of Plycon Press.

From its origin in Ethiopia (Figure 18.2), coffee has become a favorite beverage around the world and is served in many different ways to suit different national palates. Greeks and Turks savor a very strong, sweet, almost syrup-like coffee that is boiled, while Syrians add cracked cardamom seed and rosewater or orange blossom water to boiled coffee. The distinctive coffee served by Italians is prepared from darkly roasted coffee beans, which are ground very fine. Café au lait, the French way of serving coffee, is a combination of equal parts of strong coffee and hot milk. The Spanish version uses boiled milk to brew the coffee. And it comes as no surprise that coffee is served with a generous dollop of whipped cream in Vienna. Even in the United States, various versions of coffee are prepared, including the distinctive coffee in the South, which combines chicory with coffee. These are but some of the ways coffee is prepared and served around the world.

Production

The coffee available in orderly bags in the supermarket has come a long way from its original habitat. The five main coffee-growing areas around the world are located in the Equatorial Zone (between the Tropic of Cancer and the Tropic of Capricorn): East Africa, Brazil and Colombia in South America, the mountains of Central America, the islands of Southeast Asia, and the West Indies and Hawaii.

The varieties of coffee differ from one locale to another, but the climate particularly favorable to raising coffee is warm and moist, with the temperature hovering around 70°F (21°C), with daily sun and frequent showers. **Robusta** is a coffee variety that is rather hardy and can survive when conditions are a bit dry or too chilly. Its beans are rather light and acidic, characteristics that are suited to darker roasts. Robusta coffee is grown in West Africa and Southeast Asia, and some is grown in Brazil.

Arabica is a variety of coffee that is appreciated for its full body and mild aroma. Ethiopia may be the origin of this variety, but it is grown in Kenya, as well as Central America, Colombia and Brazil in South America, Hawaii (Kona), and islands in the West Indies.

Coffee beans are produced on trees, beginning with the blooming of the tree and followed by formation of the fruit, called a cherry (Figure 18.3). When the cherry is about six months old and turns to a deep purple or red color, it is harvested. Inside the cherries are the coffee beans. After being separated from the cherry pulp, the beans are dried and shipped to ports around the world.

Nations import green coffee beans from many different locales in order to obtain the desired characteristics that will be popular within that country. From these different varieties of coffee, blends of the beans will be made to achieve the desired mix of characteristics.

Following blending, the green beans are roasted to the extent preferred in the country where the coffee will be sold and used to ensure that the flavor will be appropriate to the palates of the nation. For example, Brazilians and Italians prefer a dark-roasted coffee bean, whereas many Americans, particularly on the West Coast, prefer a much lighter roast. A medium roast is used commonly in the East, while the people in the South choose a darker one. This is why roasting is done near the specific market.

Roasting accomplishes far more than simply a change in the color of the coffee beans. The browning of the beans is a sign of the chemical breakdown or caramelizing of some of the sugars and dextrinizing of some of the starch. These chemical reactions produce not only color changes but also flavor changes and a distinctive aroma of the beans. Roasting also causes an appreciable loss of moisture (about 16 percent) and a limited loss of other volatile compounds. These combined changes create the desired flavor in coffee, a flavor that is at its peak immediately after roasting.

The roasted beans are ground to create a large surface area to facilitate the extraction of flavoring compounds during brewing. Unfortunately, this also creates the opportunity for loss of the volatile flavoring compounds during storage. Particular attention must be devoted to airtight packaging once the coffee has been ground. Although there is some loss of volatile substances even from the whole roasted beans, the loss is really quite small compared with the extreme losses occurring if ground beans are not stored carefully. Flavor retention is maximized and oxidative changes are minimized by quickly packaging the ground coffee in hermetically sealed cans. For the maximum flavor, beans should be ground just before the brewing of the coffee.

http://www.howtobrewcoffee.com/Turkish.htm
—How to brew Turkish coffee in an ibrik.

http://www.ico.org/
—International Coffee Organization website.

robusta coffee Variety of coffee that is somewhat acidic and suited to dark roasts; grown primarily in West Africa and Southeast Asia.

arabica coffee Variety of coffee preferred by people who want a full-bodied, aromatic coffee.

http://www.coffeeresearch.org/agriculture/harvesting.htm
—Harvesting of coffee.

Figure 18.3
Coffee cherries will be ready for picking from the trees in Tanzania in about six months. Courtesy of Plycon Press.

Constituents of Coffee

Natural oils contribute significantly to the full, pleasing flavor of coffee because they carry and hold the volatile flavoring compounds. Unfortunately, the oils can become rancid during prolonged storage, particularly if oxygen is present. The stale flavor of coffee that has been stored carelessly or too long is partially the result of oxidized oils, a change that can begin as soon as the surfaces of the ground coffee beans are exposed to the air. Fortunately, vacuum packaging of the ground coffee is an effective deterrent. If unsealed coffee packages are kept tightly closed, the shelf life of coffee will be enhanced. Storage at a cool temperature, either in the refrigerator or the freezer if the coffee will be used only occasionally, also extends shelf life.

Caffeine the stimulating substance in coffee, is found in abundance in the green coffee bean, but roasting volatilizes some of it. Nevertheless, brewing the beverage extracts a considerable amount of caffeine from the ground coffee into the actual beverage. It is the caffeine that is credited with creating the stimulating quality of coffee. The type of coffeemaker used for brewing influences the actual amount of caffeine in a cup of coffee. Coffee brewed in a dripolator contains appreciably more caffeine per cup than does coffee prepared in a percolator (Table 18.1). Caffeine contributes to the somewhat bitter flavor of coffee.

caffeine Compound in coffee credited with contributing the stimulating effect of the beverage and also giving a touch of bitterness.

TABLE 18.1
CAFFEINE CONTENT OF COFFEE AND OTHER BEVERAGES

Beverage	Serving Size (ml)[a]	Mean Caffeine Content[b] (mg)	Caffeine per 100 ml
Coffee			
Percolator			
Nonautomatic			
5 min	150	107	70
10 min	150	118	77
Automatic	150	104	69
Dripolator			
Nonautomatic	150	142	95
Automatic	150	151	100
Instant	150	66	44
Tea[c]			
Bagged			
Black	140	28	20
Oolong	140	13	9
Green	140	14	10
Leaf			
Black	140	31	22
Oolong	140	17	12
Green	140	28	20
Cocoa			
Dutch process	150	14	10
Carbonated Beverages			
Coca-Cola	360	65	18
Pepsi Cola	360	43	12

[a]Coffee and tea measures are about 2/3 of a measuring cup; cola beverages are about 1 1/2 cups.
[b]Means of coffees represent seven brands; of bagged black teas, three brands; of bagged green teas, two brands; and of cocoa, two brands. All other data are for single brands.
[c]Brewed 1 minute.

The flavor of coffee is extremely complex and is derived from many compounds in addition to caffeine. Chromatographic analyses have revealed the presence of more than a hundred compounds contributing to the aroma and flavor of the beverage. Among these are sulfur-containing compounds, including hydrogen sulfide, dimethyl sulfide, and several others. Various organic acids and phenolic compounds also are credited with contributing to the flavor. Chlorogenic acid is the most abundant of the acids. Carbon dioxide also is found in freshly brewed coffee, which accounts for part of the sparkling quality of the beverage.

Some of the flavoring and aromatic substances are very volatile and can be noted when coffee is ground or when a sealed can is opened. However, the polyphenols are extracted from the grounds, along with the caffeine and many other compounds, when boiling water is present. By using temperatures slightly below boiling, the astringent quality of the polyphenols can be kept to a minimum.

The techniques for brewing influence the flavor of the beverage. Generally, the methods for brewing coffee used in the United States are directed toward minimizing the extraction of the polyphenols and optimizing some of the other delicate and pleasing volatiles. However, the preparation of Italian espresso is designed specifically to extract the bitter phenols by forcing steam through finely ground, dark-roasted coffee.

theobromine Stimulant contained in cocoa and chocolate.

chlorogenic acid Most abundant acid in coffee; contributes some of the sour and bitter quality to coffee flavor.

SCIENCE NOTE
CHEMICAL CONSTITUENTS IN BEVERAGES

Although there are far too many compounds contributing to the flavor and aroma of coffee and other brewed beverages to permit an in-depth study of all of them, there are some key substances to be examined. Caffeine, known for its stimulating effect, heads the list of substances of possible concern. The possible involvement of caffeine in heart disease, hypertension, bladder cancer, cancer of the pancreas, breast disease, and peptic ulcers has been the subject of considerable research. Concern has also been expressed about the possible teratogenic effects of caffeine when consumed by pregnant women because of the ease of passage through the placenta to the infant, who metabolizes caffeine quite slowly. Sensitivity to caffeine appears to vary considerably between individuals, but consumption of four or more cups of coffee can cause such symptoms as sleeplessness, an upset stomach, feelings of anxiety and depression, or even a rapid heartbeat. Probably pregnant and lactating women should restrict their intake of caffeine to avoid transmitting the stimulant to their offspring. However, proof of definite correlation between serious health problems and caffeine intake is still lacking.

The formula for caffeine and the formula for **theobromine** are given below. Note that the two compounds actually are quite similar. Theobromine is the primary stimulant in cocoa and chocolate, while caffeine is more abundant in coffee and tea, as well as in cola beverages.

Acids are important constituents in coffee. The most abundant acid is **chlorogenic acid**, but there are other organic acids, including formic acid, acetic acid, propionic acid, and butyric acid. The flavor contribution of this particular acid adds to the bitter and slightly sour characteristics in the coffee beverage.

Chlorogenic acid

Chlorogenic acid also is the parent of some key aromatic compounds contributing to the characteristic aroma and flavor of coffee. Among these compounds are furfural and many related compounds, such as 5-methylfuran and 5-methylfurfural, to name just a couple. Guaiacol is yet another derivative of chlorogenic acid. As can be seen from the structures of furfural and guaiacol, the furfural is a five-membered ring, while the guaiacol is a six-membered ring.

Caffeine   Theobromine   Furfural   Guaiacol

(Continued)

(Continued)

Another abundant bitter compound in coffee is trigonelline. Trigonelline can be converted to niacin, which accounts for the fact that coffee does contain a bit of this B vitamin. Pyridine and pyridinic substances are apparently derived from trigonelline when coffee is roasted.

Trigonelline   Niacin   Pyridine

In tea, some other polyphenolic compounds occur in significant amounts, contributing to the characteristics of the beverage. Chlorogenic acid actually is present in only rather minor quantities in tea, but **catechin** and related **polyphenols** are quite abundant in tea, accounting for much of the astringent character of brewed green tea.

An important enzyme, polyphenolase, is active during the fermentation of black tea leaves; the **theaflavins** resulting from the action of polyphenolase, although very astringent, apparently combine with caffeine in black tea to produce the pleasing briskness associated with this fermented type of tea.

Catechin

---

catechin A prominent polyphenol in green tea.

polyphenols Compounds containing more than one six-membered phenolic ring; contribute astringency to tea.

theaflavins Extremely astringent compounds in black tea which, in combination with caffeine, provide the brisk quality of black tea.

instant coffee Soluble coffee solids remaining after the water vapor has been removed from brewed coffee; often made by spray drying.

freeze-dried coffee Soluble coffee product made by freezing brewed coffee and sublimating the aqueous portion to obtain dry solids.

sublimation Change of state from ice directly to water vapor without passing through the liquid water state.

Selecting Coffee

The coffee section in most grocery stores now is quite an exciting spot, for there are numerous choices among brands, among grinds, among ground coffees and soluble coffees, and even among caffeine-containing and decaffeinated coffees. Start by deciding between soluble coffees and coffees that need to be brewed. The soluble coffees have the advantages of not requiring any special equipment and also of saving time. However, ground coffees that require brewing time and equipment for brewing have a fuller flavor than the soluble products, despite significant improvements in the soluble coffees.

Another choice is the flavor that is desired. There may be choices in degree of roasting, from light to dark roast. Frequently, flavor notes may be a choice, such as vanilla, hazelnut, and chocolate. Add the choice of caffeinated or decaffeinated, and it is clear that it may be necessary to keep an inventory of several choices to assure that the preference of the moment is available for brewing.

Soluble Coffee The array of soluble coffee products (flakes, crystals, and powders) suggests that soluble coffees are a modern product; surprisingly, the earliest version of soluble coffees has been traced back to 1771 in England. Records in the United States also indicate that a soluble coffee was field-tested during the Civil War in the 19th century. Considerable research has resulted in some soluble coffee products that are accepted quite widely by consumers.

Soluble coffees are marketed as **instant** and **freeze-dried coffees**. Spray drying can be used for producing soluble instant coffee. Freeze-drying is a four-step process that begins with freezing, followed by heat transfer of the heat of **sublimation**, movement of water vapor through the dried portions from the subliming ice crystals, and finally taking away the water vapor that emerges above the surface.

One of the problems encountered in developing a soluble coffee product was to attain a product that was dissolved very easily in hot water when being reconstituted. Fine particles presented a solubility problem because of the tendency to lump rather than dissolve readily. This problem was overcome by producing the soluble coffee in large particles that sank toward the bottom of a cup, dissolving on the way. These large particles are the result of agglomeration, or clustering, of the fine particles of coffee solids.

Retention of the volatile flavoring components in soluble coffees has been a subject of considerable effort by researchers. Now techniques have been developed to recover many of the aromatic volatiles lost during processing and then add them to freeze-dried coffee. By this technique, a freeze-dried product can be produced that approaches the flavor characteristics of the freshly brewed beverage.

Decaffeinated soluble coffees are marketed for people who want to reduce their intake of caffeine but still enjoy the flavor of the beverage. Caffeine is removed either from the green beans or from the liquid beverage prior to drying. The extraction process is so effective that only 2 percent or less of the original caffeine remains in the final product. Some loss of volatile flavoring components occurs during this step, however.

Public taste in coffee is becoming increasingly cosmopolitan, a fact that is reflected in the types of soluble coffees seen in markets today. Special flavors can be purchased for those who like the flavor of almond or another overtone blended with coffee. These soluble coffees gain their inspiration from the beverages served in Vienna and many other exotic locations where food specialties are noteworthy.

Ground Coffee Coffee connoisseurs usually prefer to brew their beverage rather than consume the soluble coffees. They may buy the roasted coffee beans and grind them themselves, or they may purchase coffee that has been ground already. Specialty shops often display a wide choice of coffee varieties, the beans being representative of coffee-producing regions of the world and of various degrees of roasting. Although the range may not be as dazzling in the supermarket as in gourmet shops, consumers can still choose among brands and among grinds. The grinds vary in particle size to meet specific brewing conditions in different types of coffeepots (Table 18.2).

The terms for grinds in Table 18.2 are described as follows:

- Turkish—powdered
- Fine—finer than granular sugar
- Medium—coarse sand
- Extra fine—finer than sugar, but not quite powdered. Grains should still be discernable to the touch
- Coarse—like heavy-grained kosher salt.

For instance, coarse grind is designed for use in percolators, while medium or fine grind is intended for use in dripolators, depending on the shape of the filter. Coarse grind provides a slightly limited surface area, which is compatible with the extensive recirculation of water in the grounds during percolation. The rather small particle size of drip grind provides an extensive surface area, thus permitting adequate extraction during the limited contact time between water and coffee grounds.

http://www. ineedcoffee.com/03/cof-feegrind/

—Description of grinds of coffee.

TABLE 18.2 SUGGESTED GRINDS FOR DIFFERENT COFFEEMAKERS	
Drip coffeemakers (flat-bottomed filters)	Medium
Drip coffeemakers (cone filters)	Fine
Plunger pot/French press	Coarse
Percolator	Coarse
Espresso machines (pump or steam)	Extra fine
Vacuum coffeepot	Coarse
Ibrik	Turkish

Preparing the Beverage

There are four requirements for making an excellent cup of coffee: (1) fresh coffee of the grind appropriate for the pot being used, (2) water with a pleasing flavor that is not hard, (3) a clean coffeemaker, and (4) controlled heat. If any of these essentials is missing, the quality of the finished beverage will be adversely affected. Fortunately, these conditions can be controlled.

Coffee beans or ground coffee may suffer flavor impairment by two routes of particular significance. Because much of the flavor in coffee is contributed by volatile flavor constituents, flavor loss may occur during storage, simply because of vaporization of key components from the dry coffee. The second problem with flavor concerns the fact that coffee contains some oils, and oils become rancid as they take up oxygen. Fortunately, both these difficulties can be reduced by careful storage. To prevent loss of volatiles and entry of oxygen in the storage container, coffee needs to be stored in a tightly sealed container. By keeping packages tightly closed except when actually measuring coffee, the original flavor can be maintained satisfactorily for at least two weeks after the package has been opened. Changes can be retarded and quality maintained for a reasonably extended period if the coffee is tightly enclosed and stored in the refrigerator or freezer.

Not surprisingly, the flavor of water used to brew coffee influences the flavor of the brewed beverage. Sulfur overtones or other distinctive characteristics of the water are transmitted to the beverage, despite the rather strong flavor of the coffee itself; water with heavy mineral content affects the clarity of the beverage; and hard water causes precipitation of the polyphenols extracted from the coffee during the brewing period. The murky appearance of the coffee is undesirable. If tap water is not of sufficient quality to produce a good cup of coffee, bottled water may be used. However, most commercial water supplies are satisfactory for making coffee of excellent quality.

Coffeepots must not only look clean but also smell clean if a beverage of high quality is to be produced. Coffeemakers need to be washed with soapy water to remove any of the oils from the beverage that are clinging to the pot. Of course, a very thorough rinsing is needed after the washing has been completed. This eliminates the soapy flavor overtones that come from traces of soap or detergent. Particular attention during washing needs to be directed toward the pouring spout and any seams or joints where an oily film might collect. To be sure a coffeepot is clean enough to make a quality cup of coffee, check the aroma just as the cover is being removed. A stale aroma is a clear indication that additional cleaning should be done before the pot is used. Special coffeepot cleaners can eliminate the oily film in spots that are difficult to reach.

The optimum temperature range for brewing coffee is 185°–203°F (85°–95°C). At temperatures slightly below boiling, the bitter polyphenols are extracted less readily than when the brew actually is boiling. This circumstance exists in a dripolator, but not in a percolator.

Yet another aid to producing an excellent coffee is to use filter paper for holding the grounds. Filter papers designed for specific coffeemakers prevent even the finest particles of the ground coffee from collecting in the beverage and affecting the desired clarity.

The amount of grounds to use in brewing coffee is a subject open to debate, because people's tastes in the strength they desire cover quite a wide range. Cookbooks suggest using 2 tablespoons of coffee grounds per cup of the brewed beverage (3/4 cup of water). However, some people prefer the weaker beverage that results from using 1 tablespoon per cup. Less than 2 tablespoons per cup probably will be appropriate when coffee is being prepared in large quantities, but the exact amount to use will be determined by the strength preferred in the beverage and by the type of equipment being used. Whether making coffee in quantity or in a small pot, the best results usually are obtained if the pot is filled to at least three-fourths of its capacity.

In making coffee, two basic designs of pots are available to consumers: percolators and dripolators. A simple kettle can be used to make steeped (also called boiled) coffee when no coffeepot is available. Various ways of preparing coffee are described in the paragraphs that follow.

Dripolator   The traditional design of a **dripolator** is composed of three parts: a pot to collect the beverage, a center container for holding the coffee grounds, and an upper unit to hold the heated water (Figure 18.4). An automatic variation of the dripolator is used extensively for

dripolator   Coffeemaker with a unit for the heated water, a section for the coffee grounds, and a pot at the bottom to collect the coffee.

Figure 18.4
Diagram of a dripolator.

brewing coffee today. This unit differs in that it has a compartment to hold the water while it is being heated to the brewing temperature, at which time the water exits into the coffee grounds en route to the collecting pot. Another version of the dripolator has a conical-shaped upper unit, which is lined with filter paper to contain the coffee grounds and prevent them from falling into the pot below.

Preparation of dripolator coffee begins with heating the water for the beverage to the boiling point. The coffee grounds are placed in the perforated basket designed for them. The upper unit and the drip-grind coffee grounds are measured and positioned above the pot in readiness for brewing the beverage. Just as soon as the water comes to a rolling boil, the measured amount of water is poured into the top unit of the assembled pot. A cover should be placed on the unit containing the water to help retain the heat while the water is being held and passed through the grounds. When all the water has drained through the coffee grounds, the upper assembly and the grounds are removed, and the cover is placed on the pot containing the beverage. If necessary, the beverage is reheated to bring it to the desired serving temperature.

Automatic dripolators are popular because of their convenience and the excellent quality of the brewed coffee. Preparation requires adding a measured amount of water to the water compartment, placing the desired amount of coffee grounds (medium or fine grind, depending on the filter) in the basket that has been lined with filter paper, and then turning on the heating element to brew the beverage. The heat can be left on to keep the coffee hot, but the flavorful volatiles will begin to vanish if the beverage is kept warm for an extended period.

Dripolator coffee is stimulating because of the high caffeine content and is flavorful without being bitter. The pleasing flavor is developed because the water passing through the grounds is a little cooler than boiling and has been in contact with the grounds only briefly. This combination extracts the desirable flavor components and only a minimal bitterness.

Cone-topped dripolators in which the coffee grounds are placed in the same unit with the boiling water permit a longer contact period between water and the coffee grounds than occurs in the standard dripolator. In this pot design, the entire quantity of water is in contact with the grounds until it drains through. This permits extraction of the bitter components. There also will be loss of some of the volatile desirable flavor compounds unless the pot has a cover. Although these pots have been marketed as the gourmet version of the dripolator, they can produce a less desirable product than is obtained with the traditional dripolator.

Coffee Press   A **coffee press** consists of a tall glass or ceramic cylinder fitted with a handle, a lid, and a filter on a long handle. Coffee is brewed by pouring boiling water into the press and stirring in coarsely ground coffee before covering and letting the beverage brew two to three minutes. Then the filter is pressed straight down carefully to force the grounds to the bottom, leaving the clear beverage ready to be poured and enjoyed. Although a coffee press is a convenient way to brew coffee, the beverage may be a bit cool by the time it is ready to be served. It also may have some sediment that escapes as the filter is being pressed downward.

Percolator   **Percolators** consist of a single unit in which a perforated basket containing the measured regular grind coffee is placed, suspended on a hollow stem (Figure 18.5). The water is measured into the pot, the lid is placed firmly on the assembly, and heat is applied rapidly until water begins to pass up through the stem, hitting the lid and falling onto the basket containing the coffee grounds. When this "perking" action begins, the heat is adjusted to maintain a slow, but continuing, action.

This form of brewing circulates water continuously through the grounds at a very high temperature, with the result that bitter compounds are extracted to a greater extent than ordinarily occurs in making dripolator coffee. The longer the period of percolation, the stronger the brewed beverage will be. Often coffee is percolated for five minutes, but some people prefer the beverage resulting from a brewing period of as little as three minutes. When the desired strength has been achieved, the basket with the coffee grounds and the stem holding the basket are removed from the pot, and the lid is replaced on the pot to help retain heat. If desired, the pot may be heated at a low setting to maintain a serving temperature for up to an hour without an undue loss of quality.

coffee press   Cylindrical container equipped with a handle, lid, and long-handled filter for brewing coffee.

percolator   Coffeepot containing a basket for ground coffee that is suspended on a hollow stem above the water in the pot, a design that allows the water to recirculate continuously through the grounds.

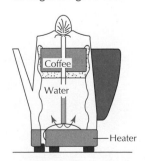

Figure 18.5
Diagram of a percolator.
Courtesy of Plycon Press.

Automatic percolators can be set to the desired length of percolating time, thus eliminating the need for careful timing during brewing. Most automatic percolators need to be started with cold water so that the high heat needed for the percolation will be triggered to brew the beverage.

Percolator coffee has slightly different flavor characteristics from dripolator coffee as a result of the differences in the brewing techniques. The circulating action in a percolator introduces air into the beverage to a far greater extent than occurs in a dripolator, and this causes some loss of flavor in percolator coffee. The recirculation of water through the grounds over and over again during the brewing period enhances the bitter overtones of coffee made in a percolator, while dripolator coffee has only a limited opportunity to extract these components. Generally, dripolator coffee will be superior to percolator coffee.

Steeped Coffee   Even when a coffeepot is not available, it is possible to make coffee by placing the coffee grounds directly in water heated almost to boiling. The grounds should be tied in a cloth bag so that they can be removed following the steeping period. Optimal quality of steeped coffee is achieved by being careful not to boil the water during the steeping period and by being sure to keep the grounds in the pot only as long as is needed to achieve the desired strength and flavor.

The fact that this version of coffee frequently is called boiled coffee reveals that such temperature control often is not maintained during the brewing period. When regular coffee is measured into a bag and allowed to steep with the appropriate amount of water just under boiling for five minutes, steeped coffee should be of acceptable quality. However, if boiled or if allowed to steep too long, steeped coffee can be distinctly inferior to either percolator or dripolator coffee. The addition of some egg white or even just the egg shell is useful in binding loose coffee grounds in steeped coffee.

Evaluating Coffee

The diverse cultural patterns influencing coffee brews around the world make it difficult to define a "good" cup of coffee. U.S. consumers generally prefer a clear beverage with a delightful, full aroma and a rich flavor free of any bitterness. The color desired is a deep, lively brown, and the beverage should be free of any suggestion of sediment or particles of grounds.

For optimum enjoyment, hot coffee should be served steaming. Freshly made coffee is at its peak of flavor and aroma. When held at serving temperature for an extended period of time, the flavor gradually will be lost, due to the volatilization of some of the key aromatic compounds. To alleviate this problem when coffee is desired throughout the day, simply heat a cup of coffee in a microwave oven as needed, leaving the remainder of the pot at room temperature.

Iced Coffee

Sometimes coffee is served iced rather than hot. The preparation of iced coffee involves simply brewing a strong pot of coffee and then pouring the hot beverage over an excess of ice, part of which melts and dilutes the beverage to the normal strength. Preferences regarding the strength of iced coffee vary, but the usual practice is to prepare the hot coffee half again or even twice as strong as the beverage. This increased strength is achieved by extra grounds, not extra brewing time. In other words, coffee to be iced should be made with 3–4 tablespoons of ground coffee per cup of the hot beverage desired. The iced coffee resulting from this level of grounds should have a pleasing flavor, with no bitterness and with a deep color.

JUDGING POINTS
COFFEE

- Pleasing aroma
- Clear and free of sediment
- Deep brown color
- Rich, full flavor free of bitterness

As people have had increasing opportunities for experiencing specialties from other countries, the variety available in food products has mushroomed, and variety in coffee reflects this trend. A particularly popular version of coffee that has been adopted from Europe is **espresso**, a strong coffee with its roots in Italy. Some people are certain that espresso is only for the hardy, the adventurous, and the mechanically competent. This last requirement stems from the need to be able to operate an espresso machine, complete with its pressurized steam. Espresso gets its impact because it is brewed using a dark-roasted, finely ground coffee subjected to steam under pressure. This combination is guaranteed to produce a very strong, somewhat bitter beverage. The fact that it is served black heightens the intense impact of espresso.

Italians also deserve credit for **cappuccino**, a close relative of espresso, that announces itself loudly when being brewed, because it is espresso topped with steamed milk foam. A dusting of sweetened cocoa powder or cinnamon often caps this dramatic presentation. A foam mustache may be the reward for those who drink cappuccino.

Europeans are noted for starting the day with **café au lait**. This beverage is brewed quietly, its scalded milk being added without the dramatic flourish of steam. Nutritionally, this is an improvement over espresso or black coffee because it usually is made with equal parts of coffee and milk.

Iced coffee can also be prepared by pouring coffee of regular strength into ice cube trays and freezing them. For use, these cubes are placed in a glass, and then coffee of regular strength is poured over the coffee cubes. When these melt, the coffee still maintains its desired strength. A convenient variation involves dissolving instant or freeze-dried coffee in hot water and pouring this mixture over ice.

Regardless of the technique used in making iced coffee, the end product should have a distinct, coffee-like flavor, and the beverage should be sparklingly translucent.

TEA

The leaves from a shrub (*Camellia sinensis*) in the Theaceae family serve as the base for a beverage that has been popular since about 350 A.D., at which time the Chinese were known to have included this brewed product in their diet. The spread of the knowledge of this brew touched key points throughout the world, beginning with adoption of the drink in Japan and then spreading to the Arabs, Venetians, English, and Portuguese. By the mid-17th century, tea had even made its way to the United States. Perhaps the most notable mention of tea was in America, when the colonists angrily staged the Boston Tea Party, a party quite different from the traditional high tea found in the British Commonwealth.

Tea bushes thrive in a tropical climate and at altitudes up to about 6,000 feet, conditions found in Japan, India, Sri Lanka, and the East Indies, as well as in part of China (Figure 18.6). Surprisingly, research on the agricultural and production problems of tea is being conducted in the United States to determine the feasibility of producing tea here. Although *Camellia sinensis*

espresso Extremely strong and rather bitter Italian coffee resulting from brewing finely ground, dark-roasted coffee with steam.

cappuccino Espresso topped with steamed milk foam, sometimes garnished with a dusting of sweetened cocoa powder or cinnamon.

café au lait Coffee with an equal amount of scalded milk.

Camellia sinensis Shrub in the Theaceae family, the leaves of which are plucked and used to make tea.

Figure 18.6
Men and women are harvesting the bud and next two leaves of new growth at the tips of the branches, a technique that assures that the tea from the mountains of southern India will be of high quality. Courtesy of Plycon Press.

http://www.tea.co.uk/tea-and-business

—Background information on tea.

http://www.pureceylontea.com/

—Sri Lanka Tea Board website.

orange pekoe   Top grade of black tea.

http://www.kaburagien.co.jp/museum/english/museum/index.php

—Historical information and description of a museum about green tea.

green tea   Somewhat astringent tea that has not been fermented.

bushes thrive on a rainfall of up to 68 inches annually, irrigation appears to be a satisfactory substitute for rain.

A pound of tea may appear insignificant when held in the hand, but considerable human labor is required to produce even this small quantity. The bushes have to be cultivated and pruned carefully for three years before the first crop can even be harvested. Fortunately, the shrubs may remain productive for as long as 50 years if they are kept pruned to a height of between three and five feet. Plucking of the tea leaves is done exclusively by hand, a slow task yielding at most only about nine pounds of marketable leaves a day per picker. Only the bud and next two leaves are picked from the tips of the branches when high-quality tea is the goal.

Types of Tea

Teas are marketed under many different, often romantic-sounding names, but all of these are categorized under three main types: green, oolong, and black. All three can be produced from the same tea leaves, the difference being created in the processing of the leaves. Black tea is the most popular of the three types in the United States, but green and oolong teas also are available in most markets.

The grades of tea are indicated by names familiar and meaningful to people in the business, but which carry little meaning to consumers. For example, the top grade of black tea leaves is designated as **orange pekoe**. In descending order, the other grades of black tea leaves are pekoe, souchong, broken orange pekoe, broken pekoe, broken pekoe souchong, fannings, and dust. The tea found in markets in the United States usually is a blend of more than one grade. However, in Darjeeling in northern India or in other regions famous for their tea, it is possible to purchase the desired single grade.

Specialty teas are other choices available in the market. A familiar illustration is jasmine tea, so named because of the dried jasmine petals added to the tea leaves to modify the flavor. Orange rind and cinnamon are other flavoring agents. These are only a few of the dried food and spice ingredients that are included in special tea blends. Choices are available to please any palate and to suit any occasion.

Green tea   **Green tea** is the simplest of the three types of tea to produce. The initial step in processing the freshly picked tea leaves to make green tea is to steam the leaves (Figure 18.7). The heat involved in steaming is sufficient to inactivate the enzymes in the leaves so that chemical changes are halted. Following steaming, green tea leaves are rolled to break the leaves and then are fired. Firing is the drying process in which the leaves are subjected first to a temperature of 200°F (93°C) and finally to a lower temperature of about 120°F (49°C). This results in a moisture level of only about 3 percent in the tea leaves, which makes it possible to store the leaves for extended periods of time when packaged properly.

Figure 18.7
Freshly picked tea leaves are ready for steaming to inactivate enzymes, the first step in processing to produce green tea. Courtesy of Plycon Press.

Green tea leaves have a soft, greenish-gray color. Green tea is produced in several Asian countries, but it is especially popular in Japan (Figure 18.8). The beverage characteristics of green tea, notably the very delicate green color and slightly **astringent** quality, complement the foods of Japan particularly well.

Oolong Tea Production of **oolong tea** begins by allowing the leaves to wither slowly until they are ready to be rolled to release some of the fluid and enzymes from the cells in the leaves. During the subsequent fermentation period, the enzymes begin to catalyze chemical changes, the result of which is a darkening of the leaf and a milder, less astringent flavor in the brewed beverage. This fermentation period is quite brief and is done on the tea farms where the leaves are harvested. The subsequent firing to halt the enzymatic changes is done in towns. Taiwan is recognized as a producer of particularly fine oolong tea.

Black Tea The production of **black tea** begins just like that of oolong tea, namely, by spreading the leaves on racks to wither slowly before being rolled to break open the cells and release the juices and enzymes (Figure 18.9). As soon as rolling is completed, the leaves are sifted and spread thinly on trays to ferment. During the fermentation process, the various polyphenols are oxidized to produce the dark color of the leaves and the rich, deep amber color characteristic of the brewed beverage. Oxidation of the polyphenols gives rise to theaflavins, which are astringent alone, but simply provide briskness to the brewed beverage when in the presence of caffeine.

Figure 18.8
Green tea is the preferred type of tea in Japan. Courtesy of Plycon Press.

astringent Characteristic of drawing together or puckering; green tea is noted for causing a puckering and rather dry mouthfeel if the leaves are steeped more than five minutes.

Oolong tea Tea that has undergone limited fermentation, resulting in characteristics intermediate between green and black tea.

black tea Brisk, rather mild, deep amber-colored tea produced by an extended fermentation period during the processing of tea leaves.

Figure 18.9
The steps in producing black tea are summarized in this sign at a tea factory in Sri Lanka. Courtesy of Plycon Press.

Figure 18.10
Firing and drying follow the conclusion to conclude the manufacturing of black tea.
Courtesy of Plycon Press.

tannins   Another term for polyphenols.

The fermentation of black tea is done at a moderate temperature (70°–80°F [21°–27°C]) for a long period of time. Finally, the fermented leaves are fired to dry them for packaging and storage. Some caramelization occurs during the drying (Figure 18.10), a chemical change contributing to the characteristic color and flavor of black tea.

Quality in black tea is related directly to the polyphenol content and the enzyme activity upon the polyphenols during processing. The importance attached to using the buds and next two leaves derives from the fact that these are higher in both polyphenol content and the copper-containing polyphenolase needed for optimum flavor development in black tea. The other leaves, being lower in the polyphenols and polyphenolase, develop slightly less desirable qualities in black tea than can be achieved by using orange pekoe (the desired bud and two leaves) to produce black tea.

Preparing the Beverage

Tea is prepared in different ways and is intended to meet the preferences of the group being served. In Japan and China, tea is intended primarily as a thirst quencher. The tea leaves are allowed to steep in the pot with the water until all of the beverage has been poured, which results in increasing astringency as the pot sits. In comparison with the U.S. version of tea, the British and nations that have been under the influence of England brew a very strong and stimulating beverage by using a longer and hotter steeping period than is used in the United States.

Tea of high quality is needed for brewing a beverage of excellence. This means buying a high grade of tea and then handling it appropriately after purchase. Fortunately, tea does not contain oils, nor does it rely heavily on volatile components for its flavor; this is quite a different circumstance from that of coffee. Storage of tea can be quite long in the home if the package is fairly airtight to keep volatile losses reduced and prevent entry of moisture. Refrigerated storage is not necessary, even when the tea will be held on the shelf for many weeks.

Tea preparation by American practices is quite simple, requiring only a high quality of tea, good water, and a china or glass teapot with a lid. The best appearance can be obtained by using distilled water, but the flavor of distilled water creates a less interesting tea than can be prepared with water possessing a pleasing flavor. Water should not be hard, for the resulting beverage will be cloudy and form a film on the cup due to precipitated polyphenols (sometimes called **tannins**). The water selected should be brought to a rolling boil and then used immediately to avoid loss of oxygen from the water. This helps to promote the desired fresh flavor of the beverage.

While the tea water is being brought to a boil, the pot should be filled with very hot water to warm the pot, and the tea leaves should be measured into a tea ball or bagged tea should be readied. Only 1 teaspoon of the dry tea leaves is needed for each cup of brewed tea (actually, 3/4 cup of water). As soon as the water starts to boil, the teapot is drained of the water used to preheat it. Then the tea ball or bag is inserted, and the boiling water is poured over the tea. By quickly replacing the lid, the preheated teapot should be able to maintain the steeping tea within the desired temperature range of 180°–211°F (82°–99°C) during the three to five-minute brewing period. At these temperatures, the tea leaves open out, exposing a maximum surface area for extraction of the flavor components.

A three-minute extraction period is sufficient to obtain maximum caffeine extraction, while keeping the undesirable polyphenols at a minimum level. This results in a tea with a brisk and stimulating quality, but without astringency. However, more flavor is developed by a five-minute than by a three-minute steeping period. The choice really is an individual matter, either time being acceptable for a quality product.

JAPANESE TEA CEREMONY

For centuries, tea (usually green tea) has been a popular beverage in Japan. When it is consumed simply as a beverage at meals there, tea is brewed efficiently by putting tea leaves in a pot, pouring boiling water over them, and steeping until served. An elaborate, beautiful tradition, the ceremonial preparation of tea is a cherished part of Japanese life even in today's hectic scene.

All movements involved in the Japanese tea ceremony are carefully prescribed to emphasize the beauty of all aspects of tea from preparing and serving to drinking it (Figure 18.11). Whether the tea ceremony is done by Japanese men, which was the tradition in the past, or by women, the pace is very relaxing and slow. Time is taken for guests to admire the beauty of the cup being used. Then the pulverized tea leaves are placed in the cup and boiling water is added. The final step is to whisk the beverage thoroughly to create some froth on top and suspend the tea leaf particles. A ceremonial presentation of the finished tea to the guest then allows the guest to partake of this special beverage. The guest expresses much appreciation regarding the beauty of the ceremony and the excellent quality of the beverage. This elaborate tradition provides today's Japanese with a tangible link to their rich cultural heritage.

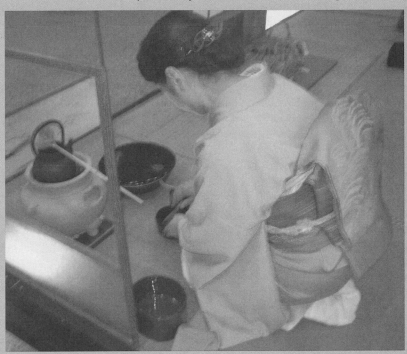

Figure 18.11
The Japanese tea ceremony is a very important cultural tradition in Japan. Courtesy of Plycon Press.

Evaluating Tea

A cup of tea of high quality will be sparklingly clear, with no suggestion of a film. Black tea will be a deep amber color, oolong will be only slightly lighter, and green tea will have a rather pale yellowish-green color. *Full, rich,* and *brisk* are adjectives describing the desired flavor of black tea. There should be no trace of bitterness or astringency. The aroma is mild, yet tempting. Oolong tea is similar to black tea, and although the characteristics should parallel those of black tea, oolong does carry overtones of the character of green tea. Green tea has little aroma, and its flavor is slightly bitter, lacking the fullness associated with the fermented teas (black and oolong). The astringency of green tea should be kept to a minimum, although there always will be some astringency associated with green tea.

Iced Tea

Iced tea is a very popular beverage in warm weather, far exceeding the consumption of iced coffee in the United States. To prepare a high-quality iced tea, two different methods may be used. Hot tea may be prepared and allowed to cool thoroughly before being poured over ice. For this method, the normal concentration of tea leaves (one teaspoon per cup) is brewed three to five minutes, just as in the preparation of hot tea.

The other method of preparing iced tea begins with the preparation of a tea of double strength and then pouring this strong infusion of hot tea directly over ice. The double strength is achieved by using twice as many tea leaves (two teaspoons per cup) and maintaining the three to five minutes of brewing time. The strong, hot tea is diluted by the melting ice to produce iced tea of the desired strength. This is a quick method, but the quickest is to stir instant tea into water and then add ice cubes.

Cloudiness often is something of a problem in making iced tea, for the polyphenols tend to precipitate in an iced product, causing the cloudy appearance. Soft water for brewing helps to reduce this problem, and distilled water usually avoids the difficulty. The addition of lemon juice helps to eliminate cloudiness, while lightening the color and altering the flavor a bit.

In some locales, the water simply is inappropriate for making a high-quality iced tea. However, sun tea (also called sunshine tea) can be prepared, usually with considerable success. Sun tea is made by adding the tea leaves directly to tap water and allowing the product to steep in the sun for an hour or at room temperature for 12 hours or slightly longer. At the comparatively low temperature of this brewing technique, there is greatly reduced extraction of the polyphenols, which virtually eliminates the problems with a cloudy tea.

Instant Tea

Instant tea is rather widely utilized for hot tea as well as for iced tea, the treatment for manufacturing instant tea being comparable to the technology used in making instant coffee. It is marketed as a powder soluble in either hot or cold water, for the very fine particles of the tea solids are quite soluble even in cold water. Because of its convenience, instant tea has attracted a broad consumer base.

Herb Teas

Technically, *tea* is a term used to designate a beverage brewed by steeping a substance in water. Of course, the beverage simply called tea fits this definition, but so do several other products found in the marketplace today. For example, herb teas fit the broad definition of tea, although they do not include leaves from the *Camellia sinensis*, as do the traditional teas. Instead, herb teas containing such diverse items as roasted carob, malted barley, cinnamon bark, orange peel, orange petals, fennel seeds, chamomile, rose hips, licorice root, roasted chicory root, and many other ingredients are blended to make products for consumers who are seeking hot beverages free of caffeine.

These beverages have no known curative powers, nor do they appear to have nutritional benefits over tea, aside from the possible benefit of not containing caffeine. However, regular teas are not very high in caffeine and do not seem to be any more harmful or unsafe than the herbal teas. In fact, some question has been raised regarding the occasional inclusion of some desert and other plants in herb teas that could cause harm. At the present time, there are more accusations than facts regarding the safety and/or benefits of tea versus herb teas. This issue may indeed be the proverbial tempest in the teapot.

COCOA AND CHOCOLATE

Processing of Cocoa and Chocolate

Cocoa and hot chocolate are popular beverages, particularly in the cold winter months. The main ingredient in these beverages is **chocolate**, the flavorful substance obtained from the beans contained in the pods that form on the *Theobroma cacao* tree (Figure 18.12). Sri Lanka, which is south of India, and Java and Samoa in the South Pacific are leading sources of the cacao beans.

After the beans have been removed from the mature cacao pods, roasting is done to develop the characteristic aroma of the nibs, the fleshy part of the beans (Figure 18.13). The heat during roasting is effective in driving off some of the moisture and in developing compounds with minimum astringency. The roasted nibs from various lots of chocolate are blended together and then are stone ground to produce a chocolate liquor in preparation for further processing. Ultimately, the chocolate may be made into not only bitter chocolate, but also semisweet, sweet, or milk chocolate can be produced by adding varying amounts of sugar, fat, and even milk solids (Table 18.3).

Nibs contain cocoa butter, starch, theobromine, caffeine, and pigments of the anthocyanin group identified as cocoa red and cocoa purple. Four fatty acids (oleic, stearic, palmitic, and linoleic) are particularly prominent in products from the roasted nibs, the concentration ranging from a mere 2 percent of linoleic acid to about 38 percent in the case of oleic acid.

The pressed ground nibs are used to make both cocoa and chocolate products. Cocoa is made by removing much of the cocoa butter, resulting in a fat content of at least 22 percent in breakfast cocoa; some of the surplus cocoa butter remaining after making cocoa is added to chocolate to raise the fat content of bitter chocolate to between 50 and 56 percent. Milk and sugar are added when milk chocolate is the end product. White chocolate contains cocoa butter, but not the dark solids in the nibs.

Figure 18.12
These cacao pods have been dried for display in a pastry shop; the beans inside them are what will be processed to be used in chocolate recipes. Courtesy of Plycon Press.

chocolate Flavorful substance derived by grinding the roasted beans from the pods of the *Theobroma cacao* tree.

Figure 18.13
Cacao beans are ready for roasting in this chocolate factory in Sri Lanka. Courtesy of Plycon Press.

TABLE 18.3
FAT AND CARBOHYDRATE CONTENT OF SOME CHOCOLATE

Type	Fat (%)	Carbohydrate (%)
Bitter	54	28
Semisweet	36	57
Milk	32	57

Source: Data from Nutritive Value of Foods, Home and Garden Bulletin No. 72, USDA, Washington, DC. 1978.

Dutch process chocolate
Chocolate treated with alkali to produce a pH between 6.0 and 8.8, causing the chocolate to be darker, less acidic, and less susceptible to settling out than chocolate processed without adding alkali.

conching Processing step in which melted chocolate is kept in constant motion for 36–72 hours at temperatures ranging from 110°–210°F (43°–99°C), a process that helps to avoid bloom.

tempering Carefully controlled cooling of conched chocolate to develop fine fat crystals, which help to avoid development of bloom during storage.

bloom White or light gray discoloration on the surface of chocolate where it has softened and moisture has collected during storage; tempering helps to avoid bloom.

Any of these chocolate derivatives can be made into either natural or Dutch process chocolates. The addition of alkali produces a pH of 6.0 to 8.8 in **Dutch process chocolate**. In contrast, the pH range without the Dutching process is about 5.2 to 6.9. This low pH is the result of not adding an alkaline ingredient; hence, chocolate products without added alkali are referred to as natural chocolate. One of the benefits of Dutch cocoa or chocolate is its reduced tendency to settle out when combined with liquids. Dutch chocolate is less tart and also is a darker color than the chocolate made without added alkali.

The appearance and texture of chocolate are important characteristics that influence consumer acceptance. To enhance the physical appearance of chocolate and its acceptability following storage, chocolate is subjected to two processing steps: **conching** and **tempering**. These steps involve keeping melted chocolate in continuous, slow movement for 36–72 hours in machines called conches (Figure 18.14) that hold the chocolate within the temperature range of 110°–210°F (43°–99°C). Then the chocolate is tempered by cooling the chocolate very gradually, with agitation, to help to maintain a chocolate containing very fine crystals of cooled fat. The end result is a chocolate capable of resisting modest temperature changes during storage, leading to **bloom** on the chocolate. When chocolate is exposed to warm temperatures, the fat softens in untempered chocolate, causing light gray or white areas on the surface of the chocolate where moisture has collected. By tempering chocolate, much of this problem is avoided.

Preparing the Beverage

The preparation of cocoa and hot chocolate is designed to minimize the tendency to sedimentation. Since chocolate and cocoa contain starch, it is possible to get some leverage against sedimentation by gelatinizing the starch in the chocolate products. When chocolate is being used, the solid chocolate must first be melted carefully to avoid scorching. This can be done easily by placing the chocolate in the top of a double boiler over boiling water, a step appropriate any time chocolate is being melted. Melting chocolate without scorching can also

Figure 18.14
Conching of chocolate is important to controlling the crystal formation during processing. Courtesy of Plycon Press.

INDUSTRY INSIGHT
QUENCHING THIRST

Commercial beverages occupy considerable shelf space in today's grocery stores, with the products ranging from bottled waters to special drinks for athletes. Although many people drink tap water and also lemons sometimes are squeezed at home to make lemonade, the preponderance of beverages is prepared commercially. The market for colas and sodas is very active throughout most parts of the world. Carbonation, sweetness, and flavorings are the basic qualities that are so popular with the public. However, the food industry is very active in other beverage products, as well (Hollingsworth, 1997). For example, fruit drinks of various types are found in abundance, some being the pure juice and others being processed and modified to meet particular product definitions. A contrast to these sweet beverages is available in the form of canned iced coffee and iced tea.

Beverages for sport have presented some significant research challenges because of the competition to formulate a beverage that will support an athlete's performance rather than interfering with it. Energy needs and the ability to derive energy from beverages are determined by the type and duration of physical activity being undertaken. Therefore, carbohydrate quantity and type will be important. One of the key concerns is being certain that fluid is replenished at adequate levels and frequencies. The rate at which an athlete's beverage can leave the stomach and be absorbed will be studied when a sports beverage is being formulated. Sodium is also considered important in sports beverages to help replace the salt lost in perspiration. Drinks for athletes will vary, but a low level of carbonation (no more than 1.3 percent), 11 mg sodium per 8 ounces of beverage, and 6–8 percent carbohydrate would be considered rather typical. However, many athletes prefer to drink plain water.

be accomplished in the microwave oven, although this requires accurate timing. Packets of fluid chocolate afford yet another alternative to obtaining liquid chocolate for making the beverage.

When the chocolate is melted, the sugar, salt, and water are mixed together and are heated to boiling while stirring. This gelatinizes the starch in preparation for adding the milk. The milk is added gradually to the gelatinized chocolate mixture and stirred while being heated to serving temperature. This procedure eliminates the undesirable raw starch flavor, minimizes sedimentation in the finished beverage, and produces a minimum amount of scum from the precipitation of milk proteins. The shorter the length of time the hot beverage must be held before serving, the less scum will form. Whipping up some foam on the surface just prior to serving also helps to avoid scum formation.

Evaluating the Beverage

Ideally, hot chocolate or cocoa will have a pleasing flavor entirely free of any suggestion of scorching. The minimum amount of sediment is achieved by the gelatinization of the starch, thus helping to achieve suspension of the chocolate or cocoa particles in the beverage. Sediment is considered undesirable in these beverages. Extensive scum formation can be caused by an extended heating period or by too high a temperature. This problem always is present, but it can be alleviated by avoiding a long heating period and by whipping up some foam on the surface. When hot chocolate or cocoa is garnished with either a dollop of whipped cream or a marshmallow, the topping provides a protective coating, thus removing the problem of scum formation, but adding calories.

Substitution

Cocoa can be substituted for chocolate in a recipe, providing that fat is added in an appropriate amount. An ounce (a square) of chocolate can be replaced by 3 1/2 tablespoons of cocoa plus 1/2 tablespoon margarine or butter.

FRUIT BEVERAGES

Fruit juices and combinations of juices are popular beverages at meal and snack times (Figure 18.15). Often these are purchased ready to drink, although they may require reconstituting with water to the normal strength. The various concentrations of juices and the use of real or synthetic juice components are covered by federal regulations and are discussed in Chapter 6.

Figure 18.15
Lemons, limes, and mangoes are just some of the fruits that can provide juice for flavorful beverages. Many fruit juices are excellent sources of vitamin C. Courtesy of Plycon Press.

The main concern in combining various juices to make a mixed fruit beverage is the effect on color. Although orange and yellow fruit juices do not undergo significant color changes when combined with other juices, the juices containing anthocyanin pigments can and do create some surprising colors in mixtures. The inclusion of lemon juice or other rather acidic juice helps to retain the desired reddish tone in anthocyanins rather than promote a muddy blue tone.

If fruit juices are being served with ice, they may get quite dilute as a result of the water introduced from the melting ice. This problem can be avoided by planning ahead and freezing some of the juice in a ring mold or ice cube trays so that the frozen juice can be used to chill the rest of the juice at the time it is served.

ALCOHOLIC BEVERAGES

Alcoholic beverages have been made from a variety of foods for countless centuries. Early evidence of wine making has been found in many parts of the Middle East, including bas reliefs and paintings showing grapevines and large containers that were used for storing wine. Wine, however, is only one of the alcoholic beverages that have been developed in various cultures. Beers and whiskeys are made from grains. Various fruits are used to make ciders, and sugarcane is the crop used to make rum.

There are many different alcoholic beverages, but they generally can be categorized as beer, wine, or distilled spirits. Beers are made by soaking barley to germinate it. After drying, water is added to the barley and heated to make wort, a mash, which is fermented with yeast in the brewing process. Hops, the leaves of a variety of mulberry vine, are added to contribute to the characteristic odor and flavor of beer. The mixture is boiled to release some of the flavor of the hops and kill undesirable microorganisms. Fermentation proceeds for more than a week of cold storage during which the action of a yeast (*Saccharomyces carlsbergensis*) produces enough alcohol to the desired level (usually 3 to 8 percent). Lager is a bottom-fermented beer held in cool conditions and is light in color, whereas ale is a stronger, darker beer that is top-fermented at warm temperatures.

Grape juice usually is the fruit used in making wines (Figure 18.16), although other fruits sometimes are used. Yeast is allowed to ferment the juice to produce alcohol from the sugars naturally present. Table wines vary in their sweetness, depending upon how much unfermented sugar is present. Dry wines have a slightly higher alcohol content and less sugar than the sweet wines, which still contain unfermented sugar. Red wines have somewhat more complex aromas and flavors than white wines, and they gain an even more interesting bouquet when they have been aged for several years. Their lovely deep red color is from the skin of the grapes used in making the wines. White wines are made without using the skins, which produce wines that are light in color and less complex in flavor. The variety of grape and the climate where wine grapes are grown are key factors in producing good wines (Figure 18.17). France has several different regions where different outstanding wines are produced, such as Bordeaux and Burgundy. Considerable competition is developing in the world's wine market, with vintners marketing their wares from Australia to South Africa to Chile and several states in the United States.

The alcoholic content (expressed either as a **percentage** or as **proof**) varies with the specific type of beverage. Beers usually vary from 3 to 6 percent, and wines typically are 12.5 percent. Both beer and wine are fermented beverages, which result in comparatively low alcohol levels. Distilled beverages are considerably higher in alcohol content. Liqueurs, and such spirits as brandy, gin, rum, bourbon, rye whiskey, Scotch whiskey, and vodka are considerably higher in alcohol than are fermented beverages. The alcohol levels of distilled spirits vary considerably (e.g., between 40 and 60 percent for single malt whiskey, 95 percent for vodka). When alcohol

http://whatscookingamerica.net/WineInCooking.htm
—Information on cooking with wine.

percentage   Measure of alcohol by volume.

proof   Expression commonly used to indicate the alcohol content of distilled beverages; proof is double the percent content.

Figure 18.16
Grapes are the source of juice for many of the world's wines. The Greeks also use the leaves as wrappers for dolmas and in some other dishes. Courtesy of Plycon Press.

level is stated as proof, the number is two times the percent figure (e.g., vodka can be 95 percent or 190 proof).

Alcoholic beverages sometimes are used in food preparation to add flavors to cooked dishes. When they are being used, they are heated for several minutes after being added so that the flavors are concentrated and all of the alcohol is evaporated from the product. Wines sometimes are added to meat, poultry, and fish dishes, and beer can be found as an ingredient in some batters and other recipes. Distilled beverages such as rum and brandy are ingredients that may be found in various desserts, ranging from English plum pudding to bananas Foster.

Figure 18.17
Wine and artisanal cheeses are two flavorful products from Greece. Courtesy of Plycon Press.

INGREDIENT HIGHLIGHT
CANADIAN WINE?

Thoughts of wine often conjure up images of vineyards in Italy, France, and other warm and sunny regions noted for their prize-winning vintages. Certainly, the idea of producing wines in British Columbia, Canada, seems like a far-fetched possibility to be pursued only by dreamers. However, the weather situation has been changing in the Okanagan Valley in inland southern British Columbia. Recently, winters have been slightly warmer, and optimistic vintners are betting that temperatures in the valley region will not drop lower than –4°F (–20°C), the coldest that most grape varieties can survive.

In the last 60 years there, the average temperature in the valley has warmed by 5°F (–3°C), the growing season has extended by 11 days, and the coldest temperature in the last

10 years was just above 0°F (–18°C). The somewhat warmer (about 4°F [2°C]) days of summer have also helped to assure that the grapes will be ripe enough to harvest before a freeze. Apparently, the optimists are winning their bets, and wines from British Columbia wineries in the Okanagan Valley near Tappen are emerging as contenders in the marketplace.

In contrast, climate change may be creating problems for vintners in the premier wine regions of the world. It is too early to tell if European, Chilean, Australian, and northern California vintners will be confronted with challenges associated with grapes affected by too much heat. Unfortunately, the sugar level and flavor components of grapes are influenced significantly by the weather during the growing season.

---

http://recline-ridge.bc.ca/ /
—Canadian winery information.

Sometimes distilled spirits are heated before being added to a dessert and quickly ignited to "flame" the dessert. The proof of the distilled beverage to be flamed is important. A beverage that is 180 proof is rather easy to ignite, but lower levels are harder to light because there is less alcohol in them. When desserts or other dishes are flamed, the flame should be allowed to keep burning until it dies out so that the alcohol is gone. Alcohol burns at a temperature low enough to avoid burning the food being flamed.

SUMMARY

Coffee and other beverages are symbols of hospitality, providing social pleasure and stimulation. Coffee gains its flavor and aroma from a wide array of volatile substances and oils found in coffee following roasting. Caffeine is the stimulant in coffee, and it is present most abundantly in coffee made by the dripolator method, although percolator coffee also has significantly more caffeine than tea or hot chocolate.

Coffee may be purchased in a soluble form (usually freeze-dried), as grounds, and sometimes as roasted beans. The recommended amount of ground coffee for preparing the beverage is two tablespoons of grounds per beverage cup, although many people prefer a weaker brew than this makes. Dripolators are recommended because of the mild, full-flavored coffee they produce; water circulates only once through the grounds, and this water is not quite boiling by the time it has filtered through. Caffeine extraction from coffees is greatest when brewing is done by the drip method. Coffee presses are convenient to use, but the beverage may not be quite hot enough when brewing is finished by pressing the filter down. Percolators extract less caffeine than dripolators, but the flavor of percolator coffee tends to have a somewhat bitter aftertaste, a consequence of the repeated recycling of the boiling hot water through the coffee grounds. Steeped coffee is made in a large kettle by maintaining the temperature of the water in the kettle just below boiling while steeping coarse grind coffee. Coffee grounds are removed when the steeping period is over. Coffee should be clear and sparkling. Espresso and iced coffee are but a couple of the variations afforded by creative marketing today.

Tea ranges from rather astringent to brisk and full in flavor, depending on the quality of the tea leaves themselves, as well as on their preparation into the beverage. Green tea is steamed to halt possible enzyme action and quickly moved through the processing steps to drying without having fermentation occur. This results in a delicately colored, very slightly astringent beverage. Oolong tea has been allowed to ferment briefly, resulting in a rather dark leaf and a somewhat mild flavor. Black tea has a long fermentation period, which permits the development of numerous flavoring compounds to heighten the flavor interest in black tea and to develop a relatively dark amber color. Only one teaspoon of tea per cup of beverage being brewed is necessary for brewing tea. Unlike coffee, tea contains essentially no oils; the flavoring compounds in tea are less likely to be lost during storage than are those of coffee. Instant teas and iced teas are popular variations of the brewed beverage. Although not tea from *Camellia sinensis*, the herb teas, with their mainstays of chamomile and other herbs, are becoming quite popular among people striving to reduce their intake of caffeine, for the herb teas usually contain no caffeine.

Cocoa and hot chocolate are prepared from the roasted beans contained in the pods of the *Theobroma cacao* tree. Both regular and Dutch process cocoa or chocolate contain some starch, which is gelatinized during the early part of the preparation. The increased viscosity of the gelatinized starch aids in preventing the formation of sediment in the bottom of a cup of cocoa or hot chocolate. A short heating period, just long enough to bring the beverage to serving temperature, is appropriate after the milk has been added; this measure helps to minimize scum formation.

Fruit juices in combination or alone are served as beverages, too. The main concerns are to avoid diluting the juice with melting ice and to prevent unfortunate color changes when mixing juices containing anthocyanins with other juices.

Alcoholic beverages may be fermented or distilled, the latter being higher in alcohol content. Wines and beers are examples of fermented alcoholic beverages; whiskey, liqueurs, rum, and vodka are among the many distilled beverages. The alcoholic content of wine and beer usually is expressed as a percentage, and the level in distilled beverages is in proof, a value twice as great as the percentage. Alcoholic beverages may be used in cooking and for flaming.

STUDY QUESTIONS

1. Describe the preparation of coffee using a dripolator and a percolator. What grind should be used in each pot? Why?
2. What are the advantages and disadvantages of a dripolator? Of a percolator?
3. Which method of making coffee results in the highest caffeine? Compare the caffeine levels of various types of tea with coffee.
4. What is the stimulant predominating in cocoa? In coffee? In tea?
5. Compare the color, flavor, and aroma of black, oolong, and green teas. Explain the reasons for these differences.
6. Compare the methods for storing coffee and tea. Why are they stored differently?
7. What is the difference between Dutch process and plain cocoa?
8. Why is it necessary to be concerned about combining fruit juices containing anthocyanin pigments? Are the same problems encountered when combining juices containing carotenoid pigments? If not, why not?

SELECTED REFERENCES

Berry, D. 2010. Still-beverage surge. *Food Product Design 20*(3): 38.

Bond, T. 2004. Tea: Nectar and ambrosia. *Food Product Design 14*(5): 76.

Bunker, M. L., and M. McWilliams. 1979. Caffeine content of common beverages. *J. Am. Dietet. Assoc. 74*: 28.

Burrington, K. J. 2005. Pouring out blended beverages. *Food Product Design 15*(1): 31.

Coleman, E. 1991. Sports drink research. *Food Technol. 45*(3): 104.

Crandall, P. G., et al. 1990. Viscosity reduction of orange juice concentrate by pulp reduction vs. enzyme treatment. *Food Technol. 44*(4): 126.

Decker, K. J. 2006. Juice drinks for the next generation. *Food Product Design 15*(10): 24.

Fass, P., and M. Jones. 2005. Functional-beverage bonanza. *Food Product Design 15*(1): 66.

Giese, J. H. 1992. Hitting the spot: Beverages and beverage technology. *Food Technol. 46*(7): 69.

Grenus, K. 2005. Beverage a day keeps the pounds away. *Food Product Design 14*(12): 87.

Hahne, B. P. 2005. Legendary chocolate. *Food Product Design 14*(10): 68.

Hasler, C. M. 2009. Exploring the health benefits of wine. *Food Technol. 63*(9): 21.

Hazen, C. 2009. Targeting beverages for demographics. *Food Product Design 19*(12): 28.

Hazen, C. 2011. Dairy-based beverages. *Food Product Design 21*(1): 32.

Hollingsworth, P. 1997. Beverages: Redefining new age. *Food Technol. 51*(8): 44.

Kundrat, S. 2004. Studying sports drinks. *Food Product Design 14*(1): 29.

Kuntz, L. A. 2010. Natural colors for beverages: A rainbow of possibilities. *Food Product Design 20*(11): 36.

Leviton, A. 1983. Caffeine: Behavioral effects. *Food Technol. 37*(9): 44.

Mermelstein, N. H. 2010. Analyzing wine. *Food Technol. 64*(2): 62.

Ohr, L. M. 2004. All tea'd up. *Food Technol. 58*(7): 71.

Palmer, S. 2005. Talking tea. *Food Product Design 14*(10): 87.

Roberts, H. W., and J. J. Barone. 1983. Caffeine: History and use. *Food Technol. 37*(9): 32.

Rockwell, B. P. 2010. Healthier kid's beverages. *Food Product Design 20*(10): 88.

Tarver, T. 2011. Healthy beverages: Back to the basics. *Food Technol. 65*(1): 33.

Turner, J. 2004. Caffeine buzz. *Food Product Design 14*(11): 14.

Von Borstel, R. W. 1983. Caffeine: Metabolism. *Food Technol. 37*(9): 40.

Zoumas, B. L., et al. 1980. Theobromine and caffeine content of chocolate products. *J. Food Sci. 45*: 324.

Sun drying, an ancient means of food preservation, is a practical way to preserve chile peppers and other spices in southern India. Courtesy of Plycon Press.

19

Preserving Food

Chapter Contents

HISTORICAL PERSPECTIVE

A basic goal of preserving food is to avoid future hunger, a motivating force that is centuries old. Drying of food was done by the ancient Egyptians, Greeks, and Persians. The Old Testament of the Bible contains references to dried food. Marco Polo noted the use of sun-dried milk by the Mongols in the 13th century. Before the time of Columbus, Native Americans were drying pemmican (meat mixed with fat) for use when fresh food was not available.

Salting and smoking were two other techniques that were developed hundreds of years ago as a means of preserving meat. Many centuries later when sugar became readily available, it was used to preserve fruits. These basic techniques created environments that were hostile to microorganisms, making reproduction and survival impossible because of dehydration of their cells.

Safely preserved food has been a major concern for the military. Napoleon offered a prize of 12,000 francs to anyone devising a technique for preserving food for his troops. The winner was Nicolas Appert, who in 1809 developed the techniques and materials needed for canning foods safely. Preservation in canning is accomplished by killing microorganisms with heat. Although many refinements have been made, canning technology still utilizes the principles put forth by Appert.

The first patent for freezing as a means of food preservation was granted in England in 1842 to H. Benjamin for his process of freezing by immersing fish or meat in an ice–salt brine solution. Freezing gradually developed as a food preservation technique, but it was not used widely until the early part of the 20th century. In the United States, Clarence Birdseye is credited with being the pioneer who brought frozen foods to the retail industry.

Food preservation affords a means of having favorite foods available to eat when they are not in season. This is not basic to survival, but it does enhance dining pleasures. For instance, a person who is very fond of the flavor of fresh strawberries may be highly motivated to have frozen strawberries to eat when the fresh berries are not available. Despite the drastic textural changes resulting from freezing, the flavor of frozen strawberries remains quite similar to the fresh berries.

Anyone who cooks doubtless has been involved in food preservation, whether consciously or unconsciously. At the very least, some leftovers have been

Key Concepts

1. Food can be preserved for later use by processing it to kill microorganisms and then storing under appropriate conditions to maintain safety of the preserved product.

2. Home food preservation techniques include canning, freezing, preserving with sugar, curing, and drying.

3. Commercial food preservation methods include irradiation and high pressure processing, as well as the procedures that can be done at home (canning, freezing, preserving with sugar, and drying).

http://www.brooklyn.cuny.edu/bc/ahp/MBG/MBG4/Appert.html
—Background on Nicolas Appert.

http://www.uga.edu/nchfp/
—National Center for Home Food Preservation.

409

packaged and placed in the freezer; at the other extreme, for some people, entire days have been devoted to canning seemingly endless jars of produce or tending grapes that were drying to become raisins. Home food preservation is an important aspect of managing the family's food supply for some people, but for others, the primary responsibility for preserving food is given willingly to the food industry.

Saving money also may be a motivating force for preserving food. If fresh produce is available for the picking, a considerable amount of food can be preserved for future use at very little cost. Even if foods to be preserved need to be purchased, wise food buying can translate into real savings in the food budget because of the comparatively low cost of foods at the height of their harvest season.

PRESERVATION METHODS

Food preservation can be done very satisfactorily in the home if safe procedures are followed carefully. Drying is the oldest means of preserving food, but interest in this form of preservation is rather limited. Presently, people who go backpacking and camping account for much of the growth in popularity of dried foods. Home gardens create a need for preserving the harvest in some form—most commonly by canning or freezing.

Whereas drying preserves foods by providing too little moisture for microorganisms to survive, canning uses heat to kill microorganisms in the container, and freezing kills some microorganisms and greatly slows some deteriorative changes. Yet another technique, preserving with sugar, creates unfavorable osmotic pressure for microorganisms, thus preventing their survival in jams and jellies. Salting and smoking also are able to aid in preservation by altering the environment so it inhibits growth and reproduction of microorganisms. The addition of acid in the form of vinegar enables pickles to be kept for long periods because the environment is too acidic for microorganisms to reproduce readily; sometimes pickles have some salt added and then they are canned to augment the preserving action of the acid.

Many different types of bacteria, molds, and yeasts can cause food spoilage. In most instances, the greatest problems stem from bacteria, although molds are the microorganisms causing the primary losses in dried foods. Interestingly, all three types of microorganisms are added deliberately to certain foods to create such popular products as yogurt, Roquefort cheese, and sourdough bread. The important fact is that the growth of microorganisms must be recognized as a potential risk in food, although some microorganisms may be desirable in specific foods.

Canning

There are two basic ways in which foods may be canned in the home, the choice between the two being based on the food being canned. Fruits of all types and usually tomatoes, foods high in acids, can be canned safely by processing in a **boiling water bath**. Foods low in acids cannot be processed to a high enough temperature by this technique to ensure a product safe for human consumption after extended room temperature storage. A **pressure canner** is needed for these low-acid foods so that the contents of the jars can be heated to a high enough temperature to assure the destruction of even the spores of *Clostridium botulinum*.

Unless processing times are controlled carefully and the right equipment is used, canned foods (particularly low-acid foods) may spoil and can even be fatal to eat. The importance of careful attention to processing techniques during canning cannot be overstated, particularly for vegetables, meats, and other low-acid foods. The danger from inadequate processing of these foods is due to the toxin produced by *C. botulinum*, which is discussed in Chapter 3.

Boiling Water Bath   Processing using a boiling water bath is suitable only for canning fruits, pickles, and tomatoes because the temperature is inadequate to destroy bacterial spores that may be present in foods with comparatively low acidity. Actually, some varieties of tomatoes are not sufficiently acidic; 1/2 teaspoon of citric acid per quart of tomatoes or 2 teaspoons of vinegar or lemon juice in each quart should be added to these to ensure that they are sufficiently acidic to be processed safely by the boiling water bath method.

boiling water bath (water bath canning)
Preservation by packing high-acid foods (e.g., fruits, tomatoes) into canning jars or cans, covering with water, and heat processing at atmospheric pressure for the appropriate length of time.

pressure canner   Large, heavy kettle with tight-fitting lid capable of withstanding internal pressure of at least 20 pounds; used for canning low-acid foods.

SCIENCE NOTE
ACIDITY AND CANNING METHODS

The pH of a food is very important in determining the viability of microorganisms during the heat processing used in canning. The break point for using water bath or pressure canning is a pH of 4.5. Below pH 4.5, a safe canning technique is provided by the use of a water bath canner, with its maximum processing temperature of 212°F (100°C). However, at pH 4.5 and higher, an unreasonably long processing time is required to ensure against botulism unless a higher processing temperature is used. This increase in temperature can only be obtained by increasing the pressure in the canner. At 10 pounds of pressure, the processing temperature is increased to 240°F (116°C), an adequate temperature for safe processing.

Since knowledge of the pH of a food is essential to determining the processing technique to use, some appreciation of the approximate pH of some of the foods commonly canned is helpful. The accompanying chart indicates the approximate pH of many different types of foods. The fruits range from very tart plums at a pH of less than 3 to pears, which have a pH approaching 4. Tomatoes are generally in the critical area around a pH of 4.5, with the actual pH being influenced considerably by the variety of tomato. Beefsteak tomatoes are one of the most acidic varieties; their average pH of 4.23 is safely in the pH range for water bath canning. However, several other varieties of tomatoes are in the pH range requiring pressure canning. Fireball tomatoes have an average pH of 4.50, and Royal Chico (pH 4.58) and San Marzano (pH 4.68) have even higher pH values. Since the pH of tomatoes usually is not known in the home, the addition of acid to any tomatoes being canned is recommended at the level of 2 teaspoons of lemon juice per quart of tomatoes or 1/2 teaspoon of citric acid (USP) per quart.

The pH of vegetables other than tomatoes ranges from the high 4 range for okra and pumpkin to peas and corn with values over 6. With these high pH values, it is easy to see why pressure canning is needed for all vegetables.

Tomatoes often are canned with other ingredients, as is done when stewed tomatoes are canned with added green pepper and onion. The addition of vegetables causes the pH of the combined food mixture to rise a little. When tomatoes already are at the pH critical to the decision about pressure canning, the added vegetables make a crucial difference. For instance, chili sauce needs pressure canning and so do salsa-type products. If there is any doubt about pH, pressure canning should be the method chosen.

pH	
2.5	Plums
	Gooseberries
	Prunes
	Dill pickles, rhubarb, apricots
3.0	Apples, blackberries
	Sour cherries, strawberries
	Peaches
	Sauerkraut, raspberries
	Blueberries
	Sweet cherries
	Pears
4.0	
	Tomatoes
	Okra
5.0	Pumpkin, carrots
	Pimiento (lye peeled)
	Turnips, cabbage
	Parsnips, beets, string beans, green peppers
	Sweet potatoes, baked beans
	Spinach
	Asparagus, cauliflower
	Red kidney beans
	Lima beans
	Succotash, meats, poultry
6.0	
	Peas
	Corn, hominy, salmon
	White fish
	Shrimp, wet pack
7.0	Lye hominy

The equipment needed for canning with a boiling water bath includes a large kettle with a cover and rack, as well as canning jars with smooth glass all around the lip of the jar and appropriate closures (Figure 19.1). The kettle must be at least an inch and a half deeper than the height of the jars. The rack to hold the jars needs to keep the jars at least a quarter of an inch above the bottom of the pan so that the boiling water can circulate under them.

In preparation for the actual canning process, enough water is brought to a boil in the boiling water bath canner to rise an inch above the jars when they are placed on the rack in the water bath canner. This water is brought to a boil while the jars are being washed and rinsed thoroughly and the fruit is being prepared for placement in the jars.

After their preliminary preparation, fruits and tomatoes are packed efficiently into jars to a level no higher than half an inch below the top of the jar. Boiling syrup, juice, or water then

http://www.versatilevinegar.org/
—Information about vinegars.

Figure 19.1
A water bath canner equipped with a rack is recommended for processing fruits and acidic tomatoes when doing canning at home.
Courtesy of Plycon Press.

is poured to within an inch and a half of the top if the fruit has not been heated prior to being placed in the jar, or to within half an inch of the top if the fruit is packed hot. The syrup may be thin, medium, or heavy, depending on preference. Syrups of varying viscosities can be made by boiling the following solutions five minutes or less:

Thin syrup: 2 cups sugar, 4 cups water
Medium syrup: 3 cups sugar, 4 cups water
Heavy syrup: 4 3/4 cups sugar, 4 cups water

A narrow rubber spatula is moved gently through the jar to release any pockets of air that may be trapped, and additional syrup is added if necessary. Then the lid is tightened firmly by hand. If the lid is tightened too much, the sealing compound in the rim may fail to achieve a good seal. The closed jars are lifted with tongs and are placed in the boiling water bath. When the designated processing period in boiling water is completed, the jars are removed and cooled upright on several thicknesses of cloth so that they cool slowly to room temperature.

The following day the seal should be checked before the jars are placed in the cupboard for extended storage. The center of the lid of a two-piece closure is flexed downward if the container is sealed. Check zinc closures by noting evidence of any leakage while tilting and rotating the jars. If the seal is not good, canned foods should be reprocessed or else stored in the refrigerator and served within a day or two. In the event that the closures being used are different in design from these types of lids, the manufacturer's directions should be followed for that specific closure design. The instructions given here are general in nature.

INGREDIENT HIGHLIGHT
VINEGARS AND PICKLES

Pickles are popular accompaniments to add piquancy to a menu. They often are made from vegetables, which naturally are low in acid. Because of their high pH, vinegar traditionally is added when making pickles. This lowers the pH and slows spoilage. The additional step of canning assures safety and quality over extended storage.

Production of vinegar from a food begins with fermentation of sugar to ethanol, a reaction promoted by the yeast *Saccharomyces cerevisiae*. The second step is formation of acetic acid from ethanol by the action of *Acetobacter*. Although vinegars can be produced from a wide range of foods (e.g., cider, rice, wines, alcohol), federal regulations for vinegars require an acetic acid content between 4 and 7 percent. Despite the limitations on acidity for any vinegar, flavor and color vary significantly depending on the food from which they are made. The choice of vinegar for a particular use should be based on flavor and color.

Pressure Canning The spores formed by *C. botulinum* are extremely heat resistant, and these can thrive in canned low-acid foods, such as meats and vegetables. Fortunately, the high temperature (about 240°F [116°C]) achieved in a pressure canner at 10 pounds of pressure is sufficient to inactivate the spores of *C. botulinum* in a reasonable length of time (Figure 19.2).

Preparation of food to be canned by pressure canning is done as follows. While the vegetables or other foods are being prepared, 2 inches of water needs to be heated to boiling in the pressure canner. The vegetables are packed into jars to within an inch of the top of the jar and boiling water is added, leaving half an inch of headspace in the jar. Immediately, the filled jars are closed according to the manufacturer's instructions and placed on the rack in the pressure canner.

When the pressure canner is full of jars, the cover of the canner is fastened securely, and the petcock is left open while heating for 7–10 minutes to exhaust the canner. Then the petcock is closed, causing pressure to begin to mount in the canner. High heat is maintained while developing the desired 10 pounds of pressure (or more, if at higher elevations). The heat is adjusted then to maintain the desired pressure, and the processing time is begun (Figure 19.3).

When processing has been completed, the heat is turned off, and the pressure canner is allowed to cool at room temperature without disturbance until the pressure has been reduced to atmospheric pressure. Then the petcock is opened gradually to allow the steam to escape before the lid is removed. The jars are held in the canner until the liquid in them stops boiling to avoid unnecessary thermal shock to the jars. The cooling and checking for sealing then follow the same routine used for jars processed in the boiling water bath.

In preparing to serve home-canned vegetables and meats, it is vital to boil these foods actively for at least 15 minutes before even tasting. This precaution is sufficient to eliminate the risk of botulism, which can result in death if even a tiny amount of viable toxin from the spores of *C. botulinum* is ingested. This procedure is necessary even when jars look normal. Furthermore, any jars with bulging lids should be discarded without even being opened.

Figure 19.2
A pressure canner, with its strong construction and pressurized seal, is needed for home canning vegetables and other low-acid foods. The high temperatures that can be reached in a pressure canner are adequate to eliminate the potential problem of botulism from *C. botulinum* spores and their toxin. Courtesy of Plycon Press.

Freezing

Freezing is a food preservation technique used in almost all homes in the United States today as a means of preserving food at least for a few days. Many cooked foods can be frozen with the simple step of wrapping them tightly in plastic wrap or aluminum foil and placing them in the freezer. No special equipment (except for the usual freezer in a refrigerator) is needed, and only the time required for wrapping is necessary. Freezing is the simplest way possible to preserve food. However, the length of time that extremely high quality is maintained in automatically defrosting freezers in refrigerators is limited in comparison with the storage time possible in free-standing freezers or in foods preserved by canning or drying.

Packaging is an important aspect of successful freezing, for the surface of frozen foods needs to be protected from the extremely dry air in the freezer unit. Extreme desiccation or drying occurs as ice crystals are sublimated wherever air comes in contact with frozen surfaces. This leaves unattractive, tough, and dry areas on the surface, a defect referred to as

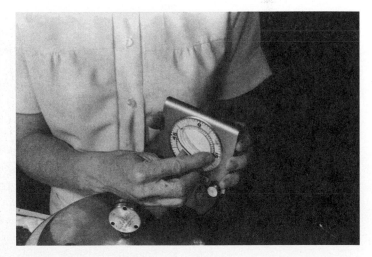

Figure 19.3
Processing time when pressure canning is being done should begin only when the correct pressure has been reached. A timer is recommended for this purpose. The time needs to be increased when canning is done at high elevations. Courtesy of Plycon Press.

freezer burn Frozen food with dessication on part of the surface.

freezer burn. A clear illustration of freezer burn can be seen on the breast of frozen turkeys if the freezer bag has even a small tear in the bag covering the turkey.

Plastic freezer cartons that are stackable and have lids that fit tightly are excellent for freezer storage. Other alternatives are plastic bags or aluminum foil that are closed securely. Glass jars *with wide mouths can be used if there is no shoulder on the jar. Otherwise, the contents of the jar may be very difficult to remove before being thawed completely. The possibility of breakage is* another disadvantage of using glass jars.

Vegetables Frozen foods are never any better than they were before freezing. Therefore, only vegetables or other foods of highest quality are suggested for freezing and frozen storage. Freezing is a means of preserving foods that requires adequate maintenance of cold temperatures to assure that deteriorative changes are kept to an absolute minimum throughout the storage period. This method of storage carries some cost because of the power needed to maintain the necessary storage temperature of 0°F (−18°C) or lower. Comparatively warm temperatures in the freezer during storage (20°F [−7°C]) may allow quality to deteriorate within only five weeks, while storage at −10°F (−23°C) permits high quality to be maintained during a storage period of six months.

The slow deterioration of the quality of frozen foods during storage is an indication of the fact that freezing is not an effective means of completely preventing food losses due to spoilage; it merely retards losses. Enzymatic reactions and growth of microorganisms account for the deterioration over time. Vegetables are fairly susceptible to enzymatic changes unless they are blanched prior to freezing. Blanching, a short heating period in boiling water or steam, inactivates enzymes as well as helps to reduce the final volume of the food being frozen. Only a short blanching period (Table 19.1) is needed to inactivate and appropriately retard enzyme action in frozen vegetables. In fact, the short blanching period is preferable to a longer cooking period because of the better texture in the finished product compared with vegetables cooked until done before being frozen.

Since overcooking during blanching is detrimental to the final texture, blanched vegetables are immersed immediately in ice water to halt the cooking. As soon as the food has been cooled in this way, vegetables are drained thoroughly, packaged, labeled, and placed immediately in the freezer. Best results are obtained when only a small amount of food is frozen at any one time. This permits the freezer to maintain a temperature sufficiently cold to freeze the package of food very fast. Very small ice crystals form when freezing is rapid, which helps to avoid serious disruption of the cell walls in vegetables and improves texture in the final product.

Fruits Best results in freezing fruit are obtained when only a small quantity is being frozen at one time, just as is true in freezing vegetables. The preparation of fruits for freezing actually is

TABLE 19.1
PROCEDURES FOR PREPARING SELECTED VEGETABLES FOR FREEZING

Vegetable	Preparation Instructions	Scalding Time[a] (min)
Asparagus	Wash, drain, and trim.	3
Beans, lima	Shell, wash, and drain.	3
Beans, green and wax	Wash, drain, and cut if desired.	3
Broccoli	Cut into sections, wash, and drain.	3
Brussels sprouts	Trim, wash, and drain.	3
Cauliflower	Cut into sections, wash, and drain.	3
Peas	Shell, wash, and drain.	2
Spinach	Wash and drain.	2
Corn	Boil 3–4 minutes, dip in cold water, cut from cob, rinse in cold water. Drain.	Done in preparation

[a]For altitudes above 5,000 feet, increase the scalding time 1 minute.

even easier and faster than is the time required to prepare vegetables. Fruits are washed, sorted, and cut (if desired), but they are not blanched. They are packed plain, sprinkled with dry sugar, or packed in syrup in most instances, with ascorbic acid or vitamin C sometimes being added to help retard discoloration.

Fruits (such as pineapple, plums, raspberries, rhubarb, strawberries, blackberries, blueberries, and gooseberries) can be frozen immediately after they are cleaned thoroughly and packaged without sugar or syrup, although use of sugar or syrup often is the method chosen (Table 19.2). A sugar pack is done simply by sprinkling about 3/4 cup of sugar on each quart of tart fruit or 1/2 cup on sweet fruits per quart of fruit. Fruits susceptible to browning should be combined with a solution of 1/4 teaspoon of vitamin C or ascorbic acid in 1/4 cup of water to coat the surface and prevent enzymatic oxidation and browning.

Syrups of varying sweetness can be used to pack fruits for freezing. Most fruits are satisfactory when the syrup contains 3 cups of sugar to 1 quart of water; very tart fruits need 4 3/4 cups of sugar to 1 quart of water. After the fruit and any sugar or syrup to be used have been added, the lid is positioned and secured snugly to keep deteriorative changes to a minimum, and the product is labeled carefully, with the date being a prominent part of the label. Careful and thorough labeling helps to ensure maximum maintenance of quality in storage and proper inventory control. Frozen fruits held at a steady temperature of 0°F (−18°C) or colder can be stored for a year.

Other Foods   Meats, poultry, and fish freeze well when wrapped tightly in airtight packaging. As with fruits and vegetables, meats will maintain structural integrity best when the rate of freezing is very fast, thus minimizing drip loss upon thawing. When meats are frozen very slowly, large ice crystals form and break through some of the cell walls. It is these breaks in the walls that permit considerable drip loss when some meats are thawed.

Casseroles and stews can be frozen after they are prepared. The major problem with the freezing of starch-thickened mixtures is the retrogradation of the starch that occurs during frozen storage. Retrogradation in stews can be reversed by heating and stirring. However, puddings thickened with starch and other comparable items that cannot be reheated and stirred do not freeze well because the starch retrogrades, causing a somewhat gritty texture in the thawed product. The use of waxy rice flour in place of wheat or cornstarch minimizes the problem of retrogradation, which helps to produce an acceptable frozen pudding (Chapter 10).

Typically, baked products freeze well. Rolls and breads of all types may be baked, cooled, and then frozen in plastic or other airtight wrap. Cakes, cookies, cream puffs, and doughnuts also are baked and cooled before being frozen. Powdered sugar icings freeze reasonably well, but more elaborate icings on cakes may be poor following frozen storage. The best method with frozen fruit pies is to freeze the unbaked pie and then bake it close to the time it will be served. Soft meringues do not freeze well, but hard meringues can be frozen following baking.

TABLE 19.2
PROCEDURES FOR FREEZING FRUIT

Fruit	Preparation Instructions	Type of Pack	Vitamin C
Apricots	Scald apricot halves 30 seconds, chill in ice water.	Syrup or dry sugar	Yes
Blackberries	Sort, wash, drain.	Syrup, dry sugar, or no sugar	No
Cherries	Sort and wash.	Syrup or dry sugar	Yes
Peaches	Wash and peel, halve or slice.	Syrup or dry sugar	Yes
Raspberries	Sort, wash, drain.	Syrup, dry sugar, or no sugar	No
Rhubarb	Wash, cut into short pieces, blanch 1 minute, cool in ice water.	Syrup	No
Strawberries	Sort, wash, remove cap, drain.	Syrup, dry sugar, or no sugar	No

jelly   Pectin gel made with fruit juice to yield a clear gel.

jam   Pectin gel with pieces of fruit plus the juice.

preserves   Pectin gel with juice and fruit pieces larger than the pieces used in jam.

conserves   Preserves with nuts added.

marmalade   Citrus preserves.

fruit butter   Cooked fruit purée.

pectin   Pectic substances in barely ripe fruit; capable of forming a gel.

pectinic acid   A form of pectin, a pectic substance.

protopectin   Pectic substance in very green fruit; incapable of forming a gel.

pectic acid   Pectic substance in overly ripe fruit; incapable of forming a gel.

Preserving with Sugar

Sugar can be an effective preservative for foods, its action being the result of the disturbance of osmotic pressure and the consequent loss of necessary fluid from microorganisms. Several different products can be made using fruit and sugar. **Jelly** is the pectin gel made using fruit juice to produce a clear product. **Jams** and **preserves** are two virtual synonyms for pectin gels containing both juice and pieces of fruit. Preserves are pectin gels consisting of some juice and very large pieces of fruit. **Conserves** are merely preserves with nuts added. **Marmalades** are preserves made with citrus fruits. **Fruit butters** are semisolid, somewhat viscous purées of fruit cooked with spices.

Fruit Selection   The best fruits for making **pectin** gels are those with a high pectin content and a rather low (acidic) pH. Tart apples, berries, citrus fruits, and grapes are fruits that contain a useful level of acid. Citrus fruits and apples are good sources of pectin.

Fortunately, pectin can be purchased to help in making gels that are sufficiently strong to be served easily. Pectin is prepared for commercial sale from the skins and cores of apples and from the albedo (white portion) of the skin of citrus fruits. This pectin is marketed as the fluid pectin or as powdered pectin, either one being effective in forming an appropriate gel structure.

The pectic substances (various chemical relatives of pectin) undergo some changes during the ripening of fruit, and these changes determine the effectiveness of pectic substances in achieving gelation. The desired form of pectic substances for making gels is pectin or **pectinic acid,** the form found in fruit that is barely ripe. Of the various pectic substances, only pectin is capable of participating in the formation of a gel in combination with fruit juices. The **protopectin** in very green fruit and the **pectic acid** that forms as fruits become overly ripe are not able to form a gel. For this reason, only barely ripe fruit is recommended for making jams, jellies, and preserves.

Fruits for Jams and Jellies   The type of fruit desired for making jams and jellies needs to be decided. Then the fruits to select are those that are barely ripe because they contain the maximum amount of pectin. However, many fruits are not high enough in pectin to form a gel, so commercial pectins ordinarily are added to the mixture to ensure that a gel will result.

Acid also is important in the gel-forming process. Some fruits are quite acidic, but others need added acids to achieve the necessary acidic pH for gel formation.

Preparation   Jelly is prepared by boiling the ingredients rapidly to bring the sugar to a concentration of 60–65 percent. During this boiling period, some breakdown of the sugar occurs, the extent being determined by the length of time the mixture is boiled. Some of the sugar is changed by acid hydrolysis to invert sugar, which is an aid in preventing the formation of sugar crystals in the finished product during storage. The other change is the caramelizing of sugar, which can occur if the cooking period is too long. The color darkens and the odor begins to change as sugar caramelizes during prolonged boiling. Caramelizing should be avoided.

For both maximum yield and general desirability of a jelly, sufficient sugar needs to be used in the recipe so that long boiling will not be required to reach the necessary concentration of sugar between 60–65 percent. A short boiling time avoids unnecessary loss of volatile flavors. Using adequate sugar keeps the boiling period as short as possible, which helps to avoid the rubbery texture that results if the pectin becomes too concentrated as water is boiled away. The short boiling period also prevents much hydrolysis of pectin. Some breakdown (hydrolysis) of pectin will occur while the jelly mixture is boiling, but the amount of change is not significant unless boiling is extended. With considerable chemical change in pectin, the final jelly will be softer than it should be because of loss of some of the gel-forming capability of the original pectin.

Various tests for doneness are possible when making jellies. A thermometer can be used to determine when the right concentration of sugar has been reached. The temperature should be 9°F (5°C) higher than the boiling point of water when cooking stops, for this indicates a sugar concentration of 65 percent. A visual test for this is to let the hot jelly flow from a spoon. At the correct end point, the jelly will "sheet off" the spoon because of its viscosity. Commercial jelly makers use the refractive index of the boiling liquid to determine when the correct concentration has been reached.

As soon as jelly is removed from the heat, it should be poured into the glasses. This achieves the maximum gel structure. Pouring after gelation begins causes disruption of the developing gel structure and weakens the final product. A good jelly is strong enough to retain the outline of the glass when it is unmolded, yet is flexible enough to sway when the dish is moved. When spread with a knife, jelly breaks into pieces that yield under pressure. The flavor should be fresh and characteristic of the fruit, and the color should be bright. No sugar crystals should be evident, and there should not be any mold.

A very soft or fluid jelly can be caused by several errors. An imbalance in the ratio of pectin, sugar, or acid and the liquid can be the result of an error in the recipe or too little evaporation of water during cooking. Too little pectin in the fruit itself can be corrected by the addition of commercial pectin. Citric or tartaric acid can be added if needed to reach the desired pH of 3.3.

SCIENCE NOTE
PECTIC SUBSTANCES

The pectic substances, a family of polysaccharides that are a part of the cellular composition of fruits, are found in cell walls and also between cells. These substances undergo chemical changes as fruits ripen. However, they all have the same underlying structure composed of repeating units of galacturonic acid. Galacturonic acid is the uronic acid derived from galactose and is present when the external (sixth) carbon of galactose is an acid functional group rather than the hydroxyl group.

Galactose   Galacturonic acid

Protopectin is a polysaccharide in which very long polymers or chains of galacturonic acid units are linked together. These cumbersome molecules contribute considerable rigidity to immature fruits. However, the acid radical on the sixth carbon is capable of forming an ester with methanol, a reaction that is catalyzed by enzymes during the ripening process.

Pectinic acid fragment

Pectin molecules vary a bit, but basically they are pectinic acid and/or pectinates, which are salts of pectinic acid. Pectin molecules that are particularly effective in forming gels are derived from apples and citrus. The molecular weight of apple pectin is approximately 280,000 and that of citrus fruit pectin is about 229,000. The concentration of pectin is greatest in fast-growing surface tissues. Polygalacturonase and pectin esterases are the enzymes catalyzing the transformation from protopectin to pectin. As this reaction gradually occurs, the texture of the fruits begins to soften.

In barely ripe fruit, enough methylation has occurred to produce pectinic acids and pectinates capable of forming gels. However, chemical reactions continue to occur in fruits, and pectin gradually changes to pectic acid, another pectic substance. Pectic acids are characterized by having fewer methyl groups esterified on the sixth carbon than are found on pectinic acids. This change in structure results in loss of gel-forming properties.

Pectin is capable of forming a gel because its colloidal-sized molecules are able to hydrogen bond to each other, forming a continuous network of pectin molecules linked to each other in a random fashion. Acid facilitates this cross-linking; at a pH of about 3.3, pectin molecules will be hydrated very little. When the usual protective coating of water on pectin is absent, the actual molecules of pectin can approach each other rather easily and form the hydrogen bonds needed for gelling. The presence of sugar in jellies also aids in gel formation because of the excellent hygroscopic nature of sugar. Sugar is quite effective in helping to bind some of the water that would otherwise tend to interfere with the formation of the gel.

A pectin gel can be visualized as being a system in which the pectin molecules, which are hydrogen bonded together, form a complex brush-like structure somewhat similar to the structure of a tumbleweed. The acid in the mixture allowed the water to be freed from the pectin sufficiently for hydrogen bonding to occur. However, the water in the fruit juice can be held in the pectin gel when the mixture is cold because the spaces between the various pectin molecules in the structural framework are quite small. This makes it possible for sugar to bind much of the water and to aid in trapping the water so that the gel structure becomes rigid.

Overcooked jellies often contain some sugar crystal aggregates that give a distinctly gritty character to the product. This usually is accompanied by a rubbery texture because of the excessive concentration of the pectin molecules. Darkening of jellies also occurs in overcooking as a result of the caramelization of some of the sugar.

Syneresis is a problem in some very acidic jellies. Cranberry jelly is particularly notorious for this problem. The loss of some of the liquid out of the gel occurs when the pH of the jelly is less than 3.3.

Salting

Salt and salt brines have been used traditionally to preserve fish and meats in many parts of the world. Salt ionizes and creates osmotic pressure unfavorable to microorganisms, which preserves the food. Other curing agents added for their preservative action include sodium nitrite and vitamin C. Nitrite is particularly important to protect against *Clostridium botulinum* in making bacon. Flavor and increased safety of bacon may be enhanced by added sugar and smoking.

Drying

Drying, the earliest method of food preservation, was first done many centuries ago, but this technique has seen limited use in recent times (Figure 19.4). However, heightened participation in camping and backpacking and the interest in "natural foods" have contributed to the swelling sales of dehydrators for drying foods at home. Although many dehydrators have been sold, there is no requirement that fancy or elaborate equipment be available for drying foods. The equipment can be as simple as some cotton cheesecloth stretched over the rack in the oven. In addition to the appeal of being able to preserve food without investing in equipment, drying of food is appealing because the finished product can be stored in tightly closed plastic bags at room temperature; campers appreciate the reduced weight and bulk of dried foods, too.

Vegetables, fruits, and meats can be dried satisfactorily in the home. Vegetables that can be dried without blanching include chives, herbs, mushrooms, okra, onions, parsley, peppers, and tomatoes. Blanching is done to asparagus, broccoli, Brussels sprouts, cabbage, carrots, cauliflower, corn, celery, greens, peas, potatoes, and squash before they are dried. Fruits that tend to brown upon standing will have a better color when dipped in an acidic fruit juice or a solution of ascorbic acid before being dried; peaches and apricots will have a brighter color if they are sulfured before drying. Meats may be marinated prior to drying, if desired.

Foods for drying are sliced thinly, with the exception of a few fruits, such as grapes, that are left whole, but are punctured with a fork. Only very lean cuts of meat are suitable

http://www.foodprocessing-technology.com/projects/directfoods/

—Story of bacon production in England.

http://www.extension.umn.edu/distribution/nutrition/DJ0974.html

—Background on production and regulation of nitrite and bacon.

Figure 19.4
Racks used for drying the catch from the Norwegian Sea in northern Norway. Courtesy of Plycon Press.

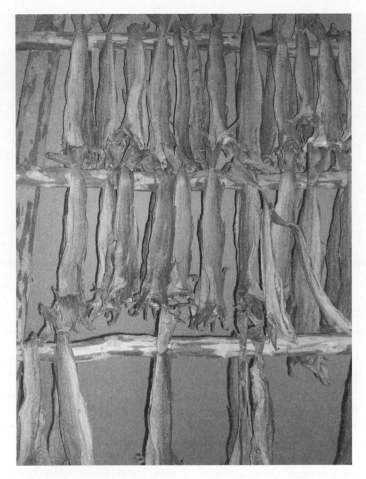

Figure 19.5
Fish dressed and hung to dry on giant racks in the sun and wind of northern Norway. Courtesy of Plycon Press.

for drying because rancidity can be a problem if fat content is very high. Moreover, the meat must be sliced very thinly so that the interior can be dried satisfactorily. The thin slices of food are placed on racks outdoors, in a dehydrator, or in an oven maintained at 200°F (93°C) (Figure 19.5). If sun drying is being done, the food must be protected from insects and animals. The food is dried until it is dry, yet pliable. Then it is placed in plastic bags that are closed tightly and labeled. Storage should be in a cool, dry, dark closet.

CULTURAL ACCENT
PEMMICAN

Pemmican was one of the most important foods of Native Americans long before pioneers pressed across the continent and settled the West. Although pemmican can be made using some variations in ingredients, the basic ingredients always are dried, powdered meat and fat plus some berries. The meats that were dried for making pemmican were those available from hunting, most commonly bison, elk, or deer. The flesh was cut in strips and hung on poles until dried. Then the meat was made into a powder so it could be stirred with almost equal parts of melted fat rendered from the inside of the animal carcasses. Berries were added to improve the flavor.

Survival during winter months and other times when fresh food supplies were limited was possible because pemmican could be stored safely for many months. This dried food was relatively light because of the low moisture content, which also made it a practical food to carry on trips.

Pemmican is a popular food among hikers and campers today for the same reason that natives counted on it. However, commercial producers of pemmican are now marketing several different flavors to appeal to the individual appetites of backpackers and other adventure seekers.

Figure 19.6
View of the Gray*Star Genesis irradiator used for irradiating food. Courtesy of Gray*Star. Inc.

Irradiation   Irradiation offers another possible way of preserving foods (Figure 19.6). When foods are subjected to gamma rays from cobalt[60] or cesium[137] microorganisms and insects are killed; storage life of grains and potatoes in particular can be extended by the use of irradiation. In 1984, the FDA proposed permitting fresh fruits and vegetables to be treated with a maximum radiation dosage of a kilogray (Table 19.3), an amount equivalent to 100 kilorads or 100,000 rads (radiation absorbed dose). A low dosage for food irradiation is considered to be up to 100 kilorads; a medium level is 100–1,000 kilorads (1 megarad); a high level is 1,000–5,000 kilorads (1–5 megarads). The FDA at the same time proposed that spices be treated at levels up to 30 kilograys because the spices often have high levels of contaminants and are eaten in extremely small quantities. These levels are designed to kill insects and other agents that could cause spoilage during room temperature storage.

National concern regarding the safety of hamburgers served in fast-food restaurants has focused on the need for care in handling and cooking perishable foods. Irradiation is a very effective means of helping to assure that food will be safe to eat when it reaches consumers. The U.S. Food and Drug Administration has approved irradiation of wheat, white potatoes, spices, pork carcasses, fresh and dried fruits and vegetables, and poultry, as well as some other products. The level of irradiation to be used for the various food items is defined and very carefully controlled. Limited marketing of several irradiated foods indicates that consumer acceptance is quite good and that the slightly higher price necessitated by the cost of irradiation is not a detriment to sales, the longer shelf life and safety of the food seemingly offsetting the small price difference.

http://www.foodirradiation.com/

—Foundation for Food Irradiation Education website.

TABLE 19.3
UNITS USED IN EXPRESSING RADIATION ENERGY

Term	Definition
Rad	Radiation absorbed dose
Gray	100 rads
Kilorad	1,000 rads
Kilogray	1,000 grays or 100 kilorads or 100,000 rads
Megarad	1,000 kilorads or 1,000,000 rads

SUMMARY

Canning, freezing, drying, freeze-drying, preserving with salt and sugar, and irradiation are techniques that are used to preserve food. Some food preservation, including canning, pickling, freezing, drying, and jam and jelly making, is done in homes; more is done commercially. All preservation techniques are directed toward preventing the growth of yeasts, molds, and bacteria that will cause food spoilage or illness. Canning utilizes high temperatures to kill microorganisms. Freezing significantly retards the growth of microorganisms. Drying promotes long storage life because microorganisms fail to thrive in an extremely low-moisture environment. Irradiation kills microorganisms, and high concentrations of salt or sugar prevent their growth. Whether preservation is done commercially or in the home, processing must be controlled conscientiously to ensure safety and long storage life of the food.

All canning needs to be done carefully, but particular attention must be given to the processing of vegetables and meats because of their low acid content. These foods must be canned in a pressure canner or pressure saucepan so that the food will reach a high enough temperature to inactivate spores of *C. botulinum*. The toxin that this bacterium can produce in these foods often is lethal to humans, even in infinitesimal amounts. If such foods are boiled for 15 minutes, they will be safe to eat.

Freezing is a quick method of preserving food. Fruits may be packed without sugar, with sugar, or with a syrup pack. Vegetables are blanched before freezing to inactivate the enzymes. Drying may be done in the oven, by sun drying, or in a dehydrator. Some fruits require sulfuring to prevent discoloration; some vegetables are blanched prior to drying.

Jams and jellies are made by using levels of pectin and sugar to gel fruits and juices at a pH of about 3.3. The high level of sugar in the cooked product prevents spoilage. Pectin and acid levels are appropriate in some fruits for making jams and jellies, but often the addition of either pectin and/or acid may be essential to the formation of a gel of satisfactory strength. Small batches should be prepared to avoid unnecessary breakdown in the sugar or pectin during the boiling period.

Pectin is the methylated galacturonic acid polymer found in the cell walls and intercellular spaces of fruits that has the ability to form gels. Protopectin (the pectic substance in unripened fruits) and pectic acids (the pectic substances in overly ripe fruits) lack the gel-forming properties of pectin. These changes in pectic substances occur as a result of enzymatic action in the maturing fruit.

Drying, the earliest method used for preserving food, is done by placing thin slices of food in a very dry environment until the moisture level drops so low that microorganisms cannot survive.

Irradiation of foods is becoming more widely approved and accepted as a means of extending shelf life and preventing some food-borne illnesses. Other commercial techniques that are being used today include freeze-drying and high pressure processing.

STUDY QUESTIONS

1. What is the oldest method of food preservation? Why do you think this method was used first?
2. Compare the advantages of canning with the advantages of freezing as preservation methods. Then contrast the disadvantages of each method. When might canning be the best method for preserving foods and when might freezing be preferred?
3. Why is dried food popular with hikers and backpackers?

4. Outline the method for drying apples in the home.

5. Explain the role of each of the following in making jelly: (a) pectin, (b) sugar, and (c) acid.

6. What is the general chemical structure of pectin? Describe the changes occurring as protopectin is transformed to pectin.

7. What foods need to be canned in a pressure canner? Why must a pressure canner be used for them?

8. What is the effect of a very slow rate of freezing on the quality of frozen foods?

9. What breads and desserts may be frozen satisfactorily after baking? Which ones should be frozen without being baked?

SELECTED REFERENCES

Blumenthal, D. 1990. Food irradiation. *FDA Consumer 24* (11): 13.

Brody, A. L. 2009. Aseptic packaging 2009. *Food Technol.* 63(9): 70.

Clark, J. P. 2006. High-pressure processing research continues. *Food Technol.* 60(2): 63.

Clark, J. P. 2006. Drying of foods. *Food Technol.* 60(12): 90.

Clark, J. P. 2007. High pressure effects on foods. *Food Technol.* 61(2): 69.

Clark, J. P. 2009. New issues with acidified foods. *Food Technol.* 6(2): 76.

Clark, J. P. 2010. Considerations on drying. *Food Technol.* 64(3): 70.

Clark, J. P. 2010. Focus on freezing. *Food Technol.* 64(11): 70.

Consumer and Food Economics Institute. 1977. *How to make jellies, jams, and preserves at home.* Home and Garden Bulletin No. 56. U.S. Dept. Agriculture. Washington, DC.

Cowell, N. D. 2007. More light on dawn of canning. *Food Technol.* 61(2): 40.

Decker, K. J. 2003. Where there's smoke, there's flavor. *Food Product Design 13*(4): 85.

Fumento, M. 1994. Irradiation—A winning recipe for wholesome beef. *Priorities 6*(2): 37.

Fumento, M. 1994. Managing technology. *Priorities 6*(2): 37.

Hoover, D. G. 1993. Pressure effects on biological systems. *Food Technol.* 47(6): 150.

Kim, H. J., and L. A. Taub. 1993. Intrinsic chemical markers for aseptic processing of particulate foods. *Food Technol.* 47(1): 91.

Lechowich, R. V. 1993. Food safety implications of high hydrostatic pressure as a food processing method. *Food Technol.* 47(6): 170.

Loaharanu, P. 1994. Cost/benefit aspects of food irradiation. *Food Technol.* 48(1): 104.

Loaharanu, P. 1994. Status and prospects of food irradiation. *Food Technol.* 48(5): 124.

McWilliams, M., and H. Paine. 1977. *Modern Food Preservation.* Plycon Press. Redondo Beach, CA.

Mertens, B., and G. Deplace. 1993. Engineering aspects of high-pressure technology in the food industry. *Food Technol.* 47(6): 164.

Miller, M. W., et al. 1977. *Drying foods at home.* Home and Garden Bulletin No. 217. U.S. Dept. Agriculture. Washington, DC.

Olson, D. G. 2004. Food irradiation future still bright. *Food Technol.* 58(7): 112.

Potkahamury, U. R., et al. 1993. Magnetic-field inactivation of microorganisms and generation of biological changes. *Food Technol.* 47(12): 85.

Pszczola, D. E. 1990. Food irradiation: Countering the tactics and claims of opponents. *Food Technol.* 44(6): 92.

Pszczola, D. E. 1993. Irradiated poultry makes U.S. debut in Midwest and Florida markets. *Food Technol.* 47(11): 89.

Rittman, A. 2003. Preserving your fruit options. *Food Product Design 13*(2): 90.

Stevenson, M. H. 1994. Identification of irradiated foods. *Food Technol.* 48(5): 41.

Teixeira, A., et al. 2006. Keeping botulism out of canned foods. *Food Technol.* 60(2): 84.

Thayer, D. W. 1994. Wholesomeness of irradiated foods. *Food Technol.* 48(5): 132.

Thomas, M. W., et al. 1981. Effect of radiation and conventional processing on the thiamin content of pork. *J. Food Sci. 46:* 824.

Wolf, I. D. 1992. Critical issues in food safety, 1991–2000. *Food Technol.* 46(1): 64.

Zimmerman, F., and C. Bergman. 1993. Isostatic high-pressure equipment for food preservation. *Food Technol.* 47(6): 162.

Section Three
Food in the Context of Life

Vegetables are a key part of healthful menus.

20

Menu Planning and Meal Preparation

CREATING TEMPTING AND HEALTHY MENUS

Good meals begin with good planning. The underlying goal in planning any meal is to meet the body's needs for the various nutrients. Fortunately, there are many ways to meet these requirements, and this is where much of the creative pleasure is found. With thoughtful planning, meals and healthful eating can be highlights of the day's activities.

Planning for Good Nutrition

A convenient and generally satisfactory way of beginning menu planning is to plan breakfast, lunch, and dinner menus for a single day and then check these menus against MyPlate. See that they include the recommended servings of cereals, vegetables, fruits, milk, and meat and meat alternatives. If any servings are missing from any of the food groups, the additional portions needed can be identified and added to the menus. For optimal nutrition without too many calories, low-fat selections may be wise choices within the milk and meat groups.

For many people, breakfast is the simplest meal of the day, yet it is a particularly important one from the perspective of nutrition. An outline of the breakfast menu appropriately includes a serving of fruit juice rich in vitamin C, a glass of milk, and a food from the cereal group (Figure 20.1). If desired, some cheese, an egg, or other food from the meat and meat alternatives group can be included.

Lunch patterns vary considerably from person to person and from family to family, due in part to the fact that lunch often is eaten away from home. For children and adults, this meal needs to be the heartiest meal of the day, hearty enough to meet energy needs during the afternoon. However, lunch for many is a moderate meal, sometimes because of lack of time or the fact that it is eaten away from home. A suggested lunch pattern includes an entrée containing the equivalent of a three-ounce serving of meat, two servings from the fruit and vegetable groups, bread or another cereal product (pasta, for example), and a glass of milk.

Key Concepts

1. Meals that are nutritionally adequate, appeal to the senses, and are adapted to cultural influences and lifestyle can be planned and served to promote good health and add pleasure to life.

2. Effective management of human energy and use of appliances can save time and energy in meal preparation without compromising food quality.

3. Food cost can be managed by (1) planning menus consistent with the food budget, (2) making a shopping list that includes all ingredients that need to be purchased to prepare the menus, and (3) shopping carefully, using nutrition and ingredient labeling, open dating, and unit pricing to select items.

4. Preparation of a meal requires that the time required to prepare each menu item is coordinated into a realistic schedule so that all foods will be ready to serve at the intended time.

5. Leftovers, including those that are preplanned, require safe food handling and very prompt refrigeration.

http://www.cnpp.usda.gov/ USDAFoodPlans CostofFood.htm

—USDA reports on food costs for families at four different income levels.

http://www.health.gov/
dietaryguidelines/

—Accesses *Dietary
Guidelines for Americans*,
2010, and related
publications.

http://www.choosemyplate.
gov/http://www.mypyramid.
gov/

—MyPlate website.

http://hp2010.nhlbihin.net/
menuplanner/menu.cgi

—Interactive menu planner.

http://www.foodandhealth.
com/leanmeals.pdf

—Ideas for lower calorie
meals.

Figure 20.1
Broiled tomato adds a bright and flavorful source of vitamin C to this
hearty breakfast.

The largest meal for many families is eaten at night; dinner serves a social function as well as a nutritional function for families who are able to eat together. In fact, dinner may be the only meal eaten during the day in an organized manner with all family members present. Because of the sociability of dinner, this meal often is the largest and most elaborate meal of the day. Emphasis on planning dinner needs to be on providing a good variety, including vegetables, a small portion of fish or other high-protein food, and also bread or rice or pasta. Time to prepare dinners like this during the week may be a major problem, but shortcuts such as picking up some prepared food on the way home or preparing items on the weekend may be the answer.

Fat content should be low. One of the easiest ways to reduce fat intake and promote good nutrition is to include a low-fat selection (poultry or fish) from the meat and meat alternatives group at least three times a week and to keep the serving sizes in this group modest (only about three ounces of cooked meat). Inclusion of another glass of milk at this meal is helpful to bone maintenance in adults and sets a good example for children in the family. In line with the recommendation to keep fat intake low, the use of non-fat (skim) milk at dinner and all other meals is recommended.

Sensory Aspects of Menu Planning

Color   Food has the potential for providing aesthetic pleasure in life, and color is a key characteristic in creating beautiful meals. When planning menus, the combination of colors in the tentative menu must be visualized. Fruits and vegetables are particularly valuable in adding color interest to a meal. They may be planned as a serving of a particular fruit or vegetable, as an ingredient in mixtures of foods, or even as a garnish to accent the appearance of a meal. To illustrate, red apples can be used in a salad with their skins left on to provide an important color highlight, or a twist of lemon or orange can be added just to garnish a meal needing a touch of excitement. Broiled salmon with a bright yellow twist of lemon, French cut green beans with toasted almonds, and a stuffed baked potato in its russet skin constitute a colorful and tempting dinner plate. Compare this with the monotonous color afforded by a plate of sliced breast of turkey, mashed potatoes, and creamed onions. This turkey menu could be enhanced considerably by changing the menu slightly to mashed sweet potatoes and adding some bright green peas to the cream sauce on the onions.

Color is a cornerstone of good menu planning. These are but a few ideas. With an awareness of the importance of thinking about color, the imagination can be exercised fully to create plates of beauty at any meal (Figure 20.2).

Shape With most menus, there are choices to be made regarding the shape of the pieces of food. Carrots provide an excellent illustration of the types of choices to be made, for they can be cooked and served whole (with only the skin and the stem and tip being removed), cut in thin slivers, in matchsticks, in thin or thick disks, grated, or even curled. When the menu simply says carrots, it is only the beginning of planning for beauty. Many other foods afford opportunities for creative planning in regard to shape.

Harmony of shape is helpful in creating a visual picture of beauty in food. Salads or casseroles containing several ingredients that are cut into pieces often are most attractive when the foods are cut into small, recognizable pieces of similar size. When planning the menu, the shapes and sizes of the foods need to be considered in relation to the other foods that will be served. If one dish is going to have comparatively small pieces, the other foods will complement this dish best if they are moderate or large slices.

Even the contour of the surface of the foods on the plate contributes to the visual effect. For example, a stalk of broccoli adds height to the area of the plate where the flower portion of the vegetable rises. Chicken wings and drumsticks are other instances of the use of food to add interesting contours. However, variety is the important feature. Not all foods on the plate should contribute height, or they will also contribute monotony.

Figure 20.2
A twist of lemon takes but an instant to prepare, yet it adds a bright touch of color as well as being a convenient way of adding a flavor accent to baked salmon. Reprinted with permission of Cargill, Inc.© 2010.

Texture The range of textural experiences available from foods adds considerable excitement to a meal. Again, contrast is the guide to success. Crisp crackers are a pleasing complement to a smooth cream soup. A steak, with its firm chewiness, gains interest when accompanied by sliced mushrooms, which contribute a smooth, slightly slippery texture. Texture is influenced by cookery techniques as well as by the natural qualities of the food. By cooking pasta just to the *al dente* stage and vegetables to the point where they retain just a suggestion of crispness, these foods retain good textural qualities to heighten palatability of meals.

Flavor The basic taste characteristics—salt, sour, sweet, bitter, and umami—can be valuable in small amounts but may be overpowering and even monotonous in large amounts (Figure 20.3). Heightened interest can be achieved in meals where additional flavoring agents are utilized. Foods themselves

Figure 20.3
Salt is harvested from ponds of saltwater as water evaporates and the sodium chloride crystallizes; it is added to foods to add flavor appeal because salt is a basic taste. Courtesy of Plycon Press.

Figure 20.4
Dried chile peppers can add plenty of heat or a hint of it, depending on the dish and the diner. Courtesy of Plycon Press.

Figure 20.5
Wiener schnitzel (breaded veal cutlet) teamed with a slice of lemon, parsley potatoes, and a salad has excellent satiety value, and the calories can be controlled by serving a portion appropriate to the size of the diner. Courtesy of Plycon Press.

should carry the primary flavor message, with spices and other seasonings being added to provide a flourish to the various recipes.

Menus will be pleasing when they present some delicate and some moderately strong flavors concurrently. This combination gives the palate a chance to rest occasionally, rather than constantly challenging the flavor receptors. However, a bland meal is monotonous. Variety is important to avoid the inevitable fatigue experienced when the same flavor keeps impacting the tongue and nasal passages. For example, a meal containing cauliflower and broccoli would be rather uninteresting, because the flavors of these two vegetables are quite similar. Familiarity with a broad array of spices is invaluable in creating flavor excitement in meals.

Temperature Perhaps the best illustration of the importance of temperature contrasts in foods is provided by a baked Alaska. Its warm meringue is a wonderful complement to the sharp coldness of the ice cream within. On a less dramatic note, the use of at least one cold food when the meal is basically a hot meal or one hot food when the meal is cold will add interest to the meal. A cold glass of milk is welcomed when hot soup is served; a hot roll is a very pleasing addition to a luncheon featuring a cold salad plate.

Some foods have a hot, burning feel (e.g., jalapeño peppers and many Indian curries), while some others are soothingly cool (e.g., peppermint). People's enjoyment of this type of heat in foods varies greatly. Some variety in temperature adds interest to a meal, but this aspect of seasoning and food selection needs to be consistent with the preferences and gastrointestinal tolerances of the people who will eat the meal (Figure 20.4).

Satiety Value The **satiety value**, or the feeling of satisfaction and fullness, is an important aspect of a meal. Although a meal may be beautiful to view and appealing to eat, it may fail to provide a feeling of satisfaction, or, conversely, it may be too filling. The inclusion of an adequate amount of protein and fat in a meal aids in providing the desired satiety value, but very rich menus can lead to discomfort following the meal (Figure 20.5).

Portion sizes are an important factor in determining the feeling of satiety following a meal. There are no rules to apply in planning portion sizes, for exact nutritional needs vary with the individual and are influenced by activity levels and basal metabolic requirements. The appropriateness of the weight of various family members is a good indication of whether or not appropriate serving sizes are the usual practice. If excess weight is evident, portion sizes need to be decreased; the reverse is true if family members are underweight.

Variety Even menus planned to satisfy the various criteria just outlined can be dull and uninteresting if they are served too frequently. Variety is needed to spark interest in food and to add zest to mealtimes. Meal planning is more exciting and less routine if an attempt is made to include new foods and recipes as time and interest dictate.

Considerable inspiration can come from browsing through cookbooks and reading articles on food in newspapers and magazines (Figure 20.6). Ideas may range from the very exotic and expensive to something as simple as using a different seasoning in a familiar food. Such explorations in the realm of food help to relieve the possible monotony of meal preparation each day, and they aid in broadening the food tastes of family members.

satiety value Ability to satisfy and provide a feeling of fullness and satisfaction.

Rosemary

Oregano

Thyme

Sage

Dill

Tarragon

Basil

Figure 20.6
Fresh herbs can add exciting flavor highlights to recipes. Courtesy of Plycon Press.

CULTURAL ACCENT
BLENDING CUISINES

Broadened horizons can inject wonderful eating pleasures into meals. Menu planning can become exciting when one or more dishes typical of an exotic cuisine are featured in a menu. Ideas may be gathered from cookbooks from distant countries, or they might be sparked by a meal eaten at an ethnic restaurant. Some of the recipes will include unique ingredients that help broaden cooking and dining experiences. Fortunately, the tremendous influx of immigrants and the nation's increasing awareness of foreign cultures have now created demand for many of these items, and local markets often carry the item that is needed.

Herbs and spices used in ethnic dishes often create exciting aromas and flavors that are quite different from typical American dishes (Figure 20.7). The flavors that help to define a cuisine vary from one culture to another. For example, rosewater is a prized ingredient in some Persian dishes. Basil is an essential herb if pesto is being prepared for an Italian meal, but Asian dishes do not require any rosewater or basil. They may rely on fish sauces, soy sauce, and seaweed, none of which would appear in typical Italian or Middle Eastern menus. Numerous other examples could be cited, but the important concept is that meals can become more exciting to prepare and eat if a broader perspective is used when planning menus. Various new dishes can be incorporated into menus gradually. Dining pleasures can provide a sense of adventure in life without even packing a suitcase.

Figure 20.7
Chicken biryani, a favorite dish in India, is served with chutney, curry, and other flavorful accompaniments. Courtesy of Plycon Press.

http://www.youtube.com/watch?v=QjvQ7T01tLo

—Video on making chicken biryani.

ENERGY MANAGEMENT

Human Energy

Wonderful menus can be developed, yet they may fail to hit the mark if the human energy factor is not considered. For example, the time and energy available for preparing a meal can make complex menus inappropriate, particularly during the week if nobody is at home during the day to do the preparation. Even on the weekend, difficult menus may prove too taxing. A warm welcome in a relaxed mealtime atmosphere is the appropriate background in which to enjoy fine food and friendship. The menu being prepared and served should be tailored to the cook(s) so that the dining experience will meet this description.

Appliances

With some thought, use of appliances can overcome some of the human energy and time constraints in preparation. For instance, a crock pot can be loaded and turned on before the cook leaves for work in the morning so that a meal is almost ready to be served the minute the front door is opened in the evening.

Judicious use of the freezer represents another approach to solving energy and time problems. Foods that freeze well can be prepared on the weekend and then frozen in serving portions, so that weeknight dinners are largely a matter of thawing and warming to serving temperature.

In some instances, meals may even be placed in the oven and the timer set to turn on the heat at an appropriate hour; when doing this, it is essential to consider the potential for food spoilage if meat is held in the oven for several hours before being heated. Frozen meats and casseroles, however, do lend themselves to this type of meal preparation.

MANAGING COSTS

Planning

Food costs and menu planning go hand in hand in the management of meals in the home (Chart 20.1). The economic situation today is placing a huge strain on personal and family budgets. Some relief may be available for those who qualify for the federal Supplemental Nutrition Assistance Program (SNAP), formerly referred to as food stamps. Sometimes decisions may need to be made regarding use of mixes, ready-to-prepare, and ready-to-eat items. Generally, the greater the amount of preparation done outside the home, the greater the cost compared with buying the basic ingredients and making the comparable item at home. However, the quality of the various choices and the availability of time to prepare the food also may be important in making the decision.

For optimum efficiency in planning and shopping, meals should be planned for a week at a time so that effective use can be made of special purchases and unnecessary shopping trips can be avoided. The simple act of limiting trips to the grocery store to one each week is a big step toward controlling food costs, for this significantly limits the opportunities for impulse buying. Rare is the shopper who refuses to buy any item not on the shopping list.

Planning for the week also can effectively reduce food waste. When the week's menus are checked over, it is easy to see whether or not leftovers have been identified and worked into subsequent meals so that they will not spoil and have to be discarded. Any necessary modifications in the menus can be made before buying the food, either reducing quantities being purchased or changing menu items to utilize leftovers.

Some flexibility in menu items is recommended so that sensible use of specials can be planned at the grocery store. Usually grocery stores run weekend specials, and these sometimes can provide substantial savings without seriously altering menu plans. However, these changes are recommended only if the substitution is compatible with family food preferences and with the other foods being planned in the meal.

The Shopping List

A shopping list is a valuable tool in managing costs, for it is prepared in concert with the weekly plan of menus. In addition, staple items, such as flour, sugar, salt, milk, and eggs, should be checked and added to the list, if needed. This list is most helpful if it is arranged in the same sequence as the floor plan of the grocery store, with the canned and non-refrigerated items being first, followed by the refrigerated and frozen items, and last, the fresh produce. This arrangement makes it possible to do one efficient tour of the store and helps maintain the quality of perishable foods.

http://www.nutrition. gov/nal_display/index. php?info_center=11&tax_ level=2&tax_ subject=391&topic_ id=1756&placement_ default=0

—Ideas for smart food shopping.

http://www.fns.usda.gov/ snap/applicant_recipients/ eligibility.htm

—SNAP information.

http://www.fns.usda. gov/snap/applicant_ recipients/10steps.htm

—Information on SNAP.

http://www.choosemyplate. gov/

—MyPyramid personal menu planner aid.

United States
Department of
Agriculture

Center for Nutrition
Policy and Promotion

3101 Park Center Drive
Alexandria, VA 22302

Official USDA Food Plans: Cost of Food at Home at Four Levels,
U.S. Average, November 2011[1]

Age-gender groups	Weekly cost[2]				Monthly cost[2]			
	Thrifty plan	Low-cost plan	Moderate-cost plan	Liberal plan	Thrifty plan	Low-cost plan	Moderate-cost plan	Liberal plan
Individuals[3]								
Child:								
1 year	21.10	28.20	32.10	38.90	91.30	122.20	139.00	168.40
2-3 years	23.00	29.10	35.20	42.90	99.50	125.90	152.40	185.90
4-5 years	24.00	30.30	37.40	45.40	103.80	131.20	162.00	196.80
6-8 years	30.60	41.90	50.90	59.90	132.40	181.50	220.60	259.30
9-11 years	34.80	45.60	59.00	68.80	151.00	197.80	255.70	298.20
Male:								
12-13 years	37.20	52.50	65.50	76.90	161.30	227.60	284.00	333.40
14-18 years	38.50	53.90	67.80	77.70	166.70	233.40	293.60	336.90
19-50 years	41.30	53.30	66.70	82.00	179.10	231.00	289.00	355.30
51-70 years	37.80	50.40	61.90	75.10	163.90	218.20	268.10	325.40
71+ years	37.90	50.00	61.70	76.10	164.40	216.70	267.40	329.60
Female:								
12-13 years	37.30	45.50	54.60	66.60	161.70	197.20	236.60	288.60
14-18 years	36.80	45.70	55.30	68.10	159.60	198.20	239.40	295.00
19-50 years	36.70	46.30	57.10	73.10	158.90	200.50	247.40	316.60
51-70 years	36.30	45.20	55.90	67.00	157.10	195.70	242.20	290.30
71+ years	35.60	44.80	55.60	66.90	154.10	194.30	240.80	289.70
Families								
Family of 2:[4]								
19-50 years	85.80	109.50	136.20	170.60	371.80	474.60	590.00	739.10
51-70 years	81.50	105.10	129.60	156.30	353.10	455.30	561.40	677.30
Family of 4:								
Couple, 19-50 years and children—								
2-3 and 4-5 years	124.90	158.90	196.30	243.40	541.40	688.60	850.70	1054.50
6-8 and 9-11 years	143.40	187.10	233.70	283.70	621.40	810.80	1012.60	1229.40

[1]The Food Plans represent a nutritious diet at four different cost levels. The nutritional bases of the Food Plans are the 1997-2005 Dietary Reference Intakes, 2005 Dietary Guidelines for Americans, and 2005 MyPyramid food intake recommendations. In addition to cost, differences among plans are in specific foods and quantities of foods. Another basis of the Food Plans is that all meals and snacks are prepared at home. For specific foods and quantities of foods in the Food Plans, see *Thrifty Food Plan, 2006* (2007) and *The Low-Cost, Moderate-Cost, and Liberal Food Plans, 2007* (2007). All four Food Plans are based on 2001-02 data and updated to current dollars by using the Consumer Price Index for specific food items.

[2]All costs are rounded to nearest 10 cents.

[3]The costs given are for individuals in 4-person families. For individuals in other size families, the following adjustments are suggested: 1-person—add 20 percent; 2-person—add 10 percent; 3-person—add 5 percent; 4-person—no adjustment; 5- or 6-person—subtract 5 percent; 7- (or more) person—subtract 10 percent. To calculate overall household food costs, (1) adjust food costs for each person in household and then (2) sum these adjusted food costs.

[4]Ten percent added for family size adjustment.

This file may be accessed on CNPP's home page at: http://www.cnpp.usda.gov.   Issued December 2011

The quantities of the various foods will vary considerably from family to family, depending on the number in the family, the age of family members, and the food-consumption patterns of the various people being served. Fortunately, patterns do develop, which simplifies this aspect of food purchasing and avoids shortages or waste. The U.S. Department of Agriculture has made a study of the amounts of foods that predictably might be utilized for good nutrition by people of various ages. This information for people on a moderate food budget is presented in Table 20.1.

TABLE 20.1
MODERATE-COST FOOD PLAN MARKET BASKETS, QUANTITIES OF FOOD PURCHASED FOR A WEEK, BY AGE–GENDER GROUP, 2007

Food Category	Males				
	12–13 Years	14–18 Years	19–50 Years	51–70 Years	71+ Years
Total Pounds	37.43	44.04	45.00	41.20	38.99
			Pounds per Week		
Grains					
Whole-grain breads, rice, pasta, and pastries (including whole-grain flours)	0.29	2.25	2.39	1.74	0.82
Whole-grain cereals (including hot cereal mixes)	0.03	0.09	0.10	0.14	1.34
Popcorn and other whole-grain snacks	1.95	0.82	0.20	0.74	0.28
Non-whole-grain breads, cereals, rice, pasta, pies, pastries, snacks, and flours	1.35	1.89	2.04	1.30	0.88
	3.62	**5.05**	**4.74**	**3.92**	**3.32**
Vegetables					
All potato products	1.61	1.81	1.61	1.20	1.84
Dark-green vegetables	0.50	1.07	1.12	1.10	2.95
Orange vegetables	1.06	0.99	0.88	0.78	0.74
Canned and dry beans, lentils, and peas (legumes)	2.21	3.11	2.64	1.61	1.51
Other vegetables	2.99	3.10	3.39	3.59	2.86
	8.37	**10.08**	**9.64**	**8.28**	**9.90**
Fruits					
Whole fruits	5.28	7.07	7.00	5.90	5.91
Fruit juices	2.22	1.80	1.68	1.74	1.70
	7.50	**8.87**	**8.68**	**7.63**	**7.61**
Milk Products					
Whole milk, yogurt, and cream	0.37	0.42	0.39	0.38	0.44
Lower fat and skim milk and low-fat yogurt	12.94	12.12	12.33	12.82	12.03
All cheese (including cheese soup and sauce)	0.08	0.11	0.13	0.06	0.11
Milk drinks and milk desserts	0.17	0.20	0.15	0.14	0.15
	13.55	**12.85**	**13.00**	**13.41**	**12.73**
Meat and Beans					
Beef, pork, veal, lamb, and game	0.78	0.88	1.04	1.02	0.87
Chicken, turkey, and game birds	0.71	2.07	2.95	3.79	2.22
Fish and fish products	0.59	0.61	0.42	0.42	0.15

(Continued)

TABLE 20.1   (CONTINUED)

Food Category	Males				
	12–13 Years	14–18 Years	19–50 Years	51–70 Years	71+ Years
Total Pounds	37.43	44.04	45.00	41.20	38.99
	Pounds per Week				
Bacon, sausages, and luncheon meats (including spreads)	0.04	0.10	0.11	0.07	0.06
Nuts, nut butters, and seeds	0.64	0.34	0.33	0.32	0.53
Eggs and egg mixtures	0.08	0.12	0.17	0.16	0.10
	2.85	4.13	5.03	5.78	3.92
Other Foods					
Table fats, oils, and salad dressings	0.25	0.44	0.47	0.31	0.39
Gravies, sauces, condiments, and spices	0.17	0.26	0.46	0.21	0.21
Coffee and tea	0.00	0.00	0.01	0.00	0.00
Soft drinks, sodas, fruit drinks, and ades (including rice beverages)	0.97	1.93	2.64	1.40	0.62
Sugars, sweets, and candies	0.06	0.14	0.13	0.11	0.07
Soups (ready-to-serve and condensed)	0.00	0.24	0.15	0.12	0.21
Soups (dry)	0.01	0.01	0.01	0.02	0.00
Frozen or refrigerated entrèe (including pizza, fish sticks, and frozen meals)	0.07	0.05	0.04	0.01	0.00
	1.53	3.06	3.91	2.18	1.51
	Females				
Total Pounds	37.56	36.49	38.94	38.53	34.58
	Pounds per Week				
Grains					
Whole-grain breads, rice, pasta, and pastries (including whole-grain flours)	1.30	1.53	1.09	2.67	2.11
Whole-grain cereals (including hot cereal mixes)	0.20	1.19	0.68	0.07	0.07
Popcorn and other whole-grain snacks	0.48	0.02	0.72	0.29	0.04
Non-whole-grain breads, cereals, rice, pasta, pies, pastries, snacks, and flours	1.31	0.90	0.92	0.28	0.55
	3.30	3.64	3.41	3.31	2.78
Vegetables					
All potato products	1.04	1.26	1.49	1.19	0.89
Dark-green vegetables	2.77	1.83	1.80	1.75	2.67
Orange vegetables	0.84	0.68	1.59	0.90	0.72
Canned and dry beans, lentils, and peas (legumes)	1.50	2.33	2.04	1.12	1.46
Other vegetables	4.04	2.72	3.54	2.62	2.83
	10.19	8.81	10.46	7.58	8.57
Fruits					
Whole fruits	5.63	5.07	5.14	7.80	4.93
Fruit juices	1.79	1.64	1.50	1.57	1.61
	7.41	6.71	6.64	9.38	6.55
Milk Products					
Whole milk, yogurt, and cream	0.76	0.58	0.40	0.06	0.22
Lower fat and skim milk and low-fat yogurt	12.12	12.59	12.86	13.25	12.80

(Continued)

(Continued)

Total Pounds	Females				
	37.56	36.49	38.94	38.53	34.58
	Pounds per Week				
All cheese (including cheese soup and sauce)	0.07	0.01	0.08	0.00	0.01
Milk drinks and milk desserts	0.10	0.06	0.05	0.02	0.04
	<u>13.05</u>	<u>13.24</u>	<u>13.40</u>	<u>13.34</u>	<u>13.08</u>
Meat and Beans					
Beef, pork, veal, lamb, and game	0.47	0.78	0.86	0.45	0.75
Chicken, turkey, and game birds	0.25	0.97	1.45	2.13	0.94
Fish and fish products	1.13	0.26	0.32	0.56	0.13
Bacon, sausages, and luncheon meats (including spreads)	0.03	0.01	0.02	0.00	0.01
Nuts, nut butters, and seeds	0.12	0.24	0.58	0.54	0.79
Eggs and egg mixtures	0.03	0.02	0.06	0.04	0.03
	<u>2.04</u>	<u>2.28</u>	<u>3.30</u>	<u>3.73</u>	<u>2.65</u>
Other Foods					
Table fats, oils, and salad dressings	0.41	0.24	0.27	0.32	0.19
Gravies, sauces, condiments, and spices	0.31	0.36	0.16	0.14	0.10
Coffee and tea	0.00	0.00	0.00	0.00	0.00
Soft drinks, sodas, fruit drinks, and ades (including rice beverages)	0.69	0.42	0.92	0.30	0.26
Sugars, sweets, and candies	0.06	0.08	0.06	0.02	0.04
Soups (ready-to-serve and condensed)	0.04	0.70	0.31	0.40	0.36
Soups (dry)	0.00	0.00	0.00	0.01	0.00
Frozen or refrigerated entrèe (including pizza, fish sticks, and frozen meals)	0.05	0.01	0.02	0.00	0.00
	<u>1.57</u>	<u>1.81</u>	<u>1.75</u>	<u>1.18</u>	<u>0.96</u>

Notes: Food in as-purchased form includes uncooked grain products; raw, canned, and frozen vegetables; fruit juice concentrates; and meat with bones. Components of the market baskets are discussed in terms of pounds; therefore, fluids such as milk are weighted more prominently than are dry foods, and juice concentrates are weighted less prominently than are their reconstituted forms.

The numbers are rounded; thus, when summed, they may not equal the respective totals.

Storage Conditions

When planning and shopping for food for a week, the storage facilities that are available in the home must be considered to avoid losses. There is a finite amount of frozen storage space in most homes, and frozen foods must either be prepared at the time of purchase or stored in a freezer. Marvelous buys on ice cream and various frozen items cease to be bargains if they cannot be held satisfactorily.

Fresh produce also requires special storage; hydrator drawers are the preferred space for some fruits and vegetables, particularly lettuce and other succulent items. Plastic bags that are closed tightly can serve as an alternative to hydrator drawers in the refrigerated storage of produce. Even winter squash, onions, and potatoes need to be able to be stored at a cool room temperature.

For large families, adequate refrigerator space for storing milk and meat may be the limiting factor in shopping. Where available, home delivery of milk two or three times a week can be a solution, but when service cannot be obtained, supplementary shopping in the middle of the week may be necessary to solve the milk supply problem. Another possible solution is to supplement the fluid milk with the use of some reconstituted dry milk solids.

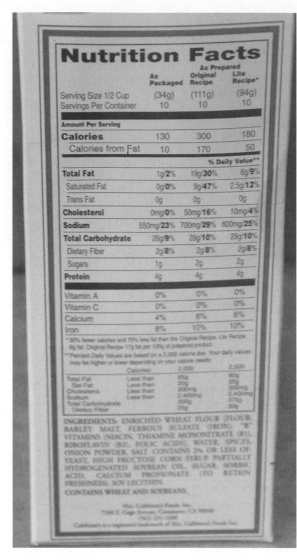

Figure 20.8
Labels stating nutrition facts and ingredients provide information important to consumers when shopping for healthful food. Courtesy of Plycon Press.

Consumer Aids

Grocery shopping can be very educational as well as time consuming. With the excellent **nutrition labeling** mandated on many foods today, a considerable amount of information regarding nutrient content and ingredients is available. However, time may limit the advantage that consumers take from labels. For items used frequently, a few minutes spent in comparing labels from different brands can serve as the basis of making informed decisions for many subsequent shopping trips (Figure 20.8).

For persons who are allergic to some ingredients or who have other health reasons for needing to avoid certain items, ingredient labeling can be a vital source of information to aid in selecting appropriate foods. **Ingredient labeling** is of considerable merit when comparing the relative cost of various brands of the same item. Because ingredients must be listed in descending order of their weight in foods, comparisons can be made between formulations. For example, a soup mixture that lists chicken before noodles would be higher in chicken than would one listing the noodles before the chicken.

Open dating of foods is another aid to consumers (Figure 20.9). Increasingly, the dates are accompanied by an explanation, such as "Best if used before Nov. 27." Dates without explanations can be confusing, for the date could mean the packing date, or it might indicate the pull date to remove the item from the grocery shelves, or it might even mean that the food should not be eaten after the date. Such vagueness is seen fairly infrequently today, although many foods still are marketed with no date at all.

Comparison Shopping

Comparisons of cost between competitive brands can save consumers a good bit of money. Because package sizes often are different, such comparative shopping can take a good bit of time unless a calculator is a part of the shopping gear. Stores provide **unit pricing** information on the shelves to let consumers know the price of an ounce or other sensible unit of measure of various products (Figure 20.10). This saves consumers a great deal of time, for comparisons can be made quickly when the shelf information can be scanned.

Even with unit pricing, consumers need to stay alert when making selections. One of the clearest examples of the need for being careful is

---

INDUSTRY INSIGHT
INGREDIENTS FOR CUSTOMERS

Today's consumers in the United States require a broad range of ingredients, whether they are needed for the food industry or in the home. The food industry is faced with the challenges of developing and producing foods that will have the quality and appeal consumers demand. Special additives often are required to achieve the performance characteristics that will provide excellent quality when consumers actually eat the product. As consumers have been developing a broader acceptance of other cuisines, the food industry also has needed to expand its ingredient repertoire to develop suitable products.

Grocery stores also are expanding their inventories to meet consumer requests for ethnic ingredients. The specific items they carry vary considerably around the country, depending in part upon the cultural demographics in the area served. Spices and sauces essential to preparing typical dishes of a cuisine need to be available. Similarly, such items as tortillas and wonton skins may be required. Fortunately, many specialty items can be kept in a store's inventory as either frozen or canned products.

Figure 20.9
Open dating statements vary in style, but are intended to give consumers information about time limits on quality. Courtesy of Plycon Press.

afforded by comparing the drained weight of canned peaches. Some packers will sell a good bit of juice and a small amount of fruit in a can, while others may have the can filled with fruit and include only a small amount of juice. If the two products were the same price, the one with the abundance of fruit clearly would be the better buy. Numerous examples of this sort can be found throughout the market.

Buying store brands rather than those that are nationally advertised often saves money. An even greater savings usually is available with basic products by buying generic equivalents. Such products bear only a label indicating what they are. The simple, uncolored label identifies the contents. Frills definitely are not added to labels on generic products. The quality of these items may be every bit as good as a leading brand in some instances, while in others consumers may find a large difference. Experience is the best criterion for making such decisions. The one clear thing is that generics are less costly than nationally advertised products.

Universal Product Code (UPC) is the name for the familiar bar coding seen on packaged food items in the market. This bar pattern was developed to aid markets in maintaining inventory information and to facilitate utilization of computers in the marketing process. An electronic scan of the UPC done at the check stand generates the cash register tape for the

Figure 20.10
Unit pricing permits easy comparisons on relative costs of various sizes and brands.
Courtesy of Plycon Press.

nutrition labeling
Nutrition Facts label required on food packages to give consumers information about the calorie and nutrient content of the serving size of the food.

ingredient labeling
Listing of ingredients beginning with the one present in the largest amount by weight and continuing in descending order.

open dating Date stating clearly the pull date or other dating message indicating whether the product is fresh.

unit pricing Cost of a designated amount of an item to make price comparisons easy for consumers.

Universal Product Code Pattern of bars (bar code) printed on packages to code inventory and cost information for translation by electronic scanning at the check stand.

consumer while also providing necessary inventory and sales records for the store. By using scanners, errors at the check stand reportedly are reduced. Consumers receive a tally of their purchases with all of the items spelled out on the slip, complete with brand, product, and price, all documented as a permanent receipt. To avoid errors, consumers are wise to do a quick scan of their receipts while at the check stand, because prices in the computer sometimes may differ from what it says on the shelf.

Time Management

One key to a successful meal is the timing of food preparation times so that everything is ready at the same time. Success in this area requires careful thought in advance. Actually, time management needs to be considered in the planning phase as well as in preparation so that the menu planned will be able to fit the time constraints of the person preparing the food. If dinner needs to be served soon after the cook returns from work, a simple meal with a brief cooking period fits the time demands. For inexperienced people, a meal with rather simple preparation requirements will help to guarantee success in preparation and timing.

When first learning to prepare meals, development of a detailed time plan will make the actual preparation proceed smoothly. Such a plan needs to anticipate all of the details that must be tended to in preparing and serving the meal, including time to set the table.

Start to develop a time plan by calculating the time needed for preparing each item in the menu. The mixing time and the time needed for assembling or cutting and washing ingredients needs to be estimated based on the speed of the worker, because the rate of productivity varies greatly from one person to another. Then the actual cooking or baking time is added to the estimated preparation time to determine the total time needed to prepare each menu item from start to actual serving.

Establish the time the meal will be served, and then work backward from the serving time to calculate precisely when preparation of each item should be started. Dishes that require long preparation and/or cooking time obviously will be started much earlier than a dish that needs only short preparation time shortly before the meal is served. After charting the time for preparing each dish, check the total schedule to see if it is realistic. Be sure that there are no conflicts that require two things to be done at the same time. If there are, adjustments will need to be made so that the work will be able to proceed smoothly.

Variables such as interruptions by small children and telephone calls can throw off the best of plans. A time plan that considers probable interruptions will reduce frustration considerably. Educated guesses regarding the amount of time needed for these distractions during meal preparation can be made and incorporated into the plan.

Adequate time needs to be allowed for arranging a centerpiece and completing other details of table arrangement. For family meals, little time will be needed for setting the table, including the centerpiece. However, company meals may require the assembling of serving dishes that are stored in a remote cupboard and may even need washing before using. Silverware may need to be polished and washed before the table can be set. Special goblets or other glassware may also need washing and drying before being used. These arrangements take a considerable amount of time. Even bringing extra chairs to the table for a company meal may be a time problem unless a detailed plan has been developed to include all aspects of setting the table. The special tasks often can be done the day before or at least earlier in the day of the special event.

When first learning to prepare meals, develop a checklist of tasks needing to be done and then plot the time plan. Be sure all the items on the checklist are included. Details such as preparing ice water are important to the success of a meal, but are likely to be forgotten in a time plan unless a checklist is utilized. Even a listing of the serving dishes and the serving silver to be used can help to bring organization to a meal plan. With experience, some of these matters will become so natural that they may be done without the formality of writing them down. However, an appreciation of the need for time to do them must be maintained if meals are to be organized, rather than chaotic.

When possible, the time plan should be evaluated after the meal to see where the planning was good and where some modifications need to be made if the time plan is to be used again. When tasks that require less time or more time than was allocated can be identified, reality can be built into the next time plan. This evaluation process, whether done informally or by writing ideas on paper, is important to the development of time-management skills. By modifying future time plans in relation to the time plan that has been tested, corrections in planning can be made, and the preparation of a meal in an organized and pleasing manner can be accomplished with increased ease.

A time plan for preparing a family meal of meat loaf, baked potato, boiled carrots with dill, Waldorf salad, and milk that will be served at 6 p.m. might have the following schedule. Adjustments probably would need to be made to fit the specific situation, depending on such variables as speed of the cook and other help that may be available to set the table and do other supporting tasks.

4:45 p.m.	Prepare meat loaf and scrub potatoes while oven is preheating
4:55 p.m.	Place meat loaf and potatoes in preheated oven
5:00 p.m.	Set the table
5:10 p.m.	Prepare salad, cover, and refrigerate it until time to serve
5:45 p.m.	Wash, pare, and cut the carrots while heating water to boiling; add carrots when water boils
5:50 p.m.	Pour water, milk, or other beverage and put on table
5:55 p.m.	Remove meat loaf and baked potatoes from oven; transfer meat loaf and potatoes to serving platter or serve on plates
5:56 p.m.	Drain and serve carrots, garnishing with fresh dill weed
5:58 p.m.	Place food on the table while diners assemble
6:00 p.m.	Dinner is served.

MANAGING LEFTOVERS

Pre-planning

Leftovers can be the result of deliberate planning or of miscalculation. If efficient use of time during the week is a goal, a pot roast may be prepared on the weekend, with the expectation that there will be enough meat left to make a vegetable beef soup and also a beef casserole during the week (Figure 20.11). Such planning allows purchase of large, but comparatively inexpensive, cuts of meat or other foods. It also saves preparation time ultimately, because little time is required to have the leftover meat ready to use in the other recipes.

If leftovers are being prepared deliberately, it is essential that the menu plans for the week provide for the utilization of the leftovers while they are of high quality and safe to eat. Leftovers that ultimately are thrown out do not represent an economy or a convenience. Frozen storage of leftovers can be a practical part of the plan for using certain leftovers.

When leftovers are not desirable, preplanning can be used to have no food left after a meal. Usually a fairly accurate calculation of the amount of food needed can be made so that extra food is not prepared. Occasionally, the diners will want more of a certain item than has been prepared, but this is only a minor problem, for many Americans tend to eat more food than they really need. However, to an energetic, athletic adolescent, too little food can be a real frustration and should be avoided. Experience quickly tells people how much food probably will be eaten.

For people who are battling the bulges, it is generally not a kindness to cook more than might be needed. Urging a small bit of extra food on someone who already has had enough to eat can lead to weight difficulties.

Figure 20.11
Pot roast can be prepared for dinner on a weekend and can easily provide planned leftovers for another meal during the week. Courtesy of Plycon Press.

This approach—of limiting the food served—is contrary to the traditional practice of showing hospitality and friendliness by serving people as much as they possibly could hold. However, awareness about weight control and desire for good nutrition have spread throughout the country, and quality is beginning to take precedence over quantity as a mark of hospitality.

Care of Leftovers

Many foods are at their height of quality when they are first prepared, and this quality can deteriorate fairly quickly if proper measures are not taken to control changes. Immediate care of leftovers after the meal has been finished can maintain quality. Protein-containing foods need to be refrigerated or frozen immediately, depending upon the food and the plans for its use.

A protective covering of plastic wrap or aluminum foil will help to prevent the absorption of other flavors and loss of moisture from the food during refrigerator storage. Foods to be frozen need to be placed in containers with tightly fitting covers to avoid desiccation during frozen storage. Leftover vegetables and fruits also should be stored covered in the refrigerator even though they will not promote growth of microorganisms nearly as readily as will the protein-containing foods.

Breads and other baked goods do not require refrigeration, but they do need to be covered to protect them from drying out. For long-term storage, leftover breads and other baked products can be wrapped tightly and stored in the freezer.

To avoid growing microbiological wonders in the refrigerator or other storage areas, the remote areas in the refrigerator need to be explored weekly. This should be done when the shopping list is being developed so that appropriate purchases will be made and edible items will not be duplicated. During this tour, food that will not be used should be discarded. Hydrator drawers and refrigerator shelves should be wiped clean in preparation for the arrival of the new food. If defrosting is needed, this also should be done before the shopping is done. This way the new food can be placed immediately into the cold storage area safely.

SUMMARY

Meal management begins with planning of the meals for the full day and a review of these menus to be sure that all of the foods needed for good health are included in the menus. Check against MyPlate recommendations to be sure that the suggested numbers of servings are being provided in each of the five groups. Breakfast may be as simple as a serving of a food high in vitamin C, a glass of milk, and a bowl of cereal. Lunch should include a source of meat or a meat substitute, a couple of servings of fruit and/or vegetables, bread or other cereal product, and a glass of milk. Dinner can follow the same pattern as lunch. Ideally, dinner will be a meal of modest size unless a person is particularly active and needs more nutrients than the average individual.

To meet these guidelines, variety in menus is recommended. The sensory qualities of food to be considered include color, shape, texture, flavor, and temperature. Meals need to be planned to provide a feeling of satiety and should have enough variety from day to day to stimulate the appetite.

Menu planning should be done with the resources of human energy and appliances being utilized appropriately. Meals should not require such elaborate preparations that those fixing them are too exhausted to be a pleasant part of the social group at the table. Some menus can be planned to utilize time-saving appliances, such as a crock pot. Food safety also needs to be considered if items are to be held at room temperature a significant period of time.

Food costs can be controlled by shopping only once a week and by utilizing special buys that can be incorporated into family meals. A shopping list can be a real money saver when it is planned well and followed. Purchase of an appropriate amount of food so that safe storage can be done and the food will be eaten while still of high quality can be an important aspect of money management. Ingredient labeling, open dating, and unit pricing are important consumer aids in the marketplace. Comparison shopping and selecting generics or other products providing adequate quality at a reasonable price are other techniques for controlling food costs.

By developing a careful time plan, you can master the task of having all foods ready at the time the meal is to be served. Concerns such as polishing silverware and arranging centerpieces also need to be considered when making the time plan. Evaluation of the plan is important after a meal so that improvements in subsequent time plans can be made. Experience is a great aid in gaining mastery of the timing of a meal.

Following a meal, proper care of leftovers is essential as a means of controlling costs and quality. Planned leftovers can be a good way of saving time in meal preparation as long as the foods are properly stored and are used while still of high quality. Freezing leftovers can sometimes help in assuring high quality in leftovers. When leftovers are not a part of the plan, appropriate amounts of food should be cooked for a meal. The practice of cooking a bit more than probably will be needed is not only costly because of food waste but may also lead to overweight in a family if the extra food is pressed on people who have already had enough to eat.

Protein-containing foods need to be covered and either refrigerated or frozen just as soon as possible after a meal to avoid spoilage. Breads and other baked products need to be covered tightly to prevent them from drying out during storage. Frozen storage is appropriate if the items will not be used soon.

Removal of unused leftovers and careful cleaning of storage areas are important steps in maintaining control over food in the kitchen. This should be done in preparation for the next shopping expedition. This allows an inventory of existing food supplies to help in the development of an appropriate shopping list.

STUDY QUESTIONS

1. What factors need to be considered in planning appealing menus? Why do these aspects of food need to be coordinated in a menu?

2. How can MyPlate be used when planning menus?

3. Plan a lunch menu for an adolescent boy. How would you vary the menu if his mother were to eat the same meal? Would any changes be needed if his father were also to eat the meal? Explain your recommendations for the mother and for the father. What considerations did you use in planning the original menu for the boy?

4. Develop a time plan to prepare the lunch you planned in the previous question. Is the menu a workable one? If so, develop the shopping list for it. If changes appear to be needed, revise the menu and develop a shopping list for the revised menu.

5. What changes would you make in this lunch menu if (a) you were attempting to keep costs as low as possible and (b) cost was not a concern?

6. Visit a supermarket and determine which foods have nutrition labels and which do not. Also examine ingredient labeling and open-dating codes on packages. Do you think that consumers in the store you visited were using the consumer information provided for them? What did you learn from examining various products?

SELECTED REFERENCES

Antonio, J. 2010. Hot and flavorful world of chiles. *Food Product Design 20*(2): 42.

Barer-Stein, T. 1999. *You Eat What You Are.* 2nd ed. Firefly Books. Richmond Hill, ON.

Berry, D. 2004. Fresh advice on herbs and spice. *Food Product Design 14*(2): 61.

Berry, D. 2009. Feeding tweens and teens. *Food Product Design 19*(5): 50.

Berry, D. 2010. Heat-and-eat meals go gourmet. *Food Product Design 20*(10): 32.

Berry, D. 2010. Diet food by any other name. *Food Product Design 20*(11): 18.

Brandt, M. B., et al. 2010. Tracking label claims. *Food Technol. 64*(2): 34.

Bertrand, K. 2005. Microwavable foods satisfy need for speed and palatability. *Food Technol. 59*(1): 30.

Cannon, R. 2008. Organic vs. natural. *Food Product Design 18*(8): 26.

Caranfa, M., and D. Morris. 2009. Putting health on the menu. *Food Technol. 63*(5): 28.

Clark, J. P. 2005. Fats and oils processors adapt to changing needs. *Food Technol. 59*(5): 74.

Clemens, R., et al. 2005. MyPyramid adds new dimension to food guidance. *Food Technol. 59*(6): 18.

Datta, A. K., et al. 2005. Microwave combination heating. *Food Technol. 59*(1): 36.

Davis, T., and W. Reinhardt. 2005. Dietary Guidelines: Where food science and nutrition converge. *Food Technol. 59*(3): 20.

Decker, K. J. 2010. Feeding healthy boomers. *Food Product Design 20*(3): 66.

Esquivel, E. 2009. Escalations in the salt debate. *Food Product Design 19*(5): 16.

Fiore, P. 2006. Consumers want clarity in labeling. *Food Technol. 60*(6): 136.

Foster, R. J. 2004. "Meating" consumer expectations. *Food Product Design 14*(9): 38.

Foster, R. J. 2008. Cholesterol control. *Food Product Design 18*(9): 56.

Foster, R. J. 2008. Morning brings the grain event. *Food Product Design 18*(12): 42.

Harding, T. B., Jr., and L. R. Davis. 2005. Organic foods marketing and labeling. *Food Technol. 59*(1): 41.

Huth, P. 2005. Dairy's fit for health. *Food Product Design 15*(7): 87.

McWilliams, M. 2009. *Fundamentals of Meal Management.* 5th ed. Prentice Hall. Upper Saddle River, NJ.

Nachay, K. 2008. Combating obesity. *Food Technol. 62*(2): 24.

Ohr, L. M. 2004. Meeting children's nutritional needs. *Food Technol. 58*(4): 65.

Pszczola, D. E. 2004. Fats: In *trans*-ition. *Food Technol. 58*(4): 52.

Reedy, J., and S. M. Krebs-Smith. 2008. Comparison of food-based recommendations and nutrient values of three food guides: USDA's MyPyramid, NHLBI's Dietary Approaches to Stop Hypertension Eating Plan, and Harvard's Healthy Eating Pyramid. *J. Am. Dietet. Assoc. 108*(3): 522.

Sloan, A. E. 2005. Cruising the center-store aisles. *Food Technol. 59*(10): 28.

Sloan, A. E. 2006. Going gourmet. *Food Technol. 60*(7): 20.

Sloan, A. E. 2006. Movable meals. *Food Technol. 60*(9): 19.

Sloan, A. E. 2010. Bridging generational food divides. *Food Technol. 64*(7): 35.

Smith, R. L., et al. 2005. GRAS flavoring substances. *Food Technol. 59*(8): 24.

A splendid dinner creates lasting memories of festive occasions. Courtesy of Plycon Press.

21

Meal Service and Hospitality

Chapter Contents

Key Concepts

1. Table linens, flatware, dishes, and glassware can be chosen to meet practical requirements (e.g., cost, maintenance) while also adding to the beauty of meals that are to be served using them.
2. Table etiquette is based on considering the pleasure of others at the table.
3. The type of meal service used should be chosen to fit the diners and the occasion.
4. Special occasions are enhanced when sufficient advance planning and preparation have been done so that the host and/or hostess will need to do only last-minute tasks and will be able to spend time with the guests.

AESTHETICS AND PRACTICALITY

A fully satisfying meal transcends the basic aspects of planning and preparation; the actual presentation of the food and the setting in which it is eaten are important to total success. As noted earlier, food provides psychological and social functions, as well as meeting nutritional needs. The total experience at the table enhances the satisfaction and pleasure provided by the food. Whether a meal is intended as a family occasion, a social gathering, or a business meeting, the setting should be compatible with the situation.

Table appointments set the tone for a meal. Sometimes informality may be the desired atmosphere (Figure 21.1); other times, a very formal occasion may be appropriate. By choosing linens, silverware, and other appointments for the table to fit the mood desired, the parameters for the meal are defined subtly. The method of service for the meal adds to this ambience desired for the group. Even the manners used at the table are a part of the total environment of the meal. These aspects of meal service are considered in this chapter.

No single definition of table setting, service, and hospitality is appropriate because the meals of different groups vary according to the occasion and the people. The intent in this chapter is to heighten awareness of the importance of creating the desired environment for a meal and using available resources to achieve the desired effect.

TABLE APPOINTMENTS

Linens

The term *table linens* is used to designate table coverings and napkins, regardless of the type of fabric used. Choices range from tablecloths to place mats or even runners. There are no set rules to follow in selecting table linens for a meal, although the appearance and condition of the table itself may dictate the use of a tablecloth. If the surface finish of a table is unattractive, a tablecloth can mask this problem, whereas place mats can be the basis of a beautiful table setting if the table that shows under the mats is attractive (Figure 21.2).

Figure 21.1
This table setting sets an informal tone for a meal.
Courtesy of Plycon Press.

Figure 21.2
Damask place mats teamed with a linen napkin bring a formal feeling to the table setting. Courtesy of Plycon Press.

silence cloth   Heavy cloth placed underneath a tablecloth to help muffle sound and also to help protect the table from hot dishes.

Figure 21.3
Tablecloths for most occasions should extend 8 to 10 inches over the edge of the table. Courtesy of Plycon Press.

Similarly, a runner can be used effectively to provide the background for two people when the table surface that shows is pleasing to see.

The fabric in linens should be suited to the occasion. For an informal occasion, a coarsely woven or informal fabric helps to set the tone; for a more formal meal, however, lace or damask is clearly appropriate. The color or pattern in a table linen should be complementary to the dishes and the food. Truly beautiful meals begin with creative selection of the linens. Often a contrasting napkin adds beauty to the setting. It is important that the linens do not compete with the food being served, for the whole purpose of table settings is to enhance the dining experience.

Tablecloths are always appropriate choices as table covers. Cloths should be large enough to extend beyond the table generously, usually about 8–10 inches on all sides (Figure 21.3). A textured fabric is a good choice for breakfast and lunch or even an informal dinner. **Silence cloths** under the solid tablecloths help to protect the table surface and also help to keep the sound level down. When a cutwork or lace tablecloth is being used, a silence cloth is not used. Part of the beauty of these openwork tablecloths is to have the grain of the table surface show through the design of the cloth.

The popularity of tablecloths is limited because they require more work in laundering than place mats do; fortunately, however, easy-care fabrics are used frequently for tablecloths so that a quick touching up with an iron is the most care required after the cloths are washed and dried. Tablecloths are pressed with a center crease extending the full length of the cloth and then are placed on the table or folded for storage without pressing in the other folds. Ideally, these softer folds will be pressed out before the cloth is used if they do show after flat storage.

Place mats are a good choice for table settings when the dining table is attractive. They are easy to care for and are available in many different colors, fabrics, and shapes to suit practically any occasion. The size of mats may vary slightly, but a convenient size for the individual place mat is about 22 inches long and 15 inches deep. The size of the table may dictate the use of slightly smaller mats. A circular table is easier to set if oval or round mats are used, rather than rectangular ones. Generally, the atmosphere for a meal is a bit less formal with mats than with a tablecloth, although delicate, lace-trimmed place mats can provide a very formal table setting.

When place mats are used, a center runner is suggested as a basis for the centerpiece. If the table is too narrow to permit the use of a runner, this may need to be omitted. Some of the table should be showing if mats are being used, and mats should not overlap each other.

The napkins selected may match the mats or cloth selected, or they may contrast, if preferred. The size varies with the meal. Breakfast napkins usually are between 11 and 13 inches square, luncheon napkins are about 16 inches square, and dinner napkins between 18 and 24 inches square. Regardless of size, napkins are folded in half, pressed, and then folded and pressed again. This results in a square one-fourth the size of the original napkin. Although cloth napkins are expected for special occasions, family meals often are served with paper napkins as a means of helping to reduce laundry duties.

Centerpieces

Artistry and imagination can be combined to develop centerpieces for various occasions. For a buffet, a large and dramatic centerpiece may suit the occasion, while somewhat smaller centerpieces are appropriate for the dining table where people will be seated. The purpose of a centerpiece is to add visual satisfaction and beauty to the occasion.

The size of a centerpiece needs to be adapted to suit the space requirements in the center of the table and also to allow direct eye contact between people seated around the table (Figure 21.4). A high centerpiece serves as a deterrent to conversation because people cannot see each other through or around the centerpiece. Consequently, centerpieces for most meals are fairly small and low. In no instance should the table appear crowded because of the centerpiece. There should be ample room for the centerpiece and any serving dishes being used at the meal.

Simple floral arrangements can be excellent centerpieces (Figure 21.5). A single flower with a touch of greenery floating in a simple bowl can be a lovely way of accenting the table appointments. Edible centerpieces featuring fruit arranged in a bowl or basket are attractive during the meal and can be functional as the dessert, if desired. Small sculptures or green plants are other possibilities. Candles often are used to heighten the sense of the occasion. If candles are used in the centerpiece, they should be lighted throughout the meal—regardless of the time of day.

Flatware

The common types of flatware are sterling silver, silver plate, and stainless steel. Each material has certain advantages and disadvantages that need to be considered when deciding what to buy. Sterling silver is surprisingly durable considering that silver is really a very soft metal. The shininess of new sterling silver gives way to a softer, more appealing look as numerous small scratches develop to impart a soft patina to the pieces.

Two drawbacks can be noted in considering selecting sterling silver flatware. Sterling silver needs to be polished occasionally to remove the tarnish that develops on the surface, particularly if egg is in contact with the silver or if the silver is not dried thoroughly after being washed. Besides the time required for caring for sterling silver, silver prices are so high that consumers may want

Figure 21.4
Although the table is set for a very formal wedding dinner, the centerpiece still is low enough for diners to see each other clearly across the table. Courtesy of Plycon Press.

http://www.towlesilver.com/
—Silver patterns and information.

http://www.gorham1831silver.com/
—Silver patterns and information.

Figure 21.5
A single rose in a bud vase is a simple, but aesthetically pleasing centerpiece in this table setting. Courtesy of Plycon Press.

Figure 21.6
Because sterling silver will last a lifetime, it is important to be sure the pattern selected is exactly the one desired before deciding to invest in it. Courtesy of Plycon Press.

to spend their money elsewhere. However, the investment in sterling silver is one that will last a lifetime, with proper care (Figure 21.6).

Silver plate resembles sterling silver because silver is plated over a base metal and the silver coating on silver plate tarnishes just like it does on sterling silver. Plate has the disadvantage that eventually the silver will wear off in certain spots on the pieces, leaving the base metal showing through. This limits the useful life of silver plate. However, the reduced cost, in comparison with the price of sterling silver, provides a motivation to consider buying silver plate.

Stainless steel flatware has grown considerably in its acceptance for daily and even special use. There is a very large range of quality in stainless steel, from stamped pieces with sharp edges that jeopardize one's mouth when using them to very costly patterns almost rivaling silver in price. A real advantage of stainless steel is its ease of care. As the name implies, stainless steel is very resistant to damage of any sort. It does not require polishing, but it never develops the rich patina seen on sterling silver (Figure 21.7).

Many flatware designs are available to suit the preferences of various people. The design should be chosen carefully because expensive flatware may be used a long time. Choices range from extremely simple to quite elaborate. Although this choice is a matter of individual preference, the flatware should be selected in relation to the dishes being selected so that the total effect will be consistent and pleasing.

Figure 21.7
Stainless steel flatware is pleasing in appearance, easy to care for, and less expensive than sterling silver. Courtesy of Plycon Press.

Once the choices of patterns are narrowed, it is wise to handle each of the different pieces of flatware in a place setting to be sure that the balance is pleasing. Note also the appearance of the various pieces, paying particular attention to the forks. The tines should be close enough together to permit food to be held easily while en route to the mouth. The tips of the tines should not feel sharp. These are details that can make quite a difference in the pleasure of eating with various flatware patterns.

DISHES

Just as was true in selecting flatware, the first decision in picking dishes is to determine the type of material desired, whether pottery or china. Even within these two major categories, there are choices of quality, with bone china being the most durable and also most costly of the alternatives. The breakable nature of dishes must be considered in making a decision about what to purchase. The initial purchase of bone china is very costly, yet the durability of this high-quality china can make this a choice that ultimately could prove to be less costly than purchasing and replacing sets of pottery over a period of years. Pottery is often much less expensive than bone china, but usually pottery is comparatively fragile.

Chipped and cracked dishes need to be discarded. They not only create an unattractive table setting, but they also present a health hazard because the defects serve as sites for the growth of some microorganisms that may be protected from destruction during dish washing. People who are particularly concerned about avoiding problems of breakage may select plastic dishes.

Stoneware offers quite a durable and attractive alternative to the use of plastic. Unfortunately, stoneware often is quite costly. It also has the disadvantage of being quite bulky and heavy to lift. Nevertheless, the many attractive designs and the solid feeling of quality found in stoneware have combined to make this type of dish quite popular, particularly for casual living.

Frequently, the patterns found in china are fairly formal, although there is a tendency recently to create some comparatively informal china patterns to add to the various product lines. On the other hand, pottery and plastic dish designs usually are quite informal. Clearly, a choice needs to be made regarding formality of design as well as formality and durability of material to be selected. If a set of dishes is to be used for all occasions in a home, a pattern that has a slight tendency toward formality without being stiff may prove to be a wise choice. An extremely informal design in dishes will prevent meals from being formal occasions. If a set of pottery and a set of china dishes will be chosen, the pottery dishes can be rather informal, while the china can be fairly formal. This arrangement makes it possible to set the table for any occasion.

Whether selecting a formal or an informal design, the appearance of the food on the plate must be visualized. Very busy designs may distract the eye from the food, yet the food should be the focal point. Often a simple, stylized design may provide a pleasing background for food. The colors in the design also should enhance the food.

Once a tentative selection has been made, check out the design of the various pieces. Of particular importance is the cup. The handle should be easy for men and women to hold. An extremely dainty handle can present a real hazard to the fingers of many men. A cup that is fairly narrow and deep is more functional than is one that is shallow and wide because the beverages will stay hot for a comparatively long time in the deep cup. The large surface area of the broad, shallow cup causes very quick heat loss; furthermore, spills also occur rather easily in cups of this design.

Ease of care is another factor to consider when picking dishes. Dishes with a sculptured, raised design are difficult to wash clean if food has been allowed to dry on the plates a bit before washing. If a dishwasher is to be used frequently for washing dishes, the dish design should have the design under the glaze so that the pigments or platinum or gold trim will be protected. In other words, dishes should be dishwasher-proof and able to withstand dishwasher temperatures. Metallic trim needs to be avoided if the dishes are possibly going to be used to heat foods in a microwave oven.

http://www.lenox.com/
—Listing of patterns by one of several manufacturers of fine china.

http://na.wwrd.com/ae/ us/wwrd/wedgwood/icat/ wedgwood/
—Listing of patterns by one of several manufacturers of fine china.

Glassware

Of the items needed to set an attractive table, glasses clearly are the least durable. The possibility of breakage definitely needs to be recognized when glassware is being selected. For optimal beauty in table settings, crystal stemware is important. Leaded crystal goblets add a regal quality to a table setting. Even though the lead in the crystal adds to the durability of this type of glassware, there still is a risk that stemware will be broken. For people wishing to set a formal table without investing such a large sum of money in glassware, considerably less expensive yet nicely designed stemware is a very satisfactory alternative.

Although stemware adds a touch of elegance to a table setting, there are many times when glasses can be used to excellent advantage. Glasses are distinctly more durable than stemware. In addition, they are less likely to be bumped and tipped over than are goblets with their tall stems. The formality and the price of glasses vary considerably. The choice of pattern and also color should be made in relation to the dishes and flatware selected. Sometimes colored glasses can add a very pleasing color accent to a table, but many times clear glass is desirable.

Practical considerations should be combined with the aesthetic when glasses are being considered. Stability is one of the key considerations. In stemware, stability is a particular problem, but it deserves some consideration in glasses, too. A broad base and/or a stem weighted toward the lower portion can be crucial to stable stemware. Glasses with heavily weighted bottoms may be a good choice, particularly if children will be at the table, for the low center of gravity of these glasses greatly reduces the likelihood of tipping. Thick glass is particularly important when young children will be using them, for they resist chipping around the edge. There even are times when plastic glasses may be the best answer.

SETTING THE TABLE

For a specific meal, place mats or a tablecloth and napkins should be selected. If it is a formal occasion and a tablecloth is being used, a silence cloth is helpful in reducing the mechanical sounds of dishes and glasses on the table, but this cloth is not used with lace cloths or cutwork. The tablecloth should be arranged carefully, being sure that the cloth is straight on the table so that all the overhanging edges are even. Place mats should be parallel with the edge of the table and about half an inch from the edge.

The specific setting for a diner at the table is often referred to as a **cover**. This cover consists of a place mat (unless a tablecloth is being used), a napkin, the flatware being used for the specific meal, and glassware, if any is being placed when the table is set. For formal occasions, a **charger** may be placed in the center of the cover, where it remains until removed before the dinner plate arrives with the entrée selected (Figure 21.8). The flatware comprising a cover or setting is arranged for orderly use in keeping with the menu. All flatware placed on either side of the plate should have the handles extending to an inch from the edge of the table so that the ends of the handles present an orderly appearance.

The fork(s) should usually be arranged to the left of the dinner plate. If a fork is to be used for dessert, that fork is placed immediately adjacent to the plate (or above the service plate). The dinner fork and the salad fork are placed to the left of the dessert fork, with the salad fork being on the extreme left. The arrangement to the right of the plate begins with the knife. The blade of

http://www.libbey.com/
—Various designs of glassware for the table.

cover   Individual place setting for a meal.

charger   Large decorative plate at the center of the cover for a formal dinner, but removed when the entrée arrives.

Figure 21.8
A charger can be used at as a dramatic background of a place setting until the entrée is served. Courtesy of Plycon Press.

the knife should be turned so that the cutting edge of the knife is facing the plate. A teaspoon is placed immediately to the right of the knife (Figure 21.9). If a soup spoon or cocktail fork is a part of the arrangement, it is positioned to the right of the teaspoon. The butter spreader is placed on the bread and butter plate at the upper edge parallel to the edge of the table. Sometimes the flatware for dessert is placed above the plate, parallel to the edge of the table. Customarily, a maximum of three pieces of flatware is placed on each side of the plate, preferably with the same number on each side to create a balanced appearance.

Certain options sometimes are followed when placing the flatware. Sometimes the soup spoon or cocktail fork simply is placed on the **liner** on which the course is served. Similarly, dessert flatware can be brought when the dessert is served (Figure 21.10).

Figure 21.9
The dinner fork is placed between the salad and dessert forks, the butter spreader is horizontal at the far edge of the bread and butter plate, and the knife and spoon are on the right, with the sharp blade pointed toward the plate. A simple bowl of lemons is the centerpiece. Courtesy of Plycon Press.

liner Plate on which a bowl or other dish containing a serving of a food is placed.

Napkins usually are placed just to the left of the forks, with the lower edge positioned an inch from the edge and parallel to the table. Before placing the napkin, it is folded over without any attempt to crease it. The open corner of the folded napkin traditionally is placed so that it is in the lower left-hand corner. This makes it convenient to pick up the napkin and partially unfold it for placing in the lap.

Sometimes napkins are folded to create different forms that serve as decorative elements until diners place them in their laps. Sometimes these decorative napkins are placed on the charger, in the empty wine glass, or above the charger. Napkin rings provide a quick way to set the table with napkins that look festive. These ideas for napkins in table settings are appropriate for fine meals, either at home or in a restaurant.

Glasses are arranged above the flatware, the water glass being positioned immediately above the knife and any other glasses being arranged in orderly fashion to the right of the water glass and slightly closer to the edge of the table. When both salad plate and a bread and butter plate are being used, the bread and butter plate is placed directly above the fork, and the salad plate is arranged to the left of the bread and butter plate and somewhat closer to the edge of the table. If a bread and butter plate is not being used, the salad plate is positioned immediately above the fork.

Figure 21.10
A liner is placed under the dessert; the spoon is placed on the liner except when the diner is eating. Courtesy of Plycon Press.

CULTURAL ACCENT
EAST MEETS WEST

The suggestions on table setting clearly are appropriate to dining in the United States. Different customs are found in other cultures. Dining in the Far East presents different traditions. Differences become apparent at the door—shoes are left neatly arranged there before entering in stocking feet. Dinner itself is served at low tables, with diners sitting on cushions, their legs tucked neatly under the table or feet pulled toward their bodies.

Table appointments also are quite different. Chopsticks replace the cutlery usually seen on Western tables. A chopstick holder is a part of the setting so that a diner will be able to put down the chopsticks without placing them directly on the table (Figure 21.11). Lacquerware, not china, is used for plates, bowls, and even cups. Almost always each diner will have a bowl of polished white rice as part of the meal. Simplicity of the table setting adds a quiet beauty to Asian dining.

Figure 21.11
Chopsticks are the preferred eating utensil in the Orient; they can rest on a chopstick holder when not in use. Courtesy of Plycon Press.

MEAL SERVICE

Various ways of serving a meal can be used to suit the occasion. Families today often dine quite informally, but special occasions may warrant taking time for a bit of traditional service. These various styles are described in this section. Of course, modifications can be made to suit the occasion and the people.

American service Method of meal service in which all of the food is placed in serving dishes on the table and passed around.

The least formal form of service is **American service**, a service in which the serving dishes are placed on the table and the dining plates are arranged at each cover. When everyone is seated, people begin to help themselves to the food placed closest to them. Then the serving dish is passed to the person to the right (counterclockwise). It is important that all the serving dishes be passed in the same direction to avoid a traffic jam of platters and serving bowls.

American service has the advantage of allowing each person to select the portion size desired. Usually the food can be kept fairly warm with American service if it is very hot when the serving dishes are filled and if the serving at the table proceeds efficiently. The disadvantage of American service is the cold food that can result if some people are slow in helping to get the food passed.

family service Service of a meal by the host, who serves all of the food onto plates stacked in front of him and then passes the served plates to the hostess and others at the table.

Family service is similar to American service. The difference is that the host serves each plate from the stack of plates in front of him. All the serving dishes are arranged conveniently around the host to facilitate rapid service of the food. After the first plate is served, it is passed along the left side of the table to the hostess. As each plate is served, it is passed along the left side of the table to serve each person, beginning with the person nearest her and moving back in sequence to the person nearest the host. Then the second side of the table is served in the same fashion. The host is the last person served.

The obvious disadvantage of this type of service is that the food often is rather cool by the time the last plate has been served. However, there is less interruption of conversation than occurs in the passing of the dishes of food in American service.

Blue-plate service is a convenient style of service that is suited well to today's lifestyles. In this service, the plates are served in the kitchen and are carried to the table. If an appetizer course is being served, this will be eaten and cleared before the dinner plates are served from the kitchen. When no appetizer is served at the table, the plates of food can be in place on the table when the diners are seated.

This form of service permits control of portion sizes, which is a distinct advantage when people are trying to restrict their food intake for weight control purposes. It also has the advantage of not using serving bowls and platters, thus reducing the tasks of the dishwasher.

English service is a somewhat more formal style of service than family service, for a waiter or waitress is used. The arrangements for English service are the same as those for placing the plates and serving dishes in family service. The host again serves the food onto the top plate of the stack placed at his cover. However, when the plate is served, the waiter or waitress takes the plate and carries it to the person for whom it is intended, starting with the hostess. The sequence of service is the same as is followed in family service.

The plates are served from the left side of the diner with beverages served from the right. The obvious advantage of English service is that the plates do not have to be passed from one person to another. However, the difficulty of serving the food while it is still pleasingly warm remains a disadvantage. Of course, the limited presence of help for serving meals frequently rules out the possibility of using English service in the home.

By far the most formal type of service is **Russian service**. This requires trained waiters or waitresses and thus fails to meet the needs of most American households today. For Russian service, a sideboard or buffet is mandatory, for this is the place where the food will be served. Each course is brought in serving dishes to the sideboard where the waiter serves it and then brings it to the individual diners.

By the time each person has been served in this fashion, the food generally is cold. However, Russian service has the advantage to the host and hostess that they can devote their full attention to their guests and to leading a stimulating conversation. When diners have all finished a course, the plates are removed in preparation for the next course. Russian service is slow, which means that the dinner often serves as the primary entertainment of the evening.

The goals in serving meals are to have all diners enjoy the meal and to have the hot foods served hot and the cold foods well chilled. The type of service used for the meal should be selected to help meet these goals. Temperature control can be aided by warming dinner plates in a warm oven or on the dry cycle in the dishwasher. The refrigerator is helpful in chilling salad plates appropriately.

TABLE ETIQUETTE

Whether dining with family, friends, or business associates, consideration for others is the underlying theme for defining rules of etiquette. Good manners at the dining table add to the pleasure and comfort of those enjoying the meal together. Table etiquette is so important at interviews and in the business world that some universities are providing guidance in etiquette to their graduating seniors.

Guidelines that help to enhance the pleasure of all at the table include the following:

- A potato chip or other food should be dipped only one time into the bowl of dip. It is unsanitary to take a bite and dip your piece of food again.
- Follow the lead of your host or hostess throughout the meal (e.g., unfolding napkin, use of silverware).

blue-plate service Dinner plates are served from the kitchen.

English service Meal service in which a waiter or waitress carries the dinner plate (served by the host) to the diner.

Russian service Very formal service in which waiters or waitresses serve the plates at a sideboard and carry them individually to the diners at the table; the meal is served in several courses, with the table being cleared between each course.

http://www.cuisinenet.com/glossary/tableman.html
—Overview of basic manners.

http://whatscookingamerica.net/Menu/DiningEtiquetteGuide.htm
—Guide to table manners.

http://www.modern-manners-and-etiquette.com/business-table-manners.html
—Guidelines for dining in business and informal settings.

http://entertaining.about.com/cs/etiquette/a/table-manners.htm
—Overview of basic manners.

- Wait to sit until all are ready to be seated.
- Wait to start eating until all at the table are served and the hostess begins to eat.
- Chew with your lips closed and avoid smacking your lips.
- Talk only when you do not have food in your mouth.
- Place used flatware on the plate, never on the table, except when using it to eat.
- Place your soup spoon or utensils used for the appetizer on the liner when you are through eating the course.
- Use the butter knife on the butter plate to transfer butter to your plate and then put the butter knife back on the butter plate.
- Use your knife to butter a small piece broken from your bread.
- Use silverware to eat most foods, but fingers may be used for exceptions such as very crisp bacon.
- Keep your elbows off the table.
- Participate in the conversation without dominating it.
- Replace your napkin at the left of your plate before rising from the table after all are through eating.

Diners can be assured that they are fitting into the expected social pattern if they will follow the example set by the hostess or host. It is the responsibility of the hostess to be certain that the people at the table have their dining needs satisfied and that they are all a part of the social occasion the meal provides (Figure 21.12).

The meal begins when the people have all been seated. The hostess places her napkin in her lap by first unfolding it so that the napkin remains folded in half. She then begins to eat with the appropriate piece of flatware. The others at the table follow this lead. The hostess should eat at a rate that results in her completing a course at the same time that the slowest diner finishes. This is a mark of hospitality, for it says that there is no need to hurry.

The flatware used in eating the appetizer should be placed on the liner used for serving that course when a person finishes the course. When the main course is finished, the knife and fork should be arranged parallel to each other and from the right side of the plate, with both the knife and the fork resting in the center of the plate and the handles extending a bit beyond the right edge of the plate. This arrangement makes it easy to remove plates without having the silverware fall off.

Figure 21.12
The host and hostess share responsibility for making guests comfortable and keeping the conversation interesting. Courtesy of Plycon Press.

When a course is finished, the table is prepared for the next course. Often the table is cleared only between the main course and dessert. When everyone has finished eating, the salt and pepper, butter plate, and any other serving items no longer needed are cleared first. When this has been done, the plates are removed. Plates should be carried to the kitchen without stacking them in the dining area. Although this means a few more trips, the reduced confusion is well worth the extra effort.

At this point, water glasses and other beverages may need to be refilled. Service of beverages ordinarily is done from the right side of the diner. Sometimes crowded dining areas make it necessary to deviate from the pattern of placing and clearing plates from the left and serving beverages from the right. Common sense and practicality need to be used when accessibility is a problem.

A bit of practice with these rather basic guidelines will make it easy to be comfortable at the dining table. The emphasis really needs to be on being a contributing and congenial person at the table. All people, whether a family member or a guest, should participate in the conversation and help to make the meal a pleasant experience for everyone. Sometimes it is helpful to identify some topics that would be interesting conversation items for the group at the table. This is a particular help when one is the host or hostess, but it also is a useful idea when one is a guest.

SPECIAL TYPES OF HOSPITALITY

Buffets

When a large group of people is to be served, **buffet service** is often used (Figure 21.13). There are different procedures that may be used with buffet service. If sufficient tables can be arranged for everyone to be seated, individual places can be set at the tables, with linens, flatware, and glasses already set before the guests arrive. In this arrangement, guests need only to fill their plates at the buffet table and then proceed to a place at one of the tables. This avoids the problem of needing to try to juggle too many items en route to the table. The alternative is to place the flatware and napkins at the far end of the buffet table for guests to pick up after they have selected their food. Guests then proceed to find a chair or other place to sit with their food. Small tables can be positioned around the room so that each person can reach one. Beverages can then be placed on these tables.

With buffet service, appetizers usually are served prior to the actual beginning of buffet service. The main course is served in appropriate serving dishes on the buffet table. The table

buffet service
Arrangement of the dinner plates and the food on a buffet table, with guests helping themselves to their food as they move along the table.

Figure 21.13
Buffet service is efficient for serving a large group; hot dishes need to have a candle or other method of heating underneath to maintain the food at serving temperature. Courtesy of Plycon Press.

for this type of service can be arranged in a dramatic style. Sometimes a runner is used as the linen for a buffet table, while a tablecloth may be more appropriate in some other situations. If a runner is to be used, the table surface needs to be pretty, for it will become part of the overall effect of the buffet table.

A fairly large, high centerpiece can be used because people will not need to be able to see above it while seated. The size of the centerpiece is dictated primarily by the size of the table in relation to the amount of food being served. There should be enough room so that the centerpiece can be seen well, without the plates of food overlapping with it.

Buffet service can be arranged so that people pass along both sides of the table, or it may be set up for only one line of service. In the former case, the centerpiece needs to be placed in the center of the table and be arranged so that both sides are attractive. For one-sided service, the centerpiece can be placed at the back of the table, with only one side being visible. When a large group is being served, the service will be speeded significantly by having the same food arranged on both sides of the table. This makes it possible for half of the people to go through each side, thus cutting serving time approximately in half.

Once the linen and centerpiece have been arranged, the arrangement of the rest of the table can be planned. The dinner plates need to be placed at the beginning of the line. The food then is arranged along the side of the table so that it can be served easily with one hand as people move along. Meats should be arranged on a platter in individual slices or servings. Sometimes it is practical to have someone carve a roast or a turkey as people pass by that part of the table. If a sauce or other garnish accompanies a specific food, the accompaniment should be placed right beside the food it is to augment. This placement helps to clarify the intended use of accompaniments.

Often all of the hot foods are placed at the beginning of the food line, and the salads and rolls are toward the end. Each item on the line should have appropriate serving silver placed with it so that the service is easy for individuals. If a large group of people is being served by buffet style, it will be necessary to replenish serving dishes of food occasionally during the service. Sometimes the serving dishes are refilled when the last person has gone through the line so that people can return for additional servings if they wish.

Dessert in buffet service can be handled in any of several different ways. One is to clear the buffet table of all main course serving dishes and to arrange the dessert, either on a serving platter or in individual servings, on the table (Figure 21.14). This can be quite attractive because the centerpiece shows off particularly well when there is only the dessert course on the table with it. The other approach is to serve the dessert to the guests where they are seated. The choice between these two methods of service is often dictated by the amount of help available for service. Regardless of which method is used for serving the dessert, the dishes from the main course need to be cleared before the dessert is served. The beverages also need to be refilled when the dessert is served. Following completion of the dessert course, all of the glasses and dishes are cleared.

Figure 21.14
Desserts may be arranged on the dessert table for guests to help themselves.
Courtesy of Plycon Press.

Teas and Coffees

Some social occasions are held in the middle of the morning or afternoon, making a complete meal inappropriate, but nevertheless suggesting the need for some refreshments. In the morning, such informal gatherings in a neighbor's home or even in a business setting often are called coffees. The usual beverage served is coffee, but any hot beverage may be offered. A hot bread provides an excellent accompaniment for the steaming hot beverage. On special occasions, fruit might be added to the menu.

In serving the refreshments, arrange the cups and coffee service from a cart or table that has been prepared with a simple cloth and a touch of decoration, perhaps a rose in a simple rose bowl. The cups are placed on the left side of the coffeepot with the handles turned so that the hostess can reach them easily. If convenient, the first cup is placed on a small tray in front of the hostess so that she can pour the beverage easily into the cup. Then the filled cup is placed on a saucer and is passed to a guest. Guests then help themselves to the platter of food and a napkin. The entire arrangement is planned for ease of service and maximum comfortable social conversation.

In contrast to a morning coffee, afternoon tea may be a formal social event, complete with silver tea service and rather elaborate foods. If there are several people attending the tea, a buffet table may be the best way to serve. The table for a formal tea is set with beautiful linens, often an elaborate floral centerpiece, and either silver or other formal candelabra. The beverage, usually hot tea, is arranged at one end of the table.

The tea service ordinarily includes a large silver platter on which the silver teapot and the silver creamer and sugar bowl are placed. The cups are placed just to the left or slightly in back of the platter, and the stack of saucers or small plates is adjacent to the cups. If several cups are needed, the cups may be stacked two high to save space. If space is limited, additional cups will need to be brought from the kitchen as needed during the tea.

Although the food for some teas may be very simple, the menu frequently is quite elaborate. Fancy tea sandwiches may be prepared in pinwheels, stacked to make ribbon sandwiches, or perhaps cut into special shapes with sandwich or cookie cutters (Figure 21.15). Small cookies and cakes may be arranged on another platter. Tarts, candies, and nuts are other foods popular at a tea. On the buffet table, the sandwiches are the first item the guest selects, followed by the dessert items, and finally the candies and nuts. The last items are the silverware and napkins.

Figure 21.15
Accompaniments for high tea sometimes are quite varied and tempting. Courtesy of Plycon Press.

SUMMARY

Table appointments cover a wide range of styles to fit the tastes and needs of many different people. Tablecloths of easy-care fabrics provide a colorful background for virtually any occasion. Place mats are convenient to use and can be excellent for meal service ranging from very informal to rather formal, providing the dining table used has a pleasing surface to enhance the appearance of the mats. Matching or contrasting napkins complete the linens needed.

Centerpieces can be varied to suit the formality or informality of the occasion. It is important that the centerpiece complement the other pieces being used on the table and that the arrangement be low enough that people can see all of the other diners seated at the table. Elaborate arrangements can be used to advantage on a formal tea table.

Choices among flatware are sterling silver, silver plate, and stainless steel. Either of the silver products will need occasional polishing to remove tarnish. Sterling is attractive, yet costly, flatware that can be used for many years; silver plate costs less than sterling, but the plating will wear off at certain key pressure points in a few years of wear.

The price and durability of dishes are key considerations when selecting dishes. Bone china is particularly durable, but it is costly to buy. Pottery is of limited sturdiness, which may result in chips. However, the comparatively low cost of pottery helps to make it a sensible choice for many people.

The patterns on dishes are very important in selecting a set of dishes, for they influence the formality of the table setting. Glassware should be compatible with the designs of the flatware and dishes. Because of the risk of breakage, decisions on glassware are not necessarily choices that must be lived with 10 years later, which provides an opportunity for a bit of experimentation or variety.

Table settings should be done carefully, with the flatware being arranged so that the handles are an inch from the edge of the table. Careful attention to arranging the flatware neatly and according to well-defined standards is essential to presentation of a meal of high quality in the home.

The same meal may be served in a variety of styles, the simplest of which is American service. The serving dishes are passed around the table, with each person serving his or her own plate. Family service is done by the host serving each of the plates from his post at the end of the table. English service is very similar to family service. However, English service requires that a waiter or waitress carry the served plates from the host to the diner. For blue-plate service, the dinner plates are served in the kitchen and then placed at each setting. Russian service requires that two people serve the food and otherwise wait on the guests. This very formal service is inconsistent with the lifestyles of many U.S. households today.

The host and hostess are involved very directly with the development of excellent table manners for all family members. It is the hostess who carries the brunt of this assignment. She is the one who signals the beginning of the meal by lifting her fork to take the first bite. It also is her responsibility to be sure that she is eating at approximately the same pace as the slowest eater.

Buffets are a good way to serve large groups. In fact, a double line can be set up on the two sides of the table to save time. Once the buffet line has been toured, guests may be seated at tables equipped with the table service needed for gracious dining. Another service style is to have guests seated away from a regular dining table, but with a small table within reach to hold the beverages conveniently.

Teas and coffees are popular in the United States as a social gathering. Coffees usually are rather informal occasions at which coffee and perhaps a bread are served. Teas **ordinarily** are held in the afternoon and boast rather elaborate dainty foods and formal service.

STUDY QUESTIONS

1. What criteria are important in selecting linens for the table?
2. Why is china more expensive to purchase than pottery?
3. Why is bone china more durable than pottery?
4. What are the advantages and disadvantages of sterling silver, silver plate, and stainless steel flatware?
5. Sketch a place setting, being sure to show how the knife is oriented.
6. What are the basic elements of each of the following forms of service: family, American, English, Russian, and blue plate?
7. What guidance would you give to a student who is going on an interview that will involve a meal?

SELECTED REFERENCES

Baldridge, L. 2003. *Letitia Baldridge's New Manners for New Times.* Scribner. New York.

Bryant, C., and P. Gilchrist. 2001. *New Book of Table Settings.* Lark Books. Ashville, NC.

Evelegh, T. 2000. *Table Settings: 100 Inspirational Stylings, Themes and Layouts.* Lorenz Books. Lanham, MD.

Hoppen, K., and K. Phillips. 1997. *Table Chic.* Thunder Bay Press. San Diego, CA.

McWilliams, M. 2008. *Fundamentals of Meal Management.* 5th ed. Prentice Hall. Upper Saddle River, NJ.

Meyer, D. 2006. *Setting the Table: The Transforming Power of Hospitality in Business.* Harper Collins. New York.

Ohrbach, B. M. 1997. *Tabletops: Easy, Practical, Beautiful Ways to Decorate the Table*. Clarkson Potter. New York.

Post, P. 1998. *Emily Post's Entertaining*. Harper Collins. New York.

Post, P. 2004. *Emily Post's Etiquette*. 17th ed. Harper Collins. New York.

Rosen, S. 2007. *Elements of the Table: A Simple Guide for Hosts and Guests*. Clarkson Potter. New York.

Stern, T., and C. Matheson. 2007. *Tea Party: 20 Themed Teas*. Clarkson Potter. New York.

Tuckerman, N., and N. Dunnan. 1995. *Amy Vanderbilt's Complete Book of Etiquette*. Doubleday. New York.

Wolfman, P. 2000. *The Perfect Setting*. Harry N. Abrams. New York.

Yeaward, W., and R. Main. 2006. *Perfect Tables: Tabletop Secrets, Settings and Centerpieces for Delicious Dining*. Cico Books. London.

Appendix A
The Metric System

The metric system is the system used in food research and other sciences. Therefore, professionals need to be familiar with this system and be able to convert between the customary and metric systems.

The metric system is based on units of 10, with prefixes providing the necessary information about size and root words indicating the type of unit: volume, weight, or distance. Specifically, the root words are *liter (l)* for volume, *gram (g)* for weight, and *meter (m)* for distance.

The prefixes attached to these root words define each unit of 10, making it possible to describe metric measures in comparatively simple numbers. Table A.1 presents the common prefixes for metrics.

Measures in metric are expressed by combining the appropriate prefix with the type of measurement being made. For example, volume might be expressed in milliliters. In this system, half a liter would be expressed as 0.5 liter, or 500 milliliters (note that 1 liter equals 1000 milliliters or 10 centiliters). Similarly, 1 kilogram is the same as 1000 grams (10^3 grams).

Not only do food scientists need to be able to work within the metric system, but they also need to be able to convert between these laboratory units and household measures. This is a matter of simple arithmetic if certain equivalent measures are known. It is helpful to know that there are about 236 milliliters in a common measuring cup and that there are approximately 454 grams in a pound. With these equivalencies and others provided in the table, calculations can be done quickly (Table A.2).

Yet another type of measurement done in the laboratory is that of determining temperatures used in food preparation. Consumers in the United States ordinarily use the Fahrenheit scale, while U.S. scientists use Celsius. Conversions may need to be made between the two scales. Comparisons are shown in Figure A.1. Familiar reference points are the boiling point of water (212°F [100°C]).

To convert from the Fahrenheit (F) scale to the Celsius (C) temperature, the following equation is used:

$$5/9(\underline{\quad}°F - 32) = \underline{\quad}°C$$

TABLE A.1
COMMON PREFIXES IN THE METRIC SYSTEM

Prefix	Symbol	Definition
Tera	T	$1,000,000,000,000 = 10^{12}$
Giga	G	$1,000,000,000 = 10^9$
Mega	M	$1,000,000 = 10^6$
Kilo[a]	k	$1,000 = 10^3$
Hecto	h	$100 = 10^2$
Deka	da	$10 = 10^1$
Deci[a]	d	$0.1 = 10^{-1}$
Centi[a]	c	$0.01 = 10^{-2}$
Milli[a]	m	$0.001 = 10^{-3}$
Micro[a]	μ	$0.000,001 = 10^{-6}$
Nano	n	$0.000,000,001 = 10^{-9}$
Pico	p	$0.000,000,000,001 = 10^{-12}$

[a]Prefixes used commonly in food and nutrition.

TABLE A.2
COMMON EQUIVALENT MEASURES AND CONVERSION FACTORS

Equivalents	Conversion Factors
Weights	
1 kilogram = 2.2 pounds	Ounces (avdp) × 28.35 = grams
454 grams = 1 pound	Pounds (avdp) × 0.454 = kilograms
28.35 grams = 1 ounce	Grams × 0.035 = ounces (avdp)
1 gram = 0.035 ounce	Kilograms × 2.2 = pounds (avdp)
Measures	
1 liter = 1.06 quarts	Quarts × 0.946 = liters
1 gallon = 3.79 liters	Gallons × 0.0037 = cubic meters
1 quart = 946.4 milliliters	Liters × 1.056 = quarts
1 cup = 235.6 milliliters	Cubic meters × 264.172 = gallons
1 fluid ounce = 29.6 milliliters	
1 tablespoon = 14.8 milliliters	

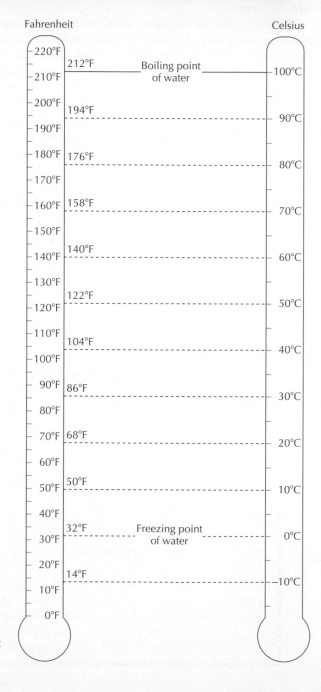

Figure A-1
Comparison of the Fahrenheit and Celsius scales.

For example, to convert 140°F to the Celsius scale:

$$5/9(140°F - 32) = \underline{\quad}°C$$

$$5/9(108) = 60°C$$

Conversion from Celsius to Fahrenheit is done by using this equation:

$$(9/5 \times \underline{\quad}°C) + 32 = \underline{\quad}°F$$

Thus, 60°C is converted to the Fahrenheit scale as follows:

$$(9/5 \times 60°C) + 32 = \underline{\quad}°F$$

$$108 + 32 = 140°F$$

Appendix B
Some Food Additives

Additive	Functions
Acacia gum	Stabilizer, thickener, surface finisher
Acetanisole	Flavoring agent (nutty flavors)
Acetic acid	Acidulant, antimicrobial agent (bacteria and yeast)
Acetone peroxide	Flour bleaching and maturing agent, solvent, oxidizing agent
Acetophenone	Flavoring agent (fruity flavors)
Adipic acid	pH control
Agar agar	Thickener
Alanine	Nutrient enrichment (amino acid)
Alcohol	Solvent
Allyl disulfide	Flavoring agent (garlic, onion)
Aluminum phosphate	Anticaking agent
Aluminum sodium sulfate	Buffer
Aluminum stearate	Defoamer
Aluminum sulfate	Firming agent
Ammonium alginate	Stabilizer, thickener, texturizer
Amylase	Enzyme (digests starch)
Amyl propionate	Flavoring agent (fruity)
Annatto	Food coloring (used in cheese)
Arabic, gum (acacia gum)	Stabilizer, thickener, surface finisher
Arabinogalactan	Stabilizer, thickener, texturizer
Arginine	Nutrient enrichment (amino acid)
Ascorbic acid	Antioxidant (to prevent enzymatic browning in fruits, color retention, curing, nutrient enrichment)
Aspartic acid	Nutrient enrichment (amino acid)
Azodicarbonamide	Flour bleaching and maturing agent
Baking powder	Leavening agent
Baking soda	Texturizing agent, pH modifier, leavener with acid
Beeswax	Surface finisher
Bentonite	Protein absorber
Benzoic acid	Antimicrobial agent (yeast and bacteria)
Benzoyl acetate	Flavoring agent (fruity flavor)
Benzoyl isoeugenol	Flavoring agent (spicy)
Benzoyl peroxide	Flour bleaching and maturing agent, oxidizing agent
BHA (butylated hydroxyanisole)	Antioxidant
BHT (butylated hydroxytoluene)	Antioxidant
Bisulfite salts	Antioxidants
Black pepper	Flavoring agent
Butyl paraben	Preservative
Butyl stearate	Defoaming agent
Calcium bromate	Maturing agent, bleaching
Calcium carbonate	Acidity control, leavening
Calcium chloride	Firming agent
Calcium citrate	Buffer, chelating agent
Calcium dioxide	Effervescent
Calcium disodium EDTA	Chelating agent
Calcium gluconate	Buffer, chelating agent
Calcium lactate	Preservative
Calcium lactobionate	Foaming agent
Calcium oxide	Acidity control
Calcium peroxide	Oxidizing agent
Calcium phosphate	Buffer, chelating agent, leavener
Calcium pyrophosphate	Buffer
Calcium silicate	Anticaking agent

Additive	Functions
Calcium sorbate	Preservative
Calcium stearate	Anticaking agent
Calcium stearoyl-2-lactylate	Emulsifier
Calcium sulfate	Processing aid
Carnauba wax	Surface finisher
Carob bean gum (acacia gum)	Stabilizer, thickener, texturizer
Carotenes	Coloring agents
Carrageenan	Thickener, stabilizer, emulsifier
Cellulose	Stabilizer, thickener, texturizer
Cholic acid	Emulsifier
Citric acid	Acidifying agent, synergist, chelating agent, preservative, antioxidant
Citrus Red No. 2	Color
Cobalt sulfate	Source of cobalt and sulfur in diet
Cochineal	Beverage color
Cornstarch	Anticaking, thickener
Corn syrup	Formulation aid, texturizing agent, sweetener
Cupric chloride	Copper source
Cyclamates	Non-nutritive sweeteners (banned in the United States)
Decanoic acid	Defoaming agent
Desoxycholic acid	Emulsifier
Dextrin	Stabilizer
Dextrose	Formulation aid, sweetener (glucose)
Dicalcium phosphate	Acidity control, leavening, anticaking
Diglycerides	Emulsifiers
Dimagnesium phosphate	Anticaking agent
Dimethylpolysiloxane	Defoamer
Dioctyl sodium sulfosuccinate	Emulsifier
Disodium EDTA	Chelating agent
Disodium guanylate	Flavor potentiator
Disodium inosinate	Flavor potentiator
Disodium phosphate	Emulsifier
EDTA (ethylenediaminetetra acetate)	Sequestrant used in salad dressings, antioxidant
Ethyl caproate	Artificial fruit flavor
Ethylene oxide	Antimicrobial agent
Ethylpelargonate	Alcoholic beverage flavor
Ethyl phenylacetate	Honey flavor
Ethyl vanillin	Chocolate and vanilla flavoring
Eugenol	Defoaming agent
Fatty acids	Emulsifiers
F. D. & C. Blue No. 1	Coloring agent
F. D. & C. Red No. 3	Red coloring agent used in baked goods
F. D. & C. Yellow No. 5	Yellow coloring agent
Ferrous gluconate	Nutrient enrichment, iron source
Ferrous sulfate	Nutrient enrichment, iron source
Fructose	Sweetener, monosaccharide
Fumaric acid	Acidity control
Furcelleran	Texturizer
Gelatin	Thickening agent
Gibberellic acid	Fermentation aid
Glucose oxidase	Oxygen scavenger
Glycerine	Solvent, texturizer, humectant
Glycerol mono- and diesters	Emulsifiers
Glycerol monostearate	Dough conditioner
Glycocholic acid	Emulsifier
Guar gum	Thickener
Gum guiac	Antioxidant
Heptylparaben	Preservative
Honey	Sweetener, texturizer
Hydrochloric acid	Acidifying agent
Hydrogen peroxide	Bleaching, antimicrobial agent, oxidizing agent

Additive	Functions
Hydrolyzed vegetable protein	Stabilizer, thickener
Invert sugar	Sweetener
Iodate, potassium	Nutrient enrichment, iodine source
Iron oxide	Color
Karaya gum	Stabilizer, thickener, texturizer
Lactylic acid esters of fatty acids	Surface active agents, emulsifiers
Larch gum	Stabilizer, thickener, texturizer
Lauric acid	Defoaming agent
Lecithin	Emulsifier (from corn and soybeans)
Lipase	Dairy flavor developer
Locust bean gum (carob bean)	Dough conditioner
Magnesium carbonate	Anticaking
Magnesium silicate	Anticaking
Magnesium stearate	Formulation aid, anticaking
Magnesium sulfate	Nutrient enrichment, magnesium source
Manganese citrate	Nutrient enrichment, manganese source
Mannitol	Formulation aid, sweetener, anticaking, stabilizer, thickener, texturizer
Methyl bromide	Kills undesirable organisms
Methyl cellulose	Bulking agent
Methyl glucoside	Clouding and crystallization inhibitor
Methylparaben	Preservative
Mineral oil	Defoaming agent
Modified food starch	Stabilizer, thickener, texturizer
Monocalcium phosphate	Leavening, dough conditioner
Monoglycerides	Emulsifiers
Monosodium glutamate (MSG)	Flavor enhancer
Mustard	Flavoring agent
Nickel sulfate	Nutrient enrichment, nickel source
Nicotinamide	Nutrient enrichment, niacin source
Nitrates	Antimicrobial action, effective against spores of *C. botulinum*
Nitrites	Antimicrobial action, effective against spores of *C. botulinum*
Oleic acid	Defoaming agent
Oxystearin	Clouding and crystallization inhibitor, defoaming agent
Palmitic acid	Defoaming agent
Papain	Proteolytic enzyme used in meat tenderizer
Pectin	Stabilizer, thickener, texturizer
Pectinase	Clarifying agent for beverages (enzyme)
Peroxidase	Enzyme used to destroy glucose in dried egg white
Petroleum waxes	Defoaming agents
Phosphates	Acidity control
Phosphoric acid	Chelating agent, sequestrant, acidity control
Phostoxin	Fumigant
Polysorbate 60, 65, and 80	Emulsifiers
Polyvinyl pyrrolidine	Surface finisher
Potassium acid citrate	Buffer
Potassium alginate	Stabilizer, thickener, texturizer
Potassium bromide	Bleach and maturing agent for flour, dough conditioner, fermentation aid
Potassium citrate	Chelating agent
Potassium gibberellate	Fermentation aid
Potassium iodide	Nutrient enrichment, source of iodine
Potassium phosphate	Chelating agent, emulsifier
Potassium polymetaphosphate	Emulsifier
Potassium propionate	Emulsifier
Potassium pyrophosphate	Emulsifier
Propylene glycol	Formulation aid, humectant, solvent
Propylene glycol monostearate	Humectant
Propylene oxide	Antimicrobial agent
Propyl gallate	Antioxidant
Propylparaben	Preservative

Additive	Functions
Red No. 40	Color
Rennin	Enzyme, used to clot milk
Resins	Insoluble materials used to remove ions from water, juices, and other liquids; forms are acrylate-acrylamide, sulfonated copolymers of styrene, sulfonated anthracite coal
Rice wax	Surface finishing
Saccharin	Non-nutritive sweetener
Saffron	Colorizer
Shellac wax	Surface finish
Silica aerogel	Anticaking agent
Silicon dioxide	Defoaming agent, anticaking
Sodium acetate	Acidity control
Sodium acid phosphate	Leavening
Sodium acid pyrophosphate	Buffer, chelating agent
Sodium alginate	Stabilizer, thickener, texturizer
Sodium aluminum citrate	Anticaking
Sodium aluminum phosphate	Leavening, emulsifier in cheese
Sodium aluminum silicate	Anticaking
Sodium aluminum sulfate	Leavening
Sodium benzoate	Preservative
Sodium bicarbonate	Texturizer, pH influence
Sodium calcium alginate	Texturizer, stabilizer, thickener
Sodium carbonate	Acidity control, leavening
Sodium carboxymethylcellulose	Bulking agent
Sodium caseinate	Formulation aid
Sodium chloride	Flavor enhancer
Sodium citrate	Acidity control
Sodium diacetate	Chelating agent
Sodium erythorbate	Curing agent, preservative
Sodium gluconate	Chelating agent
Sodium hexametaphosphate	Chelating agent
Sodium hydroxide	pH control
Sodium lauryl sulfate	Surface active agent
Sodium metaphosphate	Sequestrant, curing agent, emulsifier
Sodium nitrate	Curing agent, prevent formation of toxin from *C. botulinum* spores
Sodium nitrite	Curing agent, prevent formation of toxin from *C. botulinum* spores
Sodium potassium tartrate	Buffer, chelating agent
Sodium propionate	Preservative
Sodium silicoaluminate	Anticaking agent
Sodium sorbate	Preservative
Sodium stearyl fumarate	Maturing, bleaching, conditioning agent
Sodium tartrate	Chelating agent
Sodium tripolyphosphate	Curing agent, humectant, chelating agent
Sorbic acid	Mold and yeast inhibitor
Sorbitan monooleate	Emulsifier
Sorbitan monostearate	Emulsifier
Sorbitan tristearate	Emulsifier
Sorbitol	Chelating agent, humectant, sweetener
Starch	Thickener, moisture retention, bulking
Stearic acid	Defoaming agent
Sucrose	Flavoring agent, preservative
Sugar	Flavoring agent, preservative
Sulfites	General antimicrobial agent
Sulfur dioxide	Preservative
Sulfuric acid	Acidity control
Tannic acid	Complexes protein
Tartartic acid	Chelating agent, acidity control
Tertiary butyl hydroquinone (TBHQ)	Antioxidant
Thiamin hydrochloride	Nutrient enrichment, thiamin

Additive	Functions
Thiodopropionic acid	Decomposes hydroperoxide
Thiosulfate	Reducing agent
Titanium dioxide	Color
α-Tocopherol	Reducing agent
Tragacanth gum	Stabilizer, thickener, texturizer
Triacetin	Solvent
Tricalcium phosphate	Synergist, anticaking
Triethyl citrate	Solvent
Turmeric	Flavor, color
Ultramarine blue	Color, animal feed only
Xanthan gum	Body, bulking agent
Yeasts	Leavening agents
Yellow No. 5	Color
Yellow prussiate of soda	Anticaking

Glossary

Acid hydrolysis Cleavage of a molecule by utilizing a molecule of water in the presence of an acid, which serves as a catalyst.

Acidophilus milk Milk containing a culture of *Lactobacillus acidophilus,* which splits the lactose in milk into galactose and glucose.

Acrolein Aldehyde formed when glycerol loses two molecules of water during frying.

Acrylamide Potential carcinogen that forms when meats, vegetables, and baked products reach extremely high temperatures.

Actomyosin Complex muscle protein composed of actin and myosin formed during muscle contraction.

Additive Substance added into foods by intent or by accident.

Aerobic Needing oxygen for survival and reproduction.

Aflatoxin Mycotoxin produced by the growth of *Aspergillus flavus* or *Aspergillus parasiticus;* molds sometimes growing on peanuts, corn, seeds, or nuts that are not stored in a sufficiently dry environment or are grown in mold-containing soil.

Aged beef Prime beef that has been held in very cold storage for 15–40 days to intensify flavor, darken the color, and tenderize the muscles.

All-purpose flour Flour from hard or hard and soft wheat blended; protein content of about 10.5 percent and suitable for making most baked products.

American service Method of meal service in which all of the food is placed in serving dishes on the table and passed around.

Amino acid Subunit of protein; contains an amino ($-NH_2$) group and an organic acid group ($-COOH$).

Amorphous candies Candies with such a high sugar content that they are too viscous to permit an organized crystal structure to develop; very hard to extremely chewy candies.

Amphoteric Ability to act as an acid (carrying a + charge) or a base (a − charge). Their carboxyl and amino groups permit proteins to do this.

Amylopectin The rather insoluble fraction of starch; contains both 1,4- and 1,6-α-glucosidic linkages, resulting in a bulky, branching molecule that does not form a gel.

Amylose Linear starch fraction (1,4-α-glucosidic linkages) that is soluble and capable of forming gels.

Anadromous Fish living part of their lives in freshwater and part in saltwater.

Anaerobic Capable of surviving in an oxygen-free environment.

Angel food cake Foam cake consisting primarily of egg white foam, sugar, and cake flour, with no fat or baking powder.

Anthocyanins Group of flavonoids providing the reddish to bluish hues of fruits and vegetables.

Anthoxanthins Group of flavonoids providing the white or creamy colors in fruits and vegetables.

Arabica coffee Variety of coffee preferred by people who want a full-bodied, aromatic coffee.

Aroma Volatile compounds perceived by the olfactory receptors.

Astringent Characteristic of drawing together or puckering; green tea is noted for making the mouthfeel a bit puckered and almost dry, particularly if the leaves have steeped more than five minutes.

Atmospheric pressure The pressure of the atmosphere pressing downward on the surface of a liquid; varies with changes in elevation.

Bacteria Microscopic organisms, often single-celled and of varied shapes (filamentous, rod-like, round, or spiral), some of which are causes of food-borne illnesses.

Baking soda Bicarbonate of soda; an alkaline ingredient ($NaHCO_3$).

Beading Droplets of moisture on a meringue due to overbaking.

Beating Very vigorous agitation of food mixtures using an electric mixer at high speed or a wooden spoon to trap air and/ or to develop gluten.

Beta (β) amylase Enzyme prominent in the catalytic release of maltose and glucose from starch to provide food for yeast.

Biscuit Quick bread made by cutting in the solid shortening and using a ratio of flour to liquid of 3:1, which results in a dough that is able to be kneaded, rolled, and cut into the desired round disk for baking.

Black tea Brisk, rather mild, deep amber-colored tea produced by an extended fermentation period during the processing of tea leaves.

Blanching Boiling or steaming for a brief period to inactivate enzymes prior to freezing.

Blastoderm Germ spot in the egg yolk.

Bloom White or light gray discoloration on chocolate where the chocolate has softened and moisture has collected during storage; tempering is helpful in avoiding the development of bloom.

Blue-plate service The service of dinner plates from the kitchen.

Boiling　Active agitation of liquid and transition of some liquid to the vapor state; occurs when vapor pressure just exceeds atmospheric pressure.

Boiling water bath (water bath canning)　Preservation by packing high-acid foods, including fruits and tomatoes, into canning jars, covering closed jars with water, and heat processing for the appropriate time.

Botulism　Type of food poisoning caused by eating the toxin produced by *C. botulinum.*

Bound water　Water held so tightly by other substances that it cannot flow.

Braising　Cooking meat slowly in a small amount of liquid in a covered pan until the meat is fork tender, usually a matter of two hours or more.

Bread　A baked mixture containing a flour or meal (usually wheat) as its primary ingredient.

Broiling　Cooking by direct heat, usually at a distance of about three inches; fat is allowed to drain away from the meat.

Bromelain　Enzyme that digests protein; fresh or frozen pineapple contains active bromelain, but canning destroys the action.

BSE　Abbreviation for bovine spongiform encephalopathy, a fatal brain disease that can occur in cattle.

Buffet service　Arrangement of the dinner plates and the food on a serving table, with guests helping themselves to their food as they move along the table.

Bulgur　Parboiled, cracked wheat; chewy and nut-like.

Café au lait　Coffee with an equal amount of scalded milk.

Caffeine　Compound in coffee credited with contributing the stimulating effect of the beverage and a touch of bitterness.

Cake flour　Flour from soft wheat; contains about 7.5 percent protein.

Calories　Unit of energy provided in a food. One calorie (also called kilocalorie) is the amount of heat energy required to raise a kilogram of water 1° Celsius.

Camellia sinensis　Shrub in the Theaceae family, the leaves are plucked and dried to make tea.

Campylobacter jejuni　Type of bacteria sometimes found in poultry and meats.

Candling　Grading procedure based on silhouetting eggs in the shell.

Cappuccino　Espresso topped with steamed milk foam, sometimes garnished with a dusting of sweetened cocoa powder or cinnamon.

Carbohydrase　General term for enzyme that catalyzes the digestion of carbohydrate.

Carbohydrate　Organic compounds containing carbon, hydrogen, and oxygen, with the hydrogen and oxygen being the ratio of water (H_2O); category includes sugars, starches, pectic substances, cellulose, gums, and other complex substances.

Carcinogen　Substance that is capable of causing cancer.

Carotenoids　Carotenes and related compounds producing the orange pigments in fruits and vegetables.

Casein　Chief protein in milk, precipitated in the manufacturing of cheese from milk.

Catechin　A prominent polyphenol of green tea.

Cellulose　Complex carbohydrate in cell walls of plant foods, particularly in the dermal cells.

Chalazae　Fibrous structures at the sides of the yolk, aiding in centering the yolk within the egg.

Charger　Large decorative plate at the center of the cover for a formal dinner, but removed when the entrée arrives.

Chiffon cake　Foam cake containing oil and baking powder, as well as the ingredients used in other foam cakes, which are combined together and folded into an egg white foam beaten until the peaks just stand up straight.

Chlorogenic acid　Most abundant acid in coffee; contributes some of the sour and bitter quality to coffee flavor.

Chlorophyll　Green, magnesium-containing pigment in fruits and vegetables.

Chloroplasts　Plastids containing chlorophylls in the cytoplasm of parenchyma cells.

Chocolate　Flavorful substance derived by grinding the roasted beans from the pods of the *Theobroma cacao* tree.

Chromoplasts　Plastids containing carotenoids (orange pigments) in parenchyma cells.

Cis　Configuration at the double bond of an unsaturated fatty acid resulting in a change in the direction of the chain of a fatty acid.

Clostridium botulinum　Type of bacteria producing a toxin that is highly poisonous and frequently fatal to humans when consumed.

Clostridium perfringens　Anaerobic, spore-forming bacteria that multiply readily at room temperature; ingestion can result in perfringens poisoning.

Coagulation　The clumping together of partially denatured protein molecules into a relatively insoluble protein mass.

Coarse suspension　Dispersion of particles larger than colloidal size mixed in water or other liquid.

Co-crystallization　Addition of gum or other ingredient to a highly concentrated sugar solution just before beating very fast, a process that traps the second substance in a mass of micro crystals.

Coddling　Simmering of fruit in a sugar syrup.

Coffee press　Cylindrical container equipped with a handle, lid, and long-handled filter for brewing coffee.

Coldpack (club) cheese　Mixture of natural cheeses with an added emulsifier, but without heating.

Collagen　White connective tissue in meats; fibrous structural protein encasing muscle proteins.

Colloidal dispersion System containing protein or other molecules or particles between 1 and 100 millimicrons in size dispersed in a continuous phase.

Conching Processing step in making chocolate in which the melted chocolate is held in constant motion for between 36 and 72 hours at temperatures ranging from 110° to 210°F (43°C to 99°C), a process helpful in avoiding bloom during storage.

Conduction Transfer of heat from one molecule to the next.

Conserves Preserves with nuts added.

Continuous phase Liquid surrounding the suspended droplets in an emulsion.

Convection Transfer of heat throughout a system by movement of currents of heated air, water, or other liquid.

Conventional method Method of preparing shortened cakes, in which the fat and sugar are creamed, the beaten eggs are added, and the sifted dry ingredients are added (in thirds) alternately with the liquid (in halves).

Conventional sponge method Method of mixing shortened cakes, differing from the conventional method by separating the eggs and using part of the sugar to make a meringue to fold in at the end of mixing.

Couscous Wheat cereal product made by adding a small amount of water to a mixture of semolina and a little flour and then rubbing it together into small granules that are subsequently steamed or simmered in water.

Cover Individual place setting for a meal.

Creaming Mixing fat and sugar together vigorously to create an air-in-fat foam.

Cream puff Quick bread used as a container for dessert fillings or main course mixtures; characterized by a very large cavity resulting from an appropriate combination of butter, water, and egg, in conjunction with flour, and baked in a hot oven.

Cross contamination Introduction of microorganisms to a food when it comes in contact with a surface contaminated previously by another food.

Cross-linked starches Starches treated with various phosphate compounds prior to gelatinization to reduce rupturing of the starch granules.

Crustaceans Shellfish covered by a horny protective layer; shrimp, lobsters, and crabs are familiar examples.

Creutzfeldt–Jakob disease Fatal brain disease in humans that can be contracted by eating beef from cattle with mad cow disease.

Cryophilic Thriving at temperatures well below room temperature; cold loving.

Crystalline candies Candies with an organized crystal structure; easily bitten into or cut with a knife.

Cultured buttermilk Cultured skim milk that sometimes contains flecks of butter.

Curing Treating of meats with salt, sodium nitrate, and heat to achieve color and flavor changes and to promote shelf life and reduce spoilage.

Cutting in Process of cutting solid fats into small pieces with the use of a pastry blender or two table knives.

Cyclospora cayetanensis Protozoan (type of parasite) that can cause cyclosporiasis if it is consumed on infected produce.

Cyclosporiasis Food-borne illness caused by eating produce contaminated with *Cyclospora cayetanensis.*

Cytoplasm Viscous layer just inside the cell wall of the parenchyma cell; contains plastids.

Dark-cutting beef Darkly colored beef with a sticky and gummy character, the result of too little glycogen at slaughter, usually due to exhaustion or inadequate feeding at dispatch.

Deep-fat frying Dry heat method in which meat is immersed in very hot fat.

Delaney clause Clause in the Food Additives Amendment mandating that additives shown to cause cancer at any level must be removed from the marketplace.

Denaturation A physical change in proteins, resulting in a change from native to denatured protein to decrease the solubility and alter the flow properties of food proteins.

Devil's food cake Chocolate cake made with some excess of soda to achieve the desired deep mahogany color.

Dextrin Polysaccharide made of glucose units; smaller and more soluble than starch and with reduced thickening ability.

Dextrinization Chemical breakdown of starch to a more soluble carbohydrate as a result of intense, dry heat.

***Dietary Guidelines for Americans*, 2010** USDHHS and USDA dietary recommendations developed in 2010.

Dietary reference intakes (DRIs) Recommended intakes of nutrients needed by most healthy people on a daily basis to maintain healthy bodies.

Disaccharide Sugars occurring frequently in foods and more complex than monosaccharides, for instance, sucrose, maltose, and lactose.

Discontinuous (dispersed) phase Droplets in an emulsion.

Double-acting baking powder Baking powder containing an acid salt that reacts at room temperature (phosphate salt) and one requiring heat for reaction (sulfate salt); common type of baking powder in the retail market.

Double boiler Two-part pan and lid designed to hold water in the bottom pan and the food in the top; its French name is *bain-marie.*

Dressed fish Fish from which the gills, fins, head, tail, and entrails have been removed.

Dripolator Coffeemaker with a unit for the heated water, a section for the coffee grounds, and a pot to collect the coffee.

Drupes Fruit with a single seed surrounded by edible pulp; cherry is an example.

Dry stage   Point at which beaten egg white foam becomes brittle and loses the sheen normally seen on egg white foam; no longer useful in food preparation.

Durum wheat   A very hard, high-protein wheat grown primarily in North Dakota and particularly well suited to the production of pastas.

Dutch process chocolate   Chocolate manufactured with the addition of alkali to produce a pH between 6.0 and 8.8, causing the chocolate to be dark in color, less acidic, and less susceptible to settling out than is true of chocolate made without adding alkali.

Edible starch films   Films made from special starches containing about 80 percent amylose.

Elastin   Extremely strong connective tissue; a yellow-colored protein in meat that is not tenderized by cooking.

Emulsifying agent   Substance forming a protective coating on the surface of droplets (the interface) in an emulsion.

Emulsion   Colloidal dispersion of two immiscible liquids, with one type of liquid being dispersed as droplets in the other type of liquid.

English service   Meal service in which a waiter or waitress carries the dinner plate, which the host has served, to the diner.

Enriched cereals   Refined cereals to which thiamin, riboflavin, niacin, folate, and iron have been added at specified levels.

Escherichia coli (E. coli)   Group of bacteria often found as the cause of food-borne illnesses.

Espresso   Extremely strong and rather bitter Italian coffee resulting from brewing finely ground dark-roasted coffee with steam.

Essential amino acid   Amino acid that must be provided in the diet to maintain life and promote growth; unable to be synthesized in the body.

Evaporated milk   Canned milk product in which about half of the water content has been evaporated prior to canning; available in varying levels of fat, that is, ranging from non-fat to whole.

Family service   Service of a meal by the host, who serves all of the food onto plates stacked in front of him and then passes the served plates to the hostess and others at the table.

Fat-free or non-fat milk   Milk that has been skimmed to a fat level of 0.1 percent or less.

Fatty acid   Organic acid containing between 2 and 24 carbon atoms; combines with glycerol to form a fat.

FDA   Food and Drug Administration; the federal agency regulating food additives.

Ferrous sulfide   Iron-sulfur compound formed on the surface of the yolk of hard-cooked eggs if eggs are of low quality or are held at high temperatures too long a time.

Fiber   Components of food not digested and absorbed; cellulose, pectic substances, and gums are some carbohydrates contributing to the fiber content of the diet.

Fight Bac®   FDA's food safety education program based on four points: clean; separate; cook; and chill.

Fillet   Lengthwise piece of fish free of the backbone and associated bones.

Fish   Cold-blooded aquatic animal; term usually used to designate those with fins, a backbone, skull, and gills.

Flavonoids   Class of pigments contributing white and red to blue colors in fruits and vegetables; two main divisions are anthoxanthins and anthocyanins.

Flavor   Combination of aroma and taste perceived in the trigeminal cavity.

Flour   Finely ground cereal grains; often used to imply wheat as the grain.

Foamy stage   Transparent, coarse, somewhat fluid foam; stage appropriate for adding the acid and starting to add the sugar to egg whites, but not suitable for use in food mixtures.

Folding   Very gentle manipulation with a rubber spatula, narrow metal spatula, wire whisk, or whip to bring ingredients up from the bottom of the mixing bowl and to spread them over the upper surface to aid in blending them uniformly.

Food Additives Amendment of 1958   Amendment to the Food, Drug, and Cosmetic Act of 1938; regulates food additive usage.

Food and Drug Administration (FDA)   The federal agency regulating food additives.

Food and nutrition board   A group operating under the auspices of the Institutes of Medicine, National Academy of Sciences; members appointed to the group are nationally recognized researchers in nutrition.

Food Code   Code issued jointly by FDA, CDC, and FSIS that guides government agencies overseeing safety in food-service operations.

FOS   Fructooligosaccharide, non-nutritive, sweet carbohydrate comprised of one molecule of sucrose and two or three fructose units.

Freeze- dried coffee   Soluble coffee product made by freezing brewed coffee and sublimating the aqueous portion to obtain dry solids.

Freeze-drying   Process of drying frozen foods.

Freezer burn   Desiccation or drying of part of the surface of frozen food where air contacts the surface.

Fruit butter   Cooked fruit purée with spices.

Gel   A colloidal dispersion in which the solid is the continuous phase and the liquid is the dispersed or discontinuous phase; a starch gel is an example.

Gelatinization   Physical change in starch when heated sufficiently in the presence of water; swelling of starch granules because of the entry of water.

Gelation   Formation of a colloidal dispersion in which the solid forms a continuous phase and liquid forms the discontinuous or dispersed phase; a gelatinized starch system that does not flow.

Genetically modified organism (GMO)   Plants (and food) that have been modified by genetic engineering to enhance desired characteristics.

Ghee   Very carefully clarified butter from which the water and milk solids have been removed by heating and filtering; pronounced with a hard *g*.

Gliadin   Sticky fraction of gluten.

Gluten   Protein complex formed in batters and doughs when wheat flour is mixed with water (or other aqueous liquid).

Glutenin   Very large, elastic component of gluten.

Glycerol   Alcohol containing three carbon atoms and three hydroxyl (—OH) groups; common to the fats used in food preparation.

Glycogen   Polysaccharide in muscle, which breaks down to produce energy and lactic acid in the carcass following slaughter.

Gonyaulax catanella   One-celled organism in red tide that produces saxitoxin in infected shellfish.

GRAS list   List of many additives considered to be safe and legal to use based on a long history of safe use.

Green tea   Somewhat astringent tea that has not been fermented.

Grits   Coarsely chopped hominy.

Hazard analysis and critical control points (HACCP)   Seven-point system developed by each food company to create its own food safety program.

Heat of crystallization   Heat energy released when a viscous sugar solution crystallizes and forms a solid mass.

Heat of solidification   Heat given off when water is transformed into ice; 80 kilocalories per gram of water.

Heat of vaporization   Energy required to convert boiling water into steam; 540 kilocalories per gram of water.

Hedonic   Pertaining to pleasure.

Hemicellulose   Complex carbohydrate contributing to the strength of cell walls that is particularly abundant in the walls of vascular and parenchyma cells.

Herb tea   Beverage made by steeping herbs and other ingredients in water; chosen by some people because of absence of caffeine.

High-fructose corn syrup   Corn syrup in which isomerase has converted some of the sugar to fructose.

Hominy   Endosperm product made by soaking corn in lye.

Hydrogenation   Process of adding hydrogen to polyunsaturated fatty acids to change oils into solid fats.

Hydrolysis   Chemical reaction in which a molecule of water is used to split a compound into two molecules.

Hydrolytic rancidity   Release of free fatty acids due to lipase action during storage of fats.

Hygroscopic   Water attracting.

Incidental contaminants   Any substance that accidentally is contained in a food product.

Ingredient labeling   Listing of ingredients, beginning with the one present in the largest amount by weight and continuing in descending order.

Instant coffee   Soluble coffee solids remaining after the water vapor has been removed from brewed coffee; often made by spray drying.

Instant hot cereals   Cereals that have been precooked to gelatinize the starch and then dehydrated to produce a product requiring only rehydration to serve.

Interfering agent   Butter, corn syrup, or other ingredient inhibiting crystal formation in candies.

Inversion   Specific term for the hydrolysis of sucrose to glucose and fructose.

Invertase   Enzyme catalyzing the inversion of sucrose to glucose and fructose.

Invert sugar   A mixture of equal amounts of glucose and fructose resulting from the hydrolysis of sucrose.

Isoelectric point   pH at which a protein molecule is essentially neutral, resulting in easy aggregation of protein molecules to form curds.

Isomerase   Enzyme utilized to convert glucose to fructose in making high-fructose corn syrup.

Jam   Pectin gel with pieces of fruit plus the juice.

Jelly   Pectin gel made with fruit juice to yield a clear gel.

Kasha   Buckwheat groats (hulled and fragmented particles).

Kneading   Folding over a ball of dough and pressing it with either the fingertips or the heels of both hands, depending upon the amount of gluten needing to be developed and the ratio of ingredients.

Lactase   Enzyme needed for digesting lactose.

Lard   Fat rendered from the fatty tissue of pigs.

Leaf lard   Fat obtained from the abdominal cavity of hogs; the premium type of lard.

Lecithin   Compound in egg yolk that is attracted to both oil and water, making it a very effective emulsifying agent.

Leucoplasts   Plastids serving as the site for formation and storage of starch in cytoplasm in parenchyma cells.

Liner   Plate on which a bowl or other dish containing a serving of a food is placed.

Lipase   Enzyme catalyzing the release of fatty acids from fats.

Lipids   Compounds containing mostly carbon and hydrogen, plus a small proportion of oxygen, to provide concentrated sources of energy.

Listeria monocytogenes   Type of bacteria that can cause listeriosis; sometimes found in unpasteurized milk.

Listeriosis   Potentially very serious food-borne illness caused by ingesting viable *L. monocytogenes*.

Low-fat or light milk   Milk from which part of the fat has been skimmed, resulting in a product with fat usually at the level of 1 or 2 percent.

Lukewarm Approximately body temperature; about 100°F (37.8°C).

Lysozyme Protein involved in egg white foams; isoelectric point is pH 10.7.

Macronutrients Nutrients needed in large quantities: carbohydrates, lipids (fats), and proteins.

Mad cow disease Fatal disease of the central nervous system sometimes occurring in cows caused by eating feed containing infected meat and bone meal; another name for bovine spongiform encephalopathy (BSE).

Magnetron tube Tube generating the microwaves in a microwave oven.

Maillard reaction Browning reaction in food caused by reaction between protein and a sugar.

Marbling Deposition of fat within the muscles of meats.

Market order Regulations for the marketing of specific food products under the guidance of a board, which is authorized by the U.S. Department of Agriculture.

Marmalade Citrus preserves.

Mellorine Frozen ice cream–like dessert in which the fat is not the original milk fat.

Metabolism Chemical reactions in the body; the release of energy from carbohydrates is but one example.

Microwave oven Special type of oven that is able to heat food by sending waves of 915 or 2450 megahertz from a magnetron directly into foods, where water and/or fat molecules vibrate and heat foods.

Microwaves Form of electromagnetic energy; 915 and 2450 megahertz are the assigned frequencies for microwave ovens.

Milling Grinding and separating of the desired fractions of the cereal kernel to produce flour.

Minerals Natural elements in foods that remain as ash as a food is burned; many are essential nutrients.

Modified conventional method Method of mixing a cake utilizing the conventional method, but separating the eggs and adding the whites as a foam folded in at the end of mixing.

Molds Multiple-celled microorganisms capable of forming heads with spores that scatter and are viable even in moisture levels as low as 13 percent.

Mollusks Shellfish protected by an outer shell; scallops, clams, and oysters are common examples.

Mono-, di-, triglycerides Fat molecules containing, respectively, one, two, or three fatty acids esterified with glycerol.

Monosaccharide The simplest of the sugars; common examples include glucose, fructose, and galactose.

Mother liquor Saturated sugar solution between the crystals in crystalline candies.

Mouthfeel The term food professionals use to describe textural properties of a food.

MSG Monosodium glutamate, a by-product of sugar processing, is a flavor enhancer often used in Asian cuisines.

Muffin method Method in which melted fat or oil is blended with other liquids, added all at once to the well-mixed dry ingredients, and stirred just enough to blend the ingredients.

Muffins Quick bread with a cauliflower-like, rounded surface resulting from careful mixing and baking of a batter with a 2:1 ratio of flour to liquid.

Muskmelon One of two general subdivisions of melons; includes cantaloupe, honeydew, and other melons characterized by having a thick pulp surrounding a large central cavity full of small seeds.

Mycotoxin Poisonous substance produced by the growth of some molds.

Myoglobin Pigment in meat; compound similar to hemoglobin and capable of reacting with various substances to effect color changes in muscle.

Myosin Key, elongated, and large protein molecule in muscle.

MyPlate Visual representing the relative amounts of foods from each of the five food groups that should be eaten daily.

National Organic Program Legislation defining the production standards for produce (at least 95 percent of produce must not have been treated with sewage-sludge–based or petroleum-based fertilizers, conventional pesticides, ionizing radiation, or bioengineering) to be labeled organic.

Natural cheese Concentrated curd of milk; ripening is optional.

Nitric oxide myochrome Compound contributing pink color to cured meats.

Non-fat milk Milk resulting when almost all of the fat has been removed, leaving a maximum fat content of 0.5 percent, and usually the level is 0.1 percent or less.

Non-waxy potatoes Potatoes with a low sugar content and high starch level; best suited for baking, mashing, and frying.

Noroviruses Virus that can cause hepatitis A; spread easily through contaminated water and by infected unsanitary food handlers who fail to wash their hands adequately in hot, soapy water.

Nutrient density The amount of nutrients in relation to the calories in a food; high nutrient density means a food is high in nutrients when compared with the caloric content.

Nutrition labeling Label on packaged foods indicating the caloric and nutritive content of a serving of the item according to specific federal guidelines.

Objective evaluation Evaluation of physical and chemical aspects using equipment for measuring specific aspects of a food.

Omega-3 fatty acids Polyunsaturated fatty acids essential in the diet: α-linolenic acid (ALA), eicosapentaenoic acid (EPA), and docosahexaenoic acid (DHA).

Oolong tea   Tea that has undergone limited fermentation, resulting in characteristics intermediate between green and black tea.

Open dating   Date clearly stating pull date or other freshness date.

Orange pekoe   Top grade of black tea.

Organic seal   Seal used to designate food that meets the standards required by the National Organic Program.

Osmotic pressure   The pressure exerted to move water in or out of cells to equalize the concentration of solute in the cell and in the surrounding medium.

Ovalbumin   Heat-sensitive, abundant protein in egg white.

Oven spring   Sharp increase in volume in early phase of baking due to accelerated carbon dioxide production in a hot oven.

Overrun   The increase in volume of ice creams during freezing as a result of expansion as water turns into ice and the incorporation of air during freezing.

Ovomucin   Structural protein abundant in thick egg white.

Oxidative rancidity   Uptake of oxygen with loss of hydrogen at points of unsaturation in a fatty acid, causing undesirable flavor and aroma changes.

Pan broiling   Cooking meat in a skillet, being careful to keep removing the fat as it drains from the meat.

Pan frying   Cooking meat in a frying pan and allowing the fat to accumulate in the pan.

Parasite   Organism living within another organism and deriving its sustenance from the host; worms such as *Trichinella spiralis* can cause weight loss and other health problems.

Parenchyma cell   Type of cell comprising most of the pulp of a vegetable or fruit.

Parevine   Frozen imitation ice cream made without any dairy products.

Pasta   Various dough pastes containing durum wheat and water and sometimes egg and shaped in a variety of flat and rounded or twisted shapes.

Pasteurization   Heat treatment to kill disease-producing microorganisms in milk; usually heated to 161°F (71.6°C) and held there for 15 seconds before cooling to less than 50°F (10°C).

Pastry flour   Moderately fine-textured soft wheat flour; about 7.5 percent protein.

Pectic acid   Pectic substance in overly ripe fruit; incapable of forming a gel.

Pectic substances   Complex carbohydrates acting as cementing substances between cells; sequence of change during ripening is protopectin to pectin to pectic acid.

Pectin   Pectic substances in barely ripe fruit; capable of forming a gel.

Pectinic acid   A form of the pectic substance, pectin.

Peptide bond   Bond formed between the carboxyl of one amino acid and the amino group of a second amino acid with loss of water.

Percentage   Measure of alcohol by volume.

Percolator   Coffeepot containing a basket for coffee grounds that is suspended on a hollow stem above the water in the pot.

Perfringens poisoning   Food-borne illness caused by eating food containing viable *Clostridium perfringens*.

Permanent emulsion   Viscous emulsion containing an emulsifying agent and that rarely separates into two layers.

Peroxide value   Content of peroxides in a fat; a measure of oxidative rancidity.

Petcock   Small opening in the cover of a pressure saucepan to let steam escape and on which the pressure gauge is placed.

pH   Hydrogen ion potential; values less than 7 are acidic, while those above 7 are alkaline.

Phytochemicals   Substances contained in plants that provide some protection against heart disease and certain cancers.

Phytosterol or stanol ester   Plant compounds occurring naturally in some plant oils that can help reduce LDL and total cholesterol levels.

Plasticity   Ability of a fat to be spread easily into quite thin films.

Plastids   Special structures within the cytoplasm of parenchyma cells.

Poaching   Simmering a food in water or other liquid just below boiling until the food is tender.

Polymerization   The joining together of free fatty acids to make long chains; occurs in heated oils.

Polyphenolase   Enzyme active in converting polyphenols into theaflavins during fermentation of black tea leaves.

Polyphenols   Compounds containing more than one six-membered phenolic ring; contribute astringency to tea.

Polysaccharide   Complex carbohydrate made up of many units of monosaccharides joined together into single molecules.

Pome   Fruit with a core containing five seeds and surrounded by thick, edible pulp; apples, pears, and quince are examples.

Popovers   Quick bread made with a flour-to-liquid ratio of 1:1 and with egg and baked in deep cups in an oven heated to at least 425°F (218°C) to generate steam for leavening.

Pour batter   Flour mixture with approximately equal amounts of flour and liquid (1:1 ratio); popovers and shortened cakes are examples.

Preserves   Pectin gel with juice and fruit pieces larger than the pieces used in jam.

Pressure canner   Large, heavy kettle with tight-fitting lid capable of withstanding internal pressure of at least 20 pounds; used for canning low-acid foods.

Primal cuts   First cuts (wholesale cuts) to provide large sections, yet small enough to be handled by the butcher.

Prion   Abnormal agent that is transmitted to cause a fatal condition characterized by abnormal folding of prion proteins in the brain, as in BSE.

Process cheese   Blend of natural cheeses heated to at least 145°F (62.8°C), with the addition of an emulsifying agent and water; cheese that is not ripened.

Process cheese food   Process cheese product with about 4 percent more water than in process cheese.

Process cheese spread   Process cheese product with about 4 percent more water than in process cheese food, or about 8 percent more water than in process cheese.

Proof   Expression of alcohol content commonly used to indicate the alcohol content of distilled beverages; proof is double the percent content.

Proofing   Fermentation of a yeast-leavened batter or dough to produce the necessary carbon dioxide; usually controlled at a temperature of 85°–95°F (29°–35°C) for about an hour to double the volume.

Proteolytic enzyme   Enzyme capable of catalyzing a break in a protein at a peptide linkage.

Protopectin   Pectic substance in very green fruit; incapable of forming a gel.

Quick bread   Bread leavened with steam or carbon dioxide produced by a chemical reaction; a bread that does not require time for biological agents to generate carbon dioxide.

Quick-cooking cereals   Cereals treated with disodium phosphate to hasten softening during cooking.

Quick-rise active dry yeast   New strain of yeast capable of reducing rising time by half in yeast-leavened products.

Radiation   Transfer of energy directly from the source to the food being heated.

RDA   Recommended dietary allowances specified by the Food and Nutrition Board to provide standards for professionals to utilize in planning diets and projects for groups of people in normal good health.

Rearranged lard   Lard that has had special processing to remove the fatty acids from the glycerol and then to reunite them in a somewhat different configuration to achieve a product that tends to form beta prime (β′) crystals.

Reduced-fat milk   Milk with its fat content reduced 25 percent (to a level of about 2 percent fat).

Registered Dietitian (R.D.)   Person who has completed a specified academic program in food and nutrition, an approved clinical experience, and the registration examination.

Re-greening   Reversal of color to green on some ripe oranges if chlorophyll becomes dominant over carotenoids.

Rennin   Protein-digesting enzyme from calves' stomachs.

Resistant starch   Starch that passes out of the small intestine without being digested.

Retail cuts   Meat cuts available to consumers.

Retrogradation   Formation of crystalline areas due to aggregation of amylose molecules in a starch gel, a physical process that can be reversed by heating.

Reversion   Development of a fishy quality in poly-unsaturated fats.

Rheology   Flow properties.

Rigor mortis   Series of chemical changes occurring in the carcass following slaughter.

Robusta coffee   Variety of coffee that is somewhat acidic and suited to dark roasts; grown primarily in West Africa and Southeast Asia.

Roux method   Preparation of gravy by stirring starch into the measured drippings from fried or roasted meats.

Russian service   Very formal form of service in which the waiter or waitress serves the plates at a sideboard and carries them individually to the diners at the table; the meal is served in several courses, with the table being cleared between each course.

Saccharomyces cerevisiae   Strain of yeast used to produce carbon dioxide in yeast-leavened products.

Saccharomyces exiguus   Yeast primarily responsible for the production of carbon dioxide in acidic sourdough breads.

Salmonellae   Bacteria capable of causing severe gastrointestinal upset when ingested in large quantities of food.

Salmonellosis   Condition characterized by fever, nausea, abdominal cramps, and diarrhea resulting from ingestion of viable salmonellae.

Satiety value   Ability to satisfy and provide feeling of fullness.

Saturated solution   Homogeneous mixture that has as much solute in solution as is possible at that temperature.

Saxitoxin   Poison secreted by *Gonyaulax catanella* within a shellfish host; capable of being concentrated enough to kill a person.

Scalding   Temperature used to loosen fruit skins and perform other similar functions; about 150°F (65.5°C).

Scoring   Cutting the fat and connective tissue at intervals of about an inch around the edge of a muscle to prevent curling of meat during broiling.

Self-rising flour   Flour containing a blend of hard and soft wheats, plus an acid salt, baking soda, and salt, making it necessary to eliminate these ingredients from recipes using self-rising flour.

Semipermanent emulsion   Emulsion that is quite viscous and separates into two layers very slowly.

Semolina   Granular, milled durum wheat, with a maximum of 3 percent flour.

Shellfish   Subcategory of fish; equipped with shell or horny outer covering.

Shellfish poisoning Life-threatening poisoning from saxitoxin produced in shellfish feeding on *Gonyaulax catanella*; characterized by loss of strength and respiratory failure.

Shigella boydii Bacteria spread by fecal contamination in water or food.

Shortened cake Cake containing a solid fat (usually creamed with sugar), sugar, leavening agent, flour, and liquid.

Shortening value Ability of a fat to interfere with gluten development and tenderize a baked product.

Silence cloth Heavy cloth placed underneath a tablecloth to help muffle sound and also to help protect the table from hot dishes.

Simmering Range of temperatures of 180°–211°F (82°–99°C); bubbles form and rise, but rarely break the surface; more gentle heat treatment than boiling.

Single-stage method Method combining all of the ingredients except the egg and possibly part of the liquid, mixing, and then adding the egg and any remaining liquid with beating.

Sinigrin Compound contained in plants in the cabbage family that ultimately is converted to hydrogen sulfide, causing an unpleasant flavor.

Skim milk Milk resulting when almost all of the fat has been removed, leaving a maximum fat content of 0.5 percent; usually the level is 0.1 percent or less.

Slurry Starch paste.

Smoke point Temperature at which a fat smokes due to chemical breakdown to free fatty acids and acrolein.

Smoking Means of helping to promote shelf life of meat by hanging it in a smokehouse to dry out the surface and add flavor to the meat.

Soft batter Flour mixture with twice as much flour as liquid (2:1 ratio); muffins and drop cookies are examples.

Soft dough Flour mixture with approximately three times as much flour as liquid (3:1 ratio); biscuit and bread doughs are examples.

Soft peak stage Egg white foam beaten until the peaks just bend over, a point noted for ease of blending with other ingredients and for stability during mixing and baking.

Sol Colloidal dispersion in which the solid is the discontinuous phase or the dispersed phase and the liquid is the continuous phase; a gelatinized starch paste is an example of a sol.

Sour cream Viscous, acidic cream containing at least 18 percent fat; acidified by action of lactic acid bacteria on lactose.

Sponge cake Foam cake comprised of an egg yolk foam and an egg white foam, plus a small amount of cake flour, water, lemon, and sugar, and usually baked in a tube pan.

Sponge method Method of preparing a yeast dough, in which the salt and part of the flour are withheld until the batter has generated enough carbon dioxide to give a sponge-like quality to the mixture; addition of the rest of the flour and the salt precedes the completion of the kneading and subsequent steps.

Stabilized starches Starches resistant to retrogradation and syneresis because of formation of phosphate or acetyl esters of starch; often called modified starches.

Staphylococcal poisoning Food poisoning due to ingestion of the enterotoxin produced by *Staphylococcus aureus*; violent disturbance of gastrointestinal tract for one to two days and occurring usually within eight hours of eating the contaminated food.

Starch Complex carbohydrate (polysaccharide) made of glucose units; valued as a thickening agent.

Starch granule Units of starch (usually consisting of about 20 percent amylose and 80 percent amylopectin) deposited in concentric layers within the leucoplasts in cells.

Steak Cross-sectional slice of a uniform thickness.

Stiff dough Flour mixture with about eight times as much flour as liquid (8:1 ratio); pastry and pasta doughs are examples.

Stiff peak stage Point at which egg white peaks stand up straight, but the foam does not break apart; used in making hard meringues and chiffon cakes.

Stirring Gentle blending of ingredients when trapping of air and development of gluten are not necessary.

Straight dough method Method of making a yeast bread dough by combining all of the ingredients (scalded milk, sugar, salt, butter, and egg, with softened yeast added after mixture is sufficiently cool, and the flour) and kneaded prior to the proofing period.

Subjective (sensory) evaluation Evaluation using the senses.

Sublimation Change of state from ice directly to water vapor without passing through the liquid water state.

Sucrase Enzyme in yeast that catalyzes breakdown of sucrose to glucose and fructose to initiate the production of carbon dioxide in batters and doughs containing yeast.

Supersaturated solution Solution in which more solute is dissolved than theoretically can be dissolved; created by boiling a true solution to a high temperature and then cooling very carefully.

Surface tension Tendency of a liquid to present the least possible surface area (to form a sphere rather than to spread into a film); low surface tension is essential to foam formation and stability.

Sweetened condensed milk Canned milk product made by evaporating about half of the water and adding a high percentage (44 percent) of sugar.

Syneresis Separation of liquid from a gel.

Tallow Fat rendered from the fatty tissue of cattle.

Tannins Previous term for polyphenols.

Tapioca Starch from the root of cassava (also called manioc).

Taste Sweet, sour, salt, bitter, and umami; basic tastes detected by the taste buds on the tongue.

Tempering Carefully controlled cooling of conched chocolate to develop fine fat crystals, which helps to avoid development of bloom during storage.

Temporary emulsion   Emulsion that separates very quickly into two layers.

Textured soy protein (TSP)   Concentrated soy protein product from defatted soy flour; plant protein meat substitute.

Theaflavins   Extremely astringent compounds in black tea that, in combination with caffeine, provide the brisk quality to black tea.

Theobromine   Stimulant prominent in cocoa and chocolate.

Thermophilic   Thriving at temperatures above room temperature; heat loving.

Thin-boiling starch   Starch that has undergone limited acid hydrolysis, resulting in a product that is fluid when the gelatinized mixture is hot, but forms quite a rigid gel when cooled.

Toxin   Poisonous substance produced by metabolic reactions; *S. aureus* and *C. botulinum* are the bacteria most commonly responsible for food poisoning from toxins.

Trans   Configuration at the double bond of an unsaturated fatty acid resulting in a continuation of the linear chain.

Trans fatty acid   Form of fatty acid sometimes created when hydrogen is added to a double bond in an unsaturated fatty acid.

Trichinella spiralis   Parasite sometimes found in pork; causes trichinosis in humans.

Trichinosis   Illness caused by the presence of viable *Trichinella spiralis,* a parasite sometimes found in pork and transmitted to humans if pork is heated inadequately.

Trigeminal cavity   Space including olfactory receptors, taste buds, and oral cavity, where flavor is perceived.

Triglyceride   Fat containing three fatty acids.

Triticale   Grain produced by crossing rye and wheat; its flour has a protein mixture with some potential for making good baked products.

Turgor   The tension in cells caused by water pressing against cell walls; a desirable characteristic in salad ingredients.

UHT   Ultrahigh-temperature pasteurization of milk (280°F (137.7°C) for 2 seconds) to make the milk sterile, permitting storage at room temperature when UHT-treated milk is aseptically packaged.

Umami   Savory quality that contributes to the taste of some foods.

Unit pricing   Cost of a designated amount of an item to make price comparisons easy for consumers.

Universal Product Code   Pattern of bars printed on packages to code inventory and cost information for translation by electronic scanning at the check stand.

Vacuole   Largest region of the parenchyma cell; the portion encircled by the cytoplasm.

Vapor pressure   Pressure within a liquid for individual molecules to escape from the liquid; varies with the temperature of the liquid and with dissolved substances.

Vegetable   Herbaceous plant containing an edible portion suitably served with the main course of a meal.

Vibrio cholerae   Bacterium sometimes found in foods and water with fecal contamination; causes cholera.

Virus   Submicroscopic molecules composed of genetic material surrounded by a protein coat; some can cause diseases in their host.

Vitamin   Organic compound needed in very small amounts by the body to maintain life and promote growth; must be included in the diet.

Vitelline membrane   Membrane surrounding the yolk of an egg.

Water-holding capacity   Ability of muscles to hold water; an important contribution to juiciness of meats.

Waxy potatoes   Potatoes with a high content of sugar and low amount of starch; best suited for boiling and other preparations where shape is important.

Waxy starches   Starches from plants bred to produce a starch that is virtually all amylopectin and is free of amylose; valued for use in products where a gel is not desirable.

Weeping   Leakage or collection of fluid between the filling and meringue due to failure to denature the protein in the egg white.

Whey   Liquid removed from clotted milk in cheese manufacturing.

Whipping cream   Cream capable of being whipped into a foam because of its fat content of at least 30 percent.

Whole wheat flour   Flour containing the bran and germ, as well as the endosperm.

Winterizing   Process of chilling an oil to 45°F (7.2°C) and then filtering to remove any fat crystals.

Wok   Metallic bowl-shaped pan developed in Asia for stir-frying.

Yeast   Single-celled fungus that reproduces by budding.

Yersinia enterocolitica   Bacteria sometimes found in raw and undercooked pork and raw milk, which cause yersiniosis.

Yogurt   Milk-based food produced when milk is clotted by lactic acid–producing bacteria.

Yolk index   Measure of egg quality out of the shell; height of the yolk divided by the diameter.

Index

• • • Figure C-1
Squash can be found in a wide range of colors and shapes; many not only add color to a meal but also are good sources of phytochemicals.
Courtesy of Plycon Press.

• • • Figure C-2
Spaghetti squash lives up to its name when it is easily dragged out into spaghetti-like strands after it is baked until tender. Courtesy of Plycon Press.

• • • Figure C-3
Boiled and grilled corn-on-the-cob are featured attractions at this street vendor's stall. Courtesy of Plycon Press.

• • • Figure C-4
Okra and white baby sweet corn (left) compete with red and yellow sweet peppers and peas to tempt shoppers. Courtesy of Plycon Press.

• • • Figure C-5
This Greek vegetable medley includes white potatoes, cherry tomatoes, garlic bulbs, and zucchini blossoms. Courtesy of Plycon Press.

• • • Figure C-6
This market is overflowing with tempting fresh vegetables ranging from baby carrots, all kinds of potatoes and squash, eggplant, several types of greens, tomatoes, and even hydroponic Bibb lettuce. Courtesy of Plycon Press.

••• Figure C-7
Bibb lettuce (also known as limestone lettuce) sometimes is raised hydroponically (in water with nutrients, but without dirt) and marketed in plastic containers designed so that the roots are in the lower area and the delicate leaves of the head spread loosely in the upper compartment. Courtesy of Plycon Press.

••• Figure C-8
Among the vegetables that are used to add flavor to various casseroles, soups, and other mixtures are (left to right) red onion, garlic, Spanish onion, shallot, and boiling onions.

Courtesy of Plycon Press.

••• Figure C-9
Brussels sprouts sometimes appear in the market still attached and crowded all along the thick stem. Courtesy of Plycon Press.

• • • Figure C-10
Belgian endive can add texture, a delicate color, and graceful line to a salad, or it can be cooked as a vegetable in the main course. Courtesy of Plycon Press.

• • • Figure C-11
Celeriac (also called celery root) is a sturdy vegetable that requires some determination to peel it in preparation for boiling it or including it raw for texture and a celery flavor overtone in a salad. Courtesy of Plycon Press.

• • • Figure C-12
An array of vegetables will be the source of vitamins, minerals, and phytochemicals cooked or in salads: (clockwise from top) cucumber, daikon, carrots, squash, green beans, sweet potato, green onions, ginger root, artichokes, and a lime for accent.

Courtesy of Plycon Press.

• • • Figure C-13
These carrots, green and red peppers, red cabbage, spinach, green onions, radishes, tomatoes, and mushrooms are poised to be washed, sliced, and tossed with a vinegar and oil dressing. Courtesy of Plycon Press.

• • • Figure C-14
The appearance of salads can be enhanced by carefully slicing and cutting ingredients into attractive pieces. Courtesy of Plycon Press.

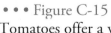

• • • Figure C-15
Tomatoes offer a variety of choices to suit the menu. including (clockwise from the rear) vine-ripened, beefsteak, plum, grape, and cherry. Courtesy of Plycon Press.

• • • Figure C-16
Fresh spinach and mandarin orange slices are highlighted by crumbled gorgonzola, a buttery cheese veined with a blue mold that adds a distinctive flavor to this healthy salad. Courtesy of Plycon Press.

• • • Figure C-17
Cherries ripening on the tree herald the season of wonderful fruit fresh from the orchard. Courtesy of Brian Jung.

• • • Figure C-18
Cherry picking has its own rewards when tasty samples are selected straight off the tree. Courtesy of Brian Jung.

• • • Figure C-19
Vineyards require careful tending, plenty of sunshine, and just enough water to grow their fruit, the first step toward producing wine. Courtesy of Plycon Press.

• • • Figure C-20
Wine grapes are full of juice when they are ready to be picked. Courtesy of Jim Bull.

• • • Figure C-21
Pomegranate juice is rapidly gaining in the marketplace because of its high levels of antioxidants and its attractive color and flavor; its seeds can be used in salads and other dishes to add a bright touch of red, as well as phytochemicals. Courtesy of Plycon Press.

• • • Figure C-22
When its thin, leathery skin is peeled,
longan (an Asian tropical tree fruit) contains
a very sweet, somewhat slippery pulp
surrounding a single seed. Courtesy of Plycon Press.

• • • Figure C-23
Asian pears, longan, and durian (bottom
shelf) vie with mangoes and oranges at this
street market. Courtesy of Plycon Press.

• • • Figure C-24
Kiwano, also called horned melon, has a tough
yellow skin with prongs and a gelatinous
interior with many soft seeds which can be
scooped out and eaten. Courtesy of Plycon Press.

• • • Figure C-25
Dragon fruit, apples, and Asian pears are arranged below mangoes and slices of melons and papaya. Courtesy of Plycon Press.

• • • Figure C-26
Dragon fruit is the fruit of a tropical cactus. Courtesy of Plycon Press.

• • • Figure C-27
Chilled tapioca pudding contrasts pleasantly with dragon fruit (the white slice with black freckles of seeds), papaya, pineapple, watermelon, and grapefruit.

Courtesy of Plycon Press.

• • • Figure C-28
Green coconuts are harvested and sold with
a straw inserted into the soft interior, which
makes it easy to suck the slightly sweet
coconut water out as a unique beverage.

Courtesy of Plycon Press.

• • • Figure C-29
Ripe coconuts are harvested when they have
matured and the shell has hardened; they
will be used to produce coconut milk or
coconut meat in slices or grated. Courtesy of
Hema Latha.

• • • Figure C-30
Cherimoyas with their cream-colored flesh,
cantaloupe, papayas, and dark-skinned
plums could be prepared together as a
colorful, vitamin-rich fruit salad. Courtesy of
Plycon Press.

• • • Figure C-31
Passion fruit is ready to spoon out for making sherbet or other delicate fruit-flavored recipe. Mangosteen, also a tropical fruit, has a thick leathery skin encasing several segments, many of which contain a seed. Courtesy of Plycon Press.

• • • Figure C-32
Starfruit (aka carambola) gets its name for the star shape when it is sliced crosswise to make a colorful tropical fruit garnish. Courtesy of Plycon Press.

• • • Figure C-33
Bananas are picked green and transported to market before they ripen. Courtesy of Plycon Press.

• • • Figure C-34
Prickly looking rambutans are surrounded by Asian pears, ripe bananas, papayas, and mangosteens. Courtesy of Plycon Press.

• • • Figure C-35
Rambutan empty skin after the fruit has been removed. Courtesy of Plycon Press.

• • • Figure C-36
Partially peeled rambutans are ready to be slipped out of their shells and eaten; each contains a large seed. Courtesy of Plycon Press.

• • • Figure C-37
Crab apples sometimes are pickled with cinnamon and served as a flavorful garnish with roast pork, while green pippin apples may end up in an apple pie, and red delicious apples may be eaten raw or made into Waldorf salad. Courtesy of Plycon Press.

• • • Figure C-38
Waldorf salad is colorful and has a contrast of textures because of the red skin on the apples and the added dried cherries, celery, and banana slices. Courtesy of Plycon Press.

• • • Figure C-39
The sweetness and acidity of the pineapple contrasts with the blandness of the cottage cheese and the bite of the bright red pomegranate seeds. Courtesy of Plycon Press.

• • • Figure C-40
This trio includes a potato salad, a mixed bean salad, and a pasta salad. Courtesy of Plycon Press.

• • • Figure C-41
Red onion, green pepper, and sliced radishes add important color, flavor, and textural contrast to the various beans, all of which have somewhat bland flavors and a fairly soft mouthfeel. Courtesy of Plycon Press.

• • • Figure C-42
Paprika and slices of hard-cooked egg are added as garnishes for this potato salad.
Courtesy of Plycon Press.

• • • Figure C-43
Balsamic vinegar and olive oil from Italy provide the perfect ingredients for a dressing to flavor this tossed salad. Courtesy of Plycon Press.

• • • Figure C-44
A salad of a wedge of lettuce accompanied by shrimp and Thousand Island dressing and a lemon wedge is not only attractive but also is wonderful to eat. Courtesy of Plycon Press.

• • • Figure C-45
Caesar salad is made with romaine, which gives a crisp texture that is augmented with toasted croutons; lemon and a tart dressing are part of the ensemble, too.

Courtesy of Plycon Press.

• • • Figure C-46
Coleslaw comprised of green and red cabbage gains added nutritional benefits from red and green peppers, slivered carrots, and a vinegar and oil dressing. Courtesy of Plycon Press.

• • • Figure C-47
Peeled, sliced fresh oranges accented with grated coconut and dried red cherries comprise a healthful, low-calorie salad that can be assembled quickly.

Courtesy of Plycon Press.

• • • Figure C-48
Special shears and a peeler are tools that speed salad preparation. Courtesy of Plycon Press.

••• Figure C-49
Cranberries are harvested in Wisconsin, the nation's biggest producer, by flooding the bogs and dragging the floating berries to the edge where they are sucked through a hose into a truck. Courtesy of Al Chavez.

••• Figure C-50
Freshly picked olives are sorted in preparation for processing. Courtesy of June Kalajian Froncillo.

••• Figure C-51
Olives (including their pits) are crushed to a pulp in this press and then a hydraulic press is used to cold-press the mass and extract extra virgin olive oil. Courtesy of June Kalajian Froncillo.

• • • Figure C-52

Sugar cane is pressed to express its sweet juice, the first step in producing cane sugar. Courtesy of June Kalajian Froncillo.

• • • Figure C-53

Several reduced and no-calorie sweeteners are marketed to satisfy consumers' desire for sweet and assist in their quest to achieve and maintain a healthy weight. Courtesy of Plycon Press.

• • • Figure C-54

In skilled hands, chocolate is transformed into delectable art atop a cake. Courtesy of Plycon Press.

• • • Figure C-55
Rice is dried after harvesting so that it can be stored without becoming spoiled due to mold growth. Courtesy of Plycon Press.

• • • Figure C-56
The outer bran layers and the germ are separated from the endosperm to produce polished rice. Courtesy of Plycon Press.

• • • Figure C-57
To make wrappers for spring rolls, rice starch is made into a paste that is spread like a pancake on a hot griddle and heated briefly to gelatinize some of the starch before being hung up to dry.

Courtesy of Plycon Press.

• • • Figure C-58
The last step in making rice paper wrappers for spring rolls is drying in the sun. Courtesy of Plycon Press.

• • • Figure C-59
Vietnamese baked rice is made by baking it in a clay pot in the oven until it is crisp and ready to garnish and eat. Courtesy of Plycon Press.

• • • Figure C-60
After the crisp, baked rice is placed upside down on a plate, it is topped with nuoc mam (Vietnamese fish sauce), black sesame seeds, and cracked black pepper.

Courtesy of Plycon Press.

• • • Figure C-61
Corn, a key cereal grain, is the source of such important ingredients as cornstarch, cornmeal, and corn oil. Courtesy of Agricultural Research Service.

• • • Figure C-62
Corn is eaten in many products, for example, as tortillas made into chips, tacos, enchiladas, and sometimes sweet corn becomes a special treat as corn-on-the-cob. Courtesy of Agricultural Research Service.

• • • Figure C-63
Wheat is the grain that is the basic ingredient of most breads, cakes, cookies, and pastries because it contains gluten, a key structural component. Courtesy of Agricultural Research Service.

• • • Figure C-64
Udon noodles (thick noodles made from a wheat flour dough) are tasty in a hot broth flavored with soy sauce. Courtesy of Plycon Press.

• • • Figure C-65
Milk from domesticated water buffalo is used to make mozzarella cheese. Courtesy of Plycon Press.

• • • Figure C-68
A Greek dairy man removes curd from the acidified whey and drains it in cheesecloth as he transforms milk from his goats into whey cheese. Courtesy of Plycon Press.

• • • Figure C-69
Whey in the kettle has a yellow-green tint because of its content of riboflavin, which is soluble in this aqueous medium; some whey proteins still are precipitating to form a curd because of the acid that has been added to make whey cheese. Courtesy of Plycon Press.

• • • Figure C-70
Ripening under controlled storage conditions is the final step in producing unique flavors in some natural cheeses. Courtesy of Plycon Press.

• • • Figure C-71
Consumers may be confronted with choices on shell color, organic, free range, fertility, size, and grade when shopping for eggs. Courtesy of Plycon Press.

• • • Figure C-72
A cheese soufflé has a light texture because of the egg white foam that is gently folded into the cheese sauce; the air expands the mixture during baking. Courtesy of Plycon Press.

• • • Figure C-73
Egg yolks are a key ingredient in puff pastries (cream puffs and gougère, for example) because they are effective in forming an emulsion with the large amount of fat in the dough. Courtesy of Plycon Press.

• • • Figure C-74
A slice of hard-cooked egg adds an attractive accent to a raw spinach salad if it does not have a dark ring of ferrous sulfide surrounding the yolk. Courtesy of Plycon Press.

• • • Figure C-75

Federally supported research on the problem of eggs infected with *Salmonella enteritidis* is ongoing as scientists try to find ways to reduce the incidence and speed identification of infection in hens and eggs. Courtesy of Agricultural Research Service.

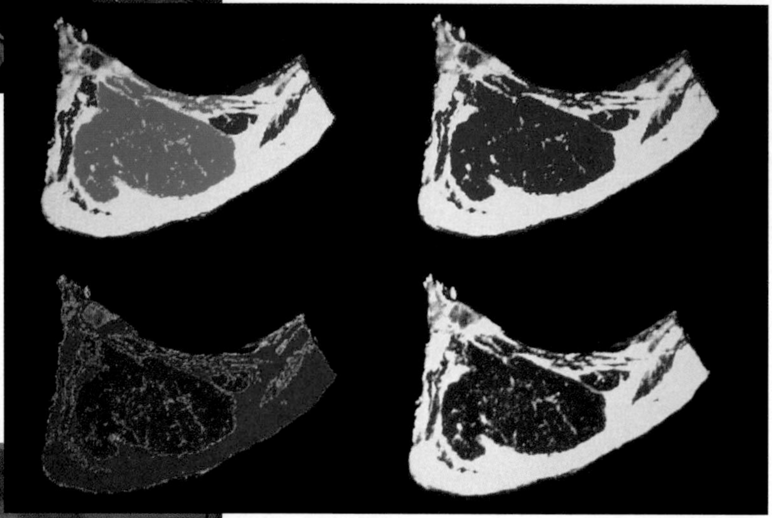

• • • Figure C-76

Analysis of computerized images of inch-thick rib-eye steak helps predict the pounds of retail beef a carcass will yield after boning and trimming. Courtesy of Agricultural Research Service.

• • • Figure C-77

Standing rib roast is a tender cut that is prepared by placing it in a shallow pan and roasting it without any cover or wrap until its interior temperature reaches the desired degree of doneness [145°F (63°C) or more].

Courtesy of Plycon Press.

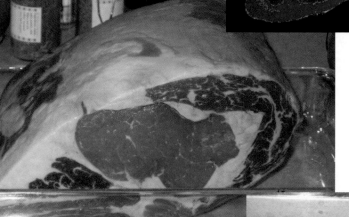

• • • Figure C-78

The roast is removed from the oven when the thermometer in the center of the cut indicates the desired temperature has been reached. The exterior is pleasingly browned because of roasting without a cover. Courtesy of Plycon Press.

Beef Made Easy

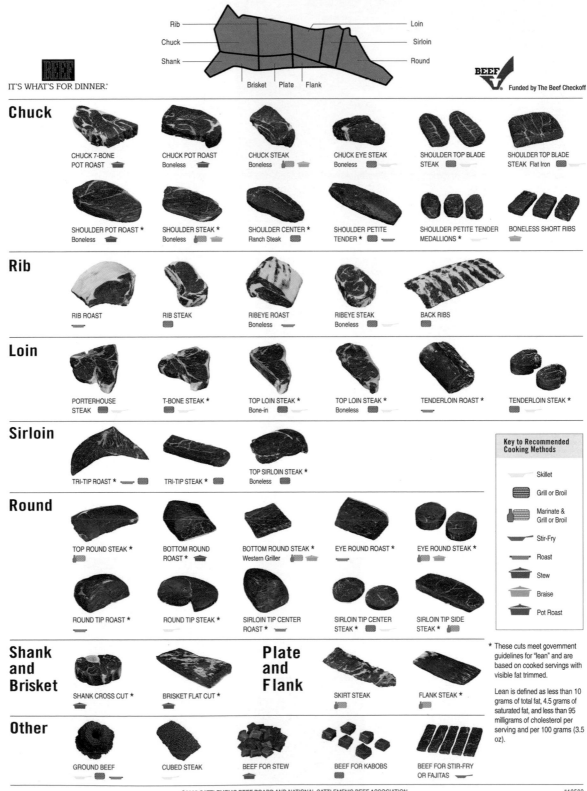

• • • Figure C-79
Primal and retail cuts and appropriate cooking methods are presented in this chart. Courtesy of the Beef Checkoff.

• • • Figure C-80
Tokyo's Tsukiji Fish Market is the place where fast-moving auctions on tuna and other prized seafood speed the day's catch to waiting restaurateurs and sushi masters who are poised to prepare it for tonight's diners. Courtesy of Plycon Press.

• • • Figure C-81
Careful chilling on ice is important to maintain the quality and safety of seafood (lobster, shrimp, and crab legs and claws) until customers take them home. Courtesy of Plycon Press.

• • • Figure C-82
Paella is being prepared over a large bed of charcoal to satisfy the appetites of guests; saffron adds a festive color to this elaborate dish containing rice, saffron, and a mixture of seafood, sausage, and chicken. Courtesy of Gary Horton.

• • • Figure C-83
Wheat harvesting begins the long process of milling the grain into flour and ultimately incorporating into a wide variety of products including breads, cakes, and pastries where the gluten in wheat flour provides a major component of the structure. Courtesy of Agricultural Research Service.

• • • Figure C-84
Breads of many types can be made using wheat as the only flour; sometimes rye, oat, barley, or other flour may be added to give variety. Courtesy of Agricultural Research Service.

• • • Figure C-85
Triticale, a grain resulting from crossbreeding wheat and rye, is harvested and made into flour with some of the characteristics of gluten that promote good texture and volume in baked products. Courtesy of Agricultural Research Service.

• • • Figure C-86

Bagels are a yeast bread that is made by boiling and then adding various types of seeds or other topping (if desired) before baking them. Courtesy of Plycon Press.

• • • Figure C-87

This corn bread has been mixed too much, as can be seen by the tunnels in it.

Courtesy of Plycon Press.

• • • Figure C-88

This torte consisting of four thin layers of chocolate cake interspersed with sweet fillings and topped with a raspberry and sweets can be a serious temptation to dieters. Courtesy of Plycon Press.

• • • Figure C-89
Rosemary is an herb that effectively blends with lamb and other entrées to add a bright flavor note. Courtesy of Plycon Press.

• • • Figure C-90
Fresh basil can be added raw to salads or to spaghetti sauce or similar recipes where it quietly enhances the flavor of the dish. Courtesy of Plycon Press.

• • • Figure C-91
A wonderful blend of aromas entices shoppers to this spice stall where a wide world of spices and herbs can be bought.

Courtesy of Plycon Press.

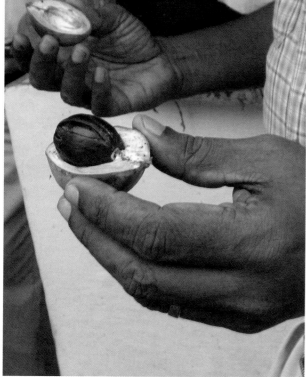

• • • Figure C-92

Saffron, the world's most expensive spice, is the dried stigmas of the crocus flower; the colorful strands add a golden color and a distinctive flavor overtone to rice, soups, and various other dishes. Courtesy of Plycon Press.

• • • Figure C-93

Nutmeg, the familiar spice sprinkled on custard, is the grated seed of a tree fruit; the lacy reddish spice on the seed is removed and sold as another spice, mace. Courtesy of Plycon Press.

• • • Figure C-94

Whole nutmeg and the dried mace removed from the surface of the seeds. Courtesy of Plycon Press.